Expert Oracle Exadata

Second Edition

Martin Bach
Karl Arao
Andy Colvin
Frits Hoogland
Kerry Osborne
Randy Johnson
Tanel Poder

⟨IOUG⟩ independent oracle users group

Apress®

Expert Oracle Exadata

ISBN-13 (pbk): 978-1-4302-6241-1

ISBN-13 (electronic): 978-1-4302-6242-8

Managing Director: Welmoed Spahr
Lead Editor: Jonathan Gennick
Development Editor: Douglas Pundick
Technical Reviewer: Frits Hoogland
Editorial Board: Steve Anglin, Louise Corrigan, Jim DeWolf, Jonathan Gennick, Robert Hutchinson, Michelle Lowman, James Markham, Susan McDermott, Matthew Moodie, Jeffrey Pepper, Douglas Pundick, Ben Renow-Clarke, Gwenan Spearing, Steve Weiss
Coordinating Editor: Jill Balzano
Copy Editor: Ann Dickson
Compositor: SPi Global
Indexer: SPi Global
Artist: SPi Global
Cover Designer: Anna Ishchenko

Distributed to the book trade worldwide by Springer Science+Business Media New York, 233 Spring Street, 6th Floor, New York, NY 10013. Phone 1-800-SPRINGER, fax (201) 348-4505, e-mail `orders-ny@springer-sbm.com`, or visit `www.springeronline.com`. Apress Media, LLC is a California LLC and the sole member (owner) is Springer Science + Business Media Finance Inc (SSBM Finance Inc). SSBM Finance Inc is a Delaware corporation.

For information on translations, please e-mail `rights@apress.com`, or visit `www.apress.com`.

Apress and friends of ED books may be purchased in bulk for academic, corporate, or promotional use. eBook versions and licenses are also available for most titles. For more information, reference our Special Bulk Sales–eBook Licensing web page at `www.apress.com/bulk-sales`.

Any source code or other supplementary materials referenced by the author in this text is available to readers at `www.apress.com/9781430262411`. For detailed information about how to locate your book's source code, go to `www.apress.com/source-code/`. Readers can also access source code at SpringerLink in the Supplementary Material section for each chapter.

Contents at a Glance

Contents

About the Authors

Martin Bach is an Oracle consultant and overall technical enthusiast. He specialized in the Oracle DBMS in 2001, with his main interests in high availability and disaster recovery solutions for mission critical 24x7 systems. For a good few years now, Martin has had a lot of fun exploring many different types of Engineered Systems from an infrastructure and performance point of view. He is an Oracle Certified Master, Oracle Ace Director, and OakTable member. Previous publications include co-authoring *Pro Oracle Database RAC 11g on Linux* and *Expert Consolidation in Oracle Database 12c*. In addition, Martin maintains a weblog on `http://martincarstenbach.wordpress.com` where additional research about this book and other topics can be found. When he expresses his thoughts in tweets, he uses the twitter handle `@MartinDBA`.

Andy Colvin is an Oracle consultant who specializes in infrastructure management. He began working in IT in 1999 as a network and systems administrator, supporting several Oracle environments. Andy joined Enkitec in 2006 and began to focus on Oracle Engineered Systems in 2010. In 2012, Andy was awarded Oracle ACE status for his online contributions, mainly found at `http://oracle-ninja.com`. When not patching or configuring an Exadata, Andy still enjoys working with networks and various operating systems. When he has something worth saying in less than 140 characters, he tweets at `@acolvin`.

Frits Hoogland is an IT professional specializing in Oracle database performance and internals. Frits frequently presents on Oracle technical topics at conferences around the world. In 2009, he received an Oracle ACE award from the Oracle Technology Network and a year later became an Oracle ACE Director. In 2010, he joined the OakTable Network. In addition to developing his Oracle expertise, Frits investigates modern operating systems. Frits currently works at the Accenture Enkitec Group. Previous involvement with publications includes being the technical reviewer for *Expert Oracle Database Architecture, Expert Consolidation in Oracle Database 12c, Expert Oracle SQL, Expert Oracle Enterprise Manager*, and *Practical Oracle Database Appliance*. Frits keeps a weblog at `http://fritshoogland.wordpress.com` where additional research can be found.

Karl Arao currently works for Accenture Enkitec Group and has nine years of Oracle database consulting experience across a broad range of industries. He specializes in Performance, Resource Management, Capacity Planning, Consolidation, and Sizing. Prior to this, he was a Solutions Architect and an R&D guy. Karl is a proud member of OCP-DBA, RHCE, Oracle ACE, and the OakTable Network. He is a frequent speaker at Oracle conferences and shares his experiences, adventures, and discoveries in his blog (`karlarao.wordpress.com`), tweets at @karlarao, and owns a wiki (`karlarao.tiddlyspot.com`) where he shares his quick guides and documentations on technologies.

The foregoing are the authors who've prepared this second edition. Also having content in this book are the first-edition authors: Kerry Osborne, Randy Johnson, and Tanel Poder. While not contributing directly to this second edition, their support and guidance have been essential to keeping this work alive.

Acknowledgments

The book you are holding in your hands, be it in electronic or printed form, has been a fair bit of work for everyone involved. The agile development on the Exadata platform was in many ways a blessing and a curse—a blessing because you could appreciate the improvements introduced with every release, and a curse because the new features should be in the book, causing more work.... This project has been one of the longest I have been involved in, and I would like to thank my family (again!) for letting me spend a lot of time researching and writing for what turned out to be a long period of time. I'll try and make up for it, promise! Personally participating in the organization and writing were hugely rewarding as they allowed me to delve into the depths of the Exadata implementation. It is probably true that only in teaching and writing do you get the most comprehensive understanding of the subject you cover. How often did I think I knew what I was about to write, only to find out I had no clue. But, thankfully, I wasn't on my own. I wouldn't have been able to do this without the support from my colleagues and my friends, who proved inspirational (sometimes even unknowingly). There are simply too many to mention on this page—I'm sure you know whom I mean when you read this paragraph. A big "thank you" to you all.

—Martin Bach

First and foremost, I would like to thank the authors of the first edition for giving us great source material to work with. To Kerry, Randy, and Tanel—for all of the times that we have heard about how great the first edition was, I hope we did it justice. This has been a long journey to say the least. It has been great to work with Martin, Frits, and Karl throughout. As Frits and Martin mentioned, this took a significant amount of time away from other priorities, mainly my family. I truly appreciate their willingness to let me spend those long nights locked away, trying to get pen to paper and work out the thoughts in my brain. This has been a revealing experience, and I have learned a lot during the writing process. Keeping up with an ever-changing platform can make for plenty of rewrites during the life of the project! I enjoyed the time spent writing this, and I hope that you are able to read this book and learn something new.

—Andy Colvin

Being a writer for a book has been a learning cycle for me, as this is my first time for actually writing, instead of "just" commenting on the work of others. I started off doing one chapter, which would have been only a modest amount of work and time, but this one chapter eventually became three chapters. Of course, having been the technical reviewer for the previous edition, I served the technical reviewer of all the chapters I didn't write. Being both a writer and technical reviewer meant I spent a tremendous amount of time creating this book. I would like to thank my family for letting me spend the countless hours writing, reviewing, researching, testing, and so on. Exactly as Martin put it, a huge part of this book came into existence because of the collaboration of colleagues and friends, in all kinds of forms. Thank you.

—Frits Hoogland

First of all, I would like to thank my parents, Denis and Nenita, and my brother, Kevin. Without you, I wouldn't be striving to be the best that I can be. I love you. To the Arao and Agustin families, my friends, and loved ones—thank you for providing support and fun moments, while keeping me sane as I wrote my chapters. To Kerry Osborne, Veronica Stigers, and Martin Paynter—thank you for always believing in me and for all the interesting challenges and rare opportunities you have given. To Dinah Salonga and SQL*Wizard Family—thank you for all the mentorship and friendship and for exposing me to a lot of difficult customer situations that helped me become a solid DBA at a young age. I will never forget all the fun sleepless nights. And thanks especially to Jonathan Gennick and the Apress team for all your patience and support. Yes, we did it! Thanks to all who helped me on my research and your valuable input. Finally, I would like to express my appreciation for the great conversations I had with the like-minded people from the Oracle community, the conferences, oracle-l mailing list, the OakTable Network, and the Oracle ACE program. Thank you for all the inspiration, learning, shared ideas, friendship, and help. Great ideas are built on the ideas of great minds and great ideas of the past. Let's keep the community spirit high all the time.

—Karl Arao

Introduction

Thank you very much for buying the second edition of *Expert Oracle Exadata*. Us current authors have been standing on the shoulders of giants while putting this together. Whenever writing a second edition of a successful book, the authors face the pressure of creating at least as good, if not better, edition than the first edition was. And good it was, the first edition. We hope that we have been able to provide you, dear reader, with a suitable introduction to Exadata. In fact, our hope is to give you enough information to get started with Exadata. It is not uncommon to find database administrators in situations where they have been introduced to Exadata. only to ask the question, "Now what?" We have tried to structure the book to help you answer this question. You will read about what Exadata is before diving into the various optimizations that make it so unique in the world of Oracle database processing hardware. While some of the material, particularly in the earlier chapters, paints a broad picture, we gradually go into a lot of detail. Access to an Exadata development system can help you a lot in understanding the more advanced material. We have tried very hard to make it possible for you to follow along, but please bear in mind that the Exadata platform is not static at all; new releases in hardware and software can change the documented outcome of commands and SQL statements. We will try to address major differences on our web site, `http://www.expertoracleexadata.com/` and our personal blogs listed in Appendix B.

Note that we have used various undocumented underscore parameters and features to demonstrate how various pieces of the software work. Do not take this as a recommended approach for managing a production system! In fact, there is usually no reason to deviate from the defaults. Setting underscore parameters is allowed only with the explicit blessings from Oracle Support and as the result of a recommendation as part of a service request you raised. Remember that we have had access to a number of systems that we could tear apart with little worry about the consequences that resulted from our actions. This gave us a huge advantage in our investigations on how Exadata works across various hardware generations.

The Intended Audience

This book assumes that you are already familiar with Oracle. We do not go into a lot of detail explaining how Oracle works except as it relates to the Exadata platform. This means that we have made some assumptions about the readers' knowledge. We do not assume, for instance, that you are an expert in Oracle performance tuning, but we expect that you are proficient writing SQL statements and have a good understanding of the Oracle architecture. Since Exadata is a hardware and software platform, you will inevitably see references to Linux administration in some of the chapters more closely related to the hardware. Do not be intimidated—as an Exadata administrator, there are only a handful of commands that you need to know in day-to-day managing of the platform.

A Moving Target

We had this exact same section in the introduction of the first edition of this book, and the message is still the same, even after all these years. What keeps us amazed to this day is the pace of development of the Exadata platform. It is not only hardware that evolves and keeps up with the development of new technologies, but also the software that is constantly pushing the limits of what is possible. A new software release does not require you to upgrade the hardware. Except for the very first Exadata system, the current Exadata software version is compatible with every hardware generation.

The changes mentioned in the previous paragraph include substantial additions of new functionality, visible in Appendix A in the *Exadata Database Machine System Overview*. As you can imagine, trying to keep track of what Oracle released at a rapid pace was the most difficult part of the project. Every chapter had to go through multiple revisions when new hardware and software was released. The latest version we try to cover in this book is Oracle 12.1.0.2.2 RDBMS with cell software 12.1.2.1.x. Unlike the first edition of this book, which came out when Oracle 11.2.0.2 was current, there are quite a few releases now that Exadata supports technically. From an Oracle Support point of view, right now you should probably be in a migration phase to Oracle 12c. This is one of the reasons we gave the latest RDBMS release so much space in the book, even though many users are yet to migrate to it. Another consideration while writing this book was that we had to be quite careful to cite the correct version when a new feature was introduced. If you only have just started with Exadata, you might find the release numbers confusing; however, once you have your first few weeks of Exadata administration under your belt, you will find that quoting Exadata cell software releases becomes second nature.

The way Exadata evolves will undoubtedly make some of the book's contents obsolete, so if you observe differences between what is covered in this book and what you see it is probably due to version differences. Nevertheless, we welcome your feedback and will address any inconsistencies that you find.

Many Thanks to Everyone Who Helped!

We have had a great deal of support from a number of people on this project. Having our official technical reviewer take on writing a few chapters is almost an occurrence of history repeating itself. Writers and reviewers swapped roles to reply to the question, "Quis custodiet ipsos custodes?" We are also very grateful for everyone at Oracle who may have even known us from the first edition of this book and helped us overcome the stumbling blocks along the way. Finally, we want to give a big "thank you" to everyone at @Enkitec who helped keep the machines up and running, patched when a new release came out, and troubleshot when something seemed broken. The list of people is really long, so we won't be able to mention everyone by name. However, it is fair to say that if you worked at @Enkitec while this book was being written, you almost certainly contributed—thank you.

The first book helped generate interest in the second edition, and we have published some research that was too comprehensive on our personal blogs and web sites, prompting e-mail, twitter, and comments to start flying our way once an article went online. The same is true for the feedback we had with the Alpha Programme; without the community's feedback, this book would probably be less complete, and we would like to explicitly thank you for your comments.

And last, but not least, we would like to give a very special "thank you" to the authors of the first edition of the book, who allowed us to update what they wrote. Kerry, Tanel, and Randy have been instrumental in understanding the intended message of the chapters as well as chapter layout and tests. Without you, we wouldn't have been able to finish the chapters while maintaining the spirit of the first book.

Who Wrote What

Following the tradition set in the first edition, we would like to list which of us worked on each chapter. The authors of the second edition (in alphabetical order) are Karl Arao, Martin Bach, Andy Colvin, and Frits Hoogland. It really was a team effort between all of us involved, and we cannot even think about counting the hours of useful conversations and instant messages exchanged among all of us to bounce off ideas and make sure that we did not overlap contents in our chapters.

Karl: contributions to Chapters 5, 6, 7, 12

Andy: Chapters 1, 8, 9, 14, 15, 16, Appendix D

Martin: Chapters 2, 3, 5, 10, 11, 12, 13, 17, Appendices A, B, C

Frits: Chapters 4, 6, 7

Have Fun!

Writing the book was, for the most part, fun for all of us—especially when we knew about a complex problem, but had trouble reproducing a situation allowing us to research it. The moment the experiment came to a successful conclusion, the moment when we had all the output and steps to reproduce it recorded in our log files, was very often a moment of great joy and also relief. We hope his book provides a platform from which you can build your own knowledge. Although having spent a lot of time with both Exadata and Oracle Database 12c, there are still things we learn every day. Somehow it still feels we are only scratching the surface, still.

CHAPTER 1

What Is Exadata?

No doubt, you already have a pretty good idea what Exadata is or you wouldn't be holding this book in your hands. In our view, it is a preconfigured combination of hardware and software that provides a platform for running Oracle Database (either version 11g Release 2 or version 12c Release 1 as of this writing). Since the Exadata Database Machine includes a storage subsystem, different software has been developed to run at the storage layer. This has allowed Oracle product development to do some things that are just not possible on other platforms. In fact, Exadata really began its life as a storage system. If you talk to people involved in the development of the product, you will commonly hear them refer the storage component as Exadata or SAGE (Storage Appliance for the Grid Environment), which was the code name for the project.

Exadata was originally designed to address the most common bottleneck with very large databases—the inability to move sufficiently large volumes of data from the disk storage system to the database server(s). Oracle has built its business by providing very fast access to data, primarily through the use of intelligent caching technology. As the sizes of databases began to outstrip the ability to cache data effectively using these techniques, Oracle began to look at ways to eliminate the bottleneck between the storage tier and the database tier. The solution the developers came up with was a combination of hardware and software. If you think about it, there are two approaches to minimize this bottleneck. The first is to make the pipe between the database and storage bigger. While there are many components involved and it's a bit of an oversimplification, you can think of InfiniBand as that bigger pipe. The second way to minimize the bottleneck is to reduce the amount of data that needs to be transferred. This they did with Smart Scans. The combination of the two has provided a very successful solution to the problem. But make no mistake—reducing the volume of data flowing between the tiers via Smart Scan is the golden goose.

In this introductory chapter, we will review the components that make up Exadata, both hardware and software. We will also discuss how the parts fit together (the architecture). In addition, we will talk about how the database servers talk to the storage servers. This is handled very differently than on other platforms, so we will spend a fair amount of time covering that topic. We will also provide some historical context. By the end of the chapter, you should have a pretty good feel for how all the pieces fit together and a basic understanding of how Exadata works. The rest of the book will provide the details to fill out the skeleton that is built in this chapter.

An Overview of Exadata

A picture is worth a thousand words, or so the saying goes. Figure 1-1 shows a very high-level view of the parts that make up the Exadata Database Machine.

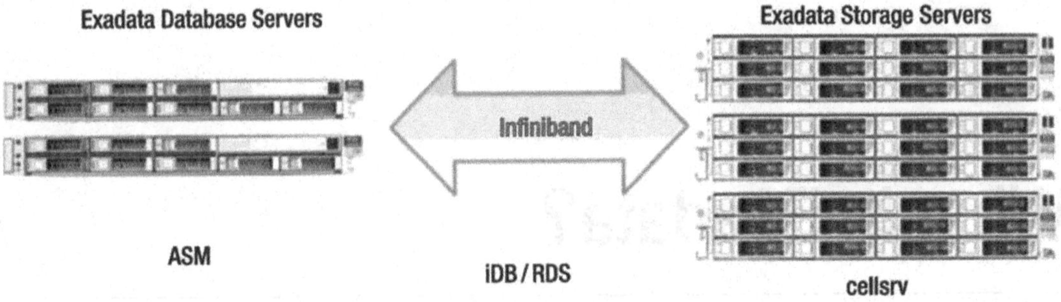

Figure 1-1. *High-level Exadata components*

When considering Exadata, it is helpful to divide the entire system mentally into two parts, the storage layer and the database layer. The layers are connected via an InfiniBand network. InfiniBand provides a low-latency, high-throughput switched fabric communications link. Redundancy is provided through multiple switches and links. The database layer is made up of multiple Sun servers running standard Oracle 11g or 12c software. The servers are generally configured in one or more Real Application Clusters (RAC), although RAC is not actually required. The database servers use Automatic Storage Management (ASM) to access the storage. ASM is required even if the databases are not configured to use RAC. The storage layer also consists of multiple Sun x86 servers. Each storage server contains 12 disk drives or 8 flash drives and runs the Oracle storage server software (`cellsrv`). Communication between the layers is accomplished via iDB, which is a network-based protocol that is implemented using InfiniBand. iDB is used to send requests for data along with metadata about the request (including predicates) to `cellsrv`. In certain situations, `cellsrv` is able to use the metadata to process the data before sending results back to the database layer. When `cellsrv` is able to do this, it is called a Smart Scan and generally results in a significant decrease in the volume of data that needs to be transmitted back to the database layer. When Smart Scans are not possible, `cellsrv` returns the entire Oracle block(s). Note that iDB uses the RDS protocol, which is a low-latency, InfiniBand-specific protocol. In certain cases, the Oracle software can set up remote direct memory access (RDMA) over RDS, which bypasses doing system calls to accomplish low-latency, process-to-process communication across the InfiniBand network.

History of Exadata

Exadata has undergone a number of significant changes since its initial release in late 2008. In fact, one of the more difficult parts of writing this book has been keeping up with the changes in the platform during the project. Following is a brief review of the product's lineage and how it has changed over time:

> **V1:** The first Exadata was released in late 2008. It was labeled as V1 and was a combination of HP hardware and Oracle software. The architecture was similar to the current X5 version, with the exception of Flash, which was added to the V2 version. Exadata V1 was marketed exclusively as a data warehouse platform. The product was interesting but not widely adopted. It also suffered from issues resulting from overheating. The commonly heard description was that you could fry eggs on top of the cabinet. Many of the original V1 customers replaced their V1s with V2s or X2-2s.

V2: The second version of Exadata was announced at Open World in 2009. This version resulted from a partnership between Sun and Oracle. By the time the announcement was made, Oracle was already in the process of attempting to acquire Sun Microsystems. Many of the components were upgraded to bigger or faster versions, but the biggest difference was the addition of a significant amount of solid state-based storage. The storage cells were enhanced with 384G of Exadata Smart Flash Cache. The software was also enhanced to take advantage of the new cache. This addition allowed Oracle to market the platform as more than a Data Warehouse platform, opening up a significantly larger market.

X2: The third edition of Exadata, announced at Oracle Open World in 2010, was named the X2. Actually, there were two distinct versions of the X2. The X2-2 followed the same basic blueprint as the V2, with up to eight dual-socket database servers. The CPUs were upgraded to hex-core models, where the V2s had used quad-core CPUs. The other X2 model was named the X2-8. It broke the small 1U database server model by introducing larger database servers with 8×8 core CPUs and a large 1TB memory footprint. The X2-8 was marketed as a more robust platform for large OLTP or mixed workload systems due primarily to the larger number of CPU cores and the larger memory footprint. In 2011, Oracle changed the hardware in the X2-8 to 8x10-core CPUs and 2TB of memory per node. For customers that needed additional storage, storage expansion racks (racks full of storage servers) were introduced. In January 2012, Oracle increased the size of the high-capacity disks from 2TB to 3TB.

X3: In 2012, Oracle announced the Exadata X3. The X3 was the natural progression of the hardware included in the X2 series. Compute node updates included eight-core Intel Sandy Bridge CPUs and increased memory, up to 256GB per server (although it originally was equipped with 128GB per server for a short time). Storage servers saw upgrades to CPUs and memory, and flash storage increased to 1.6TB per server. The X3-2 family also introduced a new size—the eighth rack. X3-8 racks saw the same improvements in the storage servers, but the compute nodes in X3-8 racks are the same as their X2-8 counterparts.

X4: Oracle released the Exadata X4 in 2013. It followed the traditional new features: processing increased to 2x12 core CPUs, the ability to upgrade to 512GB of memory in a compute node was added, and flash and disk storage increased. The X4-2 also saw a new model of high-capacity disk, trading out the 600GB, 15,000 RPM disks for 1.2TB, 10,000 RPM disks. These disks were a smaller form factor (2.5" vs 3.5"). The other notable change with the X4-2 was the introduction of an active/active InfiniBand network connection. On the X4-2, Oracle broke the bonded connection and utilized each InfiniBand port independently. This allowed for increased throughput across the InfiniBand fabric.

X5: In early 2015, Oracle announced the sixth generation of Exadata, the X5-2. The X5-2 was a dramatic change in the platform, removing the high-performance disk option in favor of an all-flash, NVMe (Non-Volatile Memory Express) model. High-capacity disk sizes were not changed, leaving them at 4TB per disk. Once again, the size of the flash cards doubled, this time to 6.4TB per storage server. Memory stayed consistent with a base of 256GB, upgradeable to 768GB, and the core count increased to 18 cores per socket. Finally, the requirement to purchase racks in predefined sizes was removed. The X5-2 rack could be purchased with any configuration required—a base rack begins with two compute nodes and three storage servers. Beyond that, any combination of compute and storage servers can be used within the rack. This removed discussions around Exadata configurations being "balanced" based on the workload. As was seen by many deployments before the X5, every workload is a little bit different and has different needs for compute and storage.

Alternative Views of What Exadata Is

We have already given you a rather bland description of how we view Exadata. However, like the well-known tale of the blind men describing an elephant, there are many conflicting perceptions about the nature of Exadata. We will cover a few of the common descriptions in this section.

Data Warehouse Appliance

Occasionally, Exadata is described as a *data warehouse appliance (DW Appliance).* While Oracle has attempted to keep Exadata from being pigeonholed into this category, the description is closer to the truth than you might initially think. It is, in fact, a tightly integrated stack of hardware and software that Oracle expects you to run without a lot of changes. This is directly in line with the common understanding of a DW Appliance. However, the very nature of the Oracle database means that it is extremely configurable. This flies in the face of the typical DW Appliance, which typically does not have a lot of knobs to turn. However, there are several common characteristics that are shared between DW Appliances and Exadata:

Exceptional Performance: The most recognizable characteristic of Exadata and DW Appliances in general is that they are optimized for data warehouse type queries.

Fast Deployment: DW Appliances and Exadata Database Machines can both be deployed very rapidly. Since Exadata comes preconfigured, it can generally be up and running within a week from the time you take delivery. This is in stark contrast to the normal Oracle clustered database deployment scenario, which generally takes several weeks.

Scalability: Both platforms have scalable architectures. With Exadata, upgrading is done in discrete steps. Upgrading from a half-rack configuration to a full rack increases the total disk throughput in lock step with the computing power available on the database servers.

Reduction in TCO: This one may seem a bit strange, since many people think the biggest drawback to Exadata is the high price tag. But the fact is that both DW Appliances and Exadata reduce the overall cost of ownership in many applications. Oddly enough, in Exadata's case, this is partially thanks to a reduction in the number of Oracle database licenses necessary to support a given workload. We have seen several situations where multiple hardware platforms were evaluated for running a company's Oracle application and have ended up costing less to implement and maintain on Exadata than on the other options evaluated.

High Availability: Most DW Appliances provide an architecture that supports at least some degree of *high availability (HA).* Since Exadata runs standard Oracle 12c or 11g software, all the HA capabilities that Oracle has developed are available out of the box. The hardware is also designed to prevent any single point of failure.

Preconfiguration: When Exadata is delivered to your data center, an Oracle engineer will be scheduled to assist with the initial configuration. This will include ensuring that the entire rack is cabled and functioning as expected. But like most DW Appliances, the work has already been done to integrate the components. Hence, extensive research and testing are not required. Having the operating system preinstalled and everything cabled and ready to go in the rack speeds up the time from delivery to implementation immensely.

Regardless of the similarities, Oracle does not consider Exadata to be a DW Appliance, even though there are many shared characteristics. Generally speaking, this is because Exadata provides a fully functional Oracle database platform with all the capabilities that have been built into Oracle over the years, including the ability to run any application that currently runs on an Oracle database and, in particular, to deal with mixed workloads that demand a high degree of concurrency, which DW Appliances are generally not equipped to handle.

OLTP Machine

This description of OLTP Machine is a bit of a marketing ploy aimed at broadening Exadata's appeal to a wider market segment. While the description is not totally off base, it is not as accurate as some other monikers that have been assigned to Exadata. It brings to mind the classic quote:

> *It depends on what the meaning of the word "is" is.*
>
> —Bill Clinton

In the same vein, OLTP (Online Transaction Processing) is a bit of a loosely defined term. We typically use the term to describe workloads that are very latency-sensitive and characterized by single-block access via indexes. But there is a subset of OLTP systems that are also very write-intensive and demand a very high degree of concurrency to support a large number of users. Exadata was not designed to be the fastest possible solution for these write-intensive workloads, although the latest flash improvements in the X5 models definitely perform better than previous generations. It is worth noting, however, that very few systems fall neatly into these categories. Most systems have a mixture of long-running, throughput-sensitive SQL statements and short-duration, latency-sensitive SQL statements—which leads us to the next view of Exadata.

Consolidation Platform

This description of Consolidation Platform pitches Exadata as a potential platform for consolidating multiple databases. This is desirable from a total cost of ownership (TCO) standpoint, as it has the potential to reduce complexity (and, therefore, costs associated with that complexity), reduce administration costs by decreasing the number of systems that must be maintained, reduce power usage and data center costs through reducing the number of servers, and reduce software and maintenance fees. This is a valid way to view Exadata. Because of the combination of features incorporated in Exadata, it is capable of adequately supporting multiple workload profiles at the same time. Although it is not the perfect OLTP Machine, the Flash Cache feature provides a mechanism for ensuring low latency for OLTP-oriented workloads. The Smart Scan optimizations provide exceptional performance for high-throughput, DW-oriented workloads. Resource Management options built into the platform provide the ability for these somewhat conflicting requirements to be satisfied on the same platform. In fact, one of the biggest upsides to this ability is the possibility of totally eliminating a huge amount of work that is currently performed in many shops to move data from an OLTP system to a DW system so that long-running queries do not negatively affect the latency-sensitive workload. In many shops, simply moving data from one platform to another consumes more resources than any other operation. Exadata's capabilities in this regard may make this process unnecessary in many cases.

Configuration Options

Since Exadata is delivered as a preconfigured, integrated system, there are very few options available. As of this writing, there are five standard versions available. They are grouped into two major categories with different model names (the X5-2 and the X4-8). The storage tiers and networking components for the two models are identical. The database tiers, however, are different.

Exadata Database Machine X5-2

The X5-2 comes in five flavors: eighth rack, quarter rack, half rack, full rack, and an elastic configuration. Table 1-1 shows the amount of storage available with each option on an Exadata X5-2. The system is built to be upgradeable, so you can upgrade later from a quarter rack to half rack, for example. Here is what you need to know about the different options:

> **Eighth Rack**: The X5-2 Eighth Rack ships with the exact same hardware as a Quarter Rack. On the database tier, half of the CPU cores are disabled via the BIOS. On the storage servers, half the hard disks, flash disks, and CPU cores are disabled as well. This gives all of the redundancy of a quarter rack for a lower cost. If customers want to upgrade from an Eighth Rack to a Quarter Rack, it is simply a matter of running a few scripts to enable the hardware. This configuration was introduced with the X3 model and was not available in the V1, V2, or X2 models. High-capacity models provide roughly 30TB of usable disk space when configured for normal redundancy (also known as double mirroring). When the extreme flash version is selected, users are provided with around 8TB of usable space with normal redundancy.
>
> **Quarter Rack**: The X5-2 Quarter Rack comes with two database servers and three storage servers. The high-capacity version provides roughly 63TB of usable disk space if it is configured for normal redundancy. The high-performance version provides roughly one-fourth of that or about 17TB of usable space, again if configured for normal redundancy.
>
> **Half Rack**: The X5-2 Half Rack comes with four database servers and seven storage servers. The high-capacity version provides roughly 150TB of usable disk space if it is configured for normal redundancy. The extreme flash version provides roughly 40TB of usable space if configured for normal redundancy.
>
> **Full Rack**: The X5-2 Full Rack comes with eight database servers and fourteen storage servers. The high-capacity version provides roughly 300TB of usable disk space if it is configured for normal redundancy. The extreme flash version provides about 80TB of usable space if configured for normal redundancy.
>
> **Elastic Configuration**: The Exadata X5-2 model removed the requirement for standard configurations and allowed customers to size an Exadata rack specific for their needs. It starts with a base rack of three storage servers and two compute servers. Beyond that, any combination of servers can be placed in the rack, with a limit of 22 compute servers or 18 storage servers. For a very small, compute-intensive database, a rack with 10 compute servers and 5 storage servers could be ordered and delivered from the factory.

Table 1-1. Usable Disk Space by Exadata Model

	X5 Full Rack	X5 Half Rack	X5 Quarter Rack	X5 Eighth Rack
HC 2x Mirror	300TB	150TB	63TB	30TB
EF 2x Mirror	80TB	40TB	17TB	8TB
HC 3x Mirror	200TB	100TB	42TB	21TB
EF 3x Mirror	53TB	26TB	11TB	5TB

Oracle offers an InfiniBand expansion switch kit that can be purchased when multiple racks need to be connected together. These configurations have an additional InfiniBand switch called a *spine switch*. This switch is used to connect additional racks. There are enough available connections to connect as many as eight racks, although additional cabling may be required depending on the number of racks you intend to connect. The database servers of the multiple racks can be combined into a single RAC database with database servers that span racks, or they may be used to form several smaller RAC clusters. Chapter 15 contains more information about connecting multiple racks

Exadata Database Machine X4-8

The Exadata X4-8 is Oracle's answer to databases that require large memory footprints. The X4-8 configuration has two database servers and an elastic number of storage cells. At the time of this writing, the X4-8 model currently in production utilizes X5-2 storage servers. It is effectively an X5-2 rack, but with two large database servers instead of the smaller database servers used in the X5-2. As previously mentioned, the storage servers and networking components are identical to the X5-2 model. There are no rack-level upgrades specific to X4-8 available. If you need more capacity, your option is to add another X4-8, a storage expansion rack, or additional storage cells.

Exadata Storage Expansion Rack X5-2

Beginning with the Exadata X2 model, Oracle began to offer storage expansion racks to customers who were challenged for space. The storage expansion racks are basically racks full of storage servers and InfiniBand switches. Just like Exadata, storage-expansion racks come in various sizes. If the disk size matches between the Exadata and storage-expansion racks, the disks from the expansion rack can be added to the existing disk groups. If customers wish to mix high-capacity and high-performance disks, they must be placed into different disk groups, due to the difference in performance characteristics between the disk types. Table 1-2 lists the amount of disk space available with each storage-expansion rack. Here is what you need to know about the different storage options:

Quarter Rack: The X5-2 quarter rack storage expansion includes four storage servers, two InfiniBand switches, and one management switch.

Half Rack: The X5-2 half rack storage expansion includes nine storage servers, three InfiniBand switches, and one management switch.

Full Rack: The X5-2 full rack storage expansion includes eighteen storage servers, three InfiniBand switches, and one management switch.

Table 1-2. Usable Disk Space by Storage Expansion Rack X5 Model

	X5 Full Expansion	X5 Half Expansion	X5 Quarter Expansion
HC 2x Mirror	301TB	150TB	66TB
EF 2x Mirror	61TB	30TB	13TB
HC 3x Mirror	200TB	100TB	44TB
EF 3x Mirror	40TB	20TB	9TB

Upgrades

Eighth racks, quarter racks, and half racks may be upgraded to add more capacity. The current price list has three options for upgrades, the half-rack to full-rack upgrade, the quarter-rack to half-rack upgrade, and the eighth-rack to quarter rack- upgrade. The options are limited in an effort to maintain the relative balance between database servers and storage servers. These upgrades are done in the field. If you order an upgrade, the individual components will be shipped to your site on a big pallet and an Oracle engineer will be scheduled to install the components into your rack. All the necessary parts should be there, including rack rails and cables. Unfortunately, the labels for the cables seem to come from some other part of the universe. When we did the upgrade on our lab system in 2010, the lack of labels held us up for a couple of days.

The quarter-to-half upgrade includes two database servers and four storage servers along with an additional InfiniBand switch, which is configured as a spine switch. The half-to-full upgrade includes four database servers and seven storage servers. Eighth-to-quarter upgrades do not include any additional hardware because it was already included in the shipment of the eighth rack. This upgrade is simply a software fix to enable the resources that were disabled during the initial configuration of the eighth rack. None of the upgrade options require any downtime, although extra care should be taken when racking and cabling the new components, as it is very easy to dislodge the existing cables, not to mention adding the InfiniBand spine switch to the bottom of the rack.

There are a couple of other things worth noting about upgrades. When customers purchase an upgrade kit, they will receive whatever the current revision of Exadata is shipping. This means it is possible to end up with a rack containing X2 and X3 components. Many companies purchased Exadata V2 or X2 systems and are now in the process of upgrading those systems. Several questions naturally arise with regard to this process. One question is whether or not it is acceptable to mix the newer X5-2 servers with the older V2 or X2 components. The answer is yes, it's OK to mix them. In the Enkitec lab environment, for example, we have a mixture of V2 (our original quarter rack) and X2-2 servers (the upgrade to a half rack). We chose to upgrade our existing system to a half rack rather than purchase another stand-alone quarter rack with X2-2 components, which was another viable option. When combining different generations into one cluster, it is important to remember that there will be different amounts of certain resources, especially on the compute nodes. Database instances running on X5 servers will have access to significantly more memory and CPU cores than they would on a V2 compute node. DBAs should take this under consideration when deciding which compute servers should host specific database services.

The other question that comes up frequently is whether or not adding additional standalone storage servers is an option for companies that are running out of space but that have plenty of CPU capacity on the database servers. If it's simply lack of space that you are dealing with, additional storage servers are certainly a viable option. With Oracle's new elastic configuration option, increasing components incrementally can be very easy.

Hardware Components

You have probably seen many pictures like the one in Figure 1-2. It shows an Exadata Database Machine X2-2 full rack. It still looks very similar to an X5-2 full rack. We have added a few graphic elements to show you where the various pieces reside in the cabinet. In this section, we will discuss those pieces.

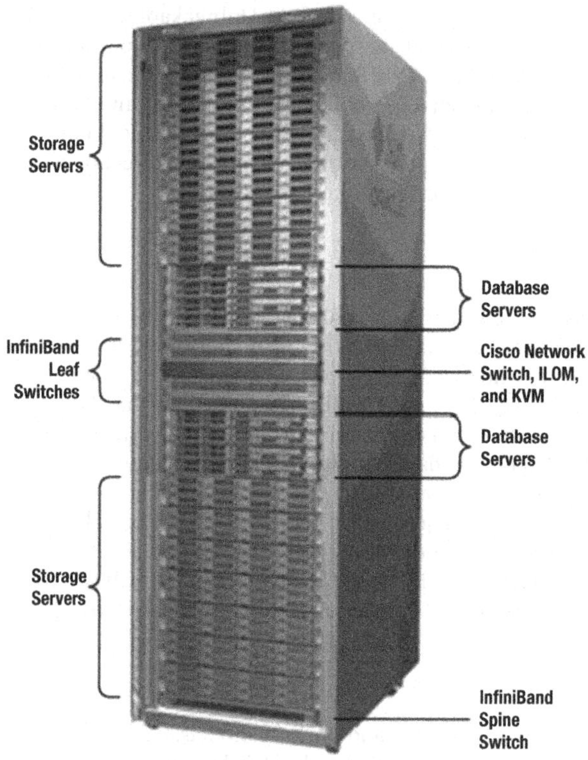

Figure 1-2. *An Exadata full rack*

As you can see, most of the networking components, including an Ethernet switch and two redundant InfiniBand switches, are located in the middle of the rack. This makes sense as it makes the cabling a little simpler. The surrounding eight slots are reserved for database servers, and the rest of the rack is used for storage servers, with two exceptions. The very bottom slot is used for an additional InfiniBand "spine" switch that can be used to connect additional racks, if so desired. It is located in the bottom of the rack, based on the expectation that your Exadata will be in a data center with a raised floor, allowing cabling to be run from the bottom of the rack. The top two slots are available for top-of-rack switches. By removing the keyboard, video, and mouse (KVM) switch in the V2 and X2-2 racks, Oracle is able to provide room for additional switches in the top of the rack.

Operating Systems

The current generation X5 hardware configurations use Intel-based Sun servers. As of this writing, all the servers come preinstalled with Oracle Linux 6. Older versions shipped with the option to choose between Oracle Linux 5 and Solaris 11. The release of the X5-2 model brought in Oracle Linux 6. Because of the overwhelming majority of customers that chose Linux, Oracle removed support for Solaris 11 on Intel-based Exadata systems. Beginning with Exadata storage server version 11.2.3.2.0, Oracle has announced that it intends to support one version of the Linux kernel—an enhanced version called the Unbreakable Enterprise Kernel (UEK). This optimized version has several enhancements that are specifically applicable to Exadata. Among these are network-related improvements to InfiniBand using the RDS protocol. One of the reasons for releasing the UEK was to speed up Oracle's ability to roll out changes/enhancements to the Linux kernel and overcome the limitations in the RedHat default kernel. Oracle has been a strong partner in the development of Linux and has made several major contributions to the code base. The stated direction is to submit all the enhancements included in the UEK version for inclusion in the standard release.

Database Servers

The current generation X5-2 database servers are based on the Sun Fire X4170 M5 (Sun Fire X5-2) servers. Each server has 2×18-core Intel Xeon E5-2699 v3 processors (2.3 GHz) and 256GB of memory. They also have four internal 600GB 10K RPM SAS drives. They have several network connections including two 10Gb fiber and four 10Gb copper Ethernet ports in addition to the two QDR InfiniBand (40Gb/s) ports. Note that the 10Gb fiber ports are open and that you need to provide the correct connectors to attach them to your existing copper or fiber network. The servers also have a dedicated ILOM port and dual hot-swappable power supplies.

The X4-8 database servers are based on the Sun Fire X4800 servers. They are designed to handle systems that require a large amount of memory. The servers are equipped with 8x15-core Intel Xeon E7-8895 v2 processors (2.8 GHz) and 2 TB of memory. The X4-8 compute nodes also include seven internal 600GB 10K RPM SAS drives, along with four QDR InfiniBand cards, eight 10Gb Ethernet fiber ports, and ten 1Gb Ethernet copper ports. This gives the full rack X4-8 a total of 240 cores and 4 terabytes of memory on the database tier.

Storage Servers

The current generation of storage servers is the same for both the X5-2 and the X4-8 models. Each storage server consists of a Sun Fire X4270 M5 (Sun Fire X5-2L) and contains either 12 hard disks or 8 flash disks. Depending on whether you have the high-capacity version or the extreme flash version, the disks will either be 4TB (originally 2TB) disks or 1.6TB flash drives. Each storage server comes with 96GB (high capacity) or 64GB (extreme flash) of memory and 2x8-core Intel Xeon E5-2630 v3 processors running at 2.4 GHz. Because these CPUs are in the Haswell family, they have built-in AES encryption support, which essentially provides a hardware assist to encryption and decryption. Each storage server also contains 1.6TB Sun Flash Accelerator F160 NVMe PCIe cards. The high-capacity version contains 4 F160 PCIe cards for the Flash Cache; the extreme flash version contains 8 F160 PCIe cards, which are used both as Flash Cache and final disk storage. The storage servers come pre-installed with Oracle Linux 6.

InfiniBand

One of the more important hardware components of Exadata is the InfiniBand network. It is used for transferring data between the database tier and the storage tier. It is also used for interconnect traffic between the database servers, if they are configured in a RAC cluster. In addition, the InfiniBand network may be used to connect to external systems for such uses as backups. Exadata provides redundant 36-port QDR InfiniBand switches for these purposes. The switches provide 40 Gb/Sec of throughput. You will occasionally see these switches referred to as "leaf" switches. In addition, each database server and each storage server are equipped with Dual-Port QDR InfiniBand Host Channel Adapters. If you are connecting multiple Oracle Engineered Systems racks together, an expansion (spine) switch is available.

Flash Cache

As mentioned earlier, each storage server comes equipped with 3.2TB of flash-based storage. This storage is generally configured to be a cache. Oracle refers to it as Exadata Smart Flash Cache (ESFC). The primary purpose of ESFC is to minimize the service time for single block reads. This feature provides a substantial amount of disk cache, about 44.8TB on a half-rack configuration.

Disks

Oracle provides two options for disks. An Exadata Database Machine may be configured with either high-capacity drives or all flash drives. As previously mentioned, the high-capacity option includes 4TB, 7200 RPM drives, while the extreme flash option includes 1.6TB NVMe flash drives. If customers wish to mix drive types, it must be accomplished using different ASM diskgroups for each storage type. With the large amount of Flash Cache available on the storage cells, it seems that the high-capacity option would be adequate for most read-heavy workloads. The Flash Cache does a very good job of reducing the single-block-read latency in the mixed-workload systems we have observed to date.

Bits and Pieces

The package price includes a 42U rack with redundant power distribution units. Also included in the price is an Ethernet switch. The spec sheets don't specify the model for the Ethernet switch, but, as of this writing, a switch manufactured by Cisco (Catalyst 4948) is being shipped. To date, this is the one piece of the package that Oracle has agreed to allow customers to replace. If you have another switch that you like better, you can remove the included switch and replace it (at your own cost). Models prior to the X3-2 included a KVM unit as well. Due to the larger database server size in the X2-8, X3-8, and X4-8, no KVM is provided. Beginning with the X3-2, Oracle has removed the KVM in favor of leaving the top two rack units available for top-of-rack switches. The package price also includes a spares kit that includes an extra flash card and an extra disk drive. The package price does not include SFP+ connectors or cables for the 10Gb Ethernet ports. These are not standard and will vary based on the equipment used in your network. These SFP+ ports are intended for external connections of the database servers to the customer's network.

Software Components

The software components that make up Exadata are split between the database tier and the storage tier. Standard Oracle database software runs on the database servers, while Oracle's disk management software runs on the storage servers. The components on both tiers use a protocol called iDB to talk to each other. The next two sections provide a brief introduction to the software stack that resides on both tiers.

Database Server Software

As previously discussed, the database servers run Oracle Linux. The database servers also run standard Oracle 11g Release 2 or Oracle 12c Release 1 software. There is no special version of the database software that is different from the software that is run on any other platform. This is actually a unique and significant feature of Exadata, compared to competing data warehouse appliance products. In essence, it means that any application that can run on Oracle 11gR2/12cR1 can run on Exadata without requiring any changes to the application. While there is code that is specific to the Exadata platform, iDB for example, Oracle chose to make it a part of the standard distribution. The software is aware of whether it is accessing Exadata storage, and this "awareness" allows it to make use of the Exadata-specific optimizations when accessing Exadata storage.

Oracle Automatic Storage Management (ASM) is a key component of the software stack on the database servers. It provides file system and volume management capability for Exadata storage. It is required because the storage devices are not visible to the database servers. There is no direct mechanism for processes on the database servers to open or read a file on Exadata storage cells. ASM also provides redundancy to the storage by mirroring data blocks, using either normal redundancy (two copies) or high redundancy (three copies). This is an important feature because the disks are physically located on multiple storage servers. The ASM redundancy provides mirroring across the storage cells, which allows for the complete loss of a storage server without an interruption to the databases running on the platform. Other than the operating system disks on the database servers, there is no form of hardware- or software-based RAID that protects the data on Exadata storage servers. The data mirroring protection is provided exclusively by ASM.

While RAC is generally installed on Exadata database servers, it is not actually required. However, RAC does provide many benefits in terms of high availability and scalability. For systems that require more CPU or memory resources than can be supplied by a single server, RAC is the path to those additional resources.

The database servers and the storage servers communicate using the Intelligent Database protocol (iDB). iDB implements what Oracle refers to as a *function shipping* architecture. This term is used to describe how iDB ships information about the SQL statement being executed to the storage cells and then returns processed data (prefiltered, for example), instead of data blocks, directly to the requesting processes. In this mode, iDB can limit the data returned to the database server to only those rows and columns that satisfy the query. The function shipping mode is only available when full scans are performed. iDB can also send and retrieve full blocks when offloading is not possible (or not desirable). In this mode, iDB is used like a normal I/O protocol for fetching entire Oracle blocks and returning them to the Oracle buffer cache on the database servers. For completeness, we should mention that it is really not a simple one-way-or-the-other scenario. There are cases where we can get a combination of these two behaviors. We will discuss that in more detail in Chapter 2.

iDB uses the Reliable Datagram Sockets (RDS) protocol and, of course, uses the InfiniBand fabric between the database servers and storage cells. RDS is a low-latency, low-overhead protocol that provides a significant reduction in CPU usage compared to protocols such as UDP. RDS has been around for some time and predates Exadata by several years. The protocol facilitates an option to use direct memory access model for interprocess communication, which allows it to avoid the latency and CPU overhead associated with traditional TCP traffic.

It is important to understand that no storage devices are directly presented to the operating systems on the database servers. Therefore, there are no operating-system calls to open files, read blocks from them, or perform the other usual tasks. This also means that standard operating-system utilities like `iostat` will not be useful in monitoring your database servers, because the processes running there will not be issuing I/O calls to the database files. Here's some output that illustrates this fact:

```
ACOLVIN@DBM011> @whoami

USERNAME              USER#         SID     SERIAL# PREV_HASH_VALUE SCHEMANAME       OS_PID
--------------- ----------- ----------- ----------- --------------- ---------- -----------
ACOLVIN                  89         591       36280      1668665417    ACOLVIN       103148

ACOLVIN@DBM011> select /* avgskew.sql */ avg(pk_col) from acolvin.skew a where col1 > 0;

...

> strace -cp 103148
Process 103148 attached - interrupt to quit
^CProcess 103148 detached
```

```
% time     seconds  usecs/call     calls    errors syscall
------ ----------- ----------- --------- --------- ----------------
 96.76    0.000358           0       750       375 setsockopt
  3.24    0.000012           0       425           getrusage
  0.00    0.000000           0        53         3 read
  0.00    0.000000           0         2           write
  0.00    0.000000           0        24        12 open
  0.00    0.000000           0        12           close
  0.00    0.000000           0       225           poll
  0.00    0.000000           0        48           lseek
  0.00    0.000000           0         4           mmap
  0.00    0.000000           0        10           rt_sigprocmask
  0.00    0.000000           0         3           rt_sigreturn
  0.00    0.000000           0         5           setitimer
  0.00    0.000000           0       388           sendmsg
  0.00    0.000000           0       976       201 recvmsg
  0.00    0.000000           0         1           semctl
  0.00    0.000000           0        12           fcntl
  0.00    0.000000           0        31           times
  0.00    0.000000           0         3           semtimedop
------ ----------- ----------- --------- --------- ----------------
100.00    0.000370                  2972       591 total
```

In this listing we have run `strace` on a user's foreground process (sometimes called a shadow process). This is the process that's responsible for retrieving data on behalf of a user. As you can see, the vast majority of system calls captured by `strace` are network-related (`setsockopt`). By contrast, on a non-Exadata platform we mostly see disk I/O-related events, primarily some form of the read call. Here's some output from a non-Exadata platform for comparison:

```
ACOLVIN@AC12> @whoami

USERNAME             USER#        SID    SERIAL#  PREV_HASH_VALUE  SCHEMANAME  OS_PID
------------- --------- ---------- ---------- ---------------  ---------- -------
ACOLVIN                103        141         13       1029988163     ACOLVIN   57449

ACOLVIN@AC12> select /* avgskew.sql */ avg(pk_col) from acolvin.skew a where col1 > 0;

AVG(PK_COL)
-----------
 16093749.8

...

[oracle@homer ~]$ strace -cp 57449
Process 57449 attached - interrupt to quit
Process 57449 detached
```

```
% time      seconds  usecs/call     calls    errors syscall
------ ----------- ----------- --------- --------- ---------------
 99.44    0.029174           4      7709              pread
  0.40    0.000117           0      3921              clock_gettime
  0.16    0.000046           0      1314              times
  0.00    0.000000           0         3              write
  0.00    0.000000           0         7              mmap
  0.00    0.000000           0         2              munmap
  0.00    0.000000           0        43              getrusage
------ ----------- ----------- --------- --------- ---------------
100.00    0.029337                 12999              total
```

Notice that the main system call captured on the non-Exadata platform is I/O-related (`pread`). The point of the previous two listings is to show that there is a very different mechanism in play in the way data stored on disks is accessed with Exadata.

Storage Server Software

Cell Services (`cellsrv`) is the primary software that runs on the storage cells. It is a multithreaded program that services I/O requests from a database server. Those requests can be handled by returning processed data or by returning complete blocks depending on the request. `cellsrv` also implements the I/O Resource Manager (IORM), which can be used to ensure that I/O bandwidth is distributed to the various databases and consumer groups appropriately.

There are two other programs that run continuously on Exadata storage cells. Management Server (MS) is a Java program that provides the interface between `cellsrv` and the Cell Command Line Interface (`cellcli`) utility. MS also provides the interface between `cellsrv` and the Grid Control Exadata plug-in (which is implemented as a set of `cellcli` commands that are run via `ssh`). The second utility is Restart Server (RS). RS is actually a set of processes that are responsible for monitoring the other processes and restarting them if necessary. ExaWatcher (previously OSWatcher) is also installed on the storage cells for collecting historical operating system statistics using standard Unix utilities such as `vmstat` and `netstat`. Note that Oracle does not authorize the installation of any additional software on the storage servers.

One of the first things you are likely to want to do when you first encounter Exadata is to log on to the storage cells and see what is actually running. Unfortunately, the storage servers are generally off-limits to everyone except the designated system administers or DBAs. Here is a quick listing showing the abbreviated output generated by a `ps` command on an active storage server:

```
> ps -eo ruser,pid,ppid,cmd

RUSER      PID  PPID CMD
root      5555  4823 /usr/bin/perl /opt/oracle.ExaWatcher/ExecutorExaWatcher.pl
root      6025  5555 sh -c /opt/oracle.ExaWatcher/ExaWatcherCleanup.sh
root      6026  6025 /bin/bash /opt/oracle.ExaWatcher/ExaWatcherCleanup.sh
root      6033  5555 /usr/bin/perl /opt/oracle.ExaWatcher/ExecutorExaWatcher.pl
root      6034  6033 sh -c /opt/oracle.cellos/ExadataDiagCollector.sh
root      6036  6034 /bin/bash /opt/oracle.cellos/ExadataDiagCollector.sh
root      6659  8580 /opt/oracle/../cellsrv/bin/cellrsomt
                     -rs_conf /opt/oracle/../cellinit.ora
                                         -ms_conf /opt/oracle/../cellrsms.state
                                         -cellsrv_conf /opt/oracle/../cellrsos.state -debug 0
```

```
root      6661  6659 /opt/oracle/cell/cellsrv/bin/cellsrv 100 5000 9 5042
root      7603     1 /opt/oracle/cell/cellofl-11.2.3.3.1_LINUX.X64_141206/../celloflsrv
                     -startup 1 0 1 5042 6661 SYS_112331_141117 cell
root      7606     1 /opt/oracle/cell/cellofl-12.1.2.1.0_LINUX.X64_141206.1/../celloflsrv
                     -startup 2 0 1 5042 6661 SYS_121210_141206 cell
root      8580     1 /opt/oracle/cell/cellsrv/bin/cellrssrm -ms 1 -cellsrv 1
root      8587  8580 /opt/oracle/../cellrsbmt
                     -rs_conf /opt/oracle/../cellinit.ora
                                         -ms_conf /opt/oracle/../cellrsms.state
                                         -cellsrv_conf /opt/oracle/../cellrsos.state -debug 0
root      8588  8580 /opt/oracle/cell/cellsrv/bin/cellrsmmt
                     -rs_conf /opt/oracle/../cellinit.ora
                                         -ms_conf /opt/oracle/../cellrsms.state
                                         -cellsrv_conf /opt/oracle/../cellrsos.state -debug 0
root      8590  8587 /opt/oracle/cell/cellsrv/bin/cellrsbkm
                     -rs_conf /opt/oracle/../cellinit.ora
                                         -ms_conf /opt/oracle/../cellrsms.state
                                         -cellsrv_conf /opt/oracle/../cellrsos.state -debug 0
root      8591  8588 /bin/sh /opt/oracle/../startWebLogic.sh
root      8597  8590 /opt/oracle/../cellrssmt
                     -rs_conf /opt/oracle/../cellinit.ora
                                         -ms_conf /opt/oracle/../cellrsms.state
                                         -cellsrv_conf /opt/oracle/../cellrsos.state -debug 0
root      8663  8591 /usr/java/jdk1.7.0_72/bin/java -client -Xms256m -Xmx512m
                     -XX:CompileThreshold=8000 -XX:PermSize=128m -XX:MaxPermSize=256m
                                         -Dweblogic.Name=msServer
                                         -Djava.security.policy=/opt/oracle/../weblogic.policy
                                         -XX:-UseLargePages -XX:Parallel
root     11449  5555 sh -c /usr/bin/mpstat -P ALL  5  720
root     11450 11449 /usr/bin/mpstat -P ALL 5 720
root     11457  5555 sh -c /usr/bin/iostat -t -x  5  720
root     11458 11457 /usr/bin/iostat -t -x 5 720
root     12175  5555 sh -c /opt/oracle/cell/cellsrv/bin/cellsrvstat
root     12176 12175 /opt/oracle/cell/cellsrv/bin/cellsrvstat
root     14386 14385 /usr/bin/top -b -d 5 -n 720
root     14530 14529 /bin/sh /opt/oracle.ExaWatcher/FlexIntervalMode.sh
                     /opt/oracle.ExaWatcher/RDSinfoExaWatcher.sh
root     14596 14595 /bin/sh /opt/oracle.ExaWatcher/FlexIntervalMode.sh
                     /opt/oracle.ExaWatcher/NetstatExaWatcher.sh 5 720
root     17315  5555 sh -c /usr/bin/vmstat  5  2
root     17316 17315 /usr/bin/vmstat 5 2
root     23881  5555 sh -c /opt/oracle.ExaWatcher/FlexIntervalMode.sh
                     '/opt/oracle.ExaWatcher/LsofExaWatcher.sh'  120  30
root     23882 23881 /bin/sh /opt/oracle.ExaWatcher/FlexIntervalMode.sh
                     /opt/oracle.ExaWatcher/LsofExaWatcher.sh 120 30
```

As you can see, there are a number of processes that look like cellrsv*XXX*. These are the processes that make up the Restart Server. The first bolded process is cellsrv itself. The next two bolded processes are the offload servers (discussed in further detail in Chapter 2), which were introduced in the 12c version of the Exadata Storage Server software. Also notice the last two bolded processes; this is the WebLogic program that we refer to as Management Server. Finally, you will see several processes associated with ExaWatcher. Note also that all the processes are started by root. While there are a couple of other semi-privileged accounts on the storage servers, it is clearly not a system that is set up for users to log on to.

Another interesting way to look at related processes is to use the ps -H command, which provides an indented list of processes showing how they are related to each other. You could work this out for yourself by building a tree based on the relationship between the process ID (PID) and parent process ID (PPID) in the previous text, but the -H option makes that a lot easier. Here's an edited snippet of output from a ps -efH command:

```
cellrssrm <= main Restart Server
   cellrsbmt
      cellrsbkm
         cellrssmt
   cellrsmmt
      startWebLogic.sh <= Management Server
         cellrsomt
            cellsrv
```

It's also interesting to see what resources are being consumed on the storage servers. Here's a snippet of output from top:

```
top - 12:01:30 up 19 days, 17:17,  1 user,  load average: 0.49, 0.26, 0.21
Tasks: 428 total,   4 running, 424 sleeping,   0 stopped,   0 zombie
Cpu(s): 11.1%us,  1.7%sy,  0.0%ni, 83.8%id,  3.3%wa,  0.0%hi,  0.0%si,  0.0%st
Mem:  65963336k total, 21307292k used, 44656044k free,   140216k buffers
Swap:  2097080k total,        0k used,  2097080k free,  1235320k cached

  PID USER      PR  NI  VIRT  RES  SHR S  %CPU  %MEM   TIME+      COMMAND
 7988 root      20   0 22.1g 7.1g  12m S 246.3  11.3   5581:38    cellsrv
 7982 root      20   0 1621m 385m  21m S   5.3   0.6   851:07.47  java
 8192 root      20   0 67960 5232  972 R   2.6   0.0     0:00.08  sh
  394 root      20   0 13016 1408  832 R   0.7   0.0     0:01.33  top
```

The output from top shows that cellsrv is using more than one full CPU core. This is common on busy systems and is due to the multithreaded nature of the cellsrv process, which makes it possible to run on multiple CPU cores at the same time.

Software Architecture

In this section, we will briefly discuss the key software components and how they are connected in the Exadata architecture. There are components that run on both the database and the storage tiers. Figure 1-3 depicts the overall architecture of the Exadata platform.

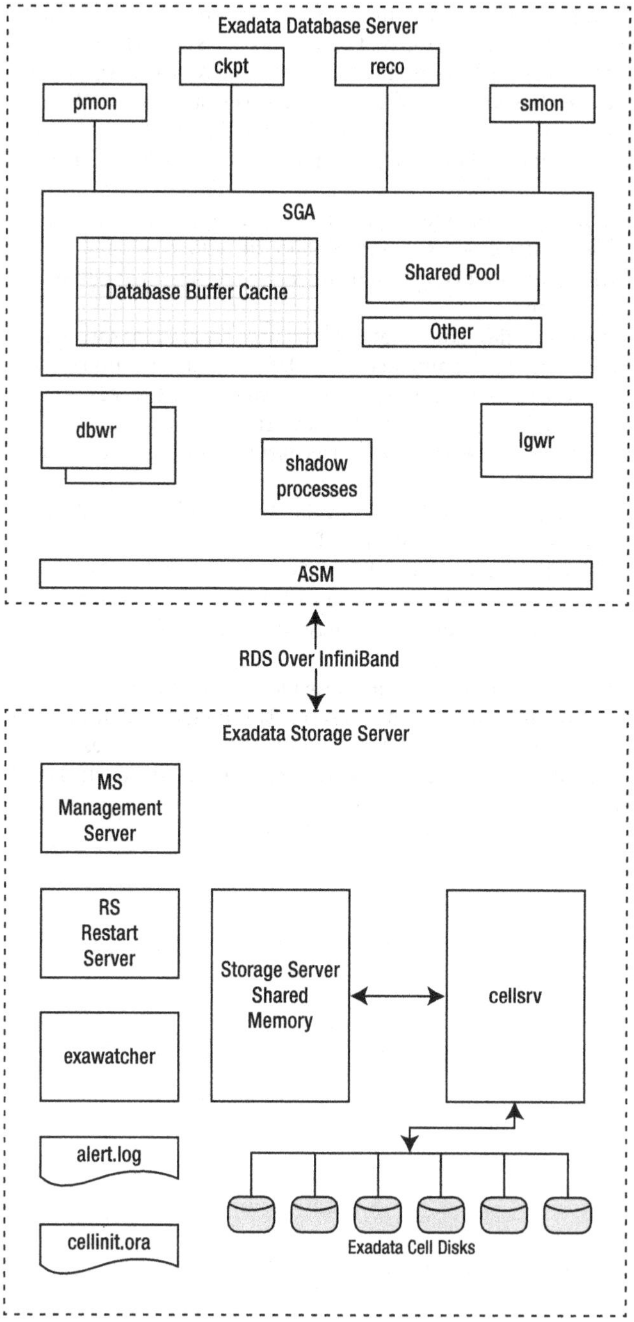

***Figure 1-3.** Exadata architecture diagram*

The top half of the diagram shows the key components on one of the database servers, while the bottom half shows the key components on one of the storage servers. The top half of the diagram should look pretty familiar, as it is standard Oracle database architecture. It shows the System Global Area (SGA), which contains the buffer cache and the shared pool. It also shows several of the key processes, such as Log Writer (LGWR) and Database Writer (DBWR). There are many more processes, of course, and much more detailed views of the shared memory that could be provided, but this should give you a basic picture of how things look on the database server.

The bottom half of the diagram shows the components on one of the storage servers. The architecture on the storage servers is pretty simple. There is one master process (`cellsrv`), and the offload servers that handle all the communication to and from the database servers. There are also a handful of ancillary processes for managing and monitoring the environment.

One of the things you may notice in the architecture diagram is that `cellsrv` uses an `init.ora` file and has an alert log. In fact, the storage software bears a striking resemblance to an Oracle database. This should not be too surprising. The `cellinit.ora` file contains a set of parameters that are evaluated when `cellsrv` is started. The alert log is used to write a record of notable events, much like an alert log on an Oracle database. Note also that Automatic Diagnostic Repository (ADR) is included as part of the storage software for capturing and reporting diagnostic information.

Also notice that there is a stand-alone process that is not attached to any database instance (`DISKMON`), which performs several tasks related to Exadata Storage. Although it is called `DISKMON`, it is really a network- and cell-monitoring process that checks to verify that the cells are alive. `DISKMON` is also responsible to propagating Database Resource Manager (DBRM) plans to the storage servers. `DISKMON` also has a single slave process per instance, which is responsible for communicating between ASM and the database it is responsible for.

The connection between the database server and the storage server is provided by the InfiniBand fabric. All communication between the two tiers is carried by this transport mechanism. This includes writes via the DBWR processes and LGWR process and reads carried out by the user foreground (or shadow) processes.

Figure 1-4 provides another systematic view of the architecture, which focuses on the software stack and how it spans multiple servers in both the database grid and the storage grid.

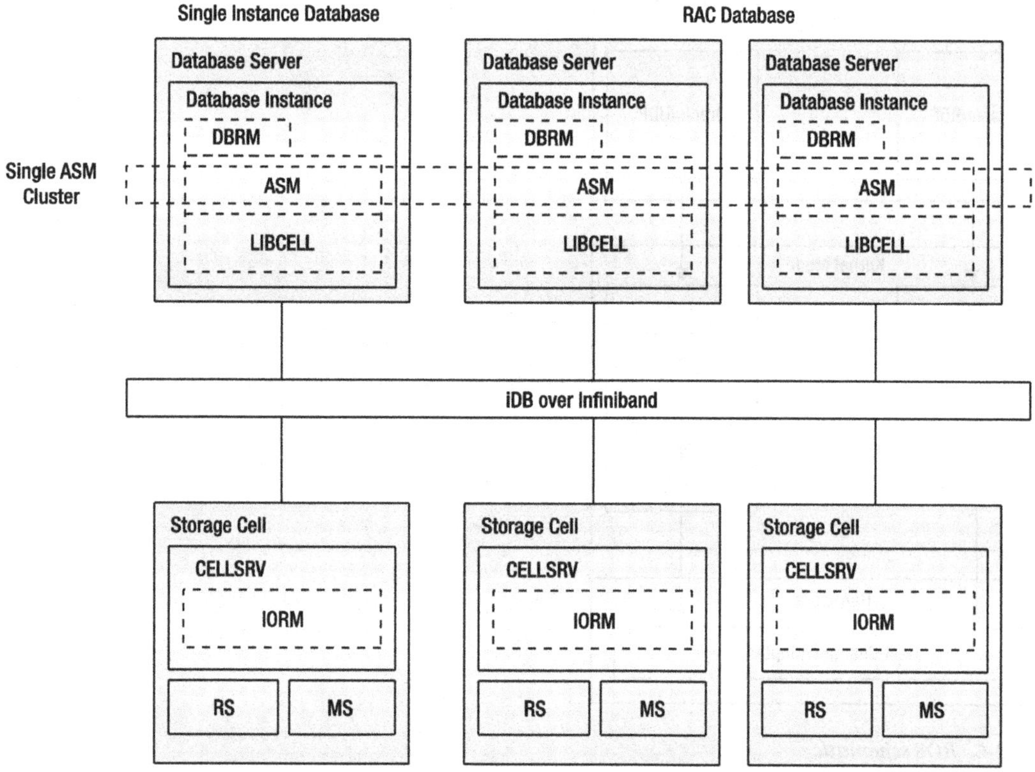

***Figure 1-4.** Exadata software architecture*

As we've discussed, ASM is a key component. Notice that we have drawn it as an object that cuts across all the communication lines between the two tiers. This is meant to indicate that ASM provides the mapping between the files and the objects that the database knows about on the storage layer. ASM does not actually sit between the storage and the database, though, and it is not a layer in the stack that the processes must touch for each "disk access."

Figure 1-4 also shows the relationship between DBRM running on the instances on the database servers and IORM, which is implemented inside `cellsrv` running on the storage servers.

The final major component in Figure 1-4 is `LIBCELL`, which is a library that is linked with the Oracle kernel. `LIBCELL` has the code that knows how to request data via iDB. This provides a very nonintrusive mechanism to allow the Oracle kernel to talk to the storage tier via network-based calls instead of operating system reads and writes. iDB is implemented on top of the RDS protocol provided by the OpenFabrics Enterprise Distribution. This is a low-latency, low-CPU-overhead protocol that provides interprocess communications. You may also see this protocol referred to in some of the Oracle marketing material as the Zero-loss Zero-copy (ZDP) InfiniBand protocol. Figure 1-5 is a basic schematic showing why the RDS protocol is more efficient than using a traditional TCP based protocol like UDP.

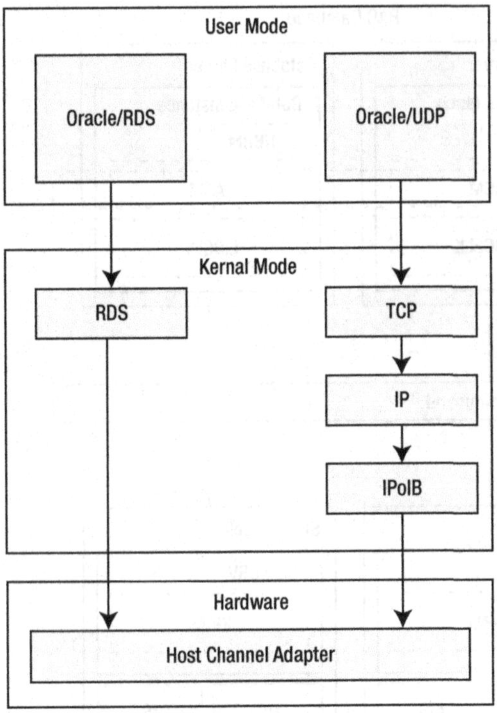

Figure 1-5. *RDS schematic*

As you can see from the diagram, using the RDS protocol to bypass the TCP processing cuts out a portion of the overhead required to transfer data across the network. Note that the RDS protocol is also used for interconnect traffic between RAC nodes.

Summary

Exadata is a tightly integrated combination of hardware and software. There is nothing magical about the hardware components. The majority of the performance benefits come from the way the components are integrated and the software that is implemented at the storage layer. In the Chapter 2, we'll delve into the offloading concept, which is what sets Exadata apart from all other platforms that run Oracle databases.

CHAPTER 2

Offloading / Smart Scan

Offloading is *the* key differentiator of the Exadata platform and has sparked excitement with us since we laid hands on our first Exadata system. *Offloading* is what makes Exadata different from every other platform that Oracle runs on. The term offloading refers to the concept of moving processing from the database layer to the storage layer. It is also the key paradigm shift provided by the Exadata platform. But it is more than just moving work in terms of CPU usage. The primary benefit of offloading is the reduction in the volume of data that must be returned to the database server—one of the major bottlenecks of most large databases.

The terms *offloading* and *Smart Scan* are used somewhat interchangeably. *Offloading* is a better description in our opinion, as it refers to the fact that part of the traditional SQL processing done by the database can be "offloaded" from the database layer to the storage layer. It is a rather generic term, though, and is used to refer to many optimizations that are not even related to SQL processing, including improving backup and restore operations, file initialization, and more.

Smart Scan, on the other hand, is a more focused term in that it refers only to Exadata's optimization of SQL statements. These optimizations come into play for scan operations—typically full segment scans. A more specific definition of a Smart Scan would be any section of the Oracle kernel code that is covered by the Smart Scan wait events. It is important to make the distinction that part of the kernel code is executed on the storage cells. There are a few wait events that include the term *Smart Scan* in their names: Cell Smart Table Scan, Cell Smart Index Scan, and, more recently, Cell External Table Smart Scan. (The latter requires additional technology outside the Exadata rack and will not be covered here.) You can read more about these wait events in detail in Chapter 10. While it is true that the term *Smart Scan* has a bit of a marketing flavor, it does have specific context when referring to the code covered by these wait events. At any rate, while the terms are somewhat interchangeable, keep in mind that *offloading* can refer to more than just speeding up SQL statement execution.

This chapter focuses on Smart Scan optimizations. We will discuss the various optimizations that can come into play with Smart Scans, the mechanics of how they work, and the requirements that must be met for them to occur. We will also give you a sneak peek at some techniques that can be used to help you determine whether Smart Scans have occurred for a given SQL statement or not. For those interested in digging deeper, Chapters 10, 11, and 12 provide a lot more background on Exadata-specific wait events, session counters, and performance investigation. The other offloading optimizations will only be mentioned briefly, as they are covered elsewhere in the book.

Why Offloading Is Important

We cannot emphasize enough how important the concept of offloading is. The idea—and actual implementation—of moving database processing to the storage tier is a giant leap forward. The concept has been around for some time. In fact, rumor has it that Oracle approached at least one of the large SAN manufacturers several years ago with the idea. The manufacturer was apparently not interested at the time, and Oracle decided to pursue the idea on its own. Oracle subsequently partnered with HP to build the original Exadata V1, which incorporated the offloading concept. Fast-forward a couple of years, and you have Oracle's acquisition of Sun Microsystems. This acquisition put the company in a position to offer an integrated stack of hardware and software and gave it complete control over which features to incorporate into the product.

Offloading is important because one of the major bottlenecks on large databases is the time it takes to transfer the large volumes of data necessary to satisfy data-warehouse (DWH)-type queries between the disk systems and the database servers (that is, because of bandwidth). These DWH-queries are sometimes referred to as *Decision Support System (DSS) queries*. You can find both terms in this book—they essentially mean the same thing. This bottleneck is partly a hardware architecture issue, but the bigger issue is the sheer volume of data that is moved by traditional Oracle databases. The Oracle database is very fast and very clever about how it processes data, but for queries that access a large amount of data, getting the data to the database can still take a long time. So, as any good performance analyst would do, Oracle focused on reducing the time spent on the thing that accounted for the majority of the elapsed time. During the analysis, the Oracle team realized that every query that required disk access was very inefficient in terms of how much data had to be returned to and processed by the database servers. Oracle has made a living by developing the best cache-management software available, but, for very large data sets, it is just not practical to keep everything in memory on the database servers. Even though modern Intel servers can accommodate multiple TB of memory, the growth of data volume has long since out-paced DRAM capacity. This does not mean that technology does not advance. Modern processors—such as the Ivy-Bridge E7-v2 Xeons found in the Exadata x4-8— support up to 6TB DRAM each for a total of 12TB DRAM in a two-node cluster. This is quite impressive!

THE IN-MEMORY COLUMN STORE

Actually, Oracle started addressing the larger memory capacity that has become available recently with the release of 12.1.0.2. This is a rather unusual patchset as it includes a lot of new functionality. One of the most heavily marketed features introduced the in-memory column store, an additional cost option. It allows the database administrator to create a new area in the SGA, named the *in-memory area*, to store information pertaining to specific segments. Unlike pure in-memory databases, Oracle's solution is a hybrid, able to access data from memory and disk if needed. The way segments are stored in the in-memory store is different from the way Oracle persists information on disk in form of the standard block. To make better use of the memory, you can elect to compress the data as well.

The in-memory feature is very exciting, but deserves its own book—we mention it only in passing in this book.

Imagine the fastest query you can think of: a single column from a single row from a single table where you actually know where the row is stored. In row-major format, the quickest way to access an individual row is by the means of using the so-called *ROWID*. Externalized as a pseudo-column, a ROWID indicates the data object number, the data file number, the data block, and the row in the block. On a traditional Oracle database, at least one block of data has to be read into memory (typically 8K) to get the one column. Assume for a moment that your table stores an average of 50 rows per block. After reading that particular block from disk, you just transferred 49 extra rows to the database server that are simply overhead for this query. Multiply that by a billion and you start to get an idea of the magnitude of the problem in a large data warehouse. Eliminating the time spent on transferring completely unnecessary data between the storage and the database tier is the main problem that Exadata was designed to solve.

Offloading is the approach that was used to solve the problem of excessive time spent moving irrelevant data between the tiers. Offloading has three design goals, although the primary goal far outweighs the others in importance:

- Reduce the volume of data transferred from disk systems to the database servers
- Reduce CPU usage on database servers
- Reduce/eliminate disk access times at the storage layer

Reducing the volume was the main focus and primary goal. The majority of the optimizations introduced by offloading contribute to this goal. Reducing CPU load is important as well, but it is not the primary benefit provided by Exadata and, therefore, takes a back seat to reducing the volume of data transferred. (As you will see, however, decompression is a notable exception to that generalization, as it is usually performed on the storage servers.) Several optimizations to reduce disk access time were also introduced. While some of the results can be quite stunning, we do not consider them to be the bread-and-butter optimizations of Exadata.

Exadata is an integrated hardware/software product that depends on both components to provide substantial performance improvement over non-Exadata platforms. However, the performance benefits of the software component dwarf the benefits provided by the hardware. Here is an example:

```
SQL> alter session set cell_offload_processing=false;

Session altered.

Elapsed: 00:00:00.00

SQL> select /*+ gather_plan_statistics monitor statement001 */
  2  count(*) from sales where amount_sold = 1;

  COUNT(*)
----------
   3006406

Elapsed: 00:00:33.15

SQL> alter session set cell_offload_processing=true;

Session altered.

SQL> select /*+ gather_plan_statistics monitor statement002 */
  2  count(*) from sales where amount_sold = 1;

  COUNT(*)
----------
   3006406

Elapsed: 00:00:04.68
```

This example shows the performance of a scan against a single, partitioned table. The SALES table has been created using Dominic Giles's shwizard, which is part of his popular Swingbench benchmark suite. In this particular case, the table has 294,575,180 rows stored in 68 partitions.

The query was first executed with offloading disabled, effectively using all the hardware benefits of Exadata and none of the software benefits. You will notice that even on Exadata hardware like this very powerful X4-2 half rack, this query took a bit more than half a minute. This is despite the fact that data is striped and mirrored across 7 cells, or in other words 7 * 12 disks, and likewise 7 * 3.2TB raw capacity for Smart Flash Cache.

After subsequent executions of the above script, more and more data was transparently cached in Smart Flash Cache, turbo-boosting the read performance to levels we did not dream of in earlier versions of the Exadata software. During the 33-second scan of the table, literally all data came from Flash Cache:

```
STAT    cell flash cache read hits              31,769
STAT    physical read IO requests               31,776
STAT    physical read bytes             15,669,272,576
```

■ **Note** You can read more about session statistics and the `mystats` script used to display them in Chapter 11.

In the first edition of this book, we used a similar example query to demonstrate the difference between offloading enabled and switched off, and the difference was larger—partially due to the fact that Smart Scans at the time did not benefit from Smart Flash Cache by default. The automatic caching of large I/O requests in Flash Cache is covered in detail in Chapter 5.

After re-enabling Offloading, the query completed in substantially less time. Obviously the hardware in play was the same in both executions. The point is that it is the software's ability via Offloading that made the difference.

A GENERIC VERSION OF EXADATA?

The topic of building a generic version of Exadata comes up frequently. The idea is to build a hardware platform that in some way mimics Exadata, presumably at a lower cost than what Oracle charges for Exadata. Of course, the focus of these proposals is to replicate the hardware part of Exadata because the software component cannot be replicated. Nevertheless, the idea of building your own Exadata sounds attractive because the individual hardware components may be purchased for less than the package price Oracle charges. There are a few points to consider, however. Before going into more detail, the two generic workload types should be named: *OLTP*, which stands for *Online Transaction Processing*, and *DSS*, which is short for *Decision Support System*. Exadata was designed with the latter when it came out, but significant enhancements allow it to compete with pure-OLTP platforms now. More importantly, though, Exadata can be used for mixed-workload environments, an area where most other platforms will struggle. Let's focus on a few noteworthy points when it comes to "rolling your own" system:

1. The hardware component that tends to get the most attention is the Flash Cache. You can buy a SAN or NAS with a large cache. The middle-sized Exadata package (half rack) in a standard configuration supplies around 44.8 terabytes of Flash Cache across the storage servers. That is a pretty big number, but what is cached is as important as the size of the cache itself. Exadata is smart enough not to cache data that is unlikely to benefit from caching. For example, it is not helpful to cache mirror copies of blocks since Oracle usually only reads primary copies (unless a corruption is detected). Oracle has a long history of writing software to manage caches. Hence, it should come as no surprise that it does a very good job of not

flushing everything out when a large table scan is processed so that frequently accessed blocks would tend to remain in the cache. The result of this database-aware caching is that a normal SAN or NAS would need a much larger cache to compete with Exadata's Flash Cache. Keep in mind also that the volume of data you will need to store will be much larger on non-Exadata storage because you won't be able to use Hybrid Columnar Compression (HCC).

2. The more important aspect of the hardware, which oddly enough is occasionally overlooked by the DIY proposals, is the throughput between the storage and database tiers. The Exadata hardware stack provides a more balanced pathway between storage and database servers than most current implementations, so the second area of focus is generally the bandwidth between the tiers. Increasing the effective throughput between storage and the database server is not as simple as it sounds. Exadata provides the increased throughput via InfiniBand and the Reliable Datagram Sockets (RDS) protocol. Oracle developed the iDB protocol to run across the InfiniBand network. The iDB protocol is not available to databases running on non-Exadata hardware. Therefore, some other means for increasing bandwidth between the tiers is necessary. For most users, this means either going down the Ethernet path (iSCSI, NFS) over 10Gbit Ethernet at the time of writing. The ever-so-present Fibre Channel offers alternatives in the range of 16Gbit/s as well. In any case, you will need multiple interface cards in the servers (which will need to be attached via a fast bus). The storage device (or devices) will also have to be capable of delivering enough output to match the pipe and consumption capabilities. (This is what Oracle means when it talks about a balanced configuration, which you get with the standard rack setup, as opposed to the X5-2 elastic configuration). You will also have to decide which hardware components to use and test the whole solution to make sure that all the various parts you pick work well together without having a major bottleneck or driver problems at any point in the path from disk to database server. This is especially true for the use of InfiniBand, which has become more commonplace. The SCSI RDMA is a very attractive protocol to attach storage effectively, but the certification from storage system to HCA to OFED drivers in the kernel can make the whole endeavor quite an effort.

3. The third component that the DIY proposals generally address is the database servers themselves. The Exadata hardware specifications are readily available, so it is a simple matter to buy exactly the same Sun models. Unfortunately, you might need to plan for more CPU power since you cannot offload any processing to the CPUs on the Exadata storage servers. This, in turn, will drive up the number of Oracle database licenses. You might also want to invest more in memory since you cannot rely on Smart Scans to reduce the amount of data from the storage solution you chose. On the other hand, when it comes to consolidating many databases on your platform, you might have found the number of CPU cores in the earlier dash two systems limited. There has, however, always been the option to use the dash eight servers that provide some of the most densely packaged systems available with the x86-64 architecture. Oracle has increased the core count with every generation, matching the advance in dual socket systems provided by Intel. The current generation of X5-2 Exadata systems offer dual-socket systems with 36 cores/72 threads.

4. And last but not least, it is again important to emphasize the benefit of HCC. As you can read in Chapter 3, HCC is well worth considering—not only from the reduction of storage point of view, but also because of the potential of scanning the data without having to decompress in the database session, again freeing CPU cycles (see point 3). Thanks to the columnar format employed in HCC segments, it can perform analytic queries very efficiently, too.

Assuming one could match the Exadata hardware performance in every area, it would still not be possible to come close to the performance provided by Exadata. That is because it is the (cell) software that provides the lion's share of the performance benefit of Exadata. The benefits of the Exadata software are easily demonstrated by disabling offloading on Exadata and running comparisons. This demonstration allows us to see the performance of the hardware without the software enhancements. A big part of what Exadata software does is eliminate totally unnecessary work, such as transferring columns and rows that will eventually be discarded back to the database servers.

As the saying goes, "The fastest way to do anything is to not do it at all!"

What Offloading Includes

There are many optimizations that can be summarized under the offloading banner. This chapter focuses on SQL statement optimizations that are implemented via Smart Scans. The major Smart Scan optimizations are column projection, predicate filtering, and storage indexes (there are of course more!). The primary goal of most of the Smart Scan optimizations is to reduce the amount of data that needs to be transmitted back to the database servers during scan execution. However, some of the optimizations also attempt to offload CPU-intensive operations—decompression, for example. We will not cover optimizations that are not related to SQL statement processing in this chapter, such as Smart File Creation and RMAN-related optimizations. Those topics will be covered in more detail elsewhere in the book. To give you a better overview of the things to come, Figure 2-1 shows the cumulative features you can see when Smart-Scanning a segment.

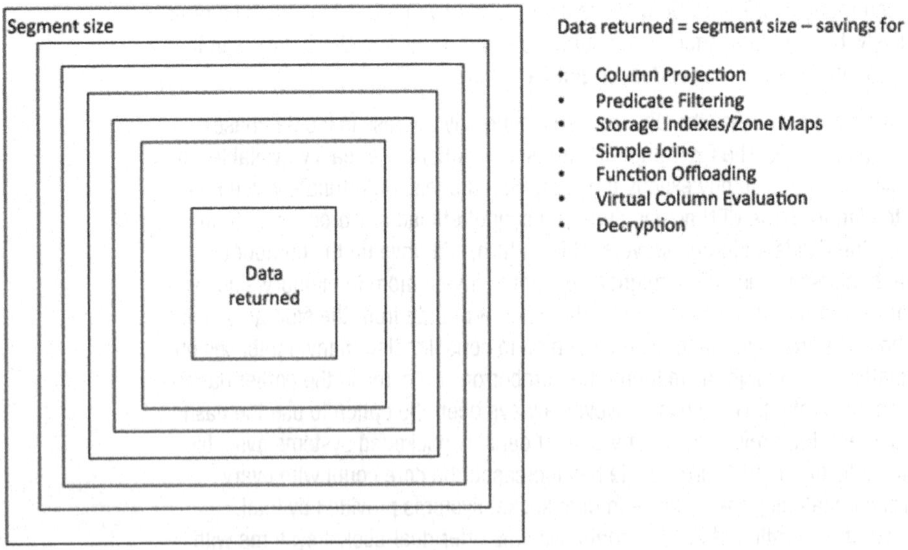

Figure 2-1. *Potential Smart Scan optimizations*

These features do not necessarily apply for every single query, and not necessarily in that order. Therefore, the amount of "data returned" is a moving target. As you can read in Chapter 10, the instrumentation of Smart Scans is not perfect and leaves some detail to be desired. The next sections will discuss the various optimizations found in Figure 2-1.

One very important change that is not listed in Figure 2-1 took place with Exadata 11.2.3.3.0. This change is termed *Automatic Flash Caching for Table Scan Workloads* and has a dramatic effect on query performance. Previously, Smart Scans would not make use of the Exadata Smart Flash Cache unless a segment was specifically marked to make use of it by changing the `cell_flash_cache` attribute set to `KEEP` to the storage clause of the segment. This served two main purposes: First, the amount of Flash Cache was not abundant in earlier Exadata generations and, secondly, the available space was better used for OLTP-style workloads where small, single block I/O dominates. In more recent Exadata generations, there is a lot more Flash Cache available; the capacity doubles with every new generation. Currently, the X5-2 high-capacity storage server feature 4 x 1.6TB F160 Flash cards attached via NVMe to the PCIe bus. The X5-2 high-performance storage server is the first one to only have PCIe Flash cards and no spinning disk.

In the following sections, we have occasionally used performance information to prove a point. Please do not let that confuse you. Chapters 10–12 will explain these in much more detail than we can provide here. When discussing offloading, the authors sometimes face the dreaded chicken-and-egg problem. On the other hand, it is not possible to write a 100-page chapter to include all the content that might be relevant, either. Please feel free to flip between this chapter and the performance chapters just mentioned, or simply take the performance counters as additional and, hopefully, useful insights.

■ **Caution** The authors will make use of underscore parameters in this section quite heavily to enable/disable certain aspects of the Exadata system. These parameters are listed here for educational and academic purposes only, as well as to demonstrate the effects of a particular optimization. Please do not set any underscore parameters in an Oracle system without explicit blessings from Oracle Support.

Column Projection

The term *column projection* refers to Exadata's ability to limit the volume of data transferred between the storage tier and the database tier by only returning columns of interest. That is, those in the select list are necessary for join operations on the database tier. If your query requests five columns from a 100-column table, Exadata can eliminate most of the data that would be returned to the database servers by non-Exadata storage. This feature is a much bigger deal than you might expect, and it can have a very significant impact on response times. Here is an example:

```
SQL> alter session set "_serial_direct_read" = always;

Session altered.

Elapsed: 00:00:00.00
SQL> alter session set cell_offload_processing = false;

Session altered.

Elapsed: 00:00:00.00
SQL> select count(distinct seller) from sales;
```

```
COUNT(DISTINCTSELLER)
---------------------
                 1000

Elapsed: 00:00:53.55
SQL> alter session set cell_offload_processing = true;

Session altered.

Elapsed: 00:00:00.01
SQL> select count(distinct seller) from sales;

COUNT(DISTINCTSELLER)
---------------------
                 1000

Elapsed: 00:00:28.84
```

This example deserves some discussion. To force direct path reads—a prerequisite for Smart Scans—the session parameter _SERIAL_DIRECT_READ is set to ALWAYS (more on that later). Next, Smart Scans are explicitly disabled by setting CELL_OFFLOAD_PROCESSING to FALSE. You can see that the test query does not have a WHERE clause. This, too, is done deliberately. It means that predicate filtering and storage indexes cannot be used to cut down the volume of data that must be transferred from the storage tier because those two optimizations can only be done when there is a WHERE clause. That leaves column projection as the only optimization in play. Are you surprised that column projection alone could cut a query's response time in half? We were the first time we saw it, but it makes sense if you think about it. And, in this particular case, the table only has 12 columns!

```
SQL> @desc sh.sales
           Name                            Null?      Type
           ------------------------------- --------   -------------
    1      PROD_ID                         NOT NULL   NUMBER
    2      CUST_ID                         NOT NULL   NUMBER
    3      TIME_ID                         NOT NULL   DATE
    4      CHANNEL_ID                      NOT NULL   NUMBER
    5      PROMO_ID                        NOT NULL   NUMBER
    6      QUANTITY_SOLD                   NOT NULL   NUMBER(10,2)
    7      SELLER                          NOT NULL   NUMBER(6)
    8      FULFILLMENT_CENTER              NOT NULL   NUMBER(6)
    9      COURIER_ORG                     NOT NULL   NUMBER(6)
   10      TAX_COUNTRY                     NOT NULL   VARCHAR2(3)
   11      TAX_REGION                                 VARCHAR2(3)
   12      AMOUNT_SOLD                     NOT NULL   NUMBER(10,2)
```

You should be aware that columns in the select list are not the only columns that must be returned to the database server. This is a very common misconception. Join columns in the WHERE clause must also be returned. As a matter of fact, in early versions of Exadata, the column projection feature was not as effective as it could have been and actually returned all the columns included in the WHERE clause, which, in many cases, included some unnecessary columns.

The DBMS_XPLAN package can display information about column projection, although by default it does not. The projection data is stored in the PROJECTION column in the V$SQL_PLAN view as well. Here is an example:

```
SQL> select /*+ gather_plan_statistics */
  2   count(s.prod_id), avg(amount_sold)
  3  from sales_nonpart s, products p
  4  where p.prod_id = s.prod_id
  5  and s.time_id = DATE '2013-12-01'
  6  and s.tax_country = 'DE';

COUNT(S.PROD_ID) AVG(AMOUNT_SOLD)
---------------- ----------------
             124       51.5241935

Elapsed: 00:00:00.09
SQL> select * from table(dbms_xplan.display_cursor(null,null,'+projection'));

PLAN_TABLE_OUTPUT
-------------------------------------
SQL_ID  69y720khfvjq4, child number 1
-------------------------------------
select /*+ gather_plan_statistics */  count(s.prod_id),
avg(amount_sold) from sales_nonpart s, products p where p.prod_id =
s.prod_id and s.time_id = DATE '2013-12-01' and s.tax_country = 'DE'

Plan hash value: 754104813

---------------------------------------------------------------------------------------------
| Id  | Operation                   | Name          | Rows  | Bytes | Cost (%CPU)| Time     |
---------------------------------------------------------------------------------------------
|   0 | SELECT STATEMENT            |               |       |       |  198K (100)|          |
|   1 |  SORT AGGREGATE             |               |     1 |    22 |            |          |
|*  2 |   HASH JOIN                 |               |   149 |  3278 |   198K   (2)| 00:00:08 |
|   3 |    TABLE ACCESS STORAGE FULL| PRODUCTS      |    72 |   288 |     3   (0)| 00:00:01 |
|*  4 |    TABLE ACCESS STORAGE FULL| SALES_NONPART|   229 |  4122 |   198K   (2)| 00:00:08 |
---------------------------------------------------------------------------------------------

Predicate Information (identified by operation id):
---------------------------------------------------

   2 - access("P"."PROD_ID"="S"."PROD_ID")
   4 - storage(("S"."TIME_ID"=TO_DATE(' 2013-12-01 00:00:00', 'syyyy-mm-dd
              hh24:mi:ss') AND "S"."TAX_COUNTRY"='DE'))
       filter(("S"."TIME_ID"=TO_DATE(' 2013-12-01 00:00:00', 'syyyy-mm-dd
              hh24:mi:ss') AND "S"."TAX_COUNTRY"='DE'))
```

```
Column Projection Information (identified by operation id):
-----------------------------------------------------------

   1 - (#keys=0) COUNT(*)[22], SUM("AMOUNT_SOLD")[22]
   2 - (#keys=1; rowset=200) "AMOUNT_SOLD"[NUMBER,22]
   3 - (rowset=200) "P"."PROD_ID"[NUMBER,22]
   4 - (rowset=200) "S"."PROD_ID"[NUMBER,22], "AMOUNT_SOLD"[NUMBER,22]

Note
-----
   - statistics feedback used for this statement

39 rows selected.

SQL> select projection from v$sql_plan
  2  where projection is not null
  3  and sql_id = '69y720khfvjq4'
  4  and child_number = 1;

PROJECTION
----------------------------------------------------------------------
(#keys=0) COUNT(*)[22], SUM("AMOUNT_SOLD")[22]
(#keys=1; rowset=200) "AMOUNT_SOLD"[NUMBER,22]
(rowset=200) "P"."PROD_ID"[NUMBER,22]
(rowset=200) "S"."PROD_ID"[NUMBER,22], "AMOUNT_SOLD"[NUMBER,22]

Elapsed: 00:00:00.00
```

As you can see, the plan output shows the projection information, but only if you use the +PROJECTION argument in the call to the DBMS_XPLAN package. Note also that the PROD_ID columns from both tables are listed in the PROJECTION section, but that not all columns in the WHERE clause are included. This becomes very apparent in the predicate output for operation ID 4. Although the query narrows the result set down by specifying TIME_ID and TAX_COUNTRY, these columns are not found anywhere in the PROJECTION. Only those columns that need to be returned to the database should be listed. Note also that the projection information is not unique to Exadata, but is a generic part of the database code.

The V$SQL family of views contain columns that define the volume of data that may be saved by offloading (IO_CELL_OFFLOAD_ELIGIBLE_BYTES) and the volume of data that was actually returned by the storage servers (IO_INTERCONNECT_BYTES, IO_CELL_OFFLOAD_RETURNED_BYTES). Note that these columns are cumulative for all the executions of the statement. These columns in V$SQL will be used heavily throughout the book because they are key indicators of offload processing. Here is a quick demonstration to show that projection does affect the amount of data returned to the database servers and that selecting fewer columns results in less data transferred:

```
SQL> select /* single-col-test */ avg(prod_id) from sales;

AVG(PROD_ID)
------------
  80.0035113

Elapsed: 00:00:14.12
SQL> select /* multi-col-test */ avg(prod_id), sum(cust_id), sum(channel_id) from sales;
```

```
AVG(PROD_ID) SUM(CUST_ID) SUM(CHANNEL_ID)
------------ ------------ ---------------
  80.0035113   4.7901E+15      1354989738

Elapsed: 00:00:25.89
SQL> select sql_id, sql_text from v$sql where regexp_like(sql_text,'(single|multi)-col-test');

SQL_ID        SQL_TEXT
------------- ----------------------------------------
8m5zmxka24vyk select /* multi-col-test */ avg(prod_id)
0563r8vdy9t2y select /* single-col-test */ avg(prod_id

SQL> select SQL_ID, IO_CELL_OFFLOAD_ELIGIBLE_BYTES eligible,
  2  IO_INTERCONNECT_BYTES actual,
  3  100*(IO_CELL_OFFLOAD_ELIGIBLE_BYTES-IO_INTERCONNECT_BYTES)
  4  /IO_CELL_OFFLOAD_ELIGIBLE_BYTES "IO_SAVED_%", sql_text
  5  from v$sql where SQL_ID in ('8m5zmxka24vyk', '0563r8vdy9t2y');

SQL_ID          ELIGIBLE     ACTUAL IO_SAVED_% SQL_TEXT
------------- ---------- ---------- ---------- ----------------------------------------
8m5zmxka24vyk 1.6272E+10 4760099744 70.7475353 select /* multi-col-test */ avg(prod_id)
0563r8vdy9t2y 1.6272E+10 3108328256 80.8982443 select /* single-col-test */ avg(prod_id

SQL> @fsx4
Enter value for sql_text: %col-test%
Enter value for sql_id:

SQL_ID         CHILD OFFLOAD IO_SAVED_%  AVG_ETIME SQL_TEXT
------------- ------ ------- ---------- ---------- ----------------------------------------
0563r8vdy9t2y      0 Yes          80.90      14.11 select /* single-col-test */ avg(prod_id
8m5zmxka24vyk      0 Yes          70.75      25.89 select /* multi-col-test */ avg(prod_id)
```

Note that the extra columns resulted in extra time required to complete the query and that the columns in V$SQL verified the increased volume of data that had to be transferred. You could also get the first glimpse at the output of a modified version of the fsx.sql script, which will be discussed in more detail later in this chapter. For now, please just accept that it shows us whether a statement was offloaded or not.

Predicate Filtering

The second of the big three Smart Scan optimizations is *predicate filtering*. This term refers to Exadata's ability to return only rows of interest to the database tier. Since the iDB protocol used to interact with the Exadata storage cells includes the predicate information in its requests, predicate filtering is accomplished by performing the standard filtering operations at the storage level before returning the data. On databases using non-Exadata storage, filtering is always done on the database servers. This generally means that a large number of records that will eventually be discarded will be returned to the database tier. Filtering these rows at the storage layer can provide a very significant decrease in the volume of data that must be transferred to the database tier. While this optimization also results in some savings in CPU usage on the database servers, the biggest advantage is generally the reduction in time needed for the data transfer.

Here is an example:

```
SQL> alter session set cell_offload_processing=false;

Session altered.

Elapsed: 00:00:00.01
SQL> select count(*) from sales;

  COUNT(*)
----------
 294575180

Elapsed: 00:00:23.17
SQL> alter session set cell_offload_processing=true;

Session altered.

Elapsed: 00:00:00.00
SQL> select count(*) from sales;

  COUNT(*)
----------
 294575180

Elapsed: 00:00:05.68
SQL> -- disable storage indexes
SQL> alter session set "_kcfis_storageidx_disabled"=true;

System altered.

Elapsed: 00:00:00.12
SQL> select count(*) from sales where quantity_sold = 1;

  COUNT(*)
----------
   3006298

Elapsed: 00:00:02.78
```

First, offloading is completely disabled using the `CELL_OFFLOAD_PROCESSING` parameter followed by an execution of a query without a `WHERE` clause ("predicate"). Without the benefit of offloading, but with the benefits of reading exclusively from Smart Flash Cache, this query took about 23 seconds. Here is proof that the data came exclusively from Smart Flash Cache, using the `mystats` script you will find detailed in Chapter 11. In this case, the "optimized" keyword indicates Flash Cache usage:

```
STAT    cell flash cache read hits                             51,483
...
STAT    physical read IO requests                              51,483
STAT    physical read bytes                            16,364,175,360
```

```
STAT    physical read requests optimized              51,483
STAT    physical read total IO requests               51,483
STAT    physical read total bytes             16,364,175,360
STAT    physical read total bytes optimized   16,364,175,360
```

Next, offloading is enabled, and the same query is re-executed. This time, the elapsed time was only about six seconds. The savings of approximately 18 seconds was due strictly to column projection (because without a WHERE clause for filtering, there were no other optimizations that could come into play). Using a trick to disable storage indexes by setting the hidden parameter, _KCFIS_STORAGEIDX_DISABLED, to TRUE (more in the next section) and by adding a WHERE clause, the execution time was reduced to about two seconds. This reduction of an additional three seconds or so was thanks to predicate filtering. Note that storage indexes had to be disabled in the example to make sure the query performance improvement was entirely due to the predicate filtering without other performance enhancements (that is, storage indexes) interfering.

Storage Indexes and Zone Maps

Storage indexes provide the third level of optimization for Smart Scans. Storage indexes are in-memory structures on the storage cells that maintain a maximum and minimum value for each 1MB disk storage unit, for up to eight columns of a table. They are created and maintained transparently on the cells after segments have been queried. Storage indexes are a little different than most Smart Scan optimizations. The goal of storage indexes is not to reduce the amount of data being transferred back to the database tier. In fact, whether they are used on a given query or not, the amount of data returned to the database tier remains constant. On the contrary, storage indexes are designed to eliminate time spent reading data from disk on the storage servers themselves. Think of this feature as a pre-filter. Since Smart Scans pass the query predicates to the storage servers and storage indexes contain a map of minimum and maximum values for up to eight columns in each 1MB storage region, any region that cannot possibly contain a matching row because it lies outside of the minimum and maximum value stored in the storage index can be eliminated without ever being read. You can also think of storage indexes as an alternate partitioning mechanism. Disk I/O is eliminated in analogous fashion to partition elimination. If a partition cannot contain any records of interest, the partition's blocks will not be read. Similarly, if a storage region cannot contain any records of interest, that storage region need not be read.

Storage indexes cannot be used in all cases, and there is little that can be done to affect when or how they are used. But, in the right situations, the results from this optimization technique can be astounding. As always, this is best shown with an example:

```
SQL> -- disable storage indexes
SQL> alter session set "_kcfis_storageidx_disabled"=true;

System altered.

Elapsed: 00:00:00.11
SQL> select count(*) from bigtab where id = 8000000;

  COUNT(*)
----------
        32

Elapsed: 00:00:22.02
SQL> -- re-enable storage indexes
SQL> alter session set "_kcfis_storageidx_disabled"=false;

System altered.
```

```
Elapsed: 00:00:00.01
SQL> select count(*) from bigtab where id = 8000000;

  COUNT(*)
----------
        32

Elapsed: 00:00:00.54
```

In this example, storage indexes have again been disabled deliberately using the aforementioned parameter `_KCFIS_STORAGEIDX_DISABLED` to remind you of the elapsed time required to read through all rows using column projection and predicate filtering only. Remember that even though the amount of data returned to the database tier is extremely small in this case, the storage servers still had to read through every block containing data for the `BIGTAB` table and then had to check each row to see if it matched the `WHERE` clause. This is where the majority of the 22 seconds was spent. After storage indexes were re-enabled and the query was re-executed, the execution time was reduced to about .05 seconds. This reduction in elapsed time is a result of storage indexes being used to avoid virtually all the disk I/O and the time spent filtering through those records.

Beginning with Exadata version 12.1.2.1.0 and database 12.1.0.2, Oracle introduced the ability to keep overall minimum and maximum values of the minimum and maximum values of a column stored in the storage indexes in the storage server. The idea is that the `min()` and `max()` functions can pick up the overall kept value and not visit the storage indexes to compute this value. This should benefit queries using `min()` and `max()` functions such as analytical workloads where dashboards are populated with these. Unfortunately, there is no extra instrumentation available at the time of writing to indicate the cached minimum or maximum value has been used. All you can see is a change in the well-known statistic "cell physical IO bytes saved by storage index."

Just to reiterate, column projection and predicate filtering (and most other Smart Scan optimizations) improve performance by reducing the volume of data being transferred back to the database servers (and thus the amount of time to transfer the data). Storage indexes improve performance by eliminating time spent reading data from disk on the storage servers and filtering that data. Storage indexes are covered in much more detail in Chapter 4.

Zone maps are new with Oracle 12.1.0.2 and conceptually similar to storage indexes. The difference is that a zone map grants the user more control over segments to be monitored. When we first heard about zone maps, we were very excited because the feature could have been seen as a port of the storage index (which requires an Exadata storage cell) to a non-Exadata platform. Unfortunately, the usage of zone maps is limited to Exadata, making it far less attractive. A *zone* in the Oracle parlance is an area of a table on disk, typically around 1024 blocks. Just as with a storage index, a zone map allows Oracle to skip areas on disk that are not relevant for a query. The big difference between zone maps and the storage indexes just discussed is that the latter are maintained on the storage servers, whereas zone maps are created and maintained under the control of the database administrator on the database level. Storage indexes reside on the cells, and the DBA has little control over them. A zone map is very similar to a materialized view, but without the need of a materialized view log. When you create a zone map, you need to decide how it is refreshed to prevent it from becoming stale. Zone-map information is also available in the database's dictionary. When a zone map is available and can be used, you will see it applied as a filter in the execution plan.

```
SQL> -- turning off storage indexes as they might interfere with the result otherwise
SQL> alter session set "_kcfis_storageidx_disabled" = true;

Session altered.
```

```
Elapsed: 00:00:00.00
SQL> select /*+ gather_plan_statistics zmap_example_001 */ count(*)
  2  from T1_ORDER_BY_ID where id = 121;

  COUNT(*)
----------
        16

Elapsed: 00:00:02.65
SQL> select * from table(dbms_xplan.display_cursor);

PLAN_TABLE_OUTPUT
-------------------------------------
SQL_ID  avt7474pb4m1m, child number 0
-------------------------------------
select /*+ gather_plan_statistics zmap_example_001 */ count(*) from
T1_ORDER_BY_ID where id = 121

Plan hash value: 775109614

-------------------------------------------------------------------------------------
| Id  | Operation                          | Name             | Rows  | Bytes | Cost (%CPU)|
-------------------------------------------------------------------------------------
|   0 | SELECT STATEMENT                   |                  |       |       |   723K(100)|
|   1 |  SORT AGGREGATE                    |                  |     1 |     5 |            |
|*  2 |   TABLE ACCESS STORAGE FULL        |                  |       |       |            |
|     |    WITH ZONEMAP                    | T1_ORDER_BY_ID   |    16 |    80 |   723K  (1)|
-------------------------------------------------------------------------------------

Predicate Information (identified by operation id):
---------------------------------------------------

   2 - storage("ID"=121)
       filter((SYS_ZMAP_FILTER('/* ZM_PRUNING */ SELECT "ZONE_ID$", CASE WHEN
              BITAND(zm."ZONE_STATE$",1)=1 THEN 1 ELSE
              CASE WHEN (zm."MIN_1_ID" > :1 OR zm."MAX_1_ID" < :2)
              THEN 3 ELSE 2 END END FROM "MARTIN"."T1_ORDER_BY_ID_ZMAP" zm
              WHERE zm."ZONE_LEVEL$"=0 ORDER BY
              zm."ZONE_ID$"',SYS_OP_ZONE_ID(ROWID),121,121)<3 AND "ID"=121))

24 rows selected.
```

When you look at the SQL traces for the statement, you will see that the zone maps are consulted for extends eligible for pruning in recursive SQL statements executed as SYS. The traced statements look just like the filter reported in the execution plan.

Simple Joins (Bloom Filters)

In some cases, join processing can be offloaded to the storage tier as well. Offloaded joins are accomplished by creating what is called a *Bloom filter*. Bloom filters have been around for a long time and have been used by Oracle since Oracle Database Version 10g Release 2. Hence, they are not specific to Exadata. One of the main ways Oracle uses them is to reduce traffic between parallel query slaves. As of Oracle 11.2.0.4 and 12c, you can also have Bloom filters in serial query processing.

Bloom filters have the advantage of being very small relative to the data set that they represent. However, this comes at a price—they can return false positives. That is, rows that should not be included in the desired result set can occasionally pass a Bloom filter. For that reason, an additional filter must be applied after the Bloom filter to ensure that any false positives are eliminated. An interesting fact about Bloom filters from an Exadata perspective is that they may be passed to the storage servers and evaluated there, effectively transforming a join to a filter. This technique can result in a large decrease in the volume of data that must be transmitted back to database servers. The following example demonstrates this:

```
SQL> show parameter bloom

PARAMETER_NAME                       TYPE        VALUE
------------------------------------ ----------- ------
_bloom_predicate_offload             boolean     FALSE

SQL> show parameter kcfis

PARAMETER_NAME                       TYPE        VALUE
------------------------------------ ----------- ------
_kcfis_storageidx_disabled            boolean     TRUE

SQL> select /* bloom0015 */ * from customers c, orders o
  2  where o.customer_id = c.customer_id and c.cust_email = 'user@example.com';

no rows selected

Elapsed: 00:00:13.57
SQL> alter session set "_bloom_predicate_offload" = true;

Session altered.

SQL> select /* bloom0015 */ * from customers c, orders o
  2  where o.customer_id = c.customer_id and c.cust_email = 'user@example.com';

no rows selected

Elapsed: 00:00:02.56
SQL> @fsx
Enter value for sql_text: %bloom0015%
Enter value for sql_id:

SQL_ID          CHILD  PLAN_HASH  EXECS  AVG_ETIME AVG_PX OFFLOAD IO_SAVED_% SQL_TEXT
------------- ------ ---------- ------ ---------- ------ ------- ---------- --------------
5n3np45j2x9vn       0  576684111      1      13.56      0 Yes          54.26 select /*
bloom0015
5n3np45j2x9vn       1 2651416178      1       2.56      0 Yes          99.98 select /*
bloom0015
```

```
SQL> --fetch first explain plan, without bloom filter
SQL> select * from table(
  2   dbms_xplan.display_cursor('5n3np45j2x9vn',0,'BASIC +predicate +partition'));

PLAN_TABLE_OUTPUT
------------------------
EXPLAINED SQL STATEMENT:
------------------------
select /* bloom0015 */ * from customers c, orders o where o.customer_id
= c.customer_id and c.cust_email = 'user@example.com'

Plan hash value: 576684111

-----------------------------------------------------------------
| Id  | Operation                    | Name      | Pstart| Pstop |
-----------------------------------------------------------------
|   0 | SELECT STATEMENT             |           |       |       |
|*  1 |  HASH JOIN                   |           |       |       |
|   2 |   PARTITION HASH ALL         |           |     1 |    32 |
|*  3 |    TABLE ACCESS STORAGE FULL| CUSTOMERS |     1 |    32 |
|   4 |   PARTITION HASH ALL         |           |     1 |    32 |
|   5 |    TABLE ACCESS STORAGE FULL| ORDERS    |     1 |    32 |
-----------------------------------------------------------------

Predicate Information (identified by operation id):
---------------------------------------------------

   1 - access("O"."CUSTOMER_ID"="C"."CUSTOMER_ID")
   3 - storage("C"."CUST_EMAIL"='user@example.com')
       filter("C"."CUST_EMAIL"='user@example.com')

25 rows selected.

Elapsed: 00:00:00.01
SQL> --fetch second explain plan, with bloom filter
SQL> select * from table(
  2  dbms_xplan.display_cursor('5n3np45j2x9vn',1,'BASIC +predicate +partition'));

PLAN_TABLE_OUTPUT
------------------------
EXPLAINED SQL STATEMENT:
------------------------
select /* bloom0015 */ * from customers c, orders o where o.customer_id
= c.customer_id and c.cust_email = 'user@example.com'

Plan hash value: 2651416178
```

```
--------------------------------------------------------------------
| Id  | Operation                      | Name       | Pstart| Pstop |
--------------------------------------------------------------------
|   0 | SELECT STATEMENT               |            |       |       |
|*  1 |  HASH JOIN                     |            |       |       |
|   2 |   JOIN FILTER CREATE           | :BF0000    |       |       |
|   3 |    PARTITION HASH ALL          |            |     1 |    32 |
|*  4 |     TABLE ACCESS STORAGE FULL| CUSTOMERS  |     1 |    32 |
|   5 |   JOIN FILTER USE              | :BF0000    |       |       |
|   6 |    PARTITION HASH ALL          |            |     1 |    32 |
|*  7 |     TABLE ACCESS STORAGE FULL| ORDERS     |     1 |    32 |
--------------------------------------------------------------------

Predicate Information (identified by operation id):
---------------------------------------------------

   1 - access("O"."CUSTOMER_ID"="C"."CUSTOMER_ID")
   4 - storage("C"."CUST_EMAIL"='user@example.com')
       filter("C"."CUST_EMAIL"='user@example.com')
   7 - storage(SYS_OP_BLOOM_FILTER(:BF0000,"O"."CUSTOMER_ID"))
       filter(SYS_OP_BLOOM_FILTER(:BF0000,"O"."CUSTOMER_ID"))

29 rows selected.
```

In this listing, the hidden parameter, _BLOOM_PREDICATE_OFFLOAD (previously in 11.2 it was named _BLOOM_PREDICATE_PUSHDOWN_TO_STORAGE), was used for comparison purposes. Notice that the test query ran in about 2 seconds with Bloom filters, and 14 seconds without. Also notice that both queries were offloaded. If you look closely at the predicate information of the plans, you will see that the SYS_OP_BLOOM_FILTER(:BF0000,"O"."CUSTOMER_ID") predicate was run on the storage servers for the second run, indicated by child cursor 1. The query that used Bloom filters ran faster because the storage servers were able to pre-join the tables, which eliminated a large amount of data that would otherwise have been transferred back to the database servers. The Oracle database engine is not limited to using a single Bloom filter, depending on the complexity of the query there can be more.

■ **Note** In-Memory Aggregation, which requires the In-Memory Option, offers another optimization similar to Bloom filters. Using it, you can benefit from offloading the key vectors that are part of the transformation.

Function Offloading

Oracle's implementation of the Structured Query Language (SQL) includes many built-in functions. These functions can be used directly in SQL statements. Broadly speaking, they may be divided into two main groups: single-row functions and multi-row functions. Single-row functions return a single result row for every row of a queried table. These single-row functions can be further subdivided into the following general categories:

- Numeric functions (SIN, COS, FLOOR, MOD, LOG, ...)
- Character functions (CHR, LPAD, REPLACE, TRIM, UPPER, LENGTH, ...)

- Datetime functions (ADD_MONTHS, TO_CHAR, TRUNC, ...)
- Conversion functions (CAST, HEXTORAW, TO_CHAR, TO_DATE, ...)

Virtually all of these single-row functions can be offloaded to Exadata storage. The second major group of SQL functions operate on a set of rows. There are two subgroups in this multi-row function category:

- Aggregate functions (AVG, COUNT, SUM, ...)
- Analytic functions (AVG, COUNT, DENSE_RANK, LAG, ...)

These functions return either a single row (aggregate functions) or multiple rows (analytic functions). Note that some of the functions are overloaded and belong to both groups. None of these functions can be offloaded to Exadata, which makes sense because many of these functions require access to the *entire set of rows*—something individual storage cells do not have.

There are some additional functions that do not fall neatly into any of the previously described groupings. These functions may or may not be offloaded to the storage cells. For example, DECODE and NVL are offloadable, but most XML functions are not. Some of the data mining functions are offloadable, but some are not. Also keep in mind that the list of offloadable functions may change as newer versions are released. The definitive list of offloadable functions for your particular version is contained in V$SQLFN_METADATA. In 11.2.0.3, for example, 393 out of 923 SQL functions 393 were offloadable.

```
SQL> select count(*), offloadable from v$sqlfn_metadata group by rollup(offloadable);

   COUNT(*) OFF
----------- ---
        530 NO
        393 YES
        923
```

In 12.1.0.2, the current release at the time of writing, the number of functions increased:

```
SQL> select count(*), offloadable from v$sqlfn_metadata group by rollup(offloadable);

  COUNT(*) OFF
---------- ---
       615 NO
       418 YES
      1033
```

Offloading functions does allow the storage cells to do some of the work that would normally be done by the CPUs on the database servers. However, the saving in CPU usage is generally a relatively minor enhancement. The big gain usually comes from limiting the amount of data transferred back to the database servers. Being able to evaluate functions contained in WHERE clauses allows storage cells to send only rows of interest back to the database tier. So, as with most offloading, the primary goal of this optimization is to reduce the amount of traffic between the storage and database tiers. If a function has been offloaded to the storage servers, you can see this in the predicate section emitted by DBMS_XPLAN.DISPLAY_CURSOR, as shown here:

```
SQL> select count(*) from sales where lower(tax_country) = 'ir';

  COUNT(*)
----------
    435700
```

```
SQL> select * from table(dbms_xplan.display_cursor(null, null, 'BASIC +predicate'));

PLAN_TABLE_OUTPUT
------------------------
EXPLAINED SQL STATEMENT:
------------------------
select count(*) from sales where lower(tax_country) = 'ir'

Plan hash value: 3519235612

---------------------------------------------
| Id  | Operation                   | Name  |
---------------------------------------------
|   0 | SELECT STATEMENT            |       |
|   1 |  SORT AGGREGATE             |       |
|   2 |   PARTITION RANGE ALL       |       |
|*  3 |    TABLE ACCESS STORAGE FULL| SALES |
---------------------------------------------

Predicate Information (identified by operation id):
---------------------------------------------------

   3 - storage(LOWER("TAX_COUNTRY")='ir')
       filter(LOWER("TAX_COUNTRY")='ir')
```

This is not to be confused with referencing a function in the select-list:

```
SQL> select lower(tax_country) from sales where rownum < 11;

LOW
---
zl
uw
...
bg

10 rows selected.

SQL> select * from table(dbms_xplan.display_cursor(null, null, 'BASIC +predicate'));

PLAN_TABLE_OUTPUT
------------------------
EXPLAINED SQL STATEMENT:
------------------------
select lower(tax_country) from sales where rownum < 11

Plan hash value: 807288713
```

```
--------------------------------------------------------
| Id  | Operation                              | Name  |
--------------------------------------------------------
|   0 | SELECT STATEMENT                       |       |
|*  1 |  COUNT STOPKEY                         |       |
|   2 |   PARTITION RANGE ALL                  |       |
|   3 |    TABLE ACCESS STORAGE FULL FIRST ROWS| SALES |
--------------------------------------------------------

Predicate Information (identified by operation id):
---------------------------------------------------

   1 - filter(ROWNUM<11)
```

As you can see, there is no reference to the `to_lower()` function in the predicate information. You will, however, benefit from column projection in this case.

Compression/Decompression

One Exadata feature that has received quite a bit of attention is HCC. Exadata offloads the decompression of data stored in HCC format during Smart Scan operations. That is, columns of interest are decompressed on the storage cells when the compressed data is accessed via Smart Scans. This decompression is not necessary for filtering, so only the data that will be returned to the database tier will be decompressed. Note that all compression is done at the database tier, however. Decompression may also be done at the database tier when data is not accessed via a Smart Scan or when the storage cells are very busy. To make it simple, Table 2-1 shows where the work is done.

Table 2-1. *HCC Compression/Decompression Offloading*

Operation	Database Servers	Storage Servers
Compression	Always	Never
Decompression	Non-Smart Scan Can help out if cells are too busy	Smart Scan

Decompressing data at the storage tier runs counter to the theme of most of the other Smart Scan optimizations. Most of them are geared to reducing the volume of data to be transported back to the database servers. Because decompression is such a CPU-intensive task, particularly with the higher levels of compression, the decision was made to do the decompression on the storage servers whenever possible. This decision is not set in stone, however, as in some situations there may be ample CPU resources available to make decompressing data on the database servers an attractive option. (That is, in some situations, the reduction in data to be shipped may outweigh the reduction in database-server CPU consumption.) In fact, as of `cellsrv` version 11.2.2.3.1, Exadata does have the ability to return compressed data to the database servers when the storage cells are busy. Chapter 3 deals with HCC in much more detail and will provide examples for such situations.

There is a hidden parameter that controls whether decompression will be offloaded at all. Unfortunately, it does not just move the decompression back and forth between the storage and database tiers. If the `_CELL_OFFLOAD_HYBRIDCOLUMNAR` parameter is set to a value of `FALSE`, Smart Scans will be completely disabled on HCC data.

Encryption/Decryption

Encryption and decryption are handled in a manner very similar to compression and decompression of HCC data. Encryption is always done at the database tier, while decryption can be done by the storage servers or by the database servers. When encrypted data is accessed via Smart Scan, it is decrypted on the storage servers. Otherwise, it is decrypted on the database servers. Note that from the X2 Exadata generation, Intel Xeon chips in the storage servers have built-in capabilities to perform cryptography in silicon. Modern Intel chips contain a special instruction set (Intel AES-NI) that effectively adds a hardware boost to processes doing encryption or decryption. Note that Oracle Database Release 11.2.0.2 or later is necessary to take advantage of the new instruction set.

Encryption and HCC compression work well together. Since compression is done first, there is less work needed for processes doing encryption and decryption on HCC data. Note that the `CELL_OFFLOAD_DECRYPTION` parameter controls this behavior, and that as it does with the hidden parameter `_CELL_OFFLOAD_HYBRIDCOLUMNAR`, setting the parameter to a value of `FALSE` completely disables Smart Scans on encrypted data, which also disables decryption at the storage layer.

Virtual Columns

Virtual columns provide the ability to define pseudo-columns that can be calculated from other columns in a table, without actually storing the calculated value. Virtual columns may be used as partition keys, used in constraints, or indexed. Column level statistics can also be gathered on them. Since the values of virtual columns are not actually stored, they must be calculated on the fly when they are accessed. Outside the Exadata platform, the database session has to calculate the values. On Exadata, these calculations can be offloaded for a segment access via Smart Scans:

```
SQL> alter table bigtab add idn1 generated always as (id + n1);

Table altered.

SQL> select column_name, data_type, data_default
  2  from user_tab_columns where table_name = 'BIGTAB';

COLUMN_NAME          DATA_TYPE            DATA_DEFAULT
-------------------- -------------------- ------------
IDN1                 NUMBER               "ID"+"N1"
ID                   NUMBER
V1                   VARCHAR2
N1                   NUMBER
N2                   NUMBER
N_256K               NUMBER
N_128K               NUMBER
N_8K                 NUMBER
PADDING              VARCHAR2

9 rows selected.
```

Now you can query the table including the virtual column. To demonstrate the effect of offloading, a random value is needed first. The combination of ID and N1 should be reasonably unique in this data set:

```
SQL> select /*+ gather_plan_statistics virtual001 */ id, n1, idn1 from bigtab where
rownum < 11;

        ID         N1       IDN1
---------- ---------- ----------
   1161826       1826    1163652
   1161827       1827    1163654
   1161828       1828    1163656
   1161829       1829    1163658
   1161830       1830    1163660
   1161831       1831    1163662
   1161832       1832    1163664
   1161833       1833    1163666
   1161834       1834    1163668
   1161835       1835    1163670

10 rows selected.
```

Here is the demonstration of how the offloaded calculation benefits the execution time:

```
SQL> select /* gather_plan_statistics virtual0002 */ count(*)
  2  from bigtab where idn1 = 1163652;

  COUNT(*)
----------
        64

Elapsed: 00:00:06.78
SQL> @fsx4
Enter value for sql_text: %virtual0002%
Enter value for sql_id:

SQL_ID         CHILD OFFLOAD IO_SAVED_%  AVG_ETIME SQL_TEXT
------------- ------ ------- ---------- ---------- ----------------------------------------
8dyyd6kzycztq      0 Yes          99.99       6.77 select /* virtual0002 */ count(*) from b

Elapsed: 00:00:00.39
SQL> @dplan
Copy and paste SQL_ID and CHILD_NO from results above
Enter value for sql_id: 8dyyd6kzycztq
Enter value for child_no:

PLAN_TABLE_OUTPUT
-------------------------------------
SQL_ID  8dyyd6kzycztq, child number 0
-------------------------------------
select /* virtual0002 */ count(*) from bigtab where idn1 = 1163652
```

```
Plan hash value: 2140185107

-------------------------------------------------------------------------------------
| Id  | Operation                  | Name   | Rows  | Bytes | Cost (%CPU)| Time     |
-------------------------------------------------------------------------------------
|   0 | SELECT STATEMENT           |        |       |       |  2780K(100)|          |
|   1 |  SORT AGGREGATE            |        |     1 |    13 |            |          |
|*  2 |   TABLE ACCESS STORAGE FULL| BIGTAB |  2560K|    31M|  2780K  (1)| 00:01:49 |
-------------------------------------------------------------------------------------

Predicate Information (identified by operation id):
---------------------------------------------------

   2 - storage("ID"+"N1"=1163652)
       filter("ID"+"N1"=1163652)
```

The amount of I/O saved is 99.99%, as calculated using the quintessential columns in V$SQL for the last execution, and the query took 6.78 seconds to finish.

As with so many features in the Oracle world, there is a parameter to influence the behavior of your session. In the next example, the relevant underscore parameter will be used to disable virtual column processing at the storage server level. This is done to simulate how the same query would run on a non-Exadata platform:

```
SQL> alter session set "_cell_offload_virtual_columns"=false;

Session altered.

Elapsed: 00:00:00.00
SQL> select /* virtual0002 */ count(*)
  2  from bigtab where idn1 = 1163652;

  COUNT(*)
----------
        64

Elapsed: 00:00:23.13
```

The execution time is visibly higher when the compute nodes have to evaluate the expression. Comparing the two statement's execution shows this:

```
SQL> @fsx4
Enter value for sql_text: %virtual0002%
Enter value for sql_id:

SQL_ID         CHILD OFFLOAD IO_SAVED_%  AVG_ETIME SQL_TEXT
------------- ------ ------- ---------- ---------- ----------------------------------------
8dyyd6kzycztq      0 Yes          99.99       6.77 select /* virtual0002 */ count(*) from b
8dyyd6kzycztq      1 Yes          94.18      23.13 select /* virtual0002 */ count(*) from b

2 rows selected.
```

You will also note the absence of the storage keyword in the predicates section when displaying the execution plan for the first child cursor:

```
SQL> @dplan
Copy and paste SQL_ID and CHILD_NO from results above
Enter value for sql_id: 8dyyd6kzycztq
Enter value for child_no: 1

PLAN_TABLE_OUTPUT
-------------------------------------
SQL_ID  8dyyd6kzycztq, child number 1
-------------------------------------
select /* virtual0002 */ count(*) from bigtab where idn1 = 1163652

Plan hash value: 2140185107

-------------------------------------------------------------------------------------
| Id  | Operation                  | Name   | Rows  | Bytes | Cost (%CPU)| Time     |
-------------------------------------------------------------------------------------
|   0 | SELECT STATEMENT           |        |       |       |  2780K(100)|          |
|   1 |  SORT AGGREGATE            |        |     1 |    13 |            |          |
|*  2 |   TABLE ACCESS STORAGE FULL| BIGTAB |    64 |   832 |  2780K  (1)| 00:01:49 |
-------------------------------------------------------------------------------------

Predicate Information (identified by operation id):
---------------------------------------------------

   2 - filter("ID"+"N1"=1163652)

Note
-----
   - statistics feedback used for this statement
```

If you are using virtual columns in WHERE clauses, you certainly get a benefit from the Exadata platform.

Support for LOB offloading

With the introduction of Exadata software 12.1.1.1.1 and RDBMS 12.1.0.2, queries against inline LOBs defined as SecureFiles can be offloaded as well. According to the documentation set, like and regexp_like can be offloaded. To demonstrate this new feature, a new table, LOBOFFLOAD ,has been created and populated with 16 million rows. This should ensure that it is considered for Smart Scans. Here is the crucial bit of information about the LOB column:

```
SQL> select table_name, column_name, segment_name, securefile, in_row
  2  from user_lobs where table_name = 'LOBOFFLOAD';

TABLE_NAME               COLUMN_NAME              SEGMENT_NAME                   SEC IN_
------------------------ ------------------------ ------------------------------ --- ---
LOBOFFLOAD               COMMENTS                 SYS_LOB0000096135C00002$$      YES YES
```

The table tries to model a common application technique where a CLOB has been defined in a table to enter additional, unstructured information related to a record. This should be OK as long as it does not circumvent the constraints in the data model and purely informational information is stored that is not needed for processing in any form. Here is the example in 12c:

```
SQL> select /*+ monitor lobofflood001 */ count(*) from lobofflood where comments like
'%GOOD%';
  COUNT(*)
----------
     15840

Elapsed: 00:00:02.93

SQL> @fsx4.sql
Enter value for sql_text: %lobofflood001%
Enter value for sql_id:

SQL_ID         CHILD OFFLOAD IO_SAVED_%  AVG_ETIME SQL_TEXT
------------- ------ ------- ---------- ---------- ----------------------------------------
18479dnagkkyu      0 Yes          98.94       2.93 select /*+ monitor lobofflood001 */ count
```

As you can see in the output of the script (which we will discuss in more detail later), the query is offloaded. This is not the case in 11.2.0.3 where the test case has been reproduced:

```
SQL> select /*+ monitor lobofflood001 */ count(*) from lobofflood where comments like
'%GOOD%';

   COUNT(*)
-----------
      15840
Elapsed: 00:01:34.04

SQL> @fsx4.sql
Enter value for sql_text: %lobofflood001%
Enter value for sql_id:

SQL_ID         CHILD OFFLOAD IO_SAVED_%  AVG_ETIME SQL_TEXT
------------- ------ ------- ---------- ---------- ----------------------------------------
18479dnagkkyu      0 No             .00      94.04 select /*+ monitor lobofflood001 */ count
```

Unlike in the first example, the second query executed on 11.2.0.3 was not offloaded. Due to the segment size, it used direct path reads, but, unlike in the first example, they did not turn into Smart Scans.

JSON Support and Offloading

With the introduction of Oracle 12.1.0.2, JSON support was added to the database layer. If you are on Exadata 12.1.0.2.1.0 or later, you can benefit from offloading some of these operators. As you saw in the section about function offloading, you can query `v$sqlfn_metadata` about a function's ability to be offloaded. Here is the result when checking for JSON-related functions and their offloading support:

```
SQL> select count(*), name, offloadable from v$sqlfn_metadata
  2  where name like '%JSON%' group by name, offloadable
  3  order by offloadable, name;
```

```
  COUNT(*) NAME                           OFF
---------- ------------------------------ ---
         1 JSON_ARRAY                     NO
         1 JSON_ARRAYAGG                  NO
         1 JSON_EQUAL                     NO
         1 JSON_OBJECT                    NO
         1 JSON_OBJECTAGG                 NO
         1 JSON_QUERY                     NO
         1 JSON_SERIALIZE                 NO
         1 JSON_TEXTCONTAINS2             NO
         1 JSON_VALUE                     NO
         2 JSON                           YES
         1 JSON_EXISTS                    YES
         1 JSON_QUERY                     YES
         1 JSON_VALUE                     YES

13 rows selected.
```

Users of 12.1.0.2.1 also benefit from the ability to offload `XMLExists` and `XMLCast` operations as per the Oracle documentation.

Data Mining Model Scoring

Some of the data model scoring functions can be offloaded. Generally speaking, this optimization is aimed at reducing the amount of data transferred to the database tier as opposed to pure CPU offloading. As with other function offloading, you can verify which data mining functions can be offloaded by querying `V$SQLFN_METADATA`. The output looks like this:

```
SQL> select distinct name, version, offloadable
  2  from V$SQLFN_METADATA
  3  where name like 'PREDICT%'
  4  order by 1,2
  5  /

NAME                           VERSION      OFF
------------------------------ ------------ ---
PREDICTION                     V10R2 Oracle YES
PREDICTION_BOUNDS              V11R1 Oracle NO
PREDICTION_COST                V10R2 Oracle YES
PREDICTION_DETAILS             V10R2 Oracle NO
PREDICTION_PROBABILITY         V10R2 Oracle YES
PREDICTION_SET                 V10R2 Oracle NO

6 rows selected.
```

As you can see, some of the functions are offloadable, and some are not. The ones that are offloadable can be used by the storage cells for predicate filtering. Here's an example query that should only return records that meet the scoring requirement specified in the WHERE clause:

```
SQL> select cust_id
  2  from customers
  3  where region = 'US'
  4  and prediction_probability(churnmod,'Y' using *) > 0.8
  5  /
```

This optimization is designed to offload CPU usage as well as reduce the volume of data transferred. However, it is most beneficial in situations where it can reduce the data returned to the database tier, such as in the previous example.

Non-Smart Scan Offloading

There are a few optimizations that are not related to query processing. As these are not the focus of this chapter, we will only touch on them briefly.

Smart/Fast File Creation

This optimization has a somewhat misleading name. It really is an optimization designed to speed up block initialization. Whenever blocks are allocated, the database must initialize them. This activity happens when tablespaces are created, but it also occurs when files are added or extended for any number of other reasons. On non-Exadata storage, these situations require the database server to format each block and then write it back to disk. All that reading and writing causes a lot of traffic between the database servers and the storage cells. As you are now aware, eliminating traffic between the layers is a primary goal of Exadata. As you might imagine, this totally unnecessary traffic has been eliminated.

This process has been further refined. Beginning with Oracle Exadata 11.2.3.3.0 (a hot contender for the authors' favorite Exadata release), Oracle introduced fast data file creation. The time it takes to initialize a data file can be further reduced by using a clever trick. The first optimization you read about in the previous paragraph was to delegate the task of zeroing out the data files to the cells, which in itself proves quite effective. The next logical step, and what you get with fast file creation, is to just write the metadata to the Write-Back Flash Cache (WBFC), thus eliminating the actual process of formatting the blocks. If WBFC is enabled in the cell, the fast data file creation will be used by default. You can read more about Exadata Smart Flash Cache in Chapter 5.

RMAN Incremental Backups

Exadata speeds up incremental backups by increasing the granularity of block change tracking. On non-Exadata platforms, block changes are tracked for groups of blocks; on Exadata, changes are tracked for individual blocks. This can significantly decrease the number of blocks that must be backed up, resulting in smaller backup sizes, less I/O bandwidth, and reduced time to complete incremental backups. This feature can be disabled by setting the _DISABLE_CELL_OPTIMIZED_BACKUPS parameter to a value of TRUE. This optimization is covered in Chapter 10 in more detail.

RMAN Restores

This optimization speeds up the file initialization portion when restoring from backup on a cell. Although restoring databases from backups is not very common, this optimization can also help speed up cloning of environments. The optimization reduces CPU usage on the database servers and reduces traffic between the two tiers. If the `_CELL_FAST_FILE_RESTORE` parameter is set to a value of `FALSE`, this behavior will be disabled. This optimization is also covered in Chapter 10.

Smart Scan Prerequisites

Smart Scans do not occur for every query run on Exadata. There are three basic requirements that must be met for Smart Scans to occur:

- There must be a full scan of a segment (table, partition, materialized view, and so forth).
- The scan must use Oracle's direct path read mechanism.
- The object must be stored on Exadata storage.

There is a simple explanation as to why these requirements exist. Oracle is a C program. The function that performs Smart Scans (`kcfis_read`) is called by the direct path read function (`kcbldrget`), which is called by one of the full scan functions. It's that simple. You can't get to the `kcfis_read` function without traversing the code path from full scan to direct read. And, of course, the storage will have to be running Oracle's software in order to process Smart Scans with all data files residing on Exadata. We will discuss each of these requirements in turn.

Full Scans

In order for queries to take advantage of Exadata's offloading capabilities, the optimizer must decide to execute a statement with a full table scan or a fast full index scan. These terms are used somewhat generically in this context. A full segment scan is a prerequisite for direct path reads as well. As you just read, there will not be a Smart Scan unless there is a direct path read decision made.

Generally speaking, the (fast) full scan corresponds to `TABLE ACCESS FULL` and `INDEX FAST FULL SCAN` operations of an execution plan. With Exadata, these familiar operations have been renamed slightly to show that they are accessing Exadata storage. The new operation names are `TABLE ACCESS STORAGE FULL` and `INDEX STORAGE FAST FULL SCAN`.

It is usually quite simple to work out if a full scan has happened, but you might need to look in more than one place. The easiest way to start your investigation is to call `DBMS_XPLAN.DISPLAY_CURSOR()` right after a query has finished executing:

```
SQL> select count(*) from bigtab;

  COUNT(*)
----------
 256000000

Elapsed: 00:00:07.98

SQL> select * from table(dbms_xplan.display_cursor(null, null));
```

```
PLAN_TABLE_OUTPUT
-------------------------------------
SQL_ID  8c9rzdry8yahs, child number 0
-------------------------------------
select count(*) from bigtab

Plan hash value: 2140185107

-------------------------------------------------------------------------------
| Id  | Operation                  | Name   | Rows  | Cost (%CPU)| Time     |
-------------------------------------------------------------------------------
|   0 | SELECT STATEMENT           |        |       |  2779K(100)|          |
|   1 |  SORT AGGREGATE            |        |     1 |            |          |
|   2 |   TABLE ACCESS STORAGE FULL| BIGTAB |  256M|  2779K  (1)| 00:01:49 |
-------------------------------------------------------------------------------
```

Alternatively, you can use the `fsx.sql` script to locate the SQL text of a query from the shared pool and invoke the `DISPLAY_CURSOR()` function with the `SQL_ID` and cursor child number. The `dplan.sql` script is a convenient way to do so.

Note that there are also some minor variations of these operations, such as `MAT_VIEW ACCESS STORAGE FULL`, that also qualify for Smart Scans of materialized views. You should, however, be aware that the fact that your execution plan shows a `TABLE ACCESS STORAGE FULL` operation does not mean that your query was performed with a Smart Scan. It merely means that this particular prerequisite has been satisfied. Later in the chapter, you will read about methods on how to verify whether a statement was actually offloaded via a Smart Scan.

Direct Path Reads

In addition to requiring full scan operations, Smart Scans also require that the read operations be executed via Oracle's direct path read mechanism. Direct path reads have been around for a long time. Traditionally, this read mechanism has been used by parallel query server processes. Because parallel queries were originally expected to be used for accessing very large amounts of data (typically much too large to fit in the Oracle buffer cache), it was decided that the parallel servers should read data directly into their own memory (also known as the program global area or PGA). The direct path read mechanism completely bypasses the standard Oracle caching mechanism of placing blocks in the buffer cache. It relies on the fast object checkpoint operation to flush dirty buffers to disk before "scooping" them up in multi-block reads. This was a very good thing for very large data sets, as it eliminated extra work that was not expected to be helpful (caching full table scan data that would probably not be reused) and kept them from flushing other data out of the cache. Additionally, the inherent latency of random seeks in hard disks was eliminated. Not inserting buffers read in the buffer cache also removes a lot of potential CPU overhead.

This was the state of play until Oracle 11g, where non-parallel queries started to use direct path reads as well. This was a bit of a surprise at the time!

As a direct consequence, Smart Scans do not require parallel execution. The introduction of the direct path reads for serial queries certainly benefits the Exadata way of reading data by means of Smart Scan. You read previously that the `kcfis` (kernel cache file intelligent storage) functions are buried under the `kcbldrget` (kernel cache block direct read get) function. Therefore, Smart Scans can only be performed if the direct path read mechanism is being used.

Serial queries do not always use Smart Scans—that would be terribly inefficient. Setting up a direct path read, especially in clustered environments, can be a time-consuming task. Therefore, direct path reads are only set up and used when the conditions are right.

A hidden parameter, _SERIAL_DIRECT_READ, controls this feature. When this parameter is set to its default value (AUTO), Oracle automatically determines whether to use direct path reads for non-parallel scans. The calculation is based on several factors including the size of the object, the size of the buffer cache, and the number of the object's blocks are already cached in the buffer cache. There is also a hidden parameter (_SMALL_TABLE_THRESHOLD) that plays a role in determining how big a table must be before it will be considered for serial direct path reads. The algorithm for determining whether to use the direct path read mechanism on non-parallel scans is not published. With a little digging, you can excavate some of the decision-making process. In recent versions of the database, you can trace a RDBMS kernel facility named NSMTIO. The low-level oradebug utility can be invoked to display traceable components in the database, and one top-level component is named KXD—Exadata specific kernel modules (kxd):

```
SQL> oradebug doc component kxd

KXD                          Exadata specific Kernel modules (kxd)
KXDAM                        Exadata Disk Auto Manage (kxdam)
KCFIS                        Exadata Predicate Push (kcfis)
NSMTIO                       Trace Non Smart I/O (nsmtio)
KXDBIO                       Exadata Block level Intelligent Operations (kxdbio)
KXDRS                        Exadata Resilvering Layer (kxdrs)
KXDOFL                       Exadata Offload (kxdofl)
KXDMISC                      Exadata Misc (kxdmisc)
KXDCM                        Exadata Metrics Fixed Table Callbacks (kxdcm)
KXDBC                        Exadata Backup Compression for Backup Appliance (kxdbc)
```

Tracing KXD.* is quite interesting from a research point of view, but it should never be done outside a lab environment due to the potentially large size trace files it generates. The NSMTIO subcomponent has interesting information about the direct path read decision. The first trace shown here is about a direct path read that turned into a Smart Scan:

```
SQL> select value from v$diag_info
  2  where name like 'Default%';

VALUE
------------------------------------------------------------------
/u01/app/oracle/diag/rdbms/dbm01/dbm011/trace/dbm011_ora_32020.trc

SQL> alter session set events 'trace[nsmtio]';

Session altered.

Elapsed: 00:00:00.00
SQL> select count(*) from bigtab;

  COUNT(*)
----------
 256000000

Elapsed: 00:00:08.10
SQL> !cat /u01/app/oracle/diag/rdbms/dbm01/dbm011/trace/dbm011_ora_32020.trc
NSMTIO: kcbism: islarge 1 next 0 nblks 10250504 type 3, bpid 65535, kcbisdbfc 0 kcbnhl
   262144 kcbstt 44648 keep_nb 0 kcbnbh 2232432 kcbnwp 3
```

```
NSMTIO: kcbism: islarge 1 next 0 nblks 10250504 type 2, bpid 3, kcbisdbfc 0 kcbnhl 262144
  kcbstt 44648 keep_nb 0 kcbnbh 2232432 kcbnwp 3
NSMTIO: kcbimd: nblks 10250504 kcbstt 44648 kcbpnb 223243 kcbisdbfc 3 is_medium 0
NSMTIO: kcbivlo: nblks 10250504 vlot 500 pnb 2232432 kcbisdbfc 0 is_large 0
NSMTIO: qertbFetch:[MTT < OBJECT_SIZE < VLOT]:
  Checking cost to read from caches(local/remote) and checking storage reduction factors
  (OLTP/EHCC Comp)
NSMTIO: kcbdpc:DirectRead: tsn: 7, objd: 34422, objn: 20491
ckpt: 1, nblks: 10250504, ntcache: 2173249, ntdist:2173249
Direct Path for pdb 0 tsn 7  objd 34422 objn 20491
Direct Path 1 ckpt 1, nblks 10250504 ntcache 2173249 ntdist 2173249
Direct Path mndb 0 tdiob 6 txiob 0 tciob 43
Direct path diomrc 128 dios 2 kcbisdbfc 0
NSMTIO: Additional Info: VLOT=11162160
Object# = 34422, Object_Size = 10250504 blocks
SqlId = 8c9rzdry8yahs, plan_hash_value = 2140185107, Partition# = 0
```

BIGTAB is relatively large at 10250504 blocks. Earlier releases of the Exadata software performed a single-block read of the segment header to determine the object size. Since 11.2.0.2, the hidden parameter `_direct_read_decision_statistics_driven` is set to `TRUE`, implying that the dictionary statistics will be consulted instead. 2173249 blocks are cached in the buffer cache, which does not seem to play a role here. However, if too many blocks are cached, a buffered access path can be chosen instead of a direct path read.

The table access function (`qertbFetch`) reports that the object is larger than the MTT or medium table threshold and smaller than the VLOT or very large object threshold. Thankfully, the `SQL_ID` and plan hash value of the statement in question are shown here, as is the partition.

Unfortunately, the medium table threshold is a bit misleading in the interval definition `[MTT < OBJECT_SIZE < VLOT]`. The MTT is calculated as five times the `_small_table_threshold` (STT), and on first glance seems to be the cut-off point from where a direct path read is considered. This is probably true for early 11.2 releases. A test in 11.2.0.3 and later, including 12c, shows that segments can be eligible for direct path reads even when they are just a bit larger than the STT. The decision is then based on the number of blocks in the buffer cache (remote and local are considered in RAC) and their type. This is indicated in the trace by the line "checking cost to read from caches (local/remote) and checking storage reduction factors...."

On the other hand, if there is no direct path read, you will see something like this for a really small table:

```
NSMTIO: kcbism: islarge 0 next 0 nblks 4 type 3, bpid 65535, kcbisdbfc 0 kcbnhl 262144
  kcbstt 48117 keep_nb 0 kcbnbh 2405898 kcbnwp 3
NSMTIO: kcbism: islarge 0 next 0 nblks 4 type 2, bpid 3, kcbisdbfc 0 kcbnhl 262144
kcbstt 48117
  keep_nb 0 kcbnbh 2405898 kcbnwp 3
NSMTIO: qertbFetch:NoDirectRead:[- STT < OBJECT_SIZE < MTT]:Obect's size: 4 (blocks),
Threshold:
  MTT(240589 blocks),
_object_statistics: enabled, Sage: enabled,
Direct Read for serial qry: enabled(::::kctfsage::), Ascending SCN table scan: FALSE
flashback_table_scan: FALSE, Row Versions Query: FALSE
SqlId: 71acyavyyg1dg, plan_hash_value: 2604480108, Object#: 25576, Parition#: 0
  DW_scan: disabled
```

In this trace, you can see that the object is far too small—only four blocks. No direct path read was chosen since the segment is smaller than the _small_table_threshold. The last argument of the trace is interesting as well: A DW_SCAN is related to the Automatic Big Table Caching (ABTC), which has nothing to do with offloading queries to the storage servers.

There is another case that could be identified. It is related to the VLOT, or very large object threshold. You could see a reference in the first NSMTIO listing, where BIGTAB was smaller than that threshold. The VLOT defaults to 500, or five times the size of the buffer cache. The additional information provided in the first NSMTIO trace reveals that the VLOT is 11162160. The instance's buffer cache is approximately 20GB in size, or 2232432 buffers. The current number of buffers in the instance's buffer cache can be retrieved from v$db_cache_advise as so:

```
SQL> select block_size,size_for_estimate,buffers_for_estimate
  2  from v$db_cache_advice where size_factor = 1 and name = 'DEFAULT';

BLOCK_SIZE SIZE_FOR_ESTIMATE BUFFERS_FOR_ESTIMATE
---------- ----------------- --------------------
      8192             20608              2232432
```

Multiplying 2232432 by 5 returns 11162160; remember that db_block_buffers are measured as blocks and not bytes.

While the ability to do serial direct path reads has been around for some time, it has only become a relatively common occurrence since Oracle 11g. Oracle Database 11gR2 has a modified version of the calculations used to determine whether to use direct path reads for non-parallel scans. The new modifications to the algorithm make the direct path read mechanism much more likely to occur than it was in previous versions. This was probably done as a result of Exadata's Smart Scan optimizations and the desire for them to be triggered whenever possible. The algorithm may be somewhat overly aggressive on non-Exadata platforms.

Exadata Storage

Of course, the data being scanned must be stored on Exadata storage in order for Smart Scans to occur. It is possible to create ASM disk groups that access non-Exadata storage on Exadata database servers. And, of course, it makes sense that any SQL statements accessing objects defined using these non-Exadata disk groups will not be eligible for offloading.

While it is unusual, it is also possible to create ASM disk groups using a combination of Exadata and non-Exadata storage. Since you cannot put Fibre Channel Host Bus Adaptors into an Exadata compute node, this leaves network-attached storage the only option. With the introduction of NAS solutions, such as the ZFS Storage Appliance, it is increasingly common to move colder data to cheaper storage, accessed via dNFS. We cover this scenario in Chapter 3 in the context of the Automatic Data Optimization (ADO).

Queries against objects whose segments reside on mixed storage are not eligible for offloading. There is actually an attribute assigned to ASM disk groups (cell.smart_scan_capable) that specifies whether a disk group is capable of processing Smart Scans. This attribute must be set to FALSE before non-Exadata storage can be assigned to an ASM disk group.

The dictionary view DBA_TABLESPACES ha a property, named PREDICATE_EVALUATION, that you can query, too. This is the output from a query against our X4-2 half-rack lab database:

```
SQL> select tablespace_name, bigfile, predicate_evaluation
  2 from dba_tablespaces;

TABLESPACE_NAME                BIG PREDICA
------------------------------ --- -------
SYSTEM                         NO  STORAGE
SYSAUX                         NO  STORAGE
UNDOTBS1                       YES STORAGE
TEMP                           YES STORAGE
UNDOTBS2                       YES STORAGE
UNDOTBS3                       YES STORAGE
UNDOTBS4                       YES STORAGE
USERS                          NO  STORAGE
SOE                            YES STORAGE
SH                             YES STORAGE
```

Smart Scan Disablers

There are situations where Smart Scans are effectively disabled. The simple case is where they have not been enabled in the code yet, so Smart Scans cannot happen at all. There are other cases where Oracle starts down the Smart Scan path, but the storage software either decides, or is forced, to revert to block shipping mode. Generally, this decision is made on a block-by-block basis. The complete list of Smart Scan disablers is found in the Exadata documentation set, which, fortunately, was publicly available at the time of writing. Refer to Chapter 7 of the *Storage Server Software User's Guide*, section "Using the SQL EXPLAIN PLAN Command with Oracle Exadata Storage Server Software." You might want to refer to it from time to time as Oracle continuously enhances the software, and current restrictions may be lifted in future releases.

Simply Unavailable

During the discussion of Smart Scan optimizations, you read about the prerequisites that must be met to enable Smart Scans. However, even when those conditions are met, there are circumstances that prevent Smart Scans. Here are a few other situations that are not related to specific optimizations, but where Smart Scans simply cannot be used:

- On clustered tables or Index Organized Tables (IOTs)
- The query scans out-of-line LOB or LONG data types
- On tables with ROWDEPENDENCIES enabled
- Instances when you query features a flashback_query_clause
- Instances when you cannot offload queries against reverse key indexes
- Instances when you are querying data on non-Exadata storage

You also saw some parameters in the previous sections that influence Smart Scan behavior. If you set CELL_OFFLOAD_PROCESSING to FALSE or maybe _SERIAL_DIRECT_READ to never, you cannot by definition have Smart Scans.

Reverting to Block Shipping

There are situations where Smart Scans are used, but for various reasons `cellsrv` reverts to block shipping mode. This is a very complex topic, and we struggled with whether to include it in an introductory chapter on offloading. But since it is a fundamental concept, we decided to discuss it here, albeit briefly. There is a lot more detail about this subject in Chapter 11.

So far, Smart Scans have been described in this chapter as a means to avoid transferring large amounts of data to the database layer by returning pre-filtered data directly to the PGA. The brunt of the work is carried out by the storage cells—the more there are, the faster the scan can be performed. Just because your query is returning only 2% of the table data does not mean that you can avoid scanning all of it, as you can see in `V$SQL` and some other places you will learn more about in this book. Remember that the storage cells operate completely independently of one another; in other words, they do not communicate during query processing, ever. Communication during query processing is limited to the information exchange between the storage servers and the compute node (or multiple nodes if you process a query in parallel across the cluster). Another important piece of information in this context is that Smart Scans will only return consistent reads, not current blocks.

Occasionally, Smart Scans can choose (or be forced) to return complete blocks to the SGA. Basically, any situation that would cause Oracle to have to read another block to complete/roll back a record to the snapshot SCN will cause this to happen. A chained row is another, and perhaps the simplest, example. When Oracle encounters a chained row, the row's headpiece will contain a pointer to the block containing the second row piece. Since the storage cells do not communicate directly with each other and it is unlikely that the chained block resides on the same storage cell, `cellsrv` simply ships the entire block and allows the database layer to deal with it.

In this very simple case, the Smart Scan is paused momentarily, and a single-block read is effectively performed, which motivates another single-block read to get the additional row piece. Keep in mind that this is a very simple case.

This same behavior comes into play when Oracle must deal with read consistency issues. For example, if Oracle notices that a block is "newer" than the current query's SCN, the process of finding an age-appropriate version of the block is left for the database layer to deal with. This effectively pauses the Smart Scan processing while the database does its traditional read consistency processing. Delayed block cleanout is a similar case that might require pausing a Smart Scan.

■ **Note** This section is far too short to convey the complete picture appropriately; there is much more to these scenarios than we wanted to cover in the introduction chapter. All the details can be found in Chapter 11.

So, is this really important, and why should you care? The answer, of course, is that it depends. In most cases, you probably do not need to be concerned. Oracle guarantees that reads will be consistent, even when doing Smart Scans. Several optimizations, such as the commit cache discussed in Chapter 11, help speed up processing. The fact that Oracle behaves exactly the same from the application standpoint, regardless of whether Smart Scans are used or not, is a big deal. Exadata is not a highly specialized analytical engine. It is still using exactly the same database software everyone else does. The fact that Oracle may do some single-block reads along with its Smart Scan is of little concern if the results are correct and the performance is not severely impacted, and in most cases it will not be. There are cases, though, where choosing to do a Smart Scan and then reverting to block shipping mode can be painful from a performance standpoint. These are the cases where it is important to understand what is going on under the covers. Again, you can find more information on this issue in Chapter 11.

Skipping Some Offloading

Another very complex behavior that we will only mention briefly is the ability of `cellsrv` to refuse to do some of the normal offload processing. This can be done to avoid overloading the CPU resources on the storage cells, for example. A good example of this behavior occurs when decompressing HCC data. Decompression is an extremely CPU-intensive task, especially for the higher levels of compression. Since Exadata storage software 11.2.2.3.0 and later, `cellsrv` can choose to skip the decompression step on some portion of the data when the CPUs on the storage cells are very busy. This effectively moves some of the workload back to the database tier by forcing the database hosts to do the decompression.

Skipping Offloading silently

Sometimes the Exadata software has to revert to what is called passthrough mode. This can be a source of concern since it is not always evident this has happened, especially in 11g Release 2. The problem is best explained with an example. The following query normally takes very little time to execute:

```
SQL> select count(*) from bigtab where id = 80000;

  COUNT(*)
----------
        32

Elapsed: 00:00:00.83
```

Assume that the statement suddenly takes 25 seconds to execute. The systematic approach would be to check for changed plans, statistics, data volume, and so on. But nothing changed (this time for real). The statement was offloaded to the storage cells when it executed in less than a second, and checking now you can see that the wait event is indicating offloading, too. If you have the licenses to use ASH, you could use a very basic query like this one to that effect:

```
SQL> select count(*), event, session_state from v$active_session_history
  2  where sql_id = '0pmmwn5xq8h9a' group by event, session_state;

  COUNT(*) EVENT                          SESSION
---------- ---------------------------- -------
        28                                ON CPU
        46 cell smart table scan          WAITING
```

Interestingly, the query is offloaded, as you can see in the presence of the Cell Smart Table Scan event. The solution to the question, "Why is it slow?," must be elsewhere. At the risk of getting a little bit ahead of us, it lies in the session statistics. Using the tools `snapper` or `mystats` described in Chapter 11, you can find out that there are lots of passthrough operations:

```
Type   Statistic Name                                                          Value
------ ---------------------------------------------------------- ----------------
STAT   cell num bytes in passthru during predicate offload          28,004,319,232
STAT   cell num smart IO sessions using passthru mode due to cellsrv             1
STAT   cell physical IO bytes eligible for predicate offload        83,886,137,344
STAT   cell physical IO bytes saved by storage index                51,698,524,160
STAT   cell physical IO interconnect bytes returned by smart scan   28,004,930,160
```

Passthrough mode implies that the cells still perform a part of the Smart Scan, but instead of applying the predicate filtering, they pass the entire block to the RDBMS layer. You can read more about passthrough mode in Chapter 11.

How to Verify That Smart Scan Is Happening

One of the most important things you can learn about Exadata is how to identify whether a query has been able to take advantage of Smart Scans. Interestingly, the normal execution plan output produced by the DBMS_XPLAN package will not show you whether a Smart Scan was used or not. Here's an example:

```
PLAN_TABLE_OUTPUT
-------------------------------------
SQL_ID  2y17pb7bnmpt0, child number 0
-------------------------------------
select count(*) from bigtab where id = 17000

Plan hash value: 2140185107

-------------------------------------------------------------------------------------
| Id  | Operation                  | Name    | Rows  | Bytes | Cost (%CPU)| Time     |
-------------------------------------------------------------------------------------
|   0 | SELECT STATEMENT           |         |       |       |  2779K(100)|          |
|   1 |  SORT AGGREGATE            |         |     1 |     6 |            |          |
|*  2 |   TABLE ACCESS STORAGE FULL| BIGTAB  |    32 |   192 |  2779K  (1)| 00:01:49 |
-------------------------------------------------------------------------------------

Predicate Information (identified by operation id):
---------------------------------------------------

   2 - storage("ID"=17000)
       filter("ID"=17000)
```

Notice that the optimizer chose a TABLE ACCESS STORAGE FULL operation and that the predicate section shows a storage() predicate associated with step 2 of the plan. Both of these characteristics indicate that a Smart Scan was possible, but neither provides a definitive verification. In fact, the statement in this listing was *not* executed with a Smart Scan. If you wonder why, we set _serial_direct_read to never in the session just prior to executing the query.

The fact that execution plans do not show whether a Smart Scan was performed is a bit frustrating. However, there are several techniques that you can use to work around this issue. The next few sections will introduce some useful techniques. Note that the topic of analyzing whether a Smart Scan happened and how effective it was is covered in much more detail in Chapters 10 and 11.

10046 Trace

One of the most straightforward ways to determine whether a Smart Scan was used is to enable a 10046 trace on the statement in question. Unfortunately, this is a bit cumbersome and does not allow you to do any investigation into what has happened with past executions. Nevertheless, tracing is a fairly foolproof way to verify whether a Smart Scan was used or not. If a Smart Scan was used, there will be CELL SMART TABLE SCAN or CELL SMART INDEX SCAN events in the trace file. Here is an excerpt from the trace file collected for the previous statement (reformatted for better readability):

```
PARSING IN CURSOR #1..4 len=44 dep=0 uid=65 oct=3 lid=65 tim=1625363834946
  hv=3611940640 ad='5e7a2e420' sqlid='2y17pb7bnmpt0'
WAIT #139856525281664: nam='cell single block physical read' ela= 1237 ...
WAIT #139856525281664: nam='cell single block physical read' ela= 651 ...
WAIT #139856525281664: nam='cell single block physical read' ela= 598 ...
...
WAIT #139856525281664: nam='cell multiblock physical read' ela= 1189 ...
WAIT #139856525281664: nam='cell single block physical read' ela= 552 ...
WAIT #139856525281664: nam='cell multiblock physical read' ela= 596 ...
WAIT #139856525281664: nam='cell multiblock physical read' ela= 612 ...
WAIT #139856525281664: nam='cell multiblock physical read' ela= 607 ...
WAIT #139856525281664: nam='cell multiblock physical read' ela= 632 ...
WAIT #139856525281664: nam='cell multiblock physical read' ela= 618 ...
[...]
```

Note that the events recorded in this part of the trace file are single-block and multi-block reads. Oracle used the opportunity to rename the db file sequential read and db file scattered read wait events to the less confusing cell single-block read and cell multi-block read. Here's an example showing a Smart Scan:

```
PARSING IN CURSOR #139856525283104 len=44 dep=0 uid=65 oct=3 lid=65 tim=1625653524727
  hv=3611940640 ad='5e7a2e420' sqlid='2y17pb7bnmpt0'
select count(*) from bigtab where id = 17000
END OF STMT
PARSE #139856525283104:c=0,e=117,p=0,cr=0,cu=0,mis=0,r=0,dep=0,og=1,plh=2140185107,...
EXEC #139856525283104:c=0,e=55,p=0,cr=0,cu=0,mis=0,r=0,dep=0,og=1,plh=2140185107,...
WAIT #139856525283104: nam='SQL*Net message to client' ela= 3 ...
WAIT #139856525283104: nam='reliable message' ela= 1049 channel context=26855200120 ...
WAIT #139856525283104: nam='enq: KO - fast object checkpoint' ela= 298 ...
WAIT #139856525283104: nam='enq: KO - fast object checkpoint' ela= 156 ...
WAIT #139856525283104: nam='cell smart table scan' ela= 151 ...
WAIT #139856525283104: nam='cell smart table scan' ela= 168 ...
WAIT #139856525283104: nam='cell smart table scan' ela= 153 ...
WAIT #139856525283104: nam='cell smart table scan' ela= 269 ...
WAIT #139856525283104: nam='cell smart table scan' ela= 209 ...
WAIT #139856525283104: nam='cell smart table scan' ela= 231 ...
WAIT #139856525283104: nam='cell smart table scan' ela= 9 ...
[...]
```

In the second example, you can see many cell Smart Table Scan events, indicating that processing has been offloaded to the storage tier.

Session Performance Statistics

Another possibility is to look at some of the performance views such as V$SESSSTAT and V$MYSTAT. This is often overlooked but very helpful as you saw in the section about passthrough mode. An excellent way to investigate what is happening with a session that is currently executing a SQL statement is Tanel Poder's Snapper script. It provides a great way to see what wait events are being generated while a statement is running. In addition, it can capture the change in session counters during the period the SQL statement is observed. Snapper focuses on actively executing SQL statements; it is not meant to go back in time.

Performance statistics provide a reliable source of data as long as you can access the system during the execution of the statement you are investigating. Here is an example using `V$MYSTATS`, which is simply a version of `V$SESSSTAT` that limits data to your current session. For this example, the focus is on the `cell scans` statistic, which is incremented when a Smart Table Scan occurs on a segment:

```
SQL> @mystat
Enter value for name: cell scans

NAME                             VALUE
--------------------------------
cell scans                           0

Elapsed: 00:00:00.04
SQL> select count(*) from bigtab where id = 17001;

  COUNT(*)
----------
        32

Elapsed: 00:00:00.44
SQL> @mystat
Enter value for name: cell scans

NAME                             VALUE
--------------------------------
cell scans                           1

Elapsed: 00:00:00.02
SQL>
```

As you can see, the query has triggered the incrementing of the session counter. It is safe to say that there has been a Smart Scan between the two executions of the `mystats` script.

■ **Note** This script is not to be confused with another script named `mystats`, also referenced in this chapter. The `mystat` script selects from `v$mystat` and prints the current value for a given session counter. `mystats`, written by Adrian Billington and available from `oracle-developer.net`, calculates the change in session counters during the execution of a SQL statement, similar to Snapper in default mode but from begin to finish.

There is a lot more to say about session counters, and we do so in Chapter 11.

Offload Eligible Bytes

There is another clue to whether a statement used a Smart Scan or not. As you saw in previous sections, the `V$SQL` family of views contain a column called `IO_CELL_OFFLOAD_ELIGIBLE_BYTES`, which shows the number of bytes that are eligible for offloading. This column can be used as an indicator of whether a statement used a Smart Scan. It appears that this column is set to a value greater than 0 only when a Smart Scan is used.

You can make use of this observation to write a little script (`fsx.sql`) that returns a value of YES or NO, depending on whether that column in V$SQL has a value greater than 0. The output of the script is a little too wide to fit in a book format, which is why there are a couple of cut-down versions in the examples. And, of course, all of the versions will be available in the online code repository. You have already seen the script in action in several of the previous sections. The script is shown here for your convenience, along with an example of its use:

```
> !cat fsx.sql
----------------------------------------------------------------------------------------
--
-- File name:   fsx.sql
--
-- Purpose:     Find SQL and report whether it was Offloaded and % of I/O saved.
--
-- Usage:       This scripts prompts for two values.
--
--              sql_text: a piece of a SQL statement like %select col1, col2 from skew%
--
--              sql_id: the sql_id of the statement if you know it (leave blank to ignore)
--
-- Description:
--
--              This script can be used to locate statements in the shared pool and
--              determine whether they have been executed via Smart Scans.
--
--              It is based on the observation that the IO_CELL_OFFLOAD_ELIGIBLE_BYTES
--              column in V$SQL is only greater than 0 when a statement is executed
--              using a Smart Scan. The IO_SAVED_% column attempts to show the ratio of
--              of data received from the storage cells to the actual amount of data
--              that would have had to be retrieved on non-Exadata storage. Note that
--              as of 11.2.0.2, there are issues calculating this value with some queries.
--
--              Note that the AVG_ETIME will not be acurate for parallel queries. The
--              ELAPSED_TIME column contains the sum of all parallel slaves. So the
--              script divides the value by the number of PX slaves used which gives an
--              approximation.
--
--              Note also that if parallel slaves are spread across multiple nodes on
--              a RAC database the PX_SERVERS_EXECUTIONS column will not be set.
--
---------------------------------------------------------------------------------------
set pagesize 999
set lines 190
col sql_text format a70 trunc
col child format 99999
col execs format 9,999
col avg_etime format 99,999.99
col "IO_SAVED_%" format 999.99
col avg_px format 999
col offload for a7
```

```
select sql_id, child_number child, plan_hash_value plan_hash, executions execs,
(elapsed_time/1000000)/decode(nvl(executions,0),0,1,executions)/
decode(px_servers_executions,0,1,px_servers_executions/
decode(nvl(executions,0),0,1,executions)) avg_etime,
px_servers_executions/decode(nvl(executions,0),0,1,executions) avg_px,
decode(IO_CELL_OFFLOAD_ELIGIBLE_BYTES,0,'No','Yes') Offload,
decode(IO_CELL_OFFLOAD_ELIGIBLE_BYTES,0,0,
100*(IO_CELL_OFFLOAD_ELIGIBLE_BYTES-IO_INTERCONNECT_BYTES)
/decode(IO_CELL_OFFLOAD_ELIGIBLE_BYTES,0,1,IO_CELL_OFFLOAD_ELIGIBLE_BYTES))
"IO_SAVED_%", sql_text
from v$sql s
where upper(sql_text) like upper(nvl('&sql_text',sql_text))
and sql_text not like 'BEGIN :sql_text := %'
and sql_text not like '%IO_CELL_OFFLOAD_ELIGIBLE_BYTES%'
and sql_id like nvl('&sql_id',sql_id)
order by 1, 2, 3
/
```

In the fsx script, you can see that the OFFLOAD column is just a DECODE that checks to see if the IO_CELL_OFFLOAD_ELIGIBLE_BYTES column is equal to 0 or not. The IO_SAVED_% column is calculated using the IO_INTERCONNECT_BYTES field, and it attempts to show how much data was returned to the database servers.

The script can be used for many useful purposes. The author primarily uses it to find the SQL_ID and child cursor number of SQL statements in the shared pool. In this example, it is used to determine if a statement has been offloaded or not:

```
SQL> select /*+ gather_plan_statistics fsx-example-002 */
  2 avg(id) from bigtab where id between 1000 and 50000;

   AVG(ID)
----------
     25500

Elapsed: 00:00:00.64
SQL> alter session set cell_offload_processing=false;

Session altered.

Elapsed: 00:00:00.00
SQL> select /*+ gather_plan_statistics fsx-example-002 */
  2 avg(id) from bigtab where id between 1000 and 50000;

   AVG(ID)
----------
     25500

Elapsed: 00:00:53.88
SQL> @fsx4
Enter value for sql_text: %fsx-example-002%
Enter value for sql_id:
```

```
SQL_ID        CHILD OFFLOAD IO_SAVED_% AVG_ETIME SQL_TEXT
------------- ------ ------- ---------- ---------- ----------------------------------------
cj0p52wha5wb8      0 Yes          99.97        .63 select /*+ gather_plan_statistics fsx-ex
cj0p52wha5wb8      1 No             .00      53.88 select /*+ gather_plan_statistics fsx-ex

2 rows selected.
```

The elapsed times are a bit of a giveaway as to whether the statement was offloaded or not, but if you are called in after the fact, the output of the `fsx` script clearly shows that the `child_number` 1 has not been offloaded. The fact that a new child cursor has been created is very important in this example. When setting `CELL_OFFLOAD_PROCESSING` to `FALSE`, the optimizer created a new child cursor due to a mismatch. Reasons why child cursors are created can be found in `v$sql_shared_cursor`. This view contains a long list of flags that allow you to identify differences between child cursors but is very hard to read in SQL*Plus. Oracle added a CLOB containing XML data in 11.2.0.2 that makes it easier to spot the difference. Using the SQL ID from the previous example, this is put to use. Note that I cast the CLOB to XML for better readability:

```
SQL> select xmltype(reason) from v$sql_shared_cursor
  2   where sql_id = 'cj0p52wha5wb8' and child_number = 0;

XMLTYPE(REASON)
---------------------------------------------------------------------------
<ChildNode>
  <ChildNumber>0</ChildNumber>
  <ID>3</ID>
  <reason>Optimizer mismatch(12)</reason>
  <size>2x356</size>
  <cell_offload_processing> true     false  </cell_offload_processing>
</ChildNode>
```

Translating the XML output into plain English, you can see that there was an optimizer mismatch: The parameter `cell_offload_processing` has changed from `TRUE` to `FALSE`.

It is not always the case for child cursors to be created after changing parameters. Certain underscore parameters such as `_SERIAL_DIRECT_READ` will not cause a new child cursor to be created. Some executions of the same cursor might be offloaded, others not. This can be quite confusing, although this should be a very rare occurrence! Here is an example to demonstrate the effect:

```
SQL> select /*+ gather_plan_statistics fsx-example-004 */ avg(id)
  2  from bigtab where id between 1000 and 50002;

   AVG(ID)
----------
     25501

Elapsed: 00:00:00.68
SQL> alter session set "_serial_direct_read" = never;

Session altered.
```

```
Elapsed: 00:00:00.00
SQL> select /*+ gather_plan_statistics fsx-example-004 */ avg(id)
  2  from bigtab where id between 1000 and 50002;

   AVG(ID)
----------
     25501

Elapsed: 00:04:50.32
SQL> SQL> alter session set "_serial_direct_read" = auto;

Session altered.

Elapsed: 00:00:00.00
SQL> select /*+ gather_plan_statistics fsx-example-004 */ avg(id)
  2  from bigtab where id between 1000 and 50002;

   AVG(ID)
----------
     25501

Elapsed: 00:00:00.63
SQL> @fsx4
Enter value for sql_text: %fsx-example-004%
Enter value for sql_id:

SQL_ID         CHILD OFFLOAD IO_SAVED_%  AVG_ETIME SQL_TEXT
------------- ------ ------- ---------- ---------- ----------------------------------------
6xh6qwv302p13      0 Yes          55.17      97.21 select /*+ gather_plan_statistics fsx-ex
```

As you can see, there are three executions using the same child cursor (no new child cursor has been created). The statistics about I/O saved and execution time now have little value: Two executions completed in less than a second, and one took almost five minutes. This is the well-known problem with averages: They obfuscate detail.

SQL Monitoring

There is one other tool that is very useful for determining whether a SQL statement was offloaded, which is pretty cool for all performance investigations actually. The REPORT_SQL_MONITOR procedure is part of the Real Time SQL Monitoring functionality that was added with 11g. It is built into the DBMS_SQLTUNE package and provides a great deal of information, provided you have the license to use it. Not only does it provide information whether a statement was offloaded, but also on which steps in a plan were offloaded. Here is an example of an offloaded statement. Unfortunately the output is too wide—it has been condensed a little bit, but still has the essential information:

```
SQL> select /*+ gather_plan_statistics monitor sqlmonexample001 */
  2  count(*) from bigtab where id between 1000 and 50000;

  COUNT(*)
----------
   1568032
```

```
Elapsed: 00:00:00.66

SQL> @report_sql_monitor
Enter value for sid:
Enter value for sql_id:
Enter value for sql_exec_id:

REPORT
------------------------------
SQL Monitoring Report

SQL Text
------------------------------
select /*+ gather_plan_statistics monitor sqlmonexample002 */ count(*) from bigtab where id
between 1000 and 50000

Global Information
------------------------------
 Status              :  DONE (ALL ROWS)
 Instance ID         :  1
 Session             :  MARTIN (1108:55150)
 SQL ID              :  0kytf1zmdt5f1
 SQL Execution ID    :  16777216
 Execution Started   :  01/22/2015 05:59:26
 First Refresh Time  :  01/22/2015 05:59:26
 Last Refresh Time   :  01/22/2015 05:59:36
 Duration            :  10s
 Module/Action       :  SQL*Plus/-
 Service             :  SYS$USERS
 Program             :  sqlplus@enkdb03.enkitec.com (TNS V1-V3)
 Fetch Calls         :  1

Global Stats
================================================================================
| Elapsed |   Cpu   |    IO    | Application | Fetch | Buffer | Read  | Read  |  Cell   |
| Time(s) | Time(s) | Waits(s) |  Waits(s)   | Calls |  Gets  | Reqs  | Bytes | Offload |
================================================================================
|      11 |    4.03 |     7.25 |        0.00 |     1 |    10M | 80083 |  78GB |  99.96% |
================================================================================

SQL Plan Monitoring Details (Plan Hash Value=2140185107)
====================================================================================
| Id |        Operation          |  Name  | Cost |   Time    | Activity | Activity Detail |
|    |                           |        |      | Active(s) |   (%)    |   (# samples)   |
====================================================================================
|  0 |SELECT STATEMENT           |        |      |         9 |          |                 |
|  1 | SORT AGGREGATE            |        |      |         9 |          |                 |
|  2 |  TABLE ACCESS STORAGE FULL | BIGTAB |   3M |         9 |   100.00 | Cpu (3)         |
|    |                           |        |      |           |          | cell smart table |
|    |                           |        |      |           |          | scan (6)        |
====================================================================================
```

You can see that the report shows a Cell Offload percentage for the entire statement in the global section. In the details section, it also shows which steps were offloaded and what they did (Activity Detail) based on ASH samples. It also shows where the statement spent its time (Activity %). This can be extremely useful with more complex statements that have multiple steps eligible for offloading. Statements that are executed in parallel have that information listed per query server process, which leads to the next point worth mentioning: The text version of the SQL Monitor report can become difficult to read for more complex statements. The most useful output format you can get is by passing `ALL` to `REPORT_LEVEL` and `ACTIVE` as the `TYPE` parameter. The resulting output is an HTML file you can open in a browser and enjoy. Oracle Enterprise Manager offers GUI access to the SQL Monitor output as well. You can learn a lot more about all aspects around SQL Monitor in Chapter 12.

Note that monitoring occurs automatically on parallelized statements and on statements that the optimizer anticipates will run for a long time. If Oracle is not automatically choosing to monitor a statement that is of interest, you can use the `MONITOR` hint to tell Oracle to monitor the statement, as seen in the example. You can check `V$SQL_MONITOR` to see if you can create a report on your `SQL_ID`.

Parameters

There are several parameters that apply to offloading. The main one is `CELL_OFFLOAD_PROCESSING`, which turns offloading on and off. There are several others that are of less importance. Table 2-2 shows a list of the non-hidden parameters that affect offloading (as of Oracle database version 12.1.0.2). Note that we have also included the hidden parameter, `_SERIAL_DIRECT_READ`, which controls this very important feature.

Table 2-2. *Important Database Parameters Controlling Offloading*

Parameter	Default	Description
`cell_offload_decryption`	`TRUE`	Controls whether decryption is offloaded. Note that when this parameter is set to `FALSE`, Smart Scans are completely disabled on encrypted data.
`cell_offload_plan_display`	`AUTO`	Controls whether Exadata operation names are used in execution plan output from `DBMS_XPLAN.DISPLAY%` functions.
`cell_offload_processing`	`TRUE`	Turns offloading on or off.
`_serial_direct_read`	`AUTO`	Controls the serial direct path read mechanism. The valid values are `ALWAYS`, `AUTO`, `TRUE`, `FALSE`, and `NEVER`.

In addition to the normal Oracle-approved parameters, there are a number of so-called hidden parameters that affect various aspects of offloading. You can view them using the `parms.sql` script provided in the online code repository by connecting as SYSDBA and specifying both `kcfis` (for kernel file intelligent storage) and `cell` (for all cellsrv related parameters). As always, note that hidden parameters should not be used on Oracle systems without prior discussion and consent from Oracle support, but they do provide valuable clues about how some of the Exadata features work and are controlled.

Summary

Offloading really is the secret sauce of Exadata. While the hardware architecture does a good job of providing more balance between the storage layer's ability to deliver data and the database layer's ability to consume it, the bulk of the performance gains are provided by the software. Smart Scans are largely responsible for these gains. The primary focus of most of these optimizations is to reduce the amount of data transferred between the storage tier and the database tier. If you have read the whole chapter from beginning to end, you will undoubtedly have noticed that there is a lot of ground to cover. Where possible, we stayed with the fundamentals necessary to understand offloading. Chapters 10–11 go into a lot more detail on the various important aspects. They introduce all the relevant Exadata wait events and most of the performance counters that Oracle tracks for each session. Chapter 12 finally gives you the overview of the tools needed to analyze Exadata query performance.

■ **Note** This page could be intentionally left blank because every chapter should end on an *even* numbered page, *even* if a blank needs to be added at the end.

CHAPTER 3

Hybrid Columnar Compression

Hybrid Columnar Compression, or (E)HCC for short, was, and probably still is, one of the most misunderstood features in Exadata. This has not really changed since the first edition of this book, which is why we place such an emphasis on it. HCC started out as an Exadata-only feature, but its use is now available to a more general audience. Anyone who wants to use HCC at the time of this writing will have to either use Exadata or the Oracle ZFS Storage Appliance. The Pillar Axiom series of storage arrays also support working with HCC compressed data natively, without having to decompress it first. Oracle's most recent storage offering, the FS1 array, also features HCC on its data sheet. Offloading scans of HCC data remains the domain of the Exadata storage cells though.

This chapter has been divided into three major areas:

- An introduction to how Oracle stores data physically on disk
- The concepts behind HCC and their implementation
- Common use cases and automating data lifecycle management

In the first part of this chapter, you will read more about the way the Oracle database stores information in what is referred to as the "Row Major" format. It explains the structure of the Oracle database block and two of the available compression methods: BASIC and ADVANCED.

Understanding the anatomy of the Oracle block is important before moving on to the next part of the chapter, which introduces the "Column Major" format unique to HCC. And in case you wondered about the "hybrid" in HCC, we will explain this as well. We will then discuss how the data is actually stored on disk, and when and where compression and decompression will occur. We will also explain the impact of HCC compressed data on Smart Scans as opposed to traditional ways of performing I/O.

The final part of this chapter is dedicated to the new Automatic Data Optimization option that helps automating and enforcing data lifecycle management.

Oracle Storage Review

As you probably already know, Oracle stores data in a block structure. These blocks are typically 8k nowadays. You define the default block size during the database creation. It is very difficult if not impossible to change the default block size after the database is created. There is good reason to stay with the 8k block size in a database as Oracle appears to perform most of its regression testing against that block size. And, if you really need to, you can still create tablespaces with different—usually bigger—block sizes.

Where does the database block fit into the bigger picture? The block is the smallest physical storage unit in Oracle. Multiple blocks form an extent, and multiple extents make up a segment. Segments are objects you work with in the database such as tables, partitions, and subpartitions.

Simplistically speaking, the block consists of a header, the table directory, a row directory, row data, and free space. The row header starts at the top of the block and works its way down, while the row data starts at the bottom and works its way up. Figure 3-1 shows the various components of a standard Oracle block in its detail.

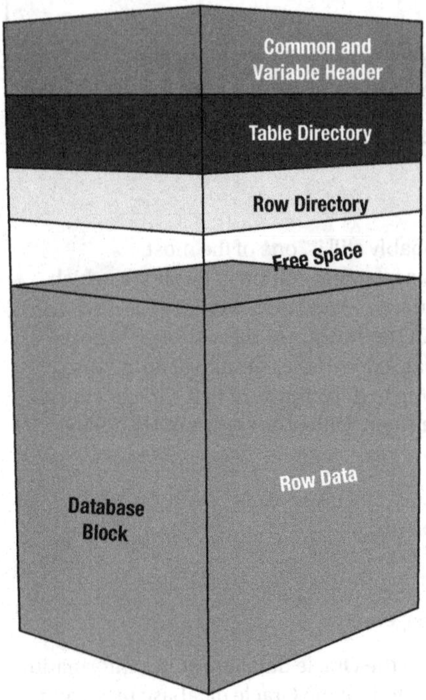

***Figure 3-1.** The standard Oracle block format (row-major storage)*

Rows are stored in no specific order, but columns are generally stored in the order in which they were defined in that table. For each row in a block there will be a row header, followed by the column data for each column. Figure 3-2 shows how the pieces of a row are stored in a standard Oracle block. Note that it is called a row piece because, occasionally, a row's data may be stored in more than one chunk. In this case, there will be a pointer to the next row piece. Chapter 11 will introduce the implications of this in great detail.

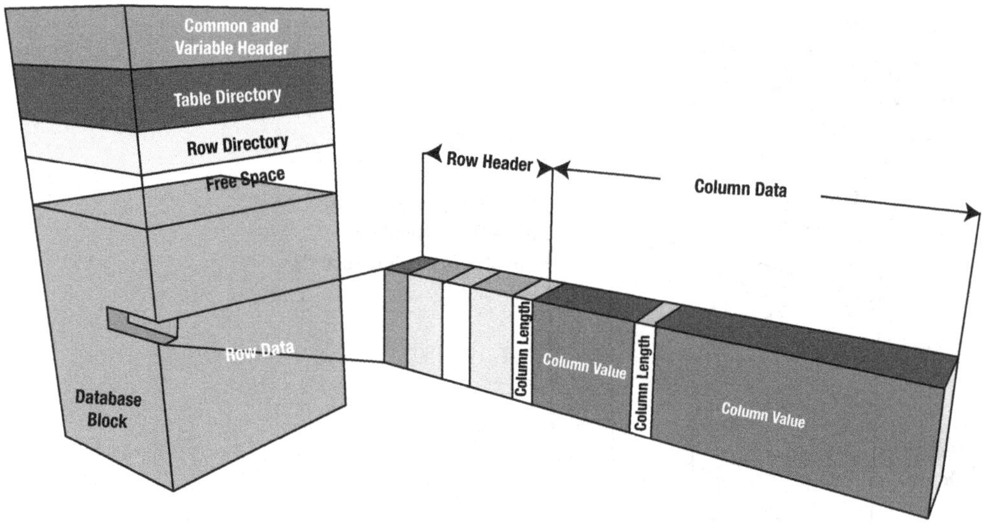

Figure 3-2. *The standard Oracle row format (row-major storage)*

Note that the row header may contain a pointer to another row piece. More on this will follow a little later, but for now, just be aware that there is a mechanism to point to another location. Also note that each column is preceded by a separate field, indicating the length of the column. Nothing is actually stored in the column value field for NULL values. The presence of a null column is indicated by a value of 0 in the column length field. Trailing NULL columns do not even store the column length fields, as the presence of a new row header indicates that there are no more columns with values in the current row.

PCTFREE is a key value associated with blocks; it controls how much space is used in a block when inserting data before it is considered full. Its purpose is to reserve some free space in each block for (future) updates. This is necessary to prevent row migration (moving rows to new blocks) that would be caused by lack of space in the row's original block when a row increases in size. When rows are expected to be updated with values requiring more space, more space in form of a higher PCTFREE setting can be reserved by the database administrator. When rows are not expected to increase in size because of updates, values as low as 0 may be specified by PCTFREE. With compressed blocks, it is common to use very low values of PCTFREE because the goal is to minimize space usage and rows are generally not expected to be updated. Figure 3-3 shows how free space is reserved based on the value of PCTFREE.

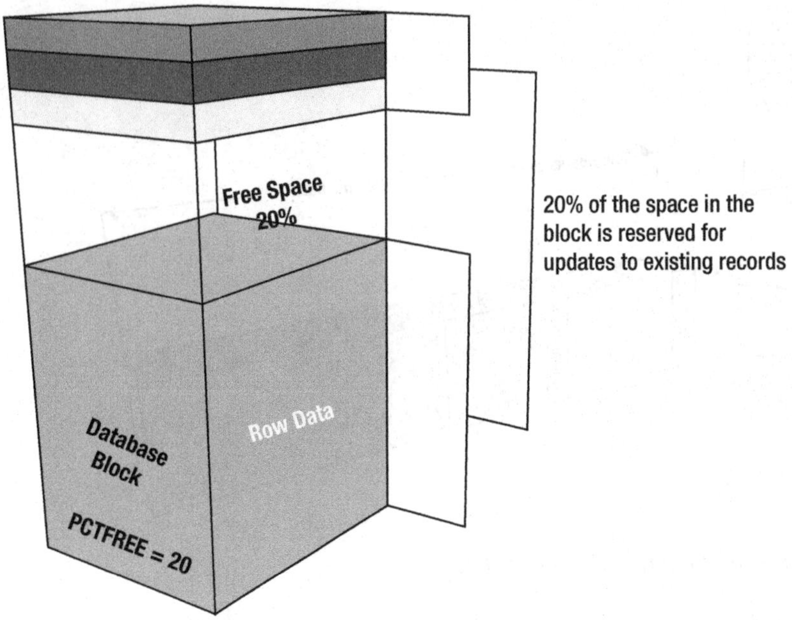

Figure 3-3. *Block free space controlled by PCTFREE*

Figure 3-3 shows a block that reserves 20 percent of its space for updates. A block with a PCTFREE setting of 0 percent would allow inserts to fill the block almost completely. When a record is updated and the new data will not fit in the available free space of the block where the record is stored, the database will move the row to a new block. This process is referred to as the said *row migration*. It does not completely remove the row from the original block but leaves a reference to the newly relocated row so that it can still be found by its original ROWID. The ROWID format defines how the database has to look up a row. It consists of the data object number, data file number, the data block, and finally the row in the block. The ROWID can be externalized by specifying the ROWID pseudo-column when querying a table. Oracle provides a package named DBMS_ROWID that allows you to parse the ROWID and extract the relevant bits of information you are after. The ROWID format will become important when you want to investigate the internals of a database block by dumping it into a trace file.

Note that the more generic term for storing rows in more than one piece is *row chaining*. Row migration is a special case of row chaining in which the entire row is relocated. Examples for row chaining and migration are presented in Chapter 11 of this book.

Disassembling the Oracle Block

So far you have only read about the concepts, but we intend to prove them as well, wherever possible. When you start looking at block dumps, then you can find all the cases of row chaining in the row headers. You can dump a block using the `alter system dump datafile x block y` syntax. Although the command is not documented officially, there are many sources that explain the technique. Here is an example of a small snippet from a block dump where the row is entirely contained in the same block. Most of the block dump information has been removed for clarity.

```
block_row_dump:
tab 0, row 0, @0x1f92
tl: 6 fb: --H-FL-- lb: 0x2  cc: 1
```

```
col  0: [ 2]  c1 02
tab 0, row 1, @0x1f8c
tl: 6 fb: --H-FL-- lb: 0x0  cc: 1
col  0: [ 2]  c1 03
```

The table definition has deliberately kept to the bare minimum, and there is just one column (named "ID") of data type NUMBER in the table. The crucial information in this dump with regards to this discussion is the flag in the row header: According to David Litchfield's article "The Oracle Database Block," the flag byte (fb) in the row header can have the following bits set:

- K = Cluster Key
- C = Cluster table member
- H = Head piece of row
- D = Deleted row
- F = First data piece
- L = Last data piece
- P = First column continues from previous piece
- N = Last column continues in next piece

In the context of the block dump, the bits H, F, and L are set, translating to the head piece, first piece, and last piece. In other words, the column data that follows is sufficient to read the whole row. But how does Oracle know what to read in the block when it comes to row lookups? Oracle records in every block how many tables are to be found. Normally, you would only find one in there, but in some special cases such as BASIC/ADVANCED compressed blocks or clustered tables you can find two. The line starting "tab 0, row 0..." references the first table in the block, and row 0 is self-explanatory. The hexadecimal number following the @-sign is the offset within the block.

To better understand the importance of the offset, you need to look at the header structures preceding the row directory. The table-directory, which precedes the row directory in the block, lists the rows in the block and their location. Consulting the table directory together with the row directory allows Oracle to find the row in question and directly jump to the offset in the row directory shown above in the output from the block dump—one of the reasons why the lookup by ROWID is so efficient! The table directory (plus some detail from the data header) looks like this for the block dump shown above:

```
ntab=1
nrow=2
frre=-1
fsbo=0x16
fseo=0x1f8c
avsp=0x1f70
tosp=0x1f70
0xe:pti[0]      nrow=2  offs=0
0x12:pri[0]     offs=0x1f92
0x14:pri[1]     offs=0x1f8c
```

To locate the row, Oracle needs to find the offset to table 0 in the block and locate the row by means of the offset. In case of the first row, the offset is 0x1f92. This is found in the row data:

```
tab 0, row 0, @0x1f92
```

This explains why a table lookup by ROWID is so fast and efficient. Migrated rows, on the other hand, merely have the head piece set and none of the other flags. Here is an example from a different table:

```
block_row_dump:
tab 0, row 0, @0x1f77
tl: 9 fb: --H----- lb: 0x3  cc: 0
nrid:  0x00c813b6.0
tab 0, row 1, @0x1f6e
tl: 9 fb: --H----- lb: 0x3  cc: 0
nrid:  0x00c813b6.1
```

If you look carefully at the dump, you notice an additional piece of information. These rows have a NRID or next ROWID. This is the said pointer to the block where the row continues. A NRID pointer exists for all chained rows, including migrated rows. To decode the NRID, you can use the DBMS_UTILITY package. Careful though—the NRID is encoded in a hexadecimal format and first needs to be converted to a decimal value. Also, there is a limitation, even in 12c, that it does not seem to work with big file tablespaces. The NRID format finishes with a ".x" where x is the row number. To locate the block for NRID 0x00c813b6.0, you could use this script (the table resides on a smallfile tablespace):

```
SQL> !cat nrid.sql
select
     dbms_utility.data_block_address_file(to_number('&1','xxxxxxxxxxxx')) file_no,
     dbms_utility.data_block_address_block(to_number('&1','xxxxxxxxxxxx')) block_no
from dual;

SQL> @nrid 00c813b6

   FILE_NO   BLOCK_NO
---------- ----------
         7     529334
```

So the row continues in data file 7, block 529334.

A row can start in one block and continue in another bock (or even blocks), a phenomenon known as *chained row*. An example is shown here. The row begins in the block with DBA (Data Block Address) 0x014000f3:

```
tab 0, row 0, @0x30
tl: 8016 fb: --H-F--N lb: 0x0  cc: 1
nrid:  0x014000f4.0
col  0: [8004]
```

You can the start of the row (*H*ead piece and *F*irst piece) and an indication that the row continues (*N*ext) elsewhere. The NRID points to a DBA of 0x014000f4 and continues in row 0.

```
tab 0, row 0, @0x1f
tl: 8033 fb: ------PN lb: 0x0  cc: 1
nrid:  0x014000f5.0
```

Here, you see that the row has a *P*revious piece and a *N*ext one to follow in DBA 0x014000f5, again row 0. This is a severe case of a chained row because it spans more than just two blocks. A few more row pieces later, we find the last remaining piece:

```
tab 0, row 0, @0x1d7c
tl: 516 fb: -----LP- lb: 0x0  cc: 1
```

The *L* in the flag byte indicates that this is the *L*ast piece; the *P* flag indicates there are *P*revious row pieces. Coincidentally, this is how a HCC super-block, a so-called Compression Unit (CU), is constructed. In the previous example, a row was "spread" over a number of blocks, which is usually undesirable in row-major format. With HCC using the column-major format, however, you will see that this is a very clever design and not at all harmful for performance. You can read more about those Compression Units later, but first let's focus on the available compression mechanics before the advent of HCC.

Compression Mechanics

HCC is a relatively new compression technology in Oracle. Before its introduction, you had different compression mechanisms available at your disposal. The naming of the technologies has changed over time, and it is admittedly somewhat confusing. The syntax for using them also seems to change with every release. To keep a common denominator, the names BASIC, OLTP, and HCC will be used.

BASIC Compression

As the name suggests, BASIC compression is a standard feature in Oracle. To benefit from BASIC compression, you have to use the direct path method of injecting rows into the table. A direct path load basically bypasses the SQL engine and the transactional mechanism built into Oracle and inserts blocks above the segment's high water mark or into an alternative "temporary" segment. More specifically, during the direct path insert, the buffer cache is not being utilized. After the direct path load operation finishes, it is mandatory to commit the transaction before anyone else can apply DML to the table. This is a concession to the faster loading process:

```
SQL> insert /*+ append */ into destination select * from dba_objects;

20543 rows created.

SQL> select * from destination;
select * from destination
              *
ERROR at line 1:
ORA-12838: cannot read/modify an object after modifying it in parallel
```

This is a major hindrance for using BASIC compression for anything but archival. Another "problem" is that updates to the data cause the updated row(s) to be stored uncompressed. The same is true for inserts not using the direct path loading mechanism.

Rows have always been stored in the format just shown in Oracle until HCC has been released—in so-called row-major format. The opposite of row-major format is the new HCC-specific column-major format you can read about later in this chapter. All BASIC compressed data will be stored self-contained within Oracle blocks. If you want to create a table with BASIC compression enabled, you can do so when you create the table or afterward:

```
SQL> create table T ... compress;

SQL> alter table T compress;
```

Note that changing a table from non-compressed to `compress` will *not* compress the data already stored in in. You first have to "move" the table, which causes the compaction of data. The command to move the table does not require the specification of a tablespace, allowing you to keep the table where it is. BASIC compression has been introduced in Oracle 9i. This form of compression is also known as Decision Support System (DSS) Compression. In fact, the term *compression* is slightly misleading. BASIC compression (and OLTP compression, for that matter) uses a de-duplication approach to reducing the amount of data to store. The details about this compression algorithm will be discussed in the next section.

OLTP Compression

OLTP compression has been one of the innovative features presented with Oracle 11g Release 1, but, unlike BASIC compression, its use requires you to have the license for the Advanced Compression Option. The Advanced Compression Option is not limited to database block compression, it can do more. An Oracle white paper describes all the use cases, and you will come across it again later in this chapter. Although the feature has been renamed to Advanced Row Compression in Oracle 12c we decided to go with its former name since we have grown so accustomed to it.

Recall from the previous section on BASIC compression that you need to use direct path operations in order to benefit from any compression. This requirement made it very difficult to use compression for tables and partitions that were actively being subjected to DML operations. If you did not use direct path operations on these, then you would increase concurrency at the cost of not compressing. If you sacrificed concurrency for storage footprint, you had to change your code and commit immediately after touching the segment. Neither of the two options are a solution, especially not the last one. OLTP compression removed the pain. Using OLTP compression, you do not need to use direct path operations for inserts, yet you benefit from compression. And unlike BASIC compression, which does not leave room in the block for future updates by default (PCTREE is 0), OLTP compression does.

Conceptually you start inserting into a new block. The rows are not compressed initially. Only when a threshold is reached will the block be compressed. This should free up some space in the block, and the block might end up available for DML again. After more rows are inserted, the threshold is hit again, data is compressed, and so forth until the block is fully utilized and compressed.

The syntax for using OLTP compression has changed; here are examples for 11g Release 1 and 2, and 12c Release 1:

```
SQL> -- 11.1 syntax
SQL> create table T ... compress for all operations;
SQL> -- 11.2 syntax
SQL> create table T ... compress for OLTP;
SQL> -- 12.1 syntax
SQL> create table T ... row store compress ADVANCED;
```

The parser in 12c Release 1 is backward compatible, but you should take the effort and update your scripts to the new syntax as the old DDL statements are deprecated.

OLTP compression is very important even if you are primarily going to compress using HCC, as it is the fallback compression method for any updated rows that previously were stored in a HCC compressed segment. An update on HCC compressed data cannot be done in-place. Instead, the row is migrated to an OLTP compressed block that might not even get compressed because it is mostly empty initially.

From a technical point of view, BASIC and OLTP compression are identical. Oracle uses de-duplication, in that it replaces occurrences of identical data with a symbol. The symbol must be looked up when reading the table; that is why, technically speaking, you find two tables in an OLTP compressed block. The first table contains the symbol table, while the second table contains the "real" data. The block dump—again reduced to the minimum necessary—shows the following:

```
bdba: 0x01437a2b
...
ntab=2
nrow=320
...
        r0_9ir2=0x0
        mec_kdbh9ir2=0x1c
                      76543210
        shcf_kdbh9ir2=----------
                  76543210
        flag_9ir2=--R---OC      Archive compression: N
                fcls_9ir2[0]={ }
                perm_9ir2[18]={ 8 16 0 17 15 14 10 13 11 1 5 6 2 12 3 4 9 7 }
0x28:pti[0]     nrow=53 offs=0
0x2c:pti[1]     nrow=267        offs=53
block_row_dump:
tab 0, row 0, @0x1dd6
tl: 7 fb: --H-FL-- lb: 0x0  cc: 15
col  0: *NULL*
col  1: [ 5]  56 41 4c 49 44
col  2: [ 1]  4e
col  3: *NULL*
col  4: [ 4]  4e 4f 4e 45
col  5: [ 1]  4e
col  6: [ 1]  4e
col  7: [ 1]  59
col  8: [ 3]  53 59 53
col  9: *NULL*
col 10: [ 7]  78 71 07 11 16 3c 0a
col 11: [19]  32 30 31 33 2d 30 37 2d 31 37 3a 32 31 3a 35 39 3a 30 39
col 12: [ 2]  c1 05
col 13: [ 7]  78 71 07 11 16 3c 0a
col 14: [ 5]  49 4e 44 45 58
bindmp: 00 55 0f 0e 20 1d 23
...
tab 1, row 0, @0x1dae
tl: 14 fb: --H-FL-- lb: 0x0  cc: 18
col  0: *NULL*
col  1: [ 5]  56 41 4c 49 44
col  2: [ 1]  4e
col  3: *NULL*
```

```
col  4: [ 4]  4e 4f 4e 45
col  5: [ 1]  4e
col  6: [ 1]  4e
col  7: [ 1]  59
col  8: [ 3]  53 59 53
col  9: *NULL*
col 10: [ 7]  78 71 07 11 16 3c 09
col 11: [19]  32 30 31 33 2d 30 37 2d 31 37 3a 32 31 3a 35 39 3a 30 38
col 12: [ 2]  c1 02
col 13: [ 7]  78 71 07 11 16 3c 09
col 14: [ 5]  54 41 42 4c 45
col 15: [ 2]  c1 03
col 16: [ 5]  49 43 4f 4c 24
col 17: [ 2]  c1 15
bindmp: 2c 00 04 03 1c cd 49 43 4f 4c 24 ca c1 15...
```

Things to note in the above output are highlighted in bold typeface. First of all, you see that there are two tables with 320 rows in total in the block. The ROWIDs with pti[0] and pti[1] explain where the number of rows per table and the table offset are for each of the two. Table 0 is the symbol table, and it is referenced by the bindmp in the "real" table, table 1. The algorithm on how to use the bindmp to locate symbols in the symbol table is out of the scope of this discussion. If you want to learn more about mapping symbol table to data table and how to read the row data as Oracle does, please refer to the article series "Compression in Oracle" by Jonathan Lewis.

Hybrid Columnar Compression

Finally, after that much introduction, you have reached the main section of this chapter—Hybrid Columnar Compression. As stated before, the use of HCC requires you to either use Exadata or the Oracle ZFS Storage Appliance or either the Pillar Axiom or Oracle FS1 storage array. Remember from the chapter on Smart Scans (Chapter 2) that a tablespace must be entirely contained on an Exadata storage server to be eligible for offload processing.

While you can manipulate HCC compressed data outside Exadata with the previously mentioned storage systems, you cannot get Smart Scans on these devices. So if you are not using any of these aforementioned storage devices, then you are out of luck. Although RMAN would restore HCC compressed data happily, accessing it while compressed does not work and you have to decompress before use (space permitting). Importing HCC compressed tables is possible if you specify the TABLE_COMPRESSION_CLAUSE of the TRANSFORM parameter so as to set the table compression to NOCOMPRESS for example. However this is a 12c feature.

```
[oracle@enkdb03 ~]$ impdp ... transform=table_compression_clause:nocompress
```

On the other hand, this might require a lot of space.

What Does the "Hybrid" in "Hybrid Columnar Compression" Mean?

Most relational database systems store data in a row-oriented format. The discussion of the Oracle block illustrates that concept: The Oracle database block contains row(s). Each row has multiple columns, and Oracle accesses these columns by reading the row, locating the column, reading the value (if it exits), and displaying the value to the end user. The basic unit the Oracle database engine operates on is the row. Row lookups by ROWID—or index-based lookups—are very efficient for most general-purpose and OLTP query engines. On the other hand, if you just want a single column of a table and perhaps to perform an aggregation on all the column's values in that table, you incur significant overhead. The "wider" your table is (in other words, the more columns it has), the greater the overhead if you want to retrieve and work on just a single one.

Columnar database engines operate on columns rather than rows, reducing the overhead just mentioned. Unlike a standard Oracle block of 8kb, a columnar database will most likely employ a larger block size of multiples of those 8k we know from the Oracle engine. It might also store values for the column co-located, potentially with lots of optimizations already included in the way it stores the column. This is likely to make columnar access very fast. Instead of having to read the whole row to extract just the value of a single column, the engine can iterate over a large-ish block and retrieve many values in multi-block operations. Columnar databases, therefore, are more geared toward analytic or read-mostly workloads. Columnar databases cannot excel in row lookups by design. In order to read a complete row, multiple large-ish blocks of storage have to be read *for each column in the table*. Therefore, columnar databases are not very good for the equivalent of (full-row) ROWID lookups usually seen in OLTP workloads.

Oracle Hybrid Columnar Compression combines advantages of columnar data organization in that it stores columns separately within a new storage type, the so-called Compression Unit or CU. But unlike pure columnar databases, it does not neglect the "table access by index ROWID" path to retrieve information. The CU is written contiguously to disk in form of multiple standard Oracle blocks. Information pertaining to a given row is within the same CU, allowing Oracle to blindly issue one or two read requests matching the size of the CU and be sure that the row information has been retrieved. As you will see later in the chapter, Exadata accesses HCC compressed data in one of two modes: block oriented or via Smart Scan.

Making Use of Hybrid Columnar Compression

HCC compression requires you to use direct path operations (again!) just as with BASIC compression. This might sound like a step back from what was possible with OLTP-compression, but in our experience it is not. There are further things worth knowing about HCC that you will read about in the next few paragraphs outlining why HCC needs to be used with a properly designed data lifecycle management policy in mind. Conventional inserts and updates cause records to be stored outside the HCC specific CU while deletes simply cause the CU header information to be updated. In case of updates, rows will migrate to new blocks flagged for OLTP compression. Any of these new blocks marked for OLTP compression are not necessarily compressed straight away. If they are not filled up to the internal threshold, then nothing will happen initially, inflating the segment size proportionally to the number of rows updated.

With HCC, you can choose from four different compression types, as shown in Table 3-1. Note that the expected compression ratios are very rough estimates and that the actual compression ratio for *your* data can deviate significantly from these numbers.

Table 3-1. HCC Compression Types

Compression Type	Description	Expected Compression Ratio
Query Low	HCC Level 1 uses algorithm 1. As of Oracle 12.1, this is the LZO (Lempel-Ziv-Oberhumer) compression algorithm. This level provides the lowest compression ratios but requires the least CPU for compression and decompression operations. This algorithm is optimized for maximizing speed (specifically for row-level access). Decompression is very fast with this algorithm.	4x
Query High	HCC Level 2 uses the ZLIB (gzip) compression algorithm as of Oracle 12.1.	6x
Archive Low	HCC Level 3 uses the same compression algorithm as Query High but at a higher compression level. Depending on the data, however, the compression ratios may not exceed those of Query High by significant amounts.	7x
Archive High	HCC Level 4 compression uses the Bzip2 compression algorithm as of 12.1. This is the highest level of compression available but is far and away the most CPU intensive. Compression times are often several times slower than for level 2 and 3. But again, depending on the data, the compression ratio may not be much higher than with Archive Low. This level is for situations where the regulator requires you to keep the data online while otherwise you would have archived it off to tertiary storage. Data compressed with this algorithm is truly cold and rarely touched.	12x

COMPRESSION ALGORITHMS

The implementation details of the various compression algorithms listed in Table 3-1 are current only at the time of this writing. Oracle reserves the right to make changes to the algorithm and refers to them in generic terms. The actual implementation is of little significance to the administrator since there is no control over them anyway. What remains a fact is that the higher the compression level, the more aggressive the algorithm. Aggressive in this context refers to how effective the data volume can be shrunk, and aggressiveness is directly proportional to CPU required. You can read more about the actual mechanics of compressing data later in the chapter.

The reference to the compression algorithms (LZO, GZIP, BZIP2) are all inferred from the function names in the Oracle code. The `ORADEBUG` utility helped printing short stack traces of the session compressing the data. As an example, here is the short stack for a create table statement for ARCHIVE HIGH compression:

```
BZ2_bzCompress()+144<-kgccbzip2pseudodo()+136<-kgccdo()+51<-kdzc_comp_
buffer()+371<-kdzc_comp_colgrp()+595<-kdzc_comp_unit()+1598<-kdzc_comp_full_
unit()+80<-kdzcompress()
```

Interestingly, but on the other hand not surprisingly, the code has changed from the first edition of the book. If you find references to functions beginning with `kdz`, there is a high probability they are used for HCC.

You can enable HCC when you create the table or partition, or afterward. Here are some code examples:

```
SQL> create table t_ql ... column store compress for query low;

SQL> create table t_ah ... column store compress for archive high;

SQL> alter table t1 modify partition p_jun_2013 column store compress for query high;
```

As with all previous examples, please note that changing a table or partition's compression status using the alter table statement does not have any effect for data already stored in the segment. It applies for future (direct path) inserts only. To compress data already stored in the segment, you have to move the segment. The alter table . . . move statement does not require you to specify a destination tablespace. To query the dictionary about the current status of the segment compression, use COMPRESSION and COMPRESS_FOR columns found in DBA_TABLES, DBA_TAB_PARTITIONS, and DBA_TAB_SUBPARTITIONS, for example:

```
SQL> select table_name,compression,compress_for
  2  from user_tables;

TABLE_NAME                     COMPRESS COMPRESS_FOR
------------------------------ -------- ------------
T1                             DISABLED
T1_QL                          ENABLED  QUERY LOW
T1_QH                          ENABLED  QUERY HIGH
T1_AL                          ENABLED  ARCHIVE LOW
T1_AH                          ENABLED  ARCHIVE HIGH
```

But again, these do not reflect the actual size of the segment, or if the segment is actually compressed with that particular compression type. The impact of compression on table sizes is demonstrated using the tables above: T1 is uncompressed and serves as a baseline while the others are compressed with the different algorithms available in Oracle 12.1:

```
SQL> select s.segment_name, s.bytes/power(1024,2) mb, s.blocks,
  2  t.compression, t.compress_for, num_rows
  3  from user_segments s, user_tables t
  4  where s.segment_name = t.table_name
  5  and s.segment_name like 'T1%'
  6  order by mb;

SEGMENT_NAME                MB     BLOCKS COMPRESS COMPRESS_FOR                    NUM_ROWS
-------------------- ---------- ---------- -------- ------------------------------ ---------
T1                         3840     491520 DISABLED                                33554432
T1_QL                       936     119808 ENABLED  QUERY LOW                      33554432
T1_QH                       408      52224 ENABLED  QUERY HIGH                     33554432
T1_AL                       408      52224 ENABLED  ARCHIVE LOW                    33554432
T1_AH                       304      38912 ENABLED  ARCHIVE HIGH                   33554432
```

The compressed tables have been created using a CTAS statement on the same tablespace as the baseline table with exactly the same number of rows. Again, the compression ratios are for illustration only. Your data compression ratios are most likely different.

To find out more about the compression algorithm employed for a given row, you can use the built-in package DBMS_COMPRESSION. It features the GET_COMPRESSION_TYPE function that takes the owner, table name, and ROWID as arguments.

```
SQL> select id, rowid,
  2  dbms_compression.get_compression_type(user, 'T1_QL', rowid) compType
  3  from t1_ql where rownum < 3;

        ID ROWID                COMPTYPE
---------- ------------------ ----------
         1 AAAPAgAAKAAJogDAAA          8
         2 AAAPAgAAKAAJogDAAB          8
```

The meaning of these values is explained in the PL/SQL Packages and Types reference for the DBMS_COMPRESSION package. The compression type "8" indicates the use of the Query Low compression algorithm. If you now think you could run a running count(*) against the query to get the compression type of each block, you are mistaken—this takes far too long to be practical, even for "small" tables.

HCC Internals

The fact that data stored in the HCC format is stored in a new format—column major—has already been touched in the introduction to HCC compression. You could also read something about the way the HCC compressed data is stored internally. In this section, you can read more about the actual HCC mechanics.

First of all, the compressed data is stored in an Oracle meta-block, called a Compression Unit. This is the first and probably most visible of the innovative HCC features. It does not mean Oracle blocks as we know them are not used, just slightly differently.

Before going into more detail, I would like to present you with a symbolic block dump of a CU from Oracle 11.2.0.4, edited for brevity.

```
Block header dump:  0x014000f3
 Object id on Block? Y
 seg/obj: 0x420f  csc: 0x00.1bec83  itc: 3  flg: E  typ: 1 - DATA
...
bdba: 0x014000f3
data_block_dump,data header at 0x7f190a39b07c
===============================================
...
ntab=1
nrow=1
frre=-1
...
tosp=0x14
        r0_9ir2=0x0
        mec_kdbh9ir2=0x0
                      76543210
        shcf_kdbh9ir2=----------
                    76543210
```

```
        flag_9ir2=--R-----      Archive compression: Y
                fcls_9ir2[0]={ }
0x16:pti[0]     nrow=1  offs=0
0x1a:pri[0]     offs=0x30
block_row_dump:
tab 0, row 0, @0x30
tl: 8016 fb: --H-F--N lb: 0x0  cc: 1
nrid:  0x014000f4.0
col  0: [8004]
Compression level: 01 (Query Low)
 Length of CU row: 8004
kdzhrh: ------PC CBLK: 4 Start Slot: 00
 NUMP: 04
 PNUM: 00 POFF: 7954 PRID: 0x014000f4.0
 PNUM: 01 POFF: 15970 PRID: 0x014000f5.0
 PNUM: 02 POFF: 23986 PRID: 0x014000f6.0
 PNUM: 03 POFF: 32002 PRID: 0x014000f7.0
CU header:
CU version: 0   CU magic number: 0x4b445a30
CU checksum: 0xf47f1618
CU total length: 32502
CU flags: NC-U-CRD-OP
ncols: 6
nrows: 2459
algo: 0
CU decomp length: 32148   len/value length: 324421
row pieces per row: 1
num deleted rows: 0
START_CU:
 00 00 1f 44 0f 04 00 00 00 04 00 00 1f 12 01 40 00 f4 00 00 00 00 3e 62 01
 ...
```

This is not the entire CU, just the Head piece. The block dump for a CU looks like a block dump for a compressed Oracle block. Technically speaking, a CU is a chained row across a number of standard Oracle blocks written to disk contiguously. Every block stores one table and that table has just one row (ntab=1 and nrow=1). Even stranger, that one row just has a single column (cc: 1), even though the table DDL shows many more. The CU header identifies the block to be the CU's head piece (Head, First, Next flags are set). The header describes the compressed data in the CU, such as the total length, number of columns, number of rows, the decompressed length, and the number of deleted rows. The actual data starts within the `START_CU` tag. A lot further down you will see an `END_CPU` and `BINDMP`. The Head piece of the CU also stores information about where the actual columns are located. A bitmap is encoded within the first block's `START_CU` piece, indicating rows that have been deleted and pointers to where columns start. The row starting with `NUMP` lists the number of blocks in the CU. This CU uses Query Low as the compression algorithm, and it consists of four pieces located in blocks 0x014000f4, ...f5, ...f6, and ...f7 (= contiguously written to disk).

Conceptually, you can think about a CU as a logical concept similar to the one in Figure 3-4.

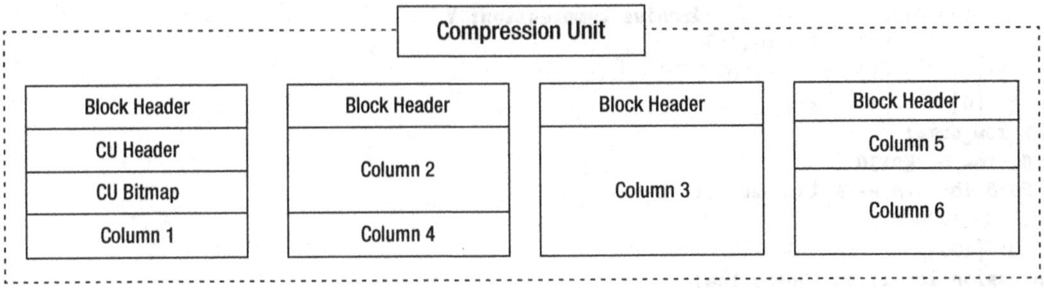

***Figure 3-4.** Schematic display of a Compression Unit*

Each block is chained to the next one using the `NRID` notation and the "next" bit set in the row header. This is the second block of the CU. Note how the DBA is the next block adjacent to the Head piece.

```
block_row_dump:
tab 0, row 0, @0x1f
tl: 8033 fb: ------PN lb: 0x0  cc: 1
nrid:  0x014000f5.0
col  0: [8021]
Compression level: 01 (Query Low)
```

Also note how each block describes the data stored in it. In this case, it is Query Low. A self-describing block allows the user to change the compression algorithm ad libitum and still gives Oracle enough information on how to decompress the block. This is why `DBMS_COMPRESSION.GET_COMPRESION_TYPE` is so useful. What you can also derive from Figure 3-4 is that the rows are no longer stored together in the same way as before in row-major format. Instead, all the data is organized by column within the CU. The bitmap in the first block of the CU, contained between `START_CU` and `END_CU` tells Oracle where to find the column and the row within it. The way the CU is laid out is not what you would find in a pure columnar database, but rather a cross ("hybrid") between the two. Remember that sorting is done only within a single CU, except for Query Low where sorting is not applied at load time to speed the process up. The next CU will start over with more data from column 1 again. The advantage of this format is that it allows a row to be read in its entirety by reading just a single CU. A pure columnar database would have to read multiple blocks, one for each column in the row. This is why Oracle can safely claim that index-based lookups to CUs are possible without the same overhead as for a pure columnar database. The disadvantage is that reading an individual record will require reading a multi-block CU instead of a single block. Of course, full table scans will not suffer because all the blocks will be read anyway. On the contrary, the full scan is most likely to benefit from the columnar storage format if your query references only the columns it actually needs. This way the code can loop through each CU in an efficient code-path referencing only columns required.

You will read more about the trade-offs a little later, but you should already be thinking that having to read the whole CU instead of just a block can be disadvantageous for tables that need to support lots of single row access. And remember that the CU is also compressed, which requires CPU cycles when decompressing it.

The sorting by columns is actually done to improve the effectiveness of the compression algorithms, not to get performance benefits of column-oriented storage. This is another contribution to the "hybrid" in HCC.

What Happens When You Create a HCC Compressed Table?

Tracing and instrumentation for HCC is embedded in the ADVCMP component. Using the new Universal Tracing Facility (UTS) for tracing Oracle, you can actually see what is happening when you are compressing a table. The syntax to enable UTS tracing for HCC is documented in ORADEBUG. Invoking ORADEBUG allows you to view what can be traced:

```
SQL> oradebug doc component ADVCMP

Components in library ADVCMP:
--------------------------------------------------------------------------
ADVCMP_MAIN              Archive Compression (kdz)
ADVCMP_COMP              Archive Compression: Compression (kdzc, kdzh, kdza)
ADVCMP_DECOMP            Archive Compression: Decompression (kdzd, kdzs)
ADVCMP_DECOMP_HPK        Archive Compression: HPK (kdzk)
ADVCMP_DECOMP_PCODE      Archive Compression: Pcode (kdp)
```

Although this component is documented even in 11g Release 2, the examples in this chapter are from 12.1.0.2. Interestingly, the `ORADEBUG doc component` command without arguments shows you code locations! From the previous code, you can derive that the KDZ* routines in Oracle seem to relate to HCC. This helps when viewing the trace file. Consider the following statement to enable tracing the compression (Warning: this can generate many gigabytes worth of trace data—do not ever run this in production, only in a dedicated lab environment. You risk filling up /u01 and causing huge problems otherwise):

```
SQL> alter session set events 'trace[ADVCMP_MAIN.*] disk=high';
```

If you are curious about the UTS syntax, just run `oradebug doc event` as described by co-author Tanel Poder on his blog. With the trace enabled, you can start compressing. Either use alter table ... move or create table ... column store compress for ... syntax to begin the operation and trace.

```
alter session set tracefile_identifier = 't2ql';
alter session set events 'trace[ADVCMP_MAIN.*] disk=high';

create table t2_ql
column store compress for query low
as select * from t2;

alter session set events 'trace[ADVCMP_MAIN.*] off';
```

■ **Note** Be warned that the trace is very, very verbose, and it easily generates many GB worth of trace data, filling up your database software mount point and thus causing all databases to grind to a halt! Again, never run such a trace outside a dedicated lab environment.

Before Oracle actually starts compressing, it analyzes the incoming data to work out the best way to compress the column. The trace will emit lines like these:

```
kdzcinit(): ctx: 0x7f9f4b7a1868  actx: (nil)  zca: (nil)  ulevel: 1  ncols: 8 totalcols: 8
kdzainit(): ctx: 7f9f4b7a2d48 ulevel 1 amt 1048576 row 4096 min 5
kdzalcd(): objn: 61487 ulevel: 1
```

```
kdzalcd(): topalgo: -1 err: 100
kdza_init_eq(): objn: 61487  ulevel: 1  enqueue state:0
kdzhDecideAlignment(): pnum: 0 min_target_size: 32000 max_target_size: 32000 ↵
  alignment_target_size: 128000 ksepec: 0 postallocmode: 0 hcc_flags: 0
kdzh_datasize(): freesz: 0 blkdtsz: 8168 flag: 1 initrans: 3 dbidl: 8050 dbhsz: 22 ↵
  dbhszz: 14 drhsz: 9 maxmult: 140737069841520
kdzh_datasize(): pnum: 0 ds: 8016 bs: 8192 ov: 20 alloc_num: 7 min_targetsz: ↵
  32000 max_targetsz: 32000 maxunitsz: 40000 delvec_size: 7954
kdzhbirc(): pnum: 0 buffer 1 rows soff: 0
...
```

It appears as if the calls to KDZA* initialize the data analyzer for object 61487 (Table T2_QL). ULEVEL in the trace possibly relates to the compression algorithm 1 (Query Low, as you will see in the block dump). The output related to kdzh_datasize() looks related to the CU header and compression information. The next lines are concerned with filling a buffer and needed to get an idea about the data to be compressed. Once that first buffer has been filled, the analyzer creates a new CU. For higher compression levels, Oracle will try to pre-sort the data before compressing it. This may not make sense in all cases—if the analyzer detects such a case, it will skip the sorting for that column. Oracle can also perform column permutation if it adds a benefit to the overall compression.

The result of this operation is presented in the analyzer context:

```
Compression Analyzer Context Dump Begin
---------------------------------------
ctx: 0x7f9f4b7a2d48  objn: 61487
Number of columns: 8
ulevel: 1
ilevel: 4645
Top algorithm: 0
Sort column: None
Total Output Size: 109435
Total Input Size: 396668
Grouping: Column-major, columns separate

Column Permutation Information
------------------------------
Columns not permuted
Total Number of rows/values  : 4096

Column Information
------------------
Col      Algo     InBytes/Row        OutBytes/Row     Ratio    Type     Name        Type Name
---      ----     -----------        ------------     -----    ----     ----        ---------
0        1025             4.0                3.01       1.3    2        NULL        NUMBER
1        257             11.0                4.11       2.7    1        NULL        CHAR
2        1025             4.0                3.01       1.3    2        NULL        NUMBER
3        1025             3.0                0.05      60.5    2        NULL        NUMBER
4        1025             5.0                4.08       1.2    2        NULL        NUMBER
5        1025             4.9                4.01       1.2    2        NULL        NUMBER
6        257              4.0                3.07       1.3    2        NULL        NUMBER
7        257             61.0                5.41      11.3    1        NULL        CHAR

Total                                        96.8            26.75         3.6
```

```
Column Metrics Information
--------------------------
Col     Unique  Repeat  AvgRun  DUnique DRepeat AvgDRun
---     ------  ------  ------  ------- ------- -------
0         4096       0     1.0        0       0     0.0
1         4096       0     1.0        0       0     0.0
2         4096       0     1.0        0       0     0.0
3           47      46    95.3        0       0     0.0
4         4082      14     1.0        0       0     0.0
5         4061      35     1.0        0       0     0.0
6         3646     408     1.0        0       0     0.0
7         3841     241     1.0        0       0     0.0

Compression Analyzer Context Dump End
-------------------------------------
```

The result of the analysis is then stored in the dictionary for reuse.

■ **Note** This step is not needed when the analysis has already been performed, such as when inserting into a HCC compressed segment.

Unfortunately, there does not seem to be an easy way to extract the analyzer information once it has been stored. Before writing the CU, you can see lots of interesting information about it in `kdzhailseb()` before the CUs are dumped for the table. The functions referenced in the trace file are also easily visible in the ORADEBUG short stack. The traces also helped confirm the various CU sizes Oracle tries to create, as found in `kdzhDecideAlignment()`. Table 3-2 lists the result of different create table statement for all four compression algorithms.

Table 3-2. *Target CU Sizes and Their Alignment Target for Oracle 12.1.0.2*

Compression Type	min_target_size	max_target_size
Query Low	32000	32000
Query High	32000	64768
Archive Low	32000	261376
Archive High	261376	261376

Remember that the same algorithm (GZIP when this text was written) is used for Query High and Archive Low. Another observation we made is that the actual CU size can vary, except for Archive High where it appears fixed.

HCC Performance

There are three areas of concern when discussing performance related to table compression. The first is *load performance*. It addresses the question how long it takes to load the data. Since compression always happens on the compute nodes and during direct path operations, it is essential to measure the impact of compression on loads. The second area of concern, *query performance*, is the impact of decompression and other side effects on queries against the compressed data. The third area of concern, *DML performance*, is the impact compression algorithms have on other DML activities such as updates and deletes.

Load Performance

As you might expect, load time tends to increase with the amount of compression applied. As the saying goes, "There is no such thing as a free lunch." Compression is computationally expensive—there is no doubt about that. The more aggressive the compression algorithm, the more CPU cycles you are going to use. The algorithms Oracle currently implements range from LZO to GZIP and BZIP2, with LZO yielding the lowest compression ratio but shortest compression time. BZIP2 can potentially give you the best compression but at the cost of huge CPU usage. There is an argument that states that data compressed with `ARCHIVE HIGH` is better decompressed to `ARCHIVE LOW` before querying it *repeatedly*. Compression ratios are hugely dependent on data-a series of the character "c", repeated a billion times can be represented with very little that is already compressed such as a JPEG image cannot be compressed further.

With this introduction, it is time to look at an example. The data in the table T3 is reasonably random. To increase the data volume, it has been copied over itself a number of times (`insert into t3 select * from t3` for a total size of 11.523 GB). The table has then been subjected to compression using BASIC, OLTP, and all HCC compression algorithms. The outcome is reported in Table 3-3.

Table 3-3. *The Effect of Compression on the Example. Table-Load Has Been Performed Serially*

Table Name	Compression	Compression Ratio	Load Time	Load Time Ratio
T3	None	1.0	00:01:16.91	1.0
T3_BASIC	BASIC	1.1	00:03:02.98	2.4
T3_OLTP	OLTP	1.0	00:03:07.22	2.4
T3_QL	Query Low	6.7	00:01:56.98	1.5
T3_QH	Query High	15.2	00:04:23.41	3.4
T3_AL	Archive Low	15.5	00:04:57.51	3.9
T3_AH	Archive High	20.6	00:17:07.17	13.4

As you can see, Query High and Archive Low yield almost identical compression ratios for this particular data set. Loading the data took roughly 30 seconds more. Loading data with compression enabled definitely has an impact—the duration to create the table is somewhere between 2.5 and 4 times longer than without compression. What is interesting is that BASIC and OLTP compression almost make no difference at all in storage space used. Not every data set is equally well compressible. Timings here are taken from an X2 system; current Exadata systems have faster and more efficient CPUs.

The compression ratios increase by a few magnitudes as soon as HCC is enabled. The load times increase in line with the storage savings except for Archive High, which we will get back to later. Loading data serially, however, is rather pedestrian in Exadata, and significant performance gains can be made by parallelizing the load operation.

■ **Note** You can read more about parallel operations in Chapter 6.

Be warned that even though Exadata is a very powerful platform, you should not overload your system with parallel queries and parallel DML! And also note you do not *have* to insert into HCC compressed segments. Depending on your strategy you can introduce compression at later stages.

Query Performance

Load time is only the first performance metric of interest. Once the data is loaded, it needs to be accessible in reasonable time as well! Most systems load data once and read it many times more often. Query performance is a mixed bag when it comes to compression. Depending on the type of query, compression can either speed it up or slow it down. Decompression can add overhead in the way of additional CPU usage, especially if it has to be performed on the compute node. The offset of using more CPU to decompress the data is on disk access. Compressed data means fewer blocks need to be physically read from disk. If the query favors the column-major format of the HCC compressed rows, additional gains are possible. These combined usually outweigh the extra cost of decompressing.

There are essentially two access patterns with HCC compressed data: Smart Scan or traditional block I/O. The importance of these lies in the way that HCC data is decompressed. For non-Smart Scans, the decompression will have to be performed on the compute node. An interesting question in this context is how long it takes to retrieve a row by its `ROWID`. It seems logical that the larger the CU, the longer it takes to decompress it. You may have asked yourself the question in previous sections of this chapter where the difference was between Query High and Archive Low, apart obviously from the CU size. The gist of it is that Archive High gives you slightly better compression and offloaded full table scans. `ROWID` access, which often is not a Smart Scan, with Archive Low is inherently a little worse due to the larger CU size. As with so many architectural decisions, it comes down again to "knowing your data."

Another important aspect is related to Lifecycle Management. Imagine a situation where the table partition in its native form is eligible for Smart Scans. Reports and any data access that relies on offloaded scans will perform at the expected speed. It is well possible that introducing compression to that partition over its lifetime will reduce the size to an extent where the segment is no longer eligible for Smart Scans. This may have a performance impact, but not necessarily so. We have seen many cases where the storage savings, in addition to the column-major format, more than outweighed the missing Smart Scans.

Returning to another set of demonstration tables that have been subject to compression, we would like to demonstrate the different types of I/O and their impact on query performance. The demonstration tables used in this section contain 128 million rows and have the following sizes:

```
SQL> select owner,segment_name,segment_type,bytes/power(1024,2) m, blocks
  2  from dba_segments
  3  where segment_name like 'T3%' and owner = 'MARTIN'
  4  order by m;

OWNER                SEGMENT_NAME                   SEGMENT_TYPE                M     BLOCKS
-------------------- ------------------------------ ------------------ ---------- ----------
MARTIN               T3_AH                          TABLE                    2240     286720
MARTIN               T3_QH                          TABLE                    3136     401408
MARTIN               T3_AL                          TABLE                    3136     401408
MARTIN               T3_QL                          TABLE                    6912     884736
MARTIN               T3_BASIC                       TABLE                   71488    9150464
MARTIN               T3_OLTP                        TABLE                   80064   10248192
MARTIN               T3                             TABLE                80100.75   10252896

8 rows selected.
```

In the first step, statistics are calculated on all of them using a call to DBMS_STATS as shown:

```
SQL> exec dbms_stats.gather_table_stats(ownname => user, tabname => 'T3', -
  2  method_opt=>'for all columns size 1', degree=>4)
```

The times per table are listed in Table 3-4.

Table 3-4. *The Effect of Compression on the Gathering Statistics*

Table Name	Compression	Compression Ratio	Run Time	Run Time Ratio
T3	None	1.0	00:01:15.60	1.0
T3_BASIC	BASIC	1.1	00:01:21.49	1.08
T3_OLTP	OLTP	1.0	00:01:21.77	1.08
T3_QL	Query Low	11.6	00:01:20.51	1.08
T3_QH	Query High	25.5	00:01:18.08	1.06
T3_AL	Archive Low	25.5	00:01:30.90	1.03
T3_AH	Archive High	35.8	00:03:00.29	1.20

Gathering statistics is certainly something that is more CPU intensive. The above examples were run with a very moderate Degree Of Parallelism (DOP) of 4. Increasing the DOP to 32 is suited to put quite a strain on the machine:

```
top - 02:41:02 up 95 days,  8:48,  5 users,  load average: 7.97, 3.34, 2.10
Tasks: 1357 total,  20 running, 1336 sleeping,   0 stopped,   1 zombie
Cpu(s): 85.8%us,  5.2%sy,  0.0%ni,  8.4%id,  0.0%wa,  0.0%hi,  0.6%si,  0.0%st
Mem:  98807256k total, 97729000k used,  1078256k free,   758456k buffers
Swap: 25165820k total,  5640088k used, 19525732k free, 13032976k cached

  PID USER      PR  NI  VIRT  RES  SHR S %CPU %MEM    TIME+  COMMAND
21209 oracle    20   0 8520m  19m  10m S 79.6  0.0   0:29.42 ora_p00k_db12c1
21239 oracle    20   0 8520m  19m  10m R 77.3  0.0   0:29.35 ora_p00r_db12c1
21247 oracle    20   0 8520m  20m  10m S 76.0  0.0   0:29.56 ora_p00v_db12c1
21110 oracle    20   0 8539m  35m  13m S 74.0  0.0  47:07.75 ora_p002_db12c1
21241 oracle    20   0 8520m  19m  10m R 73.7  0.0   0:28.33 ora_p00s_db12c1
21203 oracle    20   0 8520m  20m  10m S 73.4  0.0   0:29.35 ora_p00j_db12c1
21185 oracle    20   0 8520m  20m  10m R 71.7  0.0   0:28.86 ora_p00g_db12c1
21245 oracle    20   0 8520m  18m  10m R 71.1  0.0   0:28.66 ora_p00u_db12c1
21167 oracle    20   0 8532m  28m  11m R 69.4  0.0   3:46.38 ora_p00e_db12c1
21225 oracle    20   0 8520m  18m  10m R 69.4  0.0   0:28.43 ora_p00o_db12c1
21243 oracle    20   0 8520m  20m  10m S 69.1  0.0   0:29.29 ora_p00t_db12c1
21217 oracle    20   0 8520m  19m  10m S 68.8  0.0   0:29.68 ora_p00m_db12c1
```

As you can see, the compression slowed down the processing enough to outweigh the gains from the reduced number of data blocks that need to be read. This is due to the CPU intensive nature of the work being done.

Next up is another example that uses a very I/O intensive query. This test uses a query without a where clause that spends most of the time retrieving data from the storage layer via Smart Scans. First is the query against the baseline table—with a size of 80 GB. To negate the effect the automatic caching of data in Flash Cache has, this feature has been disabled on all tables. In addition, storage indexes have been disabled to ensure comparable results between the executions.

```
SQL> select  /*+ parallel(16) monitor gather_plan_statistics */
  2  /* hcctest_io_001 */
  3  sum(id) from t3;

   SUM(ID)
----------
1.0240E+15

Elapsed: 00:00:07.33
```

In Table 3-5, we compare this time to all the other tables.

Table 3-5. *The Effect of Compression on Full-Table Scans*

Table Name	Compression	Compression Ratio	Run Time	Run Time Ratio
T3	None	1.0	00:00:23.54	1.0
T3_BASIC	BASIC	1.1	00:00:19.27	0.82
T3_OLTP	OLTP	1.0	00:00:19.59	0.83
T3_QL	Query Low	11.6	00:00:02.64	0.11
T3_QH	Query High	25.5	00:00:01.86	0.08
T3_AL	Archive Low	25.5	00:00:01.86	0.08
T3_AH	Archive High	35.8	00:00:01.90	0.08

Automatic caching of data on Cell Flash Cache can contribute significantly to performance. Due to the fact that T3 was used as the basis for the creation of all other tables, large portions of it were found on flash cache. The initial execution time was 00:00:07.33. Cell Flash Cache as well as storage indexes were disabled when executing the queries whose runtime was recorded in Table 3-5. But since automatic caching of data is so beneficial for overall query performance, you should not disable Cell Flash Cache for a table. Leaving it at the default is usually sufficient from cell version 11.2.3.3.0 onward.

Executing these queries does not require a lot of CPU usage on the compute nodes. Since these operations were offloaded, only the cells were busy. The immense reduction in execution time is mostly due to the smaller size to be scanned. Although the Smart Scan is performed on the cells, they cannot skip reading data since storage indexes were disabled. The system had to go through roughly 80GB in the baseline and a mere 3 GB for Query High. Here is an example for the CPU usage during one of the queries:

```
top - 03:47:25 up 95 days,  9:54,  4 users,  load average: 2.23, 1.78, 1.84
Tasks: 1349 total,   5 running, 1343 sleeping,   0 stopped,   1 zombie
Cpu(s):  3.1%us,  1.3%sy,  0.0%ni, 95.5%id,  0.1%wa,  0.0%hi,  0.1%si,  0.0%st
Mem:  98807256k total, 95911576k used,  2895680k free,   356604k buffers
Swap: 25165820k total,  5731988k used, 19433832k free, 11756500k cached
```

```
  PID USER      PR  NI  VIRT  RES  SHR S %CPU %MEM    TIME+  COMMAND
21116 oracle    20   0 8551m  39m  13m R 55.6  0.0  15:14.08 ora_p005_db12c1
21153 oracle    20   0 8540m  28m  11m S 48.2  0.0   4:58.39 ora_p00c_db12c1
21108 oracle    20   0 8553m  45m  14m S 44.5  0.0  49:14.08 ora_p001_db12c1
21112 oracle    20   0 8548m  43m  13m S 44.5  0.0  47:26.76 ora_p003_db12c1
21136 oracle    20   0 8528m  28m  11m S 42.6  0.0   4:59.52 ora_p00a_db12c1
21110 oracle    20   0 8539m  35m  14m S 40.8  0.0  48:24.29 ora_p002_db12c1
21106 oracle    20   0 8539m  36m  14m S 38.9  0.0  49:21.38 ora_p000_db12c1
21122 oracle    20   0 8568m  39m  13m S 37.1  0.0  15:01.77 ora_p007_db12c1
21149 oracle    20   0 8536m  29m  11m R 37.1  0.0   4:58.12 ora_p00b_db12c1
21175 oracle    20   0 8528m  29m  11m S 37.1  0.0   5:01.79 ora_p00f_db12c1
21118 oracle    20   0 8544m  45m  13m R 35.2  0.0  14:57.77 ora_p006_db12c1
21161 oracle    20   0 8544m  30m  11m S 35.2  0.0   5:01.12 ora_p00d_db12c1
21114 oracle    20   0 8547m  42m  13m S 33.4  0.0  15:09.21 ora_p004_db12c1
21126 oracle    20   0 8544m  30m  11m S 33.4  0.0   4:55.96 ora_p008_db12c1
21130 oracle    20   0 8536m  28m  11m R 29.7  0.0   5:00.08 ora_p009_db12c1
21167 oracle    20   0 8528m  28m  11m S 27.8  0.0   5:04.26 ora_p00e_db12c1
22936 root      20   0 11880 2012  748 S 13.0  0.0   0:39.81 top
```

DML Performance

Generally speaking, records that will be updated should not be compressed. When you update a record in an HCC table, the record will be migrated to a new block that is flagged as an OLTP compressed block. Of course, a pointer will be left behind so that you can still get to the record via its old `ROWID`, but the record will be assigned a new `ROWID` as well. Since updated records are downgraded to OLTP compression, you need to understand how that compression mechanism works on updates. Figure 3-5 demonstrates how non-direct path loads into an OLTP block are processed.

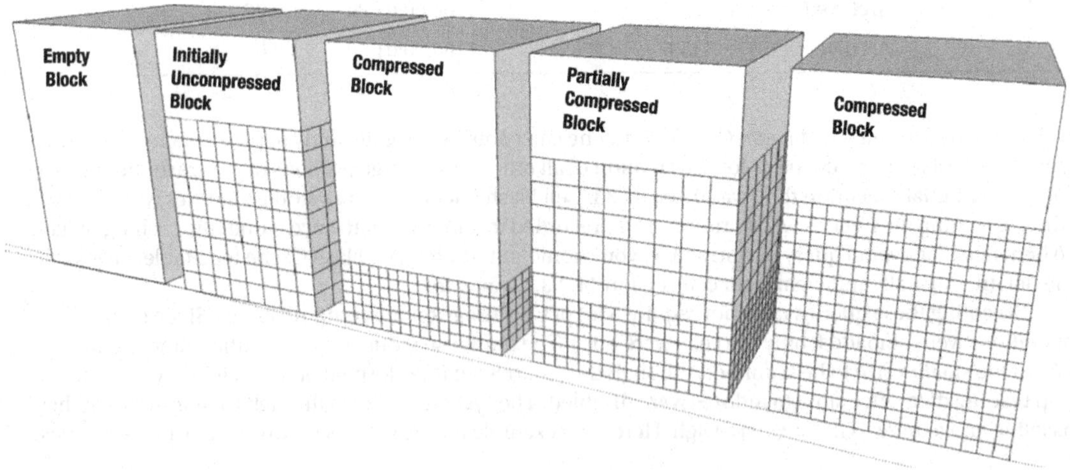

Figure 3-5. *The OLTP compression process for non-direct path loads*

The progression of states moves from left to right. Rows are initially loaded in an uncompressed state. As the block fills to the point where no more rows can be inserted, the row data in the block is compressed. The block is then made available again and is capable of accepting more uncompressed rows. This means that in an OLTP compressed table, blocks can be in various states of compression. All rows can be compressed, some rows can be compressed, or no rows can be compressed. This is exactly how records in HCC blocks behave when they are updated. A couple of examples will demonstrate this behavior. The first example will show how the size of a table can balloon with updates. Before the update, the segment was 408 MB in size. The uncompressed table is listed here for comparison:

```
SQL> select segment_name,trunc(bytes/power(1024,2)) m
  2  from user_segments where segment_name in ('T1', 'T1_QH');

SEGMENT_NAME                            M
------------------------------ ----------
T1                                   3840
T1_QH                                 408
```

Next, the entire compressed table is updated. After the update completes, you should check its size:

```
SQL> update t1_qh set id = id + 1;

33554432 rows updated.

SQL> select segment_name,trunc(bytes/power(1024,2)) m
  2  from user_segments where segment_name in ('T1','T1_QH')
  3  order by segment_name;

SEGMENT_NAME                                            M
-------------------------------------- ---------------
T1                                            3,841.00
T1_QH                                         5,123.00

2 rows selected.
```

At this point, you will notice that the updated blocks are of type 64-OLTP, compressed as a result of an update from a HCC compressed table. A call to DBMS_COMPRESSION.GET_COMPRESSION_TYPE confirms this:

```
SQL> select decode (dbms_compression.get_compression_type(user,'T1_QH',rowid),
  2      1,  'COMP_NOCOMPRESS',
  3      2,  'COMP_FOR_OLTP',
  4      4,  'COMP_FOR_QUERY_HIGH',
  5      8,  'COMP_FOR_QUERY_LOW',
  6      16, 'COMP_FOR_ARCHIVE_HIGH',
  7      32, 'COMP_FOR_ARCHIVE_LOW',
  8      64, 'COMP_BLOCK',
  9      'OTHER') type
 10  from T1_QH
 11* where rownum < 11
SQL> /
```

```
TYPE
---------------------
COMP_BLOCK
COMP_BLOCK
COMP_BLOCK
COMP_BLOCK
COMP_BLOCK
COMP_BLOCK
COMP_BLOCK
COMP_BLOCK
COMP_BLOCK
COMP_BLOCK

10 rows selected.
```

The above is an example for 11.2.0.4. The constraints in DBMS_COMPRESSION have been renamed in Oracle 12c—the "FOR" has been removed and COMP_FOR_OLTP is now known as COMP_ADVANCED. As soon as you re-compress the table, the size returns back to normal.

```
SQL> select segment_name,trunc(bytes/power(1024,2)) m
  2  from user_segments where segment_name in ('T1','T1_QH')
  3  order by segment_name;

SEGMENT_NAME                                         M
---------------------------------------- -------------
T1                                            3,841.00
T1_QH                                           546.00

2 rows selected.
```

The second example demonstrates what happens when you update a row. Unlike in previous versions of the software, the updated row is not migrated, as you will see. It is deleted from the CU, but there is no pointer left behind where the row migrated. This helps avoiding following the chained row visible in the "table fetch continued row" statistic.

Here is the table size with all rows compressed. The table needs to be on a SMALLFILE tablespace if you want to follow the example. The table does not need to contain useful information, it is merely big.

```
SQL> create table UPDTEST_QL column store compress for query low
  2  tablespace users as select * from UPDTEST_BASE;

Table created.

SQL> select segment_name, bytes/power(1024,2) m, compress_for
  2  from user_segments s left outer join user_tables t
  3  on (s.segment_name = t.table_name)
  4  where s.segment_name like 'UPDTEST%'
  5  /

SEGMENT_NAME                            M COMPRESS_FOR
------------------------------ ---------- ------------------------------
UPDTEST_QL                             18 QUERY LOW
UPDTEST_BASE                         1344
```

For the example, you need to get the first ID from the table and some other meta information:

```
SQL> select dbms_compression.get_compression_type(user,'UPDTEST_QL',rowid) as ctype,
  2  rowid, old_rowid(rowid) DBA, id from UPDTEST_QL where id between 1 and 10
  3  /

     CTYPE ROWID              DBA                          ID
---------- ------------------ -------------------- ----------
         8 AAAG6TAAFAALORzAAA 5.2942067.0                   1
         8 AAAG6TAAFAALORzAAB 5.2942067.1                   2
         8 AAAG6TAAFAALORzAAC 5.2942067.2                   3
         8 AAAG6TAAFAALORzAAD 5.2942067.3                   4
         8 AAAG6TAAFAALORzAAE 5.2942067.4                   5
         8 AAAG6TAAFAALORzAAF 5.2942067.5                   6
         8 AAAG6TAAFAALORzAAG 5.2942067.6                   7
         8 AAAG6TAAFAALORzAAH 5.2942067.7                   8
         8 AAAG6TAAFAALORzAAI 5.2942067.8                   9
         8 AAAG6TAAFAALORzAAJ 5.2942067.9                  10
```

The function `old_rowid()` is available from the Enkitec blog and the online code repository in file `create_old_rowid.sql`. It decodes the `ROWID` to get the Data Block Address or the location on disk. In the above example, ID 1 is in file 5, block 2942067, and slot 0. A compression type of 8 indicates Query Low. Let's begin the modification:

```
SQL> update UPDTEST_QL set spcol = 'I AM UPDATED' where id between 1 and 10;

10 rows updated.

SQL> commit;

Commit complete.

SQL> select dbms_compression.get_compression_type(user,'UPDTEST_QL',rowid) as ctype,
  2  rowid, old_rowid(rowid) DBA, id from updtest_ql where id between 1 and 10;

     CTYPE ROWID              DBA                          ID
---------- ------------------ -------------------- ----------
        64 AAAG6TAAFAAK4jhAAA 5.2853089.0                   1
        64 AAAG6TAAFAAK4jhAAB 5.2853089.1                   2
        64 AAAG6TAAFAAK4jhAAC 5.2853089.2                   3
        64 AAAG6TAAFAAK4jhAAD 5.2853089.3                   4
        64 AAAG6TAAFAAK4jhAAE 5.2853089.4                   5
        64 AAAG6TAAFAAK4jhAAF 5.2853089.5                   6
        64 AAAG6TAAFAAK4jhAAG 5.2853089.6                   7
         1 AAAG6TAAFAAK4jkAAA 5.2853092.0                   8
         1 AAAG6TAAFAAK4jkAAB 5.2853092.1                   9
         1 AAAG6TAAFAAK4jkAAC 5.2853092.2                  10

10 rows selected
```

As you can see, the compression type of some of the updated rows has changed to 64, which is defined as COMP_BLOCK in DBMS_COMPRESSION. This particular type is indicated in cases where an updated block is moved out of its original CU and into an OLTP compressed block. Up to Oracle 11.2.0.2, you would see a compression type of 2 or COMP_ADVANCED/COMP_FOR_OLTP. How can you tell the block has moved? Compare the new Data Block Address with the original one: Instead of file 5 block 2942067 slot 0, the block containing ID 1 is now on file 5 block 2853089 slot 0.

The question now is what happened to the data if we queried the table with the original ROWID for ID 1:

```
SQL> select id,spcol from updtest_ql where rowid = 'AAAG6TAAFAALORzAAA';

no rows selected
```

This behavior is different from when we initially described the effect of an update. You can find the original reference at Kerry Osborne's blog:

```
http://kerryosborne.oracle-guy.com/2011/01/ehcc-mechanics-proof-that-whole-cus-are-not-
decompressed/
```

The old ROWID is not accessible anymore. What about the new one? You would really hope that worked:

```
SQL> select id,spcol from updtest_ql where rowid = 'AAAG6TAAFAAK4jhAAA';

        ID SPCOL
---------- ----------------------------------------
         1 I AM UPDATED
```

During the research for this updated edition, it was not possible to create a test case where a row has been truly migrated. In other words, it was not possible to retrieve an updated row using its old ROWID. This sounds odd at first but, on the other hand, simplifies processing. If Oracle left a pointer for the new row in place, it would have to perform another lookup on the new block, slowing down processing. If we dump the new block on file 5 block 2853089, you can see that it is indeed an OLTP compressed block. Note that the rows in the next block from the above listing are not compressed. A compression type of 1 translates to uncompressed.

```
SQL> alter system dump datafile 5 block 2853089;

System altered.

SQL> @trace
SQL> select value from v$diag_info where name like 'Default%';

VALUE
---------------------------------------------------------------------
/u01/app/oracle/diag/rdbms/dbm01/dbm011/trace/dbm011_ora_53134.trc

Block header dump:  0x016b88e1
 Object id on Block? Y
 seg/obj: 0x6e93  csc: 0x00.607114  itc: 2  flg: E  typ: 1 - DATA
     brn: 0  bdba: 0x16b8881 ver: 0x01 opc: 0
     inc: 0  exflg: 0
```

```
 Itl           Xid                  Uba         Flag  Lck        Scn/Fsc
0x01   0x002c.00d.00000007  0x0020d085.0017.02  --U-    7  fsc 0x0000.00607122
0x02   0x0000.000.00000000  0x00000000.0000.00  ----    0  fsc 0x0000.00000000
bdba: 0x016b88e1
data_block_dump,data header at 0x7f5c8fb6d464
===============
tsiz: 0x1f98
hsiz: 0x34
pbl: 0x7f5c8fb6d464
     76543210
flag=-0----X-
ntab=2
nrow=11
frre=-1
fsbo=0x34
fseo=0x372
avsp=0x33e
tosp=0x33e
        r0_9ir2=0x1
        mec_kdbh9ir2=0x0
                      76543210
        shcf_kdbh9ir2=----------
                  76543210
        flag_9ir2=--R-LN-C      Archive compression: N
                fcls_9ir2[0]={ }
0x16:pti[0]     nrow=4  offs=0
0x1a:pti[1]     nrow=7  offs=4
0x1e:pri[0]     offs=0x1f7e
...
block_row_dump:
tab 0, row 0, @0x1f7e
tl: 11 fb: --H-FL-- lb: 0x0  cc: 1
col  0: [ 8]  54 48 45 20 52 45 53 54
bindmp: 00 06 d0 54 48 45 20 52 45 53 54
...
tab 1, row 0, @0x1b6f
tl: 1019 fb: --H-FL-- lb: 0x1  cc: 6
col  0: [ 2]  c1 02
col  1: [999]
 31 20 20 20 20 20 20 20 20 20 20 20 20 20 20 20 20 20 20 20 20 20 20 20 20
 20 20 20 20 20 20 20 20 20 20 20 20 20 20 20 20 20 20 20 20 20 20 20 20 20
...
col  2: [ 7]  78 71 0b 16 01 01 01
col  3: [ 7]  78 71 0b 16 12 1a 39
col  4: [ 8]  54 48 45 20 52 45 53 54
col  5: [12]  49 20 41 4d 20 55 50 44 41 54 45 44
bindmp: 2c 01 06 ca c1 02 fa 03 e7 31 20 20 20...
```

You will recognize the typical BASIC/OLTP compression meta-information in that block-a symbol table and the data table, as well as the flags in the header and a bindmp column that allows Oracle to read the data. Also notice that the `data_object_id` is included in the block in hex format (seg/obj: 0x6e93). The table has six columns. The de-duplicated values are displayed, also in hex format. Just to verify that we have the right block, we can translate the `data_object_id` and the value of the first column as follows:

```
SQL> !cat obj_by_hex.sql
col object_name for a30
select owner, object_name, object_type
from dba_objects
where data_object_id = to_number(replace('&hex_value','0x',''),'XXXXXX');

SQL> @obj_by_hex.sql
Enter value for hex_value: 0x6e93

OWNER                OBJECT_NAME                    OBJECT_TYPE
-------------------- ------------------------------ -----------------------
MARTIN               UPDTEST_QL                     TABLE

Elapsed: 00:00:00.02
```

To show you that the update did not decompress the whole CU, you can see a block dump from the original block where IDs 1 to 10 were stored:

```
data_block_dump,data header at 0x7f5c8fb6d47c
===============
tsiz: 0x1f80
hsiz: 0x1c
pbl: 0x7f5c8fb6d47c
     76543210
flag=-0------
ntab=1
nrow=1
frre=-1
fsbo=0x1c
fseo=0x30
avsp=0x14
tosp=0x14
        r0_9ir2=0x0
        mec_kdbh9ir2=0x0
                      76543210
        shcf_kdbh9ir2=----------
                  76543210
        flag_9ir2=--R-----      Archive compression: Y
                fcls_9ir2[0]={ }
0x16:pti[0]     nrow=1  offs=0
0x1a:pri[0]     offs=0x30
block_row_dump:
tab 0, row 0, @0x30
tl: 8016 fb: --H-F--N lb: 0x0  cc: 1
nrid:  0x016ce474.0
```

```
col  0: [8004]
Compression level: 01 (Query Low)
Length of CU row: 8004
kdzhrh: ------PC- CBLK: 2 Start Slot: 00
 NUMP: 02
 PNUM: 00 POFF: 7974 PRID: 0x016ce474.0
 PNUM: 01 POFF: 15990 PRID: 0x016ce475.0
*---------
CU header:
CU version: 0   CU magic number: 0x4b445a30
CU checksum: 0x504338c9
CU total length: 16727
CU flags: NC-U-CRD-OP
ncols: 6
nrows: 1016
algo: 0
CU decomp length: 16554   len/value length: 1049401
row pieces per row: 1
num deleted rows: 10
deleted rows: 0, 1, 2, 3, 4, 5, 6, 7, 8, 9,
START_CU:
...
```

Notice that this block shows that it is compressed at level 1 (`QUERY LOW`). Also notice that ten records have been deleted from this block (*moved* would be a more accurate term, as those are the record that were updated earlier). The line that says `deleted rows:` actually shows a list of the rows that have been erased.

Expected Compression Ratios

HCC can provide very impressive compression ratios. The marketing material has claimed 10× compression ratios and, believe it or not, this is actually a very achievable number for many datasets. Of course, the amount of compression depends heavily on the data and which of the four algorithms is applied. The best way to determine what kind of compression can be achieved on your dataset is to test it. Oracle also provides a utility (often referred to as the Compression Advisor) to compress a sample of data from a table in order to calculate an estimated compression ratio. This utility can even be used on non-Exadata platforms from 9i Release 2 onward. The package is included with the standard distribution for 11.2 and newer. Users of earlier versions need to download the package from Oracle's web site. This section will provide some insight into the Compression Advisor as it is provided with Oracle 12.1.

Compression Advisor

If you do not have access to an Exadata but still want to test the effectiveness of HCC, you can use the Compression Advisor functionality that is provided in the `DBMS_COMPRESSION` package. The `GET_COMPRESSION_RATIO` procedure actually enables you to compress a sample of rows from a specified table. This is not an estimate of how much compression might happen; the sample rows are inserted into a temporary table. Then a compressed version of that temporary table is created. The ratio returned is a comparison between the sizes of the compressed version and the uncompressed version.

The Compression Advisor may also be useful on Exadata platforms. Of course, you could just compress a table with the various levels to see how well it compresses. However, if the tables are very large, this may not be practical. In this case, you may be tempted to create a temporary table by selecting the records where rownum < X and do your compression test on that subset of rows. And that is basically what the Advisor does, although it is a little smarter about the set of records it chooses. Here is an example of its use in 12c:

```
SQL> ! cat get_comp_ratio_12c.sql
set sqlblanklines on
set feedback off
accept owner -
 prompt 'Enter Value for owner: ' -
 default 'MARTIN'
accept table_name -
 prompt 'Enter Value for table_name: ' -
 default 'T1'
accept comp_type -
 prompt 'Enter Value for compression_type (QH): ' -
 default 'QH'

DECLARE
   l_blkcnt_cmp      BINARY_INTEGER;
   l_blkcnt_uncmp    BINARY_INTEGER;
   l_row_cmp         BINARY_INTEGER;
   l_row_uncmp       BINARY_INTEGER;
   l_cmp_ratio       NUMBER;
   l_comptype_str    VARCHAR2 (200);
   l_comptype        NUMBER;
BEGIN

case '&&comp_type'
            when 'BASIC'        then l_comptype := DBMS_COMPRESSION.COMP_BASIC;
            when 'ADVANCED'     then l_comptype := DBMS_COMPRESSION.COMP_ADVANCED;
            when 'QL'           then l_comptype := DBMS_COMPRESSION.COMP_QUERY_LOW;
            when 'QH'           then l_comptype := DBMS_COMPRESSION.COMP_QUERY_HIGH;
            when 'AL'           then l_comptype := DBMS_COMPRESSION.COMP_ARCHIVE_LOW;
            when 'AH'           then l_comptype := DBMS_COMPRESSION.COMP_ARCHIVE_HIGH;
          END CASE;

   DBMS_COMPRESSION.get_compression_ratio (
      scratchtbsname     => 'USERS',                  -- where will the temp table be created
      ownname            => '&owner',
      objname            => '&table_name',
      subobjname         => NULL,
      comptype           => l_comptype,
      blkcnt_cmp         => l_blkcnt_cmp,
      blkcnt_uncmp       => l_blkcnt_uncmp,
      row_cmp            => l_row_cmp,
      row_uncmp          => l_row_uncmp,
      cmp_ratio          => l_cmp_ratio,
      comptype_str       => l_comptype_str
   );
```

```
  dbms_output.put_line(' ');
    DBMS_OUTPUT.put_line ('Estimated Compression Ratio using '||l_comptype_str||': '||
     round(l_cmp_ratio,3));
  dbms_output.put_line(' ');

END;
/
undef owner
undef table_name
undef comp_type
set feedback on
```

And some examples of the output:

```
SQL> @scripts/get_comp_ratio_12c.sql
Enter Value for owner: MARTIN
Enter Value for table_name: T2
Enter Value for compression_type (QH): ADVANCED

Estimated Compression Ratio using "Compress Advanced": 1.1

SQL> @scripts/get_comp_ratio_12c.sql
Enter Value for owner: MARTIN
Enter Value for table_name: T2
Enter Value for compression_type (QH): QL

Compression Advisor self-check validation successful. select count(*) on both Uncompressed
and EHCC Compressed format = 1000001 rows

Estimated Compression Ratio using "Compress Query Low": 74.8
```

Notice that the procedure can print out a validation message telling you how many records were used for the comparison. This number can be modified as part of the call to the procedure if so desired. The `get_comp_ratio_12c.sql` script prompts for a table and a Compression Type and then executes the `DBMS_COMPRESSION.GET_COMPRESSION_RATIO` procedure.

Real-World Examples

As Yogi Bear once said, you can learn a lot just by watching. Marketing slides and book author claims are one thing, but real data is often more useful. Just to give you an idea of what kind of compression is reasonable to expect, here are a few comparisons of data from different industries. The data should provide you with an idea of the potential compression ratios that can be achieved by HCC.

Custom Application Data

This dataset came from a custom application that tracks the movement of assets. The table is very narrow, consisting of only 12 columns. The table has close to one billion rows, but many of the columns have a very low number of distinct values (NDV). That means that the same values are repeated many times. This table is a prime candidate for compression. Here are the basic table statistics and the compression ratios achieved:

```
==========================================================================================
Table Statistics
==========================================================================================
TABLE_NAME                   : CP_DAILY
LAST_ANALYZED                : 29-DEC-2010 23:55:16
DEGREE                       : 1
PARTITIONED                  : YES
NUM_ROWS                     : 925241124
CHAIN_CNT                    : 0
BLOCKS                       : 15036681
EMPTY_BLOCKS                 : 0
AVG_SPACE                    : 0
AVG_ROW_LEN                  : 114
MONITORING                   : YES
SAMPLE_SIZE                  : 925241124
TOTALSIZE_MEGS               : 118019
==========================================================================================
Column Statistics
==========================================================================================
Name                      Analyzed    Null?     NDV            Density  # Nulls     # Buckets
==========================================================================================
PK_ACTIVITY_DTL_ID       12/29/2010  NOT NULL  925241124      .000000  0           1
FK_ACTIVITY_ID           12/29/2010  NOT NULL  43388928       .000000  0           1
FK_DENOMINATION_ID       12/29/2010            38             .000000  88797049    38
AMOUNT                   12/29/2010            1273984        .000001  0           1
FK_BRANCH_ID             12/29/2010  NOT NULL  131            .000000  0           128
LOGIN_ID                 12/29/2010  NOT NULL  30             .033333  0           1
DATETIME_STAMP           12/29/2010  NOT NULL  710272         .000001  0           1
LAST_MODIFY_LOGIN_ID     12/29/2010  NOT NULL  30             .033333  0           1
MODIFY_DATETIME_STAMP    12/29/2010  NOT NULL  460224         .000002  0           1
ACTIVE_FLAG              12/29/2010  NOT NULL  2              .000000  0           2
FK_BAG_ID                12/29/2010            2895360        .000000  836693535   1
CREDIT_DATE              12/29/2010            549            .001821  836693535   1
==========================================================================================

SYS@POC1> @table_size2
Enter value for owner:
Enter value for table_name: CP_DAILY_INV_ACTIVITY_DTL
```

```
OWNER                SEGMENT_NAME                   TOTALSIZE_MEGS COMPRESS_FOR
-------------------- ------------------------------ -------------- ------------
KSO                  CP_DAILY_INV_ACTIVITY_DTL           118,018.8
                                                    --------------
sum                                                      118,018.8

SYS@POC1> @comp_ratio
Enter value for original_size: 118018.8
Enter value for owner: KSO
Enter value for table_name: CP_DAILY%
Enter value for type:

OWNER      SEGMENT_NAME         TYPE               TOTALSIZE_MEGS COMPRESSION_RATIO
---------- -------------------- ------------------ -------------- -----------------
KSO        CP_DAILY_HCC1        TABLE                     7,488.1              15.8
KSO        CP_DAILY_HCC3        TABLE                     2,442.3              48.3
KSO        CP_DAILY_HCC2        TABLE                     2,184.7              54.0
KSO        CP_DAILY_HCC4        TABLE                     1,807.8              65.3
                                                   --------------
sum                                                      13,922.8
```

As expected, this table is extremely compressible. Simple queries against these tables also run much faster against the compressed tables, as you can see in this listing:

```
SQL> select sum(amount) from kso.CP_DAILY_HCC3 where credit_date = '01-oct-2010';

 SUM(AMOUNT)
------------
4002779614.9

1 row selected.

Elapsed: 00:00:02.37
SQL> select sum(amount) from kso.CP_DAILY where credit_date = '01-oct-2010';

 SUM(AMOUNT)
------------
4002779614.9

1 row selected.

Elapsed: 00:00:42.58
```

This simple query ran roughly 19 times faster using the ARCHIVE LOW compressed table than when it was run against the uncompressed table.

Telecom Call Detail Data

This table contains call detail records for a telecom company. There are approximately 1.5 billion records in the table. Many of the columns in this table are unique or nearly so. In addition, many of the columns contain large numbers of nulls. Nulls are not compressible since they are not stored in the normal Oracle block format. This is not a table we would expect to be highly compressible. Here are the basic table statistics and the compression ratios:

```
==========================================================================================
Table Statistics
==========================================================================================
TABLE_NAME                       : SEE
LAST_ANALYZED                    : 29-SEP-2010 00:02:15
DEGREE                           : 8
PARTITIONED                      : YES
NUM_ROWS                         : 1474776874
CHAIN_CNT                        : 0
BLOCKS                           : 57532731
EMPTY_BLOCKS                     : 0
AVG_SPACE                        : 0
AVG_ROW_LEN                      : 282
MONITORING                       : YES
SAMPLE_SIZE                      : 1474776874
TOTALSIZE_MEGS                   : 455821
==========================================================================================

SQL> @comp_ratio
Enter value for original_size: 455821
Enter value for owner: KSO
Enter value for table_name: SEE_HCC%
Enter value for type:

OWNER      SEGMENT_NAME         TYPE               TOTALSIZE_MEGS COMPRESSION_RATIO
---------- -------------------- ------------------ -------------- -----------------
KSO        SEE_HCC1             TABLE                   168,690.1               2.7
KSO        SEE_HCC2             TABLE                    96,142.1               4.7
KSO        SEE_HCC3             TABLE                    87,450.8               5.2
KSO        SEE_HCC4             TABLE                    72,319.1               6.3
                                                   --------------
sum                                                     424,602.1
```

Financial Data

The next table is made up of financial data—revenue accrual data from an order entry system to be exact. Here are the basic table statistics:

```
==================================================================================
Table Statistics
==================================================================================
TABLE_NAME                      : REV_ACCRUAL
LAST_ANALYZED                   : 07-JAN-2011 00:42:47
DEGREE                          : 1
PARTITIONED                     : YES
NUM_ROWS                        : 114736686
CHAIN_CNT                       : 0
BLOCKS                          : 15225910
EMPTY_BLOCKS                    : 0
AVG_SPACE                       : 0
AVG_ROW_LEN                     : 917
MONITORING                      : YES
SAMPLE_SIZE                     : 114736686
TOTALSIZE_MEGS                  : 120019
==================================================================================
```

So the number of rows is not that great, only about 115 million, but the table is wide. It has 161 columns and the average row length is 917 bytes. It is a bit of a mixed bag with regards to compressibility though. Many of the columns contain a high percentage of nulls. On the other hand, many of the columns have a very low number of distinct values. This table may be a candidate for reordering the data on disk as a strategy to improve the compression ratio. At any rate, here are the compression rates achieved on this table at the various HCC levels:

```
SQL> @comp_ratio
Enter value for original_size: 120019
Enter value for owner: KSO
Enter value for table_name: REV_ACCRUAL_HCC%
Enter value for type:

OWNER      SEGMENT_NAME         TYPE               TOTALSIZE_MEGS COMPRESSION_RATIO
---------- -------------------- ------------------ -------------- -----------------
KSO        REV_ACCRUAL_HCC1     TABLE                    31,972.6               3.8
KSO        REV_ACCRUAL_HCC2     TABLE                    17,082.9               7.0
KSO        REV_ACCRUAL_HCC3     TABLE                    14,304.3               8.4
KSO        REV_ACCRUAL_HCC4     TABLE                    12,541.6               9.6
                                                   --------------
sum                                                      75,901.4
```

Retail Sales Data

The final table is made up of sales figures from a retailer. The table contains about six billion records and occupies well over half a Terabyte. There are very few columns, and the data is highly repetitive. In fact, there are no unique fields in this table. This is a very good candidate for compression. Here are the basic table statistics:

```
==========================================================================================
Table Statistics
==========================================================================================
TABLE_NAME                     : SALES
LAST_ANALYZED                  : 23-DEC-2010 03:13:44
DEGREE                         : 1
PARTITIONED                    : NO
NUM_ROWS                       : 5853784365
CHAIN_CNT                      : 0
BLOCKS                         : 79183862
EMPTY_BLOCKS                   : 0
AVG_SPACE                      : 0
AVG_ROW_LEN                    : 93
MONITORING                     : YES
SAMPLE_SIZE                    : 5853784365
TOTALSIZE_MEGS                 : 618667
==========================================================================================
Column Statistics
==========================================================================================
Name          Analyzed    Null?    NDV            Density  # Nulls  # Buckets    Sample
==========================================================================================
TRANS_ID      12/23/2010           389808128      .000000  0        1        5853784365
TRANS_LINE_NO 12/23/2010           126            .007937  0        1        5853784365
UNIT_ID       12/23/2010           128600         .000008  0        1        5853784365
DAY           12/23/2010           3              .333333  0        1        5853784365
TRANS_SEQ     12/23/2010           22932          .000044  0        1        5853784365
BEGIN_DATE    12/23/2010           4              .250000  0        1        5853784365
END_DATE      12/23/2010           4              .250000  0        1        5853784365
UNIT_TYPE     12/23/2010           1             1.000000  0        1        5853784365
SKU_TYPE      12/23/2010           54884          .000018  0        1        5853784365
QTY           12/23/2010           104            .009615  0        1        5853784365
PRICE         12/23/2010           622            .001608  0        1        5853784365
==========================================================================================
```

Here are the compression ratios achieved for this table. As expected, they are very good:

```
SQL> @comp_ratio
Enter value for original_size: 618667
Enter value for owner: KSO
Enter value for table_name: SALES_HCC%
Enter value for type:

OWNER      SEGMENT_NAME         TYPE               TOTALSIZE_MEGS COMPRESSION_RATIO
---------- -------------------- ------------------ -------------- -----------------
KSO        SALES_HCC1           TABLE                    41,654.6              14.9
KSO        SALES_HCC2           TABLE                    26,542.0              23.3
KSO        SALES_HCC3           TABLE                    26,538.5              23.3
KSO        SALES_HCC4           TABLE                    19,633.0              31.5
                                                   --------------
sum                                                     114,368.1
```

Summary of the Real-World Examples

The examples in this section came from real applications. They show a fairly extreme variation in data compressibility. This is to be expected, as the success of compression algorithms is very dependent on the data being compressed. Table 3-6 presents the data from all four examples.

Table 3-6. *Real-World Examples Compared*

Data Type	Base Table Name	Characteristics	Compression Ratios
Asset Tracking	CP_DAILY	Skinny Table, Many Low NDV Columns	16×-65×
Call Detail Records	SEE	Many NULLs, Many Unique Columns	3×-6×
Financial Data	REV_ACCRUAL	Wide Table, Many NULLs, Many Low NDV Columns	4×-10×
Retail Sales Data	SALES	Skinny Table, Mostly Low NDV Columns	15×-32×

Hopefully, this data gives you some feel for the range of compression ratios that you can expect from HCC and the types of datasets that will benefit most. Of course, the best way to predict how compressible a particular table may be is to actually test it. This fact cannot be overemphasized.

Restrictions/Challenges

There are a few challenges with using HCC. Many of them have to do with the fact that HCC is not available on most non-Exadata platforms. This fact makes for interesting scenarios for recovery and high-availability solutions. The other major challenge is that HCC does not play well with data that is being actively updated. In particular, systems characterized by lots of single-row updates, which we often describe as OLTP workloads, will probably not work well with HCC, even in 12c, which introduced row level locking.

Moving Data to a Non-Exadata Platform

Probably the largest hurdle with using HCC has been moving the data to non-Exadata platforms. For example, while RMAN and Data Guard both support the HCC block format and will happily restore data to a non-Exadata environment, a database running on such an environment will not be able to do anything with the data until it is decompressed. The only exception to this rule is the use of Oracle's ZFS Storage Appliance, the FS1 storage system, or a Pillar Axiom array. Having to decompress data first can mean a lengthy delay before being able to access the data in a case where a failover to a standby on a non-Exadata platform occurs. The same issue holds true for doing an RMAN restore to a non-Exadata platform. The restore will work but the data in HCC formatted blocks will not be accessible until the data has been moved into a non-HCC format. This can be done with the `ALTER TABLE MOVE NOCOMPRESS` command, by the way.

■ **Note** The ability to decompress HCC data on non-Exadata platforms only became available in Oracle database version 11.2.0.2. Attempting this on version 11.2.0.1 would result in an error.

In addition to the lengthy delay associated with decompressing data before being able to access it, there is also the issue of space. If HCC is providing a 10× compression factor, for example, you will need to have 10 times the space you are currently using available on the target environment to handle the increased size of the data. For these reasons, Data Guard is rarely set up with a standby on a non-Exadata platform.

Before Oracle 12c, it was problematic to import HCC compressed data into a non-Exadata database. One long requested feature has been added to impdp, allowing the DBA to specify the compression level on the fly, as in this example:

```
[oracle@nonExadata ~]$ impdp user/password@nonExadata/testpdb1 \
> directory=data_pump_dir dumpfile=hcc_dump.dmp \
> transform=table_compression_clause:nocompress
```

Before importing the previously HCC compressed table, you need to ensure that you have enough storage space for the import to succeed. Failing to provide the transformation clause when importing to a non-Exadata system will cause the import to abort with the following error message:

```
Processing object type TABLE_EXPORT/TABLE/TABLE
ORA-39083: Object type TABLE:"MARTIN"."UPDTEST_QL" failed to create with error:
ORA-64307:  Exadata Hybrid Columnar Compression is not supported for tablespaces on
  this storage type
```

Disabling Serial Direct Path Reads

As you saw in Chapter 2, serial Direct Path Reads allow non-parallelized scan operations to use the direct path read mechanism, which is a prerequisite for enabling the Smart Scan features of Exadata. Serial Direct Path Reads are enabled based on a calculation that depends on the size of the object being scanned relative to the available buffer cache. In simplistic terms, only large objects will be considered for Serial Direct Path Reads. HCC's effectiveness can actually work against it here. Since the compression reduces the size of the objects so drastically, it can cause statements that would normally benefit from a Smart Scan to use the standard read mechanism, disabling many of Exadata's optimizations. This is generally not a huge problem because the number of blocks is considerably reduced by HCC.

The database is making the decision to use a Direct Path Read (leading to a Smart Scan) at runtime. This can become interesting when an object is compressed and partitioned. The algorithm to use a Smart Scan or not is based on the size of the object being scanned; in the case of a partitioned object, this means the size of the partition. So in cases where partitioning is used with HCC, we often see some partitions using Smart Scans and some unable to use Smart Scans. Keep in mind that not using Smart Scans also means decompression cannot be done at the storage layer, as this capability is enabled only when performing Smart Scans.

Locking Issues

The documentation used to read that updating a single row of a table compressed with HCC locks the entire CU containing the row. This can cause extreme contention issues for OLTP-type systems. Not that you would want to compress active data with HCC anyway, for reasons already laid out earlier in this chapter.

Locking the entire CU for us is the main reason that HCC is not recommended for tables (or partitions) where the data will be updated. This has changed with Oracle 12c.. If you like, you can set some space in the CU header aside for tracking DML. To enable this feature, you have to specify the new syntax for HCC, as in this example:

```
CREATE TABLE t1_ql_rll
enable row movement
column store compress for query low row level locking
AS
select * from t1_ql;

Table created.
```

Table T1_QL_RLL has been created with one million random rows using Query Low as the compression mechanism. Row level locking really works best (if you can say so) with Query Compression. Its effects are somewhat unpredictable in Archive Compression mode. But then that makes perfect sense. Archived data should not be updated in the first place, should it? Comparing the two tables yields an interesting result:

```
SQL> select table_name,compression,compress_for,last_analyzed
  2  from tabs where table_name like 'T1_QL%';

TABLE_NAME           COMPRESS COMPRESS_FOR                   LAST_ANAL
-------------------- -------- ------------------------------ ---------
T1_QL                ENABLED  QUERY LOW                      22-AUG-14
T1_QL_RLL            ENABLED  QUERY LOW ROW LEVEL LOCKING    22-AUG-14
```

First of all, you can see that row level locking has been requested and applied to the table. When you compare the table sizes, then you will notice that the extra space in the CU header, which is required to keep track of the DML operations, takes a little toll:

```
SQL> select segment_name,bytes/power(1024,2) m, blocks
  2  from user_segments
  3  where segment_name like 'T1_QL%';

SEGMENT_NAME                  M     BLOCKS
-------------------- ---------- ----------
T1_QL                       176      22528
T1_QL_RLL                   192      24576
```

In this small example with a measly one million rows, the size difference is a few MB. The information about locked rows is not hidden in the first few bytes of the CU. As one might expect, it is clearly visible in the CU header. Dumping a block with a random CU header gives it away:

```
data_block_dump,data header at 0x7efefa13407c
===============
tsiz: 0x1f80
hsiz: 0x1c
pbl: 0x7efefa13407c
     76543210
flag=-0------
ntab=1
nrow=1
frre=-1
```

```
fsbo=0x1c
fseo=0x5e8
avsp=0x5cc
tosp=0x5cc
        r0_9ir2=0x0
        mec_kdbh9ir2=0x0
                      76543210
        shcf_kdbh9ir2=----------
                  76543210
        flag_9ir2=--R-----      Archive compression: Y
                fcls_9ir2[0]={ }
0x16:pti[0]     nrow=1  offs=0
0x1a:pri[0]     offs=0x5e8
block_row_dump:
tab 0, row 0, @0x5e8
tl: 6552 fb: --H-F--N lb: 0x0  cc: 1
nrid:  0x0140219c.0
col  0: [6540]
Compression level: 01 (Query Low)
 Length of CU row: 6540
kdzhrh: ------PCL CBLK: 2 Start Slot: 00
 NUMP: 02
 PNUM: 00 POFF: 5617 PRID: 0x0140219c.0
 PNUM: 01 POFF: 13633 PRID: 0x0140219d.0
num lock bits: 7
locked rows:
*---------
CU header:
CU version: 0   CU magic number: 0x4b445a30
CU checksum: 0x22424f63
CU total length: 17189
CU flags: NC-U-CRD-OP
ncols: 6
nrows: 1015
algo: 0
CU decomp length: 17016   len/value length: 1049278
row pieces per row: 1
num deleted rows: 0
START_CU:
 00 00 19 8c 4f 02 00 00 00 02 00 00 15 f1 01 40 21 9c 00 00 00 00 35 41 01
```

In this particular CU, you can see 7 lock bits for locking rows. The next line actually shows you the locked rows (if any). Now let's try and update some rows in a compression unit and dump the block. But before that can be done, block numbers for the rows to be updated have to be found. Using the following query, they can be identified in block 192700 for IDs 1 to 78:

```
SQL> select min(id),max(id),blockn from (
  2    select id,DBMS_ROWID.ROWID_RELATIVE_FNO(rowid),
  3     DBMS_ROWID.ROWID_BLOCK_NUMBER(rowid) as blockn
  4     from martin.t1_ql_rll where id < 2500
  5  ) group by blockn order by blockn;
```

```
   MIN(ID)    MAX(ID)     BLOCKN
---------- ---------- ----------
         1         78     192700
        79        708       8603
       169        258       8689
       259        348      26064
       349        438     173609
       439        528     173715
       529        570     173860
       571        618     196434
       709       2499       8641
       841       1464       8646
      1465       2220      26012
```

In the next step, a transaction is started with an update against IDs 1 through 10:

```
SQL> update t1_ql_rll set spcol = 'me me me' where id between 1 and 10;

10 rows updated.
```

And now for the big moment—the block dump for this block shows this:

```
Block header dump:  0x01c04d40
 Object id on Block? Y
 seg/obj: 0x56ef  csc: 0x00.2385ed  itc: 3  flg: E  typ: 1 - DATA
     brn: 0  bdba: 0x1c04a03 ver: 0x01 opc: 0
     inc: 0  exflg: 0

 Itl           Xid                  Uba         Flag  Lck        Scn/Fsc
0x01   0xffff.000.00000000  0x00000000.0000.00  C---    0  scn 0x0000.002385ed
0x02   0x000a.00c.0000127a  0x000009f3.033b.0a  ----   10  fsc 0x0000.00000000
0x03   0x0000.000.00000000  0x00000000.0000.00  ----    0  fsc 0x0000.00000000
bdba: 0x01c04d40
data_block_dump,data header at 0x7f2fa276307c
[...]
tab 0, row 1, @0x2ea
tl: 3465 fb: --H-F--N lb: 0x0  cc: 1
nrid:  0x01c04d41.0
col  0: [3453]
Compression level: 01 (Query Low)
 Length of CU row: 3453
kdzhrh: ------PCL CBLK: 4 Start Slot: 00
 NUMP: 04
 PNUM: 00 POFF: 2020 PRID: 0x01c04d41.0
 PNUM: 01 POFF: 10036 PRID: 0x01c04d42.0
 PNUM: 02 POFF: 18052 PRID: 0x01c04d43.0
 PNUM: 03 POFF: 26068 PRID: 0x01c04d44.0
num lock bits: 6
locked rows: 1040(2), 1041(2), 1042(2), 1043(2), 1044(2), 1045(2), 1046(2), 1047(2),
1048(2), 1049(2),
*---------
CU header:
```

The header information reflects the updated blocks. What does this imply for concurrency? In the following example—without row level locking—the well-known behavior where the whole CU is locked can be observed:

```
Session1> update t1_ql set spcol = 'UPDATED' where id between 1 and 10;

10 rows updated.

Elapsed: 00:00:00.06

Session2> update t1_ql set spcol='UPDATED TOO' where id between 100 and 110;

-- session waits
```

As you would expect, session 2 has to wait until session 1 commits. No surprises, this is the expected behavior:

```
SQL> select sid,serial#,sql_id,seq#,event from v$session where username = 'MARTIN';

       SID    SERIAL# SQL_ID              SEQ# EVENT
---------- ---------- ------------- ---------- ---------------------------------------------
       328       1679 fvcbzbm0gak1x         91 SQL*Net message to client
      1109      13459 39pvvwpfpfcum         52 enq: TX - row lock contention
```

If you repeat the test with the table that has row level locking enabled, you will see the two updates just pass as with a regular table:

```
Session1> update t1_ql_rll set spcol = 'UPDATED' where id between 1 and 10;

10 rows updated.

Elapsed: 00:00:00.04

Session2> update t1_ql_rll set spcol='UPDATED TOO' where id between 100 and 110;

11 rows updated.

Elapsed: 00:00:00.03
```

No waits, no locks in this case. Now before you start redefining all your tables, please consider the principles around HCC and active data. Just because there is support for row level locking, other DML operations are still better not issued against HCC compressed data.

Single Row Access

HCC is built and best suited for full-table scans. Decompression is a CPU-intensive task. Smart Scans can distribute the decompression work to the CPUs on the storage cells. This makes the CPU-intensive task much more palatable. However, Smart Scans only occur when Full Scans are performed. This means that other access mechanisms, index access for example, must use the DB server CPUs to perform decompression. In extreme cases, this can put an enormous CPU load on database servers, for example in high volume OLTP-type systems. In addition, since data for a single row is spread across multiple blocks in a CU, retrieving a complete row causes the entire CU to be read. This can have a detrimental effect on the overall database efficiency for systems that tend to access data using indexes, even if the access is read-only.

Common Usage Scenarios

HCC provides such high levels of compression that it has been used as an alternative to traditional Information Lifecycle Model (ILM) strategies, which generally involve moving older historical data off the database entirely. These ILM strategies usually entail some type of date range partitioning and a purge or archiving process. This is done to free storage and, in some cases, to improve performance. Often the data must be retained in some backup format so that it can be accessed if required at some later date. With HCC, it is possible in many cases to retain data almost indefinitely by compressing the oldest partitions. This approach has many advantages over the traditional approach of moving the data.

First and foremost, the data remains available via the standard application interfaces. No additional work will need to be done to restore a backup of old data before it can be accessed. This advantage alone is often enough to justify this approach. This approach typically entails leaving active partitions uncompressed while compressing old partitions more aggressively. Here's a short example of creating a partitioned table with mixed compression modes using the 11.2 syntax:

```
SQL>   CREATE TABLE "KSO"."CLASS_SALES_P"
  2     (     "TRANS_ID" VARCHAR2(30),
  3           "UNIT_ID" NUMBER(30,0),
  4           "DAY" NUMBER(30,0),
  5           "TRANS_SEQ" VARCHAR2(30),
  6           "END_DATE" DATE,
  7           "BEGIN_DATE" DATE,
  8           "UNIT_TYPE" VARCHAR2(30),
  9           "CUST_TYPE" VARCHAR2(1),
 10           "LOAD_DATE" DATE,
 11           "CURRENCY_TYPE" CHAR(1)
 12     ) PCTFREE 10 PCTUSED 40 INITRANS 1 MAXTRANS 255  NOLOGGING
 13    STORAGE(
 14    BUFFER_POOL DEFAULT FLASH_CACHE DEFAULT CELL_FLASH_CACHE DEFAULT)
 15    TABLESPACE "CLASS_DATA"
 16    PARTITION BY RANGE ("BEGIN_DATE")
 17   (PARTITION "P1"  VALUES LESS THAN (TO_DATE
 18      (' 2008-09-06 00:00:00', 'SYYYY-MM-DD HH24:MI:SS', 'NLS_CALENDAR=GREGORIAN'))
 19  SEGMENT CREATION IMMEDIATE
 20    PCTFREE 10 PCTUSED 40 INITRANS 1 MAXTRANS 255 NOCOMPRESS NOLOGGING
 21    STORAGE(INITIAL 8388608 NEXT 1048576 MINEXTENTS 1 MAXEXTENTS 2147483645
 22    PCTINCREASE 0 FREELISTS 1 FREELIST GROUPS 1 BUFFER_POOL DEFAULT
 23    FLASH_CACHE DEFAULT CELL_FLASH_CACHE DEFAULT)
 24    TABLESPACE "CLASS_DATA" ,
 25   PARTITION "P2"  VALUES LESS THAN (TO_DATE
 26     (' 2008-09-07 00:00:00', 'SYYYY-MM-DD HH24:MI:SS', 'NLS_CALENDAR=GREGORIAN'))
 27  SEGMENT CREATION IMMEDIATE
 28    PCTFREE 0 PCTUSED 40 INITRANS 1 MAXTRANS 255 COMPRESS FOR QUERY HIGH NOLOGGING
 29    STORAGE(INITIAL 8388608 NEXT 1048576 MINEXTENTS 1 MAXEXTENTS 2147483645
 30    PCTINCREASE 0 FREELISTS 1 FREELIST GROUPS 1 BUFFER_POOL DEFAULT
 31    FLASH_CACHE DEFAULT CELL_FLASH_CACHE DEFAULT)
 32    TABLESPACE "CLASS_DATA" ,
```

```
  PARTITION "P3"  VALUES LESS THAN (TO_DATE
    (' 2008-09-08 00:00:00', 'SYYYY-MM-DD HH24:MI:SS', 'NLS_CALENDAR=GREGORIAN'))
 SEGMENT CREATION IMMEDIATE
   PCTFREE 0 PCTUSED 40 INITRANS 1 MAXTRANS 255 COMPRESS FOR ARCHIVE LOW NOLOGGING
   STORAGE(INITIAL 8388608 NEXT 1048576 MINEXTENTS 1 MAXEXTENTS 2147483645
   PCTINCREASE 0 FREELISTS 1 FREELIST GROUPS 1 BUFFER_POOL DEFAULT
   FLASH_CACHE DEFAULT CELL_FLASH_CACHE DEFAULT)
   TABLESPACE "CLASS_DATA" ) ;

Table created.
```

Oracle 12c introduces a new feature (as a cost option) to automate the data lifecycle management process, which is introduced in the next section.

Automatic Data Optimization

Oracle Data Optimization (ADO) is a new feature introduced in version 12.1.0.1. It is available for Exadata, but is not limited to it. ADO helps the administrator implement, and more importantly, enforce Information Lifecycle Management if the Advanced Compression Option is available.

What Is Data Lifecycle Management?

Data lifecycle management is an important aspect of managing data and storage effectively. In many companies you will find different tiers of storage for non-Exadata deployments. Most commonly, you find Flash memory as tier 0 or 1, depending on where you start counting. The highest-level storage tier gives the user the best possible performance while, at the same time, is not available in abundance. Most tier 0 storage is too expensive to use throughout the board. And it is not even needed: a Data Warehouse deployed entirely on Flash memory makes little sense thanks to the data access patterns we observe.

Many warehouses are (incrementally) loaded during the day. Oracle architects and application designers alike have found partitioning the tables in an Oracle Data Warehouse by range, based on a date-key, very efficient. Numerous blog posts and presentations exist demonstrating how to scale effectively with that approach. Fellow Oak-Table member Tim Gorman's paper "Scaling to Infinity: Data Warehouse on Oracle" gives a very good overview of how the partitioning option can be used to scale Oracle performance for Very Large Databases (VLDBs). So, where it is possible to partition the table into range-based segments, data lifecycle management is the natural next step to implement. It is nothing new. In fact, administrators have frequently implemented it to save costs a long time before Exadata saw the light of day.

While data is "hot," or, in other words, freshly loaded, you can expect most activity. The load itself will require sufficient bandwidth to move the data from the staging layer into the query layer where it can be accessed by end users. You need to cater not only for the load but anything Oracle will perform in order to make the data available. Creating or maintaining indexes are the most visible operations during the load, but you can equally find redo and undo generation among the tasks Oracle performs, including writing to the archived logs if the database is in archivelog mode and enforces logging. Most systems are not quiesced during the load so you need to think about query performance as well; reading from storage you are processing your ETL is most likely to happen concurrently. In summary, I/O requirements are very demanding for current data.

Once the data becomes colder over time, access to it is not as thunderous and demanding. Most query activity focuses on current data. Many architects, therefore, decide to move data, which is not as frequently queried or modified to lower tiers of storage.

Continuing with the tier-0 example (Flash memory), many users move to hard-disk-based storage. These hard disks do not offer the same high-end performance characteristics as flash memory, but they are a lot cheaper in exchange.

Finally, over time, colder data can be moved to even lower tiers of storage. This allows the administrators and architects to retain larger amounts of data at lower cost than would have been possible by keeping everything on higher tier SAN storage.

Compression

So far, we have primarily focused on how to reduce cost with longer- or long-term archiving. The topic of compression has not been touched yet, but since this book is about Exadata, it inevitably has to be mentioned.

On the Exadata platform, you do not use these storage tiers as you would on traditional hardware. The Exadata administrator does not need to worry about the exact right combination of Flash Memory/SAN based tier 2 and 3 storage/network-based solutions. Storage is provided with the system. If you want to keep everything on the storage servers, while at the same time data volumes are growing, you should seriously consider HCC. You read in the previous sections that HCC can give you very good compression ratios and, therefore, savings in your storage footprint. In addition to these, you can use Smart-Scans on HCC compressed data, enhancing throughput significantly compared to non-Exadata platforms. Accessing HCC compressed data via Infiniband should be more efficient than accessing data based on a Direct NFS (dNFS) filer, for example.

Automatic Data Optimization vs. Manual Lifecycle Management

Before Oracle 12c, it was the DBA's task to perform housekeeping. In many cases, housekeeping included implementing an ILM policy. With properly implemented change management, this used to work well. In situations where change management was not as rigorously implemented, however, it could become difficult to maintain the ILM policy.

Oracle 12c relieves the DBA from many of these tasks by allowing the application of the ILM policy to happen automatically. As you can see in the next sections, you can add a declarative policy to a segment and leave the implementation to Oracle. This feature requires the Advanced Compression License.

ADO is largely based on usage tracking. A so-called heat map tracks access and data modification at the row and segment level. Not only is the heat map the basis for ADO, it can also be queried using data dictionary views and manipulated via a set of PL/SQL Application Programming Interfaces (APIs).

The administrator—broadly speaking—is given two options that thankfully are not mutually exclusive. The first option is to compress; the other option is to use the tiering clause. The first step, though, is to enable the heat map. However, be careful: Enabling the heat map tracking already requires you to have a license for the Advanced Compression Option.

```
SQL> alter system set heat_map = on sid='*' scope=both;

System altered.
```

Oracle offers a number of views you can use to find out more about the heat map tracking in your database:

```
SQL> SELECT table_name
  2  FROM dict
  3  WHERE table_name LIKE 'V%HEAT%MAP%'
  4  OR table_name LIKE 'DBA%HEAT%MAP%';
```

```
TABLE_NAME
------------------------------
DBA_HEATMAP_TOP_OBJECTS
DBA_HEATMAP_TOP_TABLESPACES
DBA_HEAT_MAP_SEG_HISTOGRAM
DBA_HEAT_MAP_SEGMENT
V$HEAT_MAP_SEGMENT
```

V$HEAT_MAP_SEGMENT is the dictionary view that provides real-time access to the heat map, but does not feature a "owner" column such as DBA_HEATMAP_TOP_OBJECTS. You can easily join against DBA_OBJECTS on the OBJECT_ID and DATA_OBJECT_ID.

Example Use Cases for ADO

To better illustrate the concepts and implementation of ADO, the following demonstration will be used. A simple table named ADODEMO will serve for this purpose. A number of Information Lifecycle Management policies will be attached to it and their effect shown. Let's begin with the table definition:

```
CREATE TABLE adodemo (
 id, t_pad, date_created, state
)
enable row movement
partition by range (date_created)
INTERVAL(NUMTOYMINTERVAL(1, 'MONTH'))
(
 partition p_manual values less than (to_date('01.01.2005','dd.mm.yyyy'))
)
AS -- thank you Jonathan Lewis!
WITH v1 AS  (
  SELECT rownum n FROM dual CONNECT BY level <= 10000
)
SELECT
  rownum id,
  rpad(rownum,1999) t_pad,
  TRUNC(sysdate) - 180 + dbms_random.value(0,180) date_created,
  CASE
    WHEN mod(rownum,100000) = 0
    THEN CAST('RARE' AS VARCHAR2(12))
    WHEN mod(rownum,10000) = 0
    THEN CAST('FAIRLY RARE' AS VARCHAR2(12))
    WHEN mod(rownum,1000) = 0
    THEN CAST('NOT RARE' AS VARCHAR2(12))
    WHEN mod(rownum,100) = 0
    THEN CAST('COMMON' AS   VARCHAR2(12))
    ELSE CAST('THE REST' AS VARCHAR2(12))
  END state
FROM v1,
  v1
WHERE rownum <= 1e7;
```

The table has ten million rows but is rather narrow. The ADODEMO table is primarily interesting from a partitioning aspect. You read in the previous section how important partitioning was for a suitable implementation of HCC. Notice that the table does not have compression enabled at all initially. This is intentional: With ADO, you do not need to specify the compression yourself—leave that to Oracle. In our 12.1.0.2.0 test bed, the table had these physical properties:

```
SQL> select table_name,partition_name,num_rows,last_analyzed
  2  from dba_tab_partitions where table_owner = 'MARTIN' and table_name = 'ADODEMO';

TABLE_NAME                     PARTITION_NAME         NUM_ROWS LAST_ANAL
------------------------------ -------------------- ---------- ---------
ADODEMO                        P_MANUAL
ADODEMO                        SYS_P796                1721062 09-OCT-14
ADODEMO                        SYS_P797                1111364 09-OCT-14
ADODEMO                        SYS_P798                1724376 09-OCT-14
ADODEMO                        SYS_P799                1664931 09-OCT-14
ADODEMO                        SYS_P800                1720722 09-OCT-14
ADODEMO                        SYS_P801                 389333 09-OCT-14
ADODEMO                        SYS_P802                1668212 09-OCT-14

8 rows selected.
```

Thanks to the interval partitioning on MONTH, you do not need to concern yourself with the partitioning definition in too much detail. A single default partition is enough; Oracle will create new partitions when needed.

Enable ILM for Storage Tiering

You already read that Oracle allows you to automate the movement of "cold" data from tier-1 storage to lower tiers automatically based on so-called ILM policies. These policies can be assigned to a table at creation time or alternatively retrofitted. It is possible to define the policies on the row or segment.

First of all, a target to move the data to is required. In the example, it is a tablespace named ILM_COMPRESS. The source tablespace name is MARTIN_BIGFILE. Currently, every segment of table ADODEMO is found on that tablespace as a query against DBA_TAB_PARTITIONS reveals:

```
TABLESPACE_NAME                PARTITION_NAME
------------------------------ --------------
MARTIN_BIGFILE                 P_MANUAL
MARTIN_BIGFILE                 SYS_P796
MARTIN_BIGFILE                 SYS_P797
MARTIN_BIGFILE                 SYS_P798
MARTIN_BIGFILE                 SYS_P799
MARTIN_BIGFILE                 SYS_P800
MARTIN_BIGFILE                 SYS_P801
MARTIN_BIGFILE                 SYS_P802
```

Now you can add the ILM policy to the oldest partition.

```
SQL> alter table ADODEMO modify partition SYS_P797
  2  ilm add policy tier to ILM_COMPRESS;

Table altered.

SQL> select policy_name,object_name,subobject_name,enabled from user_ilmobjects;

POLICY_NAME                    OBJECT_NAME                    SUBOBJECT_NAME                 ENA
------------------------------ ------------------------------ ------------------------------ ---
P1                             ADODEMO                        SYS_P797                       YES

1 row selected.
```

You just saw one of the dictionary views related to Information Lifecycle Management in action: USER_ILMOBJECTS. This view lists all the objects to which an ILM policy has been attached. Before anything can happen to the example table, certain conditions need to be met. You can find the ILM parameters as currently defined in the view DBA_ILMPARAMETERS:

```
SQL> select * from DBA_ILMPARAMETERS;

NAME                      VALUE
-------------------- ----------
ENABLED                       1
RETENTION TIME               30
JOB LIMIT                     2
EXECUTION MODE                2
EXECUTION INTERVAL           15
TBS PERCENT USED             85
TBS PERCENT FREE             25
POLICY TIME                   0

8 rows selected.
```

With regards to storage tiering, only one parameter is of interest initially. TBS PERCENT USED is the threshold indicating when a "data move" policy should be implemented. Translated into English it means that a data move may occur when the tablespace on which the segment resides reaches more than 85% usage. Continuing the above example, the tablespace is over that threshold, which should trigger the data move.

```
Tablespace                      Size (MB)  Free (MB)     % Free     % Used
------------------------------ ---------- ---------- ---------- ----------
MARTIN_BIGFILE                     209920  6403.4375          3         97
```

The evaluation of ILM policies is performed as part of the maintenance job window overnight. For most systems, that should be 10 p.m., unless the scheduler windows have been changed. If you are in a hurry, you can speed the process on your development environment up by invoking the EXECUTE_ILM procedure in the DBMS_ILM package. One of its parameters is an out variable named task_id. It returns the automatically created name of the task associated with the execution of ILM policies.

You can use the command `print task_id` in your SQL*Plus session to get the actual value of the task. By invoking `DBMS_ILM.EXECUTE_ILM`, you execute ILM policies in the current schema. The outcome of the policy evaluation is in another new dictionary view, named `USER_ILMEVALUATIONDETAILS`:

```
SQL> select selected_for_execution, job_name, policy_name
  2  from user_ilmevaluationdetails
  3   where task_id = :task_id
  4  /

SELECTED_FOR_EXECUTION         JOB_NAME                       POLICY_NAME
------------------------------ ------------------------------ ---------------
SELECTED FOR EXECUTION         ILMJOB408                      P1
```

In this case, the policy has been selected for execution. To know more about the outcome of the data move, you can check `USER_ILMRESULTS`:

```
SQL> select job_state,start_time,completion_time from USER_ILMRESULTS
  2  where task_id = :task_id and job_name = 'ILMJOB408';

JOB_STATE                 START_TIME                     COMPLETION_TIME
------------------------- ------------------------------ ------------------------------
COMPLETED SUCCESSFULLY    08-OCT-14 10.00.42.603455 PM   08-OCT-14 10.00.55.250004 PM
```

The job's execution is also recorded in the scheduler views, such as `DBA_SCHEDULER_JOB_RUN_DETAILS`. Under the covers, Oracle executes a PL/SQL block, which is recorded in `SYS.ILM_RESULTS$` if you are interested at having a look. The actual code executed by the database is stored in the `PAYLOAD` column. The dictionary view already suggested that the job's execution succeeded, but you can see the effect yourself. Going back to `USER_TAB_PARTITIONS`, you see that the tablespace name for the partition changed:

```
SQL> select partition_name,tablespace:name from user_tab_partitions
  2  where table_name = 'ADODEMO' and partition_name = 'SYS_P797';

PARTITION_NAME                 TABLESPACE_NAME
------------------------------ ---------------
SYS_P797                       ILM_COMPRESS

1 row selected.
```

As another expected side effect, you get some more free space in the original tablespace as well. The storage tiering option is quite useful in Exadata, especially if you are using the ZFS Storage Appliance or a Pillar Axiom/FS1 array as a target for the data move. Keep in mind that neither of these allows you to Smart Scan the data on it. On the other hand, data that is moved to such a tablespace may be cold and not accessed frequently anyway.

Enable ILM for Compression

Another option that has already been alluded to allows you to compress data as it gets cold. The heat map is instrumental to this functionality. Without it, Oracle could not possibly keep track of data access and manipulation. And because Oracle kernel developers have a heart for DBAs, they even added some statistics to signal its usage to the performance architect:

```
SQL> select name from v$statname where lower(name) like '%heat%';

NAME
----------------------------------------------------------------
Heatmap SegLevel - Write
Heatmap SegLevel - Full Table Scan
Heatmap SegLevel - IndexLookup
Heatmap SegLevel - TableLookup
Heatmap SegLevel - Flush
Heatmap SegLevel - Segments flushed
Heatmap BlkLevel Tracked
Heatmap BlkLevel Not Tracked - Memory
Heatmap BlkLevel Not Updated - Repeat
Heatmap BlkLevel Flushed
Heatmap BlkLevel Flushed to SYSAUX
Heatmap BlkLevel Flushed to BF
Heatmap BlkLevel Ranges Flushed
Heatmap BlkLevel Ranges Skipped
Heatmap BlkLevel Flush Task Create
Heatmap Blklevel Flush Task Count

16 rows selected.
```

When you use co-author Tanel Poder's snapper to capture the change performance counters over time, you might actually start seeing some of these! To simulate access to the data-table ADODEMO, a small procedure has been written:

```
create or replace procedure ADODEMOPROC as
  v_id number;
  v_date date;
begin
  v_date :=  to_date('01-AUG-2014') + dbms_random.value(1,10);
  select count(id) into v_id from martin.adodemo where date_created = trunc(v_date);
end;
/
```

The intention is to use that query in a number of scheduler jobs to simulate user activity. This activity is needed for the next example to work as expected. Since the above query performed a full scan initially, an index was added on the DATE_CREATED column. The scheduler jobs are created by calling DBMS_SCHEDULER directly:

```
SQL> begin
      for i in 1..5 loop
        dbms_scheduler.create_job(
          job_name => 'ADODEMOJOB_' || i,
```

```
  5         job_type => 'STORED_PROCEDURE',
  6         job_action => 'ADODEMOPROC',
  7         start_date => systimestamp,
  8         repeat_interval => 'freq=secondly;interval=10',
  9         enabled => true);
 10     end loop;
 11  end;
 12  /

PL/SQL procedure successfully completed.
```

The ILM policy is the missing piece in the demonstration. As you can see in this example, the policy can be assigned to the table as a whole, and it will be inherited by the subpartitions:

```
SQL> alter table adodemo
  2  ilm add policy column store compress for query low
  3  segment after 30 days of no access;

Table altered.

SQL> select policy_name, subobject_name, object_type, inherited_from, enabled
  2  from user_ilmobjects where object_name = 'ADODEMO';

POLICY_NAM SUBOBJECT_NAME                 OBJECT_TYPE        INHERITED_FROM       ENA
---------- ------------------------------ ------------------ -------------------- ---
P1         SYS_P797                       TABLE PARTITION    POLICY NOT INHERITED NO
P3         P_MANUAL                       TABLE PARTITION    TABLE                YES
P3         SYS_P796                       TABLE PARTITION    TABLE                NO
P3         SYS_P797                       TABLE PARTITION    TABLE                YES
P3         SYS_P798                       TABLE PARTITION    TABLE                YES
P3         SYS_P799                       TABLE PARTITION    TABLE                YES
P3         SYS_P800                       TABLE PARTITION    TABLE                YES
P3         SYS_P801                       TABLE PARTITION    TABLE                YES
P3         SYS_P802                       TABLE PARTITION    TABLE                YES
P3                                        TABLE              POLICY NOT INHERITED YES

10 rows selected.
```

Policy P1 is the data-move policy implemented and executed in the previous section. Policy names are not user-definable. In other words, Oracle assigns them. Policy P3 is the new policy just added with the above command. As described in the previous paragraph, you can see the partitions have inherited the policy that has been assigned to the table. The scope of the policy is the data segment, or the partition in the case of a heap table. Just as with the storage tiering policy the new policy is evaluated with the opening of the maintenance window.

The outcome of the evaluation is again recorded in USER_ILMEVALUATIONDETAILS. It is possible that your segment is selected for execution, as shown here:

```
SQL> select policy_name POLICY, object_name "TABLE", subobject_name "PARTITION",
  2   selected_for_execution, job_name
  3  from user_ilmevaluationdetails;
```

```
POLICY     TABLE      PARTITION      SELECTED_FOR_EXECUTION                     JOB_NAME
---------- ---------- -------------- ------------------------------------------ ----------
P3         ADODEMO    SYS_P796       SELECTED FOR EXECUTION                     ILMJOB428
P1         ADODEMO    SYS_P797       PRECONDITION NOT SATISFIED
P3         ADODEMO    SYS_P797       PRECONDITION NOT SATISFIED
P3         ADODEMO    SYS_P798       PRECONDITION NOT SATISFIED
...
```

You can verify the job's completion in USER_ILMRESULTS. The payload in SYS.ILM_RESULTS$ reveals another PL/SQL block compressing the partition. Once the job has completed successfully, you should be able to see the result in the dictionary:

```
SQL> select partition_name, table_name, compression, compress_for
  2    from user_tab_partitions
  3   where table_name = 'ADODEMO'
  4    and partition_name = 'SYS_P796';

PARTITION_NAME       TABLE_NAME                     COMPRESS COMPRESS_FOR
-------------------- ------------------------------ -------- ------------------------------
SYS_P796             ADODEMO                        ENABLED  QUERY LOW
```

This is a short introduction to what you can do with the ADO option. There are many more options available such as using custom functions for tiering. Like so many great Oracle features, the use of Automatic Data Optimization requires you to have an additional cost license (Advanced Compression).

Summary

Introduced in Oracle 11g Release 2, HCC provides exceptional compression capabilities that are far beyond anything available in prior releases. This is thanks in large part to the adoption of industry-standard compression algorithms and an increase in the size of the compression unit from a single database block (typically 8K) to a larger unit of 32K or 64K. Despite the enhancements with row level locking in 12c, the feature is only appropriate for data that is no longer being modified, because of locking issues and the fact that updated rows are moved into a much less compressed format (OLTP compression format). For this reason, HCC should only be used with data that is no longer being modified (or only occasionally modified). Since compression can be defined at the partition level, it is common to see tables that have a mixture of compressed and uncompressed partitions. This technique can, in many cases, replace ILM approaches that require moving data to alternate storage media and then purging it from the database. With Oracle 12c, the data lifecycle management process can be automated.

CHAPTER 4

Storage Indexes

Storage indexes are a useful Exadata feature that you never hear about. They are not indexes that are stored in the database like Oracle's traditional B-tree or bitmapped indexes. In fact, they are not indexes at all in the traditional sense. They are not capable of identifying a set of records that has a certain value in a given column. Rather, they are a feature of the storage server software that is designed to eliminate disk I/O. They are sometimes described as "reverse indexes." That's because they identify locations where the requested records are not, instead of the other way around. They work by storing minimum and maximum values and the existence of null values for a column for disk storage units, which are 1 megabyte (MB) by default. Because SQL predicates are passed to the storage servers when Smart Scans are performed, the storage software can check the predicates against the storage index metadata (maximum, minimum, null values) before doing the requested I/O. Any storage region that cannot possibly have a matching row is skipped. In many cases, this can result in a significant reduction in the amount of I/O that must be performed. Keep in mind that since the storage software needs the predicates to compare to the maximum and minimum values and/or null in the storage indexes, this optimization is only available for Smart Scans.

The storage software provides no documented mechanism for altering or tuning storage indexes (although there are a few undocumented parameters that can be set prior to starting `cellsrv` on the storage servers). In fact, there is not even much available in the way of monitoring. For example, there is no wait event that records the amount of time spent when a storage index is accessed or updated. Even though there are no documented commands to manipulate storage indexes, they are an extremely powerful feature and can provide dramatic performance improvements. For that reason, it is important to understand how they work.

Structure

Storage indexes consist of a minimum and a maximum value and the existence of null for up to eight columns. This structure is maintained for 1MB chunks of storage (storage regions) by default. Storage indexes are stored in memory only and are never written to disk.

Figure 4-1 shows a conceptual view of the data contained in a storage index.

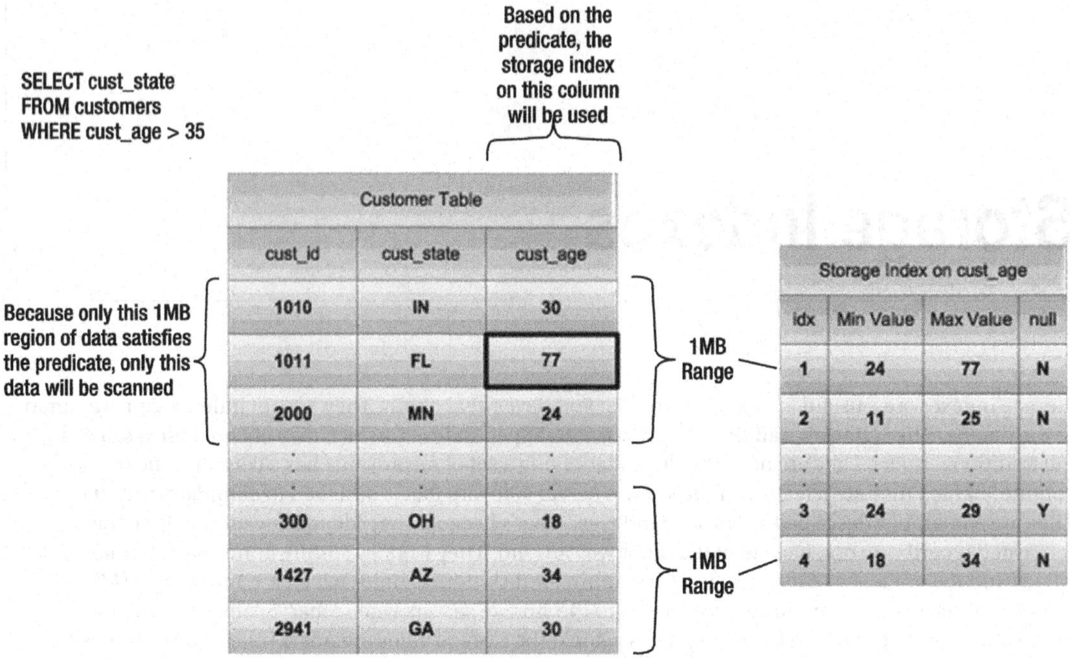

Figure 4-1. *Conceptual diagram of a storage index*

As you can see in the diagram, the first storage region in the customer table has a maximum value of 77, indicating that it's possible for it to contain rows that will satisfy the query predicate (`cust_age >35`). The other storage regions in the diagram do not have maximum values that are high enough to contain any records that will satisfy the query predicate. Therefore, those storage regions will not be read from disk.

In addition to the minimum and maximum values, there is a flag to indicate whether any of the records in a storage region contain nulls. The fact that nulls are represented at all is somewhat surprising given that nulls are not stored in traditional Oracle indexes. This ability of storage indexes to track nulls may actually have repercussions for design and implementation decisions. There are systems that don't use nulls at all. SAP, for example, uses a single space character instead of nulls. SAP does this simply to insure that records can be accessed via B-tree indexes (which do not store nulls). At any rate, storage indexes provide the equivalent of a bitmapped index on nulls, which makes finding nulls a very efficient process (assuming they represent a low percentage of the values).

Monitoring Storage Indexes

The ability to monitor storage indexes is very limited. The optimizer does not know whether a storage index will be used for a particular SQL statement. Nor do AWR or ASH capture any information about whether storage indexes were used by particular SQL statements. There is a single statistic that reports storage index usage at the database level and an undocumented tracing mechanism.

Database Statistics

There is only one database statistic directly related to storage indexes. The statistic, `cell physical IO bytes saved by storage index`, keeps track of the accumulated I/O that has been avoided by the use of storage indexes. This statistic is exposed in `v$sesstat` and `v$sysstat` and related views. It's a strange statistic that calculates a precise value for something it didn't do. Nevertheless, it is the only easily accessible indicator as to whether storage indexes have been used. Unfortunately, since the statistic is cumulative like all statistics in `v$sesstat`, it must be checked before and after a given SQL statement in order to determine whether storage indexes were used on that particular statement. Here is an example:

```
KSO@dbm2> select name, value
  2       from v$mystat s, v$statname n
  3       where s.statistic# = n.statistic#
  4       and name like '%storage index%';

NAME                                                             VALUE
---------------------------------------------------------------- ----------
cell physical IO bytes saved by storage index                             0

KSO@dbm2> select avg(pk_col) from kso.skew2 where col1 is null;

AVG(PK_COL)
-----------
   32000001

KSO@dbm2> select name, value
  2  from v$mystat s, v$statname n
  3  where s.statistic# = n.statistic#
  4  and name like '%storage index%';

NAME                                                             VALUE
---------------------------------------------------------------- ----------
cell physical IO bytes saved by storage index                    1842323456
```

As you can see, the first query asks `v$mystat` for a statistic that contains the term *storage index*. The value for this statistic will be 0 until a SQL statement that uses a storage index has been executed in the current session. In our example, the query used a storage index that eliminated about 1.8 gigabytes of disk I/O. This is the amount of additional I/O that would have been necessary without storage indexes. Note that `v$mystat` is a view that exposes cumulative statistics for your current session. As a result, if you run the statement a second time, the value should increase to twice the value it had after the first execution. Of course, disconnecting from the session (by exiting SQL*Plus, for example) resets most statistics exposed by `v$mystat`, including this one, to 0.

Tracing

There is another way to monitor what is going on with storage indexes at the individual storage cell level. The cellsrv program has the ability to create trace files whenever storage indexes are accessed. This tracing can be enabled by setting the _CELL_STORAGE_INDEX_DIAG_MODE parameter to 2 either in the cellinit.ora file to make the setting consistent across restarts of the cell server, or by changing the parameter on runtime in a cell server using the following code:

```
CellCLI> alter cell events="immediate cellsrv.cellsrv_setparam('_cell_storage_index_diag_mode',2)"
CELLSRV parameter changed: _cell_storage_index_diag_mode=2.
Modification is in-memory only.
Add parameter setting to 'cellinit.ora' if the change needs to be persistent across cellsrv reboots.
Cell enkx4cel02 successfully altered"
```

During normal use, it is obvious this parameter should be set to 0 to prevent the storage cell from the overhead of writing trace files. To make sure this parameter is set to the correct value, it can be queried from storage cell using the following:

```
CellCLI> alter cell events="immediate cellsrv.cellsrv_getparam('_cell_storage_index_diag_mode')
Parameter _cell_storage_index_diag_mode has value 0
Cell enkx4cel01 successfully altered
```

Tracing can also be enabled on all storage servers for SQL using storage indexes by setting the hidden database parameter, _KCFIS_STORAGEIDX_DIAG_MODE to a value of 2. Since these tracing mechanisms are completely undocumented, it should not be used without approval from Oracle support. Better safe than sorry.

Because the cellsrv process is multithreaded, the tracing facility creates many trace files. The result is similar to tracing a select statement that is executed in parallel on a database server in that there are multiple trace files that need to be combined to show the whole picture. The naming convention for the trace files is svtrc_, followed by a process ID, followed by a thread identifier. The process ID matches the operating system process ID of the cellsrv process. Since cellsrv enables only 100 threads by default (_CELL_NUM_THREADS), the file names are reused rapidly as requests come into the storage cells. Because of this rapid reuse, it's quite easy to wrap around the thread number portion of the file name. Such wrapping around does not wipe out the previous trace file, but rather appends new data to the existing file. Appending happens with trace files on Oracle database servers as well, but is much less common because the process ID portion of the default file name comes from the user's shadow process. By using the process ID as the identifier for the trace file with the database server, basically each session gets its own number.

Starting from the 12c release of of the storage cell software, Oracle created the concept of offload servers for the cell storage server. A cell offload server is a distinct (threaded) process started by the main cell server to have the ability to run different versions of the storage server software at the same time. The trace files that contain the information generated using above mentioned methods are the trace files generated by the offload server, not the main cell server. This also changes the trace file name—the start of the trace file name starts with celloflt rc_, and the offload server has its own diagnostic destination.

There is another related cellsrv parameter, _CELL_SI_MAX_NUM_DIAG_MODE_DUMPS, that sets a maximum number of trace files that will be created before the tracing functionality is turned off. The parameter defaults to a value of 20. Presumably, the parameter is a safety mechanism to keep the disk from getting filled by trace files since a single query can create a large number of files.

Here is a snippet from a trace file generated on our test system:

```
Trace file /opt/oracle/cell/log/diag/asm/cell/SYS_121111_140712/trace/celloflt rc_16634_15.trc
ORACLE_HOME = /opt/oracle/cell/cellofl-12.1.1.1.1_LINUX.X64_140712
System name:    Linux
```

```
Node name:       enkx4cel01.enkitec.com
Release:         2.6.39-400.128.17.el5uek
Version:         #1 SMP Tue May 27 13:20:24 PDT 2014
Machine:         x86_64
CELL SW Version:         OSS_12.1.1.1.1_LINUX.X64_140712
CELLOFLSRV SW Version:  OSS_12.1.1.1.1_LINUX.X64_140712

*** 2015-01-25 05:42:43.299
UserThread: LWPID: 16684 userId: 15 kernelId: 15 pthreadID: 140085391522112
*** 2015-01-25 06:38:55.655
4220890033:2 SIerr=0 size=1048576
2015-01-25 06:38:55.655743 :000031DA: ocl_si_ridx_pin: Pin successful for rgn_
hdl:0x6000116c1d28 rgn_index:10206 rgn_hdr:0x600085fd2de4 group_id:2 si_ridx:0x6000aa687930
4220890033:2 SIerr=0 size=1048576
2015-01-25 06:38:55.655774 :000031DB: ocl_si_ridx_pin: Pin successful for rgn_
hdl:0x6000116c1d28 rgn_index:10207 rgn_hdr:0x600085fd2df4 group_id:2 si_ridx:0x6000aa687a18
4220890033:2 SIerr=0 size=1048576
2015-01-25 06:38:55.655801 :000031DC: ocl_si_ridx_pin: Pin successful for rgn_
hdl:0x6000116c3048 rgn_index:10240 rgn_hdr:0x60008eff7004 group_id:2 si_ridx:0x6000aa687db8
4220890033:2 SIerr=0 size=1015808
2015-01-25 06:38:55.655828 :000031DD: ocl_si_ridx_pin: Pin successful for rgn_
hdl:0x6000116c3048 rgn_index:10241 rgn_hdr:0x60008eff7014 group_id:2 si_ridx:0x6000aa687b00
```

Several things are worth pointing out in this trace file:

- The first several lines are the standard trace file header with file name and software version.
- The (default) storage index tracing does contain a lot less information than used to be shown in previous (11g) versions of the storage server software, before the existence of offload servers.
- Every storage index entry describes a region of mostly 1048576 bytes (`size=1048576`).
- For every storage index entry used, the entry is "pinned" to guarantee the entry not being removed of modified during usage (`ocl_si_ridx_pin`).

For the sake of completeness, a dump of a storage index has been performed on version 11.2.3.3.1 of the storage server. The reason for using version 11 is that starting from version 12, the storage server will skip dumping the actual storage index, as can be seen in the previous dump. The 11.2.3.3.1 dump shows an actual storage index for one storage region:

```
2015-01-31 05:58:14.530028*: RIDX(0x7f07556eb1c0) : st 2(RIDX_VALID) validBitMap 0 tabn 0 id
{6507 1 964151215}
2015-01-31 05:58:14.530028*: RIDX: strt 32 end 2048 offset 86312501248 size 1032192 rgnIdx
82314 RgnOffset 16384 scn: 0x0000.00e9aa10 hist: 1
2015-01-31 05:58:14.530028*: RIDX validation history:
2015-01-31 05:58:14.530028*: 0:PartialRead 1:Undef 2:Undef 3:Undef 4:Undef 5:Undef 6:Undef
7:Undef 8:Undef 9:Undef
2015-01-31 05:58:14.530028*: Col id [1] numFilt 5 flg 2 (HASNONNULLVALUES):
2015-01-31 05:58:14.530028*: lo: c2 16 64 0 0 0 0 0
2015-01-31 05:58:14.530028*: hi: c2 19 8 0 0 0 0 0
```

```
2015-01-31 05:58:14.530028*: Col id [2] numFilt 4 flg 2 (HASNONNULLVALUES):
2015-01-31 05:58:14.530028*: lo: c5 15 4d c 22 26 0 0
2015-01-31 05:58:14.530028*: hi: c5 15 4d c 22 26 0 0
2015-01-31 05:58:14.530028*: Col id [7] numFilt 4 flg 2 (HASNONNULLVALUES):
2015-01-31 05:58:14.530028*: lo: c1 3 0 0 0 0 0 0
2015-01-31 05:58:14.530028*: hi: c1 3 0 0 0 0 0 0
```

The following items are worth pointing out:

- The storage index entry describes a region close to 1MB (`size=1032192`).
- It looks like this Storage Index entry occupies 2K of memory based on the `strt` and `end` field values.
- For each column evaluated, there is an `id` field that correlates to its position in the table.
- For each column evaluated, there is a `flg` field. It appears that it is the decimal representation of a bit mask. It also appears that the first bit indicates whether nulls are contained in the current column of the storage region. (That is, 1 and 3 both indicate that nulls are present.)
- For each column evaluated, there is a `lo` and a `hi` value (stored as hex).
- The `lo` and `hi` values are only eight bytes, indicating that the storage indexes will be ineffective on columns where the leading portion of the values are not distinct (empirical evidence bears this out, by the way).

While generating and reading trace files is very informative, it is not very easy to do and requires direct access to the storage servers. On top of that, the approach is completely undocumented. It is probably best used for investigations in nonproduction environments.

Monitoring Wrap-Up

Neither the database statistic nor the tracing is a particularly satisfying way of monitoring storage index usage. It would be nice to be able to track storage index usage at the statement level via a column in `V$SQL`, for example. In the meantime, the `cell physical IO bytes saved by storage index` statistic is the best option we have.

Controlling Storage Indexes

There is not much you can do to control storage index behavior. However, the developers have built in a few hidden parameters that provide some flexibility.

There are four database parameters that deal with storage indexes (that we're aware of):

- `_kcfis_storageidx_disabled` (default is `FALSE`)
- `_kcfis_storageidx_diag_mode` (default is 0)
- `_cell_storidx_mode` (default is `EVA`)
- `_cell_storidx_minmax_enabled` (default is `TRUE`)

None of these parameters are documented, so you need to be careful with the methods we discuss in this section. Nevertheless, we will tell you a little bit about some of these parameters and what they can do.

_kcfis_storageidx_disabled

The `_kcfis_storageidx_disabled` parameter allows storage indexes to be disabled. As with all hidden parameters, it's best to check with Oracle support before setting it, but as hidden parameters go, this one is relatively innocuous. We have used it extensively in testing and have not experienced any negative consequences.

You can set the parameter at the session level with the `alter session` statement:

```
alter session set "_kcfis_storageidx_disabled"=true;
```

Note that although setting `_kcfis_storageidx_disabled` to `TRUE` disables storage indexes for reads, the setting does not disable the maintenance of existing storage indexes. That is to say that existing storage indexes will still be updated when values in a table are changed, even if this parameter is set to `TRUE`.

_kcfis_storageidx_diag_mode

The second parameter, `__KCFIS_STORAGEIDX_DIAG_MODE`, looks eerily like the `cellinit.ora` parameter `_CELL_STORAGE_INDEX_DIAG_MODE`, which was discussed earlier. As you might expect, setting this parameter at the database layer causes trace files to be generated across all the affected storage cells. Setting it to a value of 2 enables tracing. Oddly, setting it to a value of 1 disables storage indexes. Unfortunately, the trace files are created on the storage cells, but this method of generating them is much less intrusive than restarting the `cellsrv` process on a storage server.

You can set the parameter at the session level with the `alter session` statement:

```
alter session set "_kcfis_storageidx_diag_mode"=2;
```

There may be other valid values for the parameter that enable different levels of tracing. Keep in mind that this will produce a large number of trace files on every storage cell that is involved in a query that uses storage indexes.

_cell_storidx_mode

The `_CELL_STORIDX_MODE` parameter was added in the second point release of Oracle Database 11gR2 (11.2.0.2). While this parameter is undocumented, it appears that it controls where storage indexes will be applied. There are three valid values for this parameter (`EVA,KDST,ALL`). `EVA` and `KDST` are Oracle kernel function names.

You can set the parameter at the session level with the `alter session` statement:

```
alter session set "_cell_storidx_mode"=ALL;
```

The effects of this parameter have varied across releases. As of `cellsrv` version 11.2.2.3.0, `EVA` (the default) supports all the valid comparison operators. You should note that in older versions, the `EVA` setting did not support the `IS NULL` comparison operator. It's also important to keep in mind that the database patching is tied to the storage software patching. Upgrading the version of `cellsrv` without patching the database software can result in unpredicatable behavior (disabling storage indexes, for example).

_cell_storidx_minmax_enabled

The `_CELL_STORIDX_MINMAX_ENABLED` parameter was added in the 12.1.0.2 release of Oracle Database. The default value is `TRUE`.

This parameter controls a new feature in `cellsrv` version 12.1.2.1.0 and later, for which the cell server keeps track of a running minimum and maximum of a column of a segment in addition to the ones done for the 1MB chunks. The parameter `_CELL_STORIDX_MINMAX_ENABLED` controls whether the database layer tries to use the segment's column minimum and maximum value from the storage server or tries to calculate this value at the database layer. Using the storage layer computed minimum and maximum values for a column can speed up processing of a Smart Scan because it can omit scanning storage indexes altogether for the `min()` and `max()` functions in SQL. The usage of segment level minimum and maximum values in the cell server is not reflected in the row source operator. The statistic for storage index usage (cell physical IO bytes saved by storage index) is updated just as it would with regular storage index usage, which makes the actual usage of cell kept minimum and maximum column values invisible.

Storage Software Parameters

In addition to the database parameters, there are also a number of undocumented storage software parameters that are related to storage index behavior. These parameters can be modified by adding them to the `cellinit.ora` file for setting them for all (offload) servers and then restarting `cellsrv`, or set them in the offload server specific `cellofflоadinit.ora`. Note that `cellinit.ora` will be discussed in more detail in Chapter 8. As discussed earlier in this chapter, some parameters can also be set online in the storage server using `alter cell events="immediate cellsrv.cellsrv_setparam('parameter',value)"`. Here is a list of the `cellinit.ora` storage index parameters along with their default values:

- `_cell_enable_storage_index_for_loads=TRUE`
- `_cell_enable_storage_index_for_writes=TRUE`
- `_cell_si_max_num_diag_mode_dumps=20`
- `_cell_storage_index_columns=0`
- `_cell_storage_index_diag_mode=0`
- `_cell_storage_index_partial_rd_sectors=512`
- `_cell_storage_index_partial_reads_threshold_percent=85`
- `_cell_storage_index_sizing_factor=2`
- `_cell_si_expensive_debug_tracing=FALSE`
- `_cell_si_lock_pool_num_locks=1024`
- `_si_write_diag_disable=FALSE`

You have already seen the tracing parameters (`_CELL_STORAGE_INDEX_DIAG_MODE` and `_CELL_SI_MAX_NUM_DIAG_MODE_DUMPS`) in the section Monitoring Storage Indexes. These two parameters are the most useful in our opinion, although you should get the idea from the list that there is also some built-in ability to modify behaviors such as the amount of memory to allocate for storage indexes and the number of columns that can be indexed per table.

Behavior

There is not a lot you can do to control when storage indexes are used and when they are not. Other than the parameter for disabling them, there is little you can do. There is no specific hint to enable or disable their use. And unfortunately, the `OPT_PARAM` hint does not work with the `_KCFIS_STORAGEIDX_DISABLED` parameter, either. The fact that there is no way to force the use of a storage index makes it even more important to understand when this powerful optimization will and will not be used.

In order for a storage index to be used, a query must include or make use of all the following:

Smart Scan: Storage indexes can only be used with statements that do Smart Scans. This comes with a whole set of requirements, as detailed in Chapter 2. The main requirements are that the optimizer must choose a full scan and that the I/O must be done via the direct path read mechanism.

At Least One Predicate: In order for a statement to use a storage index, there must be a `WHERE` clause with at least one predicate.

Simple Comparison Operators: Storage indexes can be used with the following set of operators:

```
=, <, >, BETWEEN, >=, <=, IN, IS NULL, IS NOT NULL
```

Mind the absense of "!=."

If a query meets the requirements of having at least one predicate involving simple comparison operators and if that query's execution makes use of Smart Scan, then the storage software can make use of storage indexes. They can be applied to any of the following aspects of the query:

Multi-Column Predicates: Storage indexes can be used with multiple predicates on the same table.

Joins: Storage indexes can be used on statements accessing multiple tables to minimize disk I/O before the join operations are carried out.

Parallel Query: Storage indexes can be used by parallel query workers. In fact, since direct path reads are required to enable storage indexes, parallel queries are very useful for ensuring that storage indexes can be used.

HCC: Storage indexes work with HCC compressed tables.

Bind Variables: Storage indexes work with bind variables. The values of the bind variables appear to be passed to the storage cells with each execution.

Partitions: Storage indexes work with partitioned objects. Individual statements can benefit from partition eliminate and storage indexes during the same execution.

Subqueries: Storage indexes work with predicates that compare a column to a value returned by a subquery.

Encryption: Storage indexes work on encrypted tables.

There are of course limitations. Following are some features and syntax that prevent the use of storage indexes:

CLOBs: Storage indexes are not created on CLOBs.

!=: Storage indexes do not work with predicates that use the != comparison operator.

Wildcards: Storage indexes do not work on predicates that use the % wildcard.

A further limitation is that storage indexes may contain up to eight columns of a table. They are created and maintained for eight-columns per table; however, this does not mean that queries with more than eight predicates cannot make use of storage indexes. In such cases, the storage software can use the indexes that exist, but by default there will be a maximum of eight columns that can be indexed. The storage servers seem to maintain a mechanism to measure popularity of the columns in the storage index and can choose to include different fields of the table in the storage index when different fields are used in predicates over time. It does appear that the developers have parameterized the setting of the number of columns in the storage index. Hence, it may be possible to change this value with help from Oracle support, although we have never heard about it being changed. Finally, bear in mind that storage indexes are not persisted to disk. The storage cell must rebuild them whenever the `cellsrv` program is restarted. They are generally created during the first Smart Scan that references a given column after a storage server has been restarted. This means it is almost certain that there will be differences in the tables and fields that are captured by storage indexes that are created after startup, unless exactly the same SQL is executed in the same sequence as after the previous startup. They can also be created when a table is created via a `CREATE TABLE AS SELECT` statement or during other direct path loads. And, of course, the storage cell will update storage indexes in response to changes that applications make to the data in the tables.

Performance

Storage indexes provide some of the most dramatic performance benefits available on the Exadata platform. Depending on the clustering factor of a particular column (that is, how well the column's data is sorted on disk), the results can be spectacular. Here is a typical example showing the performance of a query with and without the benefit of storage indexes:

```
KSO@dbm2> alter session set cell_offload_processing=false;

Session altered.

KSO@dbm2> alter session set "_kcfis_storageidx_disabled"=true;

Session altered.

KSO@dbm2> select count(*) from skew3;

  COUNT(*)
----------
 716798208

Elapsed: 00:00:22.82

KSO@dbm2> alter session set cell_offload_processing=true;

Session altered.

Elapsed: 00:00:00.00

KSO@dbm2> select count(*) from skew3;
```

```
  COUNT(*)
----------
 716798208

Elapsed: 00:00:05.77

KSO@dbm2> select count(*) from skew3 where pk_col = 7000;

  COUNT(*)
----------
        80

Elapsed: 00:00:02.32

KSO@dbm2> alter session set "_kcfis_storageidx_disabled"=false;

Session altered.

Elapsed: 00:00:00.00

KSO@dbm2> select count(*) from skew3 where pk_col = 7000;

  COUNT(*)
----------
        80

Elapsed: 00:00:00.14
```

At the start of this demonstration, all offloading was disabled via the database initialization parameter, CELL_OFFLOAD_PROCESSING. Storage indexes were also disabled via the hidden parameter _KCFIS_STORAGEIDX_DISABLED. A query without a WHERE clause was run and completed using direct path reads, but without offloading. That query took 22 seconds to do the full table scan and returned entire blocks to the database grid, just as it would on non-Exadata storage environments. Offloading was then re-enabled and the query was repeated. This time it completed in about five seconds. The improvement in elapsed time was primarily due to column projection since the storage layer only had to return a counter of rows instead of returning any of the column values.

A very selective WHERE clause was then added to the query; it reduced the time to about two seconds. This improvement was thanks to predicate filtering and the storage server Flash Cache starting to cache the data used in the scan. Remember that storage indexes were still turned off. A counter for only 80 rows had to be returned to the database machine, but the storage cells still had to read all the data to determine which rows to return. Finally, the storage indexes were re-enabled by setting _KCFIS_STORAGEIDX_DISABLED to FALSE, and the query with the WHERE clause was executed again. This time the elapsed time was only about 140 milliseconds. While this performance improvement seems extreme, it is relatively common when storage indexes are used.

Special Optimization for Nulls

Nulls are a special case for storage indexes. There is a separate flag in the storage index structure that is used to indicate whether a storage region contains nulls or not. This separate flag makes queries looking for nulls (or the absence of nulls) even more efficient than the normal minimum and maximum comparisons that are typically done. Here's an example comparing typical performance with and without the special null optimization:

```
KSO@dbm2> set timing on
KSO@dbm2> select count(*) from skew3 where col1=1000;

  COUNT(*)
----------
         0

Elapsed: 00:00:01.96

KSO@dbm2> select name, value
  2  from v$mystat s, v$statname n
  3  where s.statistic# = n.statistic#
  4  and name like '%storage index%';

NAME                                                                      VALUE
---------------------------------------------------------------- --------------
cell physical IO bytes saved by storage index                        2879774720

Elapsed: 00:00:00.00

KSO@dbm2> select count(*) from skew3 where col1 is null;

  COUNT(*)
----------
        16

Elapsed: 00:00:00.13

KSO@dbm2> select name, value
  2  from v$mystat s, v$statname n
  3  where s.statistic# = n.statistic#
  4  and name like '%storage index%';

NAME                                                                      VALUE
---------------------------------------------------------------- --------------
cell physical IO bytes saved by storage index                       32299237376

Elapsed: 00:00:00.00
```

In this example, you can see that retrieval of a few nulls was extremely fast. This is because there is no possibility that any storage region that doesn't contain a null will have to be read, so no false positives requiring reading the actual data will slow down this query. With any other value (except the minimum or maximum value for a column), there will most likely be storage regions that can't be eliminated, even though they don't actually contain a value that matches the predicates. This is exactly the case in the previous example, where no records were returned for the first query even though it took two seconds to read all the data from disk. Notice also that the amount of I/O saved by the null query is a little more than 27 gigabytes (GB), while the amount saved by the first query was *only* about 2.5GB. That means that the first query found way fewer storage regions that it could eliminate.

Physical Distribution of Values

Storage indexes behave very differently from normal indexes. They maintain a fairly coarse picture of the values that are stored on disk. However, their mechanism can be very effective at eliminating large amounts of disk I/O in certain situations while still keeping the cost of maintaining them relatively low. It is important to keep in mind that the physical distribution of data on disk will have a large impact on how effective the storage indexes are. An illustration will make this clearer.

Suppose you have a table that has a column with unique values (that is, no value is repeated). If the data is stored on disk in such a manner that the rows are ordered by that column, there will be one and only one storage region for any given value of that column. Any query with an equality predicate on that column will have to read, at most, one storage region. Figure 4-2 shows a conceptual picture of a storage index for a sorted column.

Storage Index			
idx	Min Value	Max Value	null
1	1	100	N
2	101	200	N
⋮	⋮	⋮	⋮
3	10,000	10,100	Y
4	10,101	10,200	N

Figure 4-2. *A storage index on a sorted column*

As you can see from Figure 4-2, if you wanted to retrieve the record where the value was 102, you would only have one storage region that could possibly contain that value.

Suppose now that the same data set is stored on disk in a random order. How many storage regions would you expect to have to read to locate a single row via an equality predicate? It depends on the number of rows that fit into a storage region, but the answer is certainly much larger than the one storage region that would be required with the sorted data set.

It's just that simple. Storage indexes will be more effective on sorted data. From a performance perspective, the better sorted the data is on disk, the faster the average access time will be when using storage indexes. For a column that is completely sorted, the access time should be very fast and there should be little variation in the access time, regardless of what values are requested. For unsorted data, the access times will be faster toward the ends of the range of values (because there are not many storage regions that will have ranges of values containing the queried value). The average access times for values in the middle of the distribution will vary widely. Figure 4-3 is a chart comparing access times using storage indexes for sorted and unsorted data.

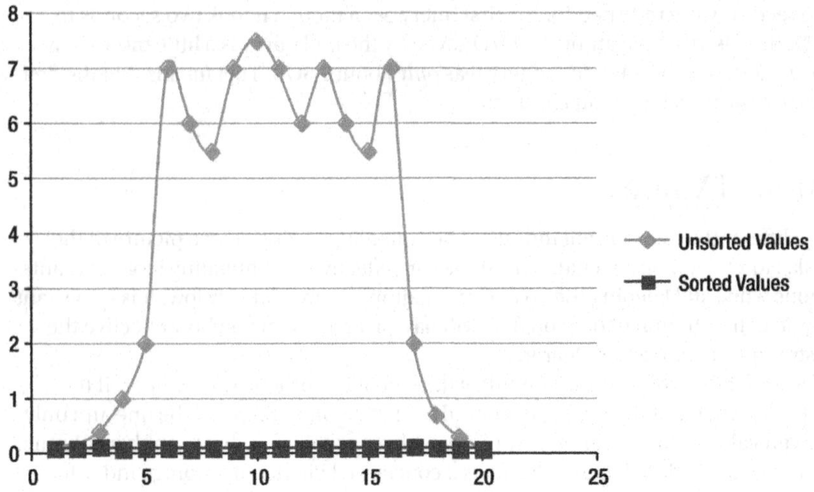

***Figure 4-3.** Storage index access times—sorted vs. unsorted*

As you can see, sorted data will provide better and more consistent results. While we are on the subject, I should point out that there are many cases where several columns will benefit from this behavioral characteristic of storage indexes. It is common in data warehouse environments to have data that is partitioned on a date column, and there are often many other columns that track the partition key such as associated dates (order date, ship date, insert date, return date for example) or sequentially generated numbers like order numbers. Queries against these column are often problematic due the fact that partition eliminate cannot help them. Storage indexes will provide a similar benefit to partition elimination as long as care is taken to ensure that the data is pre-sorted prior to loading. This means sorting of table or partition data should be considered as part of moving or loading of data to increase efficiency of not only storage indexes, but Hybrid Columnar Compression, too. However, a given table or partition can only be sorted and stored on one column.

Potential Issues

There's no such thing as a free puppy. As with everything in life, there are a few issues with storage indexes that you should be aware of.

Incorrect Results

By far, the biggest issue with storage indexes has been that in early releases of the Exadata Storage Software, there were a handful of bugs regarding incorrect results. That is to say that in certain situations, usage of storage indexes could eliminate storage regions from consideration that actually contained records of interest. This incorrect elimination could occur due to timing issues with concurrent DML while a Smart Scan was being done using storage indexes. These bugs have been addressed in 11.2.0.2 and the patches on the storage servers of that time. At current times (Oracle 11.2.0.4/12.1.0.2), the chances of incorrect results are highly unlikely, which means not higher than would occur in other parts of the Oracle database. If you run into this issue or suspect you are running in this issue, disabling storage index usage via the hidden parameter, `_KCFIS_STORAGEIDX_DISABLED` by setting it to `TRUE` may be an option to diagnose differences in query results. If queries actually do produce different results with storage indexes, you can use this parameter to disable the usage of storage indexes either by setting it systemwide or by setting it for sessions until the proper patches are applied. This parameter can be set with an `alter session` command so that only problematic queries are affected. Of course, you should check with Oracle Support before enabling any hidden parameters. Also MOS note 1260804.1 (How to diagnose Smart Scan and wrong results) can be of help diagnosing potential Exadata/Smart-Scan-related issues, including storage indexes returning incorrect results.

Moving Target

Storage indexes can be a little frustrating because they do not always kick in when you expect them to. And because you cannot tell Oracle that you really want a storage index to exist and be used, there is little you can do other than try to understand why they are not there or used in certain circumstances so you can avoid those conditions in the future.

In early versions of the storage server software, one of the main reasons that storage indexes were disabled was due to implicit data type conversions. Over the years, Oracle has gotten better and better at doing "smart" data type conversions that do not have negative performance consequences. For example, if you write a SQL statement with a `WHERE` clause that compares a date field to a character string, Oracle will usually apply a `to_date` function to the character string instead of modifying the date column (which could have the unpleasant side effect of disabling an index). Unfortunately, when the Exadata storage software was relatively new, all the nuances had not been worked out, at least to the degree we're used to from the database side. Dates have been particularly persnickety. Here is an example using `cellsrv` 11.2.1.2.6:

```
SYS@EXDB1> select count(*) from kso.skew3 where col3 = '20-OCT-05';

  COUNT(*)
----------
         0

Elapsed: 00:00:14.00
SYS@EXDB1> select name, value
  2  from v$mystat s, v$statname n
  3  where s.statistic# = n.statistic#
  4  and name like '%storage index%';

NAME                                                        VALUE
---------------------------------------------- --------------
cell physical IO bytes saved by storage index                   0

Elapsed: 00:00:00.01

SYS@EXDB1> select count(*) from kso.skew3 where col3 = '20-OCT-2005';

  COUNT(*)
----------
         0

Elapsed: 00:00:00.07

SYS@EXDB1> select name, value
  2  from v$mystat s, v$statname n
  3  where s.statistic# = n.statistic#
  4  and name like '%storage index%';
```

```
NAME                                                                 VALUE
---------------------------------------------------------------- ---------------
cell physical IO bytes saved by storage index                  15954337792

Elapsed: 00:00:00.01
```

In this very simple example, there is a query with a predicate comparing a date column (col3) to a string containing a date. In one case, the string contained a four-digit year. In the other, only two digits were used. Only the query with the four-digit-year format used the storage index. Let's look at the plans for the statements to see why the two queries were treated differently:

```
SYS@EXDB1> @fsx2
Enter value for sql_text: select count(*) from kso.skew3 where col3 = %
Enter value for sql_id:
Enter value for inst_id:

SQL_ID          AVG_ETIME  PX OFFLOAD IO_SAVED% SQL_TEXT
------------- ------------ --- ------- --------- ----------------------------------------
2s58n6d3mzkmn          .07   0 Yes        100.00 select count(*) from kso.skew3 where
                                                 col3 = '20-OCT-2005'

fuhmg9hqdbd84        14.00   0 Yes         99.99 select count(*) from kso.skew3 where
                                                 col3 = '20-OCT-05'

2 rows selected.

SYS@EXDB1> select * from table(dbms_xplan.display_cursor('&sql_id','&child_no','typical'));
Enter value for sql_id: fuhmg9hqdbd84
Enter value for child_no:

PLAN_TABLE_OUTPUT
-----------------------------------------------------------------------------------------
SQL_ID  fuhmg9hqdbd84, child number 0
-------------------------------------
select count(*) from kso.skew3 where col3 = '20-OCT-05'

Plan hash value: 2684249835

----------------------------------------------------------------------------
| Id|Operation                    |Name  | Rows|Bytes|Cost (%CPU)|Time     |
----------------------------------------------------------------------------
|  0|SELECT STATEMENT             |      |     |     | 535K(100)|          |
|  1| SORT AGGREGATE              |      |    1|   8 |          |          |
|* 2|  TABLE ACCESS STORAGE FULL|SKEW3 |  384|3072 | 535K  (2)|01:47:04|
----------------------------------------------------------------------------

Predicate Information (identified by operation id):
---------------------------------------------------

   2 - storage("COL3"='20-OCT-05')
       filter("COL3"='20-OCT-05')
```

```
20 rows selected.

SYS@EXDB1> /
Enter value for sql_id: 2s58n6d3mzkmn
Enter value for child_no:

PLAN_TABLE_OUTPUT
-----------------------------------------------------------------------------------------
SQL_ID  2s58n6d3mzkmn, child number 0
-------------------------------------
select count(*) from kso.skew3 where col3 = '20-OCT-2005'

Plan hash value: 2684249835

-----------------------------------------------------------------------------------
| Id  | Operation                  | Name  | Rows  | Bytes | Cost (%CPU)| Time     |
-----------------------------------------------------------------------------------
|   0 | SELECT STATEMENT           |       |       |       |   531K(100)|          |
|   1 |  SORT AGGREGATE            |       |     1 |     8 |            |          |
|*  2 |   TABLE ACCESS STORAGE FULL| SKEW3 |   384 |  3072 |   531K  (1)| 01:46:24 |
-----------------------------------------------------------------------------------

Predicate Information (identified by operation id):
---------------------------------------------------

   2 - storage("COL3"=TO_DATE(' 2005-10-20 00:00:00', 'syyyy-mm-dd
              hh24:mi:ss'))
       filter("COL3"=TO_DATE(' 2005-10-20 00:00:00', 'syyyy-mm-dd
              hh24:mi:ss'))

22 rows selected.
```

It appears that the optimizer did not recognize the two-digit date as a date. At the very least, the optimizer failed to apply the `to_date` function to the literal, so the storage index was not used. Fortunately, most of these types of data conversion issues have been resolved with the later releases. Here is the same test using `cellsrv` 11.2.2.2.0:

```
SYS@SANDBOX> @si

NAME                                                                       VALUE
---------------------------------------------------------------- --------------
cell physical IO bytes saved by storage index                                  0

SYS@SANDBOX> select count(*) from kso.skew3 where col3 = '20-OCT-05';

  COUNT(*)
----------
         0

SYS@SANDBOX> @si
```

```
NAME                                                                      VALUE
---------------------------------------------------------------------- ---------------
cell physical IO bytes saved by storage index                          16024526848
```

As you can see, this conversion issue has been resolved. So, why bring it up? Well, the point is that the behavior of storage indexes has undergone numerous changes as the product has matured. As a result, we have built a set of test cases that we use to verify behavior after each patch in our lab. Our test cases primarily verify comparison operators (=,<,`like`, `IS NULL`, and so on) and a few other special cases such as LOBs, compression, and encryption. Of course, it is always a good practice to test application behavior after any patching, but if you have specific cases where storage indexes are critical to your application, you may want take special care to test those parts of you application.

Partition Size

Storage indexes depend on Smart Scans, which depend on direct path reads. As we discussed in Chapter 2, Oracle will generally use serial direct path reads for large objects. However, when an object is partitioned, Oracle may fail to recognize that the object is "large" because Oracle looks at the size of each individual segment. This may result in some partitions not being read via the Smart Scan mechanism and thus disabling any storage indexes for that partition. When historical partitions are compressed, the problem becomes even more noticeable, as the reduced size of the compressed partitions will be even less likely to trigger the serial direct path reads. This issue can be worked around by not relying on the serial direct path read algorithm and, instead, specifying a degree of parallelism for the object or using a hint to force the desired behavior.

Incompatible Coding Techniques

Finally, there are some coding techniques that can disable storage indexes. Here is an example showing the effect of the `trunc` function on date columns:

```
KSO@dbm2> select count(*) from skew3 where trunc(col3) = '20-OCT-2005';

  COUNT(*)
----------
         0
1 row selected.

Elapsed: 00:00:05.36

KSO@dbm2> @expl

PLAN_TABLE_OUTPUT
-----------------------------------------------------------------------------------------
----------------------------------------------------------------
SQL_ID  2mkcfrs28z393, child number 0
-------------------------------------
select count(*) from skew3 where trunc(col3) = '20-OCT-2005'

Plan hash value: 2684249835
```

```
--------------------------------------------------------------------------------------
| Id  | Operation                    | Name  | Rows  | Bytes | Cost (%CPU)| Time     |
--------------------------------------------------------------------------------------
|   0 | SELECT STATEMENT             |       |       |       |   995K(100)|          |
|   1 |  SORT AGGREGATE              |       |     1 |     8 |            |          |
|*  2 |   TABLE ACCESS STORAGE FULL| SKEW3 |  7167K|    54M|   995K  (3)| 00:00:39 |
--------------------------------------------------------------------------------------

Predicate Information (identified by operation id):
---------------------------------------------------

   2 - storage(TRUNC(INTERNAL_FUNCTION("COL3"))=TO_DATE(' 2005-10-20
              00:00:00', 'syyyy-mm-dd hh24:mi:ss'))
       filter(TRUNC(INTERNAL_FUNCTION("COL3"))=TO_DATE(' 2005-10-20
              00:00:00', 'syyyy-mm-dd hh24:mi:ss'))

22 rows selected.
```

In this example, a function was applied to a date column, which, as you might expect, disables the storage index. The fact that applying a function to a column disables the storage index is not too surprising, but application of the `trunc` function is a commonly seen coding technique. Many dates have a time component, and many queries want data for a specific day. It is well known that truncating a date in this manner will disable normal B-tree index usage. In the past, that generally did not matter. Queries in many data warehouse environments were designed to do full scans anyway, so there was really no need to worry about disabling an index. Storage indexes change the game from this perspective and may force us to rethink some of our approaches. We will discuss this issue in more detail in Chapter 16.

Summary

Storage indexes are an optimization technique that is available when the database is able to utilize Smart Table Scans. They can provide dramatic performance improvements, although the caching of Smart-Scanned data in the Flash Cache with recent cell server versions make Smart Scan performance come closer to storage index optimized performance. They are especially effective with queries that access data via an alternate key that tracks the primary partition key.

How the data is physically stored is an important consideration and has a dramatic impact on the effectiveness of storage indexes. Care should be taken when migrating data to the Exadata platform to ensure that the data is clustered on disk in a manner that will allow storage indexes to be used effectively.
It should also be considered that storage indexes are limited to eight columns and are created dependent on predicates of SQL causing Smart Scans, fully automatic.

CHAPTER 5

Exadata Smart Flash Cache

Oracle marketing must really like the term *smart*. They have applied it to numerous different features on the Exadata platform. They also seem to like the term *flash*, which is associated with at least a half dozen features as well. To add to the confusion, there are two features in Oracle Database 12c Release 1 that have *almost* exactly the same names—Database Smart Flash Cache (DBFC) and Exadata Smart Flash Cache (ESFC). While both features make use of flash-based memory devices, they are very different. In this chapter, we will focus on ESFC and the OLTP optimizations and only mention DBFC in passing.

One of the initial goals with Exadata V2, the first version to feature ESFC, was to expand Exadata's capabilities to improve its performance with OLTP workloads. To accomplish this goal, ESFC was the key component that was added to the V2 configuration. Features based on the ESFC—such as the Exadata Smart Flash Logging (ESFL) and later Write-back Flash Cache (WBFC) as well as Flash Cache compression among others—were introduced with subsequent releases. Except for the step from V2 to X2, every new generation of Exadata hardware had more flash memory available. With the current hardware generation at the time of writing, the Exadata X5-2, you can have approximately 90TB of cache in a full rack with high-capacity storage servers. Flash Cache is handled slightly differently on the all-flash, X5-2 High Performance cells. You can read more about that later in the chapter. It is important to understand that this cache is managed by Oracle software, and the software is aware of how the data is being used by the databases that the storage layer is supporting. Oracle has been working on software for effectively managing database caches for over 30 years. Since the storage software knows what the database is asking for, it has a much better idea of what should and shouldn't be cached than a conventional storage array.

DBFC VS. ESFC

DBFC and ESFC are two completely different things. DBFC is an extension of the buffer cache on the database server. It is a standard part of 11g and is implemented as a tier 2 buffer cache for an instance. It is only supported on Solaris and Oracle Linux. It is enabled by adding Flash disks (SSD) to a database server and telling a single instance to use it. If a user needs a block that is not in the buffer cache, it will look in the DBFC to see if it is there before requesting an I/O. When blocks are aged out of the buffer pool, they are moved to the DBFC instead of being simply flushed. ESFC is, of course, the disk cache on the Exadata storage servers. It caches data for all instances that access the storage cell.

Hardware

Describing hardware has been easier before the release current Exadata generation. Beginning with the V2 and up to, but not including the X5-2, every Exadata storage server can be described in the same way. Each cell has four PCI Express Cards for Smart Flash Cache plus 12 hard disks, regardless if it is a High Performance (HP) or High Capacity (HC) model. With the X5s, you need to distinguish between the HC and HP cells with regards to the number of Flash cards. The latter do not come with any hard disks, for the first time in the Exadata product history, but instead feature 8 of next generation PCIe cards for a raw capacity of 12.8TB per cell. Since the X5-2 High Performance Storage Servers do not have any hard disks for database storage, the Flash devices will be used to store database files persistently in addition to acting as a storage layer cache for the RDBMS layer I/O requests.

Each Exadata X5-2 High Capacity Storage Server has four Flash Accelerator PCIe Cards with 1.6TB raw capacity each, for a total of 6.4TB raw space per cell. Apart from the larger capacity of the Flash device used, the HC model follows the same design principles as earlier generations of the hardware.

Looking at the raw numbers of storage space per card, you need to know that these are the ones quoted in the specifications. The amount that is available for use is slightly less. The hardware design of the cards has changed over time, and the space permits us to discuss the X4 and X5 generation only in this chapter. Where applicable, references are made to the earlier hardware generations. For this chapter, the focus will be on the HC cell since this might be the more common of the two hardware choices.

Flash Memory in Exadata X4-2 Storage Servers

You have just read that the Flash Memory in both high-capacity and high-performance models of the X4-2 storage servers were identical: four cards in each. They are connected as PCI Express (version 2) expansion cards. The PCIe slots the cards sit in have eight lanes each. Oracle calls the Flash cards F80, or Sun Flash Accelerator F80 PCIe card to be more precise. The useable capacity is easy to remember at 800GB—,it is hinted at in the product name. Internally, the card is made up of four so-called Flash (memory) Modules or FMODs of 200 GB each. As a result of this, a single of the F80 cards presents itself to the operating system as four individual block devices. You can see this in the output of the `lsscsi` command, executed on an X4-2 cell:

```
[root@enkx4cel01 ~]# lsscsi
[0:0:0:0]    disk    ATA     2E256-TU2-510B00 UI03  /dev/sda
[0:0:1:0]    disk    ATA     2E256-TU2-510B00 UI03  /dev/sdb
[0:0:2:0]    disk    ATA     2E256-TU2-510B00 UI03  /dev/sdc
[0:0:3:0]    disk    ATA     2E256-TU2-510B00 UI03  /dev/sdd
[1:0:0:0]    disk    ATA     2E256-TU2-510B00 UI03  /dev/sde
[1:0:1:0]    disk    ATA     2E256-TU2-510B00 UI03  /dev/sdf
[1:0:2:0]    disk    ATA     2E256-TU2-510B00 UI03  /dev/sdg
[1:0:3:0]    disk    ATA     2E256-TU2-510B00 UI03  /dev/sdh
[2:0:0:0]    disk    ATA     2E256-TU2-510B00 UI03  /dev/sdi
[2:0:1:0]    disk    ATA     2E256-TU2-510B00 UI03  /dev/sdj
[2:0:2:0]    disk    ATA     2E256-TU2-510B00 UI03  /dev/sdk
[2:0:3:0]    disk    ATA     2E256-TU2-510B00 UI03  /dev/sdl
[3:0:0:0]    disk    ATA     2E256-TU2-510B00 UI03  /dev/sdm
[3:0:1:0]    disk    ATA     2E256-TU2-510B00 UI03  /dev/sdn
[3:0:2:0]    disk    ATA     2E256-TU2-510B00 UI03  /dev/sdo
[3:0:3:0]    disk    ATA     2E256-TU2-510B00 UI03  /dev/sdp
[4:0:20:0]   enclosu ORACLE  CONCORD14        0d03  -
[4:2:0:0]    disk    LSI     MR9261-8i        2.13  /dev/sdq
[4:2:1:0]    disk    LSI     MR9261-8i        2.13  /dev/sdr
```

```
[4:2:2:0]    disk   LSI      MR9261-8i      2.13  /dev/sds
[4:2:3:0]    disk   LSI      MR9261-8i      2.13  /dev/sdt
[4:2:4:0]    disk   LSI      MR9261-8i      2.13  /dev/sdu
[4:2:5:0]    disk   LSI      MR9261-8i      2.13  /dev/sdv
[4:2:6:0]    disk   LSI      MR9261-8i      2.13  /dev/sdw
[4:2:7:0]    disk   LSI      MR9261-8i      2.13  /dev/sdx
[4:2:8:0]    disk   LSI      MR9261-8i      2.13  /dev/sdy
[4:2:9:0]    disk   LSI      MR9261-8i      2.13  /dev/sdz
[4:2:10:0]   disk   LSI      MR9261-8i      2.13  /dev/sdaa
[4:2:11:0]   disk   LSI      MR9261-8i      2.13  /dev/sdab
[11:0:0:0]   disk   ORACLE   UNIGEN-UFD     PMAP  /dev/sdac
[root@enkx4cel01 ~]#
```

The first devices are the FMODs, four per card. The first card's modules, for example, is addressed as 0:0:0:0 through 0:0:0:3. If you want all the glorious detail, you need to check the output of `dmesg`. A case-insensitive `egrep` for "`sas|scsi`" will show you how these devices show up during the boot phase under the `mpt2sas` kernel module ("Fusion MPT SAS Host"). This is matched by the output from `cellcli`:

```
CellCLI>  list physicaldisk attributes name,deviceName,diskType,makeModel -
> where deviceName like '/dev/sd[a-p]'

         FLASH_1_0        /dev/sdi        FlashDisk        "Sun Flash Accelerator F80 PCIe Card"
         FLASH_1_1        /dev/sdj        FlashDisk        "Sun Flash Accelerator F80 PCIe Card"
         FLASH_1_2        /dev/sdk        FlashDisk        "Sun Flash Accelerator F80 PCIe Card"
         FLASH_1_3        /dev/sdl        FlashDisk        "Sun Flash Accelerator F80 PCIe Card"
         FLASH_2_0        /dev/sdm        FlashDisk        "Sun Flash Accelerator F80 PCIe Card"
         FLASH_2_1        /dev/sdn        FlashDisk        "Sun Flash Accelerator F80 PCIe Card"
         FLASH_2_2        /dev/sdo        FlashDisk        "Sun Flash Accelerator F80 PCIe Card"
         FLASH_2_3        /dev/sdp        FlashDisk        "Sun Flash Accelerator F80 PCIe Card"
         FLASH_4_0        /dev/sde        FlashDisk        "Sun Flash Accelerator F80 PCIe Card"
         FLASH_4_1        /dev/sdf        FlashDisk        "Sun Flash Accelerator F80 PCIe Card"
         FLASH_4_2        /dev/sdg        FlashDisk        "Sun Flash Accelerator F80 PCIe Card"
         FLASH_4_3        /dev/sdh        FlashDisk        "Sun Flash Accelerator F80 PCIe Card"
         FLASH_5_0        /dev/sda        FlashDisk        "Sun Flash Accelerator F80 PCIe Card"
         FLASH_5_1        /dev/sdb        FlashDisk        "Sun Flash Accelerator F80 PCIe Card"
         FLASH_5_2        /dev/sdc        FlashDisk        "Sun Flash Accelerator F80 PCIe Card"
         FLASH_5_3        /dev/sdd        FlashDisk        "Sun Flash Accelerator F80 PCIe Card"
```

The cards are addressed by the kernel as regular block devices, just as spinning hard disks since the days of the IDE disks would be. They are visible, just like any other block device in Linux. In fact, the devices starting with `/dev/sdq` are regular, spinning hard disks. There is nothing wrong with that; it has been the standard way directly attached NAND Flash has been addressed in many devices until the introduction of the Non-Volatile Memory Host Controller Interface Specification (NVMHCI) or NVMe for short. You find these on the X5-2 storage servers you can read about in the next section.

Flash Memory in Exadata X5-2 Storage Servers

Every Exadata storage server up to the X5 featured the multi-FMOD Flash cards similar to the one shown in the section above. The capacity has, of course, been different, but the design of the card remained the same. The X5-2 is the first storage server generation that changes a few of these truths:

- The new Flash cards—F160— are not made up of multiple FMODs.
- The Flash cards are addressed differently by the operating system.
- You can choose to use an all-Flash model of the storage server.

When you check the output from the `cellcli` command on the X5-2 High Capacity cell you quickly realize that there is indeed just one "card," no more modules:

```
CellCLI> list physicaldisk attributes name,deviceName,diskType,makeModel
    8:0           /dev/sda        HardDisk        "HGST    H7240AS60SUN4.0T"
    8:1           /dev/sdb        HardDisk        "HGST    H7240AS60SUN4.0T"
    8:2           /dev/sdc        HardDisk        "HGST    H7240AS60SUN4.0T"
    8:3           /dev/sdd        HardDisk        "HGST    H7240AS60SUN4.0T"
    8:4           /dev/sde        HardDisk        "HGST    H7240AS60SUN4.0T"
    8:5           /dev/sdf        HardDisk        "HGST    H7240AS60SUN4.0T"
    8:6           /dev/sdg        HardDisk        "HGST    H7240AS60SUN4.0T"
    8:7           /dev/sdh        HardDisk        "HGST    H7240AS60SUN4.0T"
    8:8           /dev/sdi        HardDisk        "HGST    H7240AS60SUN4.0T"
    8:9           /dev/sdj        HardDisk        "HGST    H7240AS60SUN4.0T"
    8:10          /dev/sdk        HardDisk        "HGST    H7240AS60SUN4.0T"
    8:11          /dev/sdl        HardDisk        "HGST    H7240AS60SUN4.0T"
    FLASH_1_1     /dev/nvme3n1    FlashDisk       "Oracle Flash Accelerator F160 PCIe Card"
    FLASH_2_1     /dev/nvme2n1    FlashDisk       "Oracle Flash Accelerator F160 PCIe Card"
    FLASH_4_1     /dev/nvme0n1    FlashDisk       "Oracle Flash Accelerator F160 PCIe Card"
    FLASH_5_1     /dev/nvme1n1    FlashDisk       "Oracle Flash Accelerator F160 PCIe Card"
```

If you look at the output carefully, you will undoubtedly notice that not only are there fewer Flash disks, but also their device names are quite different. This has to do with the new NVMHCI interface (*NVMe*, for short) these devices can use. For the longest time, high-performance Flash memory was addressed more or less in the same way as mechanical disk. With all the progress made with recent processor generations, this model of addressing Flash memory became increasingly outdated from a performance perspective, especially when connecting the storage device to the PCIe bus that has a very fast link with the processor itself. The most visible difference is the massively increased queue depth and increased number of interrupts that can be handled via NVMe devices. Just to prove the point, you will not see the NVMe devices listed under the `lsscsi` command output. So they truly represent the next generation of Flash memory in x86-64.

In addition, the F160 cards are true PCIe v3 cards, unlike the F80 that were PCIe v2 cards. The main difference is the increased bandwidth offered by PCIe v3, which almost doubled compared to the previous generation.

According to the documentation, the storage servers, theoretically, allow PCIe cards to be replaced while the system is running. However, the Oracle Exadata Storage Software User's Guide and My Oracle Support note 1993842.1 recommend powering down the storage server before replacing one of these cards. Fortunately, you can accomplish this without experiencing an outage, as ASM redundancy allows entire storage cells to be offline without affecting the databases they are supporting. Note that replacing one of the Flash cards should not require any reconfiguration.

Flash Cache vs. Flash Disk

All of the Exadata storage servers, except for the X5-2 High Performance model, allow you to define how you want to use the Flash cards in the server. This section describes the non X5-2 High Performance cells—you can read more about the all-Flash or High Performance model later. On all the other (non-X5-2 High Performance) models, the Flash memory on the storage servers can be used in two ways. It can be configured as a disk cache (ESFC), or it can be carved up and presented as solid-state (grid) disks for use with ASM for database storage. These two modes are not mutually exclusive. The Flash memory can be allocated to either format in whatever percentages are desired. The recommended configuration is to use all the Flash memory as Flash Cache. This configuration significantly speeds up random access reads and, since Exadata version 11.2.3.3, this functionality extends to multi-block reads, too. Flash Cache can be used in two configurations: write-back and write-through, both of which will be described later in the chapter. For now, it suffices to say that the default mode of operation for ESFC is write-through.

In many systems, the approach of allocating all the available Flash memory as write-through cache works very well. However, for systems that are very write-intensive, starting with Exadata storage software version 11.2.3.2.1, it may be beneficial to change from write-through to Write-back Flash Cache (WBFC). Operating in write-back mode provides the ability to cache write I/Os to the Flash device in addition to the read IOs. Enabling this feature will give you far more write IOPS than the combined local hard disks can provide.

You can also use some of the Flash memory as a grid disk. Keep in mind that depending on the ASM redundancy level used (Normal or High), choosing this option will consume two or three times the amount of Flash storage that the objects actually occupy. This fact alone makes the option less palatable, especially on Exadata hardware that does not have the same abundance of Flash memory as the X4 and later generations. Also keep in mind that writes to data files are done in the background by the DBWR processes. So choosing to use part of the Flash-based storage as a grid disk may not provide as much benefit as you might have hoped for, especially since the introduction of WBFC. Fortunately, it is pretty easy to reallocate Flash storage, so testing your specific situation should not prove too difficult unless, of course, you do not have a dedicated test environment. However, since this chapter focuses on the Exadata Smart Flash Cache feature, we will only briefly cover using the F160s as grid disks outside the X5-2 High Performance model.

■ **Note** A common misconception is that putting online redo logs on Flash storage will significantly speed up writes to redo logs and thus increase the throughput of high-transaction systems. We have come across this on Exadata systems, as well as on non-Exadata hardware. While it's true that small random writes are faster on SSD-based storage than on traditional disks, writes to redo logs on high-transaction systems generally do not fall into that bucket and actually do not benefit that much from being stored on SSD storage. In fact, these writes should just go to the array's cache and complete very quickly. In addition, SSD write mechanics can cause a lot of variability in individual write times. There may be individual writes that take orders of magnitude longer than the average, a fact known as *write cliff*. This can cause problems on very busy systems as well. To mitigate this problem, Oracle introduced Smart Flash Logging, which you will read about later.

The all-flash X5-2 High Performance cells differ from the High Capacity model. The most striking difference is the absence of mechanical, spinning disk. Each of the new cells has eight F160 cards. The F160 cards have 1.6TB capacity each for a total raw capacity of 12.8TB. In a full rack, this amounts to 179.2 TB, which is a little less capacity than the previous X4-2 High Performance cell. Although the individual disks in the X4-2 cell are smaller at 1.2TB vs. 1.6TB of the F160 card, the X4-2 cell has 12 hard disks (plus four F80 cards for caching) for approximately 200TB raw capacity on hard disk. Without spinning disk, you have no choice but to create grid disks for ASM on Flash memory. You might be asking yourself if the all-Flash cell has a cache as well and the answer is yes. When you receive shipment of the system, Oracle reserves 5% of the Flash devices for Smart Flash Cache for reasons described in the next section.

Using Flash Memory as Cache

A very simplified description of how a disk cache works goes something like this: When a read request comes in, the I/O subsystem checks the cache to see if the requested data exists in cache. If the data is in the cache, it is returned to the requesting process. If the requested data doesn't reside in the cache, it is read from disk and returned to the requesting process. In the case of uncached data, the data is later copied to the cache (after it is returned to the requesting process). This is done to ensure that populating the cache doesn't slow down I/O processing.

In most enterprise storage arrays, "the cache" is implemented in battery or otherwise protected DRAM, fronting the disks. On the Exadata platform, a different concept is implemented. Supplementing DRAM on the disk controller, Flash cards will act as cache—albeit a smart one. Figure 5-1 shows the I/O path of reads using Oracle's ESFC.

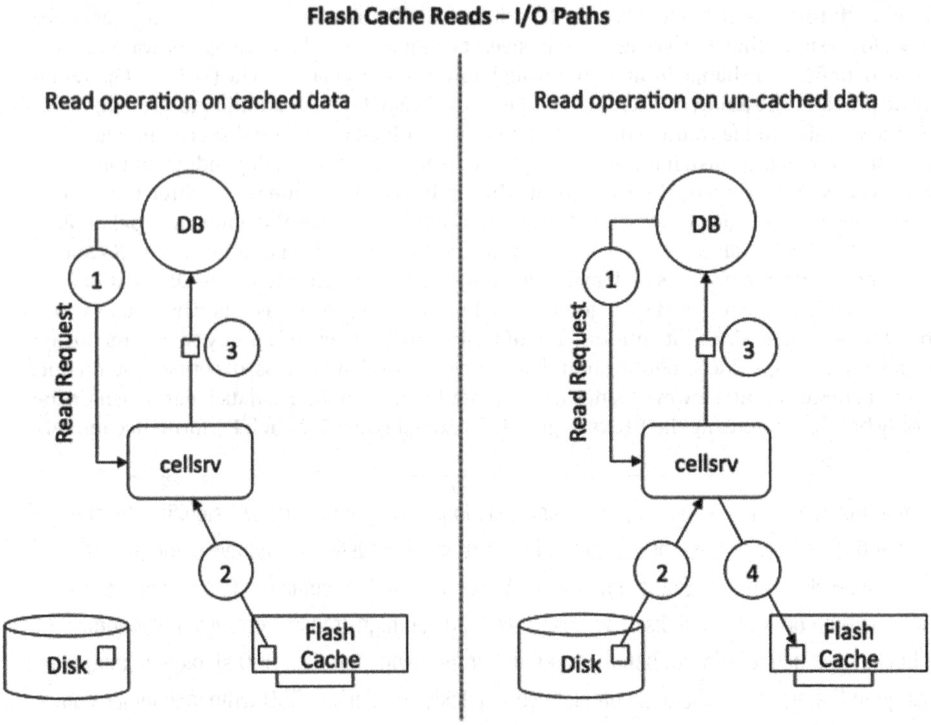

Figure 5-1. *Conceptual model of read operation I/O path*

When reading data from the persistency layer, the database session indicated as "DB" in Figure 5-1 issues a read operation, which ends up as a request in the multi-threaded `cellsrv` binary. Ignoring I/O resource management, offload servers, and the cell's ability to read from a secondary mirror copy of the extent in case of read I/O outliers for the sake of simplicity, the `cellsrv` software knows where a given block is to be read—either from Flash or from spinning disk. Depending on the data location, a read is issued. The difference between the two scenarios shown in Figure 5-1 is the non-cached read. If a chunk of data is not found in Flash Cache, the read operation is issued against the hard disk where the data resides. If it makes sense to cache the data for further operations (maybe because it can be expected to be reused in a subsequent read), the chunk of data is moved into Flash Cache, but only after it has been sent back to the requesting session.

In an ideal situation where the majority of the segment to be scanned is in Flash Cache, you can see this reflected in the sometimes drastically reduced response time for single-block reads and table scans. Regarding scans, the speedup is not limited to Smart Scans by the way. If a segment is cached in ESFC, other I/O access methods that are not offloaded will benefit as well since Exadata version 11.2.3.3.

Writes are different from the situation just described. Consider Figure 5-2, which covers both operating modes of the Smart Flash Cache: the default write-through mode as well as the write-back mode.

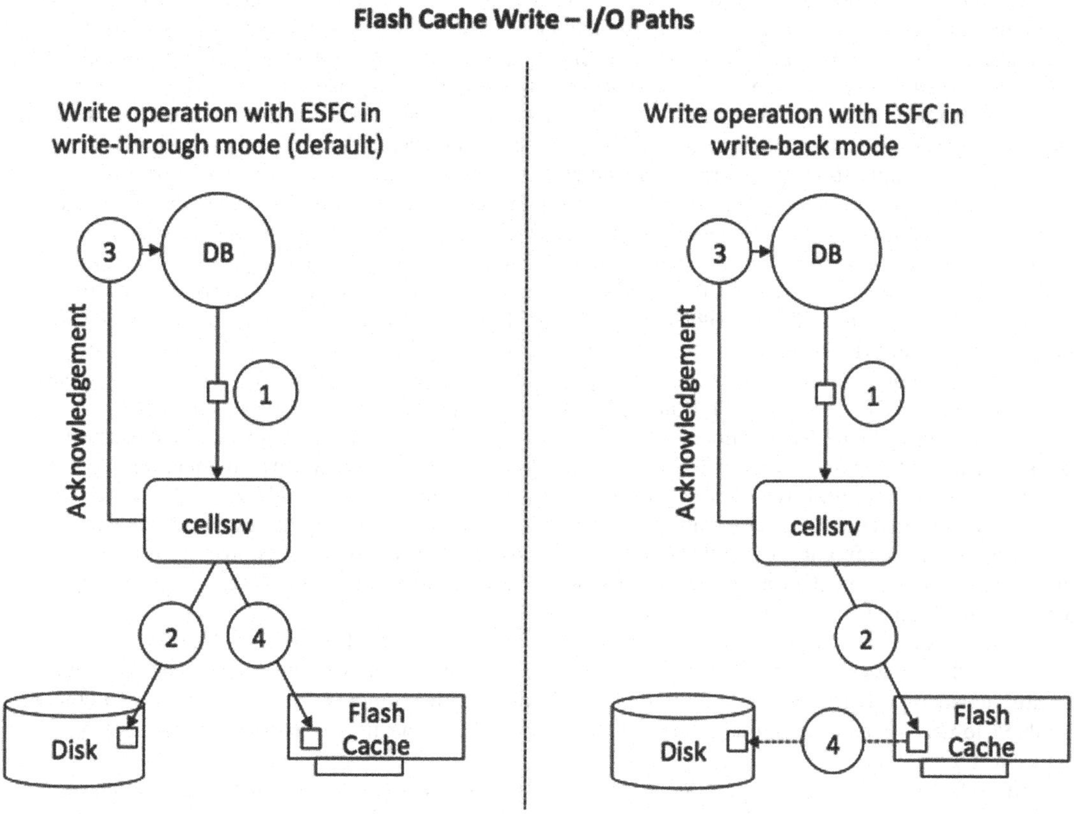

Figure 5-2. *Conceptual model of write operation I/O path in write-though and write- back mode*

■ **Note** The X5-2 High Performance cell is different again: The default mode of operation for Flash Cache is write-back. Switching back to write-through is possible, but doing so means giving up on Fast Data File Creation, for example, as the feature requires WBFC to be enabled.

Assuming here that ESFC operates in the default write-through mode, writes bypass the (Flash) cache and go directly to disk. However, after sending an acknowledgement back to the database server, Oracle's storage software then copies the data into the cache, assuming it is suitable for caching. This is a key point. The metadata that is sent with the write request lets the storage software know if the data is likely to be used again, and, if so, the data is also written to the cache. This step is done after sending an acknowledgement to the database tier in order to ensure that the write operation can complete as quickly as possible.

You can read more about the Write-back Flash Cache mode later in this section, but since it is such an important concept, the high-level steps are shown here nevertheless. When operating in write-back mode, all I/Os will go to the Flash devices first, and not to disk, at least initially. Think of the Flash Cache just as you would about the cache in an enterprise class storage array. If the Flash Cache is depleted, an algorithm will evaluate the contents and de-stage data from Flash Cache to disk. Another difference between write-through and write-back mode is that the contents of the cache is persistent across reboots. Since data may be on the Flash cards and not yet de-staged to disk, it needs to be protected from failure using ASM redundancy as well.

Beginning with Exadata software version 11.2.3.3.0, Oracle changed the way that data is scanned fundamentally. Up until then, there was a clear distinction between which component was responsible for what task. The split was as follows: The Smart Flash Cache was primarily used for single-block I/O. Smart Scans were satisfied from spinning disk. If you absolutely wanted to make use of Flash Cache for Smart Scans, you had to change the storage clause of the segment in question. The logic behind this is compelling: Different devices have different I/O queues in the operating system and, by separating single block I/O typical for OLTP applications from large, multi-block I/O operations, allowed the placement of applications with different I/O workload characteristics on the same Exadata hardware. Add in I/O Resource Manager and everyone has a well-behaved system. This worked especially well in the days of the V2 and X2, which both had very little Flash memory available compared to today's X5 system. What capacity you had was in the majority of cases probably best used for OLTP workloads. You can see this in the AWR "Wait Event Histogram" for the event "cell single block physical read." In the vast majority of cases. you should see an average wait around 1ms or less.

There is just one caveat with this: Hard-disk performance has not increased at the same speed as Flash performance, which are capable of thousands of IOPS per device with sustained throughput many times that of a hard disk. Since Flash memory is based on silicone and not magnetic recording, Flash memory undergoes much faster development cycles than hard disk, leading to faster, more resilient components that are smaller than their previous generation. In summary, Flash memory allows for larger and larger capacity, which is represented in the Exadata platform. The F160 card available in the X5 has twice the capacity of its predecessor. The amount of Flash in the X4 and X5 and to a lesser extent on the X3 now gives the architect more headroom to cache data even for full scans. All it required was a change in the `cellsrv` software, which arrived with 11.2.3.3.0.

As soon as you use this particular version (or a more recent release, of course), `cellsrv` will automatically cache popular data worth caching, full scans included. There is no change to the way small I/Os are cached as part of the new release. The main difference is that popular data can be cached and made available to Smart Scan in addition to the single block I/Os without having to change the default storage clause of a segment.

In the first edition of the book, we featured an example demonstrating how much faster a Smart Scan can be when it uses both disk and Flash Cache, but that required changing the storage clause of the segment to `CELL_FLASH_CACHE KEEP`. Since the default has changed, the demonstration has to change with it. In this example, it was necessary to explicitly forbid the use of Flash Cache for a table scan to show the difference. To this effect, two tables have been created, `BIGT` and `BIGT_ESFC`.

```
SQL> select table_name, num_rows, partitioned, compression, cell_flash_cache
  2  from tabs where table_name in ('BIGT','BIGT_ESFC');

TABLE_NAME                       NUM_ROWS PAR COMPRESS CELL_FL
------------------------------ ---------- --- -------- -------
BIGT_ESFC                       100000000 NO  DISABLED DEFAULT
BIGT                            100000000 NO  DISABLED NONE

2 rows selected.

SQL> select segment_name, blocks, bytes/power(1024,3) g
  2  from user_segments where segment_name in ('BIGT','BIGT_ESFC');
```

```
SEGMENT_NAME                       BLOCKS          G
------------------------------ ---------- ----------
BIGT                             16683456 127.284668
BIGT_ESFC                        16683456 127.284668

2 rows selected.
```

Table BIGT will act as the reference here; the first scan will make use of as little of ESFC as possible. Here is the result:

```
SQL> select /*+ gather_plan_statistics without_ESFC */ count(*) from bigt;

  COUNT(*)
----------
 100000000

Elapsed: 00:00:36.23
```

If you record the performance counters you have seen in a few places already (and can read more about in Chapter 11), you will find these interesting metrics:

```
STAT    cell IO uncompressed bytes                                      136,533,385,216
STAT    cell blocks helped by minscn optimization                            16,666,678
STAT    cell blocks processed by cache layer                                 16,666,678
STAT    cell blocks processed by data layer                                  16,666,673
STAT    cell blocks processed by txn layer                                   16,666,678
STAT    cell num smartio automem buffer allocation attempts                           1
STAT    cell physical IO bytes eligible for predicate offload           136,533,377,024
STAT    cell physical IO interconnect bytes                               2,690,691,224
STAT    cell physical IO interconnect bytes returned by smart scan        2,690,650,264
STAT    cell scans                                                                    1
...
STAT    physical read IO requests                                               130,346
STAT    physical read bytes                                             136,533,417,984
STAT    physical read total IO requests                                         130,346
STAT    physical read total bytes                                       136,533,417,984
STAT    physical read total multi block requests                                130,340
STAT    physical reads                                                       16,666,677
STAT    physical reads cache                                                          5
STAT    physical reads direct                                                16,666,672
```

Bear with us a minute—it will all become a lot clearer! After a few scans against the table with the default storage clause—all of them Smart Scans—Flash Caching becomes very apparent in the execution time:

```
SQL> select /*+ gather_plan_statistics with_ESFC */ count(*) from bigt_esfc;

  COUNT(*)
----------
 100000000

Elapsed: 00:00:13.23
```

This is a lot quicker than the 36 seconds in the non-cached table example, and the nice thing about this is that no developer or administrator had to do anything. The speedup is entirely due to the fact that Exadata decided that the object is popular and cached it. Looking at the performance counters again, you can see how many I/O operations were satisfied from Flash Cache:

```
STAT    cell IO uncompressed bytes                                          136,533,958,656
STAT    cell blocks helped by minscn optimization                                16,668,279
STAT    cell blocks processed by cache layer                                     16,668,279
STAT    cell blocks processed by data layer                                      16,666,743
STAT    cell blocks processed by txn layer                                       16,668,279
STAT    cell flash cache read hits                                                  113,612
STAT    cell num smartio automem buffer allocation attempts                               1
STAT    cell physical IO bytes eligible for predicate offload               136,533,377,024
STAT    cell physical IO interconnect bytes                                   2,690,662,344
STAT    cell physical IO interconnect bytes returned by smart scan            2,690,662,344
STAT    cell scans                                                                        1
...
STAT    physical read IO requests                                                   130,411
STAT    physical read bytes                                                 136,533,377,024
STAT    physical read requests optimized                                            113,612
STAT    physical read total IO requests                                             130,411
STAT    physical read total bytes                                           136,533,377,024
STAT    physical read total bytes optimized                                 118,944,309,248
STAT    physical read total multi block requests                                    130,343
STAT    physical reads                                                           16,666,672
STAT    physical reads direct                                                    16,666,672
```

If you compare both listings, you can see that the amount of work was almost exactly the same. The difference between the two listings can be found in the cell Flash Cache read hits and the "%physical read%optimized" statistics. Out of 130,411 I/O requests, 113,612 were optimized. The demonstration explicitly did not feature a WHERE clause to force full scans without further optimizations, such as predicate filtering or storage indexes to isolate the performance gain. Chapter 11 has a lot more information about all these counters, while Chapter 2 explains the different kinds of optimizations during a Smart Scan.

Mixed Workload and OLTP Optimizations

When the first version of the Exadata Database Machine—the so-called Exadata V1—debuted, it was very much a high performance solution to support Decision Support Systems. Flash memory, as you just read about, was absent from the very first hardware version. This has been discovered as a limitation so that the next hardware release, Exadata V2, was the first version to introduce the Flash cards. Thanks to the Flash cards and other features you read about in this book, Exadata can deliver high performance and scalability for many different types of workloads. These do not necessarily have to be uniform—the combination of high-end hardware and the optimizations found in the storage server software form a balanced combination. The key drivers for enabling OLTP workloads are the Exadata Storage Server Software and the ESFC Flash memory. Once the hardware specification is in place, the components can be put to good use. In the case of Exadata, new functionality is constantly added to the storage server software. One important OLTP optimization introduced in version 11.2.2.4.x is named Smart Flash Log.

Using Flash Memory for Database Logging

The aim of the Exadata Smart Flash Log (ESFL) is to optimize database log writes. Many DBAs with a background of managing OLTP-style applications know only too well that a low log write latency is critical. A small "hiccup" in latency can greatly impact the overall performance of an OLTP environment. Smart Flash Logging helps eliminating high-latency outliers by making use of both on-disk redo logs and a small space that is allocated on the Flash hardware for ESFC, called Flashlog. Ideally, the sequential redo log writes should all go to the disk controller's cache. Non-Exadata environments frequently use enterprise-class arrays that are fronted by more or less gracious amounts of DRAM to cache writes before they are eventually de-staged to disk. To avoid data corruption in case of power failure, these caches are backed-up by batteries or more recently, super-capacitors.

The Exadata Database Machine does not have the same amount of cache on the controller. Up to the X5-2, every disk controller had 512MB of cache, while the X5-2 has 1GB. As long as the cache is not filled up to capacity, write I/O should be able to benefit from it. In some situations, however, it is possible to deplete the cache, causing future I/O requests to pass straight through to the attached disks. This can also happen in all Exadata generations with battery-backed caches when the batteries go into a learning cycle. Long story short, it is possible that the write-back cache in the disk controllers falls back to write-through mode, which can have performance implications for (redo) writes. Smart Flash Logging is a technology developed by Oracle to counter the negative side effect of this by making the Flash cards available as alternative targets for redo log writes.

Smart Flash Logging requires Exadata Storage Software version 11.2.2.4 or later, and Oracle Database version 11.2.0.2 with Bundle Patch 11. For Oracle Database version 11.2.0.3, you need Bundle Patch 1, or a later one. The Flash Logging feature is not intrusive, even on systems with less Flash memory. On each cell, 512MB will be set aside for the temporary storage location for redo.

The Smart Flash Logging feature works as shown in Figure 5-3. When the database issues a redo log write request, the `cellsrv` software will issue the write in parallel to both the on-disk redo log and ESFL. As soon as the first write completes, `cellsrv` will send the write acknowledgement to the requesting process and the database will continue processing further transactions. In the cases where the disk controller cache is not saturated, writes to hard disk should be faster than writes to the Flash Log.

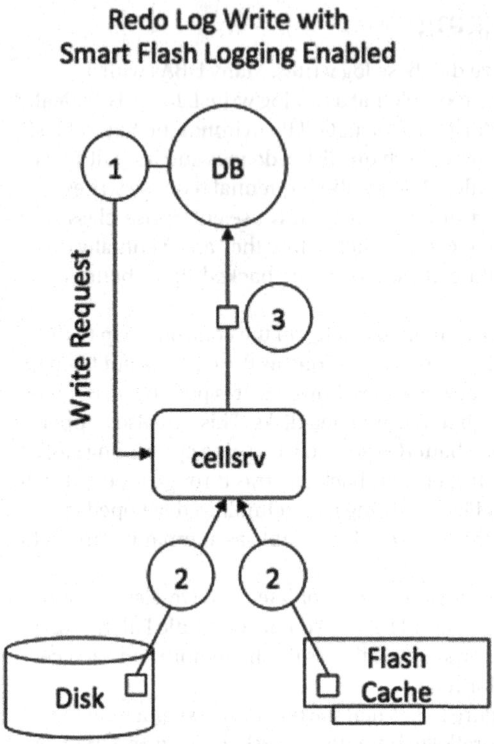

Figure 5-3. *The I/O path for redo writes with Smart Flash Log*

Thanks to the Exadata instrumentation, you can see exactly how the Flash Log was used (or not). The method to learn about the Flash Log usage is to request that information from each cell, ideally via `dcli`:

```
[oracle@enkdb03 ~]$ dcli -l cellmonitor -g ./cell_group \
> cellcli -e "list metriccurrent where name like \'FL_.*_FIRST\'"
enkcel04: FL_DISK_FIRST           FLASHLOG          10,441,253 IO requests
enkcel04: FL_FLASH_FIRST          FLASHLOG             426,834 IO requests
enkcel05: FL_DISK_FIRST           FLASHLOG          11,127,644 IO requests
enkcel05: FL_FLASH_FIRST          FLASHLOG             466,456 IO requests
enkcel06: FL_DISK_FIRST           FLASHLOG          11,376,268 IO requests
enkcel06: FL_FLASH_FIRST          FLASHLOG             456,559 IO requests
```

This is best demonstrated with an example. Figure 5-4 shows the redo log write latency before and after implementing ESFL. The data points on the graph shows 2 a.m. and 7 a.m. workload periods of one insert statement.

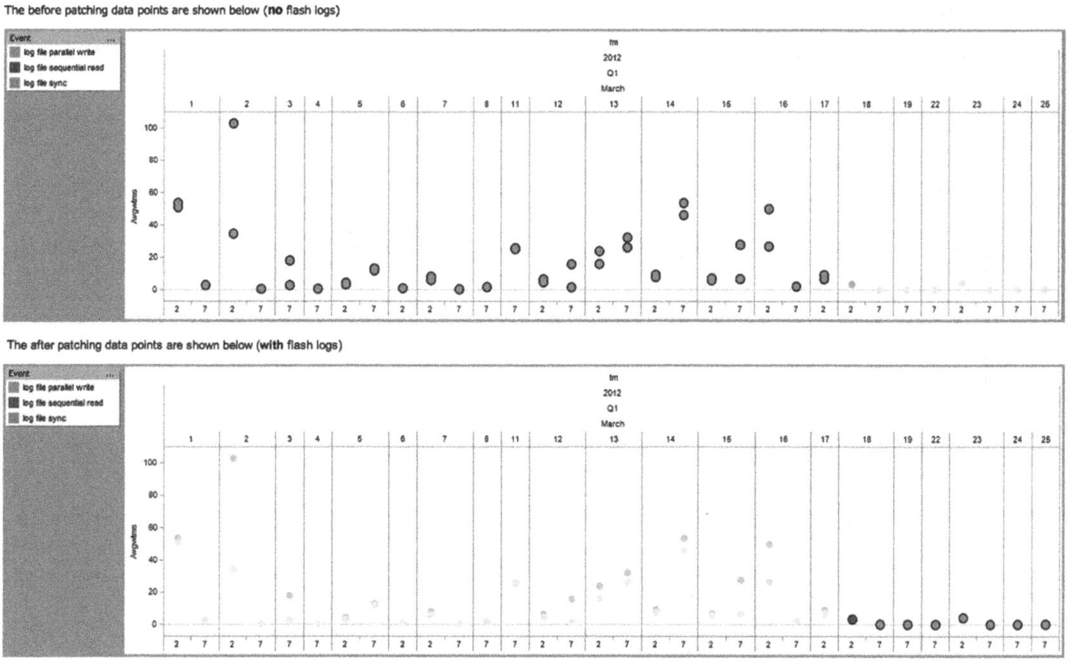

Figure 5-4. *Redo Log write latency before and after implementing Exadata Smart Flash Logging*

As you can see, the log-writer-related data points are much more in line with what you would expect. The comforting news here is that the vast majority—if not all Exadata systems—should be using Smart Flash Logging by the time this book is in print. The Smart Flash Log has removed one of the arguments for supporters of Flash used as Grid Disks for redo, allowing you to use Flash for the really important things instead. The next myth to address is that Exadata "is slow for writes." Configured correctly, it most likely is not slow, as you can read in the next section.

Using Flash Memory to Accelerate Writes

So far, this chapter has focused primarily on the default mode of operation for the Smart Flash Cache: write-through (except again, the X5-2 High Performance cell where write-back caching is the default). The cache can optionally be configured to operate in write-back mode. The Write-Back Flash Cache (WBFC) significantly increases the write IOPS capability of your current Exadata configuration. This OLTP optimization feature initially introduced in Exadata's X3 generation is backward compatible to previous generations of the Exadata Database Machine. The WBFC serves as the primary device for all write I/O requests from the database, and the cache contents are now persistent across restarts. The failure of a Flash card device is transparent to the users, as this will be automatically handled by the combination of ASM redundancy and Exadata Storage Software.

The Exadata Storage Software Version 11.2.3.2.1 is the minimum required version to enable the WBFC. My Oracle Support note 888828.1 lists further requirements for the Grid Infrastructure home and the RDBMS home. Make sure to apply these patches if you need them! Figure 5-5 and the following steps show how the WBFC works.

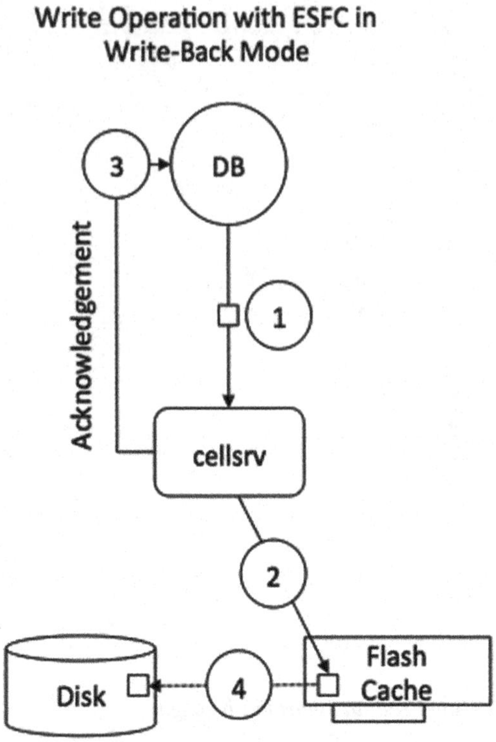

Figure 5-5. *Schematic display of the use of Flash Cache in write-back mode*

The sequence of steps as shown in Figure 5-5 is as follows:

1. When the database issues a write request, the `cellsrv` will send the write I/O directly to the Flash device (numbers 1 and 2).
2. Once the write completes, the database will immediately acknowledge the write (number 3).
3. All of the dirty blocks will be kept in the cache, which could be used for future read or write I/O. ASM provides redundancy for the Flash cards to protect the system from failure.
4. Once the block is no longer being accessed, it will eventually be aged out of the cache and written to the disk if space pressure arises (number 4). This process is generally referred to as de-staging data from cache to disk.

In order to assess the usefulness of Write-Back Flash Cache, you need to define a write-heavy I/O benchmark. The Swingbench suite is best known for the order entry benchmark. There are many more benchmarks provided in the suite worth exploring. After some more investigation, a suitable test case for this demonstration was found in the form of the *stress test*. The stress test is a relatively simple benchmark where four different potential transactions are launched against a table, aptly named STRESSTESTTABLE. The transactions unsurprisingly cover inserts, delete, updates, and selects. As it is typical for Swingbench, you can define each transaction's contribution to the load individually. If you would like to follow the testing, we defined 15% of all transactions to be inserts, 10% selects, 55% updates, and 20% deletes. As with all storage benchmarks, you need a reasonably small buffer cache to mitigate the effects of Oracle's excellent caching mechanism.

To see the benefit of what the Exadata system—in this particular case our X2-2 quarter rack—is capable of, you need to work out what the system is theoretically able to achieve. In this case, the data sheet for the X2-2 quarter rack quotes about 6,000 disk IOPS. If the benchmark, which is not RAC-optimized, can drive more than that, we can conclude that the Write-Back Flash Cache has helped. This could indeed be confirmed after executing the benchmark. Here is the I/O profile taken from the AWR report covering the benchmark's execution. The test has been conducted on a single instance of a 12.1.0.2 database using the 12.1.2.1.0 Exadata software on the X2-2 quarter rack.

```
IO Profile                  Read+Write/Second     Read/Second    Write/Second
~~~~~~~~~~                  ----------------- --------------- ---------------
            Total Requests:          22,376.6        11,088.3        11,288.3
         Database Requests:          20,799.2        11,083.9         9,715.4
        Optimized Requests:          20,684.8        11,023.8         9,661.0
             Redo Requests:           1,570.1             0.0         1,570.1
                Total (MB):             219.5            86.7           132.7
             Database (MB):             194.2            86.7           107.5
      Optimized Total (MB):             187.2            86.2           101.1
                 Redo (MB):              18.4             0.0            18.4
         Database (blocks):          24,853.6        11,094.4        13,759.3
 Via Buffer Cache (blocks):          24,844.1        11,094.3        13,749.7
           Direct (blocks):               9.5             0.0             9.5
```

As you can see, the AWR report recorded 22,376 I/O operations per second in the "total requests" category driven by a single database instance, without even optimizing the workload for use with multi-instance RAC. This is more than the data sheet quoted. Had we invested more time in tuning the benchmark, we are confident that we could have been able to create more load. Please remember from the introduction, though, that the ratio of reads to writes in this particular benchmark is 10:90, which is not necessarily your I/O distribution! The fact that there are so many reads in the I/O profile has to do with the way the update statement is performed by means of an index unique scan on the table's primary key. Later in the chapter, you can read more about monitoring the use of Flash Cache, and you will see that the `STRESSTESTTABLE` and its associated indexes are the most heavily cached objects in the Flash Cache.

Miscellaneous Other WBFC-related Optimizations

Separate space for a cache offers other benefits as well, which is the reason you still get a cache by default even on the all-Flash High Performance X5-2 cell servers. On these cells on the X5-2, the Flash Cache is set up as WBFC and it occupies about 5% of the available Flash space. One of the benefits is the advantage of Fast Data File Creation. Here is an example of the creation of a 20GB tablespace. In non-Exadata systems, your session will have to perform the data file initialization in a single thread, and that thread is at the mercy of the I/O subsystem. On Exadata, the operation is parallelized by design across all storage servers. Fast Data File Creation takes this process a step further. Using it, only the metadata about the blocks allocated in the tablespace is persisted in the Write-Back Flash Cache, the actual formatting does not take place immediately.

```
SQL> create tablespace testdata datafile size 20g;

Tablespace created.

Elapsed: 00:00:00.89
```

The elapsed time is not too bad for the creation of a 20GB data file. The session-level statistics “cell physical write bytes saved by smart file initialization” and “physical write total bytes” give you an idea about the saving you made. This feature was delivered as part of Exadata version 11.2.3.3.0.

Another interesting feature pertaining to the Write-Back Flash Cache is the ability of the storage cell to cap write-I/O outliers. According to the documentation set, write outliers caused by aging or dying Flash cards can cause slower I/O response times and can be redirected to a different card instead. You benefit from this feature with Exadata software 12.1.2.1.0 and 11.2.0.4 BP 8 or later.

How ESFC and ESFL Are Created

The Exadata Smart Flash Cache is created and managed using the `cellcli` utility on each storage server. This section merely features an example for the use of the `cellcli` command to manage Smart Flash Cache and Smart Flash Log. If you would like to learn more about these commands, please refer to Appendix A. Instead of executing `cellcli` commands locally on each cell, you can make use of the `dcli` utility, which executes commands across multiple systems (and does a lot more).

When working with the Flash disks on the storage servers, it is important to execute the commands in sequence. You start by creating the Flash Log before Flash Cache (and most Exadata users would stop there). The first example, therefore, shows you how to configure Exadata Smart Flash Log. You create it using the `CREATE FLASHLOG ALL` command, as shown here:

```
[root@enkx3cel01 ~]# cellcli -e create flashlog all
Flash log enkx3cel01_FLASHLOG successfully created
[root@enkx3cel01 ~]# cellcli -e list flashlog attributes name,size
         enkx3cel01_FLASHLOG     512M
```

The previous command automatically allocates 512MB of storage from the Exadata Flash, leaving the rest of the available space to ESFC. Remember that ESFL has to be created before ESFC or else the Flash space will only be allocated to ESFC leaving no space for the Flash Log.

The next step is to create the Flash Cache using the `CREATE FLASHCACHE` command. Here is the example for the default write-through-mode on an X3-2 storage server:

```
CellCLI> create flashcache all

Flash cache enkx3cel01_FLASHCACHE successfully created
```

This form of the command instructs the storage software to spread the cache across all the FMods on all the Flash cards. If you really, really need it and want to ignore the advice given in MOS note 1269706.1, you can specify a size instead of “all” to leave some space on the Flash cards available for use as a Flash disk. Note that the Flash Cache is automatically assigned a name that includes the name of the storage cell. To see the size of the Flash Cache, you can issue the `LIST FLASHCACHE DETAIL` command, shown here on the X3-2 cell. Remember from the introduction that the current Exadata X5-2 generation has fewer FMODs and significantly larger Flash disks. The output is reformatted for better readability. in your terminal session you will see all the Flash disks (FD) in one line:

```
[root@enkx3cel01 ~]# cellcli -e list flashcache detail
         name:                   enkx3cel01_FLASHCACHE
         cellDisk:               FD_13_enkx3cel01,FD_14_enkx3cel01,FD_12_enkx3cel01,
                                 FD_03_enkx3cel01,FD_09_enkx3cel01,FD_15_enkx3cel01,
                                 FD_11_enkx3cel01,FD_05_enkx3cel01,FD_08_enkx3cel01,
                                 FD_02_enkx3cel01,FD_04_enkx3cel01,FD_06_enkx3cel01,
```

```
                                 FD_10_enkx3cel01,FD_00_enkx3cel01,FD_01_enkx3cel01,
                                 FD_07_enkx3cel01
         creationTime:           2014-01-30T22:21:18-06:00
         degradedCelldisks:
         effectiveCacheSize:     1488.75G
         id:                     15b9e304-586c-4730-910f-0e16de67f751
         size:                   1488.75G
         status:                 normal
```

Up to the X5-2 storage server, the Flash Cache is spread across 16 cell disks. A cell disk exists for each FMod on each Flash card. To get more information about the cell disks that make up the Flash Cache, you can use the LIST CELLDISK command, shown here for an X3-2 system:

```
[root@enkx3cel01 ~]# cellcli -e list celldisk attributes name, \
> diskType, size where name like \'FD.*\'
         FD_00_enkx3cel01        FlashDisk       93.125G
         FD_01_enkx3cel01        FlashDisk       93.125G
         FD_02_enkx3cel01        FlashDisk       93.125G
         FD_03_enkx3cel01        FlashDisk       93.125G
         FD_04_enkx3cel01        FlashDisk       93.125G
         FD_05_enkx3cel01        FlashDisk       93.125G
         FD_06_enkx3cel01        FlashDisk       93.125G
         FD_07_enkx3cel01        FlashDisk       93.125G
         FD_08_enkx3cel01        FlashDisk       93.125G
         FD_09_enkx3cel01        FlashDisk       93.125G
         FD_10_enkx3cel01        FlashDisk       93.125G
         FD_11_enkx3cel01        FlashDisk       93.125G
         FD_12_enkx3cel01        FlashDisk       93.125G
         FD_13_enkx3cel01        FlashDisk       93.125G
         FD_14_enkx3cel01        FlashDisk       93.125G
         FD_15_enkx3cel01        FlashDisk       93.125G
```

Since the Flash Cache is created on cell disks, the cell disks must be created before the Flash Cache, which they usually have during the initial configuration. If not, this can be done with the CREATE CELLDISK command:

```
CellCLI> create celldisk all flashdisk
CellDisk FD_00_enkx3cel01 successfully created
CellDisk FD_01_enkx3cel01 successfully created
CellDisk FD_02_enkx3cel01 successfully created
CellDisk FD_03_enkx3cel01 successfully created
CellDisk FD_04_enkx3cel01 successfully created
CellDisk FD_05_enkx3cel01 successfully created
CellDisk FD_06_enkx3cel01 successfully created
CellDisk FD_07_enkx3cel01 successfully created
CellDisk FD_08_enkx3cel01 successfully created
CellDisk FD_09_enkx3cel01 successfully created
CellDisk FD_10_enkx3cel01 successfully created
CellDisk FD_11_enkx3cel01 successfully created
CellDisk FD_12_enkx3cel01 successfully created
```

```
CellDisk FD_13_enkx3cel01 successfully created
CellDisk FD_14_enkx3cel01 successfully created
CellDisk FD_15_enkx3cel01 successfully created
```

You can also create a Flash Cache on a limited set of FMods by specifying a specific list of cell disks. In most cases, this is not necessary, but it is possible. With only a single FMod per Flash card, this is less practical with the X5-2. Here is an example, still on the X3-2:

```
CellCLI> create flashcache celldisk='FD_00_enkx3cel01, FD_01_enkx3cel01', size=40G
Flash cache enkx3cel01_FLASHCACHE successfully created

CellCLI> list flashcache detail
         name:                   enkx3cel01_FLASHCACHE
         cellDisk:               FD_01_enkx3cel01,FD_00_enkx3cel01
         creationTime:           2014-11-09T15:29:28-06:00
         degradedCelldisks:
         effectiveCacheSize:     40G
         id:                     ad56aa9d-0de4-4713-85f2-19713a13vn3ebb
         size:                   40G
         status:                 normal
```

Once again, using cellcli is covered in more detail in Appendix A, but this section should give you a basic understanding of how the Flash Cache is created.

Enabling the Write-back Flash Cache

The Write-back Flash Cache (WBFC) is usually enabled in situations where during the average representative workload, the ratio of reads to writes tips in favor of writes. Traditionally, one would assume a workload where the number of reads has the edge over the number of writes. Another reason to enable WBFC is when you find "free buffer waits" take up a significant percentage of your wait events. Finding the event in your AWR reports or traces indicates that (one of the) database writer processes cannot keep up writing dirty blocks to disk in order to free new buffers being read into the buffer cache.

It is probably safe to say that most users operate Smart Flash Cache in the default write-through mode. Changing from write-through to write-back involves the steps explained in this section (that is, unless you are on the all-Flash cells—known as the X5-2 High Performance storage server—where write-back is already enabled by default). You can either perform the switch in a rolling or a non-rolling fashion. As a prerequisite, you have to ensure that all grid disks in the cluster are online and available:

```
[root@enkx3db01 ~]# dcli -g cell_group -l root cellcli -e list griddisk attributes \
> asmdeactivationoutcome, asmmodestatus, name, status
```

The following listings show the steps executed in order to enable the WBFC in a rolling fashion. After the first command verifying the disks on the cluster returned no problems, you should proceed by checking the status of the existing Flash Cache and Flash Log as shown. The status must not indicate any problems:

```
[root@enkx3db01 ~]# dcli -g ./cell_group -l root \
> cellcli -e list flashcache attributes name,size,status
enkx3cel01: enkx3cel01_FLASHCACHE      1488.75G        normal
enkx3cel02: enkx3cel02_FLASHCACHE      1488.75G        normal
enkx3cel03: enkx3cel03_FLASHCACHE      1488.75G        normal
```

```
[root@enkx3db01 ~]# dcli -g ./cell_group -l root \
> cellcli -e list flashlog attributes name,size,status
enkx3cel01: enkx3cel01_FLASHLOG        512M    normal
enkx3cel02: enkx3cel02_FLASHLOG        512M    normal
enkx3cel03: enkx3cel03_FLASHLOG        512M    normal
```

In the following example, the Smart Flash Cache is changed from write-through to write-back mode. Here is proof that the Flash Cache is in write-through mode:

```
[root@enkx3db01 ~]# dcli -g cell_group -l root \
> "cellcli -e list cell detail" | grep "flashCacheMode"
enkx3cel01: flashCacheMode:              WriteThrough
enkx3cel02: flashCacheMode:              WriteThrough
enkx3cel03: flashCacheMode:              WriteThrough
```

Next ,you need to drop the Flash Cache, connected as root to the first cell:

```
[root@enkx3cel01 ~]# cellcli -e drop flashcache
Flash cache enkx3cel01_FLASHCACHE successfully dropped
```

As part of the operation, ASM should stay up, tolerating the loss of the cell, thanks to the ASM normal or even high-redundancy configuration. The output of the next listing should show YES for all the disks.
To keep the chapter reasonably short, the output is truncated:

```
[root@enkx3cel01 ~]# cellcli -e list griddisk attributes name,asmmodestatus,asmdeactivation
outcome
         DATA_CD_00_enkx3cel01           ONLINE  Yes
   ...
         DATA_CD_11_enkx3cel01           ONLINE  Yes
         DBFS_DG_CD_02_enkx3cel01        ONLINE  Yes
   ...
         DBFS_DG_CD_11_enkx3cel01        ONLINE  Yes
         RECO_CD_00_enkx3cel01           ONLINE  Yes
   ...
         RECO_CD_11_enkx3cel01           ONLINE  Yes
```

Following the verification, you change the grid disks to become inactive on the cell. Again, the output is abridged for readability, and you will see one line per grid disk:

```
[root@enkx3cel01 ~]# cellcli -e alter griddisk all inactive
GridDisk DATA_CD_00_enkx3cel01 successfully altered
...
GridDisk DATA_CD_11_enkx3cel01 successfully altered
GridDisk DBFS_DG_CD_02_enkx3cel01 successfully altered
...
GridDisk DBFS_DG_CD_11_enkx3cel01 successfully altered
GridDisk RECO_CD_00_enkx3cel01 successfully altered
...
GridDisk RECO_CD_11_enkx3cel01 successfully altered
```

Now there are not too many steps remaining on the cell. In summary, you shut down the `cellsrv` process, drop the Flash Cache, set the `flashCacheMode` attribute to "WriteBack," create the Flash Cache, and bring everything back online. But, first, let's verify that the Flash Cache is really gone, using another session with a root connection on the first node in RDBMS cluster:

```
[root@enkx3db01 ~]# dcli -g ./cell_group -l root \
> cellcli -e list flashcache attributes name,size,status
enkx3cel02: enkx3cel02_FLASHCACHE      1488.75G        normal
enkx3cel02: enkx3cel03_FLASHCACHE      1488.75G        normal
```

And indeed, the first cell does not report the presence of Smart Flash Cache. The Flash Log remains unaffected, as you can see here:

```
[root@enkx3db01 ~]# dcli -g ./cell_group -l root \
> cellcli -e list flashlog attributes name,size,status
enkx3cel01: enkx3cel01_FLASHLOG        512M    normal
enkx3cel02: enkx3cel02_FLASHLOG        512M    normal
enkx3cel03: enkx3cel03_FLASHLOG        512M    normal
```

At this stage, you shut down the cell software and change the attribute to enable write-back caching before starting the service again:

```
[root@enkx3cel01 ~]# cellcli -e alter cell shutdown services cellsrv

Stopping CELLSRV services...
The SHUTDOWN of CELLSRV services was successful.

[root@enkx3cel01 ~]# cellcli -e alter cell flashCacheMode=WriteBack
Cell enkx3cel01 successfully altered

[root@enkx3cel01 ~]# cellcli -e alter cell startup services cellsrv

Starting CELLSRV services...
The STARTUP of CELLSRV services was successful.
```

Following the successful start of the `cellsrv` daemons, you bring the grid disks back into ASM:

```
[root@enkx3cel01 ~]# cellcli -e alter griddisk all active
GridDisk DATA_CD_00_enkx3cel01 successfully altered
...
GridDisk DATA_CD_11_enkx3cel01 successfully altered
GridDisk DBFS_DG_CD_02_enkx3cel01 successfully altered
...
GridDisk DBFS_DG_CD_11_enkx3cel01 successfully altered
GridDisk RECO_CD_00_enkx3cel01 successfully altered
...
GridDisk RECO_CD_11_enkx3cel01 successfully altered
```

This is not an instantaneous operation—you have to be patient for a little while and wait for the status to become ONLINE for every single grid disk. Do not proceed until every single disk is online. Here is some sample output from grid disks that are still being brought back into online state:

```
[root@enkx3cel01 ~]# cellcli -e list griddisk attributes name, asmmodestatus
         DATA_CD_00_enkx3cel01             SYNCING
         DATA_CD_01_enkx3cel01             SYNCING
         DATA_CD_02_enkx3cel01             SYNCING
         DATA_CD_03_enkx3cel01             SYNCING
         DATA_CD_04_enkx3cel01             SYNCING
         DATA_CD_05_enkx3cel01             SYNCING
         DATA_CD_06_enkx3cel01             SYNCING
         DATA_CD_07_enkx3cel01             SYNCING
         DATA_CD_08_enkx3cel01             SYNCING
         DATA_CD_09_enkx3cel01             SYNCING
         DATA_CD_10_enkx3cel01             SYNCING
         DATA_CD_11_enkx3cel01             SYNCING
         DBFS_DG_CD_02_enkx3cel01          ONLINE
         ...
         RECO_CD_11_enkx3cel01             ONLINE
```

After the disks are all back ONLINE, you can re-create the Flash Cache on the cell:

```
[root@enkx3cel01 ~]# cellcli -e create flashcache all
Flash cache enkx3cel01_FLASHCACHE successfully created
```

The result of the hard work is cell using Write-Back Flash Cache:

```
[root@enkx3db01 ~]# dcli -g cell_group -l root \
> "cellcli -e list cell detail" | grep "flashCacheMode"
enkx3cel01: flashCacheMode:              WriteBack
enkx3cel02: flashCacheMode:              WriteThrough
enkx3cel03: flashCacheMode:              WriteThrough
```

Unfortunately, you are not done yet—you have to repeat the above steps on the next Exadata storage cell node. Before taking additional cells down, however, you must be sure that this will not have an impact on the database availability. Use the command you saw in the introduction to this section listing the grid disks and ensure that the attributes `asmmodestatus` and `asmdeactivationoutcome` allow you to change the grid disk status to inactive in preparation to dropping the cell's Flash Cache. This procedure might change for future releases so please ensure you check on My Oracle Support for the latest documentation.

■ **Note** It is, of course, possible to revert back from write-back to write-through. My Oracle Support note 1500257.1 explains how to perform these steps.

Flash Cache Compression

The Oracle Exadata software 11.2.3.3.0 was the first to introduce Flash Cache compression. The F40 and F80 cards found in Exadata X3 and X4 storage cells have a built-in compression engine that allows user data to be compressed when being written into Flash Cache. Since the compression technology is built into the card's hardware, there should be less overhead associated with it compared to a software solution.

As with any compression technology, the savings are dependent on the data you want to compress. The worst compression ratio will likely be achieved with HCC Compression Units (CUs). Since these contain already compressed information, there is very little left to be squeezed out of them. Likewise, OLTP (now called "advanced") compressed blocks are not the best candidates for compression if they are already in a state where most of the block is de-duplicated. On the other hand, uncompressed blocks are good candidates for compression.

At the time of writing, My Oracle Support note 1664257.1 "EXADATA Flash Cache Compression - FAQ" states that only the F40 and F80 cards can use the compression feature and, as a prerequisite, the Advanced Compression Option must be licensed. The F160 cards in the X5-2 do not support the Flash Compression as described in this section. You should consult this note to make sure your patch levels match the minimum required. The procedure to enable Flash Cache compression is similar to enabling Write-back Flash Cache just described. In order not to repeat ourselves, we would like to refer you to the My Oracle Support note for the procedure.

When you enabled Flash Cache Compression, your Flash Cache will be reported as a lot larger than the physical device. Consider the Flash Cache on the X4-2 storage server with compression enabled:

```
[root@enkx4cel01 ~]# cellcli -e list flashcache detail
         name:                         enkx4cel01_FLASHCACHE
         cellDisk:                     FD_04_enkx4cel01,FD_06_enkx4cel01,FD_11_enkx4cel01,
                                       FD_02_enkx4cel01,FD_13_enkx4cel01,FD_12_enkx4cel01,
                                       FD_00_enkx4cel01,FD_14_enkx4cel01,FD_03_enkx4cel01,
                                       FD_09_enkx4cel01,FD_10_enkx4cel01,FD_15_enkx4cel01,
                                       FD_08_enkx4cel01,FD_07_enkx4cel01,FD_01_enkx4cel01,
                                       FD_05_enkx4cel01
         creationTime:                 2015-01-19T21:33:37-06:00
         degradedCelldisks:
         effectiveCacheSize:           5.8193359375T
         id:                           3d415a32-f404-4a27-b9f2-f6a0ace2cee2
         size:                         5.8193359375T
         status:                       normal
```

With a very keen eye, you will see that the size of the Flash Cache is 5.8TB. This is the logical cache size since the X4-2 storage server has four Flash cards of 800 GB size each for a total of 3.2 TB. In order to get these numbers, you must have Flash Cache compression enabled:

```
CellCLI> list cell attributes FlashCacheCompress
         TRUE
```

In normal circumstances, the cell disks on Flash are 186GB each, but with compression enabled will report more. This space is virtual, and Oracle manages space in the Flash Cache internally:

```
CellCLI> list celldisk attributes name,diskType,freeSpace,size,status where name like 'FD.*'
         FD_00_enkx4cel01        FlashDisk       0          372.515625G         normal
         FD_01_enkx4cel01        FlashDisk       0          372.515625G         normal
         FD_02_enkx4cel01        FlashDisk       0          372.515625G         normal
         FD_03_enkx4cel01        FlashDisk       0          372.515625G         normal
```

```
FD_04_enkx4cel01        FlashDisk     0       372.515625G       normal
FD_05_enkx4cel01        FlashDisk     0       372.515625G       normal
FD_06_enkx4cel01        FlashDisk     0       372.515625G       normal
FD_07_enkx4cel01        FlashDisk     0       372.515625G       normal
FD_08_enkx4cel01        FlashDisk     0       372.515625G       normal
FD_09_enkx4cel01        FlashDisk     0       372.515625G       normal
FD_10_enkx4cel01        FlashDisk     0       372.515625G       normal
FD_11_enkx4cel01        FlashDisk     0       372.515625G       normal
FD_12_enkx4cel01        FlashDisk     0       372.515625G       normal
FD_13_enkx4cel01        FlashDisk     0       372.515625G       normal
FD_14_enkx4cel01        FlashDisk     0       372.515625G       normal
FD_15_enkx4cel01        FlashDisk     0       372.515625G       normal
```

Flash Cache compression is a nice feature to logically extend the Flash Cache on certain models of the Exadata family.

Controlling ESFC Usage

Generally speaking, objects will be cached in the ESFC based on the storage software's automatic caching policy. However, you can override the automatic policy for individual database objects by using the CELL_FLASH_CACHE storage clause attribute, although you should probably refrain from doing so. As you have read a few times by now, the automatic caching works very well since Exadata 11.2.3.3.1 and later. If you insist on pinning objects in Flash Cache for a select few justified cases, you can set the attribute the these three valid values:

> NONE: Never cache this object.
>
> DEFAULT: The automatic caching mechanism is in effect. This is the default value.
>
> KEEP: The object should be given preferential status. Note that this designation also changes the default behavior of Smart Scans, allowing them to read from both the cache and disk.

You can specify the storage clause when an object is created. Some options of the storage clause can be modified using the ALTER command as well. Here is an example of changing the CELL_FLASH_CACHE storage clause using the ALTER command:

```
SQL> alter table martin.bigt storage (cell_flash_cache keep);
```

You can also see whether objects have been designated for more aggressive caching by looking at the cell_flash_cache column of dba_tables or dba_indexes and their partitioning-related cousins:

```
SQL> @esfc_keep_tables
SQL> select owner, table_name, status, last_analyzed,
  2  num_rows, blocks, degree, cell_flash_cache
  3  from dba_tables
  4  where cell_flash_cache like nvl('&cell_flash_cache','KEEP');
Enter value for cell_flash_cache:
old   4: where cell_flash_cache like nvl('&cell_flash_cache','KEEP')
new   4: where cell_flash_cache like nvl('','KEEP')

OWNER                TABLE_NAME      STATUS   LAST_ANAL  NUM_ROWS       BLOCKS DEGREE   CELL_FL
-------------------- --------------- -------- --------- ---------- ---------- -------- -------
MARTIN               BIGTAB_QL       VALID    28-JAN-15  256000000      890768 1        KEEP
```

You read previously that pinning objects in Flash Cache is not really needed anymore since `cellsrv` 11.2.3.3.1 and later. Upgrading to a more recent version of the storage software is a good opportunity to test if it is possible to allow Oracle to cache objects autonomously based on its algorithm. Pinning objects can be counterproductive, too, especially in the earlier Exadata hardware generations (such as the V2 and X2) due to the limited amount of Flash memory available. We still see X2 and V2 systems on sites we visit.

In Chapter 7, you can read about Resource Management. I/O Resource Manager allows the Exadata administrator to limit or even forbid the use of Smart Flash Cache.

Monitoring

You can monitor the use of Exadata Smart Flash cache in a number of places. Roughly speaking, you have the option to query certain Automatic Workload Repository (AWR) views or other dynamic performance views introduced recently. The other option is to interrogate the cell software for more information. This section can only be a teaser for the database-accessible information, you can read a lot more in Chapter 11 for session statistics and chapter 12 for graphical monitoring solutions based on Enterprise Manager 12c.

Metrics available at both cell and database level have been greatly enhanced since the first edition of this book went to print. At the end of the day the graphical tools- AWR reports, Enterprise Manager 12c and Enterprise Manager 12c Express cannot make up the numbers out of thin air-they have a clever interface to display the metrics provided by the system. To make it easier for the reader storage-server related metrics available via `cellcli` will be discussed first before changing the focus to the database layer.

At the Storage Layer

Each Exadata storage server will record its own metrics that can eventually be passed up to the RDBMS layer. If you want to dive into diagnostics based on the command line, you can do so either by connecting to each cell or alternatively by using the `dcli` tool on the compute node to harvest information from each storage server. The first option available to the performance engineer is exposed using the `cellcli` utility in the `metriccurrent` category. Regarding the Flash-related performance metrics, a number of different object types can be queried. Connected to an Exadata 12.1.2.1 storage cell, the following metric categories can be identified:

```
[root@enkx4cel01 ~]# cellcli -e list metriccurrent attributes objecttype | sort | uniq | nl
     1                  CELL
     2                  CELLDISK
     3                  CELL_FILESYSTEM
     4                  FLASHCACHE
     5                  FLASHLOG
     6                  GRIDDISK
     7                  HOST_INTERCONNECT
     8                  IBPORT
     9                  IORM_CATEGORY
    10                  IORM_CONSUMER_GROUP
    11                  IORM_DATABASE
    12                  IORM_PLUGGABLE_DATABASE
    13                  SMARTIO
```

For the purpose of this discussion only, the `objectType` highlighted in bold typeface is of interest. Since these metrics keep changing with every release, you should have a look at the output of the `list metricdefinition` command to see if there are any new ones of interest. Still connected to a 12.1.2.1 cell server, you can find the following Flash Cache related metrics:

```
CellCLI> LIST METRICDEFINITION attributes name, description WHERE objectType = 'FLASHCACHE'
```

Table 5-1 shows the output of the command limited to those statistics that had actual values associated with them. There are 111 Flash-Cache-related metrics in `cellsrv` 12.1.2.1, out of which some 54 are shown here that had values > 0 in our environment. Table 5-1 provides a brief description for each statistic tracked at the storage layer that you can report on.

Table 5-1. *A Selection of Flash Cache Metric Definitions*

Metric	Description
FC_BYKEEP_USED	Number of megabytes used for keep objects on Flash Cache
FC_BY_ALLOCATED	Number of megabytes allocated in Flash Cache
FC_BY_DIRTY	Number of unflushed megabytes in Flash Cache
FC_BY_STALE_DIRTY	Number of unflushed megabytes in Flash Cache that cannot be flushed because cached disks are not accessible
FC_BY_USED	Number of megabytes used on Flash Cache
FC_IO_BYKEEP_R	Number of megabytes read from Flash Cache for keep objects
FC_IO_BY_ALLOCATED_OLTP	Number of megabytes allocated for OLTP data in Flash Cache
FC_IO_BY_DISK_WRITE	Number of megabytes written from Flash Cache to hard disks
FC_IO_BY_R	Number of megabytes read from Flash Cache
FC_IO_BY_R_ACTIVE_SECONDARY	Number of megabytes for active secondary reads satisfied from Flash Cache
FC_IO_BY_R_ACTIVE_SECONDARY_MISS	Number of megabytes for active secondary reads not satisfied from Flash Cache
FC_IO_BY_R_DW	Number of megabytes of DW data read from Flash Cache
FC_IO_BY_R_MISS	Number of megabytes read from disks because not all requested data was in Flash Cache
FC_IO_BY_R_MISS_DW	Number of megabytes of DW data read from disk
FC_IO_BY_R_SEC	Number of megabytes read per second from Flash Cache
FC_IO_BY_R_SKIP	Number of megabytes read from disks for IO requests that bypass Flash Cache
FC_IO_BY_R_SKIP_NCMIRROR	Number of megabytes read from disk for IO requests that bypass Flash Cache as the IO is on non-primary, non-active secondary mirror
FC_IO_BY_R_SKIP_SEC	Number of megabytes read from disks per second for IO requests that bypass Flash Cache
FC_IO_BY_W	Number of megabytes written to Flash Cache
FC_IO_BY_W_FIRST	Number of megabytes that are first writes into Flash Cache
FC_IO_BY_W_FIRST_SEC	Number of megabytes per second that are first writes into Flash Cache
FC_IO_BY_W_OVERWRITE	Number of megabytes that are overwrites into Flash Cache
FC_IO_BY_W_OVERWRITE_SEC	Number of megabytes per second that are overwrites into Flash Cache

(continued)

Table 5-1. (*continued*)

Metric	Description
FC_IO_BY_W_POPULATE	Number of megabytes that are population writes into Flash Cache due to read miss
FC_IO_BY_W_SEC	Number of megabytes per second written to Flash Cache
FC_IO_BY_W_SKIP	Number of megabytes written to disk for IO requests that bypass Flash Cache
FC_IO_BY_W_SKIP_LG	Number of megabytes written to disk for IO requests that bypass Flash Cache due to the large IO size
FC_IO_BY_W_SKIP_LG_SEC	Number of megabytes written per second to disk for IO requests that bypass Flash Cache due to the large IO size
FC_IO_BY_W_SKIP_SEC	Number of megabytes written to disk per second for IO requests that bypass Flash Cache
FC_IO_RQKEEP_R	Number of requests read for keep objects from Flash Cache
FC_IO_RQ_DISK_WRITE	Number of requests written from Flash Cache to hard disks
FC_IO_RQ_R	Number of requests read from Flash Cache
FC_IO_RQ_REPLACEMENT_ATTEMPTED	Number of requests attempted to find space in the Flash Cache
FC_IO_RQ_REPLACEMENT_FAILED	Number of requests failed to find space in the Flash Cache
FC_IO_RQ_R_ACTIVE_SECONDARY	Number of requests for active secondary reads satisfied from Flash Cache
FC_IO_RQ_R_ACTIVE_SECONDARY_MISS	Number of requests for active secondary reads not satisfied from Flash Cache
FC_IO_RQ_R_DW	Number of DW IOs read data from Flash Cache
FC_IO_RQ_R_MISS	Number of read requests that did not find all data in Flash Cache
FC_IO_RQ_R_MISS_DW	Number of DW IOs read data from disk
FC_IO_RQ_R_SEC	Number of requests read per second from Flash Cache
FC_IO_RQ_R_SKIP	Number of requests read from disk that bypass Flash Cache
FC_IO_RQ_R_SKIP_NCMIRROR	Number of requests read from disk that bypass Flash Cache as the IO is on non-primary, non-active secondary mirror
FC_IO_RQ_R_SKIP_SEC	Number of requests read from disk per second that bypass Flash Cache
FC_IO_RQ_W	Number of requests that resulted in Flash Cache being populated with data
FC_IO_RQ_W_FIRST	Number of requests that are first writes into Flash Cache
FC_IO_RQ_W_FIRST_SEC	Number of requests per second that are first writes into Flash Cache
FC_IO_RQ_W_OVERWRITE	Number of requests that are overwrites into Flash Cache
FC_IO_RQ_W_OVERWRITE_SEC	Number of requests per second that are overwrites into Flash Cache
FC_IO_RQ_W_POPULATE	Number of requests that are population writes into Flash Cache due to read miss

(*continued*)

Table 5-1. *(continued)*

Metric	Description
FC_IO_RQ_W_SEC	Number of requests per second that resulted in Flash Cache being populated with data
FC_IO_RQ_W_SKIP	Number of requests written to disk that bypass Flash Cache
FC_IO_RQ_W_SKIP_LG	Number of requests written to disk that bypass Flash Cache due to the large IO size
FC_IO_RQ_W_SKIP_LG_SEC	Number of requests written to disk per second that bypass Flash Cache due to the large IO size
FC_IO_RQ_W_SKIP_SEC	Number of requests written to disk per second that bypass Flash Cache

Depending on the metrics in Table 5-1, the value can be either cumulative or instantaneous since `cellsrv` was started. The `LIST METRICCURRENT` command shows the current values of the metrics for a single storage cell. Following is an example of a `cellcli` command showing all Flash-Cache-related metrics that are currently reported with a value other than 0:

```
CellCLI> list metriccurrent attributes name,metricType,metricValue -
> where objectType = 'FLASHCACHE' and metricValue not like '0.*'
         FC_BYKEEP_USED                        Instantaneous        4,395 MB
         FC_BY_ALLOCATED                       Instantaneous        313,509 MB
         FC_BY_DIRTY                           Instantaneous        28,509 MB
         FC_BY_STALE_DIRTY                     Instantaneous        1,052 MB
         FC_BY_USED                            Instantaneous        342,890 MB
         FC_IO_BY_ALLOCATED_OLTP               Instantaneous        327,733 MB
         FC_IO_BY_DISK_WRITE                   Cumulative           39,456 MB
         FC_IO_BY_R                            Cumulative           233,829 MB
         FC_IO_BY_R_ACTIVE_SECONDARY           Cumulative           17.445 MB
         FC_IO_BY_R_ACTIVE_SECONDARY_MISS      Cumulative           5.000 MB
         FC_IO_BY_R_DW                         Instantaneous        82,065 MB
         FC_IO_BY_R_MISS                       Cumulative           19,303 MB
         FC_IO_BY_R_MISS_DW                    Instantaneous        59,824 MB
         FC_IO_BY_R_SKIP                       Cumulative           36,943 MB
         FC_IO_BY_R_SKIP_NCMIRROR              Cumulative           14,714 MB
         FC_IO_BY_W                            Cumulative           344,600 MB
         FC_IO_BY_W_FIRST                      Cumulative           86,593 MB
         FC_IO_BY_W_OVERWRITE                  Cumulative           216,326 MB
         FC_IO_BY_W_POPULATE                   Cumulative           41,680 MB
         FC_IO_BY_W_SKIP                       Cumulative           532,343 MB
         FC_IO_BY_W_SKIP_LG                    Cumulative           401,333 MB
         FC_IO_RQKEEP_R                        Cumulative           11 IO requests
         FC_IO_RQ_DISK_WRITE                   Cumulative           202,358 IO requests
         FC_IO_RQ_R                            Cumulative           20,967,497 IO requests
         FC_IO_RQ_REPLACEMENT_ATTEMPTED        Cumulative           1,717,959 IO requests
         FC_IO_RQ_REPLACEMENT_FAILED           Cumulative           427,146 IO requests
         FC_IO_RQ_R_ACTIVE_SECONDARY           Cumulative           2,233 IO requests
         FC_IO_RQ_R_ACTIVE_SECONDARY_MISS      Cumulative           80 IO requests
         FC_IO_RQ_R_DW                         Cumulative           328,018 IO requests
```

```
FC_IO_RQ_R_MISS                    Cumulative          307,935 IO requests
FC_IO_RQ_R_MISS_DW                 Cumulative          83,356 IO requests
FC_IO_RQ_R_SEC                     Rate                15.8 IO/sec
FC_IO_RQ_R_SKIP                    Cumulative          1,513,946 IO requests
FC_IO_RQ_R_SKIP_NCMIRROR           Cumulative          1,350,743 IO requests
FC_IO_RQ_R_SKIP_SEC                Rate                4.6 IO/sec
FC_IO_RQ_W                         Cumulative          26,211,256 IO requests
FC_IO_RQ_W_FIRST                   Cumulative          5,961,364 IO requests
FC_IO_RQ_W_OVERWRITE               Cumulative          19,887,434 IO requests
FC_IO_RQ_W_OVERWRITE_SEC           Rate                5.0 IO/sec
FC_IO_RQ_W_POPULATE                Cumulative          362,458 IO requests
FC_IO_RQ_W_SEC                     Rate                5.0 IO/sec
FC_IO_RQ_W_SKIP                    Cumulative          14,121,057 IO requests
FC_IO_RQ_W_SKIP_LG                 Cumulative          864,020 IO requests
FC_IO_RQ_W_SKIP_SEC                Rate                8.8 IO/sec
```

In addition to the performance metrics, you can also see what objects are in the cache. The LIST FLASHCACHECONTENT command can be used to this effect. This command shows a single entry for each cached object, the amount of space it is occupying, and various other statistics. Here is an example of looking at the Flash Cache content on a particular cell. The output of the command will list the top 20 cached objects:

```
CellCLI> list flashcachecontent where dbUniqueName like 'MBACH.*' -
> attributes objectNumber, cachedKeepSize, cachedSize, cachedWriteSize, hitCount, missCount -
> order by hitcount desc limit 20
         103456        0      2845298688      2729680896      6372231      23137
         103457        0      320430080       318562304       2031937      2293
         94884         0      32874496        12853248        664676       6569
         103458        0      103858176       101097472       662069       3051
         4294967294    0      1261568         1032192         346445       2
         4294967295    0      11259322368     5793267712      25488        440
         102907        0      404414464       154648576       21243        551
         93393         0      65232896        64184320        20019        53
         103309        0      383328256       137814016       19930        342
         102715        0      362323968       141139968       19585        273
         93394         0      73457664        71581696        19148        48
         93412         0      55427072        53739520        19122        55
         103365        0      388464640       146743296       18938        335
         103367        0      390332416       151314432       18938        347
         103319        0      385581056       149807104       18908        408
         102869        0      373628928       142901248       18596        383
         103373        0      383008768       141934592       18515        288
         103387        0      375513088       139116544       18194        427
         103323        0      354279424       129171456       18117        313
         103313        0      397303808       154607616       18018        318

CellCLI>
```

Unfortunately, the object name is still not included in the list of attributes. This means you must go back to the database to determine which object is which (by querying dba_objects, for example). Note that the ObjectNumber attribute in cellcli is equivalent to the data_object_id in the database views such as dba_objects. Here is an example how to match the cell's output with the database:

```
SQL> select owner, object_name, object_type
  2 from dba_objects where data_object_id = 103456;

OWNER      OBJECT_NAME                    OBJECT_TYPE
---------- ------------------------------ ------------------------------
SOE        STRESSTESTTABLE                TABLE
```

Given all the benchmarking performed as part of this chapter's preparation, it is not surprising that the Swingbench stress test table and its two indexes (data object IDs 103457 and 103458) are the most heavily hit and (write) cached segments.

Another useful addition of some more recent Exadata versions is the cellsrvstat tool. It is covered in detail in Chapter 11, but it is useful to mention it here as well. The command line tool allows the performance analyst to limit the output to so-called statistic groups. There are quite a few available to you, but if you would like to limit your investigation to Flash Cache, the flashcache group unsurprisingly is of most use. Here is an example of cellsrvstat output:

```
[root@enkcel04 ~]# cellsrvstat -stat_group flashcache
===Current Time===                                      Wed May  6 15:23:37 2015

== FlashCache related stats ==
Number of read hits                                            0     21065931
Read on flashcache hit(KB)                                     0    241004568
Number of keep read hits                                       0           11
Read on flashcache keep hit(KB)                                0           88
Number of read misses                                          0       307947
Total IO size for read miss(KB)                                0     19767368
Number of keep read misses                                     0            0
Total IO size for keep read miss(KB)                           0            0
Number of no cache reads                                       0      1547921
Total size for nocache read(KB)                                0     38403468
Number of keep no cache reads                                  0            0
Number of partial reads                                        0        26596
Total size for partial reads(KB)                               0      6897768
Number of optimized partial reads                              0        26528
Number of keep partial reads                                   0            0
Number of cache writes                                         0     25900731
Total size for cache writes(KB)                                0    311166944
Number of partial cache writes                                 0        15155
Number of redirty                                              0     19923003
Number of keep cache writes                                    0            0
Total size for keep cache writes(KB)                           0            0
Number of partial keep cache writes                            0            0
Number of keep redirty                                         0            0
[and many more]
```

The output of the tool is cumulative. On the left-hand side you see the metric and its name. The column of zeros here is the current value, and the large value is the one that indicates the cumulative value for the statistic. In best UNIX tradition, you can also use `cellsrvstat` to measure ongoing activity. To do so, you need to specify the interval and count parameters. If you specify an interval of, let's say, 15 seconds and a repeat count of two, you should focus on the output produced after the initial performance metrics were displayed. Similar to `iostat` and related tools, the first output represents the cumulative data since startup, whereas the second really measures the current activity during the interval specified.

At the Database Layer

Up until Oracle Database 12c, the database did not really provide much visibility into how Flash Cache is used. Worse yet, in 11.2.0.3, there were no metrics that distinguished writes from reads to (Write-back) Flash Cache—it was all a bit mixed up. Oracle 12.1.0.2.x offers the most information, closely followed by 11.2.0.4, although most of what you will read about in this section only applies to 12.1.0.2.

You can query the database in the following locations about Flash usage:

1. Session statistics as seen in `v$mystat`, `v$sesstat`, and related views
2. `V$CELL%` family of dynamic performance views
3. AWR reports

These will be discussed in the following sections.

Flash-Cache-Related Performance Counters

Performance counters are covered in Chapter 11, yet it is important to briefly list them here to give you a basic understanding of monitoring performance of Flash storage on the Exadata platform. If you need more information about any of these counters or related ones, please flip over to Chapter 11.

Before the introduction of the Write-back Flash Cache, there were really just a couple of statistics available for Flash Cache usage or efficiency: cell Flash Cache read hits and two statistics related to physical I/O. They are called physical read requests optimized and the closely related physical read total bytes optimized. The latter two can be a bit misleading since optimized I/O requests can be optimized (a)because the I/O requests benefited from a storage index and (b) when they were served from Flash Cache. Storage index savings as well as Flash Cache benefits are both rolled up in the same physical I/O statistic. If your query can make use of Flash Cache only, the statistic is relevant. Here is an example. The user in session 264 executed the following statement:

```
SQL> select /* fctest001 */ count(*) from SOE.ORDER_ITEMS where order_id < 0;

  COUNT(*)
----------
         0

Elapsed: 00:00:16.45
```

The performance analyst filtered the following statistics from the instancewide `v$sesstat` performance view:

```
SQL> select sid, name, value from v$sesstat natural join v$statname
  2  where sid = 264
  3  and name in (
  4    'cell flash cache read hits',
```

```
   'cell overwrites in flash cache',
   'cell partial writes in flash cache',
   'cell physical IO bytes saved by storage index',
   'cell writes to flash cache',
   'physical read IO requests',
   'physical read requests optimized',
   'physical read total bytes optimized',
   'physical write requests optimized',
   'physical write total bytes optimized')
 order by name;

       SID NAME                                                               VALUE
---------- ---------------------------------------------------------------- ----------
       264 cell flash cache read hits                                             5895
       264 cell overwrites in flash cache                                            0
       264 cell partial writes in flash cache                                        0
       264 cell physical IO bytes saved by storage index                             0
       264 cell writes to flash cache                                                0
       264 physical read IO requests                                              6042
       264 physical read requests optimized                                       5895
       264 physical read total bytes optimized                               810237952
       264 physical write requests optimized                                         0
       264 physical write total bytes optimized                                      0

10 rows selected.
```

Please ignore the fact that writes statistics are part of the list of statistic names—the script is generic and can be used to query foreground and background processes. As you can see from the output, the execution of the query did not benefit from a storage index, which is why the statistic *cell physical IO bytes saved by storage index* is not populated. What you can derive from the other I/O statistics, though, is that out of 6042 physical read I/O requests, 5895 or approximately 97% of all I/O requests were served from Flash Cache. If you go back a little bit to look at the statement, you can see that it queries data from the SOE schema, part of the Swingbench suite. If you have used Swingbench before, you will know that Swingbench simulates an OLTP-style workload, based on lots of indexes. And indeed, using the `fsx` (find SQL execution) and `dplan` scripts, you can see that the query was not offloaded:

```
SQL> @fsx4.sql
Enter value for sql_text: %fctest001%
Enter value for sql_id:

SQL_ID         CHILD OFFLOAD IO_SAVED_%  AVG_ETIME SQL_TEXT
------------- ------ ------- ---------- ---------- ----------------------------------------
2s4ff4z9f8q7c      0 No             .00      16.45 select /* fctest001 */ count(*) from SOE

SQL> @dplan
Enter value for sql_id: 2s4ff4z9f8q7c
Enter value for child_no: 0
```

```
PLAN_TABLE_OUTPUT
-------------------------------------------------------------------------------------------
SQL_ID  2s4ff4z9f8q7c, child number 0
-------------------------------------
select /* fctest001 */ count(*) from SOE.ORDER_ITEMS where order_id < 0

Plan hash value: 643311209

---------------------------------------------------------------------------------------
| Id  | Operation              | Name           | Rows  | Bytes | Cost (%CPU)| Time     |
---------------------------------------------------------------------------------------
|   0 | SELECT STATEMENT       |                |       |       | 26355 (100)|          |
|   1 |  SORT AGGREGATE        |                |     1 |     6 |            |          |
|*  2 |   INDEX FAST FULL SCAN| ITEM_ORDER_IX |     3 |    18 | 26355    (1)| 00:00:02 |
---------------------------------------------------------------------------------------

Predicate Information (identified by operation id):
---------------------------------------------------

   2 - filter("ORDER_ID"<0)

19 rows selected.
```

Hold on-why is that query not offloading? Aren't Index Fast Full Scans candidates? They are indeed, but what you cannot see here is that ITEM_ORDER_IX is a reverse key index, which is not offloadable in 12.1.2.1.x at least.

```
SQL> select owner, index_name, index_type, table_owner, table_name
  2  from dba_indexes
  3  where index_name = 'ITEM_ORDER_IX'
  4  and owner = 'SOE';

OWNER      INDEX_NAME           INDEX_TYPE                    TABLE_OWNER     TABLE_NAME
---------- -------------------- ----------------------------- --------------- ---------------
SOE        ITEM_ORDER_IX        NORMAL/REV                    SOE             ORDER_ITEMS
```

To finally demonstrate that the physical IO statistics can include Flash Cache hits as well as storage index savings a full scan has been forced using a hint:

```
SQL> select /*+ full(oit) */ /* fctest004  */ count(*) from SOE.ORDER_ITEMS oit
  2  where order_id < 0;

  COUNT(*)
----------
         0

Elapsed: 00:00:00.11
```

Using a slight variation of the query you saw before, you can see a different picture:

```
SQL> select sid, name, value from v$sesstat natural join v$statname
  2  where sid = (264)
  3  and name in (
  4    'cell physical IO bytes eligible for predicate offload',
  5    'cell flash cache read hits',
  6    'cell overwrites in flash cache',
  7    'cell partial writes in flash cache',
  8    'cell physical IO bytes saved by storage index',
  9    'cell writes to flash cache',
 10    'physical read IO requests',
 11    'physical read bytes',
 12    'physical read requests optimized',
 13    'physical read total bytes optimized',
 14    'physical write requests optimized',
 15    'physical write total bytes optimized')
 16  order by name;

       SID NAME                                                                          VALUE
---------- ---------------------------------------------------------------- ------------------
       264 cell flash cache read hits                                                    61.00
       264 cell overwrites in flash cache                                                  .00
       264 cell partial writes in flash cache                                              .00
       264 cell physical IO bytes eligible for predicate offload              3,050,086,400.00
       264 cell physical IO bytes saved by storage index                      3,048,513,536.00
       264 cell writes to flash cache                                                      .00
       264 physical read IO requests                                                 23,365.00
       264 physical read bytes                                                3,050,496,000.00
       264 physical read requests optimized                                          23,364.00
       264 physical read total bytes optimized                                3,050,487,808.00
       264 physical write requests optimized                                               .00
       264 physical write total bytes optimized                                            .00

12 rows selected.
```

Instead of 97% of I/O requests served by Flash, there are very few read hits. Some of these are actually caused by recursive SQL. On the other hand, you can see that out of 23,365 IO requests, 23,364 were optimized as well. Clearly, these optimizations are caused by the storage index savings.

So far in this section, you have seen cell Flash Cache read hits, but no statistics related to writes. These cannot be found in foreground processes as writes to data files are performed in batches by the database writer processes. Here is an example for the database writer statistics found on the same instance:

```
SQL> select sid, name, value from v$sesstat natural join v$statname
  2    where sid in (select sid from v$session where program like '%DBW%')
  3    and name in (
  4      'cell flash cache read hits',
  5      'cell overwrites in flash cache',
  6      'cell partial writes in flash cache',
  7      'cell physical IO bytes saved by storage index',
```

```
      'cell writes to flash cache',
      'physical read IO requests',
      'physical read requests optimized',
      'physical read total bytes optimized',
      'physical write requests optimized',
      'physical write total bytes optimized')
 order by name;

       SID NAME                                                                  VALUE
---------- ---------------------------------------------------------------- ----------
        65 cell flash cache read hits                                                0
         1 cell flash cache read hits                                                1
      1473 cell flash cache read hits                                              556
         1 cell overwrites in flash cache                                    344868411
        65 cell overwrites in flash cache                                    344836755
      1473 cell overwrites in flash cache                                    344936768
         1 cell partial writes in flash cache                                      665
        65 cell partial writes in flash cache                                      518
      1473 cell partial writes in flash cache                                      643
        65 cell physical IO bytes saved by storage index                             0
      1473 cell physical IO bytes saved by storage index                             0
         1 cell physical IO bytes saved by storage index                             0
        65 cell writes to flash cache                                        353280230
         1 cell writes to flash cache                                        353317405
      1473 cell writes to flash cache                                        353382073
      1473 physical read IO requests                                                11
        65 physical read IO requests                                                 0
         1 physical read IO requests                                                 1
         1 physical read requests optimized                                          1
        65 physical read requests optimized                                          0
      1473 physical read requests optimized                                        556
         1 physical read total bytes optimized                                    8192
      1473 physical read total bytes optimized                                 8994816
        65 physical read total bytes optimized                                       0
         1 physical write requests optimized                                 176644066
        65 physical write requests optimized                                 176625494
      1473 physical write requests optimized                                 176676770
      1473 physical write total bytes optimized                             1.5990E+12
        65 physical write total bytes optimized                             1.5981E+12
         1 physical write total bytes optimized                             1.5986E+12

30 rows selected.
```

Here you can see the Write-back Flash Cache at work.

The V$CELL% Family of Dyamic Performance Views

This section can only be an introduction to the V$CELL% family of views. They are covered in Chapter 11 as well, where you can read that the views have been greatly enhanced in Oracle 12.1.0.2 and cellOS 12.1.2.1.x and later. The most interesting views from the point of view of analyzing Flash Cache are listed in Table 5-2.

Table 5-2. *List of V$CELL Views Useful for Monitoring Flash Cache*

View Name	Contents
V$CELL_DB	Lists the I/O requests against all cells on a global level. Limit your queries to a source database to get an idea about its share on all the I/O requests.
V$CELL_DISK	Lists all the I/O-related statistics that can possibly be measured for cell disks. You should limit your query to either individual cells or, better still, individual cell disks whose name begins with *FD* for *Flash disks*. If you are using an all-Flash storage server, you should not rely on the information in this view to measure Flash Cache performance. Due to the absence of hard disks, all grid disks are created on the Flash devices and you cannot easily separate Flash Cache from grid-disk-related I/O in the view. For all other Exadata users, it is likely that all of the Flash cards are used for Flash Cache (minus the 512MB used for Flash Logging), in which case the view can show you some interesting figures about the number of I/O requests, their size, and latencies.
V$CELL_GLOBAL	One of the most interesting views in this table as it provides output very similar to the `cellcli` command "list metriccurrent" and `cellsrvstat` shown earlier. It is best explained using an example, following this table.

V$CELL_DISK and V$CELL_GLOBAL have some historization of their information in the V$CELL_DISK_HISTORY and V$CELL_GLOBAL_HISTORY, respectively. Here is the example query against V$CELL_GLOBAL to show Flash-Cache-related metrics.

```
SQL> select metric_name, metric_value, metric_type
  2  from V$CELL_GLOBAL
  3  where lower(metric_name) like '%flash cache%'
  4  and cell_name = '192.168.12.10';

METRIC_NAME                                           METRIC_VALUE METRIC_TYPE
---------------------------------------------------- ------------- ----------------
Flash cache read bytes                                358836707328 bytes
Flash cache write bytes (first writes, overwrites,    500606863872 bytes
 partial writes)

Flash cache bytes used                                360777785344 bytes
Flash cache bytes used (keep objects)                   4966318080 bytes
Flash cache keep victim bytes                                    0 bytes
Flash cache write bytes - first writes                107450368000 bytes
Flash cache write bytes - overwrites                  392564908032 bytes
Flash cache write bytes - population writes due to     50094088192 bytes
 read misses
[and many more]
```

You can find the metric definition in V$CELL_METRIC_DESC. At the time of writing, not all the metrics exposed on the cell via `cellcli` are equally exposed in the database layer, but as with all Exadata features this might change in the future.

AWR Reports

The Exadata documentation features an appendix "What's new in the Oracle Exadata Database Machine" in the Database Machine System Overview document. You should probably have a look at it from time to time—the contents are very valuable, especially since the wealth of Exadata features sometimes makes it hard to remember when a given feature was introduced. With version 12.1.2.1.0, Oracle introduced Exadata performance-related information in AWR reports. The AWR report might be better suited to display and present the performance related data. In addition to performance data, you are shown more detail about the system's configuration and a health report. The nice fact about the report is that a lot of information is applicable at a global level, so you can see information about the entire system rather than staying confined to a single database.

Summary

Exadata Smart Flash Cache provides yet another way to pare down the I/O cost associated with Oracle databases. Most of the optimizations that the Exadata platform provides require the use of Smart Scans (full table or fast full index scans). ESFC does not depend on Smart Scans and, in fact, is most useful for speeding up access on random reads of single blocks. Thanks to the transparent caching of full-scanned data introduced in Exadata 11.2.3.3.0, multi-block reads can now benefit from the Flash Cache as well. Single-block read operations are generally associated with OLTP workloads, and, as such, ESFC is the key component of Exadata for OLTP or mixed workloads. In the previous edition of this book, we argued that the fact that ESFC does not provide a write-back cache severely limited its effectiveness with systems that are bottlenecked on writes. Exadata 11.2.3.3.1 addressed this concern, and now you can operate the Flash Cache in write-back mode. This is true even for the all-Flash X5-2 arrays that come with a portion of their capacity dedicated as (write-back) Flash Cache. Write-back Flash Cache provides significant improvements with write-intensive workloads. The Flash cards in the Exadata systems provide better IOPS numbers for writes than the combined set of disks together. On an X2-2 quarter rack, that—according to the data sheet—supports 6,000 disk IOPS we managed to scale up to 22,000 IOPS without trying very hard at all. This number greatly surpasses the pure disk-based IOPS capability of the system.

The large cache and the intelligent caching algorithms used by the Oracle storage software allow ESFC to provide read performance similar to solid-state-based disk systems. Offloading large portions of random read activity from the hard disks also provides an indirect benefit to processing involving such as not-yet-cached Smart Scans. Generally speaking, the generous amount of cache available in the X4-2 and X5-2 hardware has made life a lot easier for Exadata administrators, and so has the automatic caching of data, one of this author's favorite recent Exadata features.

While ESFC was initially thought of as purely an optimization aimed at reducing latency for small reads, it now is also quite effective for large DW-type queries. In fact, the large throughput numbers that Oracle quotes depend on disk and Flash Cache being scanned concurrently when possible. The Flash Cache actually shoulders the lion's share of the burden in this case. Tweaking the storage clause to modify the caching policy should no longer be needed. Since Flash Cache has become a crucial component to the Exadata platform, it must be controlled in some form. Oracle has realized this and allows Flash Cache to be controlled using I/O Resource Manager.

CHAPTER 6

Exadata Parallel Operations

Exadata doesn't have a special way of executing parallel operations that is not available on other platforms running 11gR2 and 12c. However, parallel processing is a key component of Exadata because efficient handling of data warehouse workloads was a primary design goal for Exadata. In addition, because offloading/Smart Scan depends on direct path reads, which can be used by parallel query slaves, parallel operations take on a whole new importance. Traditionally, the efficient use of parallel query has required careful control of concurrency in order to maximize the use of available resources without overwhelming the system. Oracle's previous attempts at throttling parallel operations to allow them to be used in multiuser environments have not been entirely successful. Version 11gR2 provided some new capabilities for controlling parallel operations. In particular, a queueing mechanism has been introduced that allows the number of concurrent parallel processes to be managed more effectively. This approach appears to be much better suited to allowing a high degree of parallelism without overwhelming the available resources than previous attempts. 11gR2 also introduced the ability for Oracle to automatically calculate a degree of parallelism on a statement-by-statement basis. Version 12c introduced a Parallel Statement Queueing enhancement and process memory usage control. Also introduced in version 12c is a Database Resource Manager (DBRM) directive which allows the critical queries to bypass the parallel statement queue, and a new database parameter that limits the total Program Global Area (PGA) size, for which the idea is to avoid excessive physical memory usage that leads to high rates of swapping.

In this chapter, we will focus on parallel query. Other forms of parallelism provided by the database, such as recovery parallelism, will not be covered here. We will briefly cover parallel query mechanics and demonstrate specifically how the queueing mechanism and automatic degree of parallelism work with Exadata. We will also briefly cover the 11gR2 In-Memory Parallel Execution feature and discuss how Exadata storage parallelizes I/O operations. We will not cover all the details of parallel query or parallel DML with the assumption that the reader is familiar with basic Oracle parallel concepts. Note also that the discussion and examples will refer to behavior in Oracle Database 11g Release 2 (11.2.0.4) and 12c Release 1 (12.1.0.2.0). In most cases, the comments apply equally to version 11.2.0.1 as well. Exceptions are explicitly called out.

Parameters

Before describing the various new features and how they apply to Exadata, you should review the parameters that affect how parallel queries are handled by the database. Table 6-1 shows the parameters along with a brief description of each one's purpose.

Table 6-1. *Database Parameters Controlling 11gR2 and 12c Parallel Features*

Parameter	Default	Description
parallel_max_servers		The maximum number of parallel slave process that may be created on an instance. The default value is calculated by parallel_threads_per_cpu * cpu_count * concurrent_parallel_users * 5. The concurrent_parallel_users value is determined by: - If SGA_TARGET is set: 4. - If PGA_AGGREGATE_TARGET is set: 2. - Else 1.
parallel_servers_target		The upper limit on the number of parallel slaves that may be in use on an instance at any given time if parallel queueing is enabled. The default is calculated by parallel_threads_per_cpu * cpu_count * concurrent_parallel_users * 2. The concurrent_parallel_users value is determined by: - If SGA_TARGET is set: 4. - If PGA_AGGREGATE_TARGET is set: 2. - Else 1.
parallel_min_servers	0	The minimum number of parallel slave processes that should be kept running, regardless of usage. Usually set to eliminate the overhead of creating and destroying parallel processes.
parallel_threads_per_cpu	2	Used in various parallel calculations to represent the number of concurrent processes that a CPU can support. Please note that 2 is the Oracle default value, the Oracle Exadata recommendation is 1.
parallel_degree_policy	MANUAL	Controls several parallel features including automatic degree of parallelism (Auto DOP), Parallel Statement Queueing, and In-Memory Parallel Execution.
parallel_execution_message_size	16384	The size of parallel message buffers in bytes.
parallel_degree_level	100	New in 12c. The scaling factor for default DOP calculations. 100 represents 100%, so setting it to 50 will reduce the calculated DOP to half.
parallel_force:local	FALSE	Determines whether parallel query slaves will be forced to execute only on the node that initiated the query (TRUE), or whether they will be allowed to spread on to multiple nodes in a RAC cluster (FALSE).
parallel_instance:group		Used to restrict parallel slaves to certain instances in a RAC cluster. This is done by specifying a service name that is configured to a limited number of instances.

(*continued*)

Table 6-1. *(continued)*

Parameter	Default	Description
parallel_io_cap_enabled	FALSE	This parameter is deprecated, replaced by parallel_degree_limit when it has been set to IO. Used in conjunction with the DBMS_RESOURCE_MANAGER.CALIBRATE_IO function to limit default DOP calculations based on the I/O capabilities of the system.
parallel_degree_limit	CPU	With automatic degree of parallelism, specifies what degree of parallelism to use. When set to CPU, maximum is parallel_threads_per_cpu * cpu_count * instances. With IO, maximum is dependent on per process I/O bandwidth / total system throughput. When a number is set, it limits the maximal degree of parallelism to that number for a statement.
pga_aggregate_limit		New in 12c. This parameter limits the PGA memory usage by the instance. See chapter 7, resource management.
parallel_adaptive_multi_user	TRUE	Old mechanism of automatic parallel query usage tuning. This mechanism works by reducing the requested DOP depending on system load at query startup time.
parallel_min_time_threshold	AUTO	The minimum estimated serial execution time that will trigger Auto DOP. The default is AUTO, which translates to 10 seconds. When the PARALLEL_DEGREE_POLICY parameter is set to AUTO, ADAPTIVE, or LIMITED, parallelism is considered after the set amount of seconds. If all tables referenced use the In-Memory Column Store, this parameter defaults to 1.
parallel_server	FALSE	This parameter has nothing to do with parallel queries. Set to TRUE or FALSE depending on whether the database is RAC enabled or not. This parameter was deprecated long ago and has been replaced by the CLUSTER_DATABASE parameter.
parallel_server_instances	1	This parameter has nothing to do with parallel queries, either. This parameter is set to the number of instances in a RAC cluster.
parallel_automatic_tuning	FALSE	Deprecated since 10g. This parameter enabled an automatic DOP calculation on objects for which a parallelism attribute is set.
parallel_min_percent	0	Old throttling mechanism. When Parallel Statement Queueing is not enabled (when PARALLEL_DEGREE_POLICY is set to MANUAL or LIMITED), this represents the minimum percentage of parallel servers that are needed for a parallel statement to execute.

The parameters shown in Table 6-2 control distinct features which are enabled when automatic degree of parallelism is enabled (often referred to as "auto DOP"). The parameters are underscore parameters, which means that they should not be used in production before consulting Oracle support and getting their blessing to use them.

***Table 6-2.** Selected Underscore Database Parameters Controlling Parallel Features*

Parameter	Default	Description
`_parallel_statement_queueing`	`FALSE`	Related to automatic DOP. If set to `TRUE`, this enables Parallel Statement Queueing.
`_parallel_cluster_cache_policy`	`ADAPTIVE`	Related to automatic DOP. If set to `CACHED`, this enables In-Memory Parallel Execution.
`_parallel_cluster_cache_pct`	`80`	Percentage of the total buffer cache size in the cluster to be used for In-Memory Parallel Execution. By default, segments larger than 80% of the total buffer cache size are not considered a candidate for In-Memory Parallel Execution.

Parallelization at the Storage Tier

Exadata has a lot of processing power at the storage layer. The setup with the fixed eighth, quarter, half, or full rack configurations up to the X4 generation has more CPU resources available at the storage layer than at the computing layer. With the X5 generation, the storage server has gone from two six-core CPUs with X4 to two eight-core CPUs with X5, while the computing layer for the two socket servers has gone from two 12-core CPUs with X4 to two 18-core CPUs with X5, which means the number of cores is higher on the computing layer with the X5 generation two socket servers. Needless to say, the new "elastic configurations," meaning any kind of configuration could be created, abandons the concept of a balance between computing and storage layer altogether and should only be considered as a last resort and with great care.

Since Smart Scans offload a lot of processing to the storage cells, every query involving Smart Scans is effectively parallelized across the CPUs on the storage cells. This type of parallelization is completely independent from the traditional database parallel processing. The Smart Scan parallelization occurs even when the activity is driven by a single process on a single database server. This introduces some interesting issues that should be considered with regard to normal parallelization at the database tier. Since one of the primary jobs of a parallelized query is to allow multiple processes to participate in the I/O operations and since the I/O operations are already spread across multiple processes, the degree of parallelism required by statements running on the Exadata platform should be smaller than on other platforms.

Auto DOP

One of the major changes to parallel operations in Oracle Database 11g Release 2 was the addition of a feature affectionately known as Auto DOP (automatic degree of parallelism). It was designed to overcome the problems associated with the fact that there is rarely a single DOP value that is appropriate for all queries touching a particular object. Prior to 11gR2, the DOP could be specified at the statement level via hints or at the object level via the `DEGREE` and `INSTANCE` settings. Realistically, using hints at the statement level makes more sense in most situations for the reason just mentioned. However, it requires that the developers understand the platform that the statements will be running on and the workload that the hardware will be supporting at the time of execution, as well the concurrency of other processes requiring resources. Getting the settings correct can be a tedious trial-and-error process and, unfortunately, the DOP cannot be changed while a statement is running. Once it starts, your only options are to let it complete or kill it, change the DOP settings, and try again. This makes fine-tuning in a "live" environment a painful process.

Operation and Configuration

When Auto DOP is enabled, Oracle evaluates each statement to determine whether it should be run in parallel and, if so, what DOP should be used. Basically, any statement that the optimizer concludes will take longer than 10 seconds to run serially will be a candidate to run in parallel. The 10-second threshold can be controlled by setting the PARALLEL_MIN_TIME_THRESHOLD parameter. This decision is made regardless of whether any of the objects involved in the statement have been decorated with a parallel degree setting or not.

Auto DOP is enabled by setting the PARALLEL_DEGREE_POLICY parameter to a value of AUTO, LIMITED, or ADAPTIVE (12c). The default setting for this parameter is MANUAL, which disables all three of the new 11gR2 parallel features (Auto DOP, Parallel Statement Queueing, In-Memory Parallel Execution). Unfortunately, PARALLEL_DEGREE_POLICY is one of those parameters that control more than one thing. The following list shows the effects of the various settings for this parameter:

> **MANUAL**: If PARALLEL_DEGREE_POLICY is set to MANUAL, none of the new 11gR2 parallel features will be enabled. Parallel processing will work as it did in previous versions. That is to say, statements will only be parallelized if a hint is used or an object is decorated with a parallel setting.
>
> **LIMITED**: If PARALLEL_DEGREE_POLICY is set to LIMITED, only Auto DOP is enabled while Parallel Statement Queueing and In-Memory Parallel Execution remain disabled. In addition, only statements accessing objects that have been decorated with the default parallel setting will be considered for Auto DOP calculation.
>
> **AUTO**: If PARALLEL_DEGREE_POLICY is set to AUTO, all three of the new features are enabled. Statements will be evaluated for parallel execution regardless of any parallel decoration at the object level.
>
> **ADAPTIVE (12c)**: This new 12c parameter enables the same functionality as the previously discussed AUTO value. In addition to these, Oracle may re-evaluate the statement in order to provide a better degree of parallelism for subsequent executions based on feedback gathered during statement execution.

Although the only documented way to enable Parallel Statement Queueing and In-Memory Parallel Execution is via the all-or-nothing setting of AUTO or ADAPTIVE, the developers have thoughtfully provided hidden parameters that provide independent control of these features. Table 6-3 shows the parameters and how the settings of PARALLEL_DEGREE_POLICY alter the hidden parameters.

Table 6-3. *Hidden Parameters Affected by PARALLEL_DEGREE_POLICY*

Parallel_Degree_Policy	Parameter	Value
MANUAL	_parallel_statement_queuing	FALSE
	_parallel_cluster_cache_policy	ADAPTIVE
LIMITED	_parallel_statement_queuing	FALSE
	_parallel_cluster_cache_policy	ADAPTIVE
AUTO	_parallel_statement_queuing	TRUE
	_parallel_cluster_cache_policy	CACHED
ADAPTIVE (12c)	_parallel_statement_queuing	TRUE
	_parallel_cluster_cache_policy	CACHED

It's pretty obvious what the _PARALLEL_STATEMENT_QUEUING parameter controls. When it is set to TRUE, queueing is enabled. The purpose of the _PARALLEL_CLUSTER_CACHE_POLICY parameter is a little less obvious. It turns out that it controls In-Memory Parallel Execution. Setting the value of the _PARALLEL_CLUSTER_CACHE_POLICY parameter to CACHED enables In-Memory Parallel Execution. You should note that In-Memory Parallel Execution is arguably of less value on the Exadata platform because the Smart Scan optimizations will not be available when using this feature to use parallel processes to scan and use data in the buffer cache. We will discuss that in more detail a little later. In the meantime, here is an example showing Auto DOP in action:

```
SQL> select owner, table_name, status, last_analyzed, num_rows, blocks, degree
  2  from dba_tables where owner = 'MARTIN' and table_name = 'BIGT';

OWNER  TABLE_NAME        STATUS  LAST_ANAL   NUM_ROWS     BLOCKS   DEGREE
------ ------------- -------- --------- --------- ---------- --------
MARTIN BIGT               VALID  24-MAR-15  100000000   16683456        1

SQL> alter system set parallel_degree_policy=auto;

System altered.

SQL> select /* frits1 */ avg(id) from martin.bigt;

    AVG(ID)
-----------
  500000005

SQL> @find_sql
Enter value for sql_text: %frits1%
Enter value for sql_id:

SQL_ID        CHILD  PLAN_HASH EXECS    ETIME AVG_ETIME USERNAME SQL_TEXT
------------- ----- ---------- ----- -------- --------- -------- ---------------------------
djwmfmzgtjfqu     1 3043090422     1  1087.45   1087.45      SYS select /* frits1 */ avg(id)
                                                                 from martin.bigt
```

```
SQL> !cat dplan.sql
set verify off
set pages 9999
set lines 150
select * from table(dbms_xplan.display_cursor('&sql_id','&child_no',''))
/

SQL> @dplan
Enter value for sql_id: djwmfmzgtjfqu
Enter value for child_no:

PLAN_TABLE_OUTPUT
-----------------------------------------------------------------------------------------------------
SQL_ID  djwmfmzgtjfqu, child number 1
-------------------------------------
select /* frits1 */ avg(id) from martin.bigt

Plan hash value: 3043090422

-----------------------------------------------------------------------------------------------------
|Id|Operation                        | Name    |Rows|Bytes|Cost(%CPU)|Time     | TQ  |IN-OUT|PQ Distrib |
-----------------------------------------------------------------------------------------------------
| 0|SELECT STATEMENT                 |         |    |     | 104K(100)|         |     |      |           |
| 1| SORT AGGREGATE                  |         |  1 |   7 |          |         |     |      |           |
| 2|  PX COORDINATOR                 |         |    |     |          |         |     |      |           |
| 3|   PX SEND QC (RANDOM)           |:TQ10000|  1 |   7 |          |         |Q1,00| P->S |QC (RAND)  |
| 4|    SORT AGGREGATE               |         |  1 |   7 |          |         |Q1,00| PCWP |           |
| 5|     PX BLOCK ITERATOR           |         |100M| 667M| 104K  (1)|00:00:05 |Q1,00| PCWC |           |
|*6|      TABLE ACCESS STORAGE FULL| BIGT    |100M| 667M| 104K  (1)|00:00:05 |Q1,00| PCWP |           |
-----------------------------------------------------------------------------------------------------

Predicate Information (identified by operation id):
---------------------------------------------------

   6 - storage(:Z>=:Z AND :Z<=:Z)

Note
-----
   - automatic DOP: Computed Degree of Parallelism is 48 because of degree limit
```

As you can see, enabling Auto DOP allowed the statement to be parallelized, even though the table was not decorated with a parallel setting (which means the degree property of the table was set to 1, not an higher value or DEFAULT). Also, notice that the plan output produced by DBMS_XPLAN shows that Auto DOP was enabled and the calculated DOP was 48, and that the value 48 was limited by "degree limit." In fact, this is set by the parameter PARALLEL_DEGREE_LIMIT. In this case, the parameter PARALLEL_DEGREE_LIMIT is set to CPU (default), which means the limit is PARALLEL_THREADS_PER_CPU * CPU_COUNT * *instances*, which in this case of this example is 1 * 24 * 2, which is 48.

I/O Calibration

Oracle Database version 11.2.0.2 introduced a restriction to Auto DOP requiring that the I/O system be calibrated before statements will be automatically parallelized. This restriction is lifted with version 12c. The calibration is done by the DBMS_RESOURCE_MANAGER.CALIBRATE_IO procedure, which generates a random read-only workload and spreads it across all instances in a RAC cluster. The procedure can put a significant load on the system. The documentation recommends running it when the system is idle or very lightly loaded. Here is an example of what happens if the calibration procedure has not been run and PARALLEL_DEGREE_POLICY has been set to limited, auto, or adaptive on 11.2.0.4:

```
SQL> @dplan
Enter value for sql_id: 05cq2hb1r37tr
Enter value for child_no:

PLAN_TABLE_OUTPUT
-------------------------------------------------------------------------------------------
SQL_ID  05cq2hb1r37tr, child number 0
-------------------------------------
select avg(pk_col) from kso.skew a where col1 > 0

Plan hash value: 568322376

---------------------------------------------------------------------------
| Id | Operation            | Name |   Rows| Bytes | Cost (%CPU)| Time     |
---------------------------------------------------------------------------
|   0 | SELECT STATEMENT    |      |       |       | 44298 (100)|          |
|   1 |  SORT AGGREGATE     |      |     1 |    11 |            |          |
|*  2 |   TABLE ACCESS FULL| SKEW |    32M|   335M| 44298   (1)| 00:01:29 |
---------------------------------------------------------------------------

Predicate Information (identified by operation id):
---------------------------------------------------

   2 - filter("COL1">0)

Note
-----
   - automatic DOP: skipped because of IO calibrate statistics are missing

23 rows selected.
```

As you can see, when the I/O calibration has not been done, Auto DOP is disabled and the optimizer generates a serial execution plan. When automatic DOP is enabled on version 12.1.0.1 and above and I/O calibration has not been done, the optimizer will do the automatic DOP consideration! There are two views that provide additional information about the calibration. The V$IO_CALIBRATION_STATUS view shows whether the calibration has been done, and the DBA_RSRC_IO_CALIBRATE view shows the results of the procedure. Here is an example showing how to the calibration details, count the number of disks in the DATA disk group, and use the CALIBRATE_IO procedure:

```
SQL> select * from V$IO_CALIBRATION_STATUS;

STATUS        CALIBRATION_TIME
------------- ---------------------------------------------------------------
NOT AVAILABLE
```

If you are unsure about the number of disks, you can query the number cell disks with the DATA prefix as seen by the database to calibrate. If your DATA disk group has a slightly different name, like the rack name added to DATA, add that between DATA and CD:

```
SQL> select count(*) from v$asm_disk where path like '%DATA_CD%';

  COUNT(*)
----------
        36

SQL> !cat calibrate_io.sql
SET SERVEROUTPUT ON
DECLARE
  lat  INTEGER;
  iops INTEGER;
  mbps INTEGER;
BEGIN
-- DBMS_RESOURCE_MANAGER.CALIBRATE_IO (<DISKS>, <MAX_LATENCY>, iops, mbps, lat);
   DBMS_RESOURCE_MANAGER.CALIBRATE_IO (&no_of_disks, 10, iops, mbps, lat);

  DBMS_OUTPUT.PUT_LINE ('max_iops = ' || iops);
  DBMS_OUTPUT.PUT_LINE ('latency  = ' || lat);
  dbms_output.put_line('max_mbps = ' || mbps);
end;
/

SQL> @calibrate_io
Enter value for no_of_disks: 36
```

The database procedure will run for some time—around 15 minutes on our system. The procedure will cause the database to spawn cs*nn* processes on all instances, for which the amount of these processes is set by the the number of disks parameter. If the procedure is finished, it will show the result of the calibration. For example:

```
max_iops = 11237
latency  = 8
max_mbps = 5511

PL/SQL procedure successfully completed.

SQL> select * from V$IO_CALIBRATION_STATUS;

STATUS        CALIBRATION_TIME                                                  CON_ID
------------- ----------------------------------------------------------------- ----------
READY         24-MAY-15 07.17.45.086 AM                                                  0

SQL> select start_time, MAX_IOPS, MAX_MBPS, MAX_PMBPS, LATENCY, NUM_PHYSICAL_DISKS
     from DBA_RSRC_IO_CALIBRATE;

START_TIME                          MAX_IOPS   MAX_MBPS  MAX_PMBPS    LATENCY NUM_PHYSICAL_DISKS
------------------------------ ---------- ---------- ---------- ---------- ------------------
24-MAY-15 07.11.38.691358 AM        11237       5511        400          8                 36
```

The changes require a database restart to take effect. Once restarted, Auto DOP is using the calibration details. In certain cases, it might not be feasible to run the calibration, or a bug affecting calibration (11.2.0.2 before before bundle patch 4) to generate a too high number for Auto DOP, which means it will not consider it. In these cases, the important calibration details can be manually set. This is described in My Oracle Support (MOS) note 1269321.1. Here is how it is done:

```
SQL> delete from resource:io_calibrate$;
SQL> insert into resource:io_calibrate$ values(current_timestamp,
  2  current_timestamp, 0, 0, 200, 0, 0);
SQL> commit;
```

A database restart is required after setting the value. The value of 200 is recommended by Oracle Support for customers running on Exadata, and it is what Oracle uses to test Auto DOP on Exadata.

Auto DOP Wrap-Up

The end result of setting PARALLEL_DEGREE_POLICY to AUTO is that all kinds of statements will be run in parallel, even if no objects have been specifically decorated with a parallel degree setting. This is truly automatic parallel processing because the database decides what to run in parallel and with how many slaves. On top of that, by default, the slaves may be spread across multiple nodes in a RAC database. Unfortunately, this combination of features is a little like the Wild West with things running in parallel all over the place. However, the ability to queue parallel statements does provide some semblance of order, which leads us to the next topic.

We found Auto DOP being too optimistic about the calculated DOP in a lot of cases. A parameter worth pointing out is PARALLEL_DEGREE_LEVEL, which can be used to dial down the calculated DOP when setting the value of the parameter to a value lower than the default value 100. Other ways of limiting (Auto) DOP are PARALLEL_DEGREE_LIMIT and the database resource manager.

Parallel Statement Queueing

When Oracle first introduced the Parallel Query feature with Oracle version 7, Larry Ellison did a demo using a multiprocessor server, on which he was the only user. The individual CPU utilization was shown graphically, and all the CPUs where running full force when the Parallel Query feature was demoed. We wonder what would have happened if there were other database users in that database and what their experience would be during that demo. Probably their experience would not have been a good one. That is exactly what Parallel Statement Queueing tries to solve.

Oracle's parallel capabilities have been a great gift, but they have also been a curse because controlling the beast in an environment where there are multiple users trying to share the resources is difficult at best. There have been attempts to come up with a reasonable way of throttling big parallel statements. But to date I do not think those attempts have been overly successful.

One of the most promising aspects of Exadata is its potential to run mixed workloads (OLTP and DW) without crippling one or the other. In order to do that, Oracle needs some mechanism to separate the workloads and, just as importantly, to throttle the resource intensive parallel queries. Parallel Statement Queueing appears to be just such a tool. And when combined with the Resource Manager, it provides a pretty robust mechanism for throttling the workload to a level that the hardware can support.

The Old Way

Before we get to the new Parallel Queueing functionality, we should probably review how it was done in previous versions. The best tool we had at our disposal was Parallel Adaptive Multiuser, which provided the ability to automatically downgrade the degree of parallelism for a given statement based on the workload when a query executes. It was actually a powerful mechanism and it was the best approach we had prior to 11gR2. This feature is enabled by setting the PARALLEL_ADAPTIVE_MULTI_USER parameter to TRUE. This is still the default in 12c, by the way, so this is definitely a parameter that you may want to consider changing. The downside of this approach is that parallelized statements can have a wildly varying degree of parallism and thus execution times. As you can imagine, a statement that gets 32 slaves one time and then gets downgraded to serial execution the next time will probably not make the users very happy.

The argument for this type of approach is that queries are going to run slower if the system is busy, regardless of what you do, and that users expect it to run slower when the system is busy. The first part of that statement may be true, but I do not believe the second part is (at least in most cases). The bigger problem with the downgrade mechanism, though, is that the decision about how many slaves to use is based on a single point in time—the point when the parallel statement starts. Recall that once the degree of parallelism (DOP) is set for an execution plan, it cannot be changed. The statement will run to completion with the number of slaves it was assigned, even if additional resources become available while it is running.

Consider the statement that takes one minute to execute with 32 slaves, and suppose that same statement gets downgraded to serial due to a momentarily high load. Now say that a few seconds after it starts, the system load drops back to more normal levels. Unfortunately, the serialized statement will continue to run for nearly 30 minutes with its single process, even though on average the system is not busier than usual. This sort of erratic performance can wreak havoc for those using the system and for those supporting it.

The New Way

Now let's compare Parallel Adaptive Multi User (the old way) with the new mechanism introduced in 11gR2 that allows parallel statements to be queued. This mechanism separates long running parallel queries from the rest of the workload. The mechanics are pretty simple. Turn the feature on. Set a target number of parallel slaves using the PARALLEL_SERVERS_TARGET parameter. Run what should be a resource intensive query. If a statement that requires exceeding the target tries to start, it will be queued until the required number of slaves becomes available. There are, of course, many details to consider and other control mechanisms that can be applied to manage the process. Let's look at how it behaves:

```
SQL> alter system set parallel_degree_policy=auto;

System altered.

SQL> alter system set parallel_servers_target=10;

System altered.

SQL> @parms
Enter value for parameter: parallel%
Enter value for isset:
Enter value for show_hidden:
```

```
NAME                                               VALUE      ISDEFAUL
-------------------------------------------------- ---------  --------
parallel_adaptive_multi_user                            TRUE  FALSE
parallel_automatic_tuning                              FALSE  TRUE
parallel_degree_level                                    100  TRUE
parallel_degree_limit                                    CPU  TRUE
parallel_degree_policy                                  AUTO  FALSE
parallel_execution_message_size                        16384  FALSE
parallel_force:local                                   FALSE  TRUE
parallel_instance:group                                       TRUE
parallel_io_cap_enabled                                FALSE  TRUE
parallel_max_servers                                     240  FALSE
parallel_min_percent                                       0  TRUE
parallel_min_servers                                       0  FALSE
parallel_min_time_threshold                             AUTO  TRUE
parallel_server                                         TRUE  TRUE
parallel_server_instances                                  2  TRUE
parallel_servers_target                                   10  TRUE
parallel_threads_per_cpu                                   1  FALSE
```

In order to execute multiple SQLs that get to use automatic DOP and make them queue, we need a little script, which is shown below. The script executes 10 sqlplus processes, which are put into the background using "&." The "wait" command at the end waits for all backgrounded processes to finish.

```
T=0
while [ $T -lt 10 ]; do
  echo "select avg(id) from t1;" | sqlplus -S ts/ts &
  let T=$T+1
done
wait
echo "Finished."
```

Now the script above is executed. If we look at the DBMS_XPLAN output via we see Auto DOP calculated 10 slaves for the execution because of PARALLEL_SERVERS_TARGET set to that value above:

```
SQL> @dplan b46903fft8uz4
Enter value for sql_id: b46903fft8uz4
Enter value for child_no:

PLAN_TABLE_OUTPUT
-------------------------------------------------------------------------------------------------
SQL_ID  b46903fft8uz4, child number 2
-------------------------------------
select avg(id) from t1

Plan hash value: 3110199320
```

```
-----------------------------------------------------------------------------------------------------------
| Id | Operation                      | Name     | Rows| Bytes | Cost (%CPU)| Time     |    TQ  |IN-OUT| PQ Distrib |
-----------------------------------------------------------------------------------------------------------
|  0 | SELECT STATEMENT               |          |     |       | 64140 (100)|          |        |      |            |
|  1 |  SORT AGGREGATE                |          |   1 |     6 |            |          |        |      |            |
|  2 |   PX COORDINATOR               |          |     |       |            |          |        |      |            |
|  3 |    PX SEND QC (RANDOM)         | :TQ10000 |   1 |     6 |            |          |  Q1,00 | P->S | QC (RAND)  |
|  4 |     SORT AGGREGATE             |          |   1 |     6 |            |          |  Q1,00 | PCWP |            |
|  5 |      PX BLOCK ITERATOR         |          | 100M|  572M| 64140   (1)| 00:00:02 |  Q1,00 | PCWC |            |
|* 6 |       TABLE ACCESS STORAGE FULL| T1       | 100M|  572M| 64140   (1)| 00:00:02 |  Q1,00 | PCWP |            |
-----------------------------------------------------------------------------------------------------------

Predicate Information (identified by operation id):
---------------------------------------------------

   6 - storage(:Z>=:Z AND :Z<=:Z)

Note
-----
   - automatic DOP: Computed Degree of Parallelism is 10
```

Directly after execution of the script to start up multiple sqlplus sessions to execute the parallellized table scan, we can see the statement queueing in effect. First, if we look at the number of parallel query processes active, we see that the number of parallel query processes active does not exceed the limit of 10 set:

```
SQL> select * from v$px_process_sysstat where statistic like '%In Use%';

STATISTIC                                     VALUE     CON_ID
------------------------------ ---------- ----------
Servers In Use                                   10          0
```

If fact, the reason the limit is not exceeded is because of the Parallel Statement Queueing, which can be seen in V$SQL_MONITOR and in the wait interface:

```
SQL> select sid, sql_id, sql_exec_id, sql_text from v$sql_monitor where status='QUEUED';

  SID SQL_ID        SQL_EXEC_ID SQL_TEXT
----- ------------- ----------- ------------------------------
  588 b46903fft8uz4    16777250 select avg(id) from t1
  396 b46903fft8uz4    16777254 select avg(id) from t1
  331 b46903fft8uz4    16777251 select avg(id) from t1
  265 b46903fft8uz4    16777253 select avg(id) from t1
  463 b46903fft8uz4    16777255 select avg(id) from t1
  654 b46903fft8uz4    16777256 select avg(id) from t1
  263 b46903fft8uz4    16777252 select avg(id) from t1
  200 b46903fft8uz4    16777249 select avg(id) from t1
  166 b46903fft8uz4    16777249 select avg(id) from t1
```

```
9 rows selected.

SQL> @snapper ash=event+wait_class 1 1 all
Sampling SID all with interval 1 seconds, taking 1 snapshots...

-- Session Snapper v4.11 BETA - by Tanel Poder ( http://blog.tanelpoder.com ) - Enjoy the
Most Advanced Oracle Troubleshooting Script on the Planet! :)

---------------------------------------------------------------
Active% | EVENT                                   | WAIT_CLASS
---------------------------------------------------------------
   800% | resmgr:pq queued                        | Scheduler
   700% | cell smart table scan                   | User I/O
   300% | ON CPU                                  | ON CPU

--  End of ASH snap 1, end=2015-05-25 07:17:51, seconds=1, samples_taken=5

PL/SQL procedure successfully completed.
```

There are several things worth mentioning in this listing. To set up the desired conditions, we turned on Auto DOP, which also enables Parallel Queueing, and then set the PARALLEL_SERVER_TARGET parameter to a very low number (10) in order to trigger queueing more easily. We then used a shell script to execute 10 statements that are subject to Auto DOP. When looking at V$PX_PROCESS_SYSSTAT, there are no more than 10 parallel query servers active, as was set with the PARALLEL_SERVERS_TARGET parameter. V$SQL_MONITOR showed that the statements were indeed queueing. This is an important point. All statements using parallel query will show up in the V$SQL_MONITOR view. Please mind this view requires the tuning pack license. If they have a status of QUEUED, they are not actually executing but are instead waiting until enough parallel slaves become available. We ran Tanel Poder's Snapper script to see what event the queued statements were waiting on. As you can see, it was the `resmgr: pq queued` wait event.

■ **Note** There is one other thing you should be aware of regarding the wait events. There is a wait event change that relates to parallel queueing. This example was created using Oracle Database version 12.1.0.2. If you are using 11.2.0.1, you will see a different set of wait events (there are two). The first is `PX Queuing: statement queue`. This is the event that a statement waits on when it is next to run. The other is `enq: JX - SQL statement queue`. This event is what a statement waits on when there are other statements ahead of it in the queue. This scheme seems quite unwieldy, which is probably why it was changed in the later release.

Controlling Parallel Queueing

There are several mechanisms in place for controlling how the Parallel Statement Queueing feature behaves. The basic approach is to use a first-in, first-out queueing mechanism. But there are ways to prioritize work within the queueing framework. It is also possible to completely bypass the queueing mechanism via a hint. And, conversely, it is possible to enable queueing for a statement via a hint even when the Parallel Statement Queueing feature is not enabled at the database level. There are also a few parameters that affect the queueing behavior. And, finally, the Resource Manager has the capability to affect how statements are queued.

Controlling Queueing with Parameters

There are a handful of parameters that affect how Parallel Queueing behaves. The first two are PARALLEL_MAX_SERVERS, which sets the maximum number of parallel query slaves per instance, and the PARALLEL_SERVERS_TARGET parameter, which sets the amount of parallel query slaves to be in use after which statements that want to execute parallel need to be queued.

The default value of PARALLEL_MAX_SERVERS is calculated by:

```
parallel_threads_per_cpu * cpu_count * concurrent_parallel_users * 5
```

The default value of PARALLEL_SERVERS_TARGET is calculated by:

```
parallel_threads_per_cpu * cpu_count * concurrent_parallel_users * 2
```

Concurrent_parallel_users is determined by:

- If SGA_TARGET is set: 4.
- If PGA_AGGREGATE_TARGET is set: 2.
- Else 1.

This calculated value is almost certainly higher than you would want for most mixed workload systems, as it is geared at completely consuming the available CPU resources with parallel query processes. Allowing long-running parallel statements to consume the server completely means that response time-sensitive, OLTP-type statements could suffer. You should also note that it is possible to have more server processes active than the parameter allows. Since the number of slaves assigned to a query may be twice the DOP, the target can occasionally be exceeded.

In 12c, if the PARALLEL_STMT_CRITICAL resource management directive is used (discussed later in this chapter), it is recommended that the PARALLEL_SERVERS_TARGET be set to 50-75% of the PARALLEL_MAX_SERVERS so that critical queries that bypass the parallel queue can make use of the remaining parallel slave processes.

■ **Note** The PARALLEL_MAX_SERVERS parameter will be reduced to a value below the parameter PROCESSES if the calculated value of PARALLEL_MAX_SERVERS is greater than the value of PROCESSES parameter. You will see the occurrence of this behavior on the alert log at instance startup.

```
Mon May 06 18:43:06 2013
Adjusting the default value of parameter parallel_max_servers
from 160 to 135 due to the value of parameter processes (150)
Starting ORACLE instance (normal)
```

Another parameter that deserves some discussion is the hidden parameter, _PARALLEL_STATEMENT_QUEUING, which turns the feature on and off. As already discussed in the Auto DOP section, this parameter is set to TRUE when the PARALLEL_DEGREE_POLICY parameter is set to AUTO. However, the hidden parameter can also be set manually to turn Parallel Queueing off and on independently.

Auto DOP calculations are still a little scary, so it is nice that there is a way to turn on the Parallel Queueing feature without enabling Oracle to take complete control of which statements run in parallel. Of course, since this involves setting a hidden parameter, you should not do this in a production environment without approval from Oracle support. Nevertheless, here is another quick example showing that queueing can be turned on without enabling Auto DOP or In-Memory Parallel Execution:

```
SQL > alter system set parallel_degree_policy=manual sid='*';

System altered.

SQL > alter table ts.t1 parallel (degree 8);

Table altered.

SQL> @parms
Enter value for parameter: parallel
Enter value for isset:
Enter value for show_hidden:

NAME                                               VALUE
-------------------------------------------------- ------
parallel_adaptive_multi_user                       TRUE
parallel_automatic_tuning                          FALSE
parallel_degree_level                              100
parallel_degree_limit                              CPU
parallel_degree_policy                             MANUAL
parallel_execution_message_size                    16384
parallel_force:local                               TRUE
parallel_instance:group
parallel_io_cap_enabled                            FALSE
parallel_max_servers                               128
parallel_min_percent                               0
parallel_min_servers                               32
parallel_min_time_threshold                        AUTO
parallel_server                                    TRUE
parallel_server_instances                          2
parallel_servers_target                            10
parallel_threads_per_cpu                           1

T=0
while [ $T -lt 10 ]; do
  echo "select avg(id) from t1;" | sqlplus -S ts/ts &
  let T=$T+1
done
wait
echo "Finished."

SQL> select * from v$px_process_sysstat where statistic like '%In Use%';

STATISTIC                      VALUE     CON_ID
------------------------------ ----- ----------
Servers In Use                    80          0
```

First, we set PARALLEL_DEGREE_POLICY to manual. This disables automatic DOP and statement queueing and In-Memory Parallel Query. Next, we decorated the T1 table with a degree of eight. Then we looked at the values of the parameters that have PARALLEL in the name. For the sake of the example, we have set PARALLEL_FORCE_LOCAL to TRUE, so all the sqlplus sessions of the above script will use parallel query slaves in the current instance. Then we executed the script. As you can see, the 10 sessions all allocated their eight parallel query slaves because we see 80 servers in use.

Now set the undocumented parameter _PARALLEL_STATEMENT_QUEUING to TRUE and re-run the script to create 10 sessions:

```
SQL> alter system set "_parallel_statement_queuing"=true sid='*';

System altered.

T=0
while [ $T -lt 10 ]; do
  echo "select avg(id) from t1;" | sqlplus -S ts/ts &
  let T=$T+1
done
wait
echo "Finished."

SQL> select * from v$px_process_sysstat where statistic like '%In Use%';

STATISTIC                      VALUE     CON_ID
------------------------------ ----- ----------
Servers In Use                    12          0
```

This output shows statement queueing enabled without turning on Auto DOP. Please note that this involved a hidden parameter, which means that you should discuss setting this parameter with Oracle Support if you want to apply this technique in production.

Controlling Statement Queueing with Hints

There are two hints that can be used to control Parallel Statement Queueing at the statement level. One hint, NO_STATEMENT_QUEUING, allows the queueing process to be completely bypassed, even if the feature is turned on at the instance level. The other hint, STATEMENT_QUEUING, turns on the queueing mechanism, even if the feature is not enabled at the instance level. The STATEMENT_QUEUING hint provides a documented avenue for using the queuing feature without enabling Auto DOP.

Controlling Queueing with Resource Manager

Oracle's Database Resource Manager (DBRM) provides additional capability to control Parallel Statement Queueing. While a thorough discussion of DBRM is beyond the scope of this chapter, we will cover some specific features related to parallel query. Chapter 7 covers DBRM in more detail.

Without DBRM, the parallel statement queue behaves strictly as a first-in, first-out (FIFO) queue. DBRM provides several directive attributes that can be used to provide additional control on a consumer group basis. Many of these controls were introduced in version 11.2.0.2. Table 6-4 contains a list of additional capabilities provided by DBRM.

Table 6-4. *DBRM Parallel Statement Queueing Controls*

Control	Description
Specify a Timeout	The PARALLEL_QUEUE_TIMEOUT directive attribute can be used to set a maximum queue time for a consumer group. The time limit is set in seconds and, once it has expired, the statement will terminate with an error (ORA-07454). Note that this directive did not become available until version 11.2.0.2 of the database.
Specify Maximum DOP	The PARALLEL_DEGREE_LIMIT_P1 directive attribute sets a maximum number of parallel slaves that may be assigned to an individual statement. This is equivalent to the PARALLEL_DEGREE_LIMIT database parameter but is used to set limits for different sets of users based on consumer groups.
Manage Order of Dequeueing	The MGMT_P1, MGMT_P2, ... MGMT_P8 directive attributes can be used to alter the normal FIFO processing. This attribute allows prioritization of dequeueing aside from being used as a resource percentage allocation for CPU & I/O (Intra-database IO Resource Management). Each of the eight attributes essentially provides a distinct dequeueing priority level. All statements with an MGMT_P1 attribute will be dequeued prior to any statement with MGMT_P2. In addition to the dequeueing priority, a probability number can be assigned to regulate dequeueing of statements within the same level.
Limit Percentage of Parallel Slaves	The PARALLEL_TARGET_PERCENTAGE directive attribute can be used to limit a consumer group to a percentage of the parallel slaves available to the system. So, if a system allowed 64 slaves to be active before starting to queue and PARALLEL_TARGET_PERCENTAGE was set to 50, the consumer group would only be able to consume 32 slaves. Note that this directive did not become available until version 11.2.0.2 of the database. In 12c the PARALLEL_SERVER_LIMIT replaced this directive.
Queue Multiple SQLs as a Set	The BEGIN_SQL_BLOCK and END_SQL_BLOCK procedures in DBMS_RESOURCE_MANAGER package work with Parallel Statement Queueing by treating individual statements as if they had been submitted at the same time. The idea is that the all the statements in the block are all dequeued, preventing individual statements from being kept queued. The mechanism requires surrounding independent SQL statements with calls to the BEGIN and END procedures. Note that this procedure did not become available until version 11.2.0.2 of the database.
Critical parallel statement prioritization	With version 12c, the PARALLEL_STMT_CRITICAL directive is introduced, which can make parallel statements bypass the statement queue when the directive is set to BYPASS_QUEUE for a consumer group. All queries issued by users belonging to a consumer group where the attribute is set to BYPASS_QUEUE will bypass the parallel statement queue and execute immediately. With the bypass mechanism, the total number of parallel slaves requested may be greater than PARALLEL_SERVERS_TARGET. Please be aware the critical queries are run regardless of actual parallel query processes currently in use, which means that if current use of parallel query slaves already reached PARALLEL_MAX_SERVERS, it is possible to encounter downgrades or, even worse, serial execution. This is why you should keep some headroom between PARALLEL_SERVERS_TARGET and PARALLEL_MAX_SERVERS.

The DBRM directives can be quite involved. Here is a modified example from the *Oracle® Database VLDB and Partitioning Guide 12c Release 1 (12.1.0.2)* that shows the directives making use of the Parallel Statement Queueing features:

```
BEGIN
  DBMS_RESOURCE_MANAGER.CLEAR_PENDING_AREA();
  DBMS_RESOURCE_MANAGER.CREATE_PENDING_AREA();

--new plan
  DBMS_RESOURCE_MANAGER.CREATE_PLAN(
    'DAYTIME_PLAN',
    'Plan that priorizes short running queries'
  );
--consumer groups
  DBMS_RESOURCE_MANAGER.CREATE_CONSUMER_GROUP(
    'MEDIUM_TIME',
    'Medium: time running between 1 and 10 minutes'
  );
  DBMS_RESOURCE_MANAGER.CREATE_CONSUMER_GROUP(
    'LONG_TIME',
    'Long: time running more than 10 minutes'
  );
--directives
  DBMS_RESOURCE_MANAGER.CREATE_PLAN_DIRECTIVE(
    'DAYTIME_PLAN',
    'SYS_GROUP',
    'Directive for SYS and high priority queries',
    MGMT_P1 => 100,
    PARALLEL_STMT_CRITICAL => 'BYPASS_QUEUE'
  );
  DBMS_RESOURCE_MANAGER.CREATE_PLAN_DIRECTIVE(
    'DAYTIME_PLAN',
    'OTHER_GROUPS',
    'Directive for SQL running less than 1 minute',
    MGMT_P2 => 70,
    PARALLEL_DEGREE_LIMIT_P1 => 4,
    SWITCH_TIME => 60,
    SWITCH_ESTIMATE => TRUE,
    SWITCH_FOR_CALL => TRUE,
    SWITCH_GROUP => 'MEDIUM_TIME'
  );
  DBMS_RESOURCE_MANAGER.CREATE_PLAN_DIRECTIVE(
    'DAYTIME_PLAN',
    'MEDIUM_TIME',
    'Directive for SQL running between 1 and 10 minutes',
    MGMT_P2 => 20,
    PARALLEL_SERVER_LIMIT => 75,
    SWITCH_TIME => 600,
    SWITCH_ESTIMATE => TRUE,
    SWITCH_FOR_CALL => TRUE,
    SWITCH_GROUP => 'LONG_TIME'
  );
```

```
  DBMS_RESOURCE_MANAGER.CREATE_PLAN_DIRECTIVE(
    'DAYTIME_PLAN',
    'LONG_TIME',
    'Directive for SQL running more than 10 minutes',
    MGMT_P2 => 10,
    PARALLEL_SERVER_LIMIT => 50,
    PARALLEL_QUEUE_TIMEOUT => 3600
  );
  DBMS_RESOURCE_MANAGER.VALIDATE_PENDING_AREA();
  DBMS_RESOURCE_MANAGER.SUBMIT_PENDING_AREA();
END;
/
```

This example bears some explanation:

1. The resource plan DAYTIME_PLAN is created.
2. There are two consumer groups defined: MEDIUM_TIME and LONG_TIME. There are two other consumer groups (SYS_GROUP and OTHER_GROUPS), which are automatically created.
3. The first directive is for the SYS_GROUP consumer group. This group is assigned 100% priority as configured with MGMT_P1, which means it gets priority over the other groups. Also, this group bypasses the statement queue.
4. The second directive is for the OTHER_GROUPS consumer group, which is the default consumer group. This directive specifies that the optimizer should evaluate each SQL statement and, if the estimated execution time is longer than 60 seconds (SWITCH_TIME), the session should switched to the MEDIUM_TIME consumer group (SWITCH_GROUP=>'MEDIUM_TIME'). The session switches back to the OTHER_GROUPS consumer group once the SQL is executed (SWITCH_FOR_CALL=>TRUE). The dequeueing priority (MGMT_P2) is set to a probability of 70%, meaning that statements should be dequeued after any MGMT_P1 statement, with a probability of 70% when compared with other MGMT_P2 statements. The maximum DOP is set to 4 by the PARALLEL_DEGREE_LIMIT_P1 attribute.
5. The third directive is for the MEDIUM_TIME consumer group. This directive also includes a switch causing sessions to be moved to the LONG_TIME group if Oracle estimates the SQL statement will take longer than 10 minutes. Additionally, this directive sets the dequeueing priority to be 20% of the second priority group (MGMT_P2). This directive also puts a limit on the percentage of parallel slaves that may be used (PARALLEL_SERVER_LIMIT). In this case, 80% of the total slaves allowed on the system is the maximum that may be used by sessions in this consumer group.
6. The last directive is for the LONG_TIME consumer group. Sessions in this group have a very low dequeueing priority as compared to the others (MGMT_P2=10). It also limits the percentage of parallel slaves to 50%. Finally, since statements in this group may be queued for a long time, the PARALLEL_QUEUE_TIMEOUT attribute has been set to 14,400 seconds. Hence, if a statement is queued for four hours, it will fail with a timeout error.

There are a few additional settings that have to be done before this plan can truly work. A session needs to be granted a consumer group to be its initial consumer group if the consumer group is other than OTHER_GROUPS. This is not the case in our example, so we do not have to use the DBMS_RESOURCE_MANAGER.SET_INITIAL_CONSUMER_GROUP procedure. However, we want sessions to switch to the MEDIUM_TIME or LONG_TIME group when the rules as set in the directive apply. This means we must use the DBMS_RESOURCE_MANAGER_PRIVS.GRANT_SWITCH_CONSUMER_GROUP procedure before this plan works. In this example, the KSO user is granted the switches. This needs to be done for all the database users that are subject to this plan:

```
BEGIN
 DBMS_RESOURCE_MANAGER_PRIVS.GRANT_SWITCH_CONSUMER_GROUP('KSO','MEDIUM_TIME',FALSE);
 DBMS_RESOURCE_MANAGER_PRIVS.GRANT_SWITCH_CONSUMER_GROUP('KSO','LONG_TIME',FALSE);
END;
/
```

Parallel Statement Queueing Wrap-Up

This section has been considerably more detailed than the coverage of the other two new parallel features in 11gR2. It also contains some of the enhancements that were added in version 12c. That is because this feature is a critical component in allowing Exadata to handle mixed workloads effectively. It enables us to effectively handle a mixture of statements that are sensitive to both throughput and response time. Without this feature, it would be very difficult to provide adequate resources without severely compromising one or the other.

In-Memory Parallel Execution

Prior to 11gR2, queries that were parallelized totally ignored the buffer cache. Oracle assumed that parallel queries would only be done on very large tables that would probably never have a large percentage of their blocks in the buffer cache. This assumption led to the conclusion that it would be faster to just read the data from disk. In addition, flooding the buffer cache with a large number of blocks from a full table scan was not desirable, so Oracle developed a mechanism called *direct path reads*, which bypassed the normal caching mechanism in favor of reading blocks directly in to the user's Program Global Area (PGA).

The In-Memory Parallel Execution feature takes a different approach. It attempts to make use of the buffer cache for parallel queries. The feature is cluster-aware and is designed to spread the data across the cluster nodes (that is, the RAC database instances). The data blocks are also affinitized to a single node, reducing the number of communication and data transfers between the nodes. The goal, of course, is to speed up the parallel query by eliminating disk I/O. This can be a viable technique because many systems now have very large amounts of memory, which of course can provide a significant speed advantage over disk operations. There are some downsides to this approach though. The biggest disadvantage with regard to Exadata is that all the Smart Scan optimizations are disabled by this feature. In this respect, the new option introduced in 12c to split the buffer cache into a Big Table Scan Cache and the OLTP cache by means of an initialization parameter offers little consolation—a Smart Scan is most likely faster than an n-way scan across multiple buffer caches.

Note that we have not actually seen In-Memory Parallel Query in the wild on Exadata. This is probably good since many of the optimizations built into Exadata rely on offloading, which depends on direct path reads. Of course, direct path reads will not be done if blocks are being accessed in memory on the database servers. On most platforms, memory access would be much faster than direct path reads from disk. But with Exadata, eliminating the disk I/O also eliminates a large number of CPUs that could be applied to filtering and other operations. This means that accessing the buffer cache for parallel execution could actually be less efficient than allowing the storage servers to participate in the execution of the SQL statement.

■ **Note** The 12.1.0.2 database patchset introduced the In-Memory Option (In-Memory Column Store, Vector Processing, and In-Memory Aggregation). Version 12.1.0.1 introduced other In-Memory Caching (Automatic Big Table Caching and Full Database Caching) features, which further speeds up the analytical capabilities of Exadata while simultaneously running the OLTP. Although these are really great new features, covering them further is beyond the scope of this chapter.

A little demonstration is probably in order at this point. It is worth noting that getting this feature to kick in at all takes quite a bit of effort. Here are the basic steps we had to take in order to get it to work. First, we had to find a query that the optimizer estimated would run for longer than the number of seconds specified by the PARALLEL_MIN_TIME_THRESHOLD parameter (assuming the statement was not parallelized). The default for this parameter is AUTO, meaning 10 seconds. We set this parameter to one second to make it easier to trigger the In-Memory Parallel behavior. This query also had to be on a table that would almost completely fit in the aggregate buffer cache provided by the combination of all the participating RAC instances. To simplify things, we limited the processing to a single instance by setting the PARALLEL_FORCE_LOCAL parameter to TRUE. Of course, we had to set PARALLEL_DEGREE_POLICY to AUTO to enable the feature. We also set very low values for PARALLEL_SERVERS_TARGET and PARALLEL_DEGREE_LIMIT. Here are the parameter settings and pertinent information about the query we used to test the feature:

```
SYS@dbm2> @parms
Enter value for parameter: parallel
Enter value for isset:
Enter value for show_hidden:

NAME                                              VALUE    ISDEFAUL
-------------------------------------------------- -------- ----------
fast_start_parallel_rollback                       LOW      TRUE
parallel_adaptive_multi_user                       FALSE    FALSE
parallel_automatic_tuning                          FALSE    TRUE
parallel_degree_level                              100      TRUE
parallel_degree_limit                              8        FALSE
parallel_degree_policy                             AUTO     FALSE
parallel_execution_message_size                    16384    FALSE
parallel_force:local                               TRUE     FALSE
parallel_instance:group                                     TRUE
parallel_io_cap_enabled                            FALSE    TRUE
parallel_max_servers                               720      TRUE
parallel_min_percent                               0        TRUE
parallel_min_servers                               0        FALSE
parallel_min_time_threshold                        1        FALSE
parallel_server                                    TRUE     TRUE
parallel_server_instances                          4        TRUE
parallel_servers_target                            8        FALSE
parallel_threads_per_cpu                           1        FALSE
recovery_parallelism                               0        TRUE

19 rows selected.

SYS@dbm2> @pool_mem
```

```
AREA                                 MEGS
------------------------------ ----------
                                    384.0
free memory                       1,162.5
fixed_sga                             7.3
streams pool                           .0
log_buffer                          248.7
shared pool                       2,011.3
large pool                           26.2
buffer_cache                      4,352.0
                               ----------
sum                               8,192.0

8 rows selected.

SYS@dbm2> @table_size
Enter value for owner: KSO
Enter value for table_name: SKEWIMPQ
Enter value for type:

OWNER        SEGMENT_NAME                   TYPE           TOTALSIZE_MEGS TABLESPACE_NAME
------------ ------------------------------ -------------- -------------- ------------------
KSO          SKEWIMPQ                       TABLE                 3,577.0 USERS
                                                           --------------
sum                                                               3,577.0

SYS@dbm2> select owner, table_name, status, last_analyzed, num_rows, blocks, degree, cache
  2      from dba_tables where owner = 'KSO' and table_name = 'SKEWIMPQ';

OWNER      TABLE_NAME STATUS   LAST_ANALYZED        NUM_ROWS       BLOCKS DEGREE CACHE
---------- ---------- -------- -------------------  ---------- ---------- ------ ----
KSO        SKEWIMPQ   VALID    2015-02-14:06:52:31  89599778       451141      1     Y
```

So, the buffer cache on this instance is about 4.3G, and the table is about 3.5G. The query we used is simple and will not benefit from storage indexes, as virtually all the records satisfy the single WHERE clause:

```
SYS@dbm2> select count(*) from kso.skewimpq;

  COUNT(*)
----------
  89599778

1 row selected.

SYS@dbm2> select count(*) from kso.skewimpq where col1 > 0;

  COUNT(*)
----------
  89599776

1 row selected.
```

Now we will show some statistics prior to running the query, after running the query for the first time, and after running the query for the second time:

```
SYS@dbm2> alter system flush buffer_cache;

System altered.

SYS@dbm2> @mystats
Enter value for name: reads

NAME                                                                           VALUE
---------------------------------------------------------------------- ---------------
SecureFiles DBFS Link streaming reads                                              0
cold recycle reads                                                                 0
data blocks consistent reads - undo records applied                                0
gc cluster flash cache reads failure                                               0
gc cluster flash cache reads received                                              0
gc cluster flash cache reads served                                                0
gc flash cache reads served                                                        0
lob reads                                                                          0
physical reads                                                                     7
physical reads cache                                                               7
physical reads cache for securefile flashback block new                            0
physical reads cache prefetch                                                      0
physical reads direct                                                              0
physical reads direct (lob)                                                        0
physical reads direct for securefile flashback block new                           0
physical reads direct temporary tablespace                                         0
physical reads for flashback new                                                   0
physical reads prefetch warmup                                                     0
physical reads retry corrupt                                                       0
recovery array reads                                                               0
session logical reads                                                             14
session logical reads - IM                                                         0
session logical reads in local numa group                                          0
session logical reads in remote numa group                                         0
transaction tables consistent reads - undo records applied                         0

25 rows selected.

SYS@dbm2> select avg(pk_col) from kso.skewimpq where col1 > 0;

AVG(PK_COL)
-----------
 16228570.2

SYS@dbm2> @mystats
Enter value for name: reads
```

```
NAME                                                                       VALUE
---------------------------------------------------------------------- --------------
SecureFiles DBFS Link streaming reads                                          0
cold recycle reads                                                             0
data blocks consistent reads - undo records applied                           0
gc cluster flash cache reads failure                                           0
gc cluster flash cache reads received                                          0
gc cluster flash cache reads served                                            0
gc flash cache reads served                                                    0
lob reads                                                                      0
physical reads                                                            450216
physical reads cache                                                      450216
physical reads cache for securefile flashback block new                        0
physical reads cache prefetch                                             446512
physical reads direct                                                          0
physical reads direct (lob)                                                    0
physical reads direct for securefile flashback block new                       0
physical reads direct temporary tablespace                                     0
physical reads for flashback new                                               0
physical reads prefetch warmup                                                 0
physical reads retry corrupt                                                   0
recovery array reads                                                           0
session logical reads                                                     453226
session logical reads - IM                                                     0
session logical reads in local numa group                                      0
session logical reads in remote numa group                                     0
transaction tables consistent reads - undo records applied                     0

25 rows selected.
```

A close look at these statistics reveals all the reads that are done have gone into the cache (statistic: physical reads cache), while a "normal" full table scan on a large segment would have been done to the session's PGA via direct reads (statistic: physical reads direct). This is also visible via the wait interface, multiblock reads into the cache are visible as "db file scattered read" events on non-Exadata platforms and "cell multiblock physical read" on Exadata, while reads into the PGA are visible as "direct path read" events, which on Exadata can be offloaded as Smart Scans. This is visible via the "cell smart table scan" or "cell smart index scan" events. This scan essentially filled the buffer cache. Let's execute the same query again and see if we can use the data read into the buffer cache:

```
SYS@dbm2> select avg(pk_col) from kso.skewimpq where col1 > 0;

AVG(PK_COL)
-----------
 16228570.2

SYS@dbm2> @mystats
Enter value for name: reads
```

```
NAME                                                                          VALUE
---------------------------------------------------------------- --------------
SecureFiles DBFS Link streaming reads                                             0
cold recycle reads                                                                0
data blocks consistent reads - undo records applied                              0
gc cluster flash cache reads failure                                              0
gc cluster flash cache reads received                                             0
gc cluster flash cache reads served                                               0
gc flash cache reads served                                                       0
lob reads                                                                         0
physical reads                                                               528923
physical reads cache                                                         528923
physical reads cache for securefile flashback block new                           0
physical reads cache prefetch                                                518528
physical reads direct                                                             0
physical reads direct (lob)                                                       0
physical reads direct for securefile flashback block new                          0
physical reads direct temporary tablespace                                        0
physical reads for flashback new                                                  0
physical reads prefetch warmup                                                    0
physical reads retry corrupt                                                      0
recovery array reads                                                              0
session logical reads                                                        906435
session logical reads - IM                                                        0
session logical reads in local numa group                                         0
session logical reads in remote numa group                                        0
transaction tables consistent reads - undo records applied                        0

25 rows selected.
```

The second execution of the scan of the SKEWIMPQ table doubled the session logical reads statistics (906435/2 roughly equals 453226 as seen as logical reads after the first run), but the physical reads statistic only increased with 78707 (528923-450216), indicating all the other logical reads where satisfied by the cache.

If DBMS_XPLAN.DISPLAY_CURSOR is used to display the execution plan, Oracle reveals if In-Memory Parallel Query has been used:

```
SYS@dbm2> @dplan

PLAN_TABLE_OUTPUT
--------------------------------------------------------------------------------------
---
SQL_ID  31q77xaa06ggz, child number 2
-------------------------------------
select avg(pk_col) from kso.skewimpq where col1 > 0

Plan hash value: 3471853810
```

```
----------------------------------------------------------------------------------------------------------------
| Id  | Operation                     | Name      | Rows  | Bytes | Cost (%CPU)| Time     |    TQ  |IN-OUT| PQ Distrib |
----------------------------------------------------------------------------------------------------------------
|   0 | SELECT STATEMENT              |           |       |       | 17043 (100)|          |        |      |            |
|   1 |  SORT AGGREGATE               |           |     1 |    11 |            |          |        |      |            |
|   2 |   PX COORDINATOR              |           |       |       |            |          |        |      |            |
|   3 |    PX SEND QC (RANDOM)        | :TQ10000  |     1 |    11 |            |          |  Q1,00 | P->S | QC (RAND)  |
|   4 |     SORT AGGREGATE            |           |     1 |    11 |            |          |  Q1,00 | PCWP |            |
|   5 |      PX BLOCK ITERATOR        |           |   95M|  1002M| 17043   (1)| 00:00:01 |  Q1,00 | PCWC |            |
|*  6 |       TABLE ACCESS STORAGE FULL| SKEWIMPQ |   95M|  1002M| 17043   (1)| 00:00:01 |  Q1,00 | PCWP |            |
----------------------------------------------------------------------------------------------------------------

Predicate Information (identified by operation id):
---------------------------------------------------

   6 - storage(:Z>=:Z AND :Z<=:Z AND "COL1">0)
       filter("COL1">0)

Note
-----
   - dynamic statistics used: dynamic sampling (level=AUTO)
   - automatic DOP: Computed Degree of Parallelism is 8 because of degree limit
   - parallel scans affinitized for buffer cache

SYS@dbm2> @fsx2
Enter value for sql_text:
Enter value for sql_id: 31q77xaa06ggz

SQL_ID          AVG_ETIME       PX          OFFLOAD SQL_TEXT
-------------  ----------     ------ -------   ----------------------------------------
31q77xaa06ggz       14.37      8 No          select avg(pk_col) from kso.skewimpq
                                                       where col1 > 0

1 rows selected.
```

DBMS_XPLAN.DISPLAY_CURSOR shows the statement has been executed in parallel, as can be seen by the rowsources that start with "PX." The most interesting thing here is in the Note section of the DISPLAY_CURSOR output: The line "parallel scans affinitized for buffer cache" clearly indicates the scan used the buffer cache, which means In-Memory Parallel Query has been used.

Indirect evidence of In-Memory Parallel Query can be found using the fsx2.sql script. When the SQL_ID was entered of our query, we can see the statement was executed with eight parallel query servers (the PX column), and no Smart Scans have been used (OFFLOAD column), which must have happened with normal (non In-Memory PX) execution of parallel query scans. Note also that the fsx2.sql script reports an estimated value for the AVG_ETIME, which is way more than the actual time the execution took. This occurs because v$sql reports elapsed time as the sum of the all the elapsed times of the slave processes. Dividing this number by the number of slaves gives an estimate, but that will not be totally accurate as slaves can vary greatly in their elapsed times. Let's now compare our In-Memory Parallel Execution to how our system behaves when In-Memory Parallel Execution is not in play. We can disable this feature in a couple of ways. The documented way is to set the PARALLEL_DEGREE_POLICY parameter to MANUAL. However, this also disables Auto DOP and Parallel Statement Queueing. The other way is to set the hidden parameter _PARALLEL_CLUSTER_CACHE_POLICY to ADAPTIVE:

```
SYS@dbm2> alter system set "_parallel_cluster_cache_policy"=adaptive;

System altered.

SYS@dbm2> @mystats
Enter value for name: reads

NAME                                                                        VALUE
------------------------------------------------------------------------ --------------
SecureFiles DBFS Link streaming reads                                           0
cold recycle reads                                                              0
data blocks consistent reads - undo records applied                             0
gc cluster flash cache reads failure                                            0
gc cluster flash cache reads received                                           0
gc cluster flash cache reads served                                             0
gc flash cache reads served                                                     0
lob reads                                                                       0
physical reads                                                                  0
physical reads cache                                                            0
physical reads cache for securefile flashback block new                         0
physical reads cache prefetch                                                   0
physical reads direct                                                           0
physical reads direct (lob)                                                     0
physical reads direct for securefile flashback block new                        0
physical reads direct temporary tablespace                                      0
physical reads for flashback new                                                0
physical reads prefetch warmup                                                  0
physical reads retry corrupt                                                    0
recovery array reads                                                            0
session logical reads                                                          17
session logical reads - IM                                                      0
session logical reads in local numa group                                       0
session logical reads in remote numa group                                      0
transaction tables consistent reads - undo records applied                      0

25 rows selected.

SYS@dbm2> select avg(pk_col) from kso.skewimpq where col1 > 0;

AVG(PK_COL)
-----------
 16228570.2

SYS@dbm2> @mystats
Enter value for name: reads
```

```
NAME                                                                    VALUE
---------------------------------------------------------------------- --------------
SecureFiles DBFS Link streaming reads                                       0
cold recycle reads                                                          0
data blocks consistent reads - undo records applied                         0
gc cluster flash cache reads failure                                        0
gc cluster flash cache reads received                                       0
gc cluster flash cache reads served                                         0
gc flash cache reads served                                                 0
lob reads                                                                   0
physical reads                                                         450207
physical reads cache                                                        0
physical reads cache for securefile flashback block new                     0
physical reads cache prefetch                                               0
physical reads direct                                                  450207
physical reads direct (lob)                                                 0
physical reads direct for securefile flashback block new                    0
physical reads direct temporary tablespace                                  0
physical reads for flashback new                                            0
physical reads prefetch warmup                                              0
physical reads retry corrupt                                                0
recovery array reads                                                        0
session logical reads                                                  450895
session logical reads - IM                                                  0
session logical reads in local numa group                                   0
session logical reads in remote numa group                                  0
transaction tables consistent reads - undo records applied                  0

25 rows selected.

SYS@dbm2> @fsx2
Enter value for sql_text: %avg(pk_col)%
Enter value for sql_id:

SQL_ID               AVG_ETIME        PX   OFFLOAD SQL_TEXT
-------------       ----------    --------  ----------------------------------------
31q77xaa06ggz            14.37        8 No    select avg(pk_col) from kso.skewimpq
                                                where col1 > 0

31q77xaa06ggz             5.92        8 Yes   select avg(pk_col) from kso.skewimpq
                                                where col1 > 0
2 rows selected.
```

Notice that with In-Memory Parallel Execution disabled, the statistics show that the number of physical reads and logical reads are roughly the same, just as the previous example with the first run to populate the buffer cache. However, instead of having the statistic physical reads cache increased to the same amount as the physical reads statistic, now the statistic physical reads direct increased up to the same amount as the physical reads statistic. Notice also that the `fsx2.sql` script shows that there is a new cursor in the shared pool that was executed with eight parallel slaves, offloaded to the storage tier. This is an important point. In-Memory Parallel Execution disables the optimizations that Exadata provides via Smart Scans. That should be obvious since the disk I/O was mostly eliminated by the In-Memory Parallel Execution feature, but it is the main reason that we believe this feature will not be as useful on the Exadata platform as on other platforms. The reason the offloaded query shows less elapsed time (AVG_ETIME) is that a huge part of the processing is offloaded to the storage tier, which means the parallel process' processing is even further parallelized and only the results are sent to the database tier.

Troubleshooting Parallel Execution

In the days before Oracle version 11.2, when experiencing parallel execution issues, having a clear view of what was going on across the cluster and the corresponding workload distribution among the parallel servers was quite a challenge. Even more challenging was getting the answer to questions such as "Why is my SQL just partially parallelized?"

The introduction of the Real-Time SQL Monitoring fixed some of the instrumentation issues and allowed the DBAs and developers to analyze the parallel execution in greater detail by providing interactive display of resource consumption across the parallel servers and SQL statistics details at each step of the execution plan. In 11gR2 and 12c, it has gotten a lot better with additional columns about resource management and parallel allocation details in the V$SQL_MONITOR view. This section will not discuss in detail how to interpret a SQL Monitor report. Instead, it will focus on how to utilize the views which expose the information used by a SQL Monitor report, together with other views for quick troubleshooting and finding out when downgrades are happening and In-Memory Parallel Execution is kicking in.

Using the following SQL, you can gather extra information, like "px_in_memory" to indicate a query was affinitized for memory or, in normal speak, *doing In-Memory Parallel Query*:

```
SQL> !cat other_xml.sql
select t.*
 from v$sql_plan v,
  xmltable(
    '/other_xml/info'
    passing xmltype(v.other_xml)
    columns
        info_type varchar2(30) path '@type',
        info_value varchar2(30) path '/info'
  ) t
where v.sql_id = '&sql_id'
  and v.child_number = &child_number
  and other_xml is not null;

SQL> alter session set parallel_degree_policy=manual;

System altered.

SQL> select avg(pk_col) from kso.skew2;

AVG(PK_COL)
-----------
 62500.2406

SQL> @find_sql
Enter value for sql_text: %skew2%
Enter value for sql_id:
```

```
SQL_ID          CHILD  PLAN_HASH  EXECS   ETIME AVG_ETIME USERNAME             SQL_TEXT
------------- ------ ---------- ----- ------- --------- -------- --------------------
atb3q75xavzb6      0 4220890033     1   10.13     10.13      SYS   select avg(pk_col)
                                                                       from kso.skew2

SQL> @other_xml
Enter value for sql_id: atb3q75xavzb6
Enter value for child_number: 0

INFO_TYPE                          INFO_VALUE
------------------------------ ---------------
db_version                       12.1.0.2
parse_schema                     "SYS"
plan_hash_full                   1438813450
plan_hash                        4220890033
plan_hash_2                      1438813450
```

In this case, the extra information does not reveal a lot of extra information. In fact, there are no big surprises. However, let's turn set PARALLEL_DEGREE_POLICY to AUTO and execute the query again:

```
SQL> alter session set parallel_degree_policy=auto;

System altered.

SQL> select avg(pk_col) from kso.skew2;

AVG(PK_COL)
-----------
 62500.2406

SQL> @find_sql
Enter value for sql_text: %skew2%
Enter value for sql_id:

SQL_ID          CHILD  PLAN_HASH  EXECS   ETIME AVG_ETIME USERNAME            SQL_TEXT
------------- ------ ---------- ----- ------- --------- -------- --------------------
atb3q75xavzb6      0 4220890033     1   10.13     10.13      SYS  select avg(pk_col)
                                                                      from kso.skew2
atb3q75xavzb6      2 2117817910     1  113.39    113.39      SYS  select avg(pk_col)
                                                                      from kso.skew2

SQL> @other_xml
Enter value for sql_id: atb3q75xavzb6
Enter value for child_number: 2
```

```
INFO_TYPE                      INFO_VALUE
------------------------------ -----------
derived_cpu_dop                         15
derived_io_dop                           3
dop                                     15
px_in_memory_imc                        no
px_in_memory                           yes
io_rate                                200
derived_io_dop                           3
cpu_rate                              1000
derived_cpu_dop                         16
cpu_rate                              1000
derived_cpu_dop                         16
cpu_rate                              1000
derived_cpu_dop                         16
db_version                        12.1.0.2
parse_schema                         "SYS"
plan_hash_full                  3329629242
plan_hash                       2117817910
plan_hash_2                     3329629242
```

This child cursor shows a lot more information related to parallel query. In fact, we can now see In-Memory Parallel Query was happening, because “px_in_memory” is “yes.” Also, we can see the degree of parallelism was 15; “dop” is “15.” When not using Auto DOP, other_xml will show additional information related to parallel execution:

```
INFO_TYPE                          INFO_VALUE
------------------------------ --------------
derived_cpu_dop                             0
derived_io_dop                              0
dop_reason                     table property
dop                                         8
px_in_memory_imc                           no
px_in_memory                               no
```

Summary

Parallel execution of statements is important for maximizing throughput on the Exadata platform. Oracle database releases 11gR2 and 12c include several new features and enhancements that make the parallel execution a more controllable feature, which is especially important when using the platform with mixed workloads. The Auto DOP feature is designed to allow intelligent decisions about DOP to be made automatically based on individual statements. In-Memory Parallel Execution may not be as useful on Exadata platforms as it is on non-Exadata platforms because it disables the optimizations that come along with Smart Scans. Parallel Statement Queueing is a very useful feature as it allows a mixture of throughput-oriented work to co-exist with response-time-sensitive work. Integration with the Database Resource Manager (DBRM) further enhances this feature by providing a great deal of additional control and prioritization over the queueing mechanism.

CHAPTER 7

Resource Management

If resources were unlimited, there would be no need to manage them. We see this in all aspects of our daily lives. If your car were the only car on the road, traffic signals would not be necessary. If you were the only customer at the bank, there would be no need for the winding ropes that form orderly lines. But, as we all know, this is rarely the case, which is the same for database servers. When the load on the system is light, there is very little need for resource management. Processes complete in a fairly consistent period of time. But when the system gets busy and resources become scarce, we can find ourselves with an angry mob on our hands.

Since version 8i of the database, the Oracle Database Resource Manager has been available with features to manage resources inside the database. Without DBRM, all database connections are treated with equal priority, and they are serviced in a sort of round-robin fashion by the operating system scheduler. When the system is under heavy load, all sessions are impacted equally. Low-priority applications receive just as high a priority as business-critical applications. It is not uncommon to see a few poorly written ad-hoc queries degrade the performance of mission-critical applications using the same database. If you have been a DBA long enough, especially in data warehouse environments, you are probably familiar with the Unix `renice` command. It is a root-level command that allows you to influence the CPU priority of a process at the operating-system level. A number of years ago, we worked in a DBA group supporting a particularly heavily loaded data warehouse. The `renice` command was used frequently to throttle back CPU priority for database sessions that were dominating the system. There were a couple of obvious problems with this approach. First of all, the `renice` command is a privileged command available only to the root user and system administrators were reluctant to grant DBAs access to it. The second problem was that automating it to manage CPU resources was difficult at best. Oracle's Database Resource Manager is a much more elegant solution to the problem. It allows DBAs to address resource allocation within the domain of the database itself. It is a well-organized framework that is automated by design. It ensures that critical system resources such as CPU will be available to your important applications whenever they are needed, even when the system is under a heavy workload. This is done by creating resource allocation schemes that define priorities based on the needs of the business.

Another case for resource management is consolidation. It was inevitable that a platform with the performance, capacity, and scalability of Exadata would be viewed by many as an ideal consolidation platform. But consolidating databases is a challenge, mainly because of the difficulty of managing resources across databases. We have worked with a huge number of clients who have used Exadata to consolidate multiple database servers onto the Exadata platform. One such client consolidated 29 databases from 17 database servers onto two Exadata full racks. Needless to say, without Oracle's resource management capabilities, it would be extremely difficult, if not impossible, to balance system resources among so many database environments. Using the *database* resource manager, there is not really a way to prioritize I/O across databases. Starting from Exadata V2, Oracle introduced the I/O Resource Manager (IORM) inside the storage servers, which enables the DBA to prioritize I/O. So whether you are consolidating multiple databases onto your Exadata platform or handling resource intensive applications within a single database, effective resource management will play an important role in your success.

Beyond introducing the Exadata and non-Exadata specific options available for resource management, our goals in presenting this material are twofold. First, we want to provide enough detail to demystify resource management without overwhelming the reader. Second, we intend to demonstrate how to build a fully functional resource management model. These goals present a unique challenge. Provide too little information, and the reader will only be able to set up very simple configurations. Give too much detail, and we risk convoluting the topic and losing the audience. The most difficult part of writing this chapter has been striking a balance between the two. For that reason, we created simple, share-based single level resource plans. In fact, simple, single-level resource plans will solve a vast majority of the resource management problems we see in the real world. Moreover, multi-level resource plans can be difficult to design and test. In this chapter, we demonstrate both multi-level and single-level plans because it is important to understand how they work. However, if you are considering using the Oracle Resource Manager or other resource management options, the best approach is to keep it simple and add features only as they are needed.

Consolidation

The primary drivers of consolidation centers around cost savings. Every new generation of hardware release is typically more powerful than the previous one, and this is also true for Exadata. IT shops can take advantage of this trend by consolidating the silos of database environments into a standardized powerful platform and ultimately achieve greater efficiencies by improving the total resource utilization—in effect, lowering both capital and operational expenditures. In the following sections, we will review the types of database consolidation.

Types of Database Consolidation

Aside from resource requirements, many factors need to be considered when consolidating multiple databases. These factors include, but are not limited to, namespaces, isolation, maintenance, upgrade, backup and recovery, cloning, and service level agreements. Each approach has its own pros and cons, as you will soon see.

Server

This is probably the easiest route, which means multiple databases are put onto a single database server or servers in the case of an Oracle RAC cluster. Each application is isolated by using a dedicated database, which can be easily maintained and upgraded. But as more and more databases are moved to the server or servers, the number of resources that must be dedicated to each of them presents a practical limit to the consolidation density that can be achieved. This can also be the same from a resource standpoint for any virtualization consolidation solution, which typically has more overhead than consolidating databases on a server because every virtual machine needs resources for the operating system too. With these kinds of consolidation, especially with development environments (which means low connection count and low usage), we usually see the memory capacity being reached first.

Schema

This method puts separate application schemas coming from multiple databases into a single instance or Oracle RAC database. There is a lot more planning and due diligence that has to be done when doing this kind of consolidation than the server approach. The DBAs and the application team have to check if there are any conflicting schema names or hard-coded schema names in the SQLs and packages. If there are any conflicts, they have to be resolved with some application and database-level changes. It would be an easy consolidation if all the application schemas fit nicely with each other, meaning there are no object name collisions due to the shared data dictionary. The result of this consolidation is only one database and accompanying background processes to administer for a number of applications. This means that schema-level consolidation, if possible, reaches a way higher density than server-level consolidation.

Multitenancy

Oracle Multitenant is an option introduced with Oracle 12c with an architecture change introducing the concept of pluggable databases (PDB). This enables an Oracle database (single-instance or RAC) to be a container (CDB) which having a single set of background processes, shared memory (SGA/PGA), undo, common temp, control files, and redo log per instance, which can contain multiple isolated databases, known as PDBs. PBDs have their own set of data files. PDBs are like combining the full isolation of a dedicated database and efficient resource usage and density of schema consolidation. Although most of our customers during the time of writing are still on version 11gR2, the multitenant architecture available with version 12c could be beneficial in a lot of cases. With the multitenant option, there is only one database to administer. On the other hand, the PDBs provide isolation overcoming the problem of naming conflicts between databases, which means no application changes are needed. All PDBs can be maintained without impacting the other PDBs residing in the same CDB, and they can be easily unplugged and plugged to another CDB. There's a lot more flexibility, features, and benefits with the multitenant architecture that will be discussed in this section of this chapter. To learn more about Oracle Multitenant, visit the Part VI of the Database Concepts guide at `http://docs.oracle.com/database/121/CNCPT/part_consol.htm#CHDGDBHJ`.

Instance Caging

Instance caging provides a way to limit CPU resource usage at the instance level. It is dependent on the database resource manager to execute the throttling and, as such, needs a resource manager plan to be active. Please note that managing CPU resources for consumer groups inside the database with the database resource manager is a different feature.

There are two specific problems instance caging can address:

- Manage CPU resource usage of multiple database instances at the same host, where instance caging prevents one instance from monopolizing CPU resources for the other instances. The focus of instance caging is on guaranteeing database performance.
- Manage CPU resource usage of one or more database instances at the same host, where instance caging prevents one or more database instances from oversubscription of CPU resources. The focus of instance caging is on the prevention of long run queues for the CPUs.

Instance caging essentially works by counting the active foreground and non-critical background processes and compare this number with the number set with the `CPU_COUNT` parameter. This is done by the database resource manager, which is the reason it must be active. If the number of active processes is `CPU_COUNT` or higher, the database resource manager throttles execution of the next database process that wants to execute. The throttling is visible by the wait event `resmgr: cpu quantum`.

A less obvious benefit from instance caging is that it operates on foreground and non-critical background processes only. This means that critical background processes, like the log writer and its slaves, LMS processes, and so on, are not throttled by instance caging. Consequently, excessive activity in an instance with instance caging configured, preventing the host from oversubscription of CPU, will not lead to CPU starvation of critical background processes. Without instance caging, oversubscription of CPU resources will lead to long CPU run queues in which all database processes must wait—foreground processes and critical background processes alike. Having critical background processes waiting in a run queue can have drastic consequences: When the log writer is queued, most database processing will block, and when the LMS processes get queued, the cluster stability can be harmed, potentially leading to node evictions in extreme cases.

There is a downside to using instance caging, too. When instance caging is active, it will not use more CPU resources than is configured with the CPU_COUNT parameter, regardless of availability. This means that if the CPU_COUNT parameter is set too low, the host appears healthy and not busy, while database processing is impacted because of a lot of processes being throttled.

Configuring Instance Caging

Configuring instance caging is very simple. Set a resource plan and set CPU_COUNT to the desired number of active processes. In order to be careful, first have a look at the current contents of the parameters that are necessary to activate instance caging in the spfile:

```
SYS@v12102 AS SYSDBA> show spparameter cpu_count

SID      NAME                          TYPE        VALUE
-------- ----------------------------- ----------- ----------------------------
*        cpu_count                     integer
SYS@v12102 AS SYSDBA> show spparameter resource_manager_plan

SID      NAME                          TYPE        VALUE
-------- ----------------------------- ----------- ----------------------------
*        resource_manager_plan         string
```

By looking at the output of show spparameter, you can check the spfile for values of parameters. Checking the current setting of these parameters via show parameter will give you the value the Oracle engine filled out. In most cases, you will encounter the above situation—both CPU_COUNT and RESOURCE_MANAGER_PLAN are unset.

In order to activate instance caging, set CPU_COUNT to a value and set a resource manager plan. Both parameters can be changed at runtime:

```
SYS@v12102 AS SYSDBA> alter system set cpu_count=2 scope=both sid='*';

System altered.

SYS@v12102 AS SYSDBA> alter system set resource_manager_plan=default_plan scope=both
sid='*';

System altered.
```

If you are uncertain which resource manager plan to set, the DEFAULT_PLAN plan is usually a good choice. The DEFAULT_PLAN is a very simple plan that strongly favors the SYS_GROUP and gives a very low priority to the ORA$AUTOTASK group (used for statistics collection, space advisor, sql tuning advisor, and non-ondemand in-memory population).

```
SYS@v12102 AS SYSDBA> select group_or_subplan, mgmt_p1, mgmt_p2, mgmt_p3, mgmt_p4
  2  from dba_rsrc_plan_directives where plan = 'DEFAULT_PLAN';
```

```
GROUP_OR_SUBPLAN     MGMT_P1    MGMT_P2    MGMT_P3    MGMT_P4
---------------- ---------- ---------- ---------- ----------
SYS_GROUP                90          0          0          0
OTHER_GROUPS              9          0          0          0
ORA$AUTOTASK              1          0          0          0
```

Please note that in the maintenance window (6 a.m. - 2 a.m. on the weekends, 10 p.m. - 2 a.m. during weekdays) by default, the resource manager plan is changed to the DEFAULT_MAINTENANCE_PLAN for the duration of the window. In a lot of cases, this is not an issue. The DEFAULT_MAINTENANCE_PLAN uses a multi-level plan, where the SYS_GROUP gets 75% at level 1. The OTHER_GROUP 70% (the group in which all foreground connections will be by default), which effectively means the OTHER_GROUP, gets a little lesser priority in favor of the automatic tasks. A second important note is that with or without instance caging or a resource manager plan set, by default the default maintenance window will be set and automatic tasks be run.

However, if you run time sensitive and/or important batch processing during that time, you might want to change or disable the Oracle-provided automatic tasks in order not to run at the same time as the batch processing. For more information on changing the automatic tasks, see the Database Administrator's Guide, Managing Automated Database Maintenance Tasks at http://docs.oracle.com.

Setting CPU_COUNT

The instance caging feature depends on setting CPU_COUNT to the total amount of foreground and non-critical background processes. As has been noted earlier, CPU_COUNT can be set and changed online. A word of warning per Oracle's advice: Do not change the value too often and do not make huge changes in values. Another important warning is not to set the value of CPU_COUNT below 2, as this could prevent foreground processes from running in certain cases.

Instance Caging Usage and Results

If you have read through this chapter, you have seen we have enabled instance caging by setting CPU_COUNT to 2 and setting the DEFAULT_PLAN resource manager plan at "Configuring Instance Caging." In order to show what that means, we use a small script called burn_cpu.sql, which looks like this:

```
declare
  run boolean := true;
begin
  while run loop
    execute immediate 'select sqrt( 9999999999 ) from dual';
  end loop;
end;
/
```

If we start two normal user (which means non-SYS) sessions and let them run for a while, we can see the resource consumption and resource manager throttling using the V$RSRCMGRMETRIC view. This view is special in the sense that it shows statistics of the past one minute. After the view's contents have been refreshed, it waits for one minute, in which the view's contents do not change, and then changes with the latest minute's measurements:

```
SYS@v12102 AS SYSDBA> select consumer_group_name,
  2  cpu_consumed_time/(intsize_csec*10) "CPU_USED",
  3  cpu_wait_time/(intsize_csec*10) "CPU_WAIT"
  4  from v$rsrcmgrmetric;
```

```
CONSUMER_GROUP_NAME                CPU_USED   CPU_WAIT
------------------------------ ---------- ----------
ORA$AUTOTASK                   .000166528          0
OTHER_GROUPS                   1.91517069 .000066611
SYS_GROUP                      .000099917          0
_ORACLE_BACKGROUND_GROUP_               0          0
```

What we see is the "normal user" sessions execute in the OTHER_GROUPS consumer group and nearly use 2 CPUs,. A tiny bit of throttling is going on, which is visible in the CPU_WAIT column. The throttling happened because there was a small amount of CPU usage for the ORA$AUTOTASK and SYS_GROUPS.

What is interesting is to see what happens if we add another session executing burn_cpu.sql:

```
SYS@v12102 AS SYSDBA> select consumer_group_name,
  2  cpu_consumed_time/(intsize_csec*10) "CPU_USED",
  3  cpu_wait_time/(intsize_csec*10) "CPU_WAIT"
  4  from v$rsrcmgrmetric;

CONSUMER_GROUP_NAME                CPU_USED   CPU_WAIT
------------------------------ ---------- ----------
ORA$AUTOTASK                   .000133289          0
OTHER_GROUPS                   1.84096968 1.04265245
SYS_GROUP                      .000166611          0
_ORACLE_BACKGROUND_GROUP_               0          0
```

What we see is CPU_USED stayed a little below 2, adding a session resulted in an increase in the CPU_WAIT metric. At this point, it is important to point out that using instance caging sessions are throttled on CPU in a round-robin fashion rather than specific processes being suspended for long periods of time This is very well visible with the Linux "top" utility, which, in this case, will show a CPU percentage of the processes running the burn_cpu.sql script at around 66% (66 x 3 = 198%, so almost 200%, which is the value of CPU_COUNT).

Instance Caging and Multitenancy

When using instance caging with pluggable databases, it can only be applied on the CDB level. This sets a limitation on the total number of active processes of the CDB and all of its PDBs. Further CPU management must be done using resource manager plans.

Over-Provisioning

Over-provisioning in the area of instance caging refers to the practice of allocating more CPU resources to the databases (the sum of CPU_COUNT of all the instances on the server) than are actually available in the server. This is useful when your server hosts multiple databases with complementing peak workload schedules. For example, if one database needs a lot of CPU resources serving OLTP-like transactions during the day but is mostly idle during the night, while another database is doing data-warehouse-like transactions in the night, which requires a lot of CPU resources, but is mostly idle during day, it is the safest, but not the best-performing option, to limit both at 50% of the CPUs available. Rather, you would like to set both to, for example, 75% of the CPUs available. This introduces a risk that both databases still need to compete for CPU resources if both databases need a lot of CPU resources at the same time, despite the prognosed different peak CPU-resource usage time (75 + 75 = 150%, alias an oversubscription of 50%) but has the advantage of using a number of CPUs that otherwise would not have been available. This means that over-provisioning, like all things in life, is a trade-off.

Binding Instances to Specific CPUs Using Cgroups

The Linux "cgroups" or "control groups" feature, which provides a way to limit, account for, and isolate resource usage, was introduced with kernel version 2.6.24 and is available starting from Oracle Linux 5 with the Unbreakable Enterprise Kernel (UEK) version 2 or Oracle Linux 6 and higher. With version 12c of the Oracle database and with Oracle version 11.2.0.4, the database integrates with the cgroups feature with the `PROCESSOR_GROUP_NAME` parameter.

The cgroups feature gives you the opportunity to isolate part of the resources, specifically CPUs or specific NUMA nodes in case of the Oracle database, by assigning them to specific cgroups. One use case is to have different consolidation densities for different groups of databases by binding these groups of databases to specific CPUs. Please note that the two socket Exadata compute nodes, which are the "dash two" servers, such as X5-2, X4-2, and so on, are NUMA systems, but have NUMA turned off (numa=off) in the kernel load line in grub (`/etc/grub.conf`). This means cgroups can only be used to isolate to specific CPUs. The eight-socket Exadata compute nodes, as you might have guessed are the "dash eight" servers, have NUMA turned on, which means both isolation based on NUMA nodes and CPUs can be done.

The easiest way to use cgroups with the Oracle database is to use the script that is available in My Oracle Support note: "Using `PROCESSOR_GROUP_NAME` to bind a database instance to CPUs or NUMA nodes on Linux" (Doc ID 1585184.1).

Installation and Configuration of Cgroups

Once the script has been downloaded, the most logical place is to put it in the home directory of the root user. Any action done by the script needs to be done as root. First thing to do is look at our system:

```
# ./setup_processor_group.sh -show
This is a NUMA system.

NUMA configuration:
-------------------
Node 0
  CPUs: 0-15
  Memory Total: 75488296 kB Free: 13535460 kB

This system does not have any processor group.
```

The script is run on an Exadata V2 machine, which is the reason 75GB of memory is shown. It says it is a NUMA system and then displays one node. The reason only one node (node 0) is shown is because the Exadata dual socket compute nodes have NUMA turned off at the kernel load line (see the "kernel" line or lines in `/etc/grub.conf`, which lists the "numa=off" setting).

In order to use cgroups via the `setup_processor_group.sh` script, the system needs to be "prepared" using the script. This needs to be done only once. This is how the preparation looks like:

```
# ./setup_processor_group.sh -prepare

SUCCESS: -prepare complete
Next step: create a new proc group using option -create
```

Once this has been run, verify the preparation by running setup_processor_group.sh with the -check switch:

```
# ./setup_processor_group.sh -check

setup_processor_group.sh -prepare has been run on this system
```

The preparation modifies /etc/rc.local, and it adds the script /etc/ora_autopg. The script /etc/ora_autog mounts the cgroup pseudo filesystem at /mnt/cgroup and runs the setup_processor_group.sh script, which has been copied to /etc, together with the cgroup settings in the file /etc/auto_orapg.conf.

Now that the host is prepared, the next step is to learn how the CPU topology looks on the node. Use this script to learn what your system looks like: cpu_topo.sh.

```
echo "== summary =="
CPUINFO="/proc/cpuinfo" || CPUINFO=$1
awk -F: '/^physical/ && !ID[$2] { P++; ID[$2]=1 }; /^cpu cores/ { CORES=$2 };  /^cpu cores/
{ T++ }; END { print "sockets: "P"\ntot cores: "CORES*P"\ntot threads: "T }' $CPUINFO
echo "== cpu map =="
echo " T -  S -  C"
C=0
cat /proc/cpuinfo | egrep "processor|physical id|core id" | awk '{ print $(NF) }' | while
read V; do
        [ $C -lt 2 ] && printf "%2d - " $V || printf "%2d\n" $V
        [ $C -lt 2 ] && let ++C || C=0
done
```

This is how the output looks on my test system:

```
# ./cpu_topo.sh
== summary ==
sockets: 2
tot cores: 8
tot threads: 16
== cpu map ==
 T -  S -  C
 0 -  0 -  0
 1 -  0 -  1
 2 -  0 -  2
 3 -  0 -  3
 4 -  1 -  0
 5 -  1 -  1
 6 -  1 -  2
 7 -  1 -  3
 8 -  0 -  0
 9 -  0 -  1
10 -  0 -  2
11 -  0 -  3
12 -  1 -  0
13 -  1 -  1
14 -  1 -  2
15 -  1 -  3
```

This shows that my system has two sockets (S column, socket 0 and 1) and every socket four cores (C column, numbers 0 to 3). The thread number (T column) is the CPU number of the operating system. This means that the operating system visible CPUs on this system are actually (hyper-)threads. If you look carefully, you will see that threads number 0 and 8 are connected to the same core (both have S and C 0). In order to fully isolate workloads, it is very important to separate different cgroups based on cores. The separation is important because a CPU thread should be seen as an execution context only and requires a core to execute. This means that if one CPU thread is using the core it is connected to, the other thread has to wait for the core to become available to execute. When both threads want to execute, only one of them truly is—the other one waits. Because this waiting is an in-CPU event, it is not visible for the operating system and shows up as running on CPU. In other words, it is not visible.

Let's create a cgroup called "singlecore" and bind the group to the processor number 0 and 8, so it is bound to one core:

```
# ./setup_processor_group.sh -create -name singlecore -cpus 0,8 -u:g oracle:dba
SUCCESS: -create complete for processor group singlecore

To start an Oracle instance in this processor group,
 set the database initialization parameter:
PROCESSOR_GROUP_NAME=singlecore
```

Please note the `-u:g` switch. It is meant to set the user and the group of the Oracle executable as configured on your system. To see how it is configured, list the user and group of the of the oracle executable in `$ORACLE_HOME/bin`.

As the output of `-create` mentions, the next and last step is to set the database parameter `PROCESSOR_GROUP_NAME` in order to make the instance obey the cgroup settings it is configured for. If an instance is started with `PROCESSOR_GROUP_NAME` set for a control group, the `alert.log` file will show something like this:

```
Instance has been started in processor group singlecore (NUMA Nodes: 0 CPUs: 0,8)
```

When using cgroups and the `PROCESSOR_GROUP_NAME` database parameter with the multitenant option, the `PROCESSOR_GROUP_NAME` parameter must be set at the CDB level. Pluggable databases will inherit the cgroup properties and obey them.

Oracle 12c THREADED_EXECUTION

Oracle 12c introduced a new initialization parameter, `THREADED_EXECUTION`. This parameter, when set to `TRUE`, will make the Oracle executable run certain database processes as threads inside a process. By combining multiple database processes as threads inside an operating system process, the number of processes on the operating system level is reduced. Please note that when `THREADED_EXECUTION` is enabled, some background processes are running as a thread; however, user processes created through the listener will still be processes unless the listener parameter `DEDICATED_THROUGH_BROKER_<listener name>` is set to `ON`. Some of the critical background processes, like `PMON, DBWn, VKTM, and PSP`, still will use a dedicated process, regardless of `THREADED_EXECUTION` having been set to `TRUE`.

We have not thoroughly tested the threaded execution model. The tests we have done show both the default process model and the threaded model being in the same league with regards to performance. Both models can come out on top with the tests we performed.

There definitely is a conceptual difference between processes, being stand-alone and having their own address space, and threads sharing the address space of the process that created them. However, modern operating systems like Linux try very hard try to reduce the amount of work they need to do whenever possible. One of these optimizations is that on process creation, the address space of the new process almost entirely is shared with its parent, via pointers. Only when the new process starts writing to memory pages, new pages are allocated in a copy-on-write fashion. As such, there is no significant additional overhead in allocating memory for a process when compared with threads.

As with a lot of technical functions, it is best to choose what the majority of the users choose in order to have the most stable and most tested execution path in the Oracle kernel code. Limited tests have shown there is no significant gain in performance. These are reasons that the current advice is to use the regular process model and leave THREADED_EXECUTION at its default value, FALSE.

Managing PGA Memory

Oracle database version 12c introduced the parameter PGA_AGGREGATE_LIMIT. The purpose of this parameter seems very obvious, limiting the overall Process Global Area (PGA) memory usage of the database instance. Of course, Oracle's automatic PGA feature needs to be used before PGA_AGGREGATE_LIMIT can be used, which means the PGA_AGGREGATE_TARGET parameter needs to be set to a non-zero value. The function of the PGA_AGGREGATE_TARGET parameter is to set the desired amount of memory you want the instance's total PGA memory to take. Please note the descriptions in this paragraph are about dedicated database processes, not Shared Server/Multi-Threaded Server processes.

It is important to understand that by setting the PGA_AGGREGATE_TARGET parameter, there is no guarantee the instance will not take more memory for PGA allocations, hence the name PGA_AGGREGATE_TARGET. In essence, PGA_AGGREGATE_TARGET limits and divides work-area allocations of active processes in order to try to make overall PGA memory usage lower than the size set with PGA_AGGREGATE_TARGET. Work-area allocations are sort, hash, and bitmap memory needed during execution. Of course, there is no limit to how much a process can sort or to the size of the hash table when doing a hash join. When the amount of memory needed exceeds the work-area size, the contents are moved to the session's temporary tablespace and processing continues.

So, if PGA_AGGREGATE_TARGET works by sizing the process sort, hash ,and bitmap area, then what can cause the instance to use more memory than is set with PGA_AGGREGATE_TARGET? The following points are the ones we encountered; there could be more reasons:

- The PGA_AGGREGATE_TARGET parameter cannot just be set to a value and be respected by all sessions in the instance. Every session that is started needs a minimum memory footprint to be able to run. This means that setting the PGA target too small with respect to the number of used sessions means the instance will allocate more than is set.
- PL/SQL variables like arrays and collections can be used and extended without any restriction by any individual session. Any of these sessions can use up to 4GB with Oracle 11.2 and 32GB with Oracle 12.1 (this is specific to Linux x86-64, which commonly is used on the Exadata platform), provided the operating system limits allow this and there is enough virtual memory to accommodate this. Please note *virtual* memory—the physical memory can be exhausted way before the virtual memory is, which means the operating system needs to satisfy the memory allocations by swapping current memory contents to the swap device.
- Every cursor in a session that uses sort, hash, or bitmap memory has a minimal memory footprint, too. If a lot of cursors are allocated in the sessions that use any of these memory areas, there is a certain amount of memory that will be allocated, regardless of PGA_AGGREGATE_TARGET.

Now let's take a step back. In most cases, especially when the application allocates sessions via a connection pool, the amount of connections is static and little or no PL/SQL variables are used. This means the PGA of an instance will take the memory needed and remains at that amount for its entire duration. As a result, the actual PGA memory usage can be way lower than is actually set with PGA_AGGREGATE_TARGET, around the set value or higher, totally depending on the application's type of request, the number of cursors, and the number of connections in the database. It can be way more because, as we just described, database processes will take what is needed, regardless of what is set. It is a good practice to periodically measure the actual PGA usage in V$PGASTAT by looking at the "maximum PGA allocated" statistic after a period of normal usage to see if there is a strong difference between the high-water mark of what is actually used and what is set with PGA_AGGREGATE_TARGET.

However, sometimes the PGA usage is not that static. This can lead to problems if the memory on your system is carefully divided between the operating system, Clusterware, ASM, and database instance(s) because excessive PGA allocation means more memory is requested than is accounted for. Memory used cannot be held in main memory, and the operating system needs to resort to swapping memory contents to disk. Whenever this happens, a strong drop in performance is noticeable.

Situations as the ones described above are what the PGA_AGGREGATE_LIMIT parameter is created for. It will try to limit PGA memory allocations by terminating the current execution of a session that is doing allocations for untunable PGA once too much memory is found to be allocated to the PGA in the instance. Such a termination results in an "ORA-04036: PGA memory used by the instance exceeds PGA_AGGREGATE_LIMIT" in the session. Please note background processes and SYS connections are exempted from the limit. Parallel query processes are not considered background processes for this feature, so they could also be terminated, which is done for the entire set of parallel query processes used for a given execution.

However, testing shows that in version 12.1.0.2, PGA_AGGREGATE_LIMIT is far from a hard limit. During our research, we found that when PGA allocation exceeds PGA_AGGREGATE_LIMIT, the memory management code starts sampling sessions that are candidates for termination for 4 to 20 times before it truly terminates one or more executions to comply with PGA_AGGREGATE_LIMIT. This has the advantage that short-lived peaks of high memory usage will not immediately result in termination of execution, but it has the disadvantage that actual memory usage can go way beyond PGA_AGGREGATE_LIMIT, depending on how fast allocations are done.

The following code example allocates memory to an associative array. Because we know it will hit an ORA-4036, the exception handler prints the error code and start PGA and last PGA measurement, together with the values set for PGA_AGGREGATE_TARGET and PGA_AGGREGATE_LIMIT, in order to investigate process memory allocations:

```
pga_filler.sql:

declare
  type vc2_ar is table of varchar2(32767) index by pls_integer;
  vc vc2_ar;
  v varchar2(32767);
  target number;
  start_pga number;
  current_pga number;
  agg_target number;
  agg_limit number;
  counter number := 0;
begin
  select value into agg_target from v$parameter where name = 'pga_aggregate_target';
  select value into agg_limit from v$parameter where name = 'pga_aggregate_limit';
  select value into start_pga from v$mystat m, v$statname n where m.statistic#=n.statistic#
and name = 'session pga memory';
  for idx in 1 .. 30000000 loop
    v := rpad('x',32767,'x');
    vc(idx) := v;
    counter := counter + 1;
    if counter = 300 then
      select value into current_pga from v$mystat m, v$statname n where
        m.statistic#=n.statistic# and name = 'session pga memory';
      counter := 0;
    end if;
  end loop;
```

```
exception when others then
  dbms_output.put_line('error message :'||SQLERRM);
  dbms_output.put_line('start pga     :'||start_pga);
  dbms_output.put_line('last pga      :'||current_pga);
  dbms_output.put_line('pga agg target:'||agg_target);
  dbms_output.put_line('pga agg limit :'||agg_limit);
end;
/
```

Please do *not* to test this with the SYS user because SYS sessions will not be throttled. If the SYS user is used, the above code will either complete or give an ORA-4030 (out of process memory when trying to allocate %s bytes (%s,%s) message when 4G (oracle 11.2) or 32G (Oracle 12.1) of PGA memory has been allocated, or an operating system limit has been hit.

```
TS@v12102 > @pga_filler
error message :ORA-04036: PGA memory used by the instance exceeds PGA_AGGREGATE_LIMIT
start pga     :3338760
last pga      :807924232
pga agg target:524288000
pga agg limit :629145600

PL/SQL procedure successfully completed.
```

This example is the output of the execution of the `pga_filler.sql` script. This execution shows we had `PGA_AGGREGATE_TARGET` set to 524288000 (500M), and `PGA_AGGREGATE_LIMIT` set to 629145600 (600M). When the PL/SQL procedure began executing, the PGA had a size of 3338760 (a little more than 3M). The PL/SQL block did encounter an ORA-4036, at which time the PGA had grown to 807924232 (770M). This clearly shows the limit as set by `PGA_AGGREGATE_LIMIT` is rather a starting point for the consideration for termination rather than a hard limit.

This means that if you have the explicit need for limiting PGA memory allocations, you should set it lower than your actual needed limit for PGA memory. The most important thing is it should be very thoroughly tested in general and especially for situations where the PGA limit actually gets reached and is used to prevent your server from starting to swap, leading to a performance death spiral.

For versions prior to Oracle version 12c, Oracle introduced an (undocumented) event in a whitepaper on consolidation on Exadata to limit PGA allocations per process. This is not exactly the same as `PGA_AGGREGATE_LIMIT`, which works on the instance level. This event is event 10261, and it controls the amount of PGA a single process is allowed to allocate, including SYS connections. An ORA-600 is signaled if the amount of allocated memory exceeds the amount set as level for this event up to Oracle version 11.2.0.3 and an ORA-10260 is signaled with Oracle version 11.2.0.4. Please note this event is not a hard limit too; testing showed it could take up to approximately 100MB more than set. This is the way this event is set:

```
alter system set events = '10261 trace name context forever, level <PGA LIMIT IN BYTES>';
```

Because this is an undocumented event, this should only be a last-resort solution. If you truly need to use this way of PGA memory limiting, you should ask Oracle support for blessing and guidance specific to your case.

Database Resource Manager

Database Resource Manager (DBRM) has been around since Oracle 8i (1999) and is basically geared toward managing CPU resources at the database tier. Exadata V2 introduced a new feature called I/O Resource Manager (IORM), which, as you might expect, is geared toward managing and prioritizing I/O at the storage cell layer. When databases on Exadata request I/O from the storage cells, they send additional information along with the request that identifies the database making the request as well as the consumer group making the request. The software on the storage cells (Cellserv or `cellsrv`) knows about the consumer group priorities inside the database (DBRM) and/or at the storage cell (IORM), and it manages how I/O is scheduled. DBRM and IORM are tightly knit together, so it is important to have a solid understanding of DBRM before IORM is going to make any sense to you. Now, the Database Resource Manager is a lengthy topic and could easily justify a book all by itself. Thus, we will focus on the basic constructs that we will need to develop an effective IORM Resource Plan. If you already have experience with DBRM, you may be able to skip over this topic.

With the (Oracle 12c) multitenancy option, the database resource manager has gotten an additional layer. As described above, the traditional database resource manager manages resources within the database; however, with the multitenancy option, you essentially got "databases within a database." In order to manage resources between (pluggable) databases in the root/container database, there needs to be resource management at the root database level, which is called a CDB (container database) resource plan, and additionally resource management inside the pluggable databases, which is almost exactly the same as with a traditional non-container database, as described above.

Before we begin, let's review the terminology that will be used in this topic. Table 7-1 describes the various components of database resource manager. We will discuss these in more detail as we go along.

Table 7-1. *Resource manager component descriptions*

Name	Description
Resource consumer group Consumer group	These are the various names by which you may see resource consumer groups referred. Resource Manager allocates resources to consumer groups, rather than user sessions. A consumer group is a set of database sessions that may be grouped together based on their priority and/or resource requirements.
Resource plan directive Plan directive Directive	These are the names by which you may see resource plan directives referred. Resource allocations are not assigned directly to consumer groups. They are defined in a resource plan directive. A consumer group is then assigned to the plan directive so that resource allocations may be enforced. In the case of a CDB plan, the resource allocations are assigned to a pluggable database.
Resource plan Plan	Resource plans are sometimes referred to simply as "plans" or "the plan." Plan directives are grouped together to create a resource plan, thus defining the overarching allocation of resources to all sessions within the database. In the case of the multitenancy option, there can be CDB plans to manage resources between pluggable databases and regular plans, which act inside the pluggable database.

As shown in Table 7-2, depending on whether you use DBRM in non-CDBs or CDBs, DBRM consists of:

Table 7-2. *Resource manager component components based on tenancy*

Option	Resource manager components
Non multitenant	Plan ➤ Directive ➤ Consumer group
Multitenant	CDB: Plan ➤ Directive ➤ Pluggable database PDB: Plan ➤ Directive ➤ Consumer group

Creating a CDB Resource Plan

Support for multitenancy on the storage cell level has been introduced with cell version 12.1.1.1.0. If you have created a container database and want to do resource management, you must create A CDB resource plan first, what is what we are going to do now. Please note a CDB resource plan is required for doing resource management inside a pluggable database. If you created a regular/non-multitenant database or you are looking for a PDB resource plan, you might want to skip this part and go to the section Creating a (Pluggable) Database Resource Plan.

The next example creates a CDB resource plan, `cdb_plan`, for an imaginary container database with three pluggable databases: `database1`, `database2`, and `database3`:

```
begin
 DBMS_RESOURCE_MANAGER.CLEAR_PENDING_AREA;
 DBMS_RESOURCE_MANAGER.CREATE_PENDING_AREA;
 DBMS_RESOURCE_MANAGER.CREATE_CDB_PLAN(plan=>'cdb_plan');
 DBMS_RESOURCE_MANAGER.CREATE_CDB_PLAN_DIRECTIVE(
  plan=>'cdb_plan',
  pluggable_database=>'database1',
  shares=>4,
  utilization_limit=>null,
  parallel_server_limit=>null);
 DBMS_RESOURCE_MANAGER.CREATE_CDB_PLAN_DIRECTIVE(
  plan=>'cdb_plan',
  pluggable_database=>'database2',
  shares=>1,
  utilization_limit=>10,
  parallel_server_limit=>0);
DBMS_RESOURCE_MANAGER.CREATE_CDB_PLAN_DIRECTIVE(
  plan=>'cdb_plan',
  pluggable_database=>'database3',
  shares=>1,
  utilization_limit=>null,
  parallel_server_limit=>10);
end;
/

PL/SQL procedure successfully completed.
```

This plan requires some explanation. As you will see with (pluggable) database resource plans later on, CDB plans tend to be much simpler than database resource plans. A CDB plan simply is a plan in the root of the CDB with directives for PDBs. For every pluggable database, you can assign a number of shares, which sets the priority for a pluggable database. In this case, we got 4+1+1=6 shares; `database1` having four shares means it gets 4/6*100=66% of the CPU resources if all the pluggable databases need to contend for it. The parameter `utilization_limit` is a percentage and specifies a percentage of the total CPU capacity available a pluggable database is allowed to use. `utilization_limit` is not cumulative for the PDBs—you can give any PDB 100 (percent), which is the same as null: no limit. You can use `parallel_server_limit` to set a percentage of the number of parallel execution servers as set by the `PARALLEL_SERVERS_TARGET` parameter.

You might wonder what happens if a DBA creates a pluggable database that is not specified: Is it free to use any resource until it is specified in the CDB plan? The answer is no: If a CDB plan is enabled, a pluggable database that is not specified in a CDB plan is subject to the default directive settings. The default directive settings are: 1 share, 100(%) `utilization_limit`, and 100(%) `parallel_server_limit`. You can change the default directive settings with the `DBMS_RESOURCE_MANAGER.UPDATE_CDB_DEFAULT_DIRECTIVE()` procedure.

The plan `cdb_plan` now is created. The next step is to validate the plan and, if that completes without warnings, submit the plan:

```
begin
 DBMS_RESOURCE_MANAGER.VALIDATE_PENDING_AREA();
end;
/

PL/SQL procedure successfully completed.

begin
 DBMS_RESOURCE_MANAGER.SUBMIT_PENDING_AREA();
end;
/

PL/SQL procedure successfully completed.
```

Now the CDB plan is submitted, it is added to the data dictionary, and it can be enabled by setting the `RESOURCE_MANAGER_PLAN` parameter. A CDB plan can only be enabled in the root database of a container database. This is how a resource manager plan is enabled:

```
SQL> alter system set resource_manager_plan=cdb_plan sid='*';

System altered.
```

If this plan causes problems with the databases running in the container, another `alter system set resource_manager_plan` can be issued to revert to the old resource manager plan, or, if there was no old resource manager plan, to '' (single quote, single quote) to reset the resource manager plan.

Another caveat is the automatic maintenance jobs in the Oracle database. The automatic maintenance jobs, which are enabled by default after installation, sets the `DEFAULT_MAINTENANCE_PLAN` resource manager plan during the maintenance windows. If you rely on your own resource manager plan for meeting service levels, you can change or disable the maintenance windows or force the setting of your own resource manager plan, which is done by prefixing `FORCE:` in front of your resource manager plan when setting it with `alter system`.

If you want more information on CDB plans, the current version of Oracle 12 contains the following DBA views, accessible from the CDB root:

- `DBA_CDB_RSRC_PLANS`
- `DBA_CDB_RSRC_PLAN_DIRECTIVES`

Creating a (Pluggable) Database Resource Plan

Whether you have a pluggable database and set a CDB resource management plan and now want to manage the resources inside the individual pluggable database, or you choose not to use the multitenancy option and just want to manage resources in the database, this section will help you create a database resource management plan. When using the multitenancy option, please note that in order to set a resource manager in the pluggable database, there needs to be a CDB resource manager active already.

The following creates a database resource plan, DAYTIME_PLAN, which has consumer groups for online processing (OLTP), batch/long running jobs (BATCH) and maintenance (MAINTENANCE). You need to be connected as an administrative user in a PDB, not the CDB root for these commands to have an effect:

```
begin

 DBMS_RESOURCE_MANAGER.CLEAR_PENDING_AREA;
 DBMS_RESOURCE_MANAGER.CREATE_PENDING_AREA;

 DBMS_RESOURCE_MANAGER.CREATE_PLAN(
  plan     =>'DAYTIME_PLAN',
  mgmt_mth=>'RATIO');

 DBMS_RESOURCE_MANAGER.CREATE_CONSUMER_GROUP(
  consumer_group    => 'MAINTENANCE');
 DBMS_RESOURCE_MANAGER.CREATE_CONSUMER_GROUP(
  consumer_group    => 'OLTP');
 DBMS_RESOURCE_MANAGER.CREATE_CONSUMER_GROUP(
  consumer_group    => 'BATCH');

 DBMS_RESOURCE_MANAGER.CREATE_PLAN_DIRECTIVE(
  plan             =>'DAYTIME_PLAN',
  mgmt_p1          =>20,
  group_or_subplan=>'SYS_GROUP');
 DBMS_RESOURCE_MANAGER.CREATE_PLAN_DIRECTIVE(
  plan             =>'DAYTIME_PLAN_PLAN',
  mgmt_p1          =>10,
  group_or_subplan=>'MAINTENANCE');
 DBMS_RESOURCE_MANAGER.CREATE_PLAN_DIRECTIVE(
  plan             =>'DAYTIME_PLAN',
  mgmt_p1          =>5,
  group_or_subplan=>'OLTP');
 DBMS_RESOURCE_MANAGER.CREATE_PLAN_DIRECTIVE(
  plan             =>'DAYTIME_PLAN',
  mgmt_p1          =>3,
  group_or_subplan=>'BATCH');
 DBMS_RESOURCE_MANAGER.CREATE_PLAN_DIRECTIVE(
  plan             =>'DAYTIME_PLAN',
  mgmt_p1          =>1,
  group_or_subplan=>'OTHER_GROUPS');

 DBMS_RESOURCE_MANAGER.SET_CONSUMER_GROUP_MAPPING(
  attribute        => DBMS_RESOURCE_MANAGER.ORACLE_USER,
  value            => 'APP_ADMIN',
```

```
  consumer_group => 'MAINTENANCE');
 DBMS_RESOURCE_MANAGER.SET_CONSUMER_GROUP_MAPPING(
  attribute      => DBMS_RESOURCE_MANAGER.SERVICE_NAME,
  value          => 'OLTP',
  consumer_group => 'OLTP');
 DBMS_RESOURCE_MANAGER.SET_CONSUMER_GROUP_MAPPING(
  attribute      => DBMS_RESOURCE_MANAGER.SERVICE_NAME,
  value          => 'BATCH',
  consumer_group => 'BATCH');

end;
/

PL/SQL procedure successfully completed.
```

The resource manager plan is now created in the pending area. This is a simple plan, aimed to give you an idea on how to do it. If you choose to use the database resource manager in your database or a pluggable database, this is a good starting point. Let's go through the plan in the fashion that has been described earlier: plan, directives, and consumer groups.

The above plan is called DAYTIME_PLAN. In the plan properties, MGMT_MTH (resource allocation method) has been set from EMPHASIS (the default, which lets you use percentages at different levels) to RATIO, which lets you use single-level plans only by setting MGMT_P1 to the share it is supposed to get. By using ratio/shares-based plans, you do not have to use the emphasis/percentage-based plans, which can be hard to understand and troubleshoot. With PDB resource plans, you cannot use multi-level plans anyway.

After the creation of the plan, there are a few statements to define the consumer groups. In order to map groups of connections to the resource manager consumer group, the group first needs to exist, which is what the DBMS_RESOURCE_MANAGER.CREATE_CONSUMER_GROUP procedure does.

There are five directives in the DAYTIME_PLAN:

- The first directive is for the SYS_GROUP, aimed at prioritizing the SYS and SYSTEM users with the most resources.
- The next directive is for the MAINTENANCE group, meant to be used when doing application maintenance, which should get priority over the normal usage.
- The next directive is for the OLTP group, which is the first directive for normal usage.
- Next is the directive for the BATCH group, which should have lower priority than the OLTP group.
- The last the directive is for OTHER_GROUPS, which should give any other users the lowest priority.

If you look at the priorities, you see how the ratio/shares method is easy to read and understand:

SYS_GROUP	20	51%	(20/39*100)
MAINTENANCE	10	26%	(10/39*100)
OLTP	5	13%	(5/39*100)
BATCH	3	8%	(3/39*100)
OTHER_GROUPS	1	3%	(1/39*100)
	(39)		

A few additional remarks: If you have the need to add directives, there is no need to change anything in the other directives when using the RATIO method. You can simple add the new directive with the appropriate ratio/amount of shares set in MGMT_P1. Of course, this will change the calculation; adding the amount of shares will lower the percentages. A very important point is that the distribution of CPU as indicated with the ratio is done based on the consumer groups the current ACTIVE sessions are dedicated to. This means that if there are only active sessions in the OLTP and BATCH groups, the CPU resources will be divided based on their mutual share: 5/(5+3)*100=62.5% for the OLTP group and 3/(5+3)*100=37.5% for the BATCH group. The ratio sets the resource division; it does not keep resource groups from using CPU resource.

The last part consists of mapping rules. The mapping rules in this plan are very simple, but show the two most common ways database connections are grouped in the situations we have encountered. The first rule maps a certain database user to a group. The next two mapping rules map database connections to two groups based on the service they used to connect to the database. Services can be created using `srvctl add service ...` command line utility, which will add a "service" type cluster resource. Services can also be used to point specific use of a database to one or more instances, and they can be defined to fail over if the current instance is down.

When a non-SYS session enters the database, it belongs to the OTHER_GROUPS consumer group by default. The resource manager plan automates switching sessions to a specific consumer group and manages resources. However, sessions are not allowed to switch to any consumer group—they need to be explicitly granted to a consumer group before the resource manager plan can switch them to it. This is done with the DBMS_RESOURCE_MANAGER_PRIVS.GRANT_SWITCH_CONSUMER_GROUP procedure:

```
begin
 DBMS_RESOURCE_MANAGER_PRIVS.GRANT_SWITCH_CONSUMER_GROUP(
  grantee_name => 'APP_ADMIN',
  consumer_group => 'MAINTENANCE'
 );
 DBMS_RESOURCE_MANAGER_PRIVS.GRANT_SWITCH_CONSUMER_GROUP(
  grantee_name => 'APP_USER',
  consumer_group => 'OLTP
 );
 DBMS_RESOURCE_MANAGER_PRIVS.GRANT_SWITCH_CONSUMER_GROUP(
  grantee_name => 'APP_BATCH',
  consumer_group => 'BATCH'
 );
end;
/
```

In our example, we have an APP_ADMIN user for doing maintenance to the application schema who is granted the consumer group MAINTENANCE. The application user is APP_USER and is granted the OLTP consumer group. In the same fashion, the APP_BATCH user is granted the BATCH consumer group.

It is good practice to leave the OTHER_GROUPS (the default consumer group) out of being priorized. By priorizing specific consumer groups and granting access to the consumer groups to database users based on specific rules, any session that connects to the database outside of the rules explicitly set will automatically be left in the OTHER_GROUPS consumer group and not be priorized.

Now that we have an understanding of the resource plan, let's validate and submit it to the data dictionary:

```
begin
 DBMS_RESOURCE_MANAGER.VALIDATE_PENDING_AREA();
end;
/
```

```
PL/SQL procedure successfully completed.

begin
 DBMS_RESOURCE_MANAGER.SUBMIT_PENDING_AREA();
end;
/

PL/SQL procedure successfully completed.
```

You could set the parameter RESOURCE_MANAGER_PLAN (either in a normal database or in a PDB) to enforce the resource manager plan. However, in a lot of cases, the resource need and priorities of a database are different at different times, such as online clients having priority during the day, and batches and reports having priority during the evening and night. The next section shows how to let the database switch a resource manager plan using scheduler windows.

Using the Scheduler to Change the Resource Plan

Nearly every database has time frames in which the database is used in a totally differently way. For a lot of databases, it is common to have online users requesting information in an OLTP-like fashion during daytime, and have batch jobs for moving data in and out in the evening or night. During daytime, the online users should have the priority, and other usage like reporting and batch usage should have lower priority. However, during the evening the batches and reporting should have the highest priority. It is common that batches deliver other databases/applications with daytime transactions.

If we take the DAYTIME_PLAN, we can create a NIGHTTIME_PLAN simply by modifying the name of the plan, and change the MGMT_P1 share of the OLTP directive to 1, and change the share of the BATCH directive to 5. This way the SYS_GROUP and MAINTENANCE directives still have priority over normal usage, but now any OLTP request will have significant lower priority than the BATCH requests in this plan.

In order to change the active resource manager plan, scheduler windows can be used. The next example will make the database automatically change the resource plan based on time during the week:

```
begin
 DBMS_SCHEDULER.CREATE_WINDOW(
  window_name     => 'WEEKDAY_WINDOW',
  resource_plan   => 'DAYTIME_PLAN',
  start_date      => systimestamp at time zone 'EUROPE/AMSTERDAM',
  duration        => numtodsinterval(660, 'minute'),
  repeat_interval => 'FREQ=WEEKLY;BYDAY=MON,TUE,WED,THU,FRI;BYHOUR=7;BYMINUTE=0;BYSECOND=0',
  end_date        => null);
 DBMS_SCHEDULER.ENABLE('"SYS"."WEEKDAY_WINDOW"');
 DBMS_SCHEDULER.CREATE_WINDOW(
  window_name     => 'WEEKNIGHT_WINDOW',
  resource_plan   => 'NIGHTTIME_PLAN',
  start_date      => systimestamp at time zone 'EUROPE/AMSTERDAM',
  duration        => numtodsinterval(780, 'minute'),
  repeat_interval => 'FREQ=WEEKLY;BYDAY=MON,TUE,WED,THU,FRI;BYHOUR=18;BYMINUTE=0;BYSECOND=0',
  end_date        => null);
 DBMS_SCHEDULER.ENABLE('"SYS"."WEEKNIGHT_WINDOW"');
end;
/

PL/SQL procedure successfully completed.
```

The procedure creates two windows, WEEKDAY_WINDOW and WEEKNIGHT_WINDOW. The parameter resource_plan binds a resource plan to the window. The weekday window starts at 7 a.m.; the weeknight window starts at 18:00 (6 p.m.).

The Wait Event: resmgr: cpu quantum

The throttling by the resource manager of CPU consumption of a process will be visible by the wait event `resmgr: cpu quantum`. The throttling only happens when the database resource manager is enabled. A resource manager plan in either a regular database or a pluggable database is active because of:

- Instance caging
- A user-defined resource management plan
- The automatic maintenance jobs window turned active

■ **Tip** Without a resource manager plan, there is no way for the database to throttle CPU consumption, and thus for the wait event `resmgr: cpu quantum` to show up.

The database resource manager keeps track of database processes running and willing to run. As long as all processes can get a full time slice on the CPU, there is no need to throttle (outside of resource manager consumer groups bound to a directive with UTILIZATION_LIMIT, which we will discuss later). However, once the amount of running processes and willing to run processes exceeds the amount of CPUs visible (or number of CPUs allowed to use in the case of instance caging), the resource manager investigates the consumption groups of the running and willing to run processes and throttles the execution of the processes according to the distribution of the resources configured in the directives. The throttling is visible in the wait interface as "`resmgr: cpu quantum`." In most cases, processes in a consumer group are not throttled for extended amounts of time, but rather in a round-robin fashion among the active processes belonging to the throttled consumer group(s) for a time ("quantum") of 100ms. This means that throttled processes do not stop in most cases, but will execute slower, depending on the amount of throttling.

Where to Go from Here

As mentioned previously, the database resource manager is a topic that could easily fill a book on its own. As such, the starting point for doing database resource management has been described in the last few sections. In order to learn more on this subject and to search for specific properties, see the documentation at `http://docs.oracle.com/database/121/ADMIN/dbrm.htm`. You can also refer to Chapter 11, where you can read about the other resource manager events.

For completeness sake, this paragraph shows some specific topics on the database resource manager that have been helpful when we applied the resource manager.

Resource Mapping Priorities

You might have wondered what happens when a database user is eligible for multiple consumer groups when mapping them with the DBMS_RESOURCE_MANAGER.SET_CONSUMER_GROUP_MAPPING procedure. For example, when consumer groups are mapped like this:

```
DBMS_RESOURCE_MANAGER.SET_CONSUMER_GROUP_MAPPING(
  attribute      => DBMS_RESOURCE_MANAGER.ORACLE_USER,
  value          => 'APP_ADMIN',
  consumer_group => 'MAINTENANCE');
```

and

```
DBMS_RESOURCE_MANAGER.SET_CONSUMER_GROUP_MAPPING(
  attribute      => DBMS_RESOURCE_MANAGER.SERVICE_NAME,
  value          => 'OLTP',
  consumer_group => 'OLTP');
```

What happens when the APP_ADMIN database user logs on using the OLTP service? In that case, both the mappings apply! The answer is found in the DBA_RSRC_MAPPING_PRIORITY view, which shows which attributes are evaluated in what priority:

```
SQL> select * from dba_rsrc_mapping_priority;

ATTRIBUTE                      PRIORITY STATUS
------------------------------ ---------------
EXPLICIT                              1
SERVICE_MODULE_ACTION                 2
SERVICE_MODULE                        3
MODULE_NAME_ACTION                    4
MODULE_NAME                           5
SERVICE_NAME                          6
ORACLE_USER                           7
CLIENT_PROGRAM                        8
CLIENT_OS_USER                        9
CLIENT_MACHINE                       10
CLIENT_ID                            11

11 rows selected.
```

If the priority is not in line with your needs, you can change the priorities with the DBMS_RESOURCE_MANAGER.SET_CONSUMER_GROUP_MAPPING_PRI procedure.

Resource Limiting

The database resource plan in this chapter has the directives setup with a priority in the directive, with the intention to get a share of the CPU resources based on the set priority. Independently from the priority, the resource manager gives you the option to limit the usage of both CPU and parallel query servers.

The parameter in the directive for this is utilization_limit:

```
DBMS_RESOURCE_MANAGER.CREATE_PLAN_DIRECTIVE(
  plan              =>'DAYTIME_PLAN',
  mgmt_p1           =>3,
  utilization_limit =>10
  group_or_subplan  =>'BATCH');
```

This is one of the directives from the DAYTIME_PLAN shown earlier, but modified to include the utilization_limit directive parameter. What this does is the same as without the utilization_limit parameter, which means that it is prioritized exactly the same. However, the resource manager will limit the total CPU usage of the processes in the consumer group that uses the directive BATCH to 10%. In addition to limiting the CPU usage, it will also limit parallel query server usage with the value of this parameter as percentage of the number of parallel servers in the database parameter PARALLEL_SERVERS_TARGET. In this case, you might want to disable parallel query server usage altogether (in order not to conflict with daytime usage), in which case you could use the directive parameter parallel_server_limit and set it to zero. Setting the directive parameter parallel_server_limit overrides the value of the utilization_limit directive parameter for parallel query server usage.

Another import thing to realize when using the utilization_limit directive parameter on Exadata is that the I/O resource manager in the cell servers will take the utilization_limit directive parameter and apply the same limitation percentage, but now for limiting I/O requests from processes in the consumer group.

Other Limiting Parameters

Another resource manager option implemented as directive parameters is to set a threshold for certain conditions. Once the threshold is reached, the session will switch consumer group to the group set in the switch_group directive parameter for a number of "switch" parameters (see Table 7-3).

Table 7-3. *Resource manager directives switching parameters*

Parameter	Description
switch_io_megabytes	Specifies the amount of I/O (in MB) that a session can issue.
switch_io_reqs	Specifies the amount of I/O requests that a session can issue.
switch_io_logical	Specifies the amount of logical I/Os that a session can issue.
switch_elapsed_time	Specifies the elapsed time in the session.
switch_time	Specifies the amount of CPU time in the session.

This option provides a lot of flexibility such as whether the amount specified with the parameters is calculated for the total session or per call. If it is set to be calculated per call (switch_for_call), the consumer group is switched for the duration of the call or not (switch_for_call). Please note that for switching consumer groups, the database user must have been granted access to these groups with the DBMS_RESOURCE_MANAGER_PRIVS.GRANT_SWITCH_CONSUMER_GROUP procedure.

Another set of directive parameters to set limits for specific usage are the following:

Table 7-4. *Resource manager directives limiting parameters*

Parameter	Description
`undo_pool`	Limits the size in kilobytes of undo for a consumer group.
`max_idle_time`	Maximum session idle time in seconds.
`max_idle_blocker_time`	Maximum time a session can be idle while blocking another session.
`max_est_exec_time`	Maximum execution time (in CPU seconds) for a session. If the optimizer estimates an operation will take longer, the operation is not started and an ORA-7455 is issued.
`active_sess_pool_p1`	Specifies the maximum number of sessions that can currently have an active call.
`queueing_p1`	Specifies the time after which a call in the inactive session queue will time out. Default is `NULL`, which means unlimited.
`parallel_degree_limit_p1`	Specifies a limit on the degree of parallelism for any operation. Default is `NULL`, which means unlimited. A value of 0 means all operations will be serial.

Consumer Group Mappings Using ORACLE_FUNCTION

The resource manager provides an option to map a small number of resource intensive specific functions to consumer groups:

Table 7-5. *Resource manager mapping by function*

ORACLE_FUNCTION	Description
`BACKUP`	Backup operations using RMAN.
`COPY`	Image copies using RMAN.
`DATALOAD`	Loading data using Data Pump.

When the database has strict performance objectives, it can be beneficial to map above functions to a consumer group to manage the resource consumption. Here is how that is done:

```
BEGIN
  DBMS_RESOURCE_MANAGER.CREATE_PENDING_AREA();
  DBMS_RESOURCE_MANAGER.SET_CONSUMER_GROUP_MAPPING
    (DBMS_RESOURCE_MANAGER.ORACLE_FUNCTION, 'BACKUP', 'MAINTENANCE');

  DBMS_RESOURCE_MANAGER.SET_CONSUMER_GROUP_MAPPING
    (DBMS_RESOURCE_MANAGER.ORACLE_FUNCTION, 'COPY', 'MAINTENANCE');
DBMS_RESOURCE_MANAGER.SUBMIT_PENDING_AREA();
END;
/
```

Monitoring the Resource Manager

After you have implemented a resource manager plan, you might want to see if the resource manager plan works as intended. In order to do that, there are dynamic performance views to show you the behavior of the resource manager. One of such dynamic performance views is the V$RSRC_CONSUMER_GROUP:

Table 7-6. *V$RSRC_CONSUMER_GROUP view relevant fields*

Column	Description
NAME	The resource group name.
ACTIVE_SESSIONS	The number of active sessions in the consumer group.
EXECUTION_WAITERS	The number of active sessions waiting for a time slice in which they can use the CPU.
REQUESTS	The cumulative number of requests made by sessions in the consumer group.
CPU_WAIT_TIME	The cumulative amount of time that Resource Manager made sessions in the Resource Group wait for CPU. This wait time does not include I/O waits, delays from queue or latch contention, or the like. CPU_WAIT_TIME is the sum of the elapsed time allocated to the resmgr:cpu quantum wait event for the consumer group.
CPU_WAITS	The cumulative number of times sessions were made to wait because of resource management.
CONSUMED_CPU_TIME	The total amount of CPU time accumulated (in milliseconds) by sessions in the consumer group.
YIELDS	The cumulative number of times sessions in the consumer group had to yield the CPU to other sessions because of resource management.

The following listing is a report you may use to display the metrics collected in the V$RSRC_CONSUMER_GROUP view. These metrics are a valuable tool for determining the effect our resource allocations had on the consumer groups during the test.

```
col name                    format a12           heading "Name"
col active_sessions         format 999           heading "Active|Sessions"
col execution_waiters       format 999           heading "Execution|Waiters"
col requests                format 9,999,999     heading "Requests"
col cpu_wait_time           format 999,999,999   heading "CPU Wait|Time"
col cpu_waits               format 99,999,999    heading "CPU|Waits"
col consumed_cpu_time       format 99,999,999    heading "Consumed|CPU Time"
col yields                  format 9,999,999     heading "Yields"

SELECT DECODE(name, '_ORACLE_BACKGROUND_GROUP_', 'BACKGROUND', name) name,
       active_sessions, execution_waiters, requests,
       cpu_wait_time, cpu_waits, consumed_cpu_time, yields
  FROM v$rsrc_consumer_group
ORDER BY cpu_wait_time;
```

```
             Active Execution                 CPU Wait         CPU       Consumed
Name         Sessions   Waiters Requests          Time       Waits       CPU Time     Yields
------------ -------- --------- -------- ------------- ----------- ------------ ----------
BACKGROUND         34         0       76             0           0            0          0
APPS               30        13       30    87,157,739  11,498,286   47,963,809    365,611
REPORTS            30        27       31   145,566,524   2,476,651   10,733,274     78,950
MAINTENANCE        30        29       30   155,018,913   1,281,279    5,763,764     41,368
OTHER_GROUPS       34        29      131   155,437,715   1,259,766    5,576,621     40,168
```

If you are using the multitenant option, this view will show the resource management statistics per container/PDB. In order to relate the statistics to the pluggable database, add the con_id field in the query.

■ **Tip** The V$RSRCMGRMETRIC and V$RSRCMGRMETRIC_HISTORY views are also very useful for monitoring the effects that your DBRM resource allocations have on sessions in the database.

Resource Manager Views

Oracle supplies a number of views that report configuration, history, and metric for Resource Manager. Let's take a look at a few of the views that are useful for reviewing and monitoring resources in your DBRM configuration:

V$RSRC_PLAN: This view displays the configuration of the current active resource plan.

V$RSRC_PLAN_HISTORY: This view shows historical information, including when they were activated and deactivated and whether they were enabled by the database scheduler or scheduler windows. The history includes the latest 15 plans.

V$RSRC_CONSUMER_GROUP: This view shows information about the current active consumer groups, including performance metrics.

V$RSRC_CONS_GROUP_HIST: This view shows the historical information from the V$RSRC_CONSUMER_GROUP view, for which the SEQUENCE# column needs to be joined to the same column in the V$RSRC_PLAN in order to get plan name and times.

V$RSRC_SESSION_INFO: This view shows performance statistics for session and how they were affected by the Resource Manager.

V$SESSION: This is not really a Resource Manager view; however, the RESOURCE_CONSUMER_GROUP field is useful for determining what resource group a session is assigned to.

V$RSRCMGRMETRIC: This view contains resource usage per consumer group of a past minute and is refreshed per minute.

V$RSRCMGRMETRIC_HISTORY: This view contains one hour of history of the contents of V$RSRCMGRMETRIC.

DBA_CDB_RSRC_PLANS / CDB_CDB_RSRC_PLANS: CDB resource plans.

DBA_CDB_RSRC_PLAN_DIRECTIVES / CDB_CDB_RSRC_PLAN_DIRECTIVES: CDB resource plan directives.

CDB_RSRC_CATEGORIES: Database consumer group categories per container.

DBA_RSRC_CATEGORIES: Database consumer group categories.

DBA_RSRC_PLANS: Lists all database resource plans in the data dictionary, together with plan settings.

DBA_HIST_RSRC_PLANS: Historical information on resource manager plans (AWR; licensed view).

DBA_RSRC_CONSUMER_GROUPS: Lists all consumer groups created in the dictionary.

DBA_HIST_RSRC_CONSUMER_GROUPS: Historical information on resource manager consumer groups (AWR; licensed view).

DBA_RSRC_CONSUMER_GROUP_PRIVS: lists all the users and the consumer groups to which they have been granted access. As has been emphasized before, a user must be granted access to any other group than OTHER_GROUPS before the Resource Manager can switch a user to that group.

DBA_RSRC_PLAN_DIRECTIVES: Lists all resource manager directives stored in the data dictionary.

DBA_RSRC_GROUP_MAPPINGS: Lists session to resource group mapping rules defined in the data dictionary.

DBA_RSRC_MAPPING_PRIORITY: Lists the priority of session attributes, which is used by the Resource Manager to determine in which order to evaluate mapping rules.

DBA_USERS: This is not a resource manager view, but the field INITIAL_RSRC_CONSUMER_GROUP shows the initial resource manager group a database user is assigned to.

DBA_RSRC_IO_CALIBRATE: This view is related to the DBMS_RESOURCE_MANAGER.CALIBRATE_IO procedure and shows the outcome of the calibration.

DBA_RSRC_MANAGER_SYSTEM_PRIVS: This view shows all users and roles granted the ADMINISTER_RESOURCE_MANAGER system privilege. This privilege must be granted using the DBMS_RESOURCE_MANAGER_PRIVS package.

I/O Resource Manager

Earlier in this chapter, we discussed Oracle's Database Resource Manager, which manages CPU resources within a database through consumer groups and plan directives. Sessions are assigned to resource groups, and plan directives manage the allocation of resources by assigning values such as a CPU percentage or a share to resource management attributes like MGMT_P1. The database resource manager, however, is limited to managing resources within the database. The database resource manager actually does manage I/O resources, but in a somewhat indirect manner by limiting CPU and parallelism available to user sessions (through prioritization and limiting as set in the directives to which consumer groups are mapped). It is extremely important to realize that any session needs to be allowed to run by the database resource manager in the first place, and then needs to be able to get a timeslice to run on the CPU (on the operating system level) before it can request I/Os. In other words, CPU is the ultimate resource needed to do I/O.

Before Exadata came along, Oracle had no presence at the storage tier, and limiting CPU and parallelism to database sessions was the only way to (indirectly) manage I/O. Exadata lifts I/O Resource Management above the database tier and manages I/O at the storage cell in a very direct way. Databases installed on Exadata send I/O requests to cellsrv on the storage cells using a proprietary protocol known as Intelligent Database protocol (iDB). Using iDB, the database packs additional attributes in every I/O call to the storage cells. This additional information is used in a number of ways. For example, IORM uses the type of file (redo, undo, datafile, control file, and so on) for which the I/O was requested to determine whether caching the blocks in Flash Cache would be beneficial or not. Five attributes known to us are embedded in the I/O request: performance profile name (if set), database, container in the case of multitenancy, the consumer group, and the consumer group's category. These five bits of additional information are invaluable to Oracle's intelligent storage. Knowing which database or container is making the request allows IORM to prioritize I/O requests by database.

Categories extend the concept of consumer groups on Exadata platforms. Categories are assigned to consumer groups within the database using the Database Resource Manager. Common categories, defined in multiple databases, can then be allocated a shared I/O priority. For example, you may have several databases that map user sessions to an `INTERACTIVE` category. I/O requests coming from the `INTERACTIVE` category may now be prioritized over other categories such as `REPORTS`, `BATCH`, or `MAINTENANCE`.

Resource management profiles are a new, easy way to group databases to use a certain I/O resource management profile. Resource management profiles are introduced with Exadata version 12.1.2.1.0 and database version 12.1.0.2. Resource management profiles differ from categories in the sense resource management groups group entire databases, while categories group sessions in different databases with a the same category as set in a directive.

IORM Methods

IORM provides four distinct methods for I/O resource management: Interdatabase, Category, Intradatabase, and Resource Profile. These methods may be used individually or in combination.

Interdatabase Resource Plans

IORM determines the priority of an I/O request based on the name of the database initiating the request and its priority set in the IORM plan. Interdatabase IORM is useful when Exadata is hosting multiple databases and you need to manage I/O priorities between the databases. This is a plan created on each storage server.

Category Resource Plans

IORM determines the priority of an I/O request among multiple databases by the category that initiated the request and the priority for the category set in the plan. Managing I/O by category is useful when you want to manage I/O priorities by workload type. For example, you can create categories like `APPS`, `BATCH`, `REPORTS` and `MAINTENANCE` in each of your databases and then set an I/O allocation for these categories according to their importance to your business. If the `APPS` category is allocated 70%, then sessions assigned to the `APPS` category in all databases share this allocation. This is a plan created on each storage server, working together with a category set by the database resource manager to a consumer group in multiple databases.

Intradatabase Resource Plans

Unlike Interdatabase and Category IORM, Intradatabase IORM is configured at the database tier using DBRM. DBRM has been enhanced to work in partnership with IORM to provide fine-grained I/O resource management using resource groups defined in the database. This is done by allocating the I/O share and priority in the storage server to consumer groups using the same mechanism used to allocate CPU, the `MGMT_Pn` attribute, and the `utilization_limit` parameter. For example, the `SALES` database may be allocated 50% using an Interdatabase IORM plan. That 50% may be further distributed to the `APPS`, `REPORTS`, `BATCH`, and `OTHER_GROUPS` consumer groups within the database. This ensures that I/O resources are available for critical applications, and it prevents misbehaving or I/O-intensive processes from stealing I/O from higher-priority sessions inside the database. The management of pluggable databases also falls into the intradatabase IORM plan's responsibility.

Resource Management Profiles

Resource management profiles, fully named I/O resource management interdatabase plans, require setting a parameter in the database or container database (`DB_PERFORMANCE_PROFILE`) to a profile name defined on the storage servers. The big difference with Interdatabase plans is that instead of setting a directive for every database name in the dbplan, the names set in the dbplan now reflect profile names, to which databases are mapped by setting the `DB_PERFORMANCE_PROFILE` parameter. This is aimed at environments where the number of databases is moderate to high (10 or more) to simplify IORM by having a few profiles to which all the databases are mapped. In order for the storage server to understand it is a performance profile and not a database name, "type=profile" is added to the definition. Profiles cannot be used together with category plans.

How IORM Works

IORM manages I/O at the storage cell by organizing incoming I/O requests into queues according to the database name, category or profile, or consumer group that initiated the request. It then services these queues according to the priority defined for them in the resource plan. IORM only actively manages I/O requests when needed. This means that when a flash device or cell disk is not fully utilized, an I/O request is dispatched to the device immediately by `cellsrv`. However, when a flash device or cell disk is fully utilized, IORM will queue the I/O request in an I/O queue (per device), and schedule the I/O requests in the queues according to the priority defined in the resource manager. Please note that with storage server versions prior to 12.1.2.1.0, flash was excluded from resource management.

For example, there are two databases using a cell server, DB1 and DB2. The I/O resource plan in the cells is defined to prioritize DB1 for 75% and DB2 for 25%. When there is excess capacity available, the I/O requests will be serviced in a first-in-first-out (FIFO) manner. But when the devices on the cells begin to saturate, I/O requests will get queued. Once queued, IORM enforces the resource plan, which means the I/O requests are reordered as defined in the resource plan. Background processes are prioritized, too, based on internal resource plans with different priorities for different types of I/O. Needless to say, I/O requests of critical background processes like the log writer are given higher priority than foreground sessions (client sessions).

Please mind I/O resource management for flash and hard disks is a feature of Exadata release 12.1.2.1.0 or higher. Earlier versions of IORM only managed hard disks. Also, resource management for flash is different from resource management for hard disks. The way flash I/Os are prioritized is that small I/Os (smaller than 128K) always take priority over large I/Os, regardless of any IORM plan. Only for large I/Os, resource management plans are applied.

IORM Architecture

For every physical storage device in use by the storage server, an IORM queue is kept, regardless of the existence of any resource manager plan. The IORM queues are first organized by category or profile, depending on which type is used. This is the reason profiles and categories cannot work together. After been organized by category, the databases are organized by interdatabase plan and lastly by intradatabase plan. This is the IORM evaluation order:

1. Category/profile
2. Interdatabase plan
3. Pluggable database
4. Intradatabase plan

In order to see this for yourself, you could dump IORM information from the cell daemon. This dump is not documented and should not be done on a live system. This information is provided for completeness and educational purposes. The IORM dump information is managed and kept per cell; the cell daemons do not work together like a cluster, but work standalone.

First, log on to a cell, start cellcli, and execute: alter cell events = 'immediate cellsrv.cellsrv_statedump(2,0)':

```
CellCLI> alter cell events = 'immediate cellsrv.cellsrv_statedump(2,0)'
Dump sequence #11 has been written to /opt/oracle/cell/log/diag/asm/cell/enkcel04/trace/
svtrc_31370_114.trc
Cell enkcel04 successfully altered
```

It is very important to note the name of the trace file. The dump is very large and contains a lot of information for the purpose of bug resolving and diagnosis for Oracle development. Here is a snippet from the file, showing IORM statistics for disk /dev/sdc:

```
IORM stats for disk=/dev/sdc
Heap stats: Inuse=62KB Total=207KB
--------- IORM Workload State & Characterization ---------
IORM: Solo Workload
Solo workload (no db or cg): 0 transitions
IORM boost =429.000000 (cnt = 3395, amt = 1458813)
#Bypassedios=0 #IOs skipped for fencing=1932 #IOs cancelled=0
#served=14073 bitmap=0x0 #queued=0 adtime=0ms asmrdtime=3ms #cumulserved=56404684
#pending=0 #lpending=0
busystate=1 #max_conc_io=5 write_cache_hit_rate=98% iocost=0.66ms
#free_lrg_wrts=11 #free_sml_wrts=85728 write_cost_adjust=0%
        catidx=0 bitmap=0x0 OTHER
          SIO:#served=3249 #queued=0 Util=2% aqtime=2us ahdtime=445us afdtime=0us
                dbidx=0 bitmap=0x0 DBM01
                  SIO:#served=4 #queued=0 Util=0% aqtime=2us ahdtime=123us afdtime=0us
                      lastreqtime=Wed Jan  7 19:46:46 1970 97 msec
                        cgidx=0 bitmap=0x0 cgname=ORA$AUTOTASK limit=90
                        cgidx=1 bitmap=0x0 cgname=OTHER_GROUPS
                        cgidx=2 bitmap=0x0 cgname=SYS_GROUP
                        cgidx=3 bitmap=0x0 cgname=_ORACLE_BACKGROUND_GROUP_
                          SIO:#served=4 #queued=0 Util=0% aqtime=2us ahdtime=123us
                              afdtime=0us
                                 #concios=4, #fragios=0 #starvedios=0 #maxcapwaits=0
                        cgidx=4 bitmap=0x0 cgname=_ORACLE_MEDPRIBG_GROUP_
                        cgidx=5 bitmap=0x0 cgname=_ORACLE_LOWPRIBG_GROUP_
                        cgidx=6 bitmap=0x0 cgname=_ORACLE_LOWPRIFG_GROUP_
```

(This dump was created on a cell server version 12.1.2.1.0; this information might not be available in earlier versions.)

This dump shows that the statistics are kept per device. As indicated, this is the third physical disk, disk /dev/sdc. The first accentuated piece is "catidx=0"; this shows that first categories are evaluated. If no categories or profiles have been defined, there are two categories, OTHER and _ASM_. The second accentuated piece is "dbidx=0." This is the list of databases that the resource manager has seen for this device up until now, and the second level at which IORM can operate. The third accentuated piece is "cgidx=0" and shows the list of consumer groups in the database. Consumer group 3, 4, 5, and 6 are Oracle internal consumer groups, which have been mentioned earlier in the chapter. The _ORACLE_BACKGROUND_GROUP_ is the internal consumer group for critical I/Os of background processes. Without an intradatabase resource manager plan configured in the database, all user/foreground processes are mapped to the OTHER_GROUPS consumer group.

IORM Objective

After installation, the cell server already is running with IORM active. Versions of the storage server prior to version 11.2.3.2 were running without IORM and needed an IORM plan to be created before IORM could be enabled. Starting from version Exadata version 11.2.3.2, IORM is always enabled and running with the IORM objective 'basic.' Following is a list of the objectives that can be set:

> `low_latency`: This setting provides optimization for applications that are extremely sensitive to I/O latency. It provides the lowest possible I/O latencies by significantly limiting disk utilization. In other words, throughput-hungry applications will be significantly (negatively) impacted by this optimization objective.
>
> `high_throughput`: This setting provides the best possible throughput for DW transactions by attempting to fully utilize the I/O capacity of the storage cells. It is the opposite of `low_latency` and, as such, it will significantly (negatively) impact disk I/O latency.
>
> `Balanced`: This setting attempts to strike a balance between low latency and high throughput. This is done by limiting disk utilization for large I/O operations to a lesser degree than the `low_latency` objective described above. Use this objective when workloads are mixed and you have no applications that require extremely low latency.
>
> `Auto`: This setting allows IORM to determine the best optimization objective for your workload. `Cellsrv` continuously monitors the large/small I/O requests and applies the optimization method on a best-fit basis. If 75% or more of the I/O operations from a consumer group are small I/O (less than 128K), it is considered to be a latency-oriented consumer group and is managed accordingly.
>
> `Basic`: This setting is the default after installation. This objective means the storage server does limited optimization for low latency, but does not throttle, which the other objectives do.

The objective can be set using the `cellcli` command-line tool:

```
CellCLI> alter iormplan objective='auto';
IORMPLAN successfully altered
```

In most cases, it is beneficial to set the objective to `auto`. Doing so, IORM tries to optimize based on the usage patterns of the databases.

The objective is applied only to hard disk I/Os. For I/Os done to flash prior to storage server version 12.1.2.1.0, there was no prioritization. Starting from storage server version 12.1.2.1.0, the objective for flash I/Os is to favor small I/Os (128KB or less), regardless of the objective set.

Configuring Interdatabase IORM

An interdatabase I/O resource management plan is configured using an IORM plan. This plan determines the database I/O priorities for the storage cell. IORM plans are created using the `CellCLI` command `ALTER IORMPLAN`. There can be only one IORM plan per storage cell, regardless of how many database instances (clustered or single instance) use it for storage. Creating an interdatabase IORM plan is fairly simple. The first step is to determine what your allocation policy should be for each database. You will use these allocation policies to define the directives for your IORM plan. The `LEVEL` attribute specifies the priority a database should be given relative to other databases in the plan. The `ALLOCATION` attribute determines the percentage of I/O a database will be given out of the total I/O available on its level. There always needs to be an other directive for any database that is not listed in the plan. The following example demonstrates how you to create an IORM plan:

```
CellCLI> alter iormplan dbplan=((name=database1, level=1, allocation=60), -
> (name=database2, level=2, allocation=80), -
> (name=other, level=3, allocation=100))
IORMPLAN successfully altered
```

The CellCLI command list iormplan detail displays our new IORM plan. Notice that the catPlan attribute is empty. This is a placeholder for the Category IORM plan we will be looking at in the next section.

```
CellCLI> list iormplan detail
         name:                         enkcel04_IORMPLAN
         catPlan:
         dbPlan:                       name=database1,level=1,allocation=75
                                       name=database2,level=2,allocation=80
                                       name=other,level=3,allocation=100
         objective:                    auto
         status:                       active
```

The aggregate allocation for all databases on a level may not exceed 100%. If the sum of allocations on any level exceeds 100%, CellCLI will throw an error. For example, the following listing shows the error CellCLI produces when over 100% is allocated on level 1:

```
CellCLI> alter iormplan dbplan=((name=database1, level=1, allocation=75), -
> (name=database2, level=1, allocation=80), -
> (name=other, level=3, allocation=100))

CELL-00006: The IORMPLAN command contains an invalid allocation total at level 1.
```

Because IORM is always enabled, setting the above (correct) plan means the IORM database plan is enforced. If the plan does not work as intended, the plan can be disabled by specifying an empty database plan:

```
CellCLI> alter iormplan dbplan=''
IORMPLAN successfully altered
```

When the Data Guard option is used, the role of the database in the Data Guard setup (primary or standby) can be included in the IORM plan to specify different resource limitations for both roles:

```
CellCLI> alter iormplan dbplan=((name=database1, level=1, allocation=75, role=primary), -
> (name=database1, level=1, allocation=25, role=standby), -
> (name=database2, level=2, allocation=80), -
> (name=other, level=3, allocation=100))
IORMPLAN successfully altered
```

Because the I/O resource manager plan needs to be changed whenever a database is added that needs resource management other than set the other directive, it is a good idea to take a look at IO resource manager profiles for resource management a little later in this chapter. IORM profiles need cell server 12.1.2.1.0 or above and database version 12.1.0.2 Exadata bundle patch 4 or higher. They have the advantage that you can create a few resource profiles (High, Medium, Low, for example) and assign databases to these resource profiles by setting the parameter DB_PERFORMANCE_PROFILE to the profile name. Especially if there are new databases and old ones removed regularly, such as in a database as-a-service environment, this could save a lot of work.

Configuring Interdatabase IORM: Shares

Starting from cell server version 11.2.3.1, IORM plans can be created based on shares to express a database's relative weight instead of percentages. Percentage-based plans have a limit of 32 databases, while share-based IORM plans can support up to 1023 databases. Share-based plans cannot have multiple levels like the percentage-based plans can, and are therefore a bit more limited. However, share-based plans are easier to read and understand than percentage-based plans. Here is how a share-based plan is configured:

```
CellCLI> alter iormplan dbplan=((name=database1, share=10), -
> (name=database2, share=4))
IORMPLAN successfully altered
```

Setting this plan means that when database1 and database2 are the only databases using the cell server, database1 gets 71% (10/(10+4)*100) and database2 get 29% of the IO resources assigned in case of queueing. By default, databases that are not listed in the share plan get a share of 1. If you want to change the default settings, you can specify the change by adding a directive for name=default.

Limiting Excess I/O Utilization

Ordinarily, when excess I/O resources are available (allocated but unused by other consumer groups), IORM allows a consumer group to use more than its allocation. For example, if the database1 database is allocated 50% at level 1, it may consume I/O resources above that limit if other databases have not fully utilized their allocation. You may choose to override this behavior by setting an absolute limit on the I/O resources allocated to specific databases. This provides more predictable I/O performance for multi-database server environments. The LIMIT IORM attribute is used to set a cap on the I/O resources a database may use even when excess I/O capacity is available. The following listing shows an IORM plan that caps the database1 database at 80% of the cell's IO capacity.

```
alter iormplan dbPlan=((name=database1, level=1, allocation=50, limit=80), -
> (name=other, level=2, allocation=100))
IORMPLAN successfully altered
```

Please note that maximum I/O limits may also be defined at the consumer group level by using the UTILIZATION_LIMIT attribute in your DBRM resource plans.

Configuring Interdatabase IORM: Flash Attributes

When creating a plan, either using the allocation attribute to set percentages or the shares attribute to set relative weight, the storage server provides a number of plan attributes to manage how flash is used. The following attributes can be used to manage the use of the Flash Log feature and the Flash Cache feature:

```
CellCLI> alter iormplan dbplan=((name=database1,share=10,flashlog=on,flashcache=on), -
> (name=database2,share=4,flashlog=on,flashcache=off), -
> (name=default,share=1,flashlog=off,flashcache=off))
IORMPLAN successfully altered
```

The usage of the Flash Log and Flash Cache attributes is very straightforward and has the simple options on or off. In the above example, any other database named in the plan will have the Flash Log and Flash Cache features disabled because default is redefined in the plan line with name=default. The default setting (meaning not explicitly defined in an IORM plan) of the Flash Log and Flash Cache attributes is on.

Starting from Exadata version 12.1.2.0, IORM provides a few more flash management attributes: `flashcachemin` and `flashcachelimit`. The `flashcachemin` attribute guarantees a minimal size for database objects in the Flash Cache; `flashcachelimit` sets a maximum to the amount of space a database can use in the Flash Cache:

```
CellCLI> alter iormplan dbplan=((name=database1,share=10,flashcachemin=1G), -
> (name=database2,share=4,flashcachemin=500M,flashcachelimit=1G), -
> (name=default,share=1,flashcachelimit=500M))
IORMPLAN successfully altered
```

In this example, `database1` has a minimum size set for flash usage of 1G and no limit. `database1` could be an important database that needs flash for performance. The other named database, `database2`, also is guaranteed an amount of space in the Flash Cache, 500M, but is limited to a maximum of 1G. Any other database will have a maximum of 500M of space usage of the Flash Cache.

Category IORM

The I/O Resource Manager (IORM) extends the concept of resource groups with an attribute known as a `category`. While resource groups allow DBRM to manage resources within a database, categories provide I/O resource management among multiple databases. For example, suppose our two databases (`database1` and `database2`) have similar workloads. They both host OLTP applications that do short, time-sensitive transactions. During business hours, these transactions must take priority. These databases also do a fair amount of batch processing, such as running reports and maintenance jobs. The batch processing takes a lower priority during business hours. These two workloads can be managed and prioritized using IORM categories. The categories `APPS_CATEGORY` and `BATCH_CATEGORY` can be defined in both databases for high-priority applications and long-running, lower-priority activities, respectively. If `APPS_CATEGORY` is allocated 70% on level 1, then no matter how heavily loaded the storage grid is, sessions assigned to this category, for both databases, will be guaranteed a minimum of 70% of all I/O.

Configuring Category IORM

Setting up Category IORM is fairly straightforward. Once you have created your DBRM consumer groups, you need to create categories in the database and assign them to your consumer groups. The final step is to create an IORM plan in the storage cells to establish I/O allocation and priority for each category. You can define as many as eight levels in your Category IORM Plan.

In order to show the use of IORM category plans, we will create two new categories, `OLTP_CATEGORY`, and `BATCH_CATEGORY`, and assign them to the `OLTP`, `BATCH`, and `MAINTENANCE` consumer groups. For the sake of brevity, the creation of the consumer groups is not shown. This example uses the consumer groups created in the section Creating a (Pluggable) Database Resource Plan. The following listing creates our new categories and assigns them to the resource groups. Remember that you will need to run these commands on all databases participating in the IORM category plan. For illustration purposes, we will keep the number of categories to two. The `BATCH` and `MAINTENANCE` resource groups will be assigned to the category `BATCH_CATEGORY`:

```
BEGIN
  dbms_resource_manager.clear_pending_area();
  dbms_resource_manager.create_pending_area();

  -- Create Categories --
  dbms_resource_manager.create_category(
     category => 'OLTP_CATEGORY',
     comment  => 'Category for Interactive Applications');
```

```
  dbms_resource_manager.create_category(
     category => 'BATCH_CATEGORY',
     comment  => 'Batch and Maintenance Jobs');

  -- Assign Consumer Groups to Categories --
  dbms_resource_manager.update_consumer_group(
     consumer_group => 'OLTP',
     new_category   => 'OLTP_CATEGORY');
  dbms_resource_manager.update_consumer_group(
     consumer_group => 'BATCH',
     new_category   => 'BATCH_CATEGORY');
  dbms_resource_manager.update_consumer_group(
     consumer_group => 'MAINTENANCE',
     new_category   => 'BATCH_CATEGORY');

  dbms_resource_manager.submit_pending_area();
END;
/

PL/SQL procedure successfully completed.
```

To check your resource-group-to-category mappings, query the DBA_RSRC_CONSUMER_GROUPS view as follows. Notice that the OTHER_GROUPS consumer group was assigned to the OTHER category. That mapping is created automatically by Oracle and cannot be altered:

```
SQL> SELECT consumer_group, category
           FROM DBA_RSRC_CONSUMER_GROUPS
          WHERE consumer_group
             in ('OLTP','BATCH','MAINTENANCE','OTHER_GROUPS')
          ORDER BY category;

CONSUMER_GROUP                 CATEGORY
------------------------------ ------------------------------
OLTP                           OLTP_CATEGORY
BATCH                          BATCH_CATEGORY
MAINTENANCE                    BATCH_CATEGORY
OTHER_GROUPS                   OTHER
```

Now we can create a new IORM category plan on the storage cells and set I/O limits on these categories. Before we do, though, we will drop the Interdatabase IORM plan we created in the previous example. Remember that each storage cell maintains its own IORM plan, so you will need to run these commands on every cell in your storage grid.

```
CellCLI> alter iormplan dbplan= ''

IORMPLAN successfully altered
```

Now we are ready to create our IORM category plan. The following command creates a plan in which OLTP_CATEGORY and BATCH_CATEGORY are allocated 70% and 30%, respectively, of the total cell I/O at level 1. The default category, OTHER, is allocated 100% on level 2.

```
CellCLI> alter iormplan catplan=((name=APPS_CATEGORY, level=1, allocation=70), -
> (name=BATCH_CATEGORY, level=1, allocation=30), -
> (name=OTHER, level=2, allocation=100))
IORMPLAN successfully altered
```

Again, we will use the CellCLI command list iorm detail and confirm that our IORM category plan is configured the way we want it:

```
CellCLI> list iormplan detail
         name:                          enkcel04_IORMPLAN
         catPlan:                       name=APPS_CATEGORY,level=1,allocation=70
                                        name=BATCH_CATEGORY,level=1,allocation=30
                                        name=OTHER,level=2,allocation=100
         dbPlan:
         objective:                     auto
         status:                        active
```

Because we dropped the interdatabase plan from the previous exercise, the dbPlan field is empty. Later, in the IORM metrics section of the chapter, we will discuss how the effects of IORM can be monitored at the storage cells.

I/O Resource Manager and Pluggable Databases

With Oracle database 12c, a new architecture was implemented in the database. The new architecture has been mentioned in a number of places already and is commonly referred to as the Oracle Multitenant Option. Multitenancy has been implemented almost everywhere in the database; there are only few functional gaps between the container database and non-container database. IORM thankfully supports pluggable databases. Just like with the intradatabase IORM plan, the settings you define on the CDB level by means of the CDB resource manager plan will be sent to the cells as soon as the plan is activated on the RDBMS layer. Whichever shares are made available to the PDB are equally applicable for CPU and I/O. As with all resource management functions in the database, I/O resource management on pluggable databases will only be visible if there is an I/O constraint.

I/O Resource Manager Profiles

Exadata Storage server version 12.1.2.1.0 introduced a new mechanism to easily group databases in performance categories called *I/O resource management profiles*. The idea is to create a named performance profile on the storage servers and let the database bind to such a profile using a parameter that has been set to the name of the performance profile. The database part of this feature is a parameter named DB_PERFORMANCE_PROFILE, which is introduced with Oracle database version 12.1.0.2 Exadata bundle patch 4.

Performance profiles and category IORM plans cannot be used at the same time.

When using performance profiles, up to eight profiles can be created. Performance profiles are designed for handling large amounts of databases. In order to handle large amounts, performance profiles use the share-based prioritization method only. You might recall that interdatabase resource plans using the allocation (percentage)-based method can only handle up to 32 databases. By using the share-based prioritization method, performance profiles can handle up to 1023 databases. The database parameter DB_PERFORMANCE_PROFILE is not dynamic, which means it needs a database restart in order to set it. When using DB_PERFORMANCE_PROFILE on a container database (multitenant option), it can only be set at the CDB/root level, not at the pluggable-database level. When set at the CDB/root level, all pluggable databases inherit the DB_PERFORMANCE_PROFILE setting from the root.

This is an example on how a performance profile plan can be set:

```
CellCLI> alter iormplan dbplan=((name=gold, share=12, limit=100, type=profile), -
> (name=silver, share=5, limit=65, type=profile), -
> (name=bronze, share=3, limit=45, type=profile), -
> (name=default, share=1, limit=10))
IORMPLAN successfully altered
```

Performance profiles and interdatabase plans are two different resource management options in the storage server. This means they can be used at the same time, although we discourage this for the sake of keeping the resource management as simple as possible. Performance profiles directives are recognizable by `type=profile`; interdatabase plans do not have a type, or they have `type=database` added to the dbplan directives.

After the performance profiles have been set at all the storage servers, the `DB_PERFORMANCE_PROFILE` parameter can be set at the databases (requiring a restart) to use the profile on the storage layer. Because performance profiles have been implemented at the category (first) level, interdatabase plans can be used to divide resources inside the profile and intradatabase plans for managing resources inside the database.

■ **Note** In most cases, a single-level I/O resource plan is sufficient. As they do with DBRM, multi-level IORM resource plans increase the complexity of measuring the effectiveness of your allocation scheme.

When using multi-level allocation schemes, it's important to understand that I/O resources allocated but unused by a database, category, or consumer group on level 1 are immediately passed to the next level. For example, if you have databases A and B allocated 70%/30% on level 1, and database C is allocated 100% at level 2, then if database A uses only 50% of its allocation, the remaining 20% is passed to database C. Database B cannot capitalize on I/O resources allocated but unused by database A because A and B are on the same level. This is a subtle but important distinction of multi-level plans. If you are not careful, you can find yourself unintentionally giving excess I/O resources to less important databases at lower levels rather than making those resources available to your higher-priority databases on level 1.

The share-based resource plans are single level by design, and they are easy to create and configure. In most cases, using a share-based plan is the best way to use IORM. Unless you have a specific need that can only be solved by (multi-level) allocation (percentage)-based plans, these should be used.

Resource Management Directives Matrix

With all the features available and some of the features that cannot be used together, the following matrix tries to give an overview of which directives can and cannot be used. This might help when designing an I/O resource management strategy.

	level	allocation	shares	limit [1]	role [2]	flashcache	flashlog	flashcachemin	flashcachelimit	type	DEFAULT	OTHER	PDB
Category	yes [10]	yes [10]	no	no	no	no	no	no	no	no	no	yes	no
Profiles	no	no	yes [10]	yes [10]	no	yes	yes	yes	yes	yes	yes	no	yes [12]
Inter-DB	yes	yes	yes	yes	yes	yes	yes	yes	yes	yes [3]	yes [3]	yes [4]	no
CDB	no	no	yes	yes [5]	no	no	no	no	no	no	yes [6]	no	yes
Intra-DB [11]	yes [7]	yes [8]	yes	yes [5]	no	no	no	no	no	no	no	yes [9]	no

1. LIMIT can be used by SHARES or LEVEL and ALLOCATION
2. Should have both primary and standby directives set
3. Only if using shares
4. Only if using level and allocation
5. UTILIZATION_LIMIT and PARALLEL_SERVER_LIMIT directives
6. DEFAULT shares setting for new PDBs
7. The easiest way is to go with SHARES
8. Specified on MGMT_P1
9. OTHER_GROUPS is required
10. Category plan cannot be used when performance profiles are used (vice versa)
11. Applies to DBRM and PDB
12. DB_PERFORMANCE_PROFILE set on either non-CDB or CDB (PDBs inherit from CDB$ROOT)

IORM Monitoring and Metrics

I/O performance metrics are collected and maintained for IORM in the storage cell. These metrics may be used to determine the effects your IORM plan has on the databases, categories or profiles, and resource group resource directives you defined in your environment. For example, you can see how much I/O a particular database is using compared to other databases. By observing the actual I/O distribution for your IORM consumer groups, you can determine whether adjustments need to be made to provide adequate I/O resources for applications using your databases. In this section, we will look at how these metrics are organized and tap into the valuable information stored there. More information about Exadata monitoring, including information taken from the storage servers, is found in Chapters 11 and 12.

There are two different sources for metrics available via cellcli: METRICCURRENT, which are metrics measured over a minute after which they are available via METRICCURENT, and METRICHISTORY, which are the metrics as exposed via METRICCURRENT, which are the expired metrics of METRICCURRENT stored for a certain amount of days—seven by default. The setting can be seen by querying the metrichistorydays attribute of the cell:

```
CellCLI> list cell attributes name, metrichistorydays
         enkcel04         7
```

If there is a need to change the time, the metric history is kept. It can be done using an alter cell command:

```
CellCLI> alter cell metricHistoryDays='14'
Cell enkcel04 successfully altered

CellCLI> list cell attributes name, metricHistoryDays
         enkcel04        14
```

In most cases, seven days is enough history for the typical use of the cell metrics.

Understanding IORM Metrics

When questions on I/O throughput arise, with or without IORM plans created and set, one of the first things to check on the cell is the actual activity. The following `cellcli` command shows the current amount of requests per database grouped by the storage media used:

```
CellCLI> list metriccurrent where objecttype='IORM_DATABASE' and name like
'DB_(FC_|FD_|)IO_BY_SEC'
         DB_FC_IO_BY_SEC          ASM                      0 MB/sec
         DB_FC_IO_BY_SEC          TEST                     0 MB/sec
         DB_FC_IO_BY_SEC          COLVIN                   0 MB/sec
         DB_FC_IO_BY_SEC          MBACH                    0 MB/sec
         DB_FC_IO_BY_SEC          _OTHER_DATABASE_         0 MB/sec
         DB_FD_IO_BY_SEC          ASM                      0 MB/sec
         DB_FD_IO_BY_SEC          TEST                     0 MB/sec
         DB_FD_IO_BY_SEC          COLVIN                   0 MB/sec
         DB_FD_IO_BY_SEC          MBACH                    0 MB/sec
         DB_FD_IO_BY_SEC          _OTHER_DATABASE_         0 MB/sec
         DB_IO_BY_SEC             ASM                      0 MB/sec
         DB_IO_BY_SEC             TEST                     0 MB/sec
         DB_IO_BY_SEC             COLVIN                   0 MB/sec
         DB_IO_BY_SEC             MBACH                    0 MB/sec
         DB_IO_BY_SEC             _OTHER_DATABASE_         0 MB/sec
```

The list command lists the bandwidth used by the databases that are visible to the cell by Flash Cache (`DB_FC_IO_BY_SEC`), flash disk (`DB_FD_IO_BY_SEC`), and hard disk (`DB_IO_BY_SEC`). There are a few things worth pointing out. The database `ASM` is a special database indicator for ASM-initiated and related tasks, like rebalancing. Also `_OTHER_DATABASE_` is a special database name for IO tasks not directly related to IO on behalf of the compute layer. An example of `_OTHER_DATABASE_` IO is the destaging of Write-back Flash Cache data to disk.

IORM Metrics: metric_iorm.pl

In order to make fetching and interpreting cell I/O performance and I/O resource manager statistics on the command line easier, Oracle provides a perl script called `metric_iorm.pl` in My Oracle Support note 1337265.1 (Tool for Gathering I/O Resource Manager Metrics: `metric_iorm.pl`). This tool is very valuable for doing diagnosis on both absolute disk and flash performance, and diagnosing the effects of IO resource management. There is not much to say about this script because the My Oracle Support note is very complete on installation (the installation is done by placing the script in the home directory of the user to be used on the cell servers, which would typically be root or celladmin) and usage (essentially on how to get historical data out).

This script fetches the statistics on disk and flash I/O performance and get IORM-related statistics, and provides these in a readable way. You can read more on these statistics in the section IORM-Related Metrics Overview. Chapter 11 provides further examples and use cases for the script.

Workload Management

IORM metrics provide insight into how `cellsrv` is allocating I/O resources among the consumers in your storage grid. `Cellsrv` keeps track of I/O requests broadly categorized as "small requests" and "large requests." By comparing the large (`LG`) and small (`SM`) I/O requests in the IORM metrics, you can determine whether your databases lean more toward a DW workload (high throughput) or an OLTP workload (low latency).

By comparing the IORM_MODE with the actual workload on your storage cells, you can determine whether the current IORM objective is appropriate or not. For example, if you find that a majority of I/O operations in the storage cells are greater than 128K and thus large (LG), then you could consider setting the objective for high throughput. Likewise, if you find the majority of I/O operations in the storage cells are smaller than 128K, you could consider setting the objective for low latency. However, be aware of the implications of setting the objective to a value outside of basic or auto; the objective high_throughput can increase latency times and low_latency can decrease throughput. We find the majority of the client's to use basic or auto.

The cell server keeps track of the IORM objective set, which includes, as a quick reminder, basic, auto, low_latency, balance , and high_throughput. However, the cell server itself works with three modes of optimization for doing I/O:

- Mode 1: low_latency
- Mode 2: balanced
- Mode 3: high_throughput

In order to see what mode the cell server currently is set to, use the following command:

```
CellCLI> list metriccurrent iorm_mode
         IORM_MODE            enkcel04          2
```

When I/O latencies or bandwidth changes are influencing database processing time and the IORM objective was set to auto, the statistic IORM_MODE can be investigated for changes over time using the METRICHISTORY values:

```
CellCLI> list metrichistory where name = 'IORM_MODE' attributes name, metricvalue,
collectiontime

         IORM_MODE            2          2015-05-06T07:59:16-05:00
         IORM_MODE            2          2015-05-06T08:00:16-05:00
         IORM_MODE            2          2015-05-06T08:01:16-05:00
         IORM_MODE            2          2015-05-06T08:02:16-05:00
         IORM_MODE            2          2015-05-06T08:03:16-05:00
         IORM_MODE            2          2015-05-06T08:04:16-05:00
         IORM_MODE            2          2015-05-06T08:05:16-05:00
..snip..
```

IORM-Related Metrics Overview

The metrics we are interested in for IORM monitoring have an objectType of IORM_DATABASE, IORM_CATEGORY, IORM_PLUGGABLE_DATABASE, and IORM_CONSUMER_GROUP. These metrics are further organized by the name attribute in the METRICCURRENT object. The name of the metric is a concatenation of abbreviations that indicate the type of I/O consumer group, the type of storage device, and a descriptive name. The elements of the name attribute appear as follows:

{consumer_type}_{device type}_{metric}

Where consumer_type represents the IORM resource group and is one of these:

DB = Interdatabase IORM Plan

CT = Category IORM Plan

CG = Intradatabase IORM Plan

PDB = Pluggable database IORM Plan

And device_type is the type of storage that serviced the I/O request and is one of the following:

FC = Flash Cache

FD = Flash-based grid disk

'' = If neither of the above, then the metric represents I/O to physical disks

The last part of the attribute, {metric}, is the descriptive name of the metric. The metric name may be further qualified by SM or LG, indicating that it represents small I/O requests or large I/O requests. For example:

CG_FC_IO_RQ_LG: The total number of large I/O requests serviced from Flash Cache (FC), for DBRM consumer groups.

CG_FD_IO_RQ_LG: The total number of large I/O requests serviced from flash-based grid disks (FD), for DBRM consumer groups.

CG_IO_RQ_LG: The total number of large I/O requests serviced from physical disks (grid disks), for DBRM consumer groups.

Below is a table of metrics that interdatabase, category, intradatabase, and pluggable database resource plans have in common. This list is not exhaustive; there are many more metrics.

Name	Description
{CG, CT, DB, PDB}_IO_BY_SEC	Megabytes per second scheduled for this I/O consumer.
{CG, CT, DB, PDB}_IO_LOAD	Average I/O load for this I/O consumer. I/O load specifies the length of the disk queue. It is similar to the iostat avgqu-sz, but the value is weighted depending on type of disk; for hard disks, a large I/O has three times the weight of a small I/O. For flash disks, large and small have the same weight.
{CG, CT, DB, PDB}_IO_RQ_{SM, LG}	The cumulative number of small or large I/O requests from this I/O consumer.
{CG, CT, DB, PDB}_IO_RQ_{SM, LG}_SEC	The number of small or large I/O requests per second issued by this I/O consumer.
{CG, CT, DB, PDB}_IO_WT_{SM,LG}	The cumulative time (in milliseconds) that I/O requests from the I/O consumer have spent waiting to be scheduled by IORM.
{CG, CT, DB, PDB}_IO_WT_{SM,LG}_RQ	Derived from {CG,CT,DB}_IO_WT_{SM,LG} above. It stores the average number of waits (in milliseconds) that I/O requests have spent waiting to be scheduled by IORM in the past minute. A large number of waits indicates that the I/O workload of this I/O consumer is exceeding its allocation. For lower-priority consumers, this may be the desired effect. For high-priority consumers, it may indicate that more I/O should be allocated to the resource to meet the objectives of your organization.
{CG, CT, DB, PDB}_IO_UTIL_{SM, LG}	The percentage of total I/O resources consumed by this I/O consumer.
{CG, CT, DB, PDB}_IO_TM_{SM, LG}	The cumulative latency of reading small and large blocks by this I/O consumer.
{CG, CT, DB, PDB}_IO_TM_{SM, LG}_RQ	The average latency for reading blocks for this I/O consumer.

All cumulative metrics above are reset to 0 whenever `cellsrv` is restarted, the IORM plan is enabled, or the IORM plan changes for that I/O consumer group. For example, if the IORM category plan is changed, the following cumulative metrics will be reset:

```
CT_IO_RQ_SM
CT_IO_RQ_LG
CT_IO_WT_SM
CT_IO_WT_LG
CT_IO_TM_SM
CT_IO_TM_LG
```

These IORM metrics are further categorized using the `metricObjectName` attribute. Interdatabase resource plan metrics are stored in detail records, where `metricObjectName` is set to the corresponding database name. In a similar fashion, metrics for IORM category plans are identified with a `metricObjectName` matching the category name. IORM consumer groups are identified by a concatenation of the database name and the name of the DBRM consumer group. And, finally, IORM information related to PDBs uses the `<database name>.<PDB name>` syntax in the `metricObjectName` field.

Background Processes

As we discussed earlier, database background processes are automatically assigned to built-in (internal) IORM consumer groups according to priority. The following table shows these special IORM consumer groups, along with a description of what they are used for.

Table 7-7. *Resource manager internal consumer groups*

Consumer Group	Description
`_ASM_`	I/O related to Oracle ASM volume management
`_ORACLE_BG_CATEGORY_`	High-priority I/O requests issued from the database background processes
`_ORACLE_MEDPRIBG_CATEGORY_`	Medium-priority I/O requests issued from the database background processes
`_ORACLE_LOWPRIBG_CATEGORY_`	Low-priority I/O requests issued from the database background processes

It is important to realize that the priority for highly sensitive I/O requests, like logwriter writes, are enforced via an (internal) consumer group. But it might be too late in the chain of events. Recall the evaluation steps of IORM:

1. Category/profile
2. Interdatabase plan
3. Pluggable database
4. Intradatabase plan

You see that despite the naming high-priority I/O requests group, the evaluation of IORM is at the fourth place for the group, which means that if resources have already been given out in earlier steps, like an interdatabase plan, the database can be left with little priority. This means that even while named high-priority I/O group, it still can have very little priority in the overall situation when I/O pressure arises. Of course, it does mean that this group gets the highest priority for its I/Os with respect to I/Os done from the same database with other consumer groups.

This changes when category plans are enabled. With category plans enabled, internal category plans are created, like the above internal consumer groups, and background and ASM requests are directly prioritized. Inside the internal plans, the prioritization is done based on interdatabase plan priorities.

Summary

One of the biggest challenges for DBAs is effectively managing system resources to meet business objectives, especially when databases are consolidated. Over the years, Oracle has developed a rich set of features that make resource management a reality. Unfortunately, these features are rarely implemented due to their complexity. But make no mistake, as servers become more powerful and efficient, database consolidation is going to become increasingly common. This is especially true with the Exadata platform. Understanding how to use database and I/O resource management is going to become an increasingly important tool for ensuring your databases meet the demands of your business.

The best advice we can offer is to keep things simple. Attempting to make use of every bell and whistle in the Oracle Resource Manager can lead to confusion and undesirable results. If you do not have a specific need for multi-level resource plans, stick to the single-level approach; rather use the shares based method, which is single level by design. Category plans are another rarely needed (and used) feature. The new Exadata 12.1.2.1.0 and database 12.1.0.2 BP4 feature performance profiles looks promising and an easy approach to do resource management. A majority of the situations you will face can be resolved by implementing a simple, single-level interdatabase resource plan. This means that the best advice on resource management that we can give is start small, keep it simple, and add features as you need them.

CHAPTER 8

Configuring Exadata

Oracle offers an optional service that handles the process of installing and configuring your Exadata Database Machine from start to finish. Many companies purchase this service to speed up their implementation time and reduce the complexity of integrating Exadata into their IT infrastructure. If you're reading this chapter, you may be considering performing the configuration yourself, or perhaps you're just interested in gaining a better understanding of how it's done. The process we'll discuss here closely resembles the installation process Oracle uses largely because we will be using the same utility Oracle uses to configure Exadata. The utility is called OneCommand. It takes site-specific information you provide and performs the entire configuration from network to software to storage. When the process is complete, your Exadata Database Machine will be fully functional, including a starter database.

Exadata Network Components

Oracle database network requirements have evolved over the years, and with Exadata you will notice a few new terms as well as the addition of a new network. Traditionally, Oracle database servers required one public network link to provide administrative access (typically SSH) and database access (SQL*Net). With the introduction of 11gR2 Grid Infrastructure (formerly known as Oracle Clusterware), Oracle coined a new term for this network—the *client access network*. On the Exadata platform, administrative and database traffic have been separated with the creation of a new network for administrative access. This new network is known as the *management network*. The client access network is no longer accessible through SSH and is used only by the Oracle listener for incoming SQL*Net connections. In Exadata terms (and mostly in the context of configuration), these two networks are referred to as NET0 (management network) and BONDETH0 (client access network).

The number and type of Ethernet ports on the compute nodes and storage cells varies between the V2, X2, and X3 models of Exadata. Hardware specifications for each model are detailed in the *Exadata Database Machine Owner's Guide*. At a minimum, though, all models provide at least four embedded 1 gigabit Ethernet ports. Oracle identifies these ports as NET0, NET1, NET2, and NET3. X2-2 and newer models include a pair of 10-gigabit Ethernet connections (SFP+ modules not included) on ports NET4 and NET5. As noted, NET0 is used for the management network (ETH0), and a pair of either NET1/NET2 or NET4/NET5 is used for the client access network (BONDETH0). In RAC environments, it is a common practice to bond two Ethernet devices together to provide hardware redundancy for the client access network. These links are traditionally active/passive to provide fault tolerance. The NET3 interface is unassigned and available to be configured as an optional network.

The Management Network

Exadata Database Machines have an Ethernet switch mounted in the rack that services the management network. The management network consists of the following links:

- One uplink from the management switch to your company's management network
- One link to NET0 on each compute node and storage cell
- One link to the ILOM on each compute node and storage cell
- One link to each of the InfiniBand switches
- One link for each of the two internal power distribution units (PDUs). This is optional and is only needed if you want to monitor electrical current remotely. The PDU links do not support gigabit Ethernet, only 10/100 Ethernet.

ILOM

In addition to the management network interface (NET0), compute nodes and storage cells come equipped with an Integrated Lights Out Manager (ILOM). Commonly found in most modern servers, the ILOM is an adapter card in each compute node and storage cell that operates independently of the operating system. The ILOM boots up as soon as power is applied to the server and provides web and SSH access through the management network. The ILOM allows you to perform many of the tasks remotely that would otherwise require physical access to the servers, including gaining access to the console, powering the system off and on, and rebooting or resetting the system. If needed, the ILOM offers a serial port, which can be used to gain direct console access to the host. This serial port requires a DB-9 to RJ-45 connection. Most modern client devices will require a USB-serial port adapter, which is included with the Exadata spare parts kit. Additionally, the ILOM monitors the configuration and state of the server's internal hardware components. As noted in the table above, the ILOM is linked via its Ethernet port to the management switch within the Exadata enclosure.

The Client Access Network

The client access network is used by the Oracle listener to provide SQL*Net connectivity to the databases. This network has traditionally been referred to, in RAC terminology, as the *public network*. One or two links (NET1/NET2 or NET4/NET5) from each database server (compute node) connect directly to your corporate switches. Oracle recommends bonding the connections to provide hardware redundancy for client connections. Copper connections should be bonded on NET1 and NET2. For bonding the fiber links, utilize NET4 and NET5. If the ports are bonded, then each link should terminate at a separate switch to provide network redundancy.

The Private Network

The internal InfiniBand (IB) switches service the private network. This network manages RAC interconnect traffic (cache fusion, heartbeat), as well as iDB traffic between the database grid and the storage grid. This network is self-contained within the InfiniBand network switch fabric and has no uplink to your corporate network. The network configuration can be found in the `ifcfg-ib0` and `ifcfg-ib1` configuration files in the /etc/sysconfig/network-scripts directory. In models released before the X4, they are configured as bonded devices with a master device file ifcfg-bondib0. For example, the following listing shows the InfiniBand network configuration files from one of the X3-2 database servers in our lab. Notice how the MASTER parameter is used to map these network devices to the bondib0 device:

```
/etc/sysconfig/network-scripts/ifcfg-bondib0
DEVICE=bondib0
USERCTL=no
BOOTPROTO=none
ONBOOT=yes
IPADDR=192.168.10.1
NETMASK=255.255.252.0
NETWORK=192.168.8.0
BROADCAST=192.168.11.255
BONDING_OPTS="mode=active-backup miimon=100 downdelay=5000 updelay=5000 num_grat_arp=100"
IPV6INIT=no
MTU=65520

/etc/sysconfig/network-scripts/ifcfg-ib0
DEVICE=ib0
USERCTL=no
ONBOOT=yes
MASTER=bondib0
SLAVE=yes
BOOTPROTO=none
HOTPLUG=no
IPV6INIT=no
CONNECTED_MODE=yes
MTU=65520

/etc/sysconfig/network-scripts/ifcfg-ib1
DEVICE=ib1
USERCTL=no
ONBOOT=yes
MASTER=bondib0
SLAVE=yes
BOOTPROTO=none
HOTPLUG=no
IPV6INIT=no
CONNECTED_MODE=yes
MTU=65520
```

On X4 and X5 generation systems, each InfiniBand port is configured with its own dedicated IP address. The example below shows sample InfiniBand interface configuration files from an X4-2 compute node:

```
/etc/sysconfig/network-scripts/ifcfg-ib0
#### DO NOT REMOVE THESE LINES ####
#### %GENERATED BY CELL% ####
DEVICE=ib0
BOOTPROTO=static
ONBOOT=yes
```

```
HOTPLUG=no
IPV6INIT=no
IPADDR=192.168.12.1
NETMASK=255.255.255.0
NETWORK=192.168.12.0
BROADCAST=192.168.12.255
MTU=7000
CONNECTED_MODE=yes

/etc/sysconfig/network-scripts/ifcfg-ib1
#### DO NOT REMOVE THESE LINES ####
#### %GENERATED BY CELL% ####
DEVICE=ib1
BOOTPROTO=static
ONBOOT=yes
HOTPLUG=no
IPV6INIT=no
IPADDR=192.168.12.2
NETMASK=255.255.255.0
NETWORK=192.168.12.0
BROADCAST=192.168.12.255
MTU=7000
CONNECTED_MODE=yes
```

This configuration method provides for redundant active links. Notice that the MTU size for the IB network devices is set to 7,000 (bytes). MTU stands for *maximum transmission unit* and determines the maximum size of a network packet that may be transmitted across the network. Typical Ethernet networks are configured with an MTU size of up to 1,500 bytes. In recent years, the Jumbo Frames technology has become a popular way to improve database performance by reducing the number of network roundtrips required for cache fusion between the cluster nodes in an Oracle RAC cluster. Conventionally, Jumbo Frames support an MTU of up to 9,000 bytes, but some implementations may support an even larger MTU size.

■ **Note** Only the database servers are configured with a larger MTU size. Presumably, this is to benefit TCP/IP (IPoIB: IP over InfiniBand) traffic between the database servers and any external host that is linked to the IB switch. You may be surprised to know that the IB ports on the storage cells are configured with the standard 1,500-byte MTU size. The large MTU size is not necessary on the storage cells because most large I/O operations between the database grid and the storage grid utilize the RDS protocol, which is much more efficient for database I/O and bypasses the TCP/IP protocol stack altogether. On InfiniBand networks, the MTU size only comes into play when working with IP over InfiniBand (IPoIB)—not RDS. Processes such as backups or NFS mounts using the InfiniBand network can benefit from the larger MTU size.

About the Configuration Process

Configuring Oracle database servers has generally been a manual and somewhat error-prone process, especially for RAC environments. Exadata can be configured manually as well, but the complexities of the platform can make this a risky undertaking. Oracle has greatly simplified the configuration process by providing a utility called the Oracle Exadata Deployment Assistant (OEDA). This tool ensures that all Exadata racks are configured using the same process and toolset, which is critical for wider support of the platform. OEDA uses input parameters you provide, and it carries out all of the low-level tasks for you. Even so, gathering all the right information required by OEDA will likely be a collaborative effort, especially with the networking components. The final result of the Exadata configuration process is to leave you with a fully configured Oracle RAC system that is patched to the specified software versions with a sample database up and running. Figure 8-1 illustrates the Exadata configuration process using OEDA.

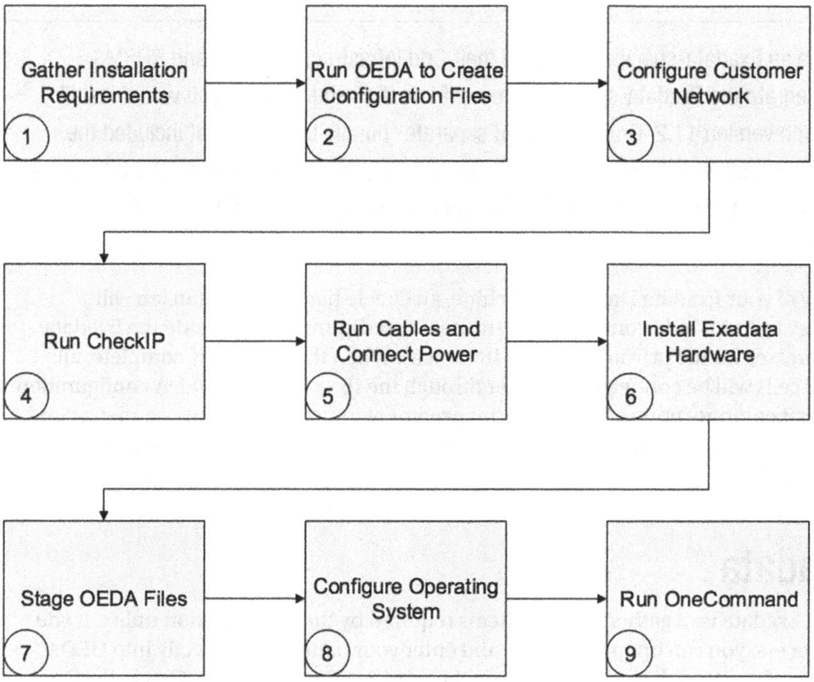

Figure 8-1. *The configuration process*

As indicated in Figure 8-1, the first step in the process is to gather the installation requirements and enter them in to the OEDA graphical utility. Exadata requires IP addresses for the three distinct networks (management, client access, and InfiniBand), as well as information for domain name service (DNS), network time protocol (NTP), automatic service request (ASR), and mail information if you wish to send out alerts. All of these items are then fed into the OEDA graphical utility. When gathering the network requirements, you will most likely need to enlist the help of your network administrator to reserve IP addresses and subnets and register new network names with the domain name server. It is important to understand how these configuration settings are used, so we will spend a considerable amount of time discussing them in "Step 2: Run OEDA."

OEDA is downloaded from My Oracle Support and can be found from MOS note # 888828.1. The person who will be performing the installation can direct you as to which files to download. OEDA contains a java-based graphical utility that is included in the larger set of files that include the OEDA configuration scripts used to install and configure the Exadata. OEDA generates all the parameter and deployment files OneCommand needs for configuring your system, along with additional files used by Oracle Enterprise Manager 12c for configuring an Exadata target, as well as configuration files used by Oracle Platinum Support for additional support. Once this is done, you are ready to upload these files to Exadata.

Before running the OEDA configuration scripts, you will need to stage the installation media for the Grid Infrastructure and the database (including any Oracle-prescribed patches). The final step of the process is to execute the OEDA configuration script. Its operation consists of multiple steps that configure all the components of your Exadata Database Machine. The top-level script that runs the OEDA configuration utility is called `config.sh`. This script can be run end-to-end, executing all of the steps automatically, or you may specify a step to run using command-line options. We strongly recommend running these steps one at a time. Doing so makes it much easier to troubleshoot if a step fails to complete successfully. Also, Exadata eighth rack configurations include several steps that will reboot the nodes.

■ **Note** Rather than create an Exadata-specific release of their Grid Infrastructure, ASM, and RDBMS products, Oracle chose to integrate the Exadata-specific code right into the same product you would install on non-Exadata platforms. With version 11.2, Oracle released separate "bundle patches" that included the standard PSU content as well as additional Exadata-specific bug fixes. Beginning with version 12.1.0.1, Oracle no longer releases separate bundle patches for Exadata, but recommends applying the standard PSU.

When you take delivery of your Exadata Database Machine, an Oracle hardware technician will complete certain tasks. These tasks include connecting all the networked components inside the Exadata rack and configuring IP addresses for the private network (IB switch). When this process is complete, all compute nodes and storage cells will be connected together through the IB switch. The OEDA configuration script is only run from the first compute node and uses the management network to execute configuration commands on other servers and storage cells, as well as to install the Grid Infrastructure and RDBMS software on all database servers.

Configuring Exadata

The first step in configuring Exadata is to gather all of the items required by the configuration utility. If you are comfortable with the process, you can opt out of step 1 and enter your parameters directly into OEDA as you gather them. The examples shown here are taken from the April 2015 version of the Oracle Exadata Deployment Assistant. As a new version of the utility is released monthly, it is very possible for there to be a variance from the images shown here.

Step 1: Gathering Installation Requirements

As always, gathering requirements is one of the most critical (and frustrating) parts of taking on any project. Because Exadata is configured in one fell swoop, everything should be ready to go at once. This means that the networks must be ready, all hostnames must be registered in DNS, and information for items such as which e-mail addresses should receive alerts all must be gathered before the system is installed. While it is possible to skip this step and move straight to the QEDA, there is no mechanism to save progress if all of the required information is not filled out. We will cover the actual items needed by walking through the configuration utility step-by-step.

Step 2: Run Oracle Exadata Deployment Assistant

Prior to the release of the X3, Oracle asked customers to fill out a lengthy document, which was sent back to Oracle. Upon receipt, Oracle would take that information and enter it all into an Excel spreadsheet (`dbm_configurator.xls`). In October 2012, Oracle combined these two steps into one java utility (OEDA) that customers could fill out directly. While it does provide less overall work, OEDA can be just as daunting for customers who are not familiar with the implications of every question being asked.

First, in order to obtain the OEDA utility, customers must download the package that will be installed on the Exadata. This can be found in the "OEDA" section of My Oracle Support note #888828.1. After the utility is downloaded, unzip the file, which will contain the configuration utility. There are separate downloads for Windows, Linux, and Mac OS X, so download the version specific to the machine where you will run the initial graphical utility. When you are ready to run the configuration utility, run `./config.sh` or `config.cmd`—depending on your operating system. The welcome screen will greet you (Figure 8-2). From here, users can click Next ➤ to move on or Import, which allows you to modify a set of existing configuration files.

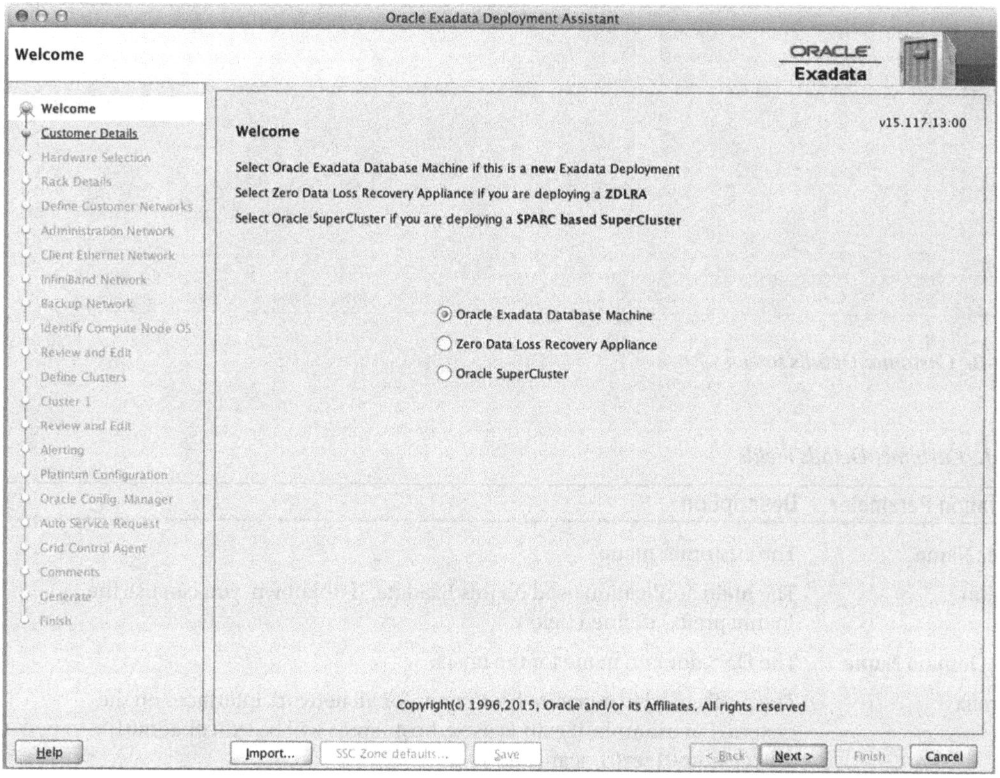

Figure 8-2. *OEDA main screen*

Customer Details

Upon clicking the Next ➤ button, the configuration utility will ask for general information about the rack that is being installed, as shown in Figure 8-3. This includes customer name, application name, region, time zone, operating system, and database name prefix. All of these fields are required and will be present in the final deployment summary. Table 8-1 defines these parameters.

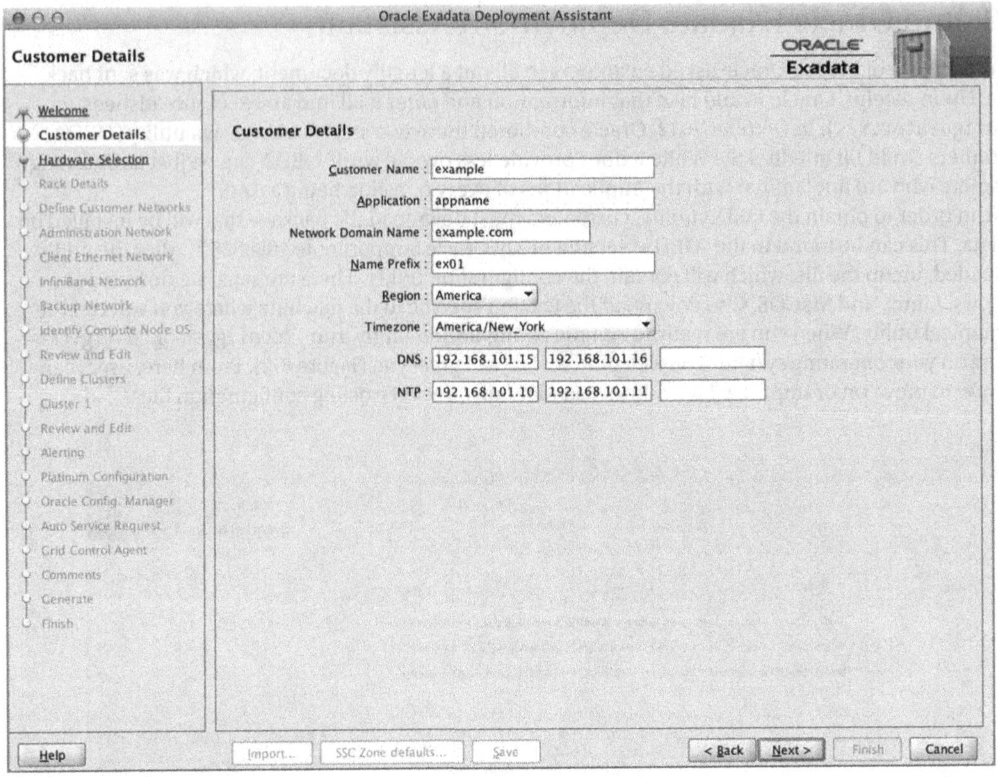

Figure 8-3. *Customer Details screen*

Table 8-1. *Customer Details Fields*

Configuration Parameter	Description
Customer Name	The customer name
Application	The main application used on this Exadata. If unknown, you can use the "name prefix" defined below.
Network Domain Name	The DNS domain name for the hosts
Name Prefix	The prefix used to generate hostnames for all network interfaces on the system. For example, if ex01 is used, hostnames will be ex01dbadm01, ex01celadm01, ex01-scan, and so on.
Region	The region that the Exadata will reside in, such as Europe or America
Time Zone	This is the time zone in which Exadata resides, for example, America/Chicago.
DNS	IP addresses for DNS servers (minimum one)
NTP	IP addresses for NTP servers (minimum one)

■ **Note** The most important field on this screen is the "Database Machine Prefix," which will be used as the basis for naming all of the hosts in the Exadata rack. Prior to the Exadata configuration utility, this prefix only supported four characters in length. With the new configuration utility, up to 16 characters are supported for the prefix. For the sake of uniformity, it is recommended to keep the hostname prefix to eight characters or less, due to the requirements for the single-client access name (SCAN). SCAN only supports hostnames up to 15 characters. Also, while many organizations are proponents of longer hostnames, the naming conventions for Exadata can be rather restrictive. While any installation may seem permanent, we have seen many Exadata racks relocated to different data centers. Because of the complexity in renaming the hosts in RAC systems—much less Exadata (which requires renaming the storage as well)—many customers decided to simply tear down and rebuild the entire cluster upon moving to the new data center. If the hostname prefix had not included the location, only the IPs would need to change—a much simpler process that is not destructive.

Hardware Selection

The "Hardware Selection" screen (Figure 8-4) is used to choose the type of Exadata rack being installed. OEDA supports Exadata racks from X2 onward and the SPARC SuperCluster platform, as well. When installing an Exadata rack, be sure to select the correct storage type and size—High Capacity models may come in 2TB, 3TB, or 4TB, depending on when the rack was purchased. Newer versions of the OEDA utility support elastic configurations found in the X5 generation of Exadata. Simply choose the "Elastic Rack" option that corresponds to your rack type—you will enter the exact number of compute or storage servers on the "Rack Details" screen.

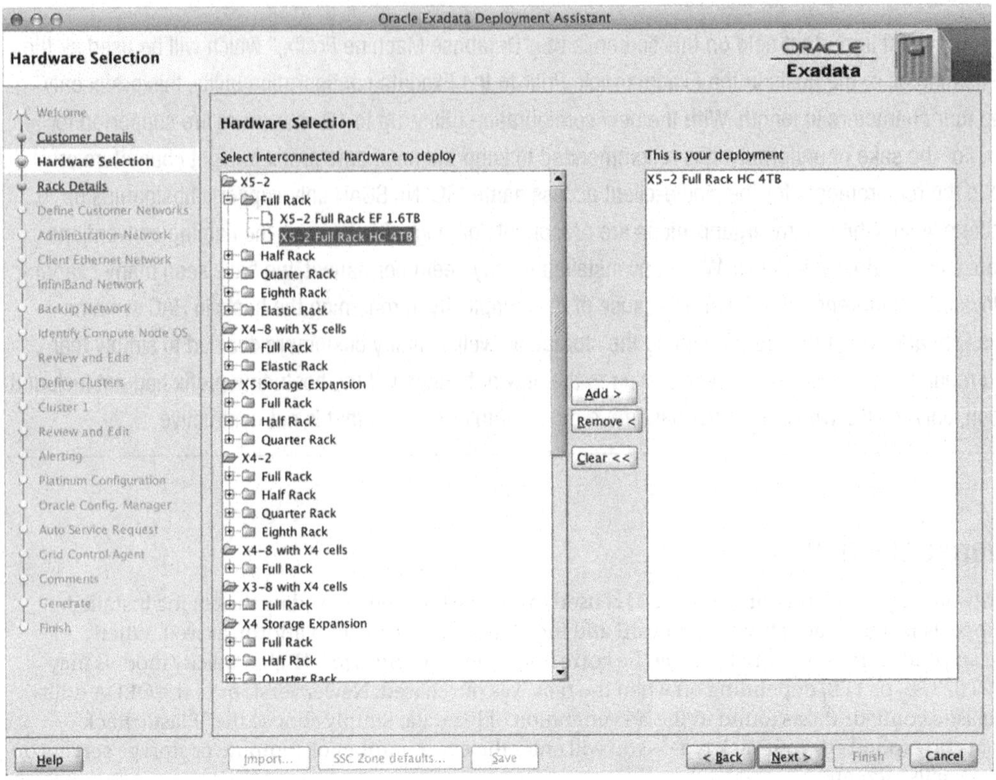

***Figure 8-4.** Hardware selection*

The "Hardware Selection" screen also allows customers to easily generate configuration files for multirack configurations by simply moving the correct rack sizes over to the right-hand pane. This will allow the multiple racks to be configured at the same time as one cluster.

Also, for customers splitting a single rack into multiple smaller racks, it is possible to generate the configuration files using OEDA. In the case of a split rack, choose the equipment size corresponding to the actual frame size (if splitting a full rack into two half racks, choose the full rack size—clusters will be defined later in the tool). We will continue the split rack topic in the "Cluster Configuration" section of the configuration utility.

Rack Details

The "Rack Details" screen shown in Figure 8-5 shows the number of compute and storage servers within the rack. Standard rack sizes (eighth, quarter, half, and full racks) will have the traditional number of servers for each option. Elastic racks allow you to set the number of compute and storage servers that are configured for your specific rack.

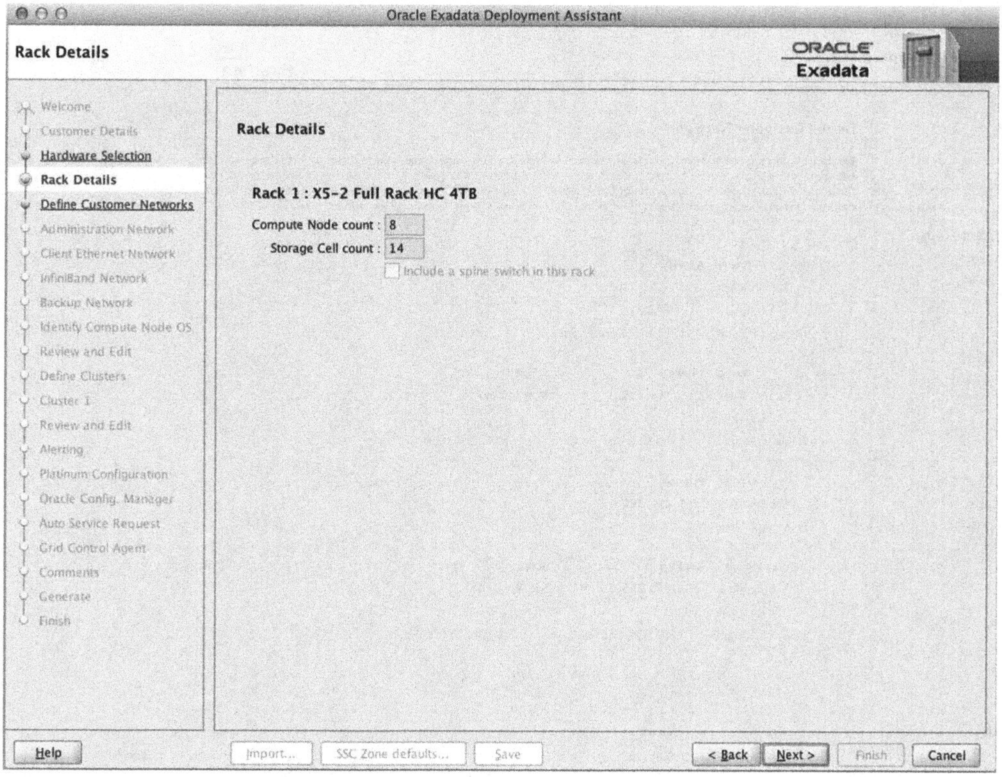

Figure 8-5. *Rack Details screen*

Define Customer Networks

The "Define Customer Networks" screen shown in Figure 8-6 requests the subnet mask and gateway information for each of the networks utilized on the Exadata rack, along with the port configuration. This is where you will specify if the connections will be bonded and whether they will use the copper or optical ports on the compute nodes. Table 8-2 defines each of the parameters listed on this screen.

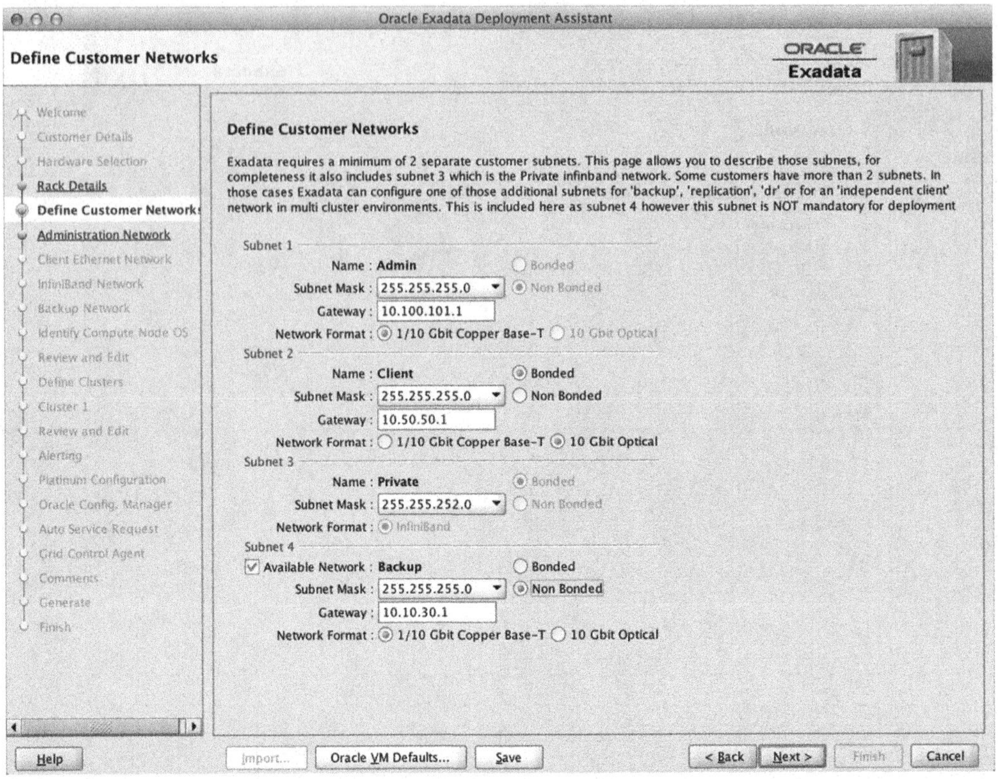

Figure 8-6. *Define Customer Networks screen*

Table 8-2. *Define Customer Networks Fields*

Configuration Parameter	Description
Admin Subnet Mask	Subnet mask for the management network
Admin Gateway	IP address of the gateway device used on the management network
Client Subnet Mask	Subnet mask for the client access network
Client Gateway	IP address of the gateway device used on the client access network
Client Bonded / Non-Bonded	Determines whether the client access network will be configured as an active/passive bond for high availability
Client Copper Base-T / Optical	Determines whether the client access network will utilize the copper connections (NET1 / NET2) or fiber connections (NET4 / NET5) for the bondeth0 interface. If bonding is not configured, NET1 or NET4 will be used.
Private Subnet Mask	Subnet mask for the InfiniBand network
Backup Subnet Mask	Subnet mask for the optional backup network
Backup Gateway	IP address of the gateway device used on the optional backup network

(*continued*)

Table 8-2. (*continued*)

Configuration Parameter	Description
Backup Bonded / Non-Bonded	Determines whether the optional backup network will be configured as an active/passive bond for high availability
Backup Copper Base-T / Optical	Determines whether the optional backup network will utilize the copper connections (NET1 / NET2 for bonded, NET3 for non-bonded) or fiber connections (NET4 / NET5) for the bondeth1 interface. If bonding is not configured, NET3 will be used.

■ **Note** The way OEDA assigns IP addresses sequentially from a base address can be problematic when adding compute nodes and storage cells to your configuration. We'll talk more about this later in the chapter when we look at upgrading Exadata.

Administration Network

The "Administration Network" screen (Figure 8-7) is used to define the management network. The fields are described in Table 8-3. The administration network (formerly known as the management network) contains IP addresses for all of the physical components in the rack, including all database and storage servers, InfiniBand switches, power distribution units, as well as the Cisco switch. You can think of this network as the SSH entry point for logging into the compute nodes, storage cells, and InfiniBand switches. The internal Cisco network switch services the management network. Only one network drop is required to uplink the Cisco management switch to your company network. The Exaconf utility requires a contiguous set of IP addresses, so only the first IP address in the range is required. Enter the subnet mask and gateway IP, and choose whether the management network will be used to define the hostname of the database servers (the default is yes). The hostnames for the management network will include <dbmachine_prefix➤ dbadm01, <dbmachine_prefix➤ celadm01, and so on. This naming convention was introduced with the Exadata configuration utility. If you still prefer the old naming convention (without the "adm"), it is possible to click the "Modify..." button and remove the "adm" entry from the hostname mask. Ensure that the "%" is still there, as it is used to enumerate the hosts, as well as the rack number (useful for multirack installations).

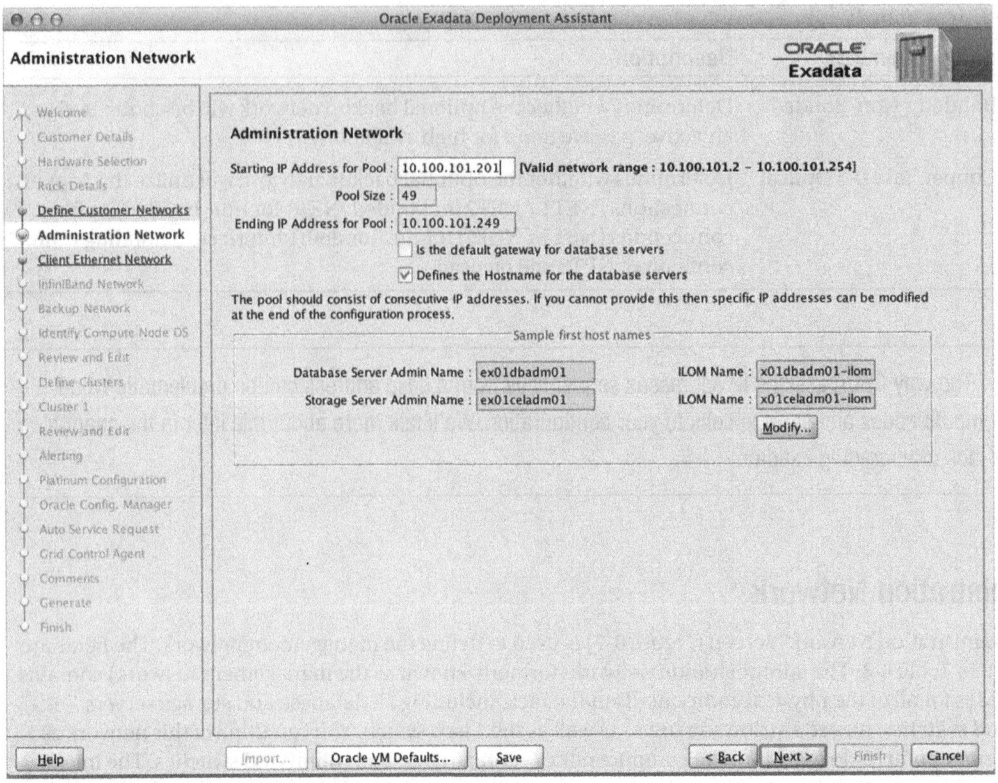

Figure 8-7. *Administration Network screen*

Table 8-3. *Administration Network Fields*

Configuration Parameter	Description
Starting IP Address for Pool	The first IP address in the range assigned to the Exadata rack for the management network
Pool Size	The number of IP addresses required for the management network. This number cannot be modified.
Ending IP Address for Pool	The last IP address used by the Exadata rack on the management network. This number cannot be modified and is computed from the starting IP address and the pool size.
Is the Default Gateway for Database Servers	If the default route for the database servers will be the management network, check this box. Default is to leave unchecked.
Defines the Hostname for the database servers	If the hostnames will be configured based on the management network, select this box. The default value is to leave this checked.

Client Ethernet Network

The "Client Ethernet Network" screen lists the configuration details for the client access network (Figure 8-8). This network is used for database traffic from application servers and includes the node virtual IP (VIP) addresses as well as the single client access name (SCAN) VIPs. Typically, this network contains the default route for the database servers. With the introduction of the OEDA utility, the default naming convention for this network changed as well. What previously was named <dbmachine_prefix><host_number> (ex0101, ex0102, etc) is now <dbmachine_prefix>client<host_number> (ex01client01, ex01client02, etc). To go back to the old naming convention, simply click the "Modify…" button and remove "client" from the name fields. Table 8-4 describes the fields for the "Client Ethernet Networks" screen.

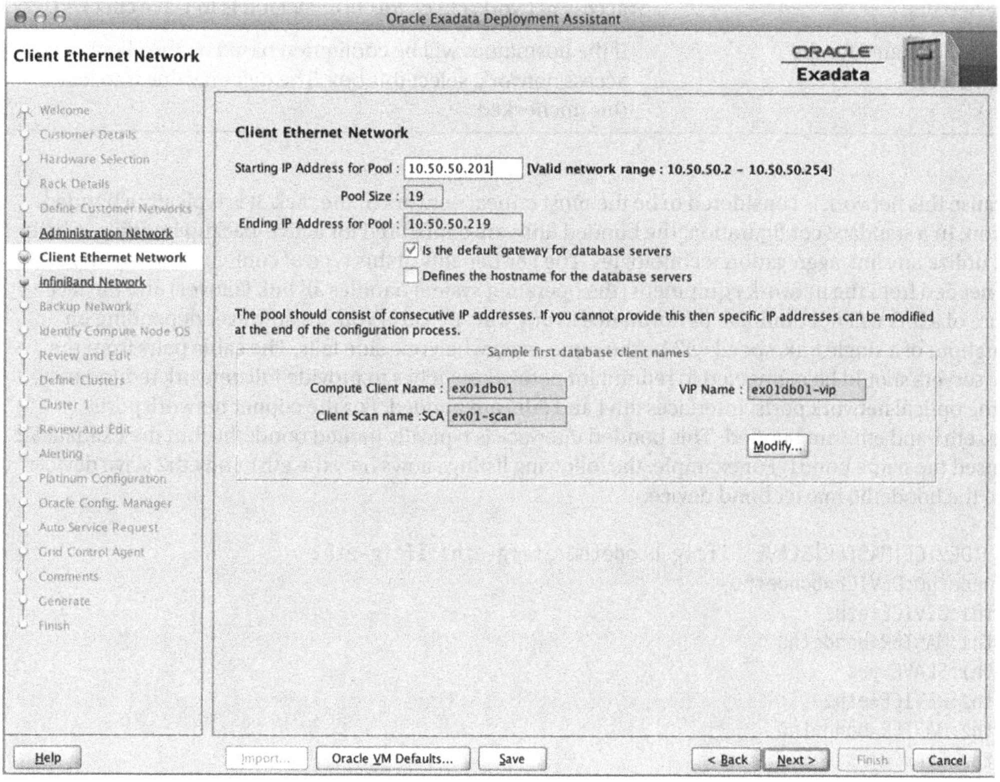

Figure 8-8. *Client Ethernet Network screen*

Table 8-4. *Client Ethernet Network Fields*

Configuration Parameter	Description
Starting IP Address for Pool	The first IP address in the range assigned to the Exadata rack for the client access network
Pool Size	The number of IP addresses required for the client access network. This number cannot be modified.
Ending IP Address for Pool	The last IP address used by the Exadata rack on the client access network
Is the Default Gateway for Database Servers	If the default route for the database servers will be the client access network, check this box. Default is to leave checked.
Defines the Hostname for the Database Servers	If the hostnames will be configured based on the client access network, select this box. The default value is to leave this unchecked.

Because this network is considered to be the most critical network in the rack, it is typically a bonded connection. In a standard configuration, the bonded links are configured for active-backup bonding, which does not utilize any link aggregation technologies. The key benefits of this type of configuration are the lack of setup needed from the network equipment (the operating system handles all link failover) and the fact that failure of a link will not diminish performance in any way. Because you are only ever depending on the throughput of a single link, speed will be the same, even when one side fails. The cable pairs from the database servers should be connected to redundant network switches to provide full network redundancy. If using the optical network ports, interfaces eth4 and eth5 are bonded. For the copper network ports, interfaces eth1 and eth2 are bonded. This bonded interface is typically named bondeth0, but the Exadata V2 models used the name bond1. For example, the following listing shows how the eth1 and eth2 slave devices reference the bondeth0 master bond device:

```
# egrep 'DEVICE|MASTER|SLAVE' ifcfg-bondeth0 ifcfg-eth1 ifcfg-eth2
ifcfg-bondeth0:DEVICE=bondeth0
ifcfg-eth1:DEVICE=eth1
ifcfg-eth1:MASTER=bondeth0
ifcfg-eth1:SLAVE=yes
ifcfg-eth2:DEVICE=eth2
ifcfg-eth2:MASTER=bondeth0
ifcfg-eth2:SLAVE=yes
```

■ **Tip** Exadata V2 systems do not include 10 gigabit Ethernet (10 GbE) interfaces, and they only support gigabit copper. Each Exadata X2-2/X3-2/X4-2/X5-2 compute node has two optical 10GbE ports, and each X3-8/X4-8 compute node has eight optical 10GbE ports.

InfiniBand Network

The "InfiniBand Network" screen (Figure 8-9) contains the configuration information for the InfiniBand network. The InfiniBand network contains a default set of IP addresses, utilizing 192.168.10.1 as the starting address, with a subnet mask of 255.255.252.0. The InfiniBand network is an internal private interconnect used to connect the database servers to the storage. Due to possible routing issues, it requires a network range that is not used anywhere else in the corporate network. Because the InfiniBand network is used as an internal network, it does not include a gateway. The OEDA configuration utility did not introduce any changes to the naming convention used on the InfiniBand network. On Exadata X4-2 racks and beyond, it is possible to choose the "active bonding" functionality. This feature breaks the previously bonded configuration and enables each of the InfiniBand ports for traffic. Selecting this option will double the number of IP addresses used on the compute nodes—X4-2 and newer storage servers will always utilize active bonding. Table 8-5 describes the fields for the "InfiniBand Network" screen.

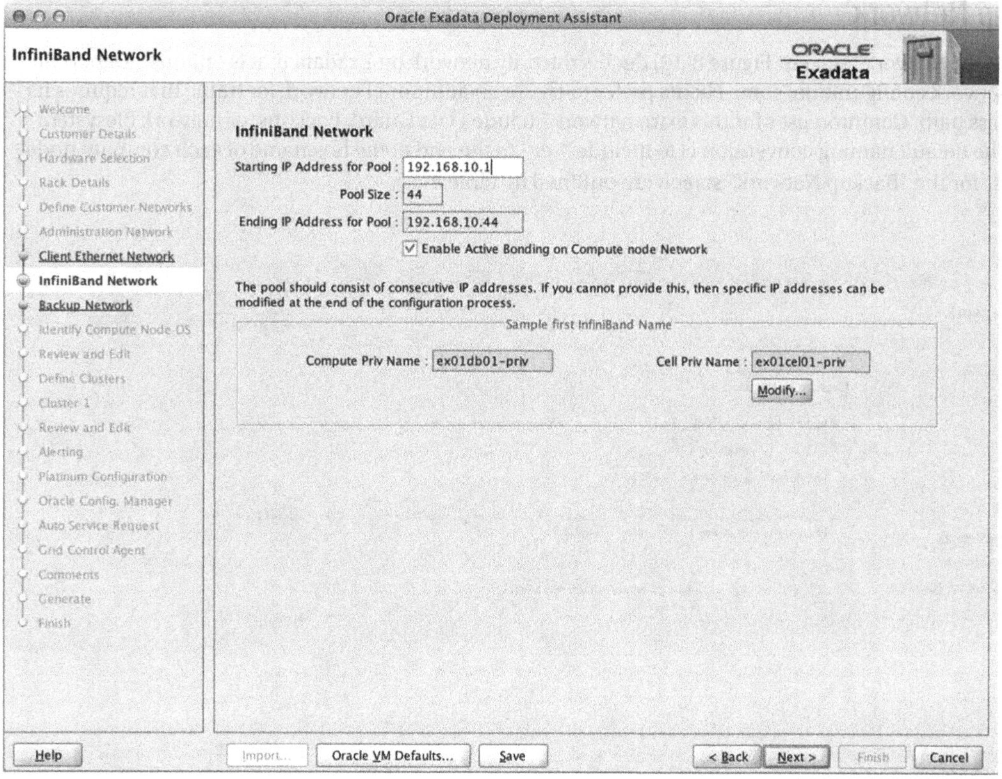

Figure 8-9. *InfiniBand Network screen*

Table 8-5. InfiniBand Network Fields

Configuration Parameter	Description
Starting IP Address for Pool	The first IP address in the range assigned to the Exadata rack for the InfiniBand network
Pool Size	The number of IP addresses required for the InfiniBand network. This number cannot be modified.
Ending IP Address for Pool	The last IP address used by the Exadata rack on the InfiniBand network
Enable Active Bonding on Compute Node Networks	Determines whether the InfiniBand ports will be configured as an active/passive bond (bondib0) or if individual network interfaces will be created. Active bonding requires Exadata X4 or newer hardware.

Backup Network

The "Backup Network" screen (Figure 8-10) details the only network on Exadata that is optional. Depending on the network configuration, some clients prefer to create an additional network for traffic that requires its own access path. Common uses for this extra network include Data Guard, backups, or network filesystem (NFS). The default naming convention is to include "-dr" to the end of the hostname of each compute node. The fields for the "Backup Network" screen are outlined in Table 8-6.

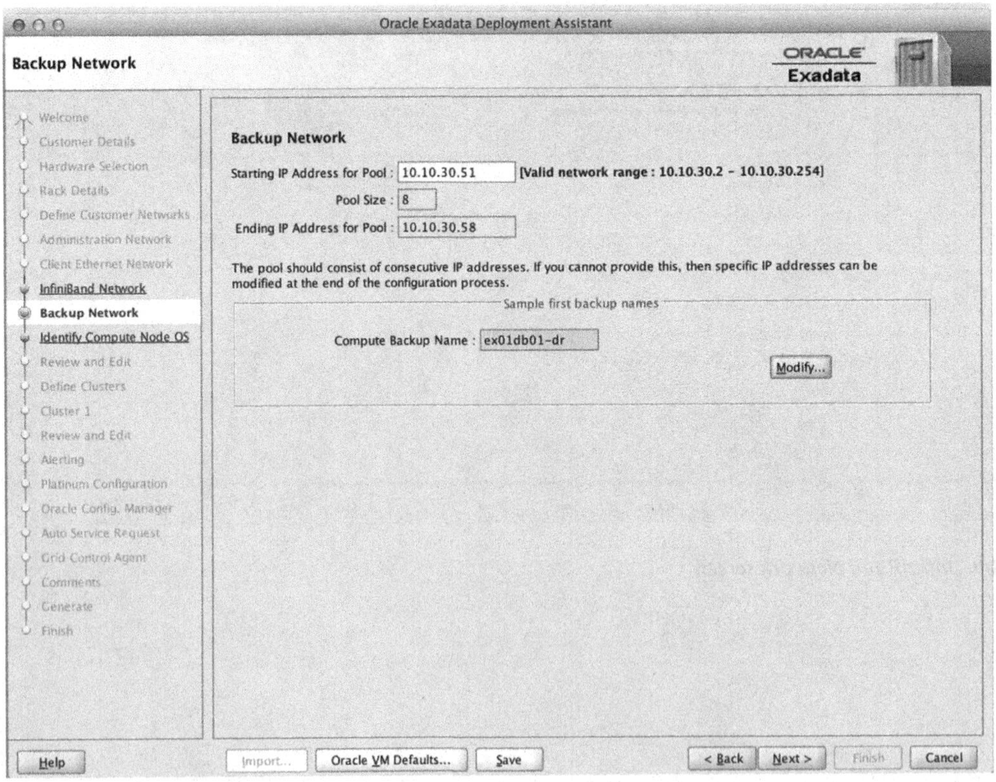

Figure 8-10. Backup / Data Guard Ethernet Network screen

Table 8-6. *Backup / Data Guard Ethernet Network Fields*

Configuration Parameter	Description
Starting IP Address for Pool	The first IP address in the range assigned to the Exadata rack for the client access network. Note that only the compute nodes will require IP addresses on this network.
Pool Size	The number of IP addresses required for the client access network. This number cannot be modified.
Ending IP Address for Pool	The last IP address used by the Exadata rack on the client access network

Identify Compute Node OS and Enable Capacity-on-Demand

The "Identify Compute Node OS and Enable Capacity-on-Demand" screen (Figure 8-11) asks standard configuration questions about the operating system environment, allowing customers to choose between a physical Linux installation or to virtualize the Exadata rack using Oracle Virtual Machine (OVM). This screen also allows customers to enable Oracle's Capacity-on-Demand feature, which disables CPU cores to save money on Oracle licenses.

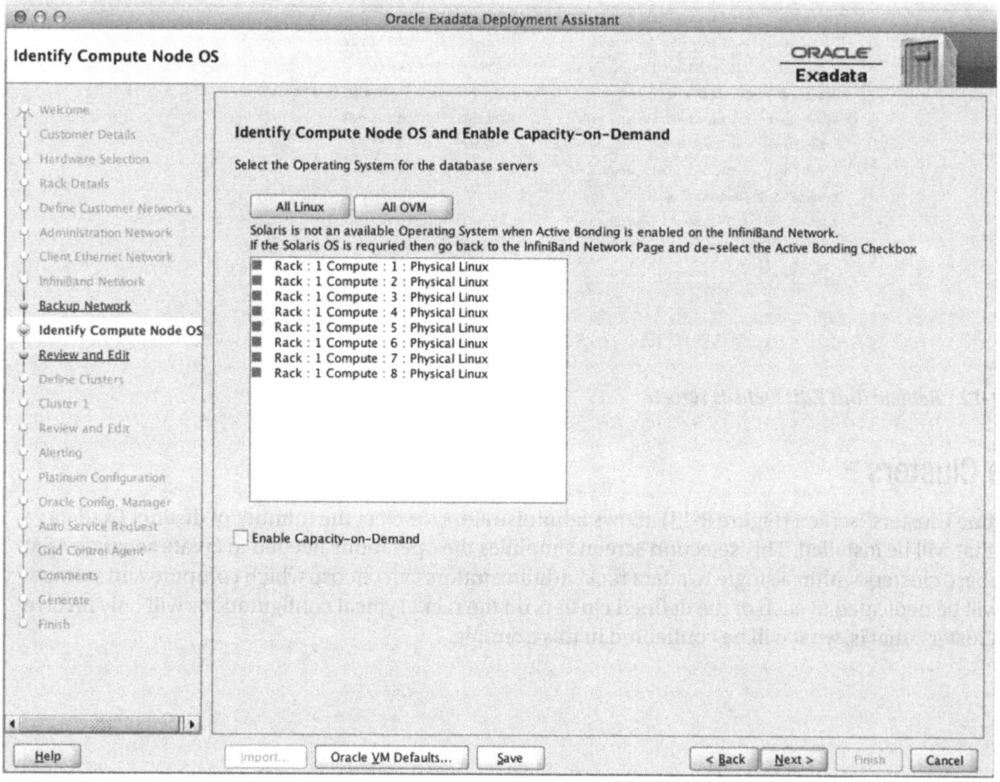

Figure 8-11. *OS configuration screen*

Review and Edit Details

The "Review and Edit Details" screen (Figure 8-12) allows users to check and modify the IP addresses for the Exadata rack on the management and private networks. In the event that you are making changes to an existing configuration, remember to click the "Re-Generate Data" button to refresh the hostnames and IP addresses.

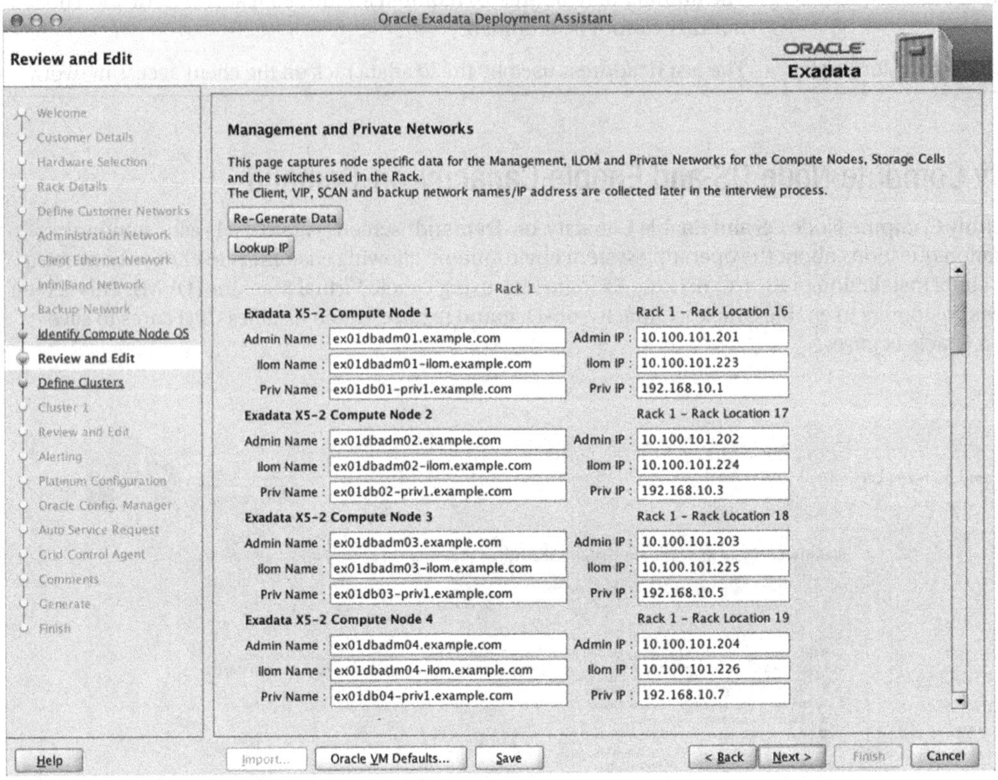

Figure 8-12. *Review and Edit Details screen*

Define Clusters

The "Define Clusters" screen (Figure 8-13) allows administrators to select the number of distinct Exadata clusters that will be installed. This selection screen simplifies the operations needed to create separate ASM and database clusters within a single Exadata rack. Administrators can choose which compute and storage servers will be dedicated to each of the defined clusters on the rack. Typical configurations will only involve a single cluster—that is, what will be configured in this example.

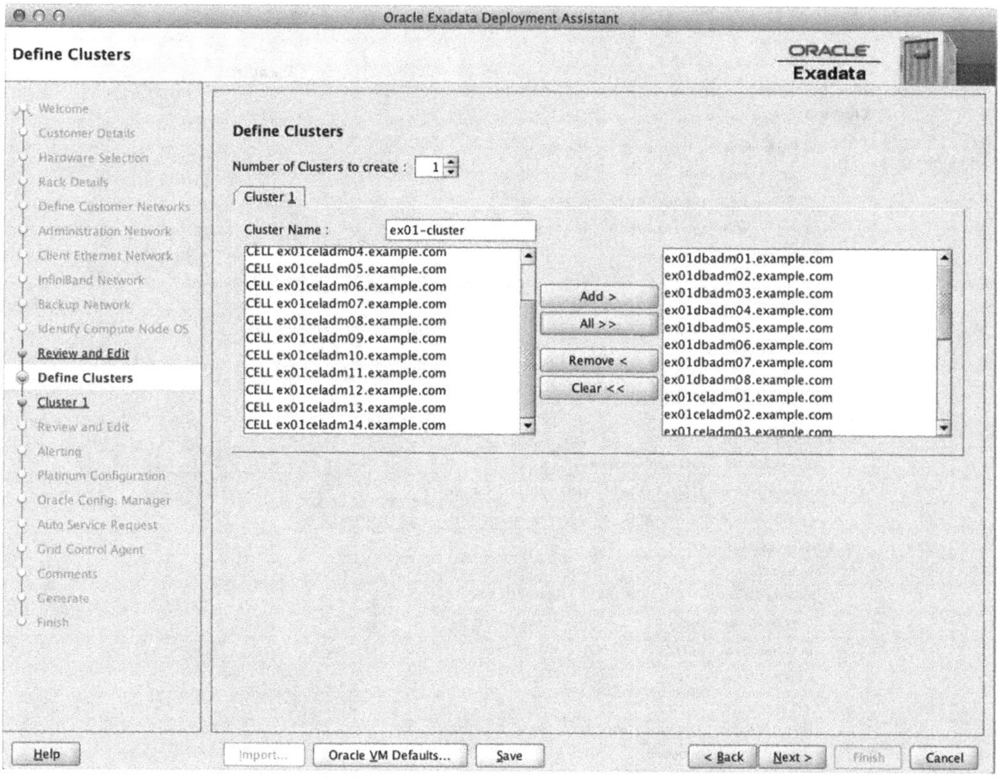

__Figure 8-13.__ Define Clusters screen

Cluster (n)

Each cluster defined in the previous screen will have its own cluster details page (Figure 8-14). The "Cluster (n)" screen asks for all of the specific details for that cluster. This includes the naming convention for all virtual IP addresses, UID and GID for the operating system accounts, Oracle software home installation details, and the ASM disk group configuration. First, the DNS and NTP servers for the compute nodes are enumerated, followed by the software account ownership details. Next, administrators define the Oracle software home directories and patch levels. By default, Oracle utilizes the Optimal Flexible Architecture (OFA) standard for naming software homes. Most Exadata installations utilize the OFA standard, as the Oracle configuration utilities are guaranteed to work properly when using OFA. It is possible to change the software locations, but remember that the factory Exadata image includes a large /u01 filesystem and a very small / filesystem. This configuration will not include adequate disk space in the event that you wish to move away from filesystems located in /u01.

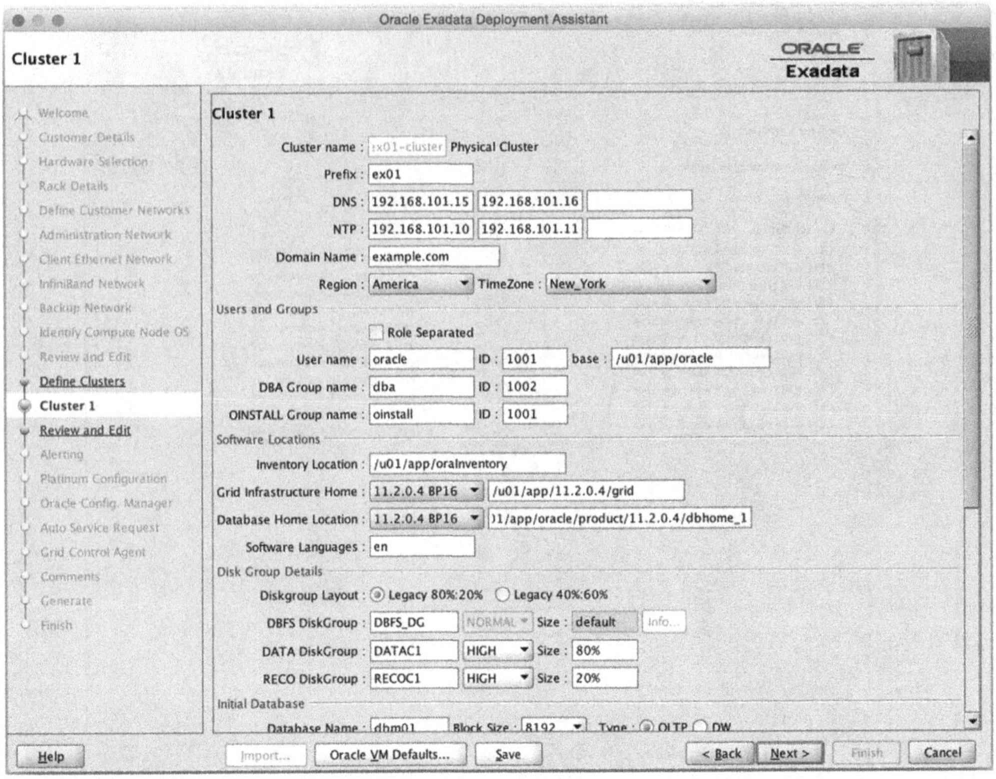

Figure 8-14. Cluster (n) screen

After the directory structure, the "cluster (n)" screen allows users to set their ASM disk group names and redundancy levels. By default, the database machine prefix (selected in the "Customer Details" screen) is appended to the end of the disk group names. As disk group redundancies are selected, the disk size settings will change dynamically. Typically, Oracle will use an 80%/20% split of DATA and RECO, assuming that the DATA disk group will be larger. For customers wishing to create a larger disk group for their fast recovery area (FRA), a check box is in place to make more space available to the RECO disk group. When planning for ASM disk group redundancy, consider the following:

> **High Redundancy**: Every extent is written with three copies. This configuration can significantly reduce available space in your disk groups. According to Oracle, it is best used when disk space is not an issue or when planning to apply all Exadata patches in a rolling fashion.
>
> **Normal Redundancy**: Every extent is written with two copies. While it provides quite a bit more usable space in the disk groups, keep in mind that the simultaneous loss of two disks containing the same data will cause ASM to dismount your disk groups. If that happens, your databases using those disk groups will also go offline. When applying rolling storage server patches, 12 disks will be taken offline at a time, leaving only one copy of data available.

As you consider which protection scheme is right for you, think about your pain tolerance when it comes to system outages. Normal redundancy provides more storage and less protection from disk/cell failures. Unless you can afford for your databases to be down for an extended period of time, you should lean toward high redundancy for the DATA disk group. If you can afford an outage while transient disk/cell failures are resolved, or in a worst-case scenario, wait for a full database recovery, then perhaps high redundancy for the RECO disk group is a better fit. If space is very tight and you can tolerate these types of outages, then you may consider setting redundancy for all disk groups to normal. It is worth saying that most Exadata customers configure their Exadata racks with normal redundancy.

The redundancy level for your DBFS_DG disk group, which stores the OCR and voting files in most configurations, will be automatically set to the normal redundancy. OneCommand will move the OCR and voting files to a high redundancy disk group, should one be available (in configurations for half racks or larger).

The name of the sample database is included (dbm), along with the block size and database type. Typically, the dbm database is dropped shortly after the system has been installed. It is common to utilize a block size of 8192—remember that Smart Scans will not return entire blocks, but only the data requested by the session. The OLTP/DW database types are mostly irrelevant, as the Exadata configuration utility creates Database Creation Assistant (DBCA) templates for both OLTP and data warehouse workloads.

Finally, the screen includes information related to the configuration of the client and backup network interfaces for the cluster members. In this section, you can define the naming standard for the virtual IP interfaces used on the client network, as well as the hostname that will be utilized by the Single Client Access Name (SCAN) feature. You are also presented with the ability to configure the naming convention used by the backup network (if utilized).

In the event that multiple clusters are configured, the next screen will request the same information for the next cluster to be configured. Repeat this process for all remaining clusters to be built. Table 8-7 details the fields on the "Cluster (n)" screen.

Table 8-7. *Cluster (n) Fields*

Configuration Parameter	Description
Prefix	The naming prefix used for the Exadata cluster
DNS	IP addresses of the DNS servers used by the cluster
NTP	IP addresses of the NTP servers used by the cluster
Domain Name	Domain name used by the hosts in the cluster
Region / Time Zone	Time zone used by the hosts in the cluster
Role Separated	Check this box if you prefer to use a role separated installation. Role separated environments create different operating system user accounts for each of the Oracle homes on the cluster.
User Name / ID	Operating system account and UID that will own the Oracle software homes
Base	Directory that will be used for the ORACLE_BASE environment variable
DBA Group Name / ID	Operating system group and GID that will be used as OSDBA when the Oracle software homes are installed
OINSTALL Group Name / ID	Operating system group and GID that will own the Oracle software inventory
Inventory Location	Directory that will be used to host the Oracle software inventory
Grid Infrastructure Home	Patch level and directory that will be used for the Grid Infrastructure Oracle home

(*continued*)

Table 8-7. *(continued)*

Configuration Parameter	Description
Database Home Location	Patch level and directory where Oracle database software will be installed
Software Install languages	Language for Oracle software installation
Disk Group Layout	Radio buttons to if you want to use one of the default storage configurations.
DBFS Disk Group	Name used for DBFS_DG ASM disk group. If running multiple clusters, this disk group may not have the same name across clusters.
DATA Disk Group / Redundancy / Size	Name used for the DATA ASM disk group. If running multiple clusters, this disk group may not have the same name across clusters. Redundancy may be either NORMAL or HIGH. Size allocations must equal 100% when complete.
RECO Disk Group / Redundancy / Size	Name used for the RECO ASM disk group. If running multiple clusters, this disk group may not have the same name across clusters. Size allocations must equal 100% when complete.
Database Name	Name of the sample database that will be created
Block Size	Block size for the sample database
OLTP/DW	Database template used for the sample database (OLTP or data warehouse)
Base Adapter (Client Network)	The network adapter defined in the "Client Ethernet Network" screen
Domain	Domain name appended to the hostnames used by the client access network
Start IP	The first IP address used for the client network by the compute nodes in the cluster
Subnet Mask	The subnet mask defined for the client access network in the "Define Customer Networks" screen
Gateway IP	The gateway IP address defined for the client access network in the "Client Ethernet Network" screen
Name Mask / Start ID	Naming convention used for hostnames on the client access network. The "%%" defined in this field will begin with the number defined in the "Start ID" field.
VIP Name Mask / Start ID	Naming convention used for the virtual IP address interfaces on the cluster. The "%%" defined in this field will begin with the number defined in the "Start ID" field.
SCAN Name	Hostname to be used by the Single Client Access Name load balancer
Base Adapter (Backup Network)	The network adapter defined in the "Backup Network" screen. If a backup network is not used, select "Not in use" and move to the next screen.
Domain	Domain name to be appended to the hostnames used by the backup network
Start IP	The first IP address used for the backup network by the compute nodes in the cluster
Name Mask / Start ID	Naming convention used for hostnames on the backup network. The "%%" defined in this field will begin with the number defined in the "Start ID" field.

Review and Edit

The "Review and Edit" screen (Figure 8-15) contains the IP addresses and hostnames that will be utilized for the cluster. Any changes from what has been automatically generated from the earlier inputs must be finalized on this screen. Typically, this screen is simply used to validate the configuration and move forward.

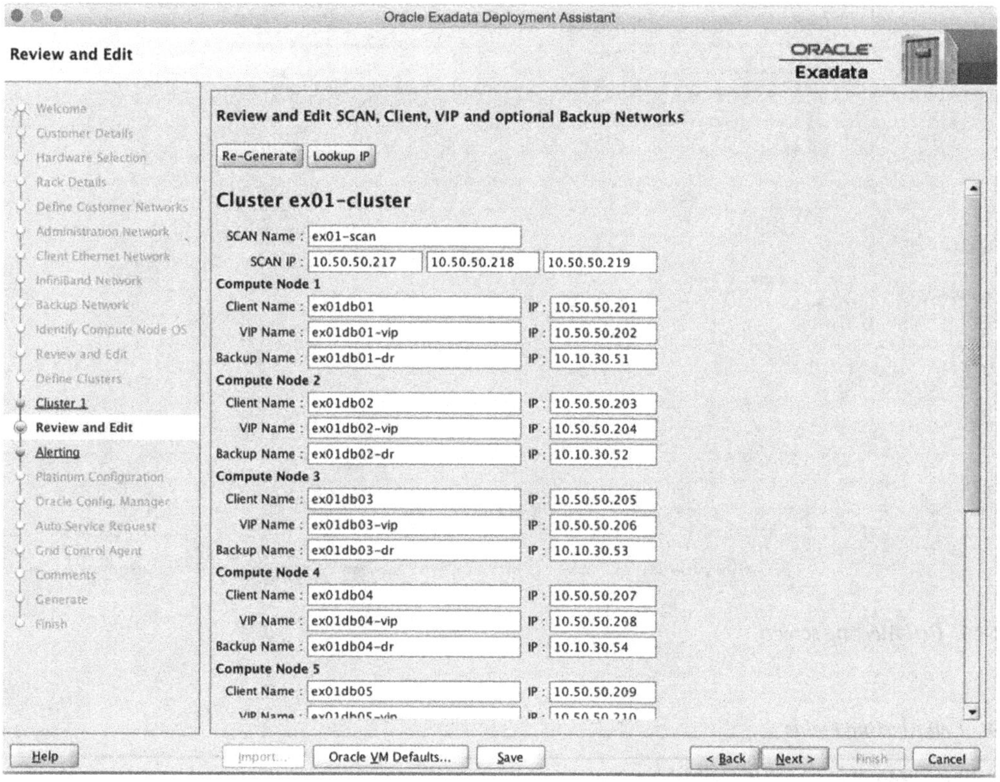

Figure 8-15. *Review and Edit screen*

Cell Alerting

The "Cell Alerting" screen (Figure 8-16) allows users to enter information that will be used to send alerts from both the storage cells and compute nodes. The `cellsrv` management service (on each storage cell) monitors the health of the storage cells and is capable of sending out notifications in the event of a problem on a storage server. Compute nodes running image version 12.1.2.1.0 and higher have a similar management service that will send alerts. Alerts can either be sent using Simple Mail Transfer Protocol (SMTP) or Simple Network Management Protocol (SNMP). SMTP alerts can be sent to multiple addresses or distribution lists. These alerts will be sent from the servers in the event that a failure occurs. Generally, most deployments only use SMTP alerting. Only select SNMP alerting at this point if using a third-party monitoring solution. Oracle Enterprise Manager and Automatic Service Request both use SNMP, but will be configured later in the process. Cell alerting is optional, but is strongly recommended, even if using other notification systems. Table 8-8 defines the fields used on this screen.

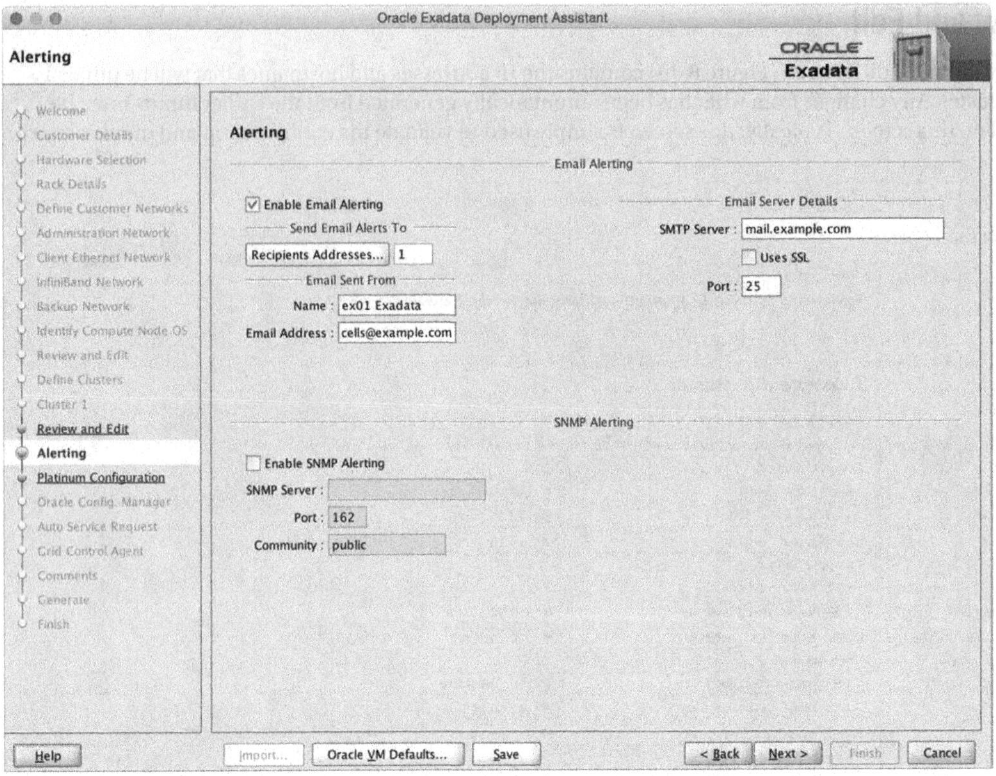

Figure 8-16. *Cell Alerting screen*

Table 8-8. *Cell Alerting Fields*

Configuration Parameter	Description
Enable Email Alerting	Check this box to enable SMTP alerts.
Recipients Addresses...	Click this box to enter e-mail addresses which will receive SMTP alerts.
SMTP Server	SMTP server used to send SMTP alerts.
Uses SSL	If using Secure Sockets Layer (SSL) to encrypt SMTP communication.
Port	SMTP port number. The default port is 25.
Name	Name that will be displayed in e-mail alerts sent by storage servers.
Email Address	E-mail address that alerts will be sent from.
Enable SNMP Alerting	Check this box to enable SNMP alerts.
SNMP Server	Server to send SNMP alerts.
Port	SNMP port number. The default port is 162.
Community	SNMP community string. The default is public.

Platinum Configuration

For customers that opt in to Oracle's "Platinum Services" offering, the "Platinum Configuration" screen (Figure 8-17) contains all questions related to the gateway server that will be used. Options include selecting whether to use an existing gateway or configure the server for a new gateway, the type of connectivity the gateway server has, and all network information relevant to the gateway server. The screen also queries for details related to the operating system user account that will be utilized to install the agent software used to provide monitoring from Oracle. Table 8-9 defines the fields in the "Platinum Configuration" screen.

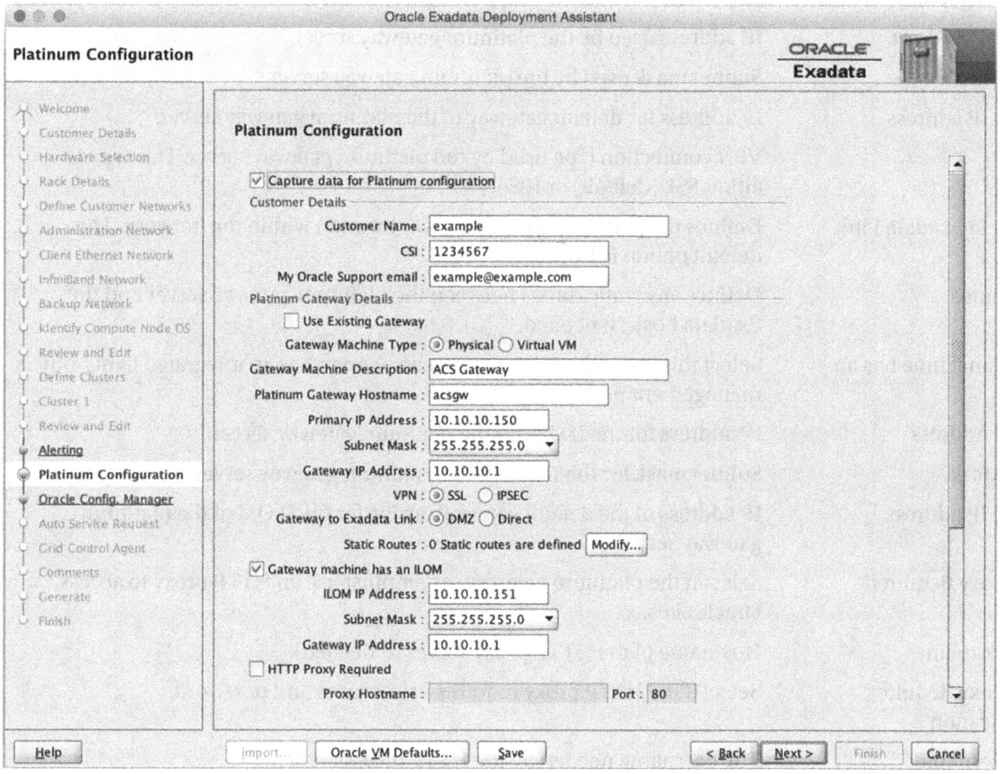

Figure 8-17. Platinum Configuration screen

Table 8-9. Platinum Configuration Fields

Configuration Parameter	Description
Capture data for Platinum configuration	Check box to determine if the system will be configured for platinum services. If not using platinum services from Oracle, uncheck the box and move to the next screen.
Customer Name	Name of the customer that owns the Exadata.
CSI	The customer support identifier for the Exadata hardware to be supported.

(continued)

Table 8-9. *(continued)*

Configuration Parameter	Description
My Oracle Support email	E-mail address for an account with access to the CSI noted above.
Use Existing Gateway	Select this box if an existing platinum services gateway will be used to monitor the system.
Gateway Machine Type	Select between a physical or virtualized gateway server installation.
Gateway Machine Description	A description of the gateway server.
Platinum Gateway Hostname	Hostname used for the platinum gateway server.
Primary IP Address	IP address used by the platinum gateway server.
Subnet Mask	Subnet mask used by the platinum gateway server.
Gateway IP address	IP address for default gateway of the platinum gateway server.
VPN	VPN connection type used by the platinum gateway server. This type is either SSL (default) or IPSec.
Gateway to Exadata Link	Defines the platinum gateway server location within the network. The default option is DMZ.
Static Routes	Defines any static routes between the platinum gateway server and the Exadata hosts, if needed.
Gateway machine has an ILOM	Select this box if the platinum gateway server has an integrated lights-out management port.
ILOM IP Address	IP address for the ILOM on the platinum gateway server.
Subnet Mask	Subnet mask for the ILOM of the platinum gateway server.
Gateway IP address	IP address of the default gateway device for the ILOM of the platinum gateway server.
HTTP Proxy Required	Select if the platinum gateway server must use an HTTP proxy to access Oracle sites.
Proxy Hostname	Hostname of the HTTP proxy server (if needed).
HTTP Proxy Requires Authentication	Select if the HTTP proxy requires a username and password.
Proxy Username	The username needed by the HTTP proxy.
Agent OS User name / ID	The operating system user name and uid that will run the platinum services monitoring agent on the Exadata hosts.
Allow agent sudo privileges	Defines whether users logging in with the agent user account can execute sudo to perform privileged actions on the Exadata hosts.
Agent OS Group name / ID	The operating system group name and gid that will run the platinum services monitoring agent on the Exadata hosts.
Agent OS User home	The operating system home directory for the agent software owner.
Agent Software home	The directory where agent software will be installed on the Exadata hosts.
Agent Port	The network port number that will be used for communications between the monitoring agent and the platinum gateway server.
SNMP Community String	The SNMP trap community string used by the platinum gateway server.

Oracle Configuration Manager

The "Oracle Configuration Manager" screen (Figure 8-18) contains all of the information needed to configure Oracle Configuration Manger (OCM). OCM is used to collect configuration information and upload it to a (Oracle Enterprise Manager) repository server. This option is not required for Exadata configuration. Oracle Platinum Services includes an installation of OCM, so this information is not needed when Platinum Services have been configured on the previous screen. If you are not using Platinum Services and wish to enable OCM, Table 8-10 includes all of the fields needed for this screen.

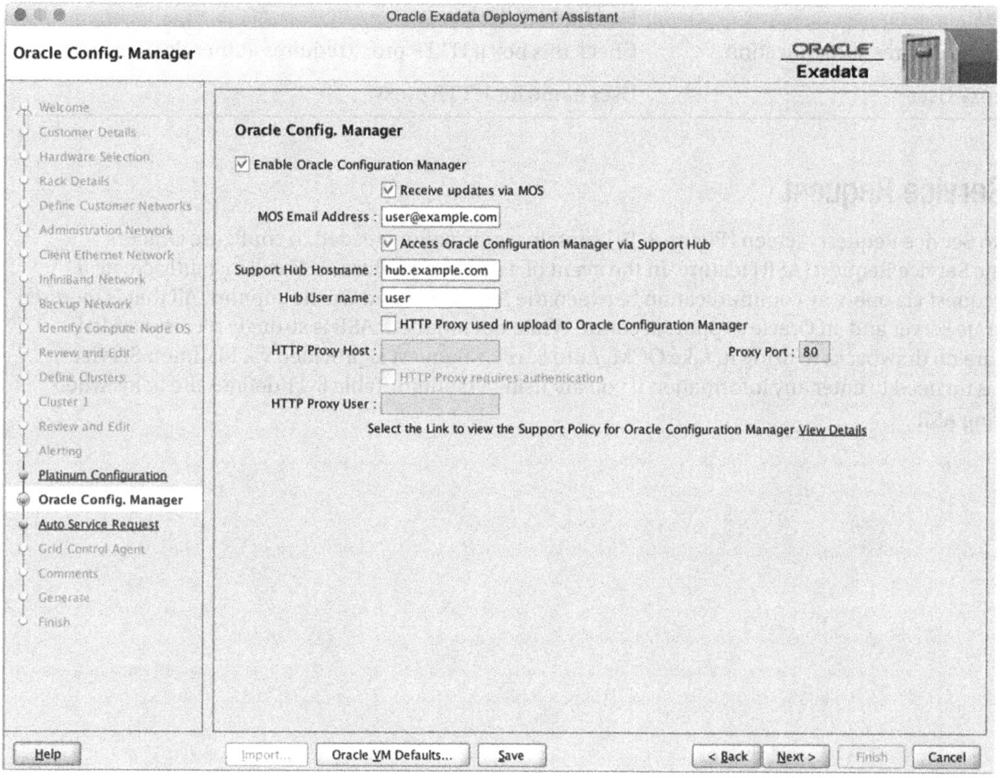

Figure 8-18. *Oracle Configuration Manager screen*

Table 8-10. *Oracle Configuration Manager Fields*

Configuration Parameter	Description
Enable Oracle Configuration Manager	Check this box to enable OCM.
Receive updates via MOS	If you plan to receive updates directly from Oracle Support, check this box.
MOS Email Address	E-mail address that receives updates from My Oracle Support.
Access Oracle Configuration Manager via Support Hub	Check this box if using a support hub.

(*continued*)

Table 8-10. (*continued*)

Configuration Parameter	Description
Support Hub Hostname	Hostname for the support hub.
Hub User Name	The operating system username for the support hub server.
HTTP Proxy used in upload to Oracle Configuration Manager	Check this box is an HTTP proxy is required to communicate with the Oracle repository.
HTTP Proxy Host	HTTP proxy hostname.
Proxy Port	HTTP proxy port.
HTTP Proxy requires authentication	Check this box if HTTP proxy requires authentication.
HTTP Proxy User	User name for HTTP proxy.

Auto Service Request

The "Auto Service Request" screen (Figure 8-19) contains information needed to configure Oracle's Automatic Service Request (ASR) feature. In the event of a hardware failure, ASR will instantly create a service request via one-way communication between the ASR server and Oracle support. All that is required is a separate server and an Oracle support account. While not required, ASR is strongly recommended, as there are no drawbacks to using it. Like OCM, Auto Service Request is provided via Platinum Services, so there is no need to enter any information if you are using Platinum. Table 8-11 defines the fields when configuring ASR.

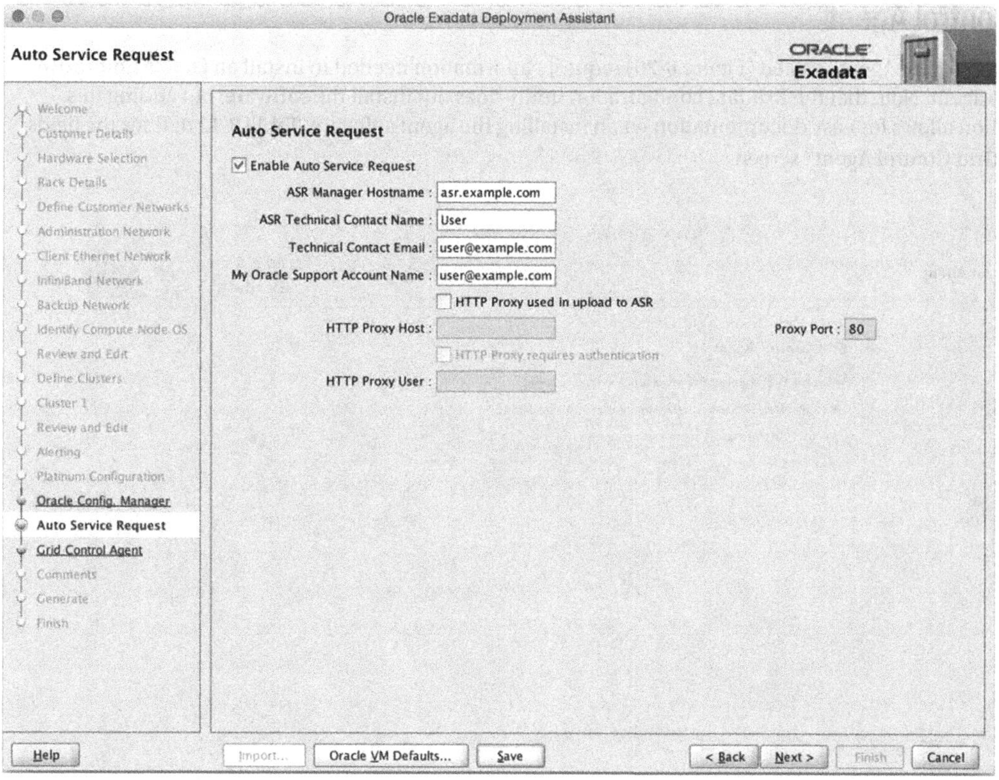

Figure 8-19. *Auto Service Request screen*

Table 8-11. *Auto Service Request Fields*

Configuration Parameter	Description
Enable Auto Service Request	Check this box if using Auto Service Request.
ASR Manager Hostname	Hostname for the ASR server.
ASR Technical Contact Name	The name of the technical contact responsible for the Exadata system.
Technical Contact Email	E-mail address of the technical contact responsible for the Exadata System.
My Oracle Support Account Name	The name for the My Oracle Support account that will create service requests when hardware failures occur.
HTTP Proxy used in upload to ASR	Check this box if the ASR server needs to utilize an HTTP proxy to communicate with Oracle support.
HTTP Proxy Host	Hostname of the HTTP proxy.
Proxy Port	HTTP proxy port.
HTTP Proxy requires authentication	Check this box if HTTP proxy requires authentication.
HTTP Proxy User	User name for HTTP proxy.

Grid Control Agent

The "Grid Control Agent" screen (Figure 8-20) requests information needed to install an Oracle Enterprise Manager agent. Note that the Exadata configuration utility does not install the software, but adding this information allows for easy documentation when installing the agent software. Table 8-12 defines the fields on the "Grid Control Agent" screen.

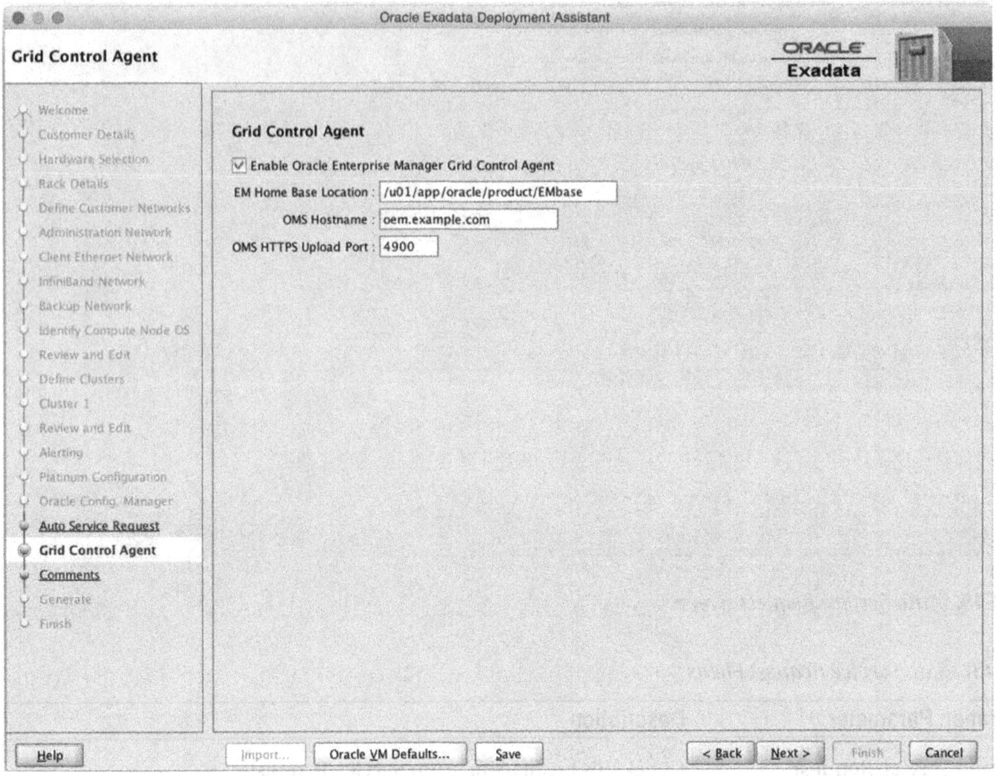

Figure 8-20. *Grid Control Agent screen*

Table 8-12. *Grid Control Agent Fields*

Configuration Parameter	Description
Enable Enterprise Manager Grid Control Agent	Check this box if you want to specify an OEM agent.
EM Home Base Location	Directory for agent installation.
OMS Hostname	Hostname of the OEM management service.
OMS HTTPS Upload Port	The port that the OEM agent should use to upload information.

Comments

The "Comments" screen (Figure 8-21) allows for Exadata administrators to enter any additional comments that may be relevant to the configuration engineer. This includes several pre-populated questions around network configurations and any custom changes that need to be applied to the Exadata rack during the configuration process. Enter any additional comments in the field shown and click the Next ➤ button. After clicking this button, the deployment assistant will ask for a location to save the documents.

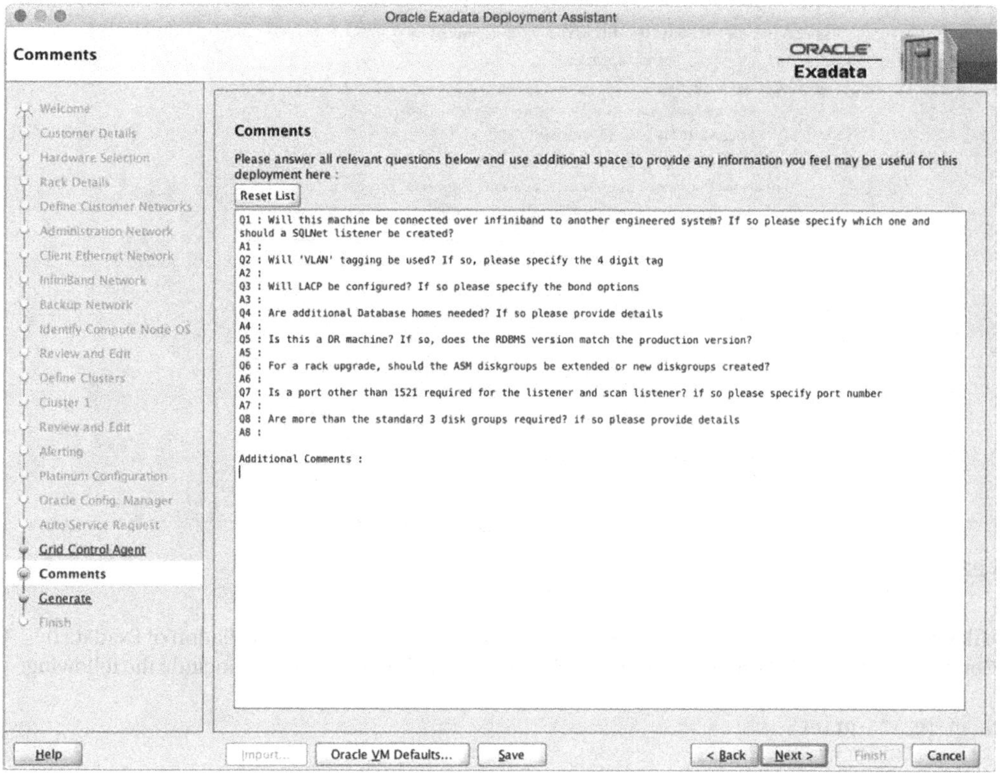

Figure 8-21. *Comments screen*

Finish

The final screen, titled "Finish," (Figure 8-22) shows the information related to the configuration files. There is also a hyperlink to load the HTML-based installation template file. When complete, click the "Finish" button, and you are ready to move to the next step.

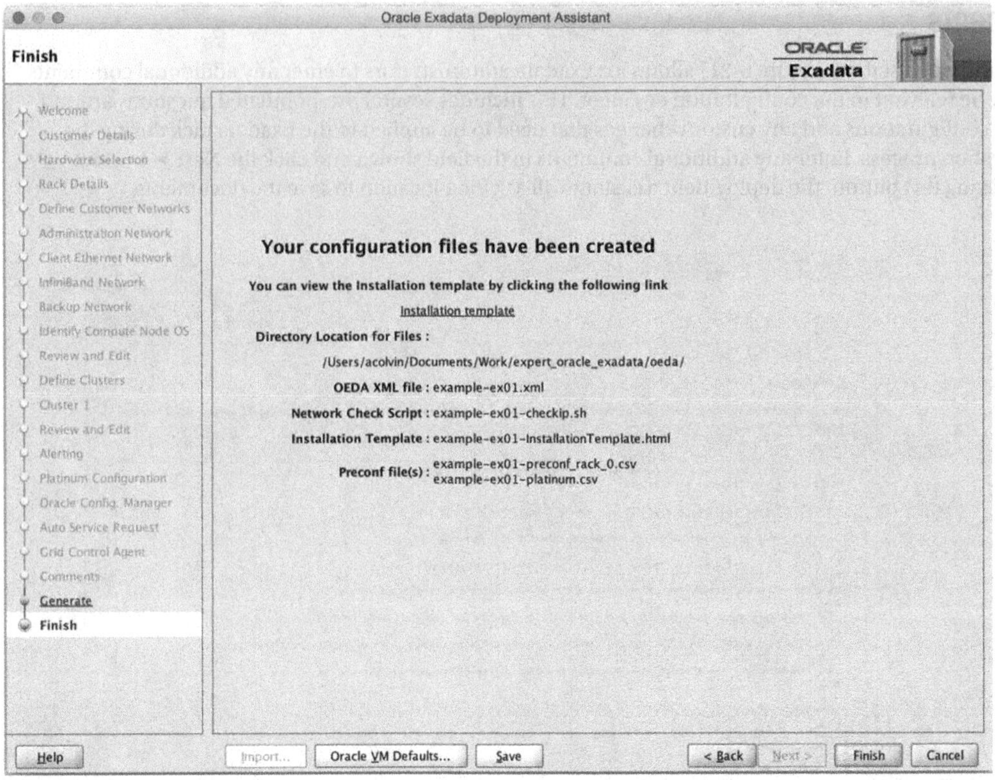

Figure 8-22. *Finish screen*

The files created by the deployment assistant are used to perform the actual installation of Exadata by the OneCommand script. A full listing of the files created by the deployment assistant include the following:

```
$ find . -name \* -print

./example-ex01-checkip.sh
./example-ex01-InstallationTemplate.html
./example-ex01-platinum.csv
./example-ex01-preconf_rack_0.csv
./example-ex01.xml
./example-ex01.zip
```

All of the files needed to install the Exadata system are included in this directory. Files will be named in the format <client>-<Exadata prefix>-<filename>. For a multirack cluster, there will be a separate XML file for each individual cluster. Table 8-13 describes the purpose of each of the files.

Table 8-13. *Parameter and Deployment Files*

File Name	Description
`checkip.sh`	This file is used to run the `checkip.sh` script that performs network readiness checks.
`InstallationTemplate.html`	The installation template is a reference file that contains all of the information provided to the deployment assistant software. This includes hostnames, IP addresses, software directories, and patch levels.
`platinum.csv`	This file is used by Oracle Platinum Services to complete their configuration tasks.
`preconf_rack_#.csv`	This file contains the network information for a specific Exadata rack. In the event that multiple Exadata racks are to be configured at once, each rack will have its own `preconf_rack_#.csv` file.
`cluster.xml`	This file contains all relevant information needed to build the cluster. The OneCommand process uses this file during the configuration process to install and configure the Oracle software stack.
`cluster.zip`	This is a zip file that contains the above files for reference.

Step 3: Create Network VLANs and DNS Entries for Hostnames

After the Exadata Deployment Assistant utility has been run, the installation template needs to be sent to the network team so that the proper network virtual LANs (VLANs) can be run. Hostnames need to be registered with your domain name system (DNS) servers as well. Because the final product of the OneCommand process is a running Oracle RAC environment, it is imperative that all hostnames be configured for both forward and reverse DNS lookups. If one hostname does not resolve correctly, issues could arise during the deployment process.

Step 4: Run CheckIP to Verify Network Readiness

One of the files created by the Exadata Deployment Assistant is the `<client>-<cluster>-checkip.sh` script. When the Oracle Exadata Deployment Assistant was rewritten in Java, this moved from being a shell script driven by a response file to a full-blown Java program. If you look inside of the shell script, you will actually see that it is just calling the Java code in the background. This script is used to validate that the network is ready and that there are no conflicts with the settings planned for the Exadata. CheckIP tests the network to confirm that the following conditions are met:

- IP addresses that should respond to a ping, do.
- IP addresses that should not respond to a ping, do not.
- Hostnames that must be registered in DNS can be both forward and reverse resolved using the information specified in the `<client>-<cluster>.xml` file.

Before running OneCommand, the `<client>-<cluster>-checkip.sh` script (CheckIP) should be run to validate the readiness of your corporate network. The script requires that the user running the script has downloaded the Oracle Exadata Deployment Assistant from the My Oracle Support site. The user will also need the `<client>-<cluster>-checkip.sh` script as well as the `<client>-<cluster>.xml` file. At this point, you should run CheckIP from a host, external to Exadata platform. The host you choose to run CheckIP from must have the same network visibility as your Exadata system will have. For example, the host must have access to the same DNS and NTP servers, and it must be able to ping the IP addresses you listed in your network settings for Exadata. After downloading the OEDA utility and copying the required files to the OEDA directory, run the following command:

```
./<client>-<cluster>-checkip.sh
```

CheckIP will print its progress out to the screen as well as build a `<client>-<cluster>-checkip.out` report file. The following listing shows sample output from the CheckIP script. The output below has been abbreviated in certain spots (FACTORY, CELL, SWITCHES, and ILOMS):

```
Executing Validate Configuration File

Checkip version: 15.141.14:00

 If this Oracle Exadata rack is to be added to an existing installation, such as Oracle
Exadata, Oracle Exalogic or Oracle Exalytics racks,
 then run the CheckIP utility from an existing machine or installation so that the private
network checks identify in-use IP addresses in the fabric, and report them.
Not identifying existing addresses may cause IP collisions after installation of the new
rack.

 Processing section NAME
 GOOD : Name Server 10.100.1.207 responds to resolve request for ex01db01.example.com
 GOOD : Name Server 10.100.1.208 responds to resolve request for ex01db01.example.com

 Processing section NTP
 GOOD : 10.100.1.208 responds to time server query
 GOOD : 10.100.148.198 responds to time server query

 Processing Section GATEWAY
 GOOD : 10.30.20.1 responds to ping
 ERROR : 10.100.233.1 responds to ping

Running checkip on cluster ex01

 Processing section SCAN
 GOOD : ex01-scan.example.com forward resolves to 3  IP adresses [10.100.233.205,
                                                     10.100.233.206, 10.100.233.207]
 GOOD : ex01-scan.example.com forward resolves to 10.100.233.205
 GOOD : 10.100.233.205 does not ping
 GOOD : ex01-scan.example.com forward resolves to 10.100.233.206
 GOOD : 10.100.233.206 does not ping
 GOOD : ex01-scan.example.com forward resolves to 10.100.233.207
 GOOD : 10.100.233.207 does not ping

 Processing section VIP
 GOOD : ex0101-vip.example.com forward resolves to 10.100.233.202
 GOOD : 10.100.233.202 does not ping
 GOOD : ex0102-vip.example.com forward resolves to 10.100.233.204
 GOOD : 10.100.233.204 does not ping
```

```
Processing section COMPUTE
GOOD : ex0101.example.com forward resolves to 10.100.233.201
GOOD : 10.100.233.201 does not ping
GOOD : ex0102.example.com forward resolves to 10.100.233.203
GOOD : 10.100.233.203 does not ping
GOOD : ex01db01.example.com forward resolves to 10.30.20.85
GOOD : 10.30.20.85 does not ping
GOOD : ex01db02.example.com forward resolves to 10.30.20.86
GOOD : 10.30.20.86 does not ping

Processing section CELL
GOOD : ex01cel01.example.com forward resolves to 10.30.20.87
GOOD : 10.30.20.87 does not ping
GOOD : ex01cel02.example.com forward resolves to 10.30.20.88
GOOD : 10.30.20.88 does not ping
...

Processing section FACTORY
GOOD : 192.168.1.1 does not ping
...
GOOD : 192.168.1.9 does not ping

Processing section SWITCHES
GOOD : ex01sw-ip.example.com forward resolves to 10.30.20.95
GOOD : 10.30.20.95 does not ping
...

Processing section ILOMS
GOOD : ex01db01-ilom.example.com forward resolves to 10.30.20.90
GOOD : 10.30.20.90 does not ping
...
Completed validation...
```

The output report generated in the `<client>-<cluster>-<checkup>.out` file contains the same information as we see in the display. If any validation errors occur, they are prefixed with "ERROR," and a message describing the failure indicates the problem encountered and what the expected results should be. For example:

```
Processing section SCAN
GOOD : exa-scan.example.com resolves to 3 IP addresses
ERROR : exa-scan. ourcompany.com forward resolves incorrectly to 144.77.43.182 144.77.43.181
144.77.43.180 , expected 144.77.43.87
...
Processing section COMPUTE
GOOD : exadb01.example.com forward resolves to 10.80.23.1
GOOD : 10.80.23.1 reverse resolves to exadb01.example.com.
ERROR : 10.80.23.1 pings
```

The output from CheckIP must contain no errors. If you see any errors in the output, they must be corrected before running OneCommand. Check the `<client>-<cluster>-checkip.out` file and make sure you did not enter an IP address incorrectly or mistype a hostname before opening a discussion with your network administrator. Sometimes a simple correction to a data entry field on the Exadata Deployment Assistant is all that is needed. If everything looks in order from your side, then send the `<client>-<cluster>-checkip.out` file to your network administrator for remediation.

Step 5: Run Cables and Power to Exadata Racks

Now that the network has been validated, it is time to run the requisite cables to where the rack will be placed. When the Exadata rack is shipped from Oracle, it comes with all internal cabling complete. This means that the number of external cables needed to connect an Exadata rack to the existing network is twice the number of compute nodes (two for each node), plus one cable for the management network.
See Figure 8-23 for an idea of what the internal cabling looks like on an Exadata rack.

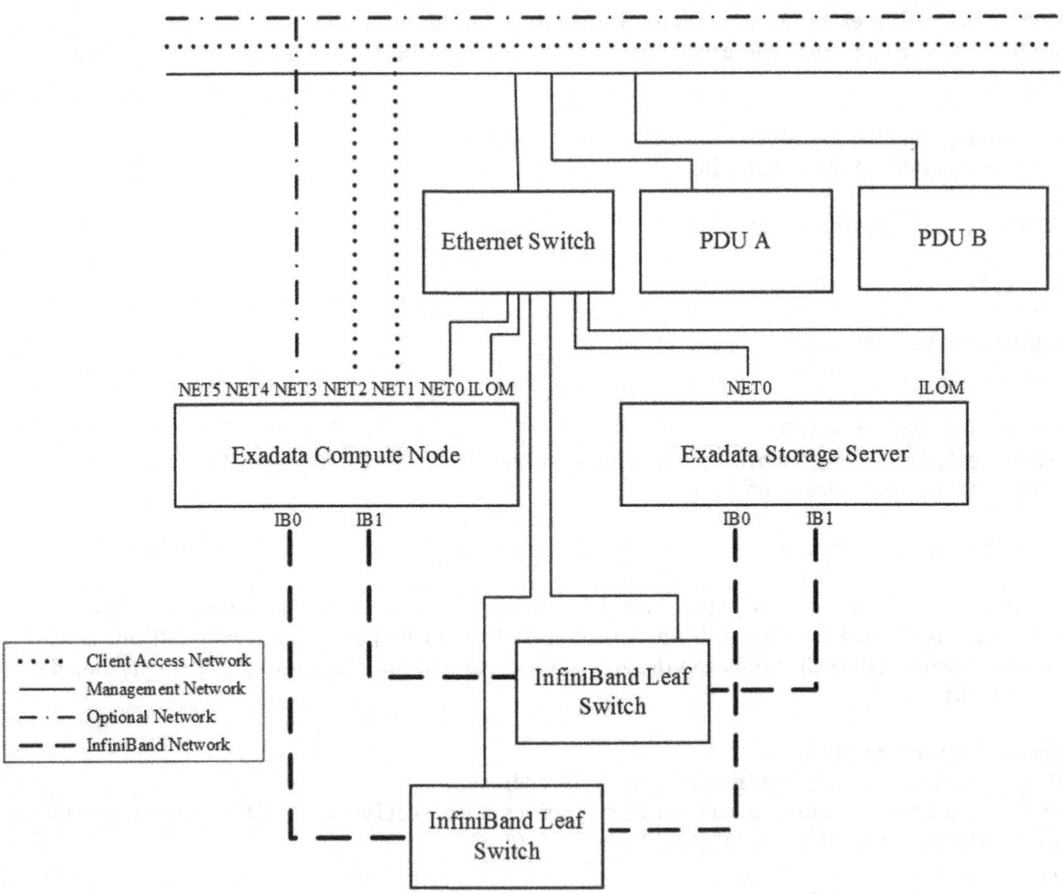

Figure 8-23. *Exadata copper networking diagram*

While the Exadata Deployment Assistant allows for the choice of whether the client access network will be bonded or not, most Exadata configurations will utilize a bonded network for high availability. Because this is considered to be a critical network on Exadata, it is a very good idea to go with the bonded client access network. In order to achieve this, each port on a particular host is connected to a different switch. On an Exadata X5-2 system utilizing copper connections for the client access network, ports NET1 and NET2 are used. For Exadata X5-2 systems using fiber connections, ports NET4 and NET5 are connected to the external switches. With either configuration, a bonded interface named `bondeth0` (the first Ethernet bond) is created for this network. See Figure 8-24 for the recommended wiring connection on a bonded client access network.

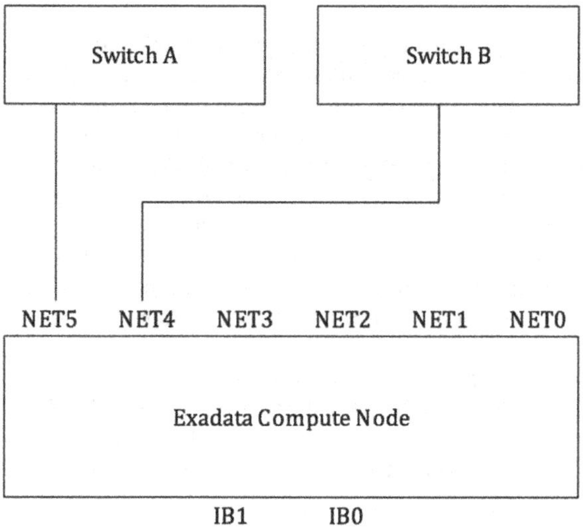

Figure 8-24. *Bonded copper client access network*

Once the cables have been run, do not plug them in to the Exadata rack. Because the rack comes preconfigured with a set of "factory" IP addresses, there is the possibility of an IP conflict if those addresses are in use elsewhere on the network. All cables will be connected after the `applyElasticConfig.sh` script has been run.

Step 6: Perform Hardware Installation

A certified Oracle Field Service Engineer (FSE) who has access to the Enterprise Installation Service checklist typically performs the hardware installation. This step in the process is fairly simple and includes powering up the Exadata rack, verifying that all of the correct components were shipped, and making sure that there was no damage to the equipment during shipment. The FSE will perform several hardware checks, and it will also configure the network equipment according to the settings specified in the `InstallationTemplate.html` file generated by the Exadata Deployment Assistant. During the installation, the FSE will configure the power distribution units, all InfiniBand switches, and the internal Ethernet switch. No network connectivity is required at this point. Also, if multiple racks are being connected into one cluster, the multirack cabling will be performed at this step in the process.

Step 7: Stage OneCommand Files and Oracle Software

Before copying the configuration files to the soon-to-be-installed Exadata compute nodes, it is required to install the latest version of the Oracle Exadata Deployment Assistant. This software is linked from My Oracle Support note #888828.1. After downloading the latest version of the Oracle Exadata Deployment Assistant, it needs to be transferred to all of the compute nodes.

There are a couple of ways to transfer the parameter and deployment files to Exadata. One method involves setting up temporary network access to the first compute node. This network configuration will be replaced with permanent network settings by `applyElasticConfig.sh` in subsequent steps. The other option is to save the files to a portable USB flash drive and then, using the USB port on the front panel of the first compute node, copy the files to the OEDA directory. The USB approach was more convenient on the older Exadata models, which contained a KVM. Because of the lack of a KVM, it's recommended to create a temporary network connection to the Exadata rack.

The factory IP setting for the Exadata rack is designed so that each rack will be in the same condition when it arrives at the customer site. All racks will be exactly the same, regardless of size—larger rack systems simply have more IP addresses in use. IP addresses are assigned based on the location in the rack and the network component type. When Oracle introduced the elastic configuration with the X5-2, the standard rack limitations were removed. Due to this flexibility, new nodes are configured to query the InfiniBand switches to determine their default IP address. The standard factory IP address scheme now is to use the 172.16.2.0/24 subnet, with the last octet determined as the InfiniBand port number, plus 36. This means that the first compute node, which is plugged in to InfiniBand port number 8, obtains a factory IP address of 172.16.2.44. The ILOM IP addresses are configured using the 192.168.1.x convention, counting up the rack. Check the Exadata Owner's guide for the InfiniBand network cabling tables in order to determine the InfiniBand port matrix for your rack.

To connect to the Exadata compute nodes from a laptop using an internal network, assign an unused IP address on the factory network (something like 172.16.2.244 with a subnet mask of 255.255.255.0 will suffice) and connect to the cable run from port 48 of the internal Ethernet switch. From this point, log in directly to the first compute node (typically 172.16.2.44) and upload the downloaded OEDA zip file via SCP. Now, it's time to stage the files across the cluster.

1. Unzip OEDA files on the first compute node in the `/opt/oracle.SupportTools/onecommand` directory.
2. Stage the configuration files on the first compute node.
3. Copy OEDA software and configuration files to all of the compute nodes.
4. Copy Oracle installation media and patches to the first compute node.

Step 7-1: Unzip OEDA

In this example, the OEDA software has been uploaded to the first compute node to `/tmp/p20974448_121211_Linux-x86-64.zip`. Unzip the file and then create a new directory for OEDA and decompress the contents of the zip file to that directory.

```
# mkdir -p /opt/oracle.SupportTools/onecommand
# chmod 777 /opt/oracle.SupportTools/onecommand
# cd /tmp
# unzip -q p20974448_121211_Linux-x86-64.zip -d /opt/oracle.SupportTools/onecommand
```

Step 7-2: Stage Configuration Files

Now that OEDA has been staged on the first compute node, upload all of the configuration files created by the Exadata Deployment Assistant to `/opt/oracle.SupportTools/onecommand/linux-x64` on the first compute node.

Step 7-3: Copy OEDA to All Compute Nodes

The contents of the /opt/oracle.SupportTools/onecommand directory need to be copied to all of the compute nodes in the rack. Because passwordless access is not configured on the hosts, you will need to copy using individual scp commands. The example below is for a half rack:

```
# scp -r /opt/oracle.SupportTools/onecommand  172.16.2.46: /opt/oracle.SupportTools
# scp -r /opt/oracle.SupportTools/onecommand  172.16.2.45: /opt/oracle.SupportTools
# scp -r /opt/oracle.SupportTools/onecommand  172.16.2.48: /opt/oracle.SupportTools
```

Step 7-4: Stage Oracle Installation Media

Finally, the software needed to perform the Oracle software installation must be uploaded to /opt/oracle.SupportTools/onecommand/linux-x64/WorkDir on the first compute node. Do not worry about staging the installation files on any other nodes—OneCommand will transfer the files as needed. The installation template should include a required-downloads section that contains the full list of files needed to perform the installation. The list typically includes the following:

- Oracle RDBMS and Grid Infrastructure media
- Quarterly database patch files for the installation media
    - OPatch files for the specified version
    - Any additional one-off patches that are recommended

Now that all files have been uploaded and staged, you are ready to start the actual configuration process.

Step 8: Configure the Operating System

When the Oracle hardware engineers complete their installation, you are ready to boot up the compute nodes and storage cells for the first time. The servers included in a new Exadata shipping from the factory will have a set of predefined IP addresses, which is referred to as the "factory configuration." For in-rack upgrades, you will have to go through an interactive Firstboot process. The Firstboot process is not well documented in the Oracle manuals, so we will take a minute to talk through the boot process and what happens the first time you boot these servers and storage cells. Typically, you will be working with a new Exadata rack, and it will take you straight to an operating system log in.

Reclaiming Disk Space

Before configuring the network settings on the compute and storage servers in the factory configuration, it is important to ensure that the compute node disk configuration is correct. X3-2 and X4-2 compute nodes were shipped with both Linux and Solaris, giving customers the choice of which operating system they would like to install. X5-2 compute nodes ship with a choice of either a physical Linux installation (the default) or an Oracle VM installation used to run virtualized environments. A script (/opt/oracle.SupportTools/reclaimdisks.sh) is installed on the compute nodes that will remove the unwanted operating system and build out a fully configured RAID-5 array on all of the disk drives. It is time to reclaim the available disk space, wiping out the unused operating system.

```
# ./reclaimdisks.sh -free -reclaim
```

The script will run in the foreground, reconfiguring the logical volume configuration. The output of the reclaimdisks.sh run on an X5-2 compute node is shown below:

```
# ./reclaimdisks.sh -reclaim -free
Model is ORACLE SERVER X5-2
Number of LSI controllers: 1
Physical disks found: 4 (252:0 252:1 252:2 252:3)
Logical drives found: 1
Linux logical drive: 0
RAID Level for the Linux logical drive: 5
Physical disks in the Linux logical drive: 4 (252:0 252:1 252:2 252:3)
Dedicated Hot Spares for the Linux logical drive: 0
Global Hot Spares: 0
[INFO     ] Check for Linux system disk
[INFO     ] Number of partitions on the system device /dev/sda: 4
[INFO     ] Higher partition number on the system device /dev/sda: 4
[INFO     ] Last sector on the system device /dev/sda: 3509760000
[INFO     ] End sector of the last partition on the system device /dev/sda: 3509759000
[INFO     ] Remove inactive system logical volume /dev/VGExaDb/LVDbSys3
[INFO     ] Remove xen files from /boot
[INFO     ] Unmount /u01 from /dev/mapper/VGExaDbOra-LVDbOra1
[INFO     ] Remove logical volume /dev/VGExaDbOra/LVDbOra1
[INFO     ] Remove volume group VGExaDbOra
[INFO     ] Remove physical volume /dev/sda4
[INFO     ] Remove partition /dev/sda4
[INFO     ] Remove device /dev/sda4
[INFO     ] Remove partition /dev/sda3
[INFO     ] Remove device /dev/sda3
[INFO     ] Create primary partition 3 using 240132160 3509759000
[INFO     ] Set lvm flag for the primary partition 3 on device /dev/sda
[INFO     ] Add device /dev/sda3
[INFO     ] Create physical volume on partition /dev/sda3
[INFO     ] Primary LVM partition /dev/sda3 has size 3269626841 sectors
[INFO     ] LVM Physical Volume /dev/sda3 has size 3269626841 sectors
[INFO     ] Size of LVM physical volume matches size of primary LVM partition /dev/sda3
[INFO     ] Extend volume group VGExaDb with physical volume on /dev/sda3
[INFO     ] Create 100Gb logical volume for DBORA partition in volume group VGExaDb
[INFO     ] Make DBORA ext4 file system on logical volume LVDbOra1
[INFO     ] Create filesystem on device /dev/VGExaDb/LVDbOra1
[INFO     ] Tune filesystem on device /dev/VGExaDb/LVDbOra1
[INFO     ] Set label DBORA for /dev/VGExaDb/LVDbOra1
[INFO     ] Mount /dev/mapper/VGExaDb-LVDbOra1 to /u01
[INFO     ] Logical volume LVDbSys2 exists in volume group VGExaDb
```

The entire process takes approximately five minutes on an X5-2 compute node. Repeat the step on all remaining compute nodes and run the `applyElasticConfig.sh` script for Exadata systems that are in the factory configuration.

The Firstboot Process

Every time a server boots up, the `/etc/init.d/precel` script is called at run level 3. This script calls the `/opt/oracle.cellos/cellFirstboot.sh` (Firstboot) script. Firstboot determines whether or not the network settings have been configured. This is undocumented, but it appears that it is triggered by the existence of the `/opt/oracle.cellos/cell.conf` file. This file is created and maintained by the `/opt/oracle.cellos/`

ipconf.pl script (ipconf) and contains all the information about your network configuration. If the file exists, it is assumed that the system is already configured and the boot cycle continues. But if the file is not found, Firstboot calls ipconf and you are led, interactively, through the network configuration process. ipconf is used to set the following network settings for your compute nodes and storage cells:

- Name server (DNS)
- Time server (NTP)
- Country code
- Local time zone
- Hostname
- IP address, netmask, gateway, *type*, and hostname for all network devices. The *type* is required and used for internal documentation in the cell.conf file. Valid types are Private, Management, SCAN, and Other.
- ILOM configuration

For example, the following listing shows the prompts for configuring the management network on a compute node:

```
Select interface name to configure or press Enter to continue: eth0
Selected interface. eth0
IP address or none: 192.168.8.217
Netmask: 255.255.255.0
Gateway (IP address or none) or none: 192.168.8.1

Select network type for interface from the list below
1: Management
2: SCAN
3: Other
Network type: 1
Fully qualified hostname or none: exadb03.ourcompany.com
```

When you have finished entering all your network settings, ipconf generates a new cell.conf file and reboots the system. Once the system has finished rebooting, it is ready for you to run the reclaimdisks.sh script and complete the software installation performed by OEDA.

applyElasticConfig

Because the hosts on the Exadata rack have factory IP settings already configured, the servers will not boot to the ipconf script. Oracle has an automated method to set all network information on all hosts in the rack via one script. The applyElasticConfig.sh script automates the process. applyElasticConfig.sh is included with the Oracle Exadata Deployment Assistant. It is a script that will determine what type of host each node is (storage or compute) and apply the specific network settings for that host. This is accomplished using the ipconf utility. Among the files created by the Exadata Deployment Assistant were the <client>-<cluster>-preconf_rack_#.csv and <client>-<cluster>.xml parameter files. The <client>-<cluster>-preconf_rack_#.csv file contains all network settings needed to create a cell.conf file for each compute node and storage cell. Because the applyElasticConfig.sh script will connect, applyElasticConfig.sh calls the ipconf script to generate these files and installs them as /opt/oracle.cellos/cell.conf in each compute node and storage cell. To run applyElasticConfig.sh, log in as root to the first compute node in your system and run applyElasticConfig.sh as follows:

```
[root@exadb01 root]# cd /opt/oracle.SupportTools/onecommand/linux-x64
[root@exadb01 linux-x64]# ./applyElasticConfig.sh -cf <client>-<cluster>.xml

Applying Elastic Config...
Applying Elastic configuration...
Searching Subnet 172.16.2.x.............
7 live IPs in  172.16.2.x..............
Exadata node found 172.16.2.44..
Configuring node : 172.16.2.46..............
Done Configuring node : 172.16.2.46
Configuring node : 172.16.2.40............
Done Configuring node : 172.16.2.40
Configuring node : 172.16.2.37...........................
Done Configuring node : 172.16.2.37
```

As each node is configured, it will reboot with the final network settings configured. Once all of the servers complete the boot cycle, Exadata should be ready to be connected to the network and configured using OneCommand. After all of the components have rebooted and the rack has been connected to the network, log in to the first compute node and run the first step in the OneCommand script to validate that everything is ready to go.

Step 9: Run OneCommand

OneCommand (included in the OEDA zip file) is the preferred method of installing Oracle software on Exadata. OneCommand is an Oracle-provided utility consisting of several configuration steps (20 as of this writing). OneCommand provides two very important benefits to Exadata customers and Oracle's support staff. First, it creates a limited number of standardized (and well-known) configurations, which makes the platform much easier to support. After all, who wants to hear, "Oh, I've never seen it configured that way before" when we finally get a support tech on the phone? This is one of Exadata's key strengths. Second, it provides a simplified and structured mechanism for configuring Exadata from start to finish. This means that with very little knowledge of Exadata internals, an experienced technician can install and configure Exadata in a matter of hours. It is unclear whether Oracle originally intended to provide support for OneCommand externally, but about the same time the X2 began shipping, Oracle began to document the OneCommand process in the *Exadata Owner's Guide*. OneCommand is a multiple-step process that is run from a shell script called install.sh. At the time of this writing, the install.sh script supports installing versions 11.2.0.3 through 12.1.0.2, including each bundle patch. These steps can be run end-to-end or one at a time. Table 8-14 shows each step in the May 2015 version, along with a brief description of what the step does.

The main script used to run OneCommand is install.sh. The 20 installation steps may be listed by running install.sh as follows:

```
# ./install.sh -cf <client>-<cluster>.xml -l
```

Table 8-14. *OneCommand Steps*

Step Number	Step Name	Description
Step 1	`Validate Configuration File`	Performs node validations, including checks to determine if all hosts are online, syntax within the `<client>-<cluster>.xml` file is correct, and all required files are available
Step 2	`Update Nodes for Eighth Rack`	Disables CPU cores on the compute nodes, removes flash cards and disk drives on the storage servers, then reboots all components
Step 3	`Setup Required Files`	Moves all files to the `/opt/oracle.SupportTools/onecommand/Software` directory, copies patch files across the cluster, then unzips all files
Step 4	`Create Users`	Creates the operating system user accounts as defined by the configuration files
Step 5	`Setup Cell Connectivity`	Creates the `/etc/oracle/cell/network-config/cellip.ora` and `/etc/oracle/cell/network-config/cellinit.ora` files
Step 6	`Verify Infiniband`	Validates the InfiniBand network using the `infinicheck` script
Step 7	`Calibrate Cells`	Checks cell disks using the `cellcli -e calibrate` command. This command tests the performance characteristics of your cell disks. If any disks are underperforming, they will be identified in this step.
Step 8	`Create Cell Disks`	Configures cell disks, Flash Cache, and Flash Log on all storage servers
Step 9	`Create Grid Disks`	Creates grid disks across all storage servers
Step 10	`Configure Alerting`	Configures SMTP and SNMP alert destinations, as defined in the configuration files
Step 11	`Install Cluster Software`	Installs Grid Infrastructure and applies patches specified in the installation template for all clusters defined in the configuration files
Step 12	`Initialize Cluster Software`	Executes `root.sh` cluster initialization scripts on all compute nodes for each cluster
Step 13	`Install Database Software`	Installs Oracle database software and applies patches specified in the installation template for all clusters defined in the configuration files
Step 14	`Relink Database with RDS`	Ensures that all database and Grid Infrastructure homes are linked to use the RDS protocol rather than UDP
Step 15	`Create ASM Diskgroups`	Creates ASM disk groups as defined by the configuration files
Step 16	`Create Databases`	Creates database as defined by the configuration files

(*continued*)

Table 8-14. *(continued)*

Step Number	Step Name	Description
Step 17	`Apply Security Fixes`	Shuts down the cluster and applies several miscellaneous fixes
Step 18	`Install Exachk`	Installs the exachk health check script
Step 19	`Create Installation Summary`	Creates a deployment summary document that includes IP addresses, hostnames, and serial numbers for the Exadata cluster
Step 20	`ResecureMachine`	Applies operating system security measures to the nodes, including setting password requirements and dropping SSH keys for the root user

```
1. Validate Configuration File
2. Update Nodes for Eighth Rack
3. Setup Required Files
4. Create Users
5. Setup Cell Connectivity
6. Verify Infiniband
7. Calibrate Cells
8. Create Cell Disks
9. Create Grid Disks
10. Configure Alerting
11. Install Cluster Software
12. Initialize Cluster Software
13. Install Database Software
14. Relink Database with RDS
15. Create ASM Disk Groups
16. Create Databases
17. Apply Security Fixes
18. Install Exachk
19. Create Installation Summary
20. Resecure Machine
```

■ **Note** OneCommand is constantly changing to improve the installation process and to support additional bundle patches. The number of steps and what they do is very likely to change with each version of Exadata. Be sure to review the README file for instructions on how to run OneCommand on your system before you begin.

There are number of ways `install.sh` may be used. For example, the following command-line options process all 20 steps of the installation process, only stopping if a step fails:

```
# ./install.sh -cf <client><cluster>.xml -r 1-20
```

Each step must complete successfully before you can proceed to the next. Oracle recommends running the steps one at a time, reviewing the output at the end of each before proceeding on to the next. `install.sh` provides this capability with the `-s` command-line option. For example, the installation procedure would look something like the following:

```
# ./install.sh -cf <client>-<cluster>.xml -s 1
```

Check output for errors...

```
# ./install.sh -cf <client>-<cluster>.xml -s 2
```

Check output for errors...

```
# ./install.sh -cf <client>-<cluster>.xml -s 3
```

Check output for errors...

```
# ./install.sh -cf <client>-<cluster>.xml -s 4
```

and so on...

`install.sh` takes as input the parameters from the files you generated earlier using the Exadata Deployment Assistant. Log files are created each time `install.sh` is called to execute a configuration step and, for some steps, it dynamically generates and executes a shell script that carries out all the tasks required. Reviewing these files can be very useful in determining why a step failed. The log files and dynamically generated shell scripts are stored in the `/opt/oracle.SupportTools/onecommand/linux-x64/log` and `/opt/oracle.SupportTools/onecommand/linux-x64/tmp` directories.

The output generated by the various installation steps varies quite a bit. But in general, `install.sh` displays some header information telling you what step it is running, where to find the log file, and whether it completed successfully. Continue through all of the steps until the deployment summary has been completed.

Upgrading Exadata

With all the companies that have adopted the Exadata platform, we have seen hardware upgrades as an increasingly popular topic. Our foray into the Exadata space began over six years ago with an Exadata V2 quarter rack configuration. Approximately a year later, we upgraded our system to a half rack. Of course, the V2s were no longer in production, so our upgrade came in the form of two X2-2 database servers and four storage cells. The configuration options we considered were as follows:

- Configure the new X2 equipment as a separate RAC cluster and storage grid, creating two somewhat asymmetric quarter rack configurations within the same Exadata enclosure. Oracle refers to this as a "split rack" configuration.
- Add the new X2 equipment to our existing quarter rack cluster, effectively upgrading it to a half rack.

Creating a New RAC Cluster

The Exadata Deployment Assistant doesn't directly support upgrading a system in this manner, but with a few adjustments it can be used to generate all the files OneCommand needs to perform the installation.

Once the parameter and deployment files are uploaded to Exadata, you should have no problem running through all of the configuration steps without impacting your existing cluster. One coworker actually used this process to create a separate Exadata configuration on the new equipment while leaving the existing system untouched.

For the most part, you simply fill in the Exadata Deployment Assistant as if you are creating a configuration that matches the total size of the rack. When choosing the components that will be in the cluster, create an additional cluster by selecting the new components. There are a few items you will need to consider when using the Exadata Deployment Assistant for this type of Exadata upgrade:

Name Prefixes: It is not required, but you may want to set your Database Machine Name, Database Server Base Name, and Storage Servers Base Names values to match your existing Exadata configuration. That way, if you ever decide to merge these servers into your old cluster, you won't have to make changes to the hostnames. For example, our quarter rack configuration had database host names of `enkdb01` and `enkdb02`. Adding the new servers continued with the names `enkdb03`, and `enkdb04`. Likewise, the storage cell host names continued with `enkcel04` through `enkcel07`.

Client Access SCAN Name: This procedure will be creating a new RAC cluster, so you will need a new SCAN name for it. You will also need to see that it and all of the other new hostnames are properly registered in your company's DNS server (just as you did when your existing Exadata system was installed).

Country Code / Time Zone: Of course, these settings should match your existing Exadata system.

NTP and DNS Servers: These should also match your existing Exadata environment.

Oracle Database Machine Model: This setting determines how many compute nodes and storage cells the configurator will use when creating host names and IP addresses.

Network IP Addresses: You should continue to use the networks you configured for the Exadata rack you are upgrading. As you enter the starting IP addresses for hosts in the Exadata Deployment Assistant, make sure that you perform the necessary IP address adjustments on the "review details" screen.

O/S User and Group Accounts: It is not required, but you should use the same user/group names and user/group IDs when configuring your new cluster. This is especially true if there is any chance these user accounts will ever interact between the new system and the old system. OneCommand will not establish user equivalency between the old and new servers for you. Hence, that must be done manually after the upgrade is complete.

When you are finished entering your settings, generate the files as you normally would. You will notice that there are separate XML files for each cluster, as well as an XML file used to define the entire rack.

From this point forward, the process is no different than it is for a fresh install. First, you will need to configure the network components using Firstboot as we discussed earlier, and then run the procedure to reclaim the disk space. Once this has completed, simply log in to the first new compute node as root and run through the `install.sh` configuration steps and call the XML file specific to the new cluster. When you are finished, you will have a new RAC cluster, complete with starter database.

Upgrading the Existing Cluster

If you are upgrading your Exadata to a half or full rack configuration and want to integrate the new servers and cells into your existing RAC cluster, you must configure the new servers and cells manually. The *Exadata Database Machine Extending and Multi-Rack Cabling Guide* has a chapter titled "Extending Oracle Database Machine" that discusses the process in detail. First, we will take a look at the basic steps for configuring the new compute nodes. Then we will take a look at how you can add the new cells to your existing storage grid.

■ **Caution** The steps in this section are not intended to be a comprehensive guide and are subject to change. Refer to your Exadata documentation for details specific to your version of Exadata.

Configuring Database Servers

The following process describes how to configure the new compute nodes:

1. Upgrade the firmware on your IB switches to the current release or latest patch. The Oracle hardware technician who installed your new hardware can do this for you or you can download the latest patch and install it yourself. Recommended firmware patches can be found in MOS note: 888828.1.
2. Update the Exadata Storage Server software release on the existing equipment to match that of the new hosts. This also includes updating the operating system on the compute nodes.
3. If possible, update the Oracle Grid Infrastructure and database software to the most current bundle patch for the version of the software your existing system is running. Ideally, the software should be running at the latest release and bundle patch.
4. Use the Exadata Deployment Assistant to generate IP addresses and hostnames for the new compute nodes and storage cells. Do not include the information related to the existing hosts.
5. Register the new hostnames and IP addresses in your DNS server.
6. Boot your new compute nodes one at a time. The first time they are booted, `ipconf` will start automatically, allowing you to enter your network settings.
7. On the database servers, copy the following files from one of your existing database servers to the new database servers:
   - `/etc/security/limits.conf`

     This file is the same on all compute nodes.
   - `/etc/profile`

     This file is the same on all compute nodes.

8. Install the version of OEDA used to run the Exadata Deployment Assistant onto the first new compute node, including the files created in step 4.
9. Run `install.sh` on the first new compute node up to, but not including, the CreateGridDisks step.
10. Follow the steps in the owner's guide for cloning the Grid Infrastructure and database homes to a new server. The procedure is similar to that of adding a new node to any Oracle RAC system.

■ **Note** The decision whether to extend an existing cluster or create a new one can be a difficult one. For many customers, the choice depends on many different factors; hardware differences between the new and existing equipment (V2/X2-2 combination vs V2/X3-2 combination), database size, consolidation workload, and outage requirements all factor in to the decision. While it is not a difficult task to reverse the decision after the fact, it does involve extra work and can be impactful for the databases that are running on the equipment that is being recommissioned. As always, sit down and weigh the pros and cons of each approach before making a decision with which direction to take your upgrade.

Expanding Exadata Storage

Adding new cells to your existing storage grid is a fairly simple process. Running the steps above will take care of most of the work. We will take a look at the remaining process so you can see the commands and files involved. The process is as follows:

1. Run the step in `install.sh` related to configuring cell alerts. If you wish to do this manually, it can be achieved using `cellcli`:

```
ALTER CELL smtpServer='mail.example.com', -
  smtpFromAddr='Exadata@example.com', -
  smtpFrom='Exadata', -
  smtpToAddr='all.dba@example.com,all.sa@example.com', -
  notificationPolicy='critical,warning,clear', -
  notificationMethod='mail'
```

2. Your current cell configuration may be displayed using the `LIST CELL DETAIL` command. Once you are finished configuring the cell, stop and restart the cell services to ensure the new settings have taken hold.
3. Using one of your old storage cells for reference, create your grid disks using the `CREATE GRIDDISK` command. We discuss using this command in Chapter 14. Be sure you create your grid disks in the proper order, as this will impact the performance of the disks. You can use the size and offset attributes of the `LIST GRIDDISK DETAIL` command to determine the proper size and creation order for the grid disks. Typically, you should create grid disks in this order: `DATA`, `RECO`, and then `DBFS_DG`.
4. Update the `/etc/oracle/cell/network-config/cellip.ora` file on all compute nodes (new and old) to reflect the InfiniBand IP addresses of all cells.

5. Add the new grid disks to ASM your existing ASM disk groups. This can be done via SQL*Plus in ASM. The following example shows adding disks to the DATA disk group in a half rack upgrade, with a rack named "dm01"—repeat the process for remaining disk groups.

```
SQL> ALTER DISKGROUP DATA ADD DISK
  2> 'o/*/DATA*dm01cel04*',
  3> 'o/*/DATA*dm01cel05*',
  4> 'o/*/DATA*dm01cel06*',
  5> 'o/*/DATA*dm01cel07*'
  6> rebalance power 32;
```

Summary

Configuring Exadata is a very detailed process, and some things tend to change somewhat as new versions of the hardware and software become available. This chapter discussed some of the main points of configuring Exadata compute nodes and storage cells, but it is not intended to be a substitute for the official Oracle documentation. Oracle has done an excellent job of documenting the platform, and you will find the *Installation and Configuration Guide* and *Storage Software User's Guide* to be invaluable assets when learning the ins and outs of configuring Exadata. There is some overlap in subject matter covered in this chapter with the topics discussed in Chapters 9 and 15, so you might find them helpful as a cross-reference for some of the configuration tasks discussed here.

CHAPTER 9

Recovering Exadata

You may have heard the saying "disk drives spin, and then they die." It's not something we like to think about, but from the moment you power up a new system, your disk drives begin aging. Disk drives have come a long way in the past 30 years, and typical life expectancy has improved dramatically. At the end of the day, though, it's a matter of "when" a disk will fail, not "if." And we all know that many disk drives fail long before they should. Knowing how to diagnose disk failures and what to do when they occur has generally been the responsibility of the system administrator or storage administrator. For many DBAs, Exadata is going to change that. Many Exadata systems out there are being managed entirely by the DBA staff. Whether or not this is the case in your data center, the procedure for recovering from a disk failure on Exadata is going to be a little different from what you are used to.

Oracle database servers have traditionally required two types of backups: operating system backups and database backups. Exadata compute nodes rely on industry standard hardware RAID and Linux logical volumes to ensure that they are resilient to hardware failures and easy to manage. Exadata adds storage cells to the mix and, with that, comes a whole new subsystem that must be protected and, on occasion, restored. The storage cell is a fairly resilient piece of hardware that employs Linux software RAID to protect the operating system filesystems. As such, it is unlikely that a single disk failure would necessitate an operating system restore. The more likely causes would be human error, a failed patch install, or a bug. Remember that these physical disk devices also contain grid disks (database volumes), so a loss of one of these disks would most likely mean a loss of database storage as well. Oracle has engineered several features into Exadata to protect your data and reduce the impact of such failures. This chapter will discuss some of the more common storage failure scenarios, how to diagnose them, and how to recover with minimal downtime.

Note One of the most challenging aspects of writing this chapter is the rapidly changing nature of the commands and scripts we will be discussing. In many cases, recovery tasks will have you working very closely with the hardware layer of Exadata. So, as you read this chapter, keep in mind that with each new version of Exadata hardware and software, the commands and scripts discussed in this chapter may change. Be sure to check the Oracle documentation for the latest updates to the commands and scripts discussed here.

Exadata Diagnostic Tools

Exadata is a highly complex blend of hardware and software that work together to produce an incredibly resilient delivery platform. The complexity of the platform can be a bit daunting at first. There are simply a lot of moving parts that one must understand in order to maintain the platform effectively. Oracle provides a wealth of diagnostic tools that can be used to verify, analyze, and report important information about the configuration and health of the system. In this section, we'll discuss some of those tools and how to use them.

Sun Diagnostics: sundiag.sh

Installed on every Exadata database server and storage cell is the `sundiag.sh` script, located in the `/opt/oracle.SupportTools` directory. On newer releases of the Exadata Storage Server software, the script is installed via the `exadata-sun-computenode` or `exadata-sun-cellnode` RPM package. If for some reason you don't find it installed on your system, you can download it from My Oracle Support. Refer to MOS Doc ID 761868.1. This script is run from the root account and collects diagnostic information needed for troubleshooting hardware failures. The files it collects are bundled in the familiar `tar` format and then compressed using bzip2.

sundiag.sh Output

The `sundiag.sh` script creates an archive with the hostname, serial number, and timestamp of the run. For example, running the script on our lab system produced an output file named as follows:

```
/tmp/sundiag_enkcel05_XXXXXXXX_2014_11_17_12_23.tar.bz2
```

Now, let's take a look at the diagnostic files collected by `sundiag.sh`. Files are compressed in an archive, with folders for the following components:

`asr`: This directory contains files associated with the configuration of Automatic Service Request.

`cell`: This directory contains output of various `CellCLI` commands as well as log files related to the Exadata Storage Server software stack. Output includes configuration information on the cell disks, grid disks, and Flash Cache, along with log files for the cellsrv and management service processes. This directory is not present when `sundiag.sh` is run on an Exadata compute node.

`disk`: This directory contains binary files related to the hard disks, generated by the LSI disk controller.

`ilom`: If the ilom or snapshot options are used, this directory will contain ILOM data collection output.

`messages`: This directory contains copies of the dmesg and messages system logs from the syslog utility.

`net`: This directory contains diagnostic information related to the assorted networks on the node. Files include a InfiniBand diagnostics, lists of any firewall rules, and network device configuration files. Additionally, the output of the `ethtool` command is also included.

`raid`: The `raid` directory contains disk controller configuration information from the `parted`, `fdisk`, and `mdstat` commands, along with RAID controller output from the `MegaCli64` command.

`sysconfig`: Files that do not fall into the other categories are left here. Files are named after the commands that generated them. Examples include `df-hl.out`, `lspci-vvv.out`, and `CheckHWnFWProfile.log`.

Some of the more important files created by the sundiag.sh script are described below. These files are found on both compute nodes and storage servers.

messages: This is a copy of the /var/log/messages file from your system. The messages file is rotated and aged out automatically by the operating system. If your system has been running for a while, you will have several of these files enumerated in ascending order from current (messages) to oldest (messages.4). This file is maintained by the syslog daemon and contains important information about the health and operation of the operating system.

dmesg: This file is created by the dmesg command and contains diagnostic kernel-level information from the *kernel ring buffer*. The kernel ring buffer contains messages sent to or received from external devices connected to the system such as disk drives, keyboard, video, and so on.

lspci: This file contains a list of all the PCI devices on the system.

lsscsi: The lsscsi file contains a list of all the SCSI devices on the system.

fdisk-l and parted: The fdisk-l and parted files contain a listing of all disk device partitions in your system.

megacli64: The sundiag.sh script runs the MegaCli64 command with various options that interrogate the MegaRAID controller for information on the configuration and status of your disk controller and attached disk drives. There is a wealth of information collected by the MegaRAID controller that can be easily tapped into using the MegaCli64 command. For example, the megacli64-PdList_short.out file shows a summary of the RAID configuration of the disk drives on a compute node:

```
Slot 00 Device 11 (HITACHI H106030SDSUN300GA3D01247NLV9ZD  ) status is: Online,
Slot 01 Device 10 (HITACHI H106030SDSUN300GA3D01247NGXRZF  ) status is: Online,
Slot 02 Device 09 (HITACHI H106030SDSUN300GA3D01246NLV1JD  ) status is: Online,
Slot 03 Device 08 (HITACHI H106030SDSUN300GA3D01247NH06DD  ) status is: Online,
```

Information in these files includes an event log and a status summary of your controller and disk drives. For example, the following listing shows a summary of the state of the physical disk drives attached to one of our database servers (from the megacli64-status.out file):

```
Checking RAID status on enkx3db01.enkitec.com
Controller a0:  LSI MegaRAID SAS 9261-8i
No of Physical disks online : 4
Degraded : 0
Failed Disks : 0
```

It is hard to say whether Exadata uses the MegaCli64 command to monitor predictive failure for disk drives or if the developers have tapped into SMART metrics through an API, but this information is available to you at the command line. There isn't a lot of information about MegaCli64 out there, but the sundiag.sh script is a good place to start if you are interested in peeking under the hood and getting a closer look at some of the metrics Exadata collects to determine the health of your disk subsystem.

If you run the sundiag.sh script on your storage cells, additional data is collected about the cell configuration, alerts, and special log files that do not exist on the database server. The following list describes these additional log files collected by sundiag.sh.

cell-detail: The cell-detail file contains detailed site-specific information about your storage cell. This is output from the CellCLI command LIST CELL DETAIL.

celldisk-detail: This file contains a detailed report of your cell disks. The report is created using the CellCLI command LIST CELLDISK DETAIL. Among other things, it shows the status, logical unit number (LUN), and physical device partition for your cell disks.

lun-detail: This report is generated using the CellCLI command LIST LUN DETAIL. It contains detailed information about the underlying LUNs on which your cell disks are configured. Included in this report are the names, device types, and physical device names (such as /dev/sdw) of your LUNs.

physicaldisk-detail: The physicaldisk-detail file contains a detailed report of all physical disks and FMODs used by the storage cell for database type storage and Flash Cache. It is generated using the CellCLI command LIST PHYSICALDISK DETAIL, and it includes important information about these devices such as the device type (hard disk or flash disk), make and model, slot address, and device status.

physicaldisk-fail: This file contains a listing of all physical disks (including flash disks) that do not have a status of Normal. This would include disks with a status of Not Present, which is a failed disk that has been replaced but not yet removed from the configuration. When a physical disk is replaced, its old configuration remains in the system for seven days, after which it is automatically purged.

griddisk-detail: This file contains a detailed report of all grid disks configured on the storage cell. It is created using the CellCLI command LIST GRIDDISK DETAIL and includes, among other things, the grid disk name, cell disk name, size, and status of all grid disks you have configured on the storage cell.

griddisk-status: This file contains the name and status of each grid disk configured on the storage cell. It is created using the CellCLI command LIST GRIDDISK ATTRIBUTES NAME, STATUS, ASMMODESTATUS, ASMDEACTIVATIONOUTCOME and includes details on the status of the grid disk from the perspective of both the storage server and ASM.

flashcache-detail: This report contains the list of all FMODs that make up the Cell Flash Cache. It is the output of the CellCLI command LIST FLASHCACHE DETAIL and includes the size and status of the Flash Cache. Also found in this report is a list of all flash cell disks that are operating in a degraded mode.

flashlog-detail: This report contains the list of all FMODs that make up the cell flash log area. It is the output of the CellCLI command LIST FLASHLOG DETAIL and includes the size and status of the flash log area. Also found in this report is a list of all flash cell disks that are operating in a degraded mode.

alerthistory: The alerthistory file contains a detailed report of all alerts that have occurred on the storage cell. It is created using the CellCLI command LIST ALERTHISTORY.

`alert.log`: The `alert.log` file is written to by the `cellsrv` process. Similar to a database or ASM alert log file, the storage cell `alert.log` contains important runtime information about the storage cell and the status of its disk drives. This file is very useful in diagnosing problems with cell storage. On Exadata storage cells running version 12c, there are multiple alert logs, one for each of the offload servers.

`ms-odl.trc`: The `ms-odl.trc` contains detailed runtime, trace-level information from the cell's management server process.

`ms-odl.log`: This file is written to by the cell's management server process. It is not included in the collection created by the `sundiag.sh` script, but we have found it very useful in diagnosing problems that occur in the storage cell. It also contains normal, day-to-day operational messages. Storage cells maintain their log files by rotating them, similar to the way the operating system rotates the system log (`/var/log/messages`). The `ms-odl.log` file records these tasks as well as more critical tasks such as disk failures.

Cell Alerts

As part of the monitoring features, Exadata tracks over 70 alert types of metrics in the storage cell. Additional alerts may be defined using Grid Control's monitoring and alerting features. Alert severities fall into four categories: Information, Warning, Critical, and Clear. These categories are used to manage alert notifications. For example, you may choose to get an e-mail alert notification for critical alerts only. The Clear severity is used to notify you when a component has returned to Normal status. The `LIST ALERTHISTORY DETAIL` command can be used to generate a detailed report of the alerts generated by the system. The following listing is an example of an alert generated by the storage cell:

```
name:                    209_1
alertMessage:            "All Logical drives are in WriteThrough caching mode.
                         Either battery is in a learn cycle or it needs to be
                         replaced. Please contact Oracle Support"
alertSequenceID:         209
alertShortName:          Hardware
alertType:               Stateful
beginTime:               2011-01-17T04:42:10-06:00
endTime:                 2011-01-17T05:50:29-06:00
examinedBy:
metricObjectName:        LUN_CACHE_WT_ALL
notificationState:       1
sequenceBeginTime:       2011-01-17T04:42:10-06:00
severity:                critical
alertAction:             "Battery is either in a learn cycle or it needs
                         replacement. Please contact Oracle Support"
```

When the battery subsequently returns to Normal status, a follow-up alert is generated with a severity of Clear, indicating that the component has returned to normal operating status:

```
name:                    209_2
alertMessage:            "Battery is back to a good state"
...
severity:                clear
alertAction:             "Battery is back to a good state. No Action Required"
```

When you review alerts, you should get in the habit of setting the examinedBy attribute of the alert so you can keep track of which alerts are already being investigated. If you set the examinedBy attribute, you can use it as a filter on the LIST ALERTHISTORY command to report all alerts that are not currently being attended to. By adding the severity filter, you can further reduce the output to just critical alerts. For example:

```
LIST ALERTHISTORY WHERE severity = 'critical' AND examinedBy = ' ' DETAIL
```

To set the examinedBy attribute of the alert, use the ALTER ALERTHISTORY command and specify the name of the alert you wish to alter. For example, we can set the examinedBy attribute for the Battery alert as follows:

```
CellCLI> alter alerthistory 209_1 examinedBy="acolvin"
Alert 209_1 successfully altered

CellCLI> list alerthistory attributes name, alertMessage, examinedby where name=209_1 detail
         name:                    209_1
         alertMessage:            "All Logical drives are in WriteThrough caching mode.
                                  Either battery is in a learn cycle or it needs to be
                                  replaced. Please contact Oracle Support"
         examinedBy:              acolvin
```

There is quite a bit more to say about managing, reporting, and customizing Exadata alerts. An entire chapter would be needed to cover the subject in detail. In this section, we've only touched on the basics. Fortunately, once you get e-mail configured for alert notification, very little must be done to manage these alerts. In many environments, e-mail notification is all that is used to catch and report critical alerts.

Backing Up Exadata

When we took delivery of our first Exadata system, one of our primary questions was, "How can we back up everything so we can restore it to working order if something goes horribly wrong?" When our Exadata arrived in May 2010, the latest version of the Cell software was 11.2.1.2.1. At the time, the only way to back up a database server was to use third-party backup software or standard Linux commands like tar. Oracle is constantly developing new features for Exadata and, less than a year later, Exadata X-2 database servers were released with the native Linux Logical Volume Manager (LVM). This was a big step forward because the LVM has built-in snapshot capabilities that provide an easy method of taking backups of the operating system. Storage cells use a built-in method for backup and recovery. In this section, we'll take a look at the various methods Oracle recommends for backing up Exadata database servers and storage cells. We'll also take a brief look at Recovery Manager (RMAN) and some of the features Exadata provides that improve the performance of database backup and recovery. After that, we'll take a look at what it takes to recover from some of the more common types of system failure. It may surprise you, but the focus of this chapter is not database recovery. There are very few Exadata-specific considerations for database backup and recovery. A majority of the product-specific backup and recovery methods pertain to backup and recovery of the system volumes containing the operating system and Exadata software. Hence, we'll spend quite a bit of time discussing recovery, from the loss of a cell disk to the loss of a system volume on the database servers or storage cells.

Backing Up the Database Servers

Exadata compute nodes have a default configuration that utilizes Linux Logical Volume Management (LVM). Logical volume managers provide an abstraction layer for physical disk partitions similar to the way ASM does for its underlying physical storage devices. LVMs have volume groups comparable to ASM disk groups. These volume groups are made up of one or more physical disks (or disk partitions), as ASM disk groups are made up of one or more physical disks (or disk partitions). LVM volume groups are carved up into logical volumes in which file systems can be created. In a similar way, databases utilize ASM disk groups for creating tablespaces that are used for storing tables, indexes, and other database objects. Abstracting physical storage from the file systems allows the system administrator to grow and shrink the logical volumes (and file systems) as needed. There are a number of other advantages to using the LVM to manage storage for the Exadata database servers, but our focus will be the new backup and restore capabilities the Linux LVM provides, namely LVM snapshots. In addition to their convenience and ease of use, LVM snapshots eliminate many of the typical challenges we face with simple backups using the `tar` command or third-party backup products. For example, depending on the amount of data in the backup set, file system backups can take quite a while to complete. These backups are not consistent to a point in time, meaning that if you must restore a file system from backup, the data in your files will represent various points in time from the beginning of the backup process to its end. Applications that continue to run during the backup cycle can hold locks on files, causing them to be skipped (not backed up). And once again, open applications will inevitably make changes to data during the backup cycle. Even if you are able to back up these open files, you have no way of knowing if they are in any usable state unless the application is shut down before the backup is taken. LVM snapshots are instantaneous because no data is actually copied. You can think of a snapshot as an index of pointers to the physical data blocks that make up the contents of your file system. When a file is changed or deleted, the original blocks of the file are written to the snapshot volume. So, even if it takes hours to complete a backup, it will still be consistent with the moment the snapshot was created. Now, let's take a look at how LVM snapshots can be used to create a consistent file system backup of the database server.

System Backup Using LVM Snapshots

Creating file system backups using LVM snapshots is a pretty simple process. First, you need to create a destination for the final copy of the backups. This can be SAN or NAS storage or simply an NFS file system shared from another server. If you have enough free space in the volume group to store your backup files, you can create a temporary logical volume to stage your backups before sending them off to tape. This can be done using the `lvcreate` command. Before creating a new logical volume, make sure you have enough free space in your volume group using the `vgdisplay` command:

```
[root@enkx4db01 ~]# vgdisplay
--- Volume group ---
  VG Name               VGExaDb
...
  VG Size               1.63 TB
  PE Size               4.00 MB
  Total PE              428308
  Alloc PE / Size       47104 / 184.00 GB
  Free  PE / Size       381204 / 1.45 TB
...
```

The `vgdisplay` command shows the size of our volume group, physical extents (PE) currently in use, and the amount of free space available in the volume group. The `Free PE/Size` attribute indicates that we have 1.45TB of free space remaining in the volume group.

First, we'll mount an NFS share from another system as the destination for our backups. We will call this `/mnt/nfs`:

```
[root@enkx4db01 ~]# mount -t nfs -o rw,intr,soft,proto=tcp,nolock <ip>/share /mnt/nfs
```

Next, we'll create and label LVM snapshots for / and /u01 using the lvcreate and e2label commands. Notice the -L1G and -L5G options we used to create these snapshots. The -L parameter determines the size of the snapshot volume. When data blocks are modified or deleted after the snapshot is created, the original copy of the block is written to the snapshot. It is important to size the snapshot sufficiently to store an original copy of all changed blocks. The snapshot will not be utilized for a long time, so typically 5GB-10GB is enough space. If the snapshot runs out of space, it will be deactivated.

```
[root@enkx4db01 ~]# lvcreate -L1G -s -n root_snap /dev/VGExaDb/LVDbSys1
  Logical volume "root_snap" created
[root@enkx4db01 ~]# e2label /dev/VGExaDb/root_snap DBSYS_SNAP
[root@enkx4db01 ~]# lvcreate -L5G -s -n u01_snap /dev/VGExaDb/LVDbOra1
  Logical volume "u01_snap" created
[root@enkx4db01 ~]# e2label /dev/VGExaDb/u01_snap DBORA_SNAP
```

Next, mount the snapshot volumes. We use the file system labels (DBSYS_SNAP and DBORA_SNAP) to ensure that the correct volumes are mounted. After they are mounted, they can be copied to the NFS mountpoint. The df command displays our new file system and the logical volumes we want to include in our system backup, VGExaDb-LVDbSys1 (logical volume of the root file system) and VGExaDb-LVDbOra1 (logical volume of the /u01 file system). Notice that the /boot file system does not use the LVM for storage. This file system must be backed up using the tar command. This isn't a problem because the /boot file system is fairly small and static so we aren't concerned with these files being modified, locked, or open during the backup cycle.

```
[root@enkx4db01 ~]# mkdir -p /mnt/snaps/u01
[root@enkx4db01 ~]# mount -L DBSYS_SNAP /mnt/snaps
[root@enkx4db01 ~]# mount -L DBORA_SNAP /mnt/snaps/u01
[root@enkx4db01 mnt]# df -h
Filesystem            Size  Used Avail Use% Mounted on
/dev/mapper/VGExaDb-LVDbSys1
                       30G   27G  1.6G  95% /
/dev/sda1             496M   40M  431M   9% /boot
/dev/mapper/VGExaDb-LVDbOra1
                       99G   53G   41G  57% /u01
tmpfs                 252G     0  252G   0% /dev/shm
192.168.10.9:/nfs/backup
                      5.4T  182G  5.2T   4% /mnt/nfs
/dev/mapper/VGExaDb-root_snap
                       30G   27G  1.4G  96% /mnt/snaps
/dev/mapper/VGExaDb-u01_snap
                       99G   53G   41G  57% /mnt/snaps/u01
```

Now that we have snapshots ensuring consistent / and /u01 file systems, we are ready to take a backup. To prove that these snapshots are consistent, we'll copy the /etc/hosts file to a test file in the /root directory. If snapshots work as they are supposed to, this file will not be included in our backup because it was created after the snapshot was created. The command looks like this:

```
[root@enkx4db01 ~]# cp /etc/hosts /root/test_file.txt
```

Because the snapshots are mounted, we can browse them just like any other file system. Snapshot file systems look and feel just like the original file systems, with one exception. If we look in the mounted snapshot for the test file we created (or any other change after the snapshot was taken), we don't see it. It's not there because the file was created after the snapshots were created:

```
[root@enkx4db01 ~]# ls -l /root/testfile
-rw-r--r-- 1 root root 1724 Nov 24 14:23 /root/test_file.txt    <- the test file we created

[root@enkx4db01 ~]# ls -l /mnt/snaps/root/test_file.txt
ls: /mnt/snaps/root/testfile: No such file or directory    <- no test file in the snapshot
```

Once the snapshots are mounted, they can be backed up using any standard Linux backup software. For this test, we'll use the `tar` command to create a tarball backup of the `/` and `/u01` file systems to the NFS share. Since we are backing up a snapshot, we don't have to worry about files that are open, locked, or changed during the backup. Notice that we've also included the `/boot` directory in this backup.

```
[root@enkx4db01 ~]# cd /mnt/snaps
[root@enkx4db01 snap]# tar -pjcvf /mnt/nfs/backup.tar.bz2 * /boot --exclude \
        nfs/backup.tar.bz2 --exclude /mnt/nfs >          \
        /tmp/backup_tar.stdout 2> /tmp/backup_tar.stderr
```

When the backup is finished, you should check the error file `/tmp/backup_tar.stderr` for any issues logged during the backup. If you are satisfied with the backup, you can unmount and drop the snapshots. You will create a new set of snapshots each time you run a backup. After the backup is copied, you can optionally unmount and drop the temporary logical volume you created:

```
[root@enkx4db01 snap]# cd /

[root@enkx4db01 /]# umount /mnt/snaps/u01
[root@enkx4db01 /]# rm -Rf /mnt/snaps/u01

[root@enkx4db01 /]# umount /mnt/snaps
[root@enkx4db01 /]# rm -Rf /mnt/snaps

[root@enkx4db01 /]# lvremove /dev/VGExaDb/root_snap
Do you really want to remove active logical volume root_snap? [y/n]: y
  Logical volume "root_snap" successfully removed

[root@enkx4db01 /]# lvremove /dev/VGExaDb/u01_snap
Do you really want to remove active logical volume u01_snap? [y/n]: y
  Logical volume "u01_snap" successfully removed
```

Early models of Exadata V2 did not implement LVM for managing file system storage. Without LVM snapshots, getting a clean system backup would require shutting down the applications on the server (including the databases), or purchasing third-party backup software. Even then, there would be no way to create a backup in which all files are consistent with the same point in time. LVM snapshots fill an important gap in the Exadata backup and recovery architecture and offer a simple, manageable strategy for backing up the database servers. Later in this chapter, we'll discuss how these backups are used for restoring the database server when file systems are lost or damaged.

Backing Up the Storage Cell

The first two disks in a storage cell contain the Linux operating system. These Linux partitions are commonly referred to as the *system volumes*. Backing up the system volumes using industry standard Linux backup software is not recommended. So, how do you back up the system volumes? Well, the answer is that you don't. Exadata automatically does this for you through the use of an internal USB drive called the *CELLBOOT USB flash drive*. If you are the cautious sort, you can also create your own cell recovery image using an external USB flash drive. In addition to the CELLBOOT USB flash drive, Exadata also maintains, on a separate set of disk partitions, a full copy of the system volumes as they were before the last patch was installed. These backup partitions are used for rolling back a patch. Now, let's take a look at how these backup methods work.

CELLBOOT USB Flash Drive

You can think of the internal CELLBOOT USB flash drive as you would any external USB drive you would plug into your laptop. The device can be seen using the parted command as follows:

```
[root@enkx4cel01 ~]# parted /dev/sdac print
Model: ORACLE UNIGEN-UFD (scsi)
Disk /dev/sdac: 4010MB
Sector size (logical/physical): 512B/512B
Partition Table: msdos

Number  Start   End     Size    Type     File system  Flags
 1      11.3kB  4008MB  4008MB  primary  ext3
```

Just for fun, we mounted the internal USB flash drive to take a peek at what Oracle included in this backup. The following listing shows the contents of this device:

```
[root@enkx4cel01 ~]# mount /dev/sdm1 /mnt/usb

[root@enkx4cel01 ~]# ls -al /mnt/usb
total 95816
drwxr-xr-x 7 root root     4096 Oct  3 21:26 .
drwxr-xr-x 9 root root     4096 Nov 23 15:49 ..
-r-xr-x--- 1 root root     2048 Aug 17  2011 boot.cat
-r-xr-x--- 1 root root       16 Oct  9  2013 boot.msg
drwxr----- 2 root root     4096 Oct  3 20:14 cellbits
drwxrwxr-x 2 root root     4096 Oct  3 20:15 grub
-rw-r----- 1 root root       16 Oct  3 20:14 I_am_CELLBOOT_usb
-rw-r----- 1 root root      805 Oct  3 19:53 image.id
-rw-r----- 1 root root      441 Oct  3 19:55 imgboot.lst
-rw-rw-r-- 1 root root  8280755 Jul 14 04:12 initrd-2.6.32-300.19.1.el5uek.img
-rw-r----- 1 root root  7381429 Oct  3 20:14 initrd-2.6.39-400.128.17.el5uek.img
-rw-r----- 1 root root 70198394 Oct  3 19:55 initrd.img
-r-xr-x--- 1 root root    10648 Aug 17  2011 isolinux.bin
-r-xr-x--- 1 root root      155 Apr 14  2014 isolinux.cfg
-rw-r----- 1 root root       25 Oct  3 20:14 kernel.ver
drwxr----- 4 root root     4096 Nov  7 16:28 lastGoodConfig
drwxr-xr-x 3 root root     4096 Oct  3 21:38 log
drwx------ 2 root root    16384 Oct  3 20:11 lost+found
```

```
-r-xr-x--- 1 root root    94600 Aug 17  2011 memtest
-r-xr-x--- 1 root root     7326 Aug 17  2011 splash.lss
-r-xr-x--- 1 root root     1770 Oct  9  2013 trans.tbl
-rwxr-x--- 1 root root  4121488 Jul 14 04:12 vmlinuz
-rwxr-xr-x 1 root root  3688864 Jul 14 04:12 vmlinuz-2.6.32-300.19.1.el5uek
-rwxr----- 1 root root  4121488 Oct  3 20:08 vmlinuz-2.6.39-400.128.17.el5uek
```

In this backup, we see the Linux boot images and all the files required to boot Linux and restore the operating system. Notice that you also see a directory called `lastGoodConfig`. This directory is a backup of the `/opt/oracle.cellos/iso/lastGoodConfig` directory on our storage cell. There is also a directory called `cellbits` containing the Cell Server software. Not only do we have a complete copy of everything needed to recover our storage cell to a bootable state on the internal USB drive, but we also have an online backup of all of our important cell configuration files and Cell Server binaries.

External USB Drive

In addition to the built-in CELLBOOT USB flash drive, Exadata also provides a way to create your own external bootable recovery image using a common 1-8GB USB flash drive you can buy at a local electronics store. Exadata will create the rescue image on the first external USB drive it finds, so before you create this recovery image, you must remove all other external USB drives from the system or the script will throw a warning and exit.

Recall that Exadata storage cells maintain two versions of the operating system and cell software: active and inactive. These are managed as two separate sets of disk partitions for the / and `/opt/oracle` file systems as can be confirmed using the `imageinfo` command, as follows:

```
[root@enkx4cel01 ~]# imageinfo | grep device
Active system partition on device: /dev/md6
Active software partition on device: /dev/md8
Inactive system partition on device: /dev/md5
Inactive software partition on device: /dev/md7
```

The `imageinfo` command shows the current (Active) and previous (Inactive) system volumes on the storage cell. Using the `df` command, we can see that we are indeed currently using the Active partitions (`/dev/md6` and `/dev/md8`) identified in the output from the `imageinfo` command:

```
[root@enkx4cel01 ~]# df | egrep 'Filesystem|md6|md8'

Filesystem           1K-blocks      Used Available Use% Mounted on
/dev/md6              10317752   6632836   3160804  68% /
/dev/md8               2063440    654956   1303668  34% /opt/oracle
```

By default, the `make_cellboot_usb` command will create a rescue image of your active configuration (the one you are currently running). The `-inactive` option allows you to create a rescue image from the previous configuration. The inactive partitions are the system volumes that were active when the last patch was installed.

The `make_cellboot_usb` command is used to create a bootable rescue image. To create an external rescue image, all you have to do is plug a USB flash drive into one of the USB ports on the front panel of the storage cell and run the `make_cellboot_usb` command.

■ **Caution** The rescue image will be created on the first external USB drive found on the system. Before creating an external rescue image, remove all other external USB drives from the system.

For example, the following listing shows the process of creating an external USB rescue image. The output from the make_cellboot_usb script is fairly lengthy, a little over 100 lines, so we won't show all of it here. Some of the output excluded from the following listing includes output from the fdisk command that is used to create partitions on the USB drive, formatting of the file systems, and the many files that are copied to create the bootable rescue disk.

```
[root@enkx4cel01 oracle.SupportTools]# ./make_cellboot_usb
[WARNING] More than one USB devices suitable for use as Oracle Exadata Cell start up boot
device.
Candidate for the Oracle Exadata Cell start up boot device     : /dev/sdad
Partition on candidate device                                  : /dev/sdad1
The current product version                                    : 12.1.1.1.1.140712
Label of the current Oracle Exadata Cell start up boot device  :
2014-11-25 10:12:27 -0600  [DEBUG] set_cell_boot_usb: cell usb        : /dev/sdad
2014-11-25 10:12:27 -0600  [DEBUG] set_cell_boot_usb: mnt sys         : /
2014-11-25 10:12:27 -0600  [DEBUG] set_cell_boot_usb: preserve        : preserve
2014-11-25 10:12:27 -0600  [DEBUG] set_cell_boot_usb: mnt usb         : /mnt/usb.make.
cellboot
2014-11-25 10:12:27 -0600  [DEBUG] set_cell_boot_usb: lock            : /tmp/usb.make.
cellboot.lock
2014-11-25 10:12:27 -0600  [DEBUG] set_cell_boot_usb: serial console  :
2014-11-25 10:12:27 -0600  [DEBUG] set_cell_boot_usb: kernel mode     : kernel
2014-11-25 10:12:27 -0600  [DEBUG] set_cell_boot_usb: mnt iso save    :
2014-11-25 10:12:27 -0600  Create CELLBOOT USB on device /dev/sdad
...
2014-11-25 10:15:11 -0600  Copying ./isolinux.cfg to /mnt/usb.make.cellboot/. ...
2014-11-25 10:15:44 -0600  Copying ./trans.tbl to /mnt/usb.make.cellboot/. ...
2014-11-25 10:15:48 -0600  Copying ./isolinux.bin to /mnt/usb.make.cellboot/. ...
2014-11-25 10:15:48 -0600  Copying ./boot.cat to /mnt/usb.make.cellboot/. ...
2014-11-25 10:15:48 -0600  Copying ./initrd.img to /mnt/usb.make.cellboot/. ...
2014-11-25 10:16:26 -0600  Copying ./memtest to /mnt/usb.make.cellboot/. ...
2014-11-25 10:16:29 -0600  Copying ./boot.msg to /mnt/usb.make.cellboot/. ...
2014-11-25 10:16:30 -0600  Copying ./vmlinuz-2.6.39-400.128.17.el5uek to /mnt/usb.make
.cellboot/. ...
2014-11-25 10:16:31 -0600  Copying ./cellbits/ofed.tbz to /mnt/usb.make.cellboot/./cellbits ...
2014-11-25 10:16:38 -0600  Copying ./cellbits/commonos.tbz to /mnt/usb.make.cellboot/
./cellbits ...
2014-11-25 10:17:51 -0600  Copying ./cellbits/sunutils.tbz to /mnt/usb.make.cellboot/
./cellbits ...
2014-11-25 10:18:11 -0600  Copying ./cellbits/cellfw.tbz to /mnt/usb.make.cellboot/
./cellbits ...
2014-11-25 10:19:30 -0600  Copying ./cellbits/doclib.zip to /mnt/usb.make.cellboot/
./cellbits ...
2014-11-25 10:20:34 -0600  Copying ./cellbits/debugos.tbz to /mnt/usb.make.cellboot/
./cellbits ...
2014-11-25 10:26:07 -0600  Copying ./cellbits/exaos.tbz to /mnt/usb.make.cellboot/
./cellbits ...
```

```
2014-11-25 10:27:19 -0600  Copying ./cellbits/cellboot.tbz to /mnt/usb.make.cellboot/
./cellbits ...
2014-11-25 10:27:26 -0600  Copying ./cellbits/cell.bin to /mnt/usb.make.cellboot/
./cellbits ...
2014-11-25 10:30:52 -0600  Copying ./cellbits/kernel.tbz to /mnt/usb.make.cellboot/
./cellbits ...
2014-11-25 10:31:37 -0600  Copying ./cellbits/cellrpms.tbz to /mnt/usb.make.cellboot/
./cellbits ...
2014-11-25 10:33:59 -0600  Copying ./initrd-2.6.39-400.128.17.el5uek.img to /mnt/usb.make.
cellboot/. ...
2014-11-25 10:34:20 -0600  Copying ./splash.lss to /mnt/usb.make.cellboot/. ...
2014-11-25 10:34:26 -0600  Copying ./image.id to /mnt/usb.make.cellboot/. ...
2014-11-25 10:34:32 -0600  Copying ./imgboot.lst to /mnt/usb.make.cellboot/. ...
2014-11-25 10:34:37 -0600  Copying ./vmlinuz to /mnt/usb.make.cellboot/. ...
2014-11-25 10:34:44 -0600  Copying lastGoodConfig/* to /mnt/usb.make.cellboot/
lastGoodConfig ...
/opt/oracle.cellos
...
2014-11-25 10:37:01 -0600  [DEBUG] set_grub_conf_n_initrd: mnt sys         : /
2014-11-25 10:37:01 -0600  [DEBUG] set_grub_conf_n_initrd: grub template   : USB_grub.in
2014-11-25 10:37:01 -0600  [DEBUG] set_grub_conf_n_initrd: boot dir        : /mnt/usb.make
.cellboot
2014-11-25 10:37:01 -0600  [DEBUG] set_grub_conf_n_initrd: kernel param    : 2.6.39-
400.128.17.el5uek
2014-11-25 10:37:01 -0600  [DEBUG] set_grub_conf_n_initrd: marker          :
I_am_CELLBOOT_usb
2014-11-25 10:37:01 -0600  [DEBUG] set_grub_conf_n_initrd: mode            :
2014-11-25 10:37:01 -0600  [DEBUG] set_grub_conf_n_initrd: sys dev         :
2014-11-25 10:37:01 -0600  [DEBUG] set_grub_conf_n_initrd: Image id file:
//opt/oracle.cellos/image.id
2014-11-25 10:37:01 -0600  [DEBUG] set_grub_conf_n_initrd: System device where image id
exists: /dev/md5
2014-11-25 10:37:01 -0600  [DEBUG] set_grub_conf_n_initrd: Kernel version:
2.6.39-400.128.17.el5uek
2014-11-25 10:37:01 -0600  [DEBUG] set_grub_conf_n_initrd: System device with image_id
(/dev/md5) and kernel version (2.6.39-400.128.17.el5uek) are in sync
2014-11-25 10:37:01 -0600  [DEBUG] set_grub_conf_n_initrd: Full kernel version:
2.6.39-400.128.17.el5uek
2014-11-25 10:37:01 -0600  [DEBUG] set_grub_conf_n_initrd: System device for the next boot:
/dev/md5
2014-11-25 10:37:01 -0600  [DEBUG] set_grub_conf_n_initrd: initrd for the next boot:
/mnt/usb.make.cellboot/initrd-2.6.39-400.128.17.el5uek.img
2014-11-25 10:37:01 -0600  [INFO] set_grub_conf_n_initrd: Set /dev/md5 in /mnt/usb.make
.cellboot/I_am_CELLBOOT_usb
2014-11-25 10:37:01 -0600  [INFO] Set kernel 2.6.39-400.128.17.el5uek and system device
/dev/md5 in generated /mnt/usb.make.cellboot/grub/grub.conf from //opt/oracle.cellos/tmpl/
USB_grub.in
2014-11-25 10:37:01 -0600  [INFO] Set /dev/md5 in /mnt/usb.make.cellboot/
initrd-2.6.39-400.128.17.el5uek.img
33007 blocks
2014-11-25 10:37:12 -0600  [WARNING] restore_preserved_cell_boot_usb: Unable to restore logs
and configs. Archive undefined
```

```
    GNU GRUB  version 0.97  (640K lower / 3072K upper memory)

 [ Minimal BASH-like line editing is supported.  For the first word, TAB
   lists possible command completions.  Anywhere else TAB lists the possible
   completions of a device/filename.]
grub> root (hd0,0)
 Filesystem type is ext2fs, partition type 0x83
grub> setup (hd0)
 Checking if "/boot/grub/stage1" exists... no
 Checking if "/grub/stage1" exists... yes
 Checking if "/grub/stage2" exists... yes
 Checking if "/grub/e2fs_stage1_5" exists... yes
 Running "embed /grub/e2fs_stage1_5 (hd0)"...  16 sectors are embedded.
succeeded
 Running "install /grub/stage1 (hd0) (hd0)1+16 p (hd0,0)/grub/stage2 /grub/grub.conf"...
succeeded
Done.
```

Here you can see that the `make_cellboot_usb` script copies over all of the storage cell software (`cellbits`) and configuration files (`lastGoodConfig`) it needs to recover the storage cell. Finally, you see that the Grub boot loader is installed on the USB drive so you can boot the system from it. When the script completes, you can remove the external USB disk from the system. This rescue disk can later be used for restoring your storage cell to working condition should the need arise.

Backing Up the Database

Exadata represents a leap forward in capacity and performance. Just a few years ago, large databases were described in terms of gigabytes. Today, it's not uncommon to find databases measured in terabytes. It wasn't long ago when a table was considered huge if it contained tens of millions of rows. Today, we commonly see tables that contain tens of billions of rows. This trend makes it clear that we will soon see databases measured in exabytes. As you might imagine, this creates some unique challenges for backup and recovery. The tools for backing up Exadata databases have not fundamentally changed, and the need to complete backups in a reasonable period of time is becoming increasingly difficult to achieve. Some of the strategies we'll discuss here will not be new; however, we will be looking at ways to leverage the speed of the platform so backup performance can keep pace with the increasing volume of your databases.

Disk-Based Backups

Oracle 10g introduced us to a new feature called the *Flash Recovery Area,* which extended Recovery Manager's structured approach to managing backups. Recently, this feature has been renamed to the *Fast Recovery Area (FRA).* The FRA is a storage area much like any other database storage. It can be created on raw devices, block devices, file systems, and, of course, ASM. Since the FRA utilizes disk-based storage, it provides a very fast storage medium for database recovery. This is especially true when using Exadata's high-performance storage architecture. Eliminating the need to retrieve backups from tape can shave hours and sometimes days off the time it takes to recover your databases. And, since the FRA is an extension of the database, Oracle automatically manages that space for you. When files in the FRA are backed up to tape, they are not immediately deleted. They are, instead, kept online as long as there is enough free space to do so. When more space is needed, the database deletes (in a FIFO manner) enough of these files to provide the needed space.

Tape-Based Backups

Using the FRA for disk-based backups can greatly improve the time it takes to recover your databases, but it does not eliminate the need for tape backups. As a matter of fact, tape-based backups are required for backing up the FRA. Moving large quantities of backup data to tape can be a challenge, and, with the volume of data that can be stored on Exadata, the need for high-performance tape backups is critical. Exadata V2 comes equipped with Gigabit Ethernet (GigE) ports that are each capable of delivering throughput up to 1000 megabits per second. Exadata X2-2 and later come with 10 Gigabit Ethernet ports, capable of delivering up to 10 times the throughput of the GigE ports of the V2. The problem is that even the 10 GigE ports between Exadata and the tape library's media server may not be fast enough to keep up.

A common solution to this problem is to install a 40 Gbps QDR InfiniBand card (or two) into the media server, allowing it to be linked directly into the spare ports on the Exadata InfiniBand network switch. Figure 9-1 illustrates a common backup configuration that leverages the high-speed InfiniBand network inside the Exadata rack to provide high-speed backups to tape.

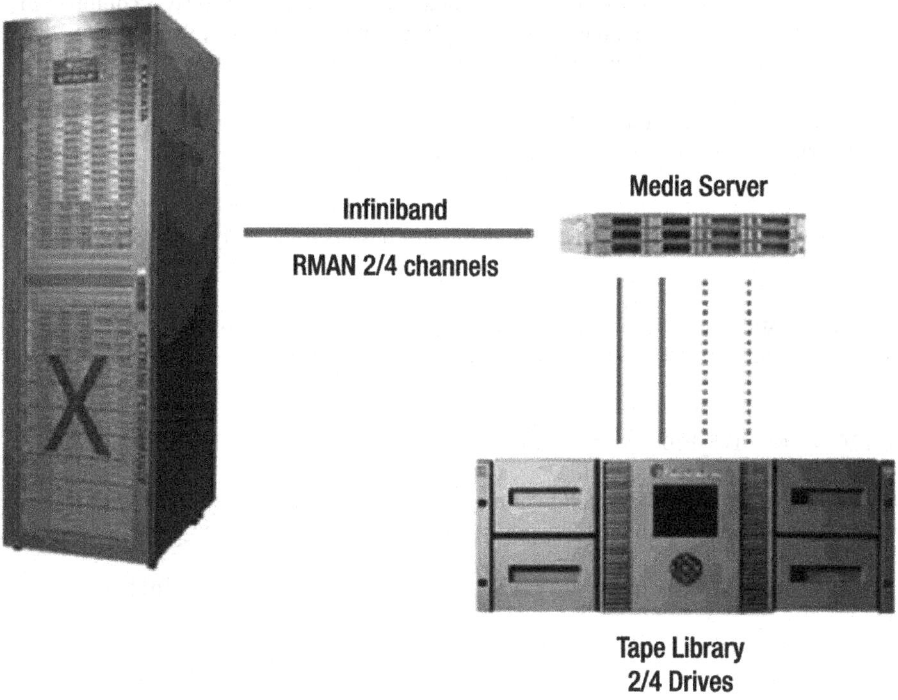

Figure 9-1. *Exadata backup architecture*

For very large databases, one InfiniBand card may not provide the throughput needed to complete backups in a reasonable time. For Oracle RAC databases, backups can be parallelized and distributed across any or all nodes in the RAC cluster. For Exadata full-rack configurations, this means you can have up to eight nodes (in a single rack) participating in the backup workload. Installing additional InfiniBand cards into the media server allows you to increase the throughput in 40 Gbps increments (3.2GB effective) up to the limits of the media server. An additional media server can be added to the configuration and load-balanced to extend performance even further. Oracle's MAA group published a very good white paper entitled "Backup and Recovery Performance and Best Practices for Exadata Cell and the Sun Oracle Database Machine," in which they reported backup rates of up to 2,509 MB/sec or 8.6 TB/hr for tape backups.

Backup from Standby Database

If you are planning to set up a disaster recovery site using Data Guard, you have the option of offloading your database backups to the standby database. This is not in any way an Exadata feature, so we will only touch briefly on the subject. The main purpose of the standby database is to take over the production load in the event that the primary database experiences a total failure. However, using a physical standby database also provides an additional backup for your primary database. If a datafile from the primary database is lost, a replacement datafile from the standby database can be used to replace it. Once the file has been restored to the primary database, archived redo logs are used to recover the datafile up to the current SCN of the database. The standby database is typically mounted (but not open) during normal operations. Cold backups can be made from the standby to the Fast Recovery Area (FRA) and then to tape. Backups from the standby database can be restored directly to the primary database. This provides three levels of recovery to choose from before deciding whether a failover to the standby is necessary.

It is best to use an Exadata platform for your standby database. This is because although tables that use Hybrid Columnar Compression (HCC) will replicate to non-Exadata databases just fine, you will not be able to read from them. Typically, the database kernel on non-Exadata databases cannot read HCC compressed data (there are a few exceptions, such as when data resides on a ZFS Storage Appliance). For example, the following error is returned when you select from an HCC table on a standard 11.2.x database:

```
SQL> select distinct segment_name from bigtab_arch_high;
 select distinct segment_name from small_table_arch_high
                              *
ERROR at line 1:
ORA-64307: hybrid columnar compression is only supported in tablespaces residing on Exadata
storage
```

Your compressed data is still intact. You just cannot read it unless you first uncompress it. HCC compressed tables can be uncompressed on non-Exadata databases using the `ALTER TABLE MOVE` command as follows:

```
SQL> alter table BIGTAB_ARCHIVE_HIGH move nocompress;
```

Partitioned tables can be uncompressed in a similar manner, and the operation can be parallelized using the `parallel` option, as you can see in the following command:

```
SQL> alter table BIGTAB_ARCHIVE_HIGH move partition JAN_2011 nocompress parallel;
```

Once the table is uncompressed, it can be read from a non-Exadata database. Keep in mind that with the high degree of compression HCC provides, you must take into consideration the additional disk storage that will be required by the uncompressed table or partition, which can be quite substantial.

Exadata Optimizations for RMAN

When RMAN performs an incremental backup on the Exadata platform, `cellsrv` filters out unwanted blocks and sends back only those that have changed since the last level 0 or level 1 backup. This improves the performance of incremental backups and reduces the workload on the database server. But even when only a relatively small number of blocks have changed, discovering them is a very I/O-intensive process because every block in the database must be examined to determine which ones have changed since the last incremental backup. This is true for both Exadata and non-Exadata databases. The only difference is where the work is done—on the database server or on the storage cells. A few years ago, Oracle 10g introduced *block change tracking* (BCT) to address this problem. Of course, this was long before Exadata came onto the scene. This feature maintains a bitmap structure in a file called the block change tracking file. Each bit in the BCT file (1 bit per 32K of data) represents a group of blocks in the database. When a data block is modified, Oracle flips a bit in the BCT file representing the group of blocks in which the changed block resides. When an incremental backup is taken, RMAN retrieves the whole group of blocks (represented by a flipped bit in the BCT file) and examines them to determine which one changed. Block change tracking introduces minimal overhead on the database server and is a very efficient way to track changed blocks. And, since it greatly reduces the number of blocks that must be examined during a backup, it improves backup performance while reducing the workload on the database server and storage grid.

For the Exadata platform, you may choose to allow `cellsrv` to do all of the block filtering for incremental backups, or you may use it in tandem with block change tracking. Block change tracking seems to provide the most benefit when fewer than 20 percent of the blocks in the database have changed since the last level 0 or level 1 backup. If your database is close to that threshold, you should do some testing to determine whether or not BCT improves incremental backup performance. The `BLOCKS_SKIPPED_IN_CELL` column of the `V$BACKUP_DATAFILE` view shows the number of blocks that were read and filtered out at the storage cell. This offloading is transparent and requires no user intervention or special parameters to be set ahead of time.

Wait Events

There are two Exadata-specific wait events that are triggered by database backup and recovery operations on the Exadata platform; `cell smart incremental backup` and `cell smart restore from backup`. These wait events are covered in more detail in Chapter 10.

> **cell smart incremental backup**: This wait event occurs when Exadata offloads incremental backup processing to the storage cells. The P1 column of the `V$SESSION_WAIT` view contains the cell hash number. This hash value can be used to compare the relative backup performance of each storage cell and determine if there is a performance problem on any of the cells.

> **cell smart restore from backup:** This wait event occurs during restore operations when Exadata offloads the task of initializing a file to the storage cells. The P1 column of `V$SESSION_WAIT` contains the cell hash number. This hash value can be used to compare the relative restore performance of each storage cell and determine if there is a performance problem on any of the cells.

Recovering Exadata

A better title for this section might be "When Things Go Wrong." After all, that's usually about the time we realize how little practical experience we have recovering our systems. As corporate America continues to squeeze every drop of productive time out of our workweek, DBAs and system administrators spend most if not all of their waking hours (and sometimes sleeping hours) just "keeping the wheels on." So, actually, practicing system recovery is more often than not treated like the proverbial "redheaded stepchild"—seldom thought about and rarely attended to. And even if we find ourselves in the enviable position of having the time to practice system recovery, it's rare to have the spare equipment to practice on. So kudos to you if you are reading this and nothing is actually broken. In this section, we'll be discussing Exadata system recovery using the backup methods we covered in the "Backing Up Exadata" section of this chapter.

Restoring the Database Server

Backing up and restoring the database servers can be done using third-party backup software or homegrown scripts using familiar commands such as `tar` and `zip`. The Linux Logical Volume Manager (LVM) provides the capability of backing up database servers via snapshots for creating point-in-time, `tar`-based backup sets. The procedure for recovering Exadata database servers is a very structured process that is specific to Exadata. In this section, we'll be stepping through this procedure, presuming the backup was taken using the backup procedure discussed earlier in this chapter. So, if you haven't read through that section of this chapter, you might want to take a look at it before continuing.

■ **Caution** Before performing any of the recovery steps listed in this section, it is a good idea to open a service request with Oracle support. Many of the tools described here will require passwords or assistance that can typically only be provided by Oracle's support organization. These steps should be performed as a last resort only.

Recovery Using LVM Snapshot-Based Backup Images

Restoring the database server using the LVM snapshot backup procedure we discussed earlier in this chapter is a fairly straightforward process. The backup image we will use in this procedure, `backup.tar.bz2`, is the one we created earlier in this chapter and includes the `/`, `/boot`, and `/u01` file systems. The first thing you need to do is stage the backup image on an NFS file system that can be mounted by the failed database server. The server is then booted from a special diagnostics ISO boot image included on all Exadata servers. When the system boots from the diagnostics ISO, you will be prompted step-by-step through the recovery process. Let's take a look at the basic steps for recovering a failed database server from the LVM snapshot-based backup we took earlier in this chapter:

1. Place the LVM snapshot backup image on an NFS shared file system that is accessible to the failed server by IP address. The file we'll be working with is named `backup.tar.bz2`.

2. Attach the `/opt/oracle.SupportTools/diagnostics.iso` boot image (obtained from a surviving server) to the failed server through the ILOM remote console.

3. Reboot the failed server and select the CD-ROM as the boot device. When the system boots from the diagnostics ISO, it will enter a special server recovery process.

4. From this point on, the recovery process will include step-by-step directions. For example, the following process recovers the database server from the backup image, `backup.tar.bz2`. Answers to the prompts are shown in ***bold_italics***:

```
Choose from following by typing letter in '()':
(e)nter interactive diagnostics shell. Must use credentials from Oracle support
to login (reboot or power cycle to exit the shell),
(r)estore system from NFS backup archive,
Select: r

Are you sure (y/n) [n]: y
```

```
The backup file could be created either from LVM or non-LVM based compute node.
Versions below 11.2.1.3.1 and 11.2.2.1.0 or higher do not support LVM based
partitioning. Use LVM based scheme(y/n): y

Enter path to the backup file on the NFS server in format:
<ip_address_of_the_NFS_share>:/<path>/:<archive_file>

For example, 10.10.10.10:/export/:operating_system.tar.bz2

NFS line: 10.160.242.200:/export/:backup.tar.bz2
IP Address of this host: 10.160.242.170
Netmask of this host: 255.255.255.0
Default gateway: 10.160.242.1
```

5. When all the above information is entered, Exadata will proceed to mount the backup image across the network and recover the system. When the recovery is finished, you will be prompted to log in. Log in as root using the password provided in the Oracle documentation.
6. Detach the diagnostics ISO from the ILOM.
7. Reboot the system using the `reboot` command. The failed server should be completely restored at this point.

When the system finishes booting, you can verify the recovery using the `imagehistory` command. The following listing shows that the image was created as a `restore from nfs backup` and was completed successfully:

```
[enkdb01:oracle:EXDB1] /home/oracle
> su -
Password:

[enkdb01:root] /root
> imagehistory
Version                              : 11.2.1.2.3
Image activation date                : 2010-05-15 05:58:56 -0700
Imaging mode                         : fresh
Imaging status                       : success
...

Version                              : 11.2.2.2.0.101206.2
Image activation date                : 2010-12-17 11:51:53 -0600
Imaging mode                         : patch
Imaging status                       : success

Version                              : 11.2.2.2.0.101206.2
Image activation date                : 2010-01-23 15:23:05 -0600
Imaging mode                         : restore from nfs backup
Imaging status                       : success
```

Generally speaking, it's a good idea not to get too creative when it comes to customizing your Exadata database server. Oracle permits you to create new LVM partitions and add file systems to your database servers, but if you do so, your recovery will require some additional steps. They aren't terribly difficult, but if you choose to customize your LVM partitions, be prepared to document the changes somewhere and familiarize yourself with the recovery procedures for customized systems in the Oracle documentation. Also, scripts that come from Oracle will not be aware of custom changes to the file system layout. This could lead to unexpected results when running those scripts—in particular, the LVM backup scripts provided in Exadata documentation.

Reimaging a Database Server

If a database server must be replaced or rebuilt from scratch and there is no backup image to recover from, an image can be created from an install image provided by Oracle Support. It is a lengthy and highly complicated process, but we'll hit the highlights here so you get a general idea of what it involves.

Before the server can be reimaged, it must be removed from the RAC cluster. This is the standard procedure for deleting a node from any 11gR2 or 12cR1 RAC cluster. First, the listener on the failed server must be shut down and disabled. Then the `ORACLE_HOME` for the database binaries is removed from the Oracle inventory. The VIP is then stopped and removed from the cluster configuration and the node deleted from the cluster. Finally, the `ORACLE_HOME` for the Grid Infrastructure is removed from the Oracle inventory.

The Oracle Software Delivery Cloud (formerly e-Delivery) hosts a `computeImageMaker` file that is used for creating an install image from one of the surviving database servers. This imagemaker file is specific to the version and platform of your Exadata system and will be named as follows:

```
computeImageMaker_{exadata_release}_LINUX.X64_{release_date}.{platform}.tar
```

An external USB flash drive is used to boot the recovery image on the failed server. The USB drive doesn't need to be very big, a 2–4GB thumb drive can be used. The next step is to unzip the imagemaker file you downloaded from Oracle Support on one of the other Exadata database servers in your rack. A similar recovery processes for storage cells uses the first USB drive found on the system so, before proceeding, you should remove all other external USB devices from the system. To create a bootable system image for recovering the failed database server, you will run the `makeImageMedia.sh` script. When the `makeImageMedia.sh` script completes, you are ready to install the image on your failed server. Remove the USB drive from the good server and plug it into the failed server. Log in to the ILOM on the failed server and reboot it. When the server boots up, it will automatically find the bootable recovery image on the external USB drive and begin the reimaging process. From this point, the process is automated. First, it will check the firmware and BIOS versions on the server and update them as needed to match them with your other database servers. Don't expect this to do anything if you are reimaging a server that was already part of your Exadata system, but it is necessary if the damaged server has been replaced with new equipment. Once the hardware components are up-to-date, a new image will be installed. When the reimaging process is complete, you can unplug the external USB drive and power cycle the server to boot up the new system image.

When the reimaging process is complete and the database server is back online, it will be set to factory defaults. For all intents and purposes, you should think of the reimaged server as a brand-new server. The server will enter the firstboot process, where it will ask you for any relevant network information required to complete the installation. This includes hostnames, IP addresses, DNS, and NTP servers. Once the operating system is configured, you will need to reinstall the Grid Infrastructure and database software and add the node back into the cluster. This is a well-documented process that many RAC DBAs refer to as the "add node" procedure. If you're not familiar with the process, let us reassure you—it's not nearly as daunting or time-consuming as you might think. Once you have the operating system prepared for the install, much of the heavy lifting is done for you by the Oracle Installer. The Exadata Owner's Guide does an excellent job of walking you through each step of the process.

Recovering the Storage Cell

Storage cell recovery is a very broad subject. It can be as simple as replacing an underperforming or failed data disk and as complex as responding to a total system failure such as a malfunctioning chip on the motherboard. In this section, we'll be discussing various types of cell recovery including removing and replacing physical disks, and failed Flash Cache modules. We will also discuss what to do if an entire storage cell dies and must be replaced.

System Volume Failure

Recall that the first two disks in the storage cell contain the Linux operating system and are commonly referred to as the "system volumes." Exadata protects these volumes using software mirroring through the Linux operating system. Even so, certain situations may require you to recover these disks from backup. Following are some reasons for performing cell recovery:

- System volumes (disks 1 and 2) fail simultaneously.
- The boot partition is damaged beyond repair.
- File systems become corrupted.
- A patch installation or upgrade fails.

If you find yourself in any of these situations, it may be necessary, or at least more expedient, to recover the system volumes from backup. As discussed earlier, Exadata automatically maintains a backup of the last good boot configuration using a 4GB internal USB flash drive called the CELLBOOT USB flash drive. Recovering the system volumes using this internal USB flash disk is commonly referred to as the *storage cell rescue procedure*. The steps for performing the cell rescue procedure basically involve booting from the internal USB drive and following the prompts for the type of rescue you want to perform. By the way, since Exadata comes equipped with an Integrated Lights Out Management module (ILOM), you can perform all cell recovery operations remotely, across the network. There is no need to stand in front of the rack to perform a full cell recovery from the internal USB flash disk.

■ **Note** In order to perform a sanity check of the USB recovery media, every Exadata storage cell is configured to use the USB device as its primary boot media. The cell will utilize a bootloader installed on the USB recovery media, which then points back to the system volumes. In the event that the USB recovery media is unavailable, the cell will revert back to boot from the system volumes and generate an alert that the USB recovery media is either not present or is damaged.

This section is not intended to be a step-by-step guide to cell recovery, so we're not going to go into all the details of cell recovery from the CELLBOOT USB flash disk. The Oracle documentation should be used for that, but we will take a look at what to consider before starting such a recovery.

> **Cell Disks and Grid Disks**: The rescue procedure restores the Linux system volumes only. Cell disks and their contents are not restored by the rescue procedure. If these partitions are damaged, they must be dropped and re-created. Once the grid disks are online, they can be added back to the ASM disk group and a subsequent rebalance will restore the data.

ASM Redundancy: Recovering a storage cell from USB backup can potentially cause the loss of all data on the system volumes. This includes your database data in the grid disks on these disk drives. If your ASM disk groups use Normal redundancy, we strongly recommend making a database backup before performing cell recovery from USB disk. With ASM High redundancy, you have a total of three copies of all your data, so it is safe to perform cell recovery without taking database backups. Even so, we'd still take a backup if at all possible. The recovery process does not destroy data volumes (cell/grid disks) unless you explicitly choose to do so when prompted by the rescue procedure.

Software and Patches: The rescue procedure will restore the cell to its former state, patches included, when the backup was taken. Also included in the restore are the network settings and SSH keys for the root, celladmin, and cellmonitor accounts.

Cell Rescue Options

In order to access the cell rescue options, connect to a virtual console from the lights-out management card and reboot the cell. When the grub menu shows on the screen, press a key to bring up the boot options. You will see several different options for the pair of system disks on the storage cell. The CELLBOOT USB device can be accessed through the final option, `CELL_USB_BOOT_CELLBOOT_usb:in_rescue_mode`. Upon booting from the CELLBOOT USB device, you have two initial options for recovery—enter a rescue shell or reimage the storage server. The rescue shell can be helpful if only a few files need to be recovered, or if the failure can be resolved via the command line. Typically, you will need to reimage the cell. While this may sound like a drastic option, Oracle has made sure that everything critical to rebuilding the operating system has been backed up. This means that you will not need to enter IP addresses, hostnames, or reset the root password. Upon choosing to reimage the storage cell, you are asked whether you would like to erase all of the data partitions and disks. This decision is based on the type of recovery that you need to perform.

Erase data partitions and data disks: If this option is chosen, the reimage procedure will drop the partitions on the system disks and remove the cell disk metadata from the nonsystem disks. This leaves the storage cell in a state with a reimaged operating system and no cell disks within the storage server configuration.

Do not erase data partitions and data disks: The storage cell will still be reimaged, but only the system volume partitions will be impacted. This option leaves all of the cell disk metadata intact, meaning that the individual cell disks will still be available and contain all of the data that resided on them before the reimage. The cell disks will still have to be imported, but that can be done with a simple `import celldisk all force` command in `CellCLI`. This option is valuable if the ASM disks for that cell have not been dropped from the ASM disk groups. Importing the cell disks will avoid the need for an I/O-intensive rebalance.

So, what happens if, for some reason, the internal CELLBOOT USB flash disk cannot be used for the rescue procedure? If this happens, you can follow the compute node reimage procedure and download the storage cell imagemaker software from the Oracle Software Delivery Cloud. Create a bootable USB device and boot the storage cell using that. Keep in mind that you will need to enter all of the network information specific to that cell because the image you are using does not have this data. All cell disks and grid disks will need to be recreated as well. Hopefully, this should never happen due to the constant validation checks performed on the storage cells. Newer versions of the Exadata Storage Server software include periodic checks of the CELLBOOT USB device and will automatically rebuild the device if it becomes corrupted.

Cell Disk Failure

ASM handles the temporary or permanent loss of a cell disk through its redundant failure group technology. As a result, the loss of a cell disk should not cause any interruption to the databases as long as the disk group is defined with Normal redundancy. If High redundancy is used, the disk group can suffer the simultaneous loss of two cell disks within the same failure group. Recall that on Exadata, each storage cell constitutes a separate failure group. This means that with Normal redundancy, you can lose an entire storage cell (12 cell disks) without impact to your databases. With High redundancy, you can lose two storage cells simultaneously and your databases will continue to service your clients without interruption. That's pretty impressive. Redundancy isn't cheap, though. For example, consider a disk group with 30 terabytes of raw space (configured for External redundancy). With Normal redundancy, that 30 terabytes becomes 15 terabytes of usable space. With High redundancy, it becomes 10 terabytes of usable storage. Also keep in mind that the database will typically read the primary copy of your data unless it is unavailable. On Oracle 12c, a disk failure will enable the even read feature, which will read from the disk with the lightest load, regardless of whether it contains a primary or mirrored copy of the data. Normal and High redundancy provide no performance benefits. They are used strictly for fault tolerance. The key is to choose a redundancy level that strikes a balance between resiliency and budget.

Simulated Disk Failure

In this section, we're going to test what happens when a cell disk fails. The system used for these tests was a quarter rack, Exadata V2. We've created a disk group called SCRATCH_DG, defined as follows:

```
SYS:+ASM2> CREATE DISKGROUP SCRATCH_DG NORMAL REDUNDANCY
  FAILGROUP CELL01 DISK 'o/192.168.12.3/SCRATCH_DG_CD_05_cell01'
  FAILGROUP CELL02 DISK 'o/192.168.12.4/SCRATCH_DG_CD_05_cell02'
  FAILGROUP CELL03 DISK 'o/192.168.12.5/SCRATCH_DG_CD_05_cell03'
  attribute 'compatible.rdbms'='12.1.0.2.0',
            'compatible.asm'  ='12.1.0.2.0',
            'au_size'='4M',
            'cell.smart_scan_capable'='true';
```

Notice that this disk group is created using three grid disks. Following Exadata best practices, we've used one grid disk from each storage cell. It's interesting to note that even if we hadn't specified three failure groups with one disk in each, ASM would have done so automatically. We then created a small, single-instance database called SCRATCH using this disk group. The disk group is configured with normal redundancy (two mirror copies for each block of data), which means our database should be able to suffer the loss of one grid disk without losing access to data or causing a crash. Since each grid disk resides on a separate storage cell, we could even suffer the loss of an entire storage cell without losing data. We'll discuss what happens when a storage cell fails later in the chapter.

In a moment, we will take a look at what happens when a grid disk is removed from the storage cell (a simulated disk failure). But before we do, there are a few things we need to do:

- Verify that no rebalance or other volume management operations are running
- Ensure that all grid disks for the SCRATCH_DG disk group are online
- Verify that taking a disk offline will not impact database operations
- Check the disk repair timer to ensure the disk is not automatically dropped before we can bring it back online again

There are a couple of ways to verify that volume management activity is not going on. First, let's check the current state of the disk groups using asmcmd. The ls -l command shows the disk groups, the type of redundancy, and whether or not a rebalance operation is currently underway. By the way, you could also get this information using the lsdg command, which also includes other interesting information such as space utilization, online/offline status, and more. The Rebal column in the following listing indicates that no rebalance operations are executing at the moment.

```
> asmcmd -p
ASMCMD [+] > ls -l
State    Type    Rebal  Name
MOUNTED  NORMAL  N      DATA_DG/
MOUNTED  NORMAL  N      RECO_DG/
MOUNTED  NORMAL  N      SCRATCH_DG/
MOUNTED  NORMAL  N      STAGE_DG/
MOUNTED  NORMAL  N      SYSTEM_DG/
```

Notice that not all volume management operations are shown in the asmcmd commands. If a grid disk has been offline for a period of time, there may be a considerable amount of backlogged data that must be copied to it in order to bring it up-to-date. Depending on the volume of data, it may take several minutes to finish resynchronizing a disk. Although this operation is directly related to maintaining balance across all disks, it is not technically a "rebalance" operation. As such, it will not appear in the listing. For example, even though the ls -l command in the previous listing showed a status of N for rebalance operations, you can clearly see that a disk is currently being brought online by running the next query:

```
SYS:+ASM2> select dg.name "Diskgroup", disk.name, disk.failgroup, disk.mode_status
       from v$asm_disk disk,
            v$asm_diskgroup dg
      where dg.group_number = disk.group_number
        and disk.mode_status <> 'ONLINE';

Diskgroup          NAME                           FAILGROUP  MODE_ST
------------------ ------------------------------ ---------- -------
SCRATCH_DG         SCRATCH_CD_05_CELL01           CELL01     SYNCING
```

Checking for the online/offline state of a disk is a simple matter of running the following query from SQL*Plus. In the following listing, you can see that the SCRATCH_CD_05_CELL01 disk is offline by its MOUNT_STATE of MISSING and HEADER_STATUS of UNKNOWN:

```
SYS:+ASM2> select d.name, d.MOUNT_STATUS, d.HEADER_STATUS, d.STATE
 from v$asm_disk d
 where d.name like 'SCRATCH%'
 order by 1;

NAME                                               MOUNT_S HEADER_STATU STATE
-------------------------------------------------- ------- ------------ ----------
SCRATCH_CD_05_CELL01                               MISSING UNKNOWN      NORMAL
SCRATCH_CD_05_CELL02                               CACHED  MEMBER       NORMAL
SCRATCH_CD_05_CELL03                               CACHED  MEMBER       NORMAL
```

Still, perhaps a better way of checking the status of all disks in the SCRATCH_DG disk group would be to check the mode_status in V$ASM_DISK_STAT. The following listing shows that all grid disks in the SCRATCH_DG disk group are online:

```
SYS:+ASM2> select name, mode_status from v$asm_disk_stat where name like 'SCRATCH%';

NAME                                                 MODE_ST
---------------------------------------------------- -------
SCRATCH_CD_05_CELL03                                 ONLINE
SCRATCH_CD_05_CELL01                                 ONLINE
SCRATCH_CD_05_CELL02                                 ONLINE
```

The next thing we'll look at is the disk repair timer. Recall that the disk group attribute disk_repair_time determines the amount of time ASM will wait before it permanently removes a disk from the disk group and rebalances the data to the surviving grid disks when read/write errors occur. Before taking a disk offline, we should check to see that this timer is going to give us enough time to bring the disk back online before ASM automatically drops it. This attribute can be displayed using SQL*Plus and running the following query. (By the way, the V$ASM views are visible whether you are connected to an ASM instance or a database instance.)

```
SYS:+ASM2> select dg.name "DiskGroup",
           attr.name,
           attr.value
      from v$asm_diskgroup dg,
           v$asm_attribute attr
     where dg.group_number = attr.group_number
       and attr.name like '%repair_time';

DiskGroup         NAME                      VALUE
----------------- ------------------------- ----------
DATA_DG           disk_repair_time          3.6h
DATA_DG           failgroup_repair_time     24.0h
DBFS_DG           disk_repair_time            3.6h
DBFS_DG           failgroup_repair_time     24.0h
RECO_DG           disk_repair_time            3.6h
RECO_DG           failgroup_repair_time     24.0h
SCRATCH_DG        disk_repair_time            8.5h
SCRATCH_DG        failgroup_repair_time       24h
STAGE_DG          disk_repair_time            72h
STAGE_DG          failgroup_repair_time       24h
```

The default value for the disk repair timer is 3.6 hours. Since this query was run on a cluster running Oracle 12c, there is also a failgroup_repair_time attribute. This is the amount of time that will be taken before the disks are dropped in the event that an entire fail group goes missing. This is useful when there is a hardware failure across the entire storage cell. These attributes are engaged when a storage cell is rebooted or when a disk is temporarily taken offline, but, on rare occasion, they can also occur spontaneously when there is an actual hardware failure. Sometimes simply pulling a disk out of the chassis and reinserting it will clear unexpected transient errors. Any data that would normally be written to the failed disk will queue up until the disk is brought back online or the disk repair time expires. If ASM drops a disk, it can be manually added back into the disk group, but it will require a full rebalance, which can be a lengthy process. The following command was used to set the disk repair timer to 8.5 hours for the SCRATCH_DG disk group:

```
SYS:+ASM2> alter diskgroup SCRATCH_DG set attribute 'disk_repair_time'='8.5h';
```

Now, let's verify whether taking a cell disk offline will affect the availability of the disk group. We can do that by checking the asmdeactivationoutcome and asmmodestatus attributes of our grid disks. For example, the following listing shows the output from the LIST GRIDDISK command when a grid disk in a normal redundancy disk group is taken offline. In this example, we have a SCRATCH_DG disk group consisting of one grid disk from three failure groups (enkcel01, enkcel02, and enkcel03). First, we'll check the status of the grid disks when all disks are active:

```
[enkdb02:root] /root
> dcli -g cell_group -l root " cellcli -e list griddisk \
    attributes name, asmdeactivationoutcome, asmmodestatus " | grep SCRATCH
enkcel01: SCRATCH_DG_CD_05_cell01   Yes     ONLINE
enkcel02: SCRATCH_DG_CD_05_cell02   Yes     ONLINE
enkcel03: SCRATCH_DG_CD_05_cell03   Yes     ONLINE
```

Now, we'll deactivate one of these the grid disks at the storage cell and run the command again:

```
CellCLI> alter griddisk SCRATCH_DG_CD_05_cell01 inactive
GridDisk SCRATCH_DG_CD_05_cell01 successfully altered

 [enkdb02:root] /root
> dcli -g cell_group -l root " cellcli -e list griddisk \
    attributes name, asmdeactivationoutcome, asmmodestatus " | grep SCRATCH
enkcel01: SCRATCH_DG_CD_05_cell01   Yes     OFFLINE
enkcel02: SCRATCH_DG_CD_05_cell02   "Cannot de-activate due to other offline disks in the
diskgroup"       ONLINE
enkcel03: SCRATCH_DG_CD_05_cell03   "Cannot de-activate due to other offline disks in the
diskgroup"       ONLINE
```

As you can see, the asmmodestatus attribute of the offlined grid disk is now set to OFFLINE, and the asmdeactivationoutcome attribute of the other two disks in the disk group warns us that these grid disks cannot be taken offline. Doing so would cause ASM to dismount the SCRATCH_DG disk group.

■ **Note** Notice that we use the dcli command to run the CellCLI command LIST GRIDDISK ATTRIBUTES on each cell in the storage grid. Basically, dcli allows us to run a command concurrently on multiple nodes. The cell_group parameter is a file containing a list of all of our storage cells.

If the output from the LIST GRIDDISK command indicates it is safe to do so, we can test what happens when we take one of the grid disks for our SCRATCH_DG disk group offline. For this test, we will physically remove the disk drive from the storage cell chassis. The test configuration will be as follows:

- For this test, we will create a new tablespace with one datafile. The datafile is set to autoextend so it will grow into the disk group as data is loaded.
- Next, we'll generate a considerable amount of data in the tablespace by creating a large table; a couple of billion rows from DBA_SEGMENTS should do it.

- While data is being loaded into the large table, we will physically remove the disk from the cell chassis.
- Once the data is finished loading, we will reinstall the disk and observe Exadata's automated disk recovery in action.

The first order of business is to identify the location of the disk drive within the storage cell. To do this, we will use the grid disk name to find the cell disk it resides on. Then we'll use the cell disk name to find the slot address of the disk drive within the storage cell. Once we have the slot address, we will turn on the service LED on the front panel so we know which disk to remove.

From storage cell 3, we can use the `LIST GRIDDISK` command to find the name of the cell disk we are looking for:

```
CellCLI> list griddisk attributes name, celldisk where name like 'SCRATCH.*' detail
         name:                    SCRATCH_DG_CD_05_cell03
         cellDisk:                CD_05_cell03
```

Now that we have the cell disk name, we can use the `LIST LUN` command to find the slot address of the physical disk we want to remove. In the following listing, we see the slot address we're looking for, 16:5.

```
CellCLI> list LUN attributes celldisk, physicaldrives where celldisk=CD_05_cell03 detail
         cellDisk:                CD_05_cell03
         physicalDrives:          16:5
```

With the slot address, we can use the `MegaCli64` command to activate the drive's service LED on the front panel of the storage cell. Note that the \ characters in the `MegaCli64` command below are used to prevent the Bash shell from interpreting the brackets ([ ]) around the physical drive address. (Single quotes work as well, by the way.)

```
/opt/MegaRAID/MegaCli/MegaCli64 -pdlocate -physdrv \[16:5\] -a0
```

The amber LED on the front of the disk drive should be flashing, as can be seen in Figure 9-2.

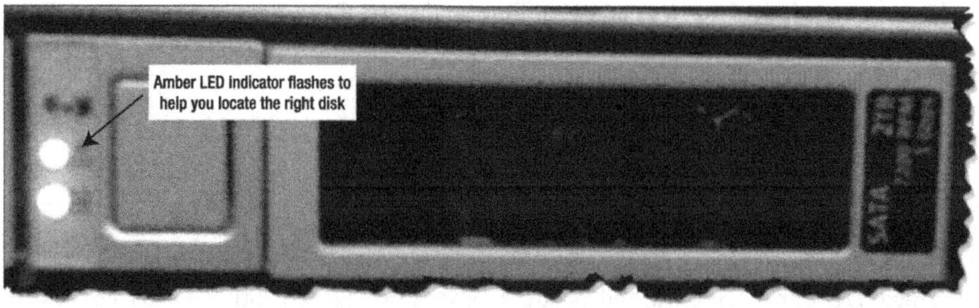

Figure 9-2. *Disk drive front panel*

And, in case you were wondering, the service LED can be turned off again using the `stop` option of the `MegaCli64` command, like this:

```
/opt/MegaRAID/MegaCli/MegaCli64 -pdlocate -stop -physdrv \[16:5\] -a0
```

Now that we've located the right disk, we can remove it from the storage cell by pressing the release button and gently pulling the lever on the front of the disk, as you can see in Figure 9-3.

Figure 9-3. *Ejected disk drive*

■ **Note** All disk drives in the storage cell are hot-pluggable and may be replaced without powering down the storage cell.

Checking the grid disk status in `CellCLI`, we see that it has been changed from Active to Inactive. This makes the grid disk unavailable to the ASM storage cluster.:

```
CellCLI> list griddisk where name = 'SCRATCH_CD_05_cell03';
         SCRATCH_CD_05_cell03     inactive
```

ASM immediately notices the loss of the disk, takes it offline, and starts the disk repair timer. The ASM alert log (`alert_+ASM2.log`) shows that we have about 8.5 hours (30596/60/60) to bring the disk back online before ASM permanently drops it from the disk group:

```
alert_+ASM1.log
--------------------
Tue Dec 28 08:40:54 2010
GMON checking disk modes for group 5 at 121 for pid 52, osid 29292
Errors in file /u01/app/oracle/diag/asm/+asm/+ASM2/trace/+ASM2_gmon_5912.trc:
ORA-27603: Cell storage I/O error, I/O failed on disk o/192.168.12.5/SCRATCH_CD_05_cell03 at
offset 4198400 for data length 4096
ORA-27626: Exadata error: 201 (Generic I/O error)
WARNING: Write Failed. group:5 disk:3 AU:1 offset:4096 size:4096
...
WARNING: Disk SCRATCH_DG_CD_05_CELL03 in mode 0x7f is now being offlined
WARNING: Disk SCRATCH_DG_CD_05_CELL03 in mode 0x7f is now being taken offline
...
Tue Dec 28 08:43:21 2010
WARNING: Disk (SCRATCH_DG_CD_05_CELL03) will be dropped in: (30596) secs on ASM inst: (2)
Tue Dec 28 08:43:23 2010
```

The status of the disk in ASM can be seen using the following query from one of the ASM instances. Notice that the SCRATCH disk group is still mounted (online):

```
SYS:+ASM2> select dg.name, d.name, dg.state, d.mount_status, d.header_status, d.state
             from v$asm_disk d,
                  v$asm_diskgroup dg
            where dg.name = 'SCRATCH_DG'
              and dg.group_number = d.group_number
            order by 1,2;

NAME          NAME                        STATE      MOUNT_S HEADER_STATU STATE
------------- --------------------------- ---------- ------- ------------ ----------
SCRATCH       SCRATCH_DG_CD_05_CELL01     MOUNTED    CACHED  MEMBER       NORMAL
SCRATCH       SCRATCH_DG_CD_05_CELL02     MOUNTED    CACHED  MEMBER       NORMAL
SCRATCH       SCRATCH_DG_CD_05_CELL03     MOUNTED    MISSING UNKNOWN      NORMAL
```

While the disk is offline, ASM continues to poll its status to see if the disk is available. We see the following query repeating in the ASM alert log:

```
alert_+ASM1.log
--------------------
WARNING: Exadata Auto Management: OS PID: 5918 Operation ID: 3015:   in diskgroup  Failed
  SQL    : /* Exadata Auto Mgmt: Select disks in DG that are not ONLINE. */
select name from v$asm_disk_stat
  where
    mode_status='OFFLINE'
      and
    group_number in
      (
       select group_number from v$asm_diskgroup_stat
         where
           name='SCRATCH_DG'
             and
           state='MOUNTED'
      )
```

Our test database also detected the loss of the grid disk, as can be seen in the database alert log:

```
alert_SCRATCH.log
-----------------------
Tue Dec 28 08:40:54 2010
Errors in file /u01/app/oracle/diag/rdbms/scratch/SCRATCH/trace/SCRATCH_ckpt_22529.trc:
ORA-27603: Cell storage I/O error, I/O failed on disk o/192.168.12.5/SCRATCH_CD_05_cell03 at
offset 26361217024 for data length 16384
ORA-27626: Exadata error: 201 (Generic I/O error)
WARNING: Read Failed. group:5 disk:3 AU:6285 offset:16384 size:16384
WARNING: failed to read mirror side 1 of virtual extent 0 logical extent 0 of file 260 in
group [5.1611847437] from disk SCRATCH_CD_05_CELL03  allocation unit 6285 reason error; if
possible, will try another mirror side
NOTE: successfully read mirror side 2 of virtual extent 0 logical extent 1 of file 260 in
group [5.1611847437] from disk SCRATCH_CD_05_CELL02 allocation unit 224
...
```

```
Tue Dec 28 08:40:54 2010
NOTE: disk 3 (SCRATCH_CD_05_CELL03) in group 5 (SCRATCH) is offline for reads
NOTE: disk 3 (SCRATCH_CD_05_CELL03) in group 5 (SCRATCH) is offline for writes
```

Notice that the database automatically switches to the mirror copy for data it can no longer read from the failed grid disk. This is ASM normal redundancy in action.

When we reinsert the disk drive, the storage cell returns the grid disk to a state of Active, and ASM brings the disk back online again. We can see that the grid disk has returned to a state of CACHED and a HEADER_STATUS of NORMAL in the following query:

```
SYS:+ASM2> select dg.name, d.name, dg.state, d.mount_status, d.header_status, d.state
             from v$asm_disk d,
                  v$asm_diskgroup dg
            where dg.name = 'SCRATCH'
              and dg.group_number = d.group_number
            order by 1,2;

NAME          NAME                      STATE      MOUNT_S HEADER_STATU STATE
------------- ------------------------- ---------- ------- ------------ ----------
SCRATCH       SCRATCH_CD_05_CELL01      MOUNTED    CACHED  MEMBER       NORMAL
SCRATCH       SCRATCH_CD_05_CELL02      MOUNTED    CACHED  MEMBER       NORMAL
SCRATCH       SCRATCH_CD_05_CELL03      MOUNTED    CACHED  MEMBER       NORMAL  ←
```

It is likely that the disk group will need to catch up on writing data that queued up while the disk was offline. If the disk was reinserted before the disk_repair_time counter hit zero, the disk will simply catch up on the writes that were missed. If not, then the entire disk group will need to be rebalanced, which can take a significant amount of time. Generally speaking, the delay is not a problem because it all happens in the background. During the resilvering process, ASM redundancy allows our databases to continue with no interruption to service. You can see the status of a resync or rebalance operation through the gv$asm_operation view in ASM. Keep in mind that resync operations are only visible in Oracle 12c and on.

If this had been an actual disk failure and we actually replaced the disk drive, we would need to wait for the RAID controller to acknowledge the new disk before it could be used. This doesn't take long, but you should check the status of the disk to ensure that its status is Normal before using it. The disk status may be verified using the CellCLI command LIST PHYSICALDISK, as shown here:

```
CellCLI> list physicaldisk where diskType=HardDisk AND status=critical detail
```

When a disk is replaced, the storage cell performs the following tasks automatically:

- The disk firmware is updated to match the other disk drives in the storage cell.
- The cell disk is re-created to match that of the disk it replaced.
- The replacement cell disk is brought online (status set to Normal).
- The grid disk (or grid disks) on the failed disk will be re-created.
- The grid disk status is set to Active.

Once the replacement grid disks are set to Active, ASM automatically opens the disk and begins the resilvering process. The Exadata Storage Server software handles all of these tasks automatically, making disk replacement a fairly painless process.

When to Replace a Cell Disk

Disk failure can occur abruptly, causing the disk to go offline immediately, or it can occur gradually, manifesting poor I/O performance. Storage cells are constantly monitoring the disk drives. This monitoring includes drive performance, in terms of both I/O and throughput, and SMART metrics such as temperature, speed, and read/write errors. The goal is to provide early warning for disks that are likely to fail before they actually do. When the storage cell detects a problem, an alert is generated with specific instructions on how to replace the disk. If the system has been configured for e-mail notification, these alerts will be e-mailed to you automatically. Alerts will also be sent using the other available notification methods, including Oracle Enterprise Manager and Automatic Service Request. Figure 9-4 shows an example of an e-mail alert from an Exadata storage cell. Note that the e-mail includes the name of the host, the disk that has failed, and even a picture of the front of a storage cell with a red ring around the disk that has failed. When the disk has been replaced and the alert has cleared, a follow up e-mail will be sent with a green ring around the new disk.

ORACLE
EXADATA

Maintenance: Hardware Stateful Alert 15_1

Event Time 2014-12-22T06:19:44-06:00

Description System hard disk failed.

Status	FAILED
Manufacturer	SEAGATE
Model Number	ST360057SSUN600G
Size	600GB
Serial Number	XXXXXXXX
Firmware	0B25
Slot Number	1
Cell Disk	CD_01_exacel05
Grid Disk	DATA_EXA01_CD_01_exacel05, RECO_EXA01_CD_01_exacel05

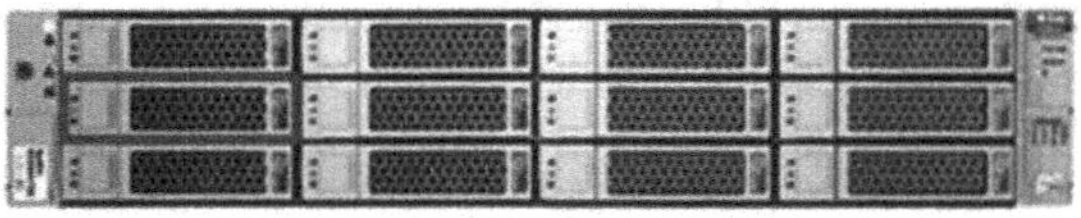

Affected Cell

Name	exacel05
Server Model	Oracle Corporation SUN FIRE X4270 M2 SERVER High Performance
Chassis Serial Number	XXXXXXXX
Release Version	11.2.3.3.0
Release Label	OSS_11.2.3.3.0_LINUX.X64_131014.1

Recommended Action The system hard disk has failed. A white cell locator LED has been lit to help locate the affected cell, and an amber service action LED and a blue ok-to-remove LED have both been lit on the drive to help locate the affected drive. Please replace the drive.
Oracle ASM rebalance will automatically restore the data redundancy.
Detailed information on this problem can be found at https://support.oracle.com/CSP/main/article?cmd=show&type=NOT&id=1112994.1

Automatic Service Request has been notified with Unique Identifier: f6b1b7ae-bf08-4b0c-98e1-0395577fdaef.

Figure 9-4. *Example of an e-mail alert from a failed disk drive*

In the previous section, we walked you through a simulated drive failure. Had this been an actual disk failure, the procedure for replacing the disk would follow the same steps we used for the simulation. But what happens when Exadata's early warning system determines that a drive is likely to fail soon? When Exadata detects drive problems, it sets the physical disk status attribute accordingly. The following CellCLI command displays the status of all disks in the storage cell:

```
CellCLI> list physicaldisk attributes name, status where disktype = 'HardDisk'
         35:0     normal
         35:1     normal
         ...
         35:11    normal
```

Table 9-1 shows the various disk status values and what they mean.

Table 9-1. *Disk Status Definitions*

Status	Description
Normal	The drive is healthy.
Predictive Failure	The disk is still working but likely to fail soon and should be replaced as soon as possible.
Poor Performance	The disk is exhibiting extremely poor performance and should be replaced.

Predictive Failure

If a disk status shows Predictive Failure, ASM will automatically drop the grid disks from the drive and rebalance data to other disks in the disk group according to the redundancy policy of the affected disk groups that use the drive. Once ASM has finished rebalancing and completed the drop operation, you can replace the disk drive. The following listing can be used to track the status of the ASM disk. A status of Offline indicates that ASM has not yet finished rebalancing the disk group. Once the rebalance is complete, the disk will no longer appear in the listing. By the way, tailing the ASM alert log is also an excellent way of checking the progress of the drop.

```
SYS:+ASM2>select name, mode_status
            from v$asm_disk_stat
           where name like 'SCRATCH%'
           order by 1;

NAME                                                   MODE_ST
------------------------------------------------------ -------
SCRATCH_CD_05_CELL01                                   ONLINE
SCRATCH_CD_05_CELL02                                   ONLINE
SCRATCH_CD_05_CELL03                                   OFFLINE
```

■ **Caution** The first two physical disks in the storage cell also contain the Linux operating system. The O/S partitions on these two disks are configured as mirrors of one another. If one of these disks fails, the data must be in sync with the mirror disk before you remove it. Use the CellCLI command `alter cell validate configuration` to verify that no `mdadm` errors exist before replacing the disk.

The CellCLI command VALIDATE CONFIGURATION performs this verification for you:

```
CellCLI> ALTER CELL VALIDATE CONFIGURATION
Cell enkcel01 successfully altered
```

Poor Performance

If a disk exhibits poor performance, it should be replaced. A single poorly performing cell disk can impact the performance of other healthy disks. When a disk begins performing extremely badly, its status will be set to Poor Performance. As is the case with Predictive Failure status, ASM will automatically drop all grid disks (on this cell disk) from the disk groups and begin a rebalance operation. Once the rebalance is complete, you can remove and replace the failing disk drive. You can use the CellCLI command CALIBRATE to manually check the performance of all disks in the storage cell. This command runs Oracle's Orion calibration tool to look at both the performance and throughput of each of the disks. Ordinarily, cellsrv should be shut down before running CALIBRATE because it can significantly impact I/O performance for databases using the storage cell. If you cannot shut down cellsrv for the test, you can run CALIBRATE using the FORCE option. As daunting as that sounds, FORCE simply overrides the safety switch and allows you to run CALIBRATE while cellsrv is up and applications are using the cell disks. The following listing shows the output from the CALIBRATE command run on a healthy set of cell disks from an Exadata X4-2 high capacity cell. The test takes about ten minutes to run.

```
CellCLI> calibrate
Calibration will take a few minutes...
Aggregate random read throughput across all hard disk LUNs: 1123 MBPS
Aggregate random read throughput across all flash disk LUNs: 8633 MBPS
Aggregate random read IOs per second (IOPS) across all hard disk LUNs: 2396
Aggregate random read IOs per second (IOPS) across all flash disk LUNs: 260102
Calibrating hard disks (read only) ...
LUN 0_0  on drive [20:0      ] random read throughput: 141.27 MBPS, and 195 IOPS
LUN 0_1  on drive [20:1      ] random read throughput: 139.66 MBPS, and 203 IOPS
LUN 0_10 on drive [20:10     ] random read throughput: 141.02 MBPS, and 201 IOPS
LUN 0_11 on drive [20:11     ] random read throughput: 140.82 MBPS, and 200 IOPS
LUN 0_2  on drive [20:2      ] random read throughput: 139.89 MBPS, and 199 IOPS
LUN 0_3  on drive [20:3      ] random read throughput: 142.46 MBPS, and 201 IOPS
LUN 0_4  on drive [20:4      ] random read throughput: 140.99 MBPS, and 203 IOPS
LUN 0_5  on drive [20:5      ] random read throughput: 141.92 MBPS, and 198 IOPS
LUN 0_6  on drive [20:6      ] random read throughput: 141.23 MBPS, and 199 IOPS
LUN 0_7  on drive [20:7      ] random read throughput: 143.44 MBPS, and 202 IOPS
LUN 0_8  on drive [20:8      ] random read throughput: 141.54 MBPS, and 204 IOPS
LUN 0_9  on drive [20:9      ] random read throughput: 142.63 MBPS, and 202 IOPS
Calibrating flash disks (read only, note that writes will be significantly slower) ...
LUN 1_0  on drive [FLASH_1_0] random read throughput: 540.90 MBPS, and 39921 IOPS
LUN 1_1  on drive [FLASH_1_1] random read throughput: 540.39 MBPS, and 40044 IOPS
LUN 1_2  on drive [FLASH_1_2] random read throughput: 541.03 MBPS, and 39222 IOPS
LUN 1_3  on drive [FLASH_1_3] random read throughput: 540.45 MBPS, and 39040 IOPS
LUN 2_0  on drive [FLASH_2_0] random read throughput: 540.56 MBPS, and 43739 IOPS
LUN 2_1  on drive [FLASH_2_1] random read throughput: 540.64 MBPS, and 43662 IOPS
LUN 2_2  on drive [FLASH_2_2] random read throughput: 542.54 MBPS, and 36758 IOPS
LUN 2_3  on drive [FLASH_2_3] random read throughput: 542.63 MBPS, and 37341 IOPS
LUN 4_0  on drive [FLASH_4_0] random read throughput: 542.35 MBPS, and 39658 IOPS
LUN 4_1  on drive [FLASH_4_1] random read throughput: 542.62 MBPS, and 39374 IOPS
```

```
LUN 4_2  on drive [FLASH_4_2] random read throughput: 542.80 MBPS, and 39699 IOPS
LUN 4_3  on drive [FLASH_4_3] random read throughput: 543.14 MBPS, and 38951 IOPS
LUN 5_0  on drive [FLASH_5_0] random read throughput: 542.42 MBPS, and 38388 IOPS
LUN 5_1  on drive [FLASH_5_1] random read throughput: 542.69 MBPS, and 39360 IOPS
LUN 5_2  on drive [FLASH_5_2] random read throughput: 542.59 MBPS, and 39350 IOPS
LUN 5_3  on drive [FLASH_5_3] random read throughput: 542.72 MBPS, and 39615 IOPS
CALIBRATE results are within an acceptable range.
Calibration has finished.
```

Cell Flash Cache Failure

Exadata X4-2 storage cells come equipped with four F80 PCIe Flash Cache cards. Each card has four Flash Cache disks (FDOMs) for a total of 16 flash disks. Exadata X5-2 high-capacity cells include four F160 PCIe Flash cards with a total of four flash disks. These Flash Cache cards occupy slots 1, 2, 4, and 5 inside the storage cell. If a Flash Cache module fails, performance of the storage cell will be degraded and should be replaced at your earliest opportunity. If you are using some of your Flash Cache for flash disk-based grid disks, your disk group redundancy will be affected as well. These Flash Cache cards are not hot-pluggable, so replacing them will require you to power off the affected cell.

If a flash disk fails, Exadata will send you an e-mail notifying you of the failure. The e-mail will include the slot address of the card. If a specific FDOM has failed, it will include the address of the FDOM on the card (1, 2, 3, or 4). The failed Flash Cache card can be seen using the `CellCLI` command `LIST PHYSICALDISK` as follows:

```
CellCLI> list physicaldisk where disktype=flashdisk and status!=normal detail

         name:                   FLASH_5_3
         diskType:               FlashDisk
         flashLifeLeft:          100
         luns:                   5_3
         makeModel:              "Sun Flash Accelerator F80 PCIe Card"
         physicalFirmware:       UIO1
         physicalInsertTime:     2014-10-03T20:08:05-05:00
         physicalSize:           372.52903032302856G
         slotNumber:             "PCI Slot: 5; FDOM: 3"
         status:                 critical
```

The `slotNumber` attribute here shows you where the card and FDOM are installed. In our case, the card is installed in PCIe slot 5. Once you have this information, you can shut down and power off the storage cell and replace the defective part. Keep in mind that when the cell is offline, ASM will no longer have access to the grid disks. So, before you shut down the cell, make sure that shutting it down will not impact the availability of the disk groups it supports. This is the same procedure we described in the "Cell Disk Failure" section of this chapter. Once the part is replaced and the cell reboots, the storage cell will automatically configure the cell disk on the replacement card and, if it was used for Flash Cache, you will see your Flash Cache return to its former size.

Cell Failure

There are two main types of cell failure—temporary and permanent. Temporary cell failures can be as harmless as a cell reboot or a power failure. Extended cell failures can also be temporary in nature. For example, if a patch installation fails or a component must be replaced, it could take the cell offline for hours or even days. Permanent cell failures are more severe in nature and require the entire cell chassis to be replaced. In either case, if your system is configured properly, there will be no interruption to ASM or your databases. In this section, we'll take a look at what happens when a cell is temporarily offline and what to do if you ever have to replace one.

Temporary Cell Failure

As discussed in Chapter 14, Exadata storage cells are Sun servers with internal disk drives running Oracle Enterprise Linux 5 or 6. If a storage cell goes offline, all the disks on that cell become unavailable to the database servers. This means that all disk groups containing database data (as well as OCR and Voting files) on that storage cell are offline for the duration of the outage. ASM failure groups provide redundancy that allows your cluster and databases to continue to run during the outage, albeit with reduced I/O performance. When grid disks are created in a storage cell, they are assigned to a failure group. Each cell constitutes a failure group, as can be seen in the following listing:

```
SYS:+ASM2> select dg.name diskgroup, d.name disk, d.failgroup
             from v$asm_diskgroup dg,
                  v$asm_disk d
            where dg.group_number = d.group_number
              and dg.name like 'SCRATCH%'
            order by 1,2,3;

DISKGROUP                      DISK                           FAILGROUP
------------------------------ ------------------------------ ------------------------------
SCRATCH_DG                     SCRATCH_DG_CD_05_CELL01        CELL01
SCRATCH_DG                     SCRATCH_DG_CD_05_CELL02        CELL02
SCRATCH_DG                     SCRATCH_DG_CD_05_CELL03        CELL03
```

Because SCRATCH_DG was created using Normal redundancy, our SCRATCH database should be able to continue even if an entire storage cell dies. In this section, we'll be testing what happens when a storage cell goes dark. We'll use the same disk group configuration we used for the disk failure simulation earlier in this chapter. To cause a cell failure, we'll log in to the ILOM on storage cell 3 and power it off. Because each storage cell constitutes an ASM failure group, this scenario is very similar to losing a single cell disk, I/O performance notwithstanding. The difference, of course, is that we are losing an entire failure group. Just as we did in our cell disk failure tests, we'll generate data in the SCRATCH database during the failure to verify that the database continues to service client requests during the cell outage.

To generate I/O for the tests, we'll be repeatedly inserting 23205888 rows from the BIGTAB table into the bigtab2 table:

```
RJOHNSON:SCRATCH> insert /*+ append */ into bigtab2 nologging (select * from bigtab);
RJOHNSON:SCRATCH> commit;
```

While the above inserts are running, let's power off Cell03 and take a look at the database alert log. As you can see, the database throws an error when reading from a disk on Cell03, "failed to read mirror side 1." A couple of lines further down in the log, you see the database successfully reading the mirror copy of the extent, "successfully read mirror side 2."

```
alert_SCRATCH.log
-----------------------
Fri Jan 16 21:09:45 2015
Errors in file /u01/app/oracle/diag/rdbms/scratch/SCRATCH/trace/SCRATCH_mmon_31673.trc:
ORA-27603: Cell storage I/O error, I/O failed on disk o/192.168.12.5/SCRATCH_CD_05_cell03 at
offset 2483044352 for data length 16384
```

```
ORA-27626: Exadata error: 12 (Network error)
...
WARNING: Read Failed. group:3 disk:2 AU:592 offset:16384 size:16384
WARNING: failed to read mirror side 1 of virtual extent 2 logical extent 0 of file 260 in
group [3.689477631] from disk SCRATCH_CD_05_CELL03  allocation unit 592 reason error; if
possible,will try another mirror side
NOTE: successfully read mirror side 2 of virtual extent 2 logical extent 1 of file 260 in
group [3.689477631] from disk SCRATCH_CD_05_CELL01 allocation unit 589
```

Turning to the ASM alert log, we see that ASM also noticed the issue with Cell03 and responds by taking grid disk `SCRATCH_CD_05_CELL03` offline. Notice further on that ASM is in the process of taking other grid disks offline as well. This continues until all grid disks on Cell03 are offline:

```
alert_+ASM2.log
-----------------------
--- Test Cell03 Failure --
Fri Jan 16 21:09:45 2015
NOTE: process 23445 initiating offline of disk 2.3915933784 (SCRATCH_CD_05_CELL03) with mask
0x7e in group 3
...
WARNING: Disk SCRATCH_CD_05_CELL03 in mode 0x7f is now being offlined
Fri Jan 16 21:09:47 2015
NOTE: process 19753 initiating offline of disk 10.3915933630 (RECO_CD_10_CELL03) with mask
0x7e in group 2
```

Checking the `V$SESSION` and `V$SQL` views, we can see that the insert is still running:

```
  SID PROG       SQL_ID        SQL_TEXT
----- ---------- ------------- -----------------------------------------
    3 sqlplus@en 9ncczt9qcg0m8  insert /*+ append */ into bigtab2 nologgi
```

So our databases continue to service client requests even when one-third of all storage is lost. That's pretty amazing. Let's power up Cell03 again and observe what happens when this storage is available again.

Looking at Cell03's alert log we see `cellsrv` bring our grid disks back online again. The last thing we see in Cell03's alert log is it rejoining the storage grid by establishing a heartbeat with the `diskmon` (disk monitor) process on the database servers:

```
Cell03 Alert log
-----------------
Storage Index Allocation for GridDisk SCRATCH_DG_CD_05_cell03 successful [code: 1]
CellDisk v0.5 name=CD_05_cell03 status=NORMAL guid=edc5f61e-6a60-48c9-a4a6-58c403a86a7c
found on dev=/dev/sdf
Griddisk SCRATCH_DG_CD_05_cell03  - number is (96)
Storage Index Allocation for GridDisk RECO_CD_06_cell03 successful [code: 1]
Storage Index Allocation for GridDisk SYSTEM_CD_06_cell03 successful [code: 1]
Storage Index Allocation for GridDisk STAGE_CD_06_cell03 successful [code: 1]
Storage Index Allocation for GridDisk DATA_CD_06_cell03 successful [code: 1]
CellDisk v0.5 name=CD_06_cell03 status=NORMAL guid=00000128-e01b-6d36-0000-000000000000
found on dev=/dev/sdg
Griddisk RECO_CD_06_cell03  - number is (100)
Griddisk SYSTEM_CD_06_cell03  - number is (104)
```

```
Griddisk STAGE_CD_06_cell03  - number is (108)
Griddisk DATA_CD_06_cell03  - number is (112)
...
Fri Jan 16 22:51:30 2015
Heartbeat with diskmon started on enkdb02.enkitec.com
Heartbeat with diskmon started on enkdb01.enkitec.com
Fri Jan 16 22:51:40 2015
...
```

Summary

Exadata is a highly redundant platform with a lot of moving parts. Businesses don't typically invest in such a platform without expectations of minimal downtime. As such, Exadata is commonly used for hosting mission-critical business applications with very stringent uptime requirements. Knowing what to do when things go wrong is critical to meeting these uptime requirements. In this chapter, we discussed the proper procedures for protecting your applications and customers from component and system failures. Before your system is rolled into production, make it a priority to practice backing up and restoring system volumes, removing and replacing disk drives, and rebooting storage cells. In addition, become familiar with what happens to your databases. Run the diagnostic tools we've discussed in this chapter and make sure you understand how to interpret the output. If you are going to be responsible for maintaining Exadata for your company, now is the time to get comfortable with the topics discussed in this chapter.

CHAPTER 10

Exadata Wait Events

The Oracle database is a very well-instrumented piece of code, and it has been so for quite a while. It keeps track of the amount of time spent in discrete operations via the use of wait events, unless the session in question is on the CPU. While the database software is quite complex, wait event analysis allows performance analysts to determine where the database is spending its time. Many difficult performance problems can be resolved by analyzing data from the wait interface and, more recently, the Active Session History (ASH). The introduction of Exadata has resulted in the creation of several new wait events to support the unique operations that are performed on the platform. This chapter will focus on describing these new events and how they relate to the activities actually being performed, while contrasting them with the wait events used by the database on non-Exadata platforms. It will also describe a few wait events that are not specific to Exadata but play an important role on Exadata platforms.

In some rare cases, the wait interface is not granular enough to allow you to work out what the database engine is spending time on. If you use your favorite search engine to search for "wait interface not enough," you will find blog posts about that exact subject, as well as how the session statistics Oracle maintains can provide further insight into what a session does. Chapter 11 will help you understand the session statistics better. In most cases, though, an analysis of the wait events will be sufficient to troubleshoot the problem. A very useful piece of advice to this chapter's author was not to get lost in the details too soon!

A wait event is actually a section of code that is timed and assigned a name. The pieces of code covered by these events are quite often discrete operating system calls, such as individual I/O requests, but some wait events cover considerably larger portions of code. The events may even include sections of code that contain other wait events. The naming of wait events has been somewhat inconsistent over the years, and many events have slightly misleading names. Even though some of the event names are acknowledged to be potentially misleading, Oracle has been understandably reluctant to change them. The Exadata platform has provided an excuse to rename some of the I/O-related events, and, as you will see shortly, the developers took the opportunity to do just that.

Wait events are externalized in many places in the database. The most common ways to view wait events are queries against V-dollar views, tracing, and SQL Monitor. Common V-dollar views used to view wait event information are `V$SESSSION` or `V$SESSION_WAIT`. These views show the current wait event for a session, but not the history of events. The introduction of Active Session History in 10g changed this for the better by sampling active sessions and recording relevant information for the performance analyst, but it requires an extra license. Always make sure that what you are doing is compliant with your licenses.

If you want to get all waits for a session, you have the option to enable SQL tracing. The well-established SQL traces allow you to record SQL statements issued against the database as well as all the associated wait events. The raw trace file, which is found in the diagnostic destination for the database, is then post-processed and transformed into something more human-readable.

An alternative to SQL tracing is the use of the SQL Monitor. Thankfully on the Exadata platform, you will not be in a position where this great tool is not technically unavailable (licensing again is a separate question). SQL Monitor was introduced in Oracle 11.1, which was the minimum supported version on Exadata. SQL Monitor allows you to peek into the execution of a single SQL statement in real time.

During the SQL statement's execution, you can see exactly where and in what row source of the SQL execution of a SQL the RDBMS engine is spending time, and you can see wait events, if applicable, as well. All of that is available even while the statement is still executing! To be able to make use of this great tool, you have to have the Diagnostic and Tuning Pack licensed for the database. The underlying technology enabling SQL Monitor again is Active Session History (ASH) and, as you just read, was introduced with Oracle 10g. ASH samples database activity every second and gathers information about active sessions, which it stores for about one hour with a one-second interval. After that, the information is aggregated and every tenth sample is preserved on disk in the `SYSAUX` tablespace. The persistent part is referred to as the Active Workload Repository (AWR). AWR resembles the `STATSPACK` tool only in that it keeps a record of database activity over time. The retention period for the information is user configurable. The amount of space it takes to store AWR information can be large, but you should not forget that more data allows you to make comparisons with past events a lot easier. As with everything, you need to find the balance between disk space usage and the advantage of comparing a perceived performance problem with past events. In my opinion, the default retention period of eight days is far too little and should be increased.

Events Specific to Exadata

There are actually no events that exist exclusively on the Exadata platform. Wait events are built into the database code. Since the compute nodes on Exadata run standard Oracle Database software, all the wait events that are used when invoking Exadata-specific features are available in databases that are running on non-Exadata platforms as well. But because the Exadata features are only available on the Exadata platform, no time is ever allocated to those events on other platforms. By way of proof, consider the following example, which compares the events from `V$EVENT_NAME` (which exposes the valid wait events) first on an Exadata Database Machine and then on a standard 12c Release 1 database on a non-Exadata platform:

```
SQL> select count(1) from v$event_name;

  COUNT(1)
----------
      1650

SQL> select count(1) from v$event_name@lab12c;

  COUNT(1)
----------
      1650

SQL> select name from v$event_name
  2  minus
  3  select name from v$event_name@lab12c;

no rows selected
```

So there are no differences in the events. This does make it a little difficult to come up with a list of "Exadata Only" events. The event names however are a good starting point.

The "cell" Events

The Oracle Exadata Storage Server Software User's Guide 12c Release 1 provides a table of wait events. All of them start with the word "cell." The manual lists ten such events. One of them (`cell interconnect retransmit during physical read`) still does not actually exist.

There is also another batch of event names with the word "cell" in their names that are not included in the documentation. Combining both the documented and undocumented events reveals the complete list of "cell" events. This list will be the starting point of this chapter. You can query V$EVENT_NAME for that list, and you will get the following results. Notice that most of the events are in one of the I/O classes. The number of wait events has not changed in 12.1.0.1.x; there are still the same 17 events as found in 11.2.0.2 used for this chapter in the first edition of the book.

```
SYS:db12c1> select name,wait_class
  2  from v$event_name
  3  where name like 'cell%'
  4  order by name;

NAME                                               WAIT_CLASS
-------------------------------------------------- --------------------
cell list of blocks physical read                  User I/O
cell manager cancel work request                   Other
cell manager closing cell                          System I/O
cell manager discovering disks                     System I/O
cell manager opening cell                          System I/O
cell multiblock physical read                      User I/O
cell single block physical read                    User I/O
cell smart file creation                           User I/O
cell smart flash unkeep                            Other
cell smart incremental backup                      System I/O
cell smart index scan                              User I/O
cell smart restore from backup                     System I/O
cell smart table scan                              User I/O
cell statistics gather                             User I/O
cell worker idle                                   Idle
cell worker online completion                      Other
cell worker retry                                  Other

17 rows selected.
```

Oracle 12.1.0.2 was the first release that added new cell-related wait events. These are as follows:

- cell external table Smart Scan
- cell list of blocks read request
- cell multi-block read request
- cell physical read no I/O
- cell single block read request

The events are covered in the later section with one exception: The external table scan event belongs to a different Oracle product and will not be covered here.

The following sections will cover all of the relevant Exadata wait events, along with a few of additional events that have special applicability to Exadata.

Plan Steps That Trigger Events

First, though, it might be interesting to see what operations (plan steps) cause the "cell" wait events to occur. Here is a query against DBA_HIST_ACTIVE_SESS_HISTORY on an active production system running on an Exadata system that shows cell events and the operations that caused them. The list is not exhaustive, of course, not every event is visible on every system!

```
SQL> select event, operation,  count(*) from (
  2  select sql_id, event, sql_plan_operation||' '||sql_plan_options operation
  3    from DBA_HIST_ACTIVE_SESS_HISTORY
  4    where event like 'cell %')
  5    group by operation, event
  6    order by 1,2,3
  7  /

EVENT                              OPERATION                                COUNT(*)
---------------------------------- ---------------------------------------- ----------
cell list of blocks physical read                                                  62
                                   DDL STATEMENT                                     2
                                   INDEX FAST FULL SCAN                              1
                                   INDEX RANGE SCAN                               3060
                                   INDEX STORAGE FAST FULL SCAN                      7
                                   INDEX STORAGE SAMPLE FAST FULL SCAN              10
                                   INDEX UNIQUE SCAN                              1580
                                   INSERT STATEMENT                                  6
                                   TABLE ACCESS BY GLOBAL INDEX ROWID              151
                                   TABLE ACCESS BY INDEX ROWID                    5458
                                   TABLE ACCESS BY LOCAL INDEX ROWID               131
                                   TABLE ACCESS STORAGE FULL                       183
                                   TABLE ACCESS STORAGE SAMPLE                       2
                                   TABLE ACCESS STORAGE SAMPLE BY ROWID RAN          1
cell multiblock physical read                                                    3220
                                   DDL STATEMENT                                   157
                                   INDEX FAST FULL SCAN                             94
                                   INDEX RANGE SCAN                                  2
                                   INDEX STORAGE FAST FULL SCAN                   6334
                                   INDEX STORAGE SAMPLE FAST FULL SCAN             429

                                   UNIQUE SCAN                                       2
                                   VIEW ACCESS STORAGE FULL                        634
                                   MAT_VIEW ACCESS STORAGE SAMPLE                   56
                                   TABLE ACCESS BY GLOBAL INDEX ROWID                5
                                   TABLE ACCESS BY INDEX ROWID                     484
                                   TABLE ACCESS BY LOCAL INDEX ROWID                 3
                                   TABLE ACCESS STORAGE FULL                     41559
                                   TABLE ACCESS STORAGE SAMPLE                    1763
                                   TABLE ACCESS STORAGE SAMPLE BY ROWID RAN         78
                                   UPDATE                                            4
```

```
cell single block physical read                                                        181186
                                  BUFFER SORT                                               1
                                  CREATE TABLE STATEMENT                                   67
                                  DDL STATEMENT                                           985
                                  DELETE                                                11204
                                  DELETE STATEMENT                                          6
                                  FIXED TABLE FIXED INDEX                                 352
                                  FOR UPDATE                                               27
                                  HASH GROUP BY                                             3
                                  HASH JOIN                                                14
                                  HASH JOIN RIGHT OUTER                                     1
                                  INDEX BUILD NON UNIQUE                                   80
                                  INDEX BUILD UNIQUE                                        6
                                  INDEX FAST FULL SCAN                                      9
                                  INDEX FULL SCAN                                        1101
                                  INDEX RANGE SCAN                                      17597
                                  INDEX RANGE SCAN (MIN/MAX)                                1
                                  INDEX RANGE SCAN DESCENDING                               6
                                  INDEX SKIP SCAN                                         691
                                  INDEX STORAGE FAST FULL SCAN                            313
                                  INDEX STORAGE SAMPLE FAST FULL SCAN                      72
                                  INDEX UNIQUE SCAN                                     30901
                                  INSERT STATEMENT                                       5174
                                  LOAD AS SELECT                                          120
                                  LOAD TABLE CONVENTIONAL                                5827
                                  MAT_VIEW ACCESS STORAGE FULL                              3
                                  MAT_VIEW ACCESS STORAGE SAMPLE                            1
                                  MERGE                                                    12
                                  PX COORDINATOR                                            1
                                  SELECT STATEMENT                                        978
                                  SORT CREATE INDEX                                         1
                                  SORT GROUP BY                                             1
                                  SORT JOIN                                                 5
                                  SORT ORDER BY                                             2
                                  TABLE ACCESS BY GLOBAL INDEX ROWID                     5812
                                  TABLE ACCESS BY INDEX ROWID                           65799
                                  TABLE ACCESS BY LOCAL INDEX ROWID                      4591
                                  TABLE ACCESS BY USER ROWID                              464
                                  TABLE ACCESS CLUSTER                                     57
                                  TABLE ACCESS STORAGE FULL                              7168
                                  TABLE ACCESS STORAGE SAMPLE                             205
                                  TABLE ACCESS STORAGE SAMPLE BY ROWID RAN                 24
                                  UNION-ALL                                                 7
                                  UPDATE                                                89353
                                  UPDATE STATEMENT                                        367
                                  WINDOW CHILD PUSHED RANK                                  2
                                  WINDOW SORT                                               1
                                  WINDOW SORT PUSHED RANK                                   1
```

```
cell smart file creation                                                        35
                                   DELETE                                        3
                                   INDEX BUILD NON UNIQUE                        5
                                   LOAD AS SELECT                                3
                                   LOAD TABLE CONVENTIONAL                       1
                                   UPDATE                                        1
cell smart incremental backup                                                  714
cell smart index scan                                                           14
                                   INDEX STORAGE FAST FULL SCAN                 42
                                   INDEX STORAGE SAMPLE FAST FULL SCAN          32
cell smart table scan                                                          163
                                   MAT_VIEW ACCESS STORAGE FULL                  1
                                   TABLE ACCESS STORAGE FULL                 12504
```

Again, this output does not show all the possible combinations, but it should give you an idea of the relative frequency of events and which operations generally motivate them.

Exadata Wait Events in the User I/O Class

The User I/O Class is far and away the most important for Exadata. The most interesting events in this category are, of course, the two Smart Scan events (`cell smart table scan` and `cell smart index scan`). These are the events that record time for the primary query offloading optimizations provided by Exadata, which primarily include predicate filtering, column projection, and storage index usage. The User I/O Class also contains three events described as physical I/O events. These three events actually measure time for physical I/O using the more familiar multi-block and single-block read mechanisms you are used to seeing on non-Exadata platforms, although their names have been changed to something a little more meaningful. Finally, there are two events that do not really seem to belong in the User I/O category at all. One has to do with initialization of blocks when file space is allocated. The other has to do with gathering statistical information from the storage cells. Oracle 12.1.2.1 and database 12.1.0.2 introduced three new minor cell events as well related to user I/O that did not exist in 12.1.0.1 or 11.2.0.3. Each of these wait events are covered in turn in the next several sections, starting with the Smart Scan events.

cell smart table scan

The `cell smart table scan` event is what Oracle uses to account for time spent waiting for full table scans that are offloaded. It is the most important event on the Exadata platform for reporting workloads. Its presence or absence can be used to verify whether a statement benefited from offloading or not. As discussed in Chapter 2, offloading only occurs when Oracle is able to do direct path reads. Consequently, this event replaces the `direct path read` event in most cases on Exadata. As with non-Exadata direct path reads, data is returned directly to the PGA of the requesting process on the database server (either the user's shadow process or a parallel slave process). Blocks are not returned to the buffer cache.

Event Meaning

Although the mechanism for performing reads across the InfiniBand network is very different from that for normal reads on non-Exadata platforms, the code path driving the Smart Scans is actually very similar to a direct path read on a non-Exadata platform. The main difference lies in the fact that each request to a storage cell contains a reference to the metadata of the statement, which in the case of Exadata includes the predicates and the list of columns to be returned, among others. Since the storage cells have access to this information, they can apply the filters and do the column projection before returning the data to the requesting process. These optimizations are applied to each set of blocks as they are requested. The processes on the database servers that request the data have access to the ASM extent map and can, therefore, request the required allocation units (AUs) from each storage cell. The storage cells read the requested AU in the absence of storage index segments and apply the predicate filters, among other tasks. If any rows satisfy the filters, the cells return the projected columns to the requesting process. The process then requests the next AU and the entire routine is repeated until all the data has been scanned. So this event will occur repeatedly in a large scan. It is important that, unlike some other I/O-related events, a single Smart Scan event cannot be used to derive I/O performance. You either use OEM 12c for that or the `cellcli` command to access metric information on the cells. We cover this in Chapter 12 in more detail.

■ **Note** Column Projection is one of the major optimizations provided by Smart Scans. The feature is slightly misunderstood. It does not pass only columns in the select list back to the database servers; it also passes back some columns from the `WHERE` clause. Older versions of `cellsrv` passed all columns specified in a `WHERE` clause back to the database tier. Later versions have corrected this behavior to include only columns that are involved in joining predicates. You can see the columns projected in the output from `DBMS_XPLAN.DISPLAY_CURSOR`, for example.

As all wait events, the `cell smart table scan` will be recorded in a SQL trace. But with Exadata, you might want to investigate further, since a trace file is not limited to contain information for a single event you set. It may not immediately be obvious that you can combine the output of multiple events in a single trace file. For Smart Scans, you could include traces for LIBCELL's client library (mainly useful for inter-system communication), the Exadata Smart Scan layer, and finally for SQL Trace to get a combined picture of everything that is happening. Consider the following snippet to enable lots of tracing. You would not normally need to trace that much information, but it is extremely useful for research! Needless to say, you do not enable these events in production. This is for a development system only, outside of production and disaster recovery environments. The amount of information in the trace can be massive, filling up the `/u01` mount point and effectively causing an outage.

```
SQL> select value from v$diag_info where name like 'Default%'

VALUE
------------------------------------------------------------------------
/u01/app/oracle/diag/rdbms/db12c/db12c1/trace/db12c1_ora_11916.trc

SQL> alter session set events 'trace[LIBCELL.Client_Library.*] disk=highest';

Session altered.

SQL> alter session set events 'sql_trace level 8';

Session altered.

SQL> alter session set events 'trace[KXD.*] disk=highest';

Session altered.

SQL> select count(*) from t1;

  COUNT(*)
----------
  33554432
```

Oracle has been so kind as to document many of its traceable components, so you can actually see the code prefixes and map them to their respective code layer. The command to get the magic documentation is oradebug. Use `oradebug doc event name` and `oradebug doc component` to get more information about what can be traced, as in this example for LIBCELL.

```
SQL> oradebug doc component libcell

Components in library LIBCELL:
--------------------------
  Client_Library              Client Library
    Disk_Layer                Disk Layer
    Network_Layer             Network Layer
    IPC_Layer                 IPC Layer
```

The asterisk in the above code example includes every sublayer without having to explicitly specify it. Be warned that the resulting trace will most likely be huge and can cause space problems in your database mount point. But let's not digress—back to the SQL Trace. When tracing SQL alone, the trace file shows the following lines:

```
=====================
PARSING IN CURSOR #140...784 len=23 dep=0 uid=198 oct=3 lid=198 tim=3471433479182
hv=4235652837 ad='808033f0' sqlid='5bc0v4my7dvr5'
select count(*) from t1
END OF STMT
PARSE #140...784:c=0,e=138,p=0,cr=0,cu=0,mis=0,r=0,dep=0,og=1,plh=3724264953,tim=3471433479181
EXEC #140...784:c=0,e=51,p=0,cr=0,cu=0,mis=0,r=0,dep=0,og=1,plh=3724264953,tim=3471433479280
WAIT #140...784: nam='SQL*Net message to client' ela= 4 driver id=1650815232 #bytes=1 p3=0
  obj#=-1 tim=3471433479330
WAIT #140...784: nam='reliable message' ela= 968 channel context=10126085744 channel
  handle=10164814784 broadcast message=10178993320 obj#=-1 tim=3471433480522
WAIT #140...784: nam='enq: KO - fast object checkpoint' ela= 194 name|mode=1263468550 2=65606
  0=1 obj#=-1 tim=3471433480789
WAIT #140...784: nam='enq: KO - fast object checkpoint' ela= 125 name|mode=1263468545 2=65606
 0=2 obj#=-1 tim=3471433480986
WAIT #140...784: nam='Disk file operations I/O' ela= 6 FileOperation=2 fileno=7 filetype=2
  obj#=-1 tim=3471433481040
WAIT #140...784: nam='cell smart table scan' ela= 145 cellhash#=3249924569 p2=0 p3=0 obj#=61471
  tim=3471433501731
WAIT #140...784: nam='cell smart table scan' ela= 149 cellhash#=674246789 p2=0 p3=0 obj#=61471
  tim=3471433511233
WAIT #140...784: nam='cell smart table scan' ela= 143 cellhash#=822451848 p2=0 p3=0 obj#=61471
  tim=3471433516295
WAIT #140...784: nam='cell smart table scan' ela= 244 cellhash#=3249924569 p2=0 p3=0 obj#=61471
  tim=3471433561706
WAIT #140...784: nam='cell smart table scan' ela= 399 cellhash#=674246789 p2=0 p3=0
...
```

Unfortunately, Oracle changed the format of the cursor names somewhere in the life cycle in Oracle 11g. This would have caused the trace lines to wrap around in the output above. This is why the full cursor identifier has been truncated.

This portion of the trace file also shows the `enq: KO - fast object checkpoint` event, which is used to ensure that any dirty blocks for the scanned object are flushed to disk prior to beginning the scan. By the way, the `direct path read` event is not completely eliminated on Exadata platforms. In fact, it is possible to use a hint to disable offloading and see how the same statement behaves without offloading:

```
=====================
PARSING IN CURSOR #140...520 len=75 dep=0 uid=198 oct=3 lid=198 tim=3471777663904
hv=2068810426 ad='9114cd20' sqlid='44xptp5xnz2pu'
select /*+ opt_param('cell_offload_processing','false') */
count(*) from t1
END OF STMT
PARSE #140...520:c=2000,e=1381,p=0,cr=0,cu=0,mis=1,r=0,dep=0,og=1,plh=3724264953,
  tim=3471777663903
EXEC #140...520:c=0,e=41,p=0,cr=0,cu=0,mis=0,r=0,dep=0,og=1,plh=3724264953,tim=3471777663997
WAIT #140...520: nam='SQL*Net message to client' ela= 4 driver id=1650815232 #bytes=1 p3=0
  obj#=61471 tim=3471777664057
WAIT #140...520: nam='enq: KO - fast object checkpoint' ela= 228 name|mode=1263468550 2=65677
  0=2 obj#=61471 tim=3471777664460
WAIT #140...520: nam='reliable message' ela= 1036 channel context=10126085744 channel
  handle=10164814784 broadcast message=10179010104 obj#=61471 tim=3471777665585
WAIT #140...520: nam='enq: KO - fast object checkpoint' ela= 134 name|mode=1263468550 2=65677
  0=1 obj#=61471 tim=3471777665771
WAIT #140...520: nam='enq: KO - fast object checkpoint' ela= 126 name|mode=1263468545 2=65677
  0=2 obj#=61471 tim=3471777665950
WAIT #140...520: nam='direct path read' ela= 807 file number=7 first dba=43778051 block cnt=13
  obj#=61471 tim=3471777667104
WAIT #140...520: nam='direct path read' ela= 714 file number=7 first dba=43778081 block cnt=15
  obj#=61471 tim=3471777668112
WAIT #140...520: nam='direct path read' ela= 83 file number=7 first dba=43778097 block cnt=15
  obj#=61471 tim=3471777668322
WAIT #140...520: nam='direct path read' ela= 617 file number=7 first dba=43778113 block cnt=15
  obj#=61471 tim=3471777669050
WAIT #140...520: nam='direct path read' ela= 389 file number=7 first dba=43778129 block cnt=15
  obj#=61471 tim=3471777669549
```

Note that we still have the `enq: KO - fast object checkpoint` events for flushing dirty blocks. So, it is clear that the `cell smart table scan` event replaces this event.

Parameters

The parameters for this event are not particularly informative. Only the object ID of the table being scanned and the cell hash number are provided:

P1 - Cell hash number

P2 - Not used

P3 - Not used

`obj#` - The data object ID of the table segment being scanned

You should use the obj# reported in the trace to look up the table name in DBA_OBJECTS. Remember that Smart Scans operate on the segment level—you will need to query for the data_object_id rather than the object_id. You will notice that the direct path read event (which cell smart table scan replaces) provides additional information including the file number, the offset into the file (first dba), and the number of contiguous blocks read (block cnt). On the other hand, with the direct path read event, there is no indication how the read requests are routed to the individual cells.

The cell hash number reported with many of the wait events can be found in the V$CELL view. This view has only two columns, CELL_PATH and CELL_HASHVAL. The CELL_PATH column actually contains the IP address of the storage cell. If you trace using the KXD and LIBCELL components, you will see a lot more information prior and post each wait event. The additional trace information is well suited to give you extremely in-depth insights in the Smart Scan processing. A full explanation of these does not fit the scope of the chapter; please refer back to Chapter 2.

Unlike some of the non-Exadata I/O events, the Smart Scan event is not really suited to time I/O completion. Remember from Chapter 2 that Smart Scans are fired off asynchronously against various threads in the cell—each is a separate logical unit of work. The Oracle software may read the results of these I/O events out of their order of execution. This, as well as the complicated nature of Smart Scan processing, makes it impossible to derive I/O latencies using this event.

cell smart index scan

Time is clocked to the cell smart index scan event when fast full index scans are performed that are offloaded. This event is analogous to cell smart table scan, except that the object being scanned is an index. This index access path is not to be confused with any of the other index access paths available, such as index unique, range, or full scan. The latter indicate single block I/O calls and by definition cannot be offloaded. The cell smart index scan wait replaces the direct path read event and returns data directly to the PGA of the requesting process as opposed to the buffer cache.

Event Meaning

This event does not show up very often on the systems we have observed, probably for several reasons:

- Exadata is quite good at doing full table scans, so the tendency is to eliminate a lot of indexes when moving to the platform. This can include making indexes invisible for the purpose of query optimization.
- Direct path reads are not done as often on index scans as they are on table scans. One of the important changes to Oracle 11.2 is the aggressiveness with which it does direct path reads on serial table scans. This enhancement was probably pushed forward specifically in order to allow Exadata to do more smart full table scans, but, regardless,, without this feature, only parallel table scans would be able to take advantage of Smart Scans. The same enhancement applies to index fast full scans. That is, they can also be done via serial direct path reads. However, the algorithm controlling when they happen appears to be less likely to use this technique with indexes (probably because the indexes can be much smaller than tables).

In addition, only fast full scans of indexes are eligible for Smart Scans (range scans and full scans are not eligible). As a result of these issues, cell smart index scans are fairly rare compared to cell smart table scans. It is, of course, possible to encourage the feature with hints (such as parallel_index) or by decorating specific indexes with a parallel degree setting of greater than 1. Here is an excerpt from a 10046 trace file showing the event:

```
=====================
PARSING IN CURSOR #140694139370464 len=100 dep=1 uid=198 oct=3 lid=198 tim=3551928848463
  hv=3104270335 ad='85f450b8' sqlid='fg97a72whftzz'
select /*+ monitor gather_plan_statistics parallel_index(t1) */
       /* ffs_test_001 */
      count(id) from t1
END OF STMT
PARSE #140694139370464:c=0,e=114,p=0,cr=0,cu=0,mis=0,r=0,dep=1,og=1,plh=3371189879,
  tim=3551928848462
WAIT #140694139370464: nam='cell smart index scan' ela= 173 cellhash#=674246789 p2=0 p3=0
  obj#=78100 tim=3551928872228
WAIT #140694139370464: nam='cell smart index scan' ela= 127 cellhash#=674246789 p2=0 p3=0
  obj#=78100 tim=3551928872442
WAIT #140694139370464: nam='cell smart index scan' ela= 8888 cellhash#=674246789 p2=0 p3=0
  obj#=78100 tim=3551928881675
WAIT #140694139370464: nam='cell smart index scan' ela= 142 cellhash#=822451848 p2=0 p3=0
  obj#=78100 tim=3551928900699
WAIT #140694139370464: nam='cell smart index scan' ela= 400 cellhash#=822451848 p2=0 p3=0
  obj#=78100 tim=3551928901202
```

Note that this trace file was produced by one of the parallel slave processes and not the requesting process. Some of the PX messages have been removed for clarity. The trace produced for the same statement when offloading is disabled should look more familiar. Here is an excerpt, again from a query slave:

```
=====================
PARSING IN CURSOR #13...92 len=158 dep=1 uid=198 oct=3 lid=198 tim=3553633447559
hv=3263861856 ad='9180bab0' sqlid='35yb4ug18p530'
select /*+ opt_param('cell_offload_processing','false') monitor
          gather_plan_statistics parallel_index(t1) */
       /* ffs_test_002 */
      count(id) from t1
END OF STMT
PARSE #13...92:c=0,e=152,p=0,cr=0,cu=0,mis=0,r=0,dep=1,og=1,plh=3371189879,tim=3553633447557
WAIT #13...92: nam='PX Deq: Execution Msg' ela= 9671 sleeptime/senderid=268566527 passes=1
  p3=9216340064 obj#=-1 tim=3553633458202
WAIT #13...92: nam='direct path read' ela= 5827 file number=7 first dba=39308443 block
cnt=128 obj#=78100 tim=3553633464791
WAIT #13...92: nam='PX Deq: Execution Msg' ela= 62 sleeptime/senderid=268566527 passes=1
  p3=9216340064 obj#=78100 tim=3553633481394
WAIT #13...92: nam='direct path read' ela= 2748 file number=7 first dba=39370251 block cnt=128
  obj#=78100 tim=3553633484390
WAIT #13...92: nam='PX Deq: Execution Msg' ela= 64 sleeptime/senderid=268566527 passes=1
  p3=9216340064 obj#=78100 tim=3553633497671
WAIT #13...92: nam='direct path read' ela= 4665 file number=7 first dba=39357143 block cnt=128
  obj#=78100 tim=3553633502565
WAIT #13...92: nam='PX Deq: Execution Msg' ela= 70 sleeptime/senderid=268566527 passes=1
  p3=9216340064 obj#=78100 tim=3553633518439
WAIT #13...92: nam='direct path read' ela= 3001 file number=7 first dba=39337739 block cnt=128
  obj#=78100 tim=3553633521674
```

Compare this to the previous example where the cells offloaded the scan. In that example the `cell smart index scan` event replaces the direct path read. The `enq: KO - fast object checkpoint` events for flushing dirty blocks prior to starting the direct path reads are still present. However, they are not shown in this excerpt because they occur in the query coordinator process, not in the parallel slave processes.

Parameters

Just as with the `cell smart table scan` event, the parameters for `cell smart index scan` do not contain a lot of details. The cell hash number and the object ID of the segment being scanned are the only information provided:

> `P1` - Cell hash number
>
> `P2` - Not used
>
> `P3` - Not used
>
> `obj#` - The object number of the index being scanned

cell single block physical read

This event is equivalent to the `db file sequential read` event used on non-Exadata platforms. Single block reads are used most often for index access paths (both the index block reads and the table block reads via rowids from the index lookups). They can also be used for a wide variety of other operations where it makes sense to read a single block.

Event Meaning

Here is the output of a query that shows the operations that resulted in the `cell single block physical read` wait event on an active production system:

```
SQL> select event, operation,  count(*) from (
  2  select sql_id, event, sql_plan_operation||' '||sql_plan_options operation
  3    from DBA_HIST_ACTIVE_SESS_HISTORY
  4    where event like 'cell single%')
  5    group by operation, event
  6    order by 1,2,3
  7  /

EVENT                             OPERATION                                  COUNT(*)
--------------------------------- ---------------------------------------- ----------
cell single block physical read                                                 13321
                                  CREATE TABLE STATEMENT                           35
                                  DDL STATEMENT                                   118
                                  DELETE                                          269
                                  FIXED TABLE FIXED INDEX                           3
                                  FOR UPDATE                                        2
                                  HASH JOIN                                         4
                                  HASH JOIN RIGHT OUTER                             8
                                  INDEX FULL SCAN                                9283
                                  INDEX FULL SCAN (MIN/MAX)                         1
```

```
INDEX RANGE SCAN                                2763
INDEX STORAGE FAST FULL SCAN                       6
INDEX STORAGE SAMPLE FAST FULL SCAN               13
INDEX UNIQUE SCAN                               1676
INSERT STATEMENT                                1181
LOAD AS SELECT                                     6
LOAD TABLE CONVENTIONAL                           92
MERGE                                            106
SELECT STATEMENT                                  41
SORT ORDER BY                                      6
TABLE ACCESS BY GLOBAL INDEX ROWID             10638
TABLE ACCESS BY INDEX ROWID                     8714
TABLE ACCESS BY LOCAL INDEX ROWID              10446
TABLE ACCESS CLUSTER                              12
TABLE ACCESS STORAGE FULL                        776
TABLE ACCESS STORAGE SAMPLE                       40
UPDATE                                          8116
```

As you can see, row access via an index is the most common operation that generates this event. You should also be aware that Exadata provides a large amount of Flash Cache on each storage cell. For that reason, physical reads (both multi-block and single-block) are considerably faster than on most disk-based storage systems, even without offloading. Here is an excerpt from an AWR report showing a histogram of single-block reads for the instance:

```
                                          % of Waits
                                          -----------------------------------------
                                  Total
Event                             Waits   <1ms  <2ms  <4ms  <8ms <16ms <32ms  <=1s   >1s
-------------------------------   -----   ----  ----  ----  ---- ----- -----  ----  ----
cell single block physical        2940K   94.4   3.2    .3    .6    .9    .5    .2    .0
```

Notice that about 95 percent of the `cell single block physical read` events take less than 1ms. This is fairly representative of several production systems that we have observed.

Parameters

The `cell single block physical read` event provides more information than most cell events. The parameters allow you to tell exactly which object was read along with providing the disk and cell where the block was stored:

P1 - Cell hash number

P2 - Disk hash number

P3 - Total bytes passed during read operation (always 8192 assuming 8K block size)

obj# - The object number of the object being read

cell multiblock physical read

This is another renamed event. It is equivalent to the less clearly named `db file scattered read` event. On non-Exadata platforms, Oracle Database 11gR2 and 12c still uses the `db file scattered read` event whenever it issues a contiguous multi-block buffered read to the operating system. The "scattered" in the old event name reflects how the data read from disk is stored in the buffer cache: scattered around. It is not a reflection of how data is read from disk, which is actually contiguous.

Event Meaning

This event is generally used with full table scans and fast full index scans, although it can be used with many other operations. The new name on the Exadata platform is much more descriptive than the older name. For reporting workloads, this wait event is not nearly as prevalent on Exadata platforms as on non-Exadata platforms, because Exadata handles many full scan operations with Smart Scans that have their own wait events (`cell smart table scan` and `cell smart index scan`). The `cell multiblock physical read` event on Exadata platforms is used for serial full scan operations on tables that are below the threshold for serial direct path reads. That is to say, you will see this event used most often on full scans of relatively small tables. On the other hand, if your queries are not offloaded (caused by a very large buffer cache, for instance) you will see lots of these events as well. The threshold before a Smart Scan or direct path read is initiated is very high in these cases.

The event is also used for fast full index scans that are not executed with direct path reads. Here is the output of a query that shows the operations that resulted in the `cell multiblock physical read` wait event on an active production system:

```
EVENT                            OPERATION                                 COUNT(*)
-------------------------------- ---------------------------------------- ---------
cell multiblock physical read                                                   764
                                 DDL STATEMENT                                   28
                                 INDEX FAST FULL SCAN                             2
                                 INDEX STORAGE FAST FULL SCAN                   657
                                 INDEX STORAGE SAMPLE FAST FULL SCAN            133
                                 TABLE ACCESS BY INDEX ROWID                     74
                                 TABLE ACCESS BY LOCAL INDEX ROWID             1428
                                 TABLE ACCESS STORAGE FULL                     5046
                                 TABLE ACCESS STORAGE SAMPLE                    916
```

Parameters

The `cell multiblock physical read` event also provides more information than most cell events. The parameters in the following list allow you to tell which object was read and identifies the disk and cell where the blocks were stored. The total bytes passed should be a multiple of the block size:

P1 - Cell hash number

P2 - Disk hash number

P3 - Total bytes passed during read operation

obj# - The object number of the object being read

cell list of blocks physical read

This event is a replacement for the `db file parallel read` event on non-Exadata platforms. It appears that the developers took the opportunity to rename some of the events that are related to disk operations, and this is one of those events. The new name is actually much more descriptive than the previous name, since the wait event has nothing whatsoever to do with parallel query or parallel DML.

Event Meaning

This event is used for a multi-block read of non-contiguous blocks. This is more effective with asynchronous I/O, which is enabled on Exadata by default. This event can be provoked by several operations. The most common are index range scans, index unique scans, and table access by index rowid. The most common reason for the event is index pre-fetching. Here is the output of a query that shows the operations that resulted in this wait event on an Exadata system:

```
SQL> select event, operation,  count(*) from (
  2  select sql_id, event, sql_plan_operation||' '||sql_plan_options operation
  3    from DBA_HIST_ACTIVE_SESS_HISTORY
  4    where event like 'cell list%')
  5    group by operation, event
  6    order by 1,2,3
  7  /

EVENT                                     OPERATION                               COUNT(*)
----------------------------------------- ----------------------------------- ------------
cell list of blocks physical read                                                        2
                                          INDEX RANGE SCAN                             156
                                          INDEX STORAGE FAST FULL SCAN                   1
                                          INDEX UNIQUE SCAN                             66
                                          TABLE ACCESS BY GLOBAL INDEX ROWID            90
                                          TABLE ACCESS BY INDEX ROWID                 1273
                                          TABLE ACCESS BY LOCAL INDEX ROWID           2593
                                          TABLE ACCESS STORAGE FULL                     20
                                          TABLE ACCESS STORAGE SAMPLE                    1
```

As you can see, the vast majority of these events were motivated by index access paths. By the way, on non-Exadata platforms, noncontiguous multi-block reads still clock time to the old `db file parallel read` event. It is also possible for this older wait event name to show up on an Exadata platform for some operations.

Parameters

The `cell list of blocks physical read` event provides more information than most cell events. The following parameters allow you to tell exactly which object was read along with identifying the disk and cell where the block was stored:

P1 - Cell hash number

P2 - Disk hash number

P3 - Number of blocks read

obj# - The object number of the object being read

cell smart file creation

Exadata has an optimization technique that allows the storage cells to do the initialization of blocks when a data file is created or extended. This occurs when a tablespace is created or a data file is manually added to a tablespace. However, it can also occur when a data file is automatically extended during DML operations.

Event Meaning

You have previously read in this chapter that this event seemed out of place in the User I/O class. However, if it occurs because of DML operations, it makes sense to have it in this category. At any rate, offloading the block formatting eliminates CPU usage and I/O from the database servers and moves it to the storage tier. When this occurs, time is collected in the `cell smart file creation` event. This event replaces the `Data file init write` event that is still used on non-Exadata platforms. Here is the output of a query from a busy production system showing operations that generated this event:

```
SYS@EXDB1> select event, operation,  count(*) from (
  2  select sql_id, event, sql_plan_operation||' '||sql_plan_options operation
  3    from DBA_HIST_ACTIVE_SESS_HISTORY
  4    where event like 'cell smart file%')
  5    group by operation, event
  6    order by 1,2,3
  7  /

EVENT                      OPERATION                  COUNT(*)
-------------------------- ------------------------- --------
cell smart file creation                                   35
                           DELETE                           3
                           INDEX BUILD NON UNIQUE           5
                           LOAD AS SELECT                   3
                           LOAD TABLE CONVENTIONAL          1
                           UPDATE                           1
```

You will notice that on this particular system, the `cell smart file creation` event was occasionally generated by a `DELETE` statement. The fact that a `DELETE` could cause this event might be a little surprising. But remember that this event is actually timing a section of code that does block formatting, not file creation.

Parameters

The only parameter of interest for this event is `P1`, which shows which cell was being accessed when this event was generated:

`P1` - Cell hash number

`P2` - Not used

`P3` - Not used

cell statistics gather

The `cell statistics gather` event records time spent reading from various V$ and X$ tables. Although the event is grouped in the User I/O category, it does not refer to I/O in the sense of reading and writing to and from disk.

Event Meaning

Time is clocked to this event when a session is reading from the V$CELL family of views and a few other X$ tables in the same category. The event is miscategorized, in our opinion, and does not really belong in the User I/O category. Here is a typical example:

```
PARSING IN CURSOR #140003020408112 len=79 dep=0 uid=0 oct=3 lid=0 tim=4163271218132
hv=2136254865 ad='a2c23650' sqlid='fcjwbgdzp9acj'
select count(cell_name),cell_name from V$CELL_THREAD_HISTORY group by cell_name
END OF STMT
PARSE #14...12:c=17997,e=23189,p=5,cr=99,cu=0,mis=1,r=0,dep=0,og=1,plh=3108513074,tim=4
WAIT #14...12: nam='Disk file operations I/O' ela= 34 FileOperation=8 fileno=0
  filetype=8 obj#=262 tim=4163271218207
EXEC #14...12:c=0,e=54,p=0,cr=0,cu=0,mis=0,r=0,dep=0,og=1,plh=3108513074,tim=4...
WAIT #14...12: nam='SQL*Net message to client' ela= 2 driver id=1650815232 #bytes=1 p3=0
   obj#=262 tim=4163271218304
WAIT #14...12: nam='cell statistics gather' ela= 162 cellhash#=0 p2=0 p3=0 obj#=262 tim=4163
WAIT #14...12: nam='cell statistics gather' ela= 248 cellhash#=0 p2=0 p3=0 obj#=262 tim=4163
WAIT #14...12: nam='cell statistics gather' ela= 236 cellhash#=0 p2=0 p3=0 obj#=262 tim=4163
WAIT #14...12: nam='cell statistics gather' ela= 250 cellhash#=0 p2=0 p3=0 obj#=262 tim=4163
```

■ **Note** You can read more about the V$CELL% family of views in Chapter 11.

Parameters

The parameters for this event provide no additional information. In fact, values are not even set for the parameters in this event. Here are the parameter definitions:

P1 - Cell hash number (always 0)

P2 - Not used

P3 - Not used

Minor Events in the User/IO Class

As you read in the introduction, Oracle 12.1.0.2 is the first release in a long time that introduces new Exadata-related wait events. To recap, here are the events again:

- cell list of blocks read request
- cell multi-block read request
- cell physical read no I/O
- cell single-block read request

Although great care has been taken when preparing this chapter, we could not find a way to generate waits for them with two exceptions: cell single block read request and cell multi-block read request have been found as part of the execution of DBMS_STATS.GATHER_SCHEMA_STATS. The corresponding SQL_IDs were a sure sign that the events have been triggered as part of the stats gathering job. The TOP_LEVEL_SQL_ID could be used to confirm this.

Exadata Wait Events in the System I/O Class

The Exadata wait events that are assigned to the System I/O class are of less importance and do not generally show up as major consumers of time. The backup events are the most interesting as they record time for sections of code that have been optimized on the Exadata platform. The others are simply housekeeping events. The non-backup events are listed in Table 10-1, while the backup events are detailed in the following sections.

Table 10-1. *Miscellaneous System I/O Class Events*

Event	Description
`cell manager closing cell`	This is a shutdown-related event. The cell hash number is contained in the `P1` column of the `v$session_wait` view for this event. The `P2` and `P3` columns are unused.
`cell manager discovering disks`	This is a startup-related event. The cell hash number is contained in the `P1` column of the `v$session_wait` view for this event. The `P2` and `P3` columns are unused.
`cell manager opening cell`	This is a startup-related event. The cell hash number is contained in the `P1` column of the `v$session_wait` view for this event. The `P2` and `P3` columns are unused.

cell smart incremental backup

This event is used to measure time spent waiting on RMAN when doing an incremental level 1 backup. Exadata optimizes incremental backups by offloading much of the processing to the storage tier. This new wait event was added to account for time spent waiting on the optimized incremental backup processing that is offloaded to the storage cells.

The processing for incremental backups in its unoptimized form is quite resource intensive. The backup process needs to capture every change to the data files after the previous incremental backup. A lot of I/O is required to preform this task as the data files have to be scanned from start to finish. To reduce the time it takes to do a level 1 backup, Oracle introduced block change tracking long before Exadata. Block change tracking is implemented using a small binary file that is updated when redo is generated. The introduction of the block-change-tracking file sped up incremental backups many times.

Event Meaning

Interestingly, an incremental level 0 backup does not result in this wait event written to a trace file even though the word "incremental" is in the RMAN command. That is because the Level 0 backup—despite the name—does not take an incremental backup at all. It generates a full backup that is flagged as a baseline for future incremental backups. Here is an excerpt from a 10046 trace file generated on a process that was creating an incremental level 1 backup, this time on 11.2.0.4 and block change tracking enabled:

```
*** 2014-07-06 15:23:11.171
*** SESSION ID:(200.471) 2014-07-06 15:23:11.171
*** CLIENT ID:() 2014-07-06 15:23:11.171
*** SERVICE NAME:(SYS$USERS) 2014-07-06 15:23:11.171
*** MODULE NAME:(backup incr datafile) 2014-07-06 15:23:11.171
*** ACTION NAME:(0000048 STARTED16) 2014-07-06 15:23:11.171
```

```
WAIT #0: nam='enq: TC - contention' ela= 30442809 name|mode=1413677062 checkpoint ID=65586 0=0
  obj#=-1 tim=1404678191171373
WAIT #0: nam='enq: CF - contention' ela= 223 name|mode=1128660997 0=0 operation=0 obj#=-1
  tim=1404678191172055
...
WAIT #0: nam='change tracking file synchronous read' ela= 523 block#=9344 blocks=64 p3=0
  obj#=-1 tim=1404678192231084
WAIT #0: nam='change tracking file synchronous read' ela= 523 block#=9472 blocks=64 p3=0
  obj#=-1 tim=1404678192231665
WAIT #0: nam='change tracking file synchronous read' ela= 501 block#=9920 blocks=64 p3=0
  obj#=-1 tim=1404678192232261
WAIT #0: nam='cell smart incremental backup' ela= 150 cellhash#=379339958 p2=0 p3=0
  obj#=-1 tim=1404678192234400
WAIT #0: nam='cell smart incremental backup' ela= 170 cellhash#=2133459483 p2=0 p3=0
  obj#=-1 tim=1404678192235378
WAIT #0: nam='cell smart incremental backup' ela= 160 cellhash#=3176594409 p2=0 p3=0
  obj#=-1 tim=1404678192237663
WAIT #0: nam='KSV master wait' ela= 70 p1=0 p2=0 p3=0 obj#=-1 tim=1404678192243295
WAIT #0: nam='KSV master wait' ela= 1438 p1=0 p2=0 p3=0 obj#=-1 tim=1404678192244762
WAIT #0: nam='ASM file metadata operation' ela= 57 msgop=33 locn=0 p3=0
  obj#=-1 tim=1404678192244786
WAIT #0: nam='KSV master wait' ela= 63 p1=0 p2=0 p3=0 obj#=-1 tim=1404678192251632
WAIT #0: nam='KSV master wait' ela= 1340 p1=0 p2=0 p3=0 obj#=-1 tim=1404678192253010
WAIT #0: nam='ASM file metadata operation' ela= 62 msgop=33 locn=0 p3=0
  obj#=-1 tim=1404678192253032
WAIT #0: nam='cell smart incremental backup' ela= 198 cellhash#=379339958 p2=0 p3=0
  obj#=-1 tim=1404678192255205
WAIT #0: nam='cell smart incremental backup' ela= 214 cellhash#=2133459483 p2=0 p3=0
  obj#=-1 tim=1404678192255495
WAIT #0: nam='cell smart incremental backup' ela= 212 cellhash#=3176594409 p2=0 p3=0
  obj#=-1 tim=1404678192255802
WAIT #0: nam='cell smart incremental backup' ela= 10 cellhash#=379339958 p2=0 p3=0
  obj#=-1 tim=1404678192256723
WAIT #0: nam='cell smart incremental backup' ela= 100 cellhash#=2133459483 p2=0 p3=0
  obj#=-1 tim=1404678192256846
```

You can see the effect of the block-change-tracking file in the change tracking file synchronous read. The actual backup work—scanning the data files for changes since the last backup—is performed on the cells as visible in the cell smart incremental backup event. You can gauge the effectiveness of the offloading to the cells in the `v$backup_datafile` view. Use the `blocks_skipped_in_cell` column and put it in relation to the `blocks_read`.

Parameters

The only parameter used for this event is `P1`, which shows which cell was responsible for generating the event:

P1 - Cell hash number

P2 - Not used

P3 - Not used

obj# - Not used

■ **Note** The obj# field is a part of many wait events, even some that are not specifically related to an individual object. Be aware that, in some cases, the value may be set by one event and then not cleared appropriately when the wait ends, resulting in meaningless values left in place for the next wait event. In the previous example, the obj# was cleared (set to a value of -1).

cell smart restore from backup

This event is used to measure time spent waiting on RMAN when doing a restore. Exadata optimizes RMAN restores by offloading processing to the storage cells.

Event Meaning

The event actually records time related to file initialization during a restore. Here's an excerpt from a 10046 trace file taken while a restore was in progress:

```
WAIT #0: nam='KSV master wait' ela= 68 p1=0 p2=0 p3=0 obj#=-1 tim=1404740066131406
WAIT #0: nam='RMAN backup & recovery I/O' ela= 3320 count=1 intr=256 timeout=4294967295
 obj#=-1 tim=1404740066135786
WAIT #0: nam='RMAN backup & recovery I/O' ela= 3160 count=1 intr=256 timeout=4294967295
  obj#=-1 tim=1404740066139862
WAIT #0: nam='RMAN backup & recovery I/O' ela= 3201 count=1 intr=256 timeout=4294967295
  obj#=-1 tim=1404740066143790
WAIT #0: nam='RMAN backup & recovery I/O' ela= 2 count=1 intr=256 timeout=2147483647
  obj#=-1 tim=1404740066143822
WAIT #0: nam='cell smart restore from backup' ela= 853 cellhash#=2133459483 p2=0 p3=0
  obj#=-1 tim=1404740066146969
WAIT #0: nam='cell smart restore from backup' ela= 137 cellhash#=379339958 p2=0 p3=0
  obj#=-1 tim=1404740066148003
WAIT #0: nam='cell smart restore from backup' ela= 167 cellhash#=3176594409 p2=0 p3=0
  obj#=-1 tim=1404740066148948
WAIT #0: nam='cell smart restore from backup' ela= 269 cellhash#=2133459483 p2=0 p3=0
  obj#=-1 tim=1404740066149335
WAIT #0: nam='cell smart restore from backup' ela= 261 cellhash#=379339958 p2=0 p3=0
  obj#=-1 tim=1404740066149767
WAIT #0: nam='cell smart restore from backup' ela= 375 cellhash#=3176594409 p2=0 p3=0
  obj#=-1 tim=1404740066150294
WAIT #0: nam='cell smart restore from backup' ela= 124 cellhash#=3176594409 p2=0 p3=0
  obj#=-1 tim=1404740066152236
```

Parameters

The only parameter used for this event is P1, which shows which cell was responsible for generating the event.

P1 - Cell hash number

P2 - Not used

P3 - Not used

Exadata Wait Events in the Other and Idle Classes

These are relatively minor events that occur primarily during startup and shutdown of storage cells and fault conditions. You will probably not see them on normally functioning systems. There is one exception to this, the `cell smart flash unkeep` event. Table 10-2 lists the "cell" wait events in the Other class along with their parameters. A separate section will cover `cell smart flash unkeep`.

***Table 10-2.** Miscellaneous Other and Idle Class Events*

Event	Description
`cell manager cancel work request`	This event is not very informative, as all three of the parameters (`P1`, `P2`, `P3`) from the `v$session_wait` view are unused.
`cell worker online completion`	This appears to be a startup event. The cell hash number is contained in the `P1` column of the `v$session_wait` view for this event. The `P2` and `P3` columns are unused.
`cell worker retry`	The cell hash number is contained in the `P1` column of the `v$session_wait` view for this event. The `P2` and `P3` columns are unused.
`cell worker idle`	The `P1`, `P2`, and `P3` columns from the `v$session_wait` view are unused in this idle event.

cell smart flash unkeep

This event records the time spent waiting when Oracle must flush blocks out of Exadata Smart Flash Cache. This can occur when a table that has a storage clause designating that it be pinned in Exadata Smart Flash Cache is truncated or dropped. This is an important distinction. Beginning with Exadata 11.2.3.3.0, the cell software will automatically cache data from single block IO as well as Smart Scans. This allows the next scan to read from disk and flash simultaneously, resulting in much better performance. Prior to 11.2.3.3.0, it was necessary to manually pin tables and partitions in Flash Cache. It is easier to understand this with an example. Consider the following use case: Table T1 in database DB12C has a data object ID of 79208. After the table has been created and light query activity against it in form of Smart Scans, you can observe a pattern similar to this one:

```
[oracle@enkdb03 ~]$ dcli -g cell_group -l cellmonitor \
> "cellcli -e list flashcachecontent where objectNumber = 79208 detail" | grep cache
enkcel04: cachedKeepSize:        0
enkcel04: cachedSize:            4374528
enkcel04: cachedWriteSize:       4358144
enkcel05: cachedKeepSize:        0
enkcel05: cachedSize:            5521408
enkcel05: cachedWriteSize:       5521408
enkcel06: cachedKeepSize:        0
enkcel06: cachedSize:            5177344
enkcel06: cachedWriteSize:       5177344
```

As you can see, the cache is already populated—thanks to the Smart Scans— without having specified the `KEEP` keyword in the `CELL_FLASH_KEEP` clause. You can also see that the `KEEP` size is 0, for the same reason.

Event Meaning

Truncating or dropping the table does not have an immediate effect for the Smart Flash Cache at this stage. So, when would you see the event?

Back to the CELL_FLASH_CACHE clause: As soon as the storage clause is changed to KEEP, the cell will cache data from the table, populating the values for cachedKeepSize. In the previous example, it required a few more queries until the keep cache is populated:

```
[oracle@enkdb03 ~]$ dcli -g cell_group -l cellmonitor \
> "cellcli -e list flashcachecontent where objectNumber = 79208 detail" | grep cache
enkcel04: cachedKeepSize:          1239744512
enkcel04: cachedSize:              1243955200
enkcel04: cachedWriteSize:         5365760
enkcel05: cachedKeepSize:          1406525440
enkcel05: cachedSize:              1410203648
enkcel05: cachedWriteSize:         5980160
enkcel06: cachedKeepSize:          1355415552
enkcel06: cachedSize:              1358880768
enkcel06: cachedWriteSize:         6381568
```

If you truncate the table now, it will show you the cell smart flash unkeep event. Here is a tkprof'd example for the truncate statement:

```
truncate table t1


call     count       cpu    elapsed       disk      query    current        rows
------- ------  -------- ---------- ---------- ---------- ----------  ----------
Parse        1      0.00       0.00          0          6          0           0
Execute      1      0.24       0.57         12        480       5667           0
Fetch        0      0.00       0.00          0          0          0           0
------- ------  -------- ---------- ---------- ---------- ----------  ----------
total        2      0.24       0.58         12        486       5667           0

Misses in library cache during parse: 1
Optimizer mode: ALL_ROWS
Parsing user id: 198

Elapsed times include waiting on following events:
  Event waited on                             Times   Max. Wait  Total Waited
  ----------------------------------------   Waited  ----------  ------------
  enq: IV -  contention                          10        0.00          0.00
  row cache lock                                  4        0.00          0.00
  Disk file operations I/O                        1        0.00          0.00
  enq: RO - fast object reuse                     6        0.00          0.00
  reliable message                                2        0.00          0.00
  log file sync                                   2        0.00          0.00
  cell smart flash unkeep                        18        0.01          0.01
  cell single block physical read                12        0.00          0.00
  local write wait                                3        0.00          0.00
```

```
  gc current grant 2-way                          16        0.00          0.00
  DFS lock handle                               1452        0.00          0.30
  gc current grant busy                            7        0.00          0.00
  SQL*Net message to client                        1        0.00          0.00
  SQL*Net message from client                      1        4.00          4.00
********************************************************************************
```

When reviewing the raw trace file, you will note that the `cell smart flash unkeep` event is preceded by a little more than a handful of `enq: RO - fast object reuse` events, which are used to mark time associated with cleaning up the buffer cache after a drop or truncate. The `cell smart flash unkeep` is basically an extension of that event to clean up the Exadata Smart Flash Cache on the storage server as well.

Parameters

The only parameter used for this event is `P1`, which shows which cell was responsible for generating the event:

`P1` - Cell hash number

`P2` - Not used

`P3` - Not used

Non-Exadata-Specific Events

In addition to the new cell events, there are also a few non-Exadata-specific wait events that you should be aware of. These are events that you may already be familiar with from managing Oracle on other platforms. They happen to also be important in an Exadata environment, so they represent cases in which your existing knowledge and skill can carry over and stand you in good stead as you move in to managing Exadata.

direct path read

`Direct path reads` are used by Oracle to read data directly into PGA memory (instead of into the buffer cache). They are an integral part of Exadata offloading because SQL processing can only be offloaded to the storage cells when the `direct path read` mechanism is used. The `direct path read` wait event is actually replaced by the `cell smart table scan` and `cell smart index scan` wait events when a query is offloaded. However, the `direct path read` mechanism is still used by the code covered by those new wait events. That is, either the plan must include a parallel (table) scan or Oracle must decide to use the serial `direct path read` mechanism as described in Chapter 2.

Event Meaning

This event records time that Oracle spends waiting on a direct path read to complete. You should know that the `direct path read` wait event can be very misleading. As with the Smart Scan events, both the number of events recorded and the timings associated with them can appear to be inaccurate. This is due to the fact that direct path reads are done in an asynchronous and overlapping fashion. In essence, this event is not an I/O latency wait because of the asynchronous/overlapping nature of how Oracle fires off I/O requests, while the classic, synchronous I/O events are. It also bears mentioning that Oracle—from 11gR2 onward—contains an enhancement that causes serial direct path reads to occur more frequently than in previous releases. See MOS Note 793845.1, which briefly mentions this change. Many DBAs must have wondered why the I/O profile changed after the database was migrated from 10.2 to 11.2 and 12c.

Although not as relevant as it is on other platforms, the direct path read wait event does still show up on the Exadata platform for various operations but generally not for full table scans unless the table (or partition) is relatively small. The other case where you might see a direct path read is when the scan of the segment in question is not offloadable, such as for an Index Organized Table (IOT). An example for a 10046 trace and direct path reads is shown in the description of cell smart table scan.

Parameters

The parameters for this event show you exactly which segment (obj) is scanned and which set of blocks were scanned during this event:

P1 - File number

P2 - First Database Block Address (DBA)

P3 - Block count

obj# - The object number of the table being scanned

As mentioned in the cell smart table scan section, the parameters contain more specific information about which file and object are being accessed. The offset into the file is also provided in the P2 parameter, along with the number of contiguous blocks read in the P3 parameter.

Enq: KO—fast object checkpoint

The enq:KO event has a very strange name. Don't be put off by that. The event is essentially an object checkpoint event. The V$LOCK_TYPE view describes the KO lock as follows:

```
SQL> select type, name, description from v$lock_type
  2  where type = 'KO';

TYPE  NAME                           DESCRIPTION
----- ------------------------------ ---------------------------------------------
KO    Multiple Object Checkpoint     Coordinates checkpointing of multiple objects
```

Event Meaning

This event is used when a session is waiting for all dirty blocks to be flushed from the buffer cache for a segment prior to starting a direct path read or cell smart table scan or cell smart index scan. This event is important because the time required to do the checkpoint may outweigh the benefit of the direct path reads. This is unlikely on Exadata storage, though, where the additional Smart Scan benefits are only enabled by the direct path read mechanism. Nevertheless, the execution engine tries to factor the checkpoint cost in before the decision is made to offload the query to the cells. Chapter 2 contains a lot more information about the mechanism.

Parameters

The parameters for this event are not overly helpful, but the event does show which object is scanned. Here are the parameter definitions:

P1 - Name/ Mode

P2 - Not used

P3 - Not used

obj# - The object number of the object being check pointed

reliable message

The reliable message event is used to record time spent communicating with background processes, like the checkpoint process (CKPT). We have included it here because of its close association with the enq: KO - fast object checkpoint event.

Event Meaning

In Oracle 11.2 and later, this event is the precursor to the enq: KO - fast object checkpoint event (among others). The communication is done using an inter-process communication channel rather than a more normal post mechanism. This communication method allows the sender to request an ACK before it continues; thus, the reason it is called a reliable message. It is generally a very short duration event as it only records time for communicating between processes. Both the users foreground process and the CKPT process will wait on this event as they communicate with each other. Here is an excerpt of a 10046 trace file showing a complete reliable message event, taken from a 11.2.0.4 database:

```
=====================
PARSING IN CURSOR #140457550697520 len=27 dep=0 uid=44 oct=3 lid=44 tim=1404832965816981
  hv=521453784 ad='25d376810' sqlid='cdjur50gj9h6s'
select count(*) from bigtab
END OF STMT
PARSE #140457550697520:c=1000,e=1072,p=0,cr=0,cu=0,mis=1,r=0,dep=0,og=1,plh=2140185107,
  tim=1404832965816980
EXEC #1...0:c=0,e=35,p=0,cr=0,cu=0,mis=0,r=0,dep=0,og=1,plh=2140185107,tim=1404832965817073
WAIT #1...0: nam='SQL*Net message to client' ela= 1 driver id=1650815232 #bytes=1 p3=0
  obj#=18532 tim=1404832965817131
WAIT #1...0: nam='reliable message' ela= 1230 channel context=10035861184 channel
  handle=10055026416 broadcast message=10199413976 obj#=18532 tim=1404832965818567
WAIT #1...0: nam='enq: KO - fast object checkpoint' ela= 189 name|mode=1263468550 2=65571 0=1
  obj#=18532 tim=1404832965818827
WAIT #1...0: nam='enq: KO - fast object checkpoint' ela= 107 name|mode=1263468545 2=65571 0=2
  obj#=18532 tim=1404832965819004
WAIT #1...0: nam='cell smart table scan' ela= 199 cellhash#=2133459483 p2=0 p3=0 obj#=18532
  tim=1404832965820790
WAIT #1...0: nam='cell smart table scan' ela= 182 cellhash#=3176594409 p2=0 p3=0 obj#=18532
  tim=1404832965821746
WAIT #1...0: nam='cell smart table scan' ela= 163 cellhash#=379339958 p2=0 p3=0 obj#=18532
  tim=1404832965822672
```

Parameters

Here are the parameters for the reliable message event:

P1 - Channel context

P2 - Channel handle

P3 - Broadcast message

obj# - The object number of the object of interest (not always set)

Resource Manager Events

Before wrapping up the chapter, we will discuss a few Resource Manager events that you should be aware of. While these are not specific to Exadata, Resource Manager provides key functionality for combining mixed workloads on Exadata. There are actually eight separate events as of release 12.1.0.2. The following query against V$EVENT_NAME shows these events and their parameters:

```
SQL> select name,parameter1,parameter2,parameter3,wait_class
  2  from v$event_name where name like 'resmgr%' order by name;

NAME                           PARAMETER1 PARAMETER2           PARAMETER3 WAIT_CLASS
------------------------------ ---------- -------------------- ---------- ------------
resmgr:become active           location                                   Scheduler
resmgr:cpu quantum             location   consumer group id               Scheduler
resmgr:internal state change   location                                   Concurrency
resmgr:internal state cleanup  location                                   Other
resmgr:large I/O queued        location                                   Scheduler
resmgr:pq queued               location                                   Scheduler
resmgr:sessions to exit        location                                   Concurrency
resmgr:small I/O queued        location                                   Scheduler

8 rows selected.
```

There are only three of these events that are of interest.

resmgr:become active

You will see this event when sessions are waiting to begin execution. Consider, for example, where you define a consumer group to have a maximum number of concurrent sessions at a given point in time. Any further session will wait on "resmgr:become active" before it can start its work.

Event Meaning

The event indicates sessions are being held back by Resource Manager from beginning execution. If you create a plan directive limiting the number of concurrent sessions in a consumer group, you will see output similar to this:

```
SQL> select sid,serial#,username,seq#,event,resource:consumer_group rsrc_cons_grp
  2  from v$session where username = 'LMTD';
```

```
       SID    SERIAL# USERNAME         SEQ# EVENT                          RSRC_CONS_GRP
---------- ---------- ---------- ---------- ------------------------------ -----------------
       916       1413 LMTD            31124 cell smart table scan          LMTD_GROUP
      1045       2667 LMTD            29480 cell smart table scan          LMTD_GROUP
      1112      20825 LMTD               42 resmgr:become active           LMTD_GROUP
      1178         91 LMTD               43 resmgr:become active           LMTD_GROUP
      1239      22465 LMTD               46 resmgr:become active           LMTD_GROUP
      1311      19703 LMTD               47 resmgr:become active           LMTD_GROUP
      1374      32129 LMTD               44 resmgr:become active           LMTD_GROUP
      1432      29189 LMTD               40 resmgr:become active           LMTD_GROUP

8 rows selected.
```

To be more precise, the number of concurrent sessions for consumer group LMTD_GROUP is set to 2. Here is the corresponding configuration example:

```
BEGIN
 dbms_resource:manager.clear_pending_area();
 dbms_resource:manager.create_pending_area();

 dbms_resource:manager.UPDATE_PLAN_DIRECTIVE(
  plan => 'ENKITEC_DBRM',
  group_or_subplan => 'LMTD_GROUP',
  new_active_sess_pool_p1 => 2);

 dbms_resource:manager.validate_pending_area();
 dbms_resource:manager.submit_pending_area();
end;
/
```

With this setting, you will never have more than the defined number of sessions performing work at the same time.

Parameters

Here are the parameters for this event. Note that the obj# parameter exists but is not used:

P1 - Location

P2 - Not used

P3 - Not used

obj# - N/A

The location parameter is a numeric value that most likely refers to a location (function) in the Oracle code. There are at least five distinct locations that we have observed. Unfortunately, Oracle does not publicly document where in the Oracle kernel these checks are performed.

resmgr:cpu quantum

This event is used to record forced idle time imposed by Database Resource Manager (DBRM) due to competition with higher priority work. Said another way, it is the time a process spent waiting for DBRM to allocate it a time slice. Interestingly, at of the time of this writing, no database event reflects throttling on the I/O Resource Manager level.

Event Meaning

DBRM behaves in an analogous manner to CPU scheduling algorithms in that it divides time into units (quantum) and either allows a process to run or not, depending on other workload on the system. Unlike CPU scheduling algorithms, though, DBRM throttling is interjected at key locations in the Oracle code to eliminate the possibility of a process being kicked off of the CPU when it is holding a shared resource such as a latch. This prevents some nasty behavior that may occur on heavily loaded systems such as priority inversion problems. In effect, the processes voluntarily go to sleep when they are not holding these shared resources. There are multiple locations in the code where these checks are implemented. Here's an excerpt of a 10046 trace file showing the `resmgr:cpu quantum` event:

```
PARSING IN CURSOR #140473587700424 len=30 dep=1 uid=208 oct=3 lid=208 tim=4695862695328
  hv=2336211758 ad='22465dc70' sqlid='gq01wgy5mzhtf'
SELECT COUNT(*) FROM MARTIN.T1
END OF STMT
EXEC #1...4:c=0,e=97,p=0,cr=0,cu=0,mis=0,r=0,dep=1,og=1,plh=3724264953,tim=4695862695326
WAIT #1...4: nam='enq: KO - fast object checkpoint' ela= 216 name|mode=1263468550 2=65683 0=2
  obj#=79208 tim=4695862695834
WAIT #1...4: nam='reliable message' ela= 1126 channel context=10126085744 channel
  handle=10164815328 broadcast message=10179052064 obj#=79208 tim=4695862697054
WAIT #1...4: nam='enq: KO - fast object checkpoint' ela= 160 name|mode=1263468550
  2=65683 0=1 obj#=79208 tim=4695862709511
WAIT #1...4: nam='enq: KO - fast object checkpoint' ela= 177 name|mode=1263468545
  2=65683 0=2 obj#=79208 tim=4695862709811
WAIT #1...4: nam='cell smart table scan' ela= 1830 cellhash#=3249924569 p2=0 p3=0
  obj#=79208 tim=4695862713420
WAIT #1...4: nam='cell smart table scan' ela= 326 cellhash#=674246789 p2=0 p3=0 obj#=79208
  tim=4695862714610
WAIT #1...4: nam='cell smart table scan' ela= 362 cellhash#=822451848 p2=0 p3=0 obj#=79208
  tim=4695862715784
WAIT #1...4: nam='resmgr:cpu quantum' ela= 278337 location=2 consumer group id=80408  =0
  obj#=79208 tim=4695863561098
WAIT #1...4: nam='cell smart table scan' ela= 2713 cellhash#=822451848 p2=0 p3=0 obj#=79208
  tim=4695863564184
```

Parameters

Here are the parameters for this event. Note that the `obj#` parameter exists but is not used:

P1 - Location

P2 - Consumer group id

P3 - Not used

obj# - N/A

The location parameter is a numeric value that most likely refers to a location (function) in the Oracle code as described above in the resmgr:become active event.

The consumer group number in the P2 parameter is pretty self-explanatory. It maps to the CONSUMER_GROUP_ID column in the DBA_RSRC_CONSUMER_GROUPS view. This parameter allows you to tell what consumer group a process was assigned to when its CPU usage was curtailed.

resmgr:pq queued

This event is used to record time spent waiting in the parallel query queue. Parallel statement queueing is a new feature introduced with 11g Release 2. One part of the new functionality that is enabled by setting parallel_degree_policy to Automatic is statement queueing. In Oracle 12c, you can also set the value to ADAPTIVE for the same purpose. Statement queuing allows you to queue for available parallel server slaves if the required degree of parallelism cannot be met instead of being downgraded, as with the old parallel automatic tuning option. Refer back to Chapter 6 for more information about parallel execution on Exadata.

Event Meaning

The parallel statement queuing feature comes with its own wait event. Statements that are queued due to insufficient parallel server processes or other directives clock time to this event. Here is an excerpt of a 10046 trace file showing the resmgr:pq queued event:

```
PARSING IN CURSOR #140583609334256 len=68 dep=0 uid=205 oct=3 lid=205 tim=4755825333777
  hv=2381215807 ad='220a20bc0' sqlid='944dxty6ywy1z'
select /*+ PARALLEL(32) STATEMENT_QUEUING */ count(*) from martin.t3
END OF STMT
PARSE #140583609334256:c=0,e=188,p=0,cr=0,cu=0,mis=0,r=0,dep=0,og=1,plh=3978228158,
  tim=4755825333776
WAIT #140583609334256: nam='resmgr:pq queued' ela= 25193140 location=1  =0  =0 obj#=-1
  tim=4755850527127
WAIT #140583609334256: nam='reliable message' ela= 889 channel context=10126085744 channel
  handle=10164818472 broadcast message=10179043672 obj#=-1 tim=4755850529508
WAIT #140583609334256: nam='enq: KO - fast object checkpoint' ela= 197 name|mode=1263468550
  2=65690 0=1 obj#=-1 tim=4755850529777
WAIT #140583609334256: nam='enq: KO - fast object checkpoint' ela= 124 name|mode=1263468545
  2=65690 0=2 obj#=-1 tim=4755850529959
WAIT #140583609334256: nam='PX Deq: Join ACK' ela= 39 sleeptime/senderid=268500992 passes=1
  p3=9216157728 obj#=-1 tim=4755850531333
WAIT #140583609334256: nam='PX Deq: Join ACK' ela= 42 sleeptime/senderid=268500993 passes=1
  p3=9216246432 obj#=-1 tim=4755850531420
WAIT #140583609334256: nam='PX Deq: Join ACK' ela= 39 sleeptime/senderid=268500994 passes=1
  p3=9216266144 obj#=-1 tim=4755850531507
```

While testing this use case, it turned out that the event is written to the tracefile only once, at the very beginning. Furthermore, the trace information about the queued statement is not emitted until the session actually starts work.

Parameters

Here are the parameters for the `resmgr:pq queued` event:

P1 - Location

P2 - Not used

P3 - Not used

obj# - NA

The location parameter is a numeric value that most likely refers to a location (function) in the Oracle code as described above in the `resmgr:become active` event.

Summary

The wait interface has been expanded to cover several Exadata-specific features. In this chapter, you read about the new wait events you should know. By far the most interesting of the new events are `cell smart table scan` and `cell smart index scan`. These events cover the time spent waiting on an offloadable read I/O request to a storage cell. There is a lot of processing that occurs at the storage layer that is lumped together under these events. It's important to understand that these events replace the `direct path read` event and that the mechanism of returning the data directly to the process PGA employed by the Smart Scan events is analogous to the way it is handled by `direct path read`.

CHAPTER 11

Exadata Performance Metrics

Oracle Exadata is a big step forward from the traditional database server architecture; however, despite all the innovative features, it is still running the standard Oracle Database software. Most of the well-versed database performance rules still apply, with the addition of some that recognize the advantage of Exadata functionality like Smart Scans, cell join filtering, and the Flash Cache. In this chapter, you can read more about the Exadata-specific and related performance topics, metrics, and some relevant internals.

Thankfully, Oracle, both at the database layer and in cells, provides lots of performance metrics for our use. However, when looking into any metric, you should know *why* you are monitoring this and what numbers are you looking for. In other words, how do you know when everything is OK and no action is needed, and how do you know when things are bad and action is needed? In order to avoid wasting effort on fixing the wrong problem, it is really important to measure *what matters*. For database performance, nothing matters more than *response time*, the actual time the end user (or connected system) has to wait for the response. So, if you want to make something faster in the database, you should focus on measuring and then optimizing the response time. All the other metrics and indicators, like the number of I/O requests or cache hits, are secondary. End users, who are waiting for their report to be generated, care about the time they have to wait only, not secondary metrics like CPU utilization or I/O rate. Nevertheless, often these secondary metrics become very useful for understanding and explaining performance issues.

The key metrics for breaking down database *response time* are the Oracle wait interface's events. Some key wait events are discussed in Chapter 10, and you will be introduced to performance monitoring tools that make use of them in Chapter 12. However, there are additional useful metrics Exadata provides, such as the number of bytes of data returned by Smart Scans and the actual amount of I/O avoided thanks to storage indexes, and many more. Such metrics give very important additional information about what is happening in the database and storage cells during SQL execution. In this chapter, you will read more about these metrics, and you will learn how to access and display them and, most importantly, what they mean. Even if you are not interested in knowing what each metric means, we still recommend you read this chapter, as it explains some important internals and design decisions in the Exadata-specific parts of the database code and the storage servers.

The information in this chapter should give you a good understanding about some key internal workings of Exadata databases and storage servers, and it should prepare you for Chapter 12, where this knowledge will be put to good use when monitoring and troubleshooting Exadata performance.

Measuring Exadata's Performance Metrics

Before examining Exadata-specific performance metrics, let's examine some internals and review some important elements of Exadata-specific features and metrics. One must understand what the performance numbers actually stand for before trying to monitor or optimize anything with this info.

By now, you know that Exadata database nodes do not perform physical disk I/O themselves, but ask the cells to execute the requests for them via the ASM layer. In the case of Smart Scans, the cell servers will also process the blocks read: extract their contents, filter rows, and so on. So, conceptually, the cells appear just like a black box from database's point of view. The database layer requests blocks or ranges of blocks of data, and the cells perform the physical I/O work transparent to the database layer and return the requested columns of matching rows. Thankfully, the Oracle Exadata architects, engineers, and developers have put a surprisingly large amount of instrumentation into `cellsrv` and related components. The cells keep track of how much work they have done and, they can also *send the metrics back to the database layer* along the results. This allows us—DBAs, developers, and troubleshooters—to have an end-to-end overview of what happened in the database *and* the cells when servicing a user's request or running a query. Try to get this amount of performance detail from your existing storage infrastructure as a DBA and you will quickly appreciate Exadata even more.

For example, when a query is executed via Smart Scan, you will still see familiar statistics such as `physical_reads` when you query `V$SQLSTATS` in the database layer, even though the database layer itself did not do any physical reads directly. Another example is the *cell physical IO bytes saved by storage index* statistic, which is counted in the cell level and not in the database. These numbers are visible in the database layer thanks to the cells sending back useful performance metrics in addition to the data queried. Some metrics currently report data at the cell and database level, and you can see some double counting on these.

In addition to the standard Oracle performance tools, this chapter will introduce two custom-built tools discussed in this chapter and Chapter 12. They are more suitable for flexible and advanced performance analysis and allow you to go beyond the standard wait events and SQL statement level statistics. The first tool, Oracle Session Snapper, is a script containing just an anonymous PL/SQL block, which measures detailed performance metrics from `V$SESSION`, `V$SESSION_EVENT`, `V$SESS_TIME_MODEL`, `V$SESSTAT`, among others. The last performance view from that list, `V$SESSTAT`, is especially important for advanced performance analysis—it contains hundreds of dynamic performance counters (over 600 in 11.2.0.2 and 1178 in Oracle 12.1.0.2) for each session in the instance. In addition to the usual monitoring using wait events, diving into `V$SESSTAT` gives us a much better idea of what kind of work Oracle sessions are doing, such as how many I/O requests per second they are doing, how many full segment scans per second, how many migrated/chained rows had to be fetched during a scan, and many more.

A BRIEF HISTORY OF SESSION COUNTERS

Oracle performance counters have been part of the database engine for a long time. The number of counters Oracle maintains for each session allows for very fine-grained analysis of what is happening. If you calculate the delta between a start and an end snapshot, you usually get a very good overview of database activity.

What is remarkable about the session performance counters is that Oracle continues to instrument the engine with every patch. You can see the numbers increasing by querying `v$statname`. It contains a column named "class," which has been documented in the Oracle Reference. As an example of the evolution of the database's instrumentation, some mainstream releases have been examined using the following query:

```
with stats as (
        select name, decode(class,
                1, 'USER',
                2, 'REDO',
                4, 'ENQUEUE',
                8, 'CACHE',
                16, 'OS',
                32, 'RAC',
                64, 'SQL',
                128, 'DEBUG',
                'MULTI-CATEGORY'
        ) as decoded_class from v$statname
)
```

```
select count(decoded_class), decoded_class
 from stats
 group by rollup(decoded_class)
 order by 1
```

The result of which was enlightening. In 11.2.0.3, the following distribution was found:

```
COUNT(DECODED_CLASS) DECODED
-------------------- -------
                   9 ENQUEUE
                  16 OS
                  25 RAC
                  32 REDO
                  47 MULTI-CATEGORY
                  93 SQL
                 107 USER
                 121 CACHE
                 188 DEBUG
                 638
```

Oracle 11.2.0.4 (which has been released after 12.1.0.1) has come out showing this:

```
COUNT(DECODED_CLASS) DECODED
-------------------- -------
                   9 ENQUEUE
                  16 OS
                  25 RAC
                  34 REDO
                  48 MULTI-CATEGORY
                  96 SQL
                 117 USER
                 127 CACHE
                 207 DEBUG
                 679
```

As you can see, there are quite a few more counters added, but nothing in comparison to 12.1.0.2:

```
COUNT(DECODED_CLASS) DECODED
-------------------- -------
                   9 ENQUEUE
                  16 OS
                  35 RAC
                  68 REDO
                  74 MULTI-CATEGORY
                 130 SQL
                 130 USER
                 151 CACHE
                 565 DEBUG
                1178
```

Nearly twice as many as with 11.2.0.3! To be fair, a large number of these are related to the in-memory option, but, nevertheless, the plus in instrumentation is a welcome addition.

Revisiting the Prerequisites for Exadata Smart Scans

In this section, you are going to be gently introduced to the metrics the Oracle Database kernel's instrumentation provides us in more detail. The focus is on the Exadata-related performance statistics. Details of the Exadata wait events are not covered here, as these are already explained in Chapter 10. Where applicable, a review of how to use wait events for a better understanding of database performance is added, and you may find some of the offloading and Smart Scan material already covered in Chapter 2. This is a refresher for the benefit of understanding the chapter and without having to go back many pages. Understanding the details is important in the context of the chapter and in the context of monitoring and troubleshooting Exadata performance.

One of the primary performance boosters for data warehousing and reporting workloads on the Exadata platform is the Exadata Smart Scan. OLTP workloads benefit greatly from the use of Exadata Smart Flash Cache. The first part of this section details how to measure whether your workload is benefitting from both of these features. This knowledge forms the building blocks for later database and query performance monitoring in subsequent sections. In the second part, you can read more about some Exadata internal performance counters.

Exadata Smart Scan Performance

Since Smart Scans are such an exciting feature, their metrics come first. Before discussing any of the metrics, let's review how the decision to do a Smart Scan is made in Oracle. Note that a Smart Scan can be used on regular table segments and also on materialized view segments—which are physically no different from regular tables. Smart Scans can also be used for full scanning through B*Tree index segments (Index Fast Full Scan) and also bitmap index segments (Bitmap Index Fast Full Scan). Scanning through index segments using the "brute force" multi-block reads as opposed to the single block I/O approach otherwise employed is very similar to how a full table scan is executed against a table. The major difference is that index segments have an additional structure called *index branch blocks*, which have to be skipped and ignored, in addition to ASSM bitmap blocks, which have to be skipped both in table and index scans. Smart Scans on partitions and subpartitions of tables and indexes are internally no different from scans on nonpartitioned objects. A partitioned segment really is just a logical grouping of smaller segments. Remember that the Smart Scans can scan a variety of segments.

Regardless of segment type, a Smart Scan always requires direct path reads to be chosen by the SQL execution engine during execution time, which is *not* an optimizer decision. So, when troubleshooting why a Smart Scan was not used, you will have to first check whether direct path reads were used or not. You should check the execution plan first, to see whether a full scan is reported there at all. Here you see simple examples showing full segment scans happening on different segment types, starting with a full table scan:

```
SELECT AVG(line) FROM t WHERE owner LIKE 'S%'

-----------------------------------------------------------------------------
| Id  | Operation                  | Name | Rows  | Bytes | Cost (%CPU)| Time     |
-----------------------------------------------------------------------------
|   0 | SELECT STATEMENT           |      |       |       |   295K(100)|          |
|   1 |  SORT AGGREGATE            |      |     1 |    11 |            |          |
|*  2 |   TABLE ACCESS STORAGE FULL| T    | 5743K|    60M|   295K  (1)| 00:59:01 |
-----------------------------------------------------------------------------
```

```
Predicate Information (identified by operation id):
---------------------------------------------------

   2 - storage("OWNER" LIKE 'S%')
       filter("OWNER" LIKE 'S%')
```

Note that the "STORAGE" in the TABLE ACCESS STORAGE FULL line here does *not* mean that Oracle is attempting to do a Smart Scan. This keyword merely indicates that Oracle knows that this segment is residing on a storage cell, not something else like an NFS mount or iSCSI device, and it is using the table scan codepath *capable of performing* a Smart Scan. Whether a Smart Scan is actually used depends on multiple other factors, which were discussed in Chapter 2 and will be also demonstrated here briefly. Whether or not the storage keyword is displayed in the execution plan also depends on the initialization parameter cell_offload_plan_display. Also, *Smart Scan* is a broad term, covering filtration (which may be able to take advantage of storage indexes), column projection, decompression of HCC compressed CUs, and hash join early elimination with bloom filters among others— all done in the cells. Even if you are not taking advantage of the filter predicate offloading to storage (filtration), the cells may be able to reduce the amount of data returned to the database. If Smart Scan is used, the column projection is done in the cells, and they return only the required columns instead of entire blocks containing the full-length rows.

In addition to finding the storage keyword in the execution plan, it is important to check whether a storage() predicate is shown in the "Predicate Information" section below the execution plan. This is a good indicator of whether the execution plan *is capable of* doing a Smart Scan's predicate offload (smart filtration). Unfortunately, this does not mean that a Smart Scan predicate offload was actually attempted. There are cases where even the presence of a storage() predicate does not guarantee that a predicate offload will take place. This is where Oracle performance metrics will be helpful, but more about them shortly.

In summary, a full segment scan access path with the STORAGE keyword *and* the storage() predicate must be present in the execution plan in order for it to *be capable of* doing a Smart Scan's predicate offload at all. If you do see the STORAGE lines in execution plan, but no storage() predicates under it, then predicate offload will not even be attempted, but you still may benefit from column projection offload, in which only the required columns are returned by the cells. You will probably see multiple storage predicates (and full scan operations) in real-life query plans, as you will be doing multi-table joins.

If you see the STORAGE option and storage() predicate in an execution plan, the odds are that a Smart Scan will be attempted. Predicate offload is possible in principle, but there is no guarantee that a Smart Scan happens every time you run the query. On the other hand, if you do not see a STORAGE keyword in the execution plan, then there is no way a Smart Scan could happen on a corresponding segment in a given execution plan step. When there is no STORAGE keyword in the execution plan line, it means that this rowsource operator is not capable of using the smart features of the storage cells, and thus is unable to push any storage() predicates into the cell either.

You read earlier that Smart Scans can be done on materialized view segments, too. This is possible because a materialized view segment is physically exactly the same as any regular table. Here is the corresponding excerpt from an execution plan:

```
select count(*) from mv1 where owner like 'S%'

-----------------------------------------------------------------------
| Id  | Operation                        | Name | E-Rows | Cost (%CPU)|
-----------------------------------------------------------------------
|   0 | SELECT STATEMENT                 |      |        |   139K(100)|
|   1 |  SORT AGGREGATE                  |      |      1 |            |
|*  2 |   MAT_VIEW ACCESS STORAGE FULL| MV1  |  2089K|   139K  (1)|
-----------------------------------------------------------------------
```

```
Predicate Information (identified by operation id):
---------------------------------------------------

   2 - storage("OWNER" LIKE 'S%')
       filter("OWNER" LIKE 'S%')
```

Following are two examples where Smart Scans can be attempted. The first is when scanning through a regular B*Tree index segment, where an Index Fast Full Scan is requested:

```
SELECT /*+ INDEX_FFS(t2) */ AVG(LENGTH(owner)) FROM t2 WHERE owner LIKE'S%'

-------------------------------------------------------------------------
| Id  | Operation                    | Name  | E-Rows | Cost (%CPU)|
-------------------------------------------------------------------------
|   0 | SELECT STATEMENT             |       |        |  5165 (100)|
|   1 |  SORT AGGREGATE              |       |      1 |            |
|*  2 |   INDEX STORAGE FAST FULL SCAN| T2_I1 |   597K|  5165   (2)|
-------------------------------------------------------------------------

Predicate Information (identified by operation id):
---------------------------------------------------

   2 - storage("OWNER" LIKE 'S%')
       filter("OWNER" LIKE 'S%')
```

In the second example, an Index Fast Full Scan is requested on a bitmap index segment:

```
SELECT /*+ INDEX_FFS(t1) */ AVG(LENGTH(owner)) FROM t1 WHERE owner LIKE'S%'

Plan hash value: 3170056527

---------------------------------------------------------------------------------------------
| Id  | Operation                           | Name        | E-Rows | Cost (%CPU)|
---------------------------------------------------------------------------------------------
|   0 | SELECT STATEMENT                    |             |        |   505 (100)|
|   1 |  SORT AGGREGATE                     |             |      1 |            |
|   2 |   BITMAP CONVERSION TO ROWIDS       |             |   597K|   505   (0)|
|*  3 |    BITMAP INDEX STORAGE FAST FULL SCAN| BI_T1_OWNER |        |            |
---------------------------------------------------------------------------------------------

Predicate Information (identified by operation id):
---------------------------------------------------

   3 - storage("OWNER" LIKE 'S%')
       filter("OWNER" LIKE 'S%')
```

In both cases, you see that the segments were scanned using a *fast full scan*, which is just like a full table scan but on index segments, and the presence of the STORAGE option and storage() predicates on the full scan operations shows that a Smart Scan predicate offload can be attempted.

You may wonder why you are repeatedly reading, "Smart Scan predicate offload can be *attempted.*" The reason for the considerate wording is simple: there are cases where a Smart Scan either is not employed or is started but does not complete during runtime. Yes, the execution plan structure may lead you to believe a Smart Scan will be used for a query, but whether the Smart Scan is actually executed depends first on whether a direct path read is chosen to scan the segment or not. Moreover, even if a direct path read *is* chosen *and* a Smart Scan is executed, then somewhere during (or at the beginning of) Smart Scan execution, a different decision may be made. This depends on multiple factors, and we will cover some of them here. At that point, the session statistics really shine and help the performance analyst to determine reasons for the observed behavior.

This rather abstract sounding paragraph is best explained with an example. You could try Smart Scan on an Index-Organized Table (IOT) segment first to see how valuable the additional Oracle metrics are. Note that as of the current Oracle version at the time of writing, Oracle has *not* implemented Smart Scan functionality on Index Organized Table segments yet. That is why this is a good example for practicing using the Smart Scan-related metrics.

Review the execution plan shown here; it is from a query using an *index fast full scan* on an Index Organized Table's index segment:

```
select avg(length(state)) from t1_iot where date_created >
to_date('07.11.2013','dd.mm.yyyy')

Plan hash value: 379056979

------------------------------------------------------------------------------------------
| Id  | Operation              | Name              | Rows  | Bytes | Cost (%CPU)| Time     |
------------------------------------------------------------------------------------------
|   0 | SELECT STATEMENT       |                   |       |       |   402 (100)|          |
|   1 |  SORT AGGREGATE        |                   |     1 |    17 |            |          |
|*  2 |   INDEX FAST FULL SCAN| SYS_IOT_TOP_19445 |  740K|    12M|   402   (6)| 00:00:01 |
------------------------------------------------------------------------------------------

Predicate Information (identified by operation id):
---------------------------------------------------

   2 - filter("DATE_CREATED">TO_DATE(' 2013-11-07 00:00:00', 'syyyy-mm-dd
              hh24:mi:ss'))
```

Unlike in plans listed earlier, there is no STORAGE option listed in the execution plan row source (line 2), and there is no storage() predicate, indicating an opportunity to push a filter predicate to the storage cells. This plan is not capable of using any Smart Scan functionality; it will do good old block I/O. Looking at additional Exadata and cell metrics can be skipped straight away, as the execution plan itself shows that it cannot use a Smart Scan-compatible row source codepath.

Understanding Exadata Smart Scan Metrics and Performance Counters

When you have an Oracle execution plan using the storage-aware row sources, you still cannot be entirely sure whether a Smart Scan really is attempted and does what you expect. The wait interface introduced in Chapter 10 is a trustworthy source of performance-related information. During the execution of your query, consult the relevant V$-views to determine what your session is waiting for. Consider the following possibilities:

- **CPU usage only:** This seems to mean that a buffered data access is used (not direct path), as visible in the absence of I/O wait events when traversing the buffer cache and all the data happens to be cached. Careful though: ASH and tools taking performance data from it uses a one-second sample interval and might miss very short physical IO events. The venerable SQL Trace or usage of snapper to capture information from `v$sesstat/v$mystat` get their data from a different source than ASH.
- **cell multiblock physical read:** Apparently buffered multi-block reads are used (looks like a full segment scan), but multi-block read waits can be reported also for LOB and SecureFile read operations, where in case of LOBs, the LOB chunk size is bigger than the block size. Otherwise, single-block reads would be reported for LOB access. With Exadata cell software 12.1.1.1.1+, inline LOBs can be offloaded.
- **cell single block physical read:** Apparently buffered single block reads are used. If these are the only I/O wait events you see (and not together with multi-block reads), then it appears you are not using a full segment scan at all. Sometimes single-block reads show up due to other operations in the execution plan (like some index range scan) or due to chained rows in data blocks.

If you see regular `cell multiblock physical read` wait events in your session, then direct path reads were clearly *not* used. This may happen mainly for serially executed operations, as if you are using `parallel_degree_policy = MANUAL` or `LIMITED`. Parallel Execution slaves will quite likely perform direct path read scans, which will then be offloaded and executed as Smart Scans. On the other hand, when you are using the new automatic parallel degree policy (`parallel_degree_policy = AUTO or ADAPTIVE`) and Oracle decides to perform an in-memory parallel query, Oracle will use reads using the buffer cache even for parallel operations, for which the wait events will show "buffered" reads as a result.

In addition to these issues, there are more reasons and special cases where Smart Scans just silently are not used or fall back to regular block I/O mode—potentially slowing down your queries and workload more than you expect. Thankfully, Oracle Exadata is very well instrumented and by using the performance framework, the analyst can review underperforming queries and optimize accordingly.

Exadata Dynamic Performance Counters

While the Oracle wait interface's wait events provide us with crucial information about where the database response time is spent, the Exadata dynamic performance counters take us one step further and explain what kind of operations or tasks the Oracle kernel is performing—and how many of them. Wait events and performance counters complement each other and should not really be used alone. Oracle dynamic performance counters are also known as `V$SESSTAT` or `V$SYSSTAT` statistics (or counters), as these views are used for accessing them. When using 12c Multi-Tenant databases, you might find `V$CON_SYSSTAT` interesting as well.

When and How to Use Performance Counters

When troubleshooting performance, you should always begin the troubleshooting process by considering the wait events and SQL ID-level activity measurements. These keep track of the *time,* which end users care about. If additional detail is needed, then proceed to reviewing performance counters. If standard wait event information does not provide enough information, the performance counters provide a very detailed insight into what Oracle sessions are doing. For example, if your session seems to be burning lots of CPU, you can see whether the *session logical reads* or *parse count (hard)* counters increase for a session more than normally. Or if you see some unexpected single-block reads during a full table scan, you can check whether the *table fetch continued row* or some statistic like *data blocks consistent reads - undo records applied* increases, which indicate either a chained/migrated row or consistent read (CR) buffer cloning plus rollback overhead. Another useful metric is *user commits,* which gives you an understanding of how many database transactions are done inside an instance (or in chosen sessions). So, the next time a session seems to be waiting for a *log file sync* wait event, you can check its *user commits* counter value from V$SESSTAT to see how frequently this session is committing its work.

Unfortunately, Oracle does not document all performance counters. The ones documented can be found in the Oracle 12c Reference, Appendix E "Statistics Descriptions." Some cell-related performance counters are documented in the Exadata documentation set in the *Exadata Storage Server Software User's Guide.* However, the level of detail in the documentation is not always enough to understand a given performance counter. Experience will teach you which ones are important and which ones are not.

Although performance statistics can also be found in AWR reports, they are most useful when used while a problem is occurring. When calculating the rate of change ("delta") of these counters, it is possible to see what your session is doing in a lot more detail.

You read earlier in this chapter that performance counters are assigned to a class. But even within these classes, you can make out groups of related counters. Think of physical I/O, for example. There are statistics for reads and writes, with the different reads shown here:

```
SQL> select name from v$statname where name like 'physical reads%' order by name;

NAME
----------------------------------------------------------------
physical reads
physical reads cache
physical reads cache for securefile flashback block new
physical reads cache prefetch
physical reads direct
physical reads direct (lob)
physical reads direct for securefile flashback block new
physical reads direct temporary tablespace
physical reads for flashback new
physical reads prefetch warmup
physical reads retry corrupt

11 rows selected.
```

Now, if you were to execute a SQL statement and capture the value of the counters at the query's start and end, you could calculate the difference between end and start. In the next example, this has been done for physical reads. The session executed the following statement:

```
SQL> select count(*) from bigtab union all select count(*) from bigtab;
```

The following statistic counters related to physical reads have changed while the query executed:

```
physical read bytes                            : 27603034112
physical read IO requests                      : 26379
physical read requests optimized               : 23671
physical reads                                 : 3369127
physical reads direct                          : 3369127
physical read total bytes                      : 27528650752
physical read total bytes optimized            : 24767488000
physical read total IO requests                : 26310
physical read total multi block requests       : 26286
```

This should give you a very exact picture over the physical reads as reported by the database layer for *this particular session and query*. Note that these are not the only physical reads accounted for—you will be introduced to the full spectrum of IO events relevant to Smart Scan processing in later sections.

The wait interface would have given you the following information, taken from a tkprof'd trace file:

```
Elapsed times include waiting on following events:
  Event waited on                             Times   Max. Wait  Total Waited
  ----------------------------------------   Waited  ----------  ------------
  Disk file operations I/O                        2        0.00          0.00
  SQL*Net message to client                       2        0.00          0.00
  enq: KO - fast object checkpoint                6        0.00          0.00
  reliable message                                2        0.00          0.00
  cell smart table scan                        2969        0.01          2.55
  SQL*Net message from client                     2        1.49          1.49
```

Both of these—statistic counters and wait interface—give you information about the session's activity. What should have become apparent, though, is how the session statistics give you more detailed information about the disk reads. Other statistics—remember that Oracle maintains 1178 for your session in 12.1.0.2—give you more insights into other aspects of the processing performed. By just looking at the wait information, you cannot determine if Flash Cache has been accessed to provide the relevant data. The performance counters allow you to confirm that Flash Cache was used for 23,671 out of 26,379 physical read requests. Storage indexes were specifically disabled for that query in the current session and, therefore, did not play a role (although, strictly speaking, this was not needed due to the lack of a where clause).

Dynamic performance counters provide important clues, which allow you to direct your troubleshooting efforts better. Note that tools like Statspack and AWR reports rely heavily on V$SYSSTAT counters. They just store values from these ever-increasing numbers (since instance start) in their repository tables. So, whenever you run a Statspack/AWR report, just deltas between values in chosen snapshots are reported. Statspack and AWR reports are all about showing you deltas between V$SYSSTAT (and other views) numbers from different snapshots of time.

While the V$SYSSTAT view is fine for monitoring and troubleshooting instance-wide performance (like AWR and Statspack reports do), its problem is that you cannot possibly use systemwide statistics to troubleshoot a single session's problem. System-level statistics aggregate all your (potentially thousands of) sessions' metrics together into one set of counters. That is why Oracle also has V$SESSTAT, which keeps track of all these individual counters for each session separately! Every single session in the instance has its own hundreds or thousands of performance counters, keeping track of only its activity. This dynamic performance view truly is a goldmine—if only a few sessions (or users) have a problem in the instance, you can monitor only their activity without being distracted by all the other users' noise in the database.

As said earlier, V$SYSSTAT accumulates instancewide performance counters; they start from zero and only increase throughout the instance lifetime. Most of the V$SESSTAT counters always increase (cumulative statistics) with some exceptions, for example *logons current* and *session pga/uga memory*. In any case, when examining the counter values, you should not just look at the *current* value of a counter, especially if your session has been connected for a while. The problem is that even if you see a big-looking number for some counter in V$SESSTAT of a long-running connection pool's session, how do you know what portion of that was incremented or added today, right now, when you have the problem, as opposed to a few weeks ago when that session logged on? In other words, when troubleshooting a problem happening right now, you should look at performance metrics for right now, in that particular time interval of the problem. A similar rule applies when troubleshooting issues of the past.

This is why coauthor Tanel Poder has written a "little" helper tool called Oracle Session Snapper, which allows its user to easily display the sessions' current activity from V$SESSTAT and various other session-level performance views. An important aspect about this tool is that it is "just" an anonymous PL/SQL block, parsed on the fly; it does not require any installation or DDL privileges in the database. This should make it easy to deploy and use. The current Snapper version is available online at ExpertOracleExadata.com. Following is one example of how to run Snapper to measure SID 789's activity (for a single five-second interval). In this example, the script has been renamed to snapper4.sql to distinguish it from previous versions. Read the Snapper header for instructions and detailed documentation. In this example, Snapper has been instructed to report any difference for the performance counters for session 789. Additionally, it samples wait-event related information from V$SESSION and presents it in an ASH-like format.

■ **Note** Unfortunately, the output Snapper produces related to session statistics is too wide for this book. A little filter trims it down to a manageable size.

```
sid username     statistic                                              delta
789 MARTIN       Requests to/from client                                    1
789 MARTIN       opened cursors cumulative                                  1
789 MARTIN       user calls                                                 2
789 MARTIN       pinned cursors current                                     1
789 MARTIN       session logical reads                                  2.59M
789 MARTIN       user I/O wait time                                       166
789 MARTIN       non-idle wait time                                       166
789 MARTIN       non-idle wait count                                    8.14k
789 MARTIN       session uga memory                                     6.23M
789 MARTIN       session pga memory                                     8.85M
789 MARTIN       enqueue waits                                              3
789 MARTIN       enqueue requests                                           2
789 MARTIN       enqueue conversions                                        4
789 MARTIN       enqueue releases                                           2
789 MARTIN       global enqueue gets sync                                   6
789 MARTIN       global enqueue releases                                    2
789 MARTIN       physical read total IO requests                       20.24k
789 MARTIN       physical read total multi block requests              20.22k
789 MARTIN       physical read requests optimized                      18.31k
789 MARTIN       physical read total bytes optimized                   19.17G
789 MARTIN       physical read total bytes                             21.18G
789 MARTIN       cell physical IO interconnect bytes                  416.83M
789 MARTIN       ges messages sent                                          3
789 MARTIN       consistent gets                                        2.59M
```

```
789 MARTIN        consistent gets from cache                                          13
789 MARTIN        consistent gets from cache (fastpath)                               13
789 MARTIN        consistent gets direct                                           2.59M
789 MARTIN        logical read bytes from cache                                   106.5k
789 MARTIN        physical reads                                                   2.59M
789 MARTIN        physical reads direct                                            2.59M
789 MARTIN        physical read IO requests                                       20.24k
789 MARTIN        physical read bytes                                             21.19G
789 MARTIN        calls to kcmgcs                                                     13
789 MARTIN        calls to get snapshot scn: kcmgss                                    1
789 MARTIN        file io wait time                                               53.16k
789 MARTIN        cell physical IO bytes eligible for predicate offload           21.19G
789 MARTIN        cell physical IO interconnect bytes returned by smart scan     417.12M
789 MARTIN        cell num smartio automem buffer allocation attempts                  1
789 MARTIN        table scans (long tables)                                            1
789 MARTIN        table scans (direct read)                                            1
789 MARTIN        table scan rows gotten                                          15.54M
789 MARTIN        table scan blocks gotten                                         2.59M
789 MARTIN        cell scans                                                           1
789 MARTIN        cell blocks processed by cache layer                             2.59M
789 MARTIN        cell blocks processed by txn layer                               2.59M
789 MARTIN        cell blocks processed by data layer                              2.59M
789 MARTIN        cell blocks helped by minscn optimization                        2.59M
789 MARTIN        cell IO uncompressed bytes                                      21.24G
789 MARTIN        session cursor cache hits                                            1
789 MARTIN        session cursor cache count                                           1
789 MARTIN        workarea memory allocated                                        3.09k
789 MARTIN        parse count (total)                                                  1
789 MARTIN        execute count                                                        1
789 MARTIN        bytes sent via SQL*Net to client                                     1
789 MARTIN        bytes received via SQL*Net from client                             298
789 MARTIN        cell flash cache read hits                                      18.41k
```

The simulated ASH information does fit within the limits and is shown here:

```
SYS@DBM011:1> @snapper4 ash 5 1 789
Sampling SID 789 with interval 5 seconds, taking 1 snapshots...

-- Session Snapper v4.12 BETA - by Tanel Poder ( http://blog.tanelpoder.com )
-- Enjoy the Most Advanced Oracle Troubleshooting Script on the Planet! :)

------------------------------------------------------------------------------------------
Active% | INST | SQL_ID          | SQL_CHILD | EVENT                              | WAIT_CLASS
------------------------------------------------------------------------------------------
    50% |    1 | cdjur50gj9h6s   | 0         | ON CPU                             | ON CPU
    28% |    1 | cdjur50gj9h6s   | 0         | cell smart table scan              | User I/O

--  End of ASH snap 1, end=2014-08-06 09:04:30, seconds=5, samples_taken=36

PL/SQL procedure successfully completed.
```

As you can see from the output, the statement captured during the five-second interval clearly performed a Smart Scan, as indicated in the simulated ASH section and confirmed in the section above with cell scans indicated as 1 (there was a single segment scan). No need to worry about ASH in this context. Quoting from the Snapper documentation, "The 'ASH' functionality in Snapper just samples GV$SESSION view, so you do NOT need Diagnostics Pack licenses to use Snapper's 'ASH' output."

This output also shows that session 789 performed 2.59M logical reads. It issued a total of 20.24k read IO requests to read 21.18G of data, almost entirely satisfied by multi-block I/O requests. In this example, the human-readable delta values have been chosen, but Snapper can, of course, print the exact values as well.

The Meaning and Explanation of Exadata Performance Counters

After the introduction about their usefulness, it is time to explore the *meaning* of performance counters. No matter how pretty the charts or pictures a performance tool draws using these metrics, if you are not aware of their meaning, they will be of limited use for troubleshooting. When writing this chapter, we faced a dilemma: There are so many interesting performance counters out there that are each worth a dedicated section. But, if we did that, this chapter would be in excess of 100 pages. To keep the chapter within reasonable limits, mostly Exadata-specific statistics are covered, and only the most relevant ones. Keep an eye out on the authors' blogs for information on the events that did not make the chapter.

Here is a script that lists all statistics related to storage cells from V$STATNAME, with the statistic class, which indicates the purposes for which Oracle kernel engineers have expected to use these counters

```
SQL> SELECT
         name
       , TRIM(
           CASE WHEN BITAND(class,  1) =   1 THEN 'USER  ' END ||
           CASE WHEN BITAND(class,  2) =   2 THEN 'REDO  ' END ||
           CASE WHEN BITAND(class,  4) =   4 THEN 'ENQ   ' END ||
           CASE WHEN BITAND(class,  8) =   8 THEN 'CACHE ' END ||
           CASE WHEN BITAND(class, 16) =  16 THEN 'OSDEP ' END ||
           CASE WHEN BITAND(class, 32) =  32 THEN 'PARX  ' END ||
           CASE WHEN BITAND(class, 64) =  64 THEN 'SQLT  ' END ||
           CASE WHEN BITAND(class,128) = 128 THEN 'DEBUG ' END
        ) class_name
     FROM
         v$statname
     WHERE
         name LIKE '%cell%'
     ORDER BY
         name
   /
```

On an Oracle 12.1.0.2 system, the above query produced the following output:

```
NAME                                                             CLASS_NAME
---------------------------------------------------------------- ---------------
cell CUs processed for compressed                                SQLT
cell CUs processed for uncompressed                              SQLT
cell CUs sent compressed                                         SQLT
cell CUs sent head piece                                         SQLT
cell CUs sent uncompressed                                       SQLT
cell IO uncompressed bytes                                       SQLT
```

```
cell XT granule bytes requested for predicate offload            DEBUG
cell XT granule predicate offload retries                        DEBUG
cell XT granules requested for predicate offload                 DEBUG
cell blocks helped by commit cache                               SQLT
cell blocks helped by minscn optimization                        SQLT
cell blocks processed by cache layer                             DEBUG
cell blocks processed by data layer                              DEBUG
cell blocks processed by index layer                             DEBUG
cell blocks processed by txn layer                               DEBUG
cell commit cache queries                                        SQLT
cell flash cache read hits                                       CACHE
cell index scans                                                 SQLT
cell interconnect bytes returned by XT smart scan                DEBUG
cell logical write IO requests                                   USER
cell logical write IO requests eligible for offload              USER
cell num block IOs due to a file instant restore in progress     SQLT
cell num bytes in block IO during predicate offload              SQLT
cell num bytes in passthru during predicate offload              SQLT
cell num bytes of IO reissued due to relocation                  SQLT
cell num fast response sessions                                  SQLT
cell num fast response sessions continuing to smart scan         SQLT
cell num smart IO sessions in rdbms block IO due to big payload  SQLT
cell num smart IO sessions in rdbms block IO due to no cell mem  SQLT
cell num smart IO sessions in rdbms block IO due to open fail    SQLT
cell num smart IO sessions in rdbms block IO due to user         SQLT
cell num smart IO sessions using passthru mode due to cellsrv    SQLT
cell num smart IO sessions using passthru mode due to timezone   SQLT
cell num smart IO sessions using passthru mode due to user       SQLT
cell num smart file creation sessions using rdbms block IO mode  SQLT
cell num smartio automem buffer allocation attempts              SQLT
cell num smartio automem buffer allocation failures              SQLT
cell num smartio permanent cell failures                         SQLT
cell num smartio transient cell failures                         SQLT
cell overwrites in flash cache                                   CACHE
cell partial writes in flash cache                               CACHE
cell physical IO bytes eligible for predicate offload            SQLT
cell physical IO bytes saved by columnar cache                   CACHE
cell physical IO bytes saved by storage index                    CACHE
cell physical IO bytes saved during optimized RMAN file restore  SQLT
cell physical IO bytes saved during optimized file creation      SQLT
cell physical IO bytes sent directly to DB node to balance CPU   SQLT
cell physical IO interconnect bytes                              SQLT
cell physical IO interconnect bytes returned by smart scan       SQLT
cell physical write IO bytes eligible for offload                USER
cell physical write IO host network bytes written during offloa  USER
cell physical write bytes saved by smart file initialization     CACHE
cell scans                                                       SQLT
cell simulated physical IO bytes eligible for predicate offload  SQLT  DEBUG
cell simulated physical IO bytes returned by predicate offload   SQLT  DEBUG
cell smart IO session cache hard misses                          SQLT
cell smart IO session cache hits                                 SQLT
```

```
cell smart IO session cache hwm                                   SQLT
cell smart IO session cache lookups                               SQLT
cell smart IO session cache soft misses                           SQLT
cell statistics spare1                                            SQLT
cell statistics spare2                                            SQLT
cell statistics spare3                                            SQLT
cell statistics spare4                                            SQLT
cell statistics spare5                                            SQLT
cell statistics spare6                                            SQLT
cell transactions found in commit cache                           SQLT
cell writes to flash cache                                        CACHE
chained rows processed by cell                                    SQLT
chained rows rejected by cell                                     SQLT
chained rows skipped by cell                                      SQLT
error count cleared by cell                                       SQLT
sage send block by cell                                           SQLT

73 rows selected.
```

If you own the first edition of this book, you will notice that there are many more cell-related counters in 12.1.0.2 than there were in 11.2.0.2, which was the standard production release at the time of the first edition's writing. Using a similar query to the one shown above, it is possible to focus on the statistics related to the HCC feature, covered in Chapter 3:

```
NAME                                                              CLASS_NAME
----------------------------------------------------------------- ---------------
EHCC Analyze CUs Decompressed                                     DEBUG
EHCC Analyzer Calls                                               DEBUG
EHCC Archive CUs Compressed                                       DEBUG
EHCC Archive CUs Decompressed                                     DEBUG
EHCC Attempted Block Compressions                                 DEBUG
EHCC Block Compressions                                           DEBUG
EHCC CU Row Pieces Compressed                                     DEBUG
EHCC CUs Compressed                                               DEBUG
EHCC CUs Decompressed                                             DEBUG
EHCC CUs all rows pass minmax                                     DEBUG
EHCC CUs no rows pass minmax                                      DEBUG
EHCC CUs some rows pass minmax                                    DEBUG
EHCC Check CUs Decompressed                                       DEBUG
EHCC Columns Decompressed                                         DEBUG
EHCC Compressed Length Compressed                                 DEBUG
EHCC Compressed Length Decompressed                               DEBUG
EHCC Conventional DMLs                                            DEBUG
EHCC DML CUs Decompressed                                         DEBUG
EHCC Decompressed Length Compressed                               DEBUG
EHCC Decompressed Length Decompressed                             DEBUG
EHCC Dump CUs Decompressed                                        DEBUG
EHCC Normal Scan CUs Decompressed                                 DEBUG
EHCC Pieces Buffered for Decompression                            DEBUG
EHCC Preds all rows pass minmax                                   DEBUG
EHCC Preds no rows pass minmax                                    DEBUG
```

```
EHCC Preds some rows pass minmax                               DEBUG
EHCC Query High CUs Compressed                                 DEBUG
EHCC Query High CUs Decompressed                               DEBUG
EHCC Query Low CUs Compressed                                  DEBUG
EHCC Query Low CUs Decompressed                                DEBUG
EHCC Rowid CUs Decompressed                                    DEBUG
EHCC Rows Compressed                                           DEBUG
EHCC Rows Not Compressed                                       DEBUG
EHCC Total Columns for Decompression                           DEBUG
EHCC Total Pieces for Decompression                            DEBUG
EHCC Total Rows for Decompression                              DEBUG
EHCC Turbo Scan CUs Decompressed                               DEBUG
EHCC Used on Pillar Tablespace                                 DEBUG
EHCC Used on ZFS Tablespace                                    DEBUG

39 rows selected.
```

All the statistics starting with `cell%` are, as the name suggests, related to storage cells. Some of these stats are measured and maintained by cells themselves and then sent back to the database sessions during any interaction over iDB protocol. Some are maintained in the Exadata-specific portion of the Oracle database kernel. Those statistics with "XT" in their name are related to a different product and out of this chapter's scope. Every database session receives the cell statistics along with the replies from their corresponding cell sessions and then updates the relevant database V$-views with it. This is how the Oracle database layer has insight into what is going on in the "black box" of a cell, like the real number of I/O operations done and the number of cell Flash Cache hits. Note that there are a few chained rows [...] cell statistics, which apparently use a different naming convention, having the "cell" in the end of the statistic name.

Statistics starting with EHCC are related to Hybrid Columnar Compression. You always see the values increasing during Smart Scans on HCC segments. During a Smart Scan, the `cell CU%`-counters are incremented on the cells while the worker threads tear through the compressed data on disk. Whenever the Smart Scan produces a match with the predicates in the query, the cells will decompress the column in the CU (not the whole Compression Unit!) and pass it to the RDBMS layer. It is during RDBMS layer processing that the EHCC counters are increased, even if the data is already uncompressed. Unfortunately, it is impossible to discuss each of the EHCC% counters in this chapter, but a quick categorization of the counters does fit in here.

Performance Counter Reference for a Selected Subset

This section explains some of the more important and interesting statistics listed in the output earlier. Since the chapter had too much content in the first edition of the book already, a careful selection was necessary to cut down on the number of counters described to make some room for the new features worth covering. We hope to have made a reasonable selection.

In many cases of performance troubleshooting, you probably do not have to delve this deeply. The wait interface and Real Time SQL Monitoring features you will read about in Chapter 12 should provide enough information. Nevertheless, understanding what happens behind the scenes and why these statistics are incremented will give you further insight into Exadata internals and enable you to troubleshoot unusual performance problems more effectively. The noteworthy statistics are covered in alphabetical order.

cell CUs sent compressed

This first statistic counter to be covered here is incremented on the cell. If you see the numbers go up here, you are witnessing memory stress on the cells. It is not the worst form of memory pressure instrumented (see next section), but, due to a memory shortage, some work the cells would do when scanning HCC compressed data cannot be performed on a storage cell. Filtering is still being done and predicates are evaluated. It's just that the column information is not decompressed on the cell. Here again, the rule laid out in Chapter 3 has a huge effect: When using HCC, you should really only ever reference the columns you intend to use, as opposed to the ubiquitous select * from table... The more columns are sent uncompressed to the RDBMS layer, the more work your session has to perform.

cell CUs sent head piece

If the cell is under more memory stress and memory allocations fail, it might not be possible for the cell to decompress anything and the whole CU must be sent to the RDBMS layer for processing. This is probably the worst-case scenario during Smart Scans of compressed data.

If you want to see the memory statistics on a cell, you can use the `cellsrvstat` utility (discussed later in this chapter) to check for a statistic group named `mem`. This chapter explains `cellsrvstat` toward the end; the memory-related statistics can be queried using `cellsrvstat -stat_group=mem`.

cell CUs sent uncompressed

After the previous counters that meant trouble, this one is what you want to see instead during Smart Scans. This is the equivalent to the ORA-00000: normal, successful completion. If you see this counter increase, the CU has been processed and was decompressed on the cell. Again, you will only see this statistic counter increase during a Smart Scan when the cells decompressed CUs. Remember that CUs span multiple Oracle blocks. When checking related statistics, you might want to check the size of the CU first.

cell blocks helped by commit cache

During a Smart Scan in the storage cell, the normal data consistency rules still need to be applied, sometimes with help of undo data. An important concept to remember is that Smart Scans produce consistent reads. Therefore, consistent read guarantees must work also for Smart Scans. There is just one difficulty: The Smart Scan works entirely in the storage cells, where it does not have access to any undo data in the database instances' buffer caches. Undo can become necessary to revert changes to a block and to get it back to a SCN from where it is safe to read, as you will see in a moment.

Remember that cells do not communicate with other cells by design during Smart Scans. An individual cell is unable to read the undo data from undo segments striped across other cells. Consistent read buffer cloning and rollbacks, whenever needed, would have to be done inside the database layer. Whenever the Smart Scan hits a row, which still has its lock byte set (the row/block has not been cleaned out for reasons explained a little later), it has to switch into block I/O mode for this particular block and send the entire data block back to the database layer for normal consistent read processing—with the help of undo data available there. The lock-byte is set on the row level in a block, as seen in this excerpt from a block dump:

```
tab 0, row 0, @0x1b75
tl: 1035 fb: --H-FL-- lb: 0x2  cc: 6
col  0: [ 2]  c1 0b
col  1: [999]
 31 20 20 20 20...
```

This is the way Oracle implements row-level locking. The lock byte (lb) points to an entry in the block's Interested Transaction List (ITL). In this example, it is the second one:

```
Itl           Xid                  Uba         Flag  Lck        Scn/Fsc
0x01   0xffff.000.00000000  0x00000000.0000.00  C---    0  scn 0x0000.01d2ab27
0x02   0x000a.001.0000920f  0x00009f97.26c9.45  --U-    6  fsc 0x0000.01d2b741
0x03   0x0000.000.00000000  0x00000000.0000.00  ----    0  fsc 0x0000.00000000
```

Without going into too much detail, the second ITL entry shows a commit (Flag = U), and the transaction indicated by the Xid-column affects six rows in total, equaling the total number of rows in the block (nrows=6 in the block dump, not shown here). It also points to the undo record address (Uba) which is required to revert that change out of the block, but not available to the cell.

Note that when a block is cleaned out correctly (in other words, the lock bytes are cleared) and its cleanout SCN in the block header is from an earlier SCN than the query start time SCN (*snapshot SCN*), the cell knows that a rollback of that block would not be needed. The cleanout SCN is named csc in the block dump and indicates the last time a block was subject to a proper cleanout:

```
Block header dump:  0x017c21c3
 Object id on Block? Y
seg/obj: 0x12075  csc: 0x00.1d2ab27  itc: 3  flg: E  typ: 1 - DATA
     brn: 0  bdba: 0x17c21c0 ver: 0x01 opc: 0
     inc: 0  exflg: 0
```

If the latest change to that block happened before the query started, the block image in the cell is valid, a good enough block to satisfy the query with the given SCN. How does the cell know the starting SCN of a query executed in the database layer? That is the task of the storage-aware row sources in the execution plans, which communicate the SCN to cells over iDB when setting up Smart Scan sessions for themselves.

Now, when some of the rows do have some lock bytes set in the block or when the cleanout SCN in a block header happens to be higher than the query's snapshot SCN, the cells cannot determine the validity of the block/data version themselves and need to ship the block back to the database layer for regular, non-Smart Scan processing. This would considerably slow down the Smart Scan processing if such check had to be done for many locked rows and not cleaned-out blocks. However, there is an optimization that helps reducing the number of times the cell has to fall back to block I/O processing in the database layer.

Whenever a Smart Scan finds a locked row during a segment scan, it will check which transaction locked that row. This can easily be achieved by reading the transaction's ITL entry in the current data block header pointed to by the lock byte. Note that bitmap index segment blocks and HCC compressed blocks do not have a lock byte for each single row in the block, but the idea remains the same: Oracle is able to find out the transaction ID of the locked row(s) from the block at hand itself.

If the locked transaction has not committed yet, the Smart Scan falls back to block I/O mode for that block and the database layer will have to go through the normal consistent read buffer cloning/rollback mechanism, and there is no workaround for that. As you can see in the example that follows, having to fall back to block mode can have a noteworthy performance impact on the first execution of the query against the table with uncommitted transactions. Subsequent queries will not have to use physical I/O anymore to read the blocks from disk but can rely on the blocks available in the buffer cache. Nevertheless, the consistent read processing requires blocks to be rolled back.

If the transaction *has* already committed, but has left the lock bytes not cleaned out in some blocks (this usually happens after large updates and is called delayed block cleanout), the Smart Scan does not have to fall back to block I/O and an in-database, consistent read mechanism. It knows that this row is not really locked anymore, as the locking transaction has committed already, even though the lock byte is still in place.

How does the cell know if a given transaction has committed on RDBMS layer? This is achieved by caching the number of recently committed transactions in what is referred to as the commit cache. Without the commit cache, performance could suffer if you had a Smart Scan going over lots of rows with their lock byte still set. You definitely do not want the Smart Scan to ship blocks to the database layer every time it hits another locked row for consistent read processing. The commit cache might probably be just an in-memory hash-table, organized by transaction ID, and it keeps track of which transactions are committed and which are not. When the cell Smart Scan encounters a locked row, it will extract the transaction ID (from the ITL section of the data block), and it checks whether there is any information about that transaction in the commit cache. This check will increment the statistic *cell commit cache queries* by one. If there is no such transaction in the commit cache, then the Smart Scan is out of luck and has to perform consistent read processing by reverting to comparatively slow single block I/O processing. A cache hit, on the other hand, will increment the statistic *cell blocks helped by commit cache* by one.

To demonstrate the effect of the commit cache on queries, we have conducted a little test. To ensure that the test results were reproducible, we had to exert a little bit of force—the situation is exaggerated and you are unlikely to see similar effects in real production environments. (Who updates a very large table without a where clause?) First, a reasonably large table has been created with a size that would guarantee a Smart Scan when querying it. Next, an update in session 1 modified all blocks of this table to ensure delayed block cleanout, followed by a command to flush the buffer cache to disk. The blocks being forced to disk are not completely "cleared" for reasons explained in the next few paragraphs. Suffice to say at this point that the blocks are "dirty" and will require processing. Additionally, the active transaction that modified the blocks has not committed yet.

If anyone would query that table in its current state (for the first time), query elapsed time will be quite high. In the example, it took about 25 seconds:

```
SQL> select count(*) from t;

  COUNT(*)
----------
   1000000

Elapsed: 00:00:25.54
```

The reason is quickly identified in single-block reads. The table has been created with the storage clause set to explicitly not cache blocks in the Smart Flash Cache to ensure consistent read times. In current production systems, it is highly likely that the Flash Cache satisfies single-block reads though. Here are some important statistics for that query:

```
Statistic Name                                                              Value
---------------------------------------------------------------- ----------------
CPU used by this session                                                       22
active txn count during cleanout                                          166,672
cell blocks helped by minscn optimization                                       4
cell blocks processed by cache layer                                      167,961
cell blocks processed by data layer                                             4
cell blocks processed by txn layer                                              4
cell commit cache queries                                                 167,957
cell physical IO bytes eligible for predicate offload               1,365,409,792
cell physical IO interconnect bytes                                 1,528,596,408
cell physical IO interconnect bytes returned by smart scan          1,365,854,136
cell scans                                                                      1
cleanouts and rollbacks - consistent read gets                            166,672
consistent gets                                                         2,044,459
```

```
consistent gets direct                                                 166,676
data blocks consistent reads - undo records applied                  1,710,729
physical read total IO requests                                         22,459
physical read total multi block requests                                 1,838
```

These show that there was a lot of read-consistency processing involved. The number of multi-block reads was also quite low. Out of 22,459 I/O requests only 1,838 were multi-block reads—the rest, therefore, single-block I/O. You can also see that the cache layer opened 167,961 blocks in preparation for Smart Scan processing, but had to abandon that in all but four cases. (These four blocks were "helped" by `minscn` optimization, which you can read more about in the next section.) Also note that the number of bytes returned by Smart Scan is almost identical to the number of bytes eligible for predicate offload. In other words, there is no saving at all in doing I/O despite using a Smart Scan to access the data (the statistic "cell scans" is 1).

Subsequent executions of the same statement will no longer have to perform single-block I/O to read the "dirty" blocks from disk, but can make use of the blocks already in the buffer cache. Execution time for the second query against the table was down to 2.96 seconds. The same consistent read processing was required and still only four blocks were processed via Smart Scan. However, since the blocks have been read into the buffer cache, at least the physical I/O could be skipped. The recorded "CPU used for this session" was down from 499 to 277, and there were just a few single-block I/O requests visible. The number of block "cleanouts and rollbacks - consistent read gets" has not changed substantially, which was to be expected since the transaction has not committed.

When the user in session 1 commits, things improve for the queries against that table executed on Exadata. Non-Exadata platforms will not see a benefit here. The first execution of the query against the table then exhibits the following characteristics:

```
SQL> select count(*) from t;

  COUNT(*)
----------
   1000000

Elapsed: 00:00:01.52
```

The most relevant stats are shown here:

```
Statistic Name                                                            Value
---------------------------------------------------------------- ---------------
CPU used by this session                                                     22
cell blocks helped by commit cache                                      166,672
cell blocks helped by minscn optimization                                     4
cell blocks processed by cache layer                                    166,676
cell blocks processed by data layer                                     166,676
cell blocks processed by txn layer                                      166,676
cell commit cache queries                                               166,672
cell physical IO bytes eligible for predicate offload             1,365,409,792
cell physical IO interconnect bytes                                  26,907,936
cell physical IO interconnect bytes returned by smart scan           26,907,936
cell scans                                                                    1
cell transactions found in commit cache                                 166,672
consistent gets                                                         167,058
consistent gets direct                                                  166,676
physical read total IO requests                                           1,308
physical read total multi block requests                                  1,308
```

In comparison to the previous two executions of the query, you can see that Smart Scans occur for all blocks—thanks to the commit cache (166,672) and the four blocks benefiting from the minscn optimization. CPU usage is down to 22 from 499 previously, and all consistent gets are in direct mode. All I/O requests are multi-block reads, and there is a substantial saving in using the Smart Scan: Out of the approximately 1.3 GB eligible for predicate offload, only 26.9 MB are returned to the RDBMS layer.

In summary, an increase in the value of *cell blocks helped by commit cache* statistic when your sessions are performing a Smart Scan indicates that the cells have some overhead due to checking whether locked rows are really still locked in the commit cache. But, at the same time, you will not see a performance degradation. Without this optimization, the whole Smart Scan would slow down, as it must interact with the database layer. You would also see more logical I/O being done at the database layer (see the statistics starting with *consistent gets from cache*), as opposed to only a single LIO per segment for reading the extent locations and number of blocks under the high water mark out from the segment header.

■ **Note** A similar optimization actually exists also in the database layer and in non-Exadata databases. Oracle can cache the committed transaction information in the database session's private memory, so it won't have to perform buffer gets on the undo segment header when hitting many locked rows. Whenever a session caches a committed transaction's state in memory, it increments the *Commit SCN cached* statistic in its `V$SESSTAT` array. Whenever it does a lookup from that cache, it increments the *Cached Commit SCN referenced* statistic.

If you are not familiar with the delayed block cleanout mechanism in Oracle, you might have been wondering how Oracle blocks can have rows with their lock bytes still set after the transaction has already committed. This is how Oracle is different from most other mainstream commercial RDBMS products. Oracle does not have to keep the blocks with uncommitted rows cached in memory; database writer (DBWR) is free to write them out to disk and release the memory for other data blocks. Now, when committing the transaction, it would be inefficient to read all the transactions back from the disk just to clean up the lock bytes. If there were many such blocks, your commit time would increase to unacceptable levels. Instead, Oracle just marks the transaction complete in its undo segment header slot. Any future block readers can just check whether the transaction in that undo segment header slot is still alive or not. If you perform block I/O to read the data blocks to the database layer later on, the reading session would clean up the block (clear the lock bytes of rows modified by committed transactions), so no further transaction status checks would be needed in future reads. This is why during some queries you can see redo being generated.

However, storage cells do not perform block cleanouts—cells do not modify data blocks on their own because database block modifications require writing of redo operations. But how would a cell write to a redo log file that is managed and striped over many cells at the database layer? There is an interesting side effect to block cleanouts and direct path reads on non-Exadata platforms as well, since direct path reads do not make use of the buffer cache.

Note that for small transactions modifying only a few blocks, with most of the modified blocks still in the buffer cache, Oracle can perform block cleanout right during the commit time. Also, the issues just discussed do not apply to databases (data warehouses usually) where tables are loaded using direct path load inserts (and index partitions are built after the table partitions are loaded) because, in the case of direct path loads, the table rows are not locked in the newly formatted table blocks. The same applies to index entries in leaf blocks if an index is created after the data load.

cell blocks helped by minscn optimization

Exadata cell server has another optimization designed to improve consistent read efficiency even more. It is called the Minimum Active SCN optimization, and it keeps track of the lowest SCN of any still active (uncommitted) transaction in the database. This allows Oracle to easily compare the SCN in the ITL entries of the locking transactions with the lowest SCN of the "oldest" active transaction in the database.

As the Oracle database is able to send this MinSCN information to the cell when starting a Smart Scan session, the cells can avoid exchanging data with the database layer whenever the known minimum active SCN passed to the cell is higher than the SCN in the transaction's ITL entry in the block. Whenever the Smart Scan processes a block and finds a locked row with an active transaction in the ITL slot, it can conclude that the transaction must have committed. Thanks to the MinSCN passed by the database session, the *cell blocks helped by minscn optimization* statistic is incremented (once for each block).

Without this optimization, Oracle would have to check the commit cache (described in the *cell blocks helped by commit cache* statistic section). If it finds no information about this transaction in the commit cache, it would interact with the database layer to find out whether the locking transaction has already committed or not. This optimization is RAC-aware; in fact, the Minimum SCN is called Global Minimum SCN, and the MMON processes in each instance will keep track of the MinSCN and keep it synced in an in-memory structure in each node's SGA. You can query the current known global Minimum Active SCN from the `x$ktumascn` fixed table as shown here (as SYS):

```
SQL> COL min_act_scn FOR 99999999999999999
SQL>
SQL> SELECT min_act_scn FROM x$ktumascn;

       MIN_ACT_SCN
------------------
     9920890881859
```

This *cell blocks helped by minscn optimization* statistic is also something you should not be worried about, but it can come in handy when troubleshooting advanced Smart Scan issues, or even bugs, where Smart Scans seem to get interrupted because they have to fall back to block I/O and talk to the database too much.

cell blocks processed by cache layer

The *cell blocks processed by ... layer* statistics are good indicators of the *depth* of offload process in the cells. The main point and advantage of the Exadata storage servers is that part of the Oracle kernel code has been ported into the `cellsrv` executable running in the storage cells. In other words, processing and intelligence is brought to storage. This is what allows the Oracle database layer to offload the data scanning, filtering, and projection work into the cells. In order to do that, the cells must be able to read and understand Oracle data block and row contents, just as the database does. The *cell blocks processed by cache layer* statistic indicates how many data blocks the *cells* have processed (opened, read, and used for Smart Scan) as opposed to just passing the blocks read up to the database layer.

When a cell just passes the blocks back to the database in block I/O mode, this statistic is not updated. But when the cell itself uses these blocks for Smart Scan, one of the first things that is done when opening a block for a consistent read is to check the block cache layer header. This is to make sure it is the correct block, is not corrupt, and is valid and coherent. These tests are done by cache layer functions (KCB for Kernel Cache Buffer management) and reported back to the database as *cell blocks processed by cache layer*.

In the database layer, with regular block I/O, the corresponding statistics are *consistent gets from cache* and *consistent gets from cache (fastpath)* depending on which buffer pinning code path is used for the consistent buffer get. Note that `cellsrv` does only consistent mode buffer gets (CR reads) and no current mode block gets. So all the current mode gets you see in stats are done in the database layer and are reported as *db block gets from cache* or *db block gets from cache (fastpath)*. This statistic is a useful and simple measure of how many logical reads the `cellsrv` does for your sessions.

Note that it is entirely OK to see some database layer I/O processing during a SQL plan execution, as the plan is probably accessing multiple tables (and joining them). So, when doing a ten-table join between a large fact and nine dimension tables, you may well see that all of the dimensions are scanned using regular, cached block I/O (and using an index, if present), and only the large fact table access path will take advantage of the Smart Scan.

cell blocks processed by data layer

While the previous statistic counts all the block gets performed by the cache layer (KCB), this statistic is similar, but counts the blocks processed in the cell by the data layer. This statistic applies specifically to reading table blocks or materialized view blocks (which are physically just like table blocks). Information is collected using a data layer module, called KDS for Kernel Data Scan, which can extract rows and columns out of table blocks and pass them on to various evaluation functions for filtering and predicate checks. As with the database layer, the data layer in the cells is able to read a block and extract the relevant parts. It is also responsible for writing the result of the operation into an Exadata-specific format to be sent up to the database layer for processing using column simple projection and filtering techniques.

If the cell Smart Scan can do all of its processing in the cell without having to fall back to database block I/O mode, this *processed by data layer* statistic plus the processed by *index layer* statistic should add up to the *processed by cache layer* value for most Smart Scan processing. This means that every block actually opened made its way through the cache and transaction layer checks and was passed to the data or index layer for row and column extraction. If the *processed by data layer* plus *processed by index layer* statistics add up to a smaller value than the *processed by cache layer* statistic, it means that the rest of the blocks were not fully processed by the cell and had to be sent back to the database for regular block I/O processing.

cell blocks processed by index layer

This statistic is just like the preceding *cell blocks processed by data layer*, but it is incremented when Smart Scanning through B*Tree or bitmap index segment blocks. The code path for extracting rows out of index blocks is different from the code path executed for extracting rows from tables. The *cell blocks processed by index layer* counts how many index segment blocks were processed by a Smart Scan.

cell blocks processed by txn layer

This statistic shows how many blocks were processed in the cell by the transaction layer. Here is a simplified explanation of the sequence of actions during a consistent read for Smart Scan in a storage cell:

1. The cache layer (KCB) opens the data block and checks its header, last modification SCN, and cleanout status.
2. If the block in the cell has not been modified after the snapshot SCN of the query running the current Smart Scan, this block can be passed to the transaction layer for processing. However, if the block image on disk (cell) has been modified after the query's snapshot SCN, the cache layer already knows that this block has to be rolled back for consistent read. In this case, the block is not passed into the cell transaction layer at all, but the cell falls back to block I/O and passes that block to the database layer for normal consistent-read processing.

3. If the block is passed to the transaction layer (KTR) by the cache layer, the transaction layer can use the commit cache and MinActiveSCN optimization to avoid performing consistent-read processing to reduce the amount of communication with the database layer if it hits locked rows and not cleaned-out blocks of committed transactions. When there is no need to perform consistent-read processing in the database layer, the consistent reads will be performed by the data layer or index layer code inside the storage cell. However, if the consistent read cannot be completed within the cell, the entire data block at hand must be transported back to the database layer and the consistent read will be performed there.

The point of this explanation is that if the Smart Scans work optimally, they do not have to interrupt their work and exchange data with the database layer during the Smart Scan processing. Ideally, all the scanning work is done in the storage cell and, once enough rows are ready to be returned, they are sent to the database in a batch. If this is the case, then the *cell blocks processed by data layer* (or *index layer)* statistic will equal to the *cell blocks processed by cache layer* (and *txn layer*), showing that all the blocks could be fully processed in the cell and rows extracted from them without having to fall back to database-layer block I/O and consistent reads.

Remember that all this complexity related to consistent reads in storage cells matters only when doing a Smart Scan. When doing regular block I/O, cells just pass the blocks read directly back to the database layer, and the consistent read logic is executed in the database layer as usual. You should not really worry about these metrics unless you see that your Smart Scan wait events tend to be interspersed with *cell single block physical reads*, consuming a significant part of your query response time.

cell commit cache queries

This is the number of times the cell Smart Scan looked up a transaction status from the cell commit cache hash table. A lookup from commit cache is normally done once per uncommitted transaction found per block scanned by Smart Scan— where the MinActiveSCN optimization has not yet kicked in and eliminated the need to check for individual transaction statuses. This is closely related to the previously discussed *cell blocks helped by commit cache* statistic.

cell flash cache read hits

This statistic shows how many I/O requests were satisfied from the Cell Flash Cache so that a hard disk read was not necessary. Emphasis here is on "hard disk read," not just physical read. Reads from the PCIe flash cards also require physical reads (system calls resulting in flash card I/O), just like any read to a block device does in Linux. When you see this number, it means that the required blocks were not in the database layer buffer cache (or the access path chose to use a direct path read), but luckily some or even all the blocks required by an I/O request were in Cell Flash Cache. (The official term is *Exadata Smart Flash Cache.*)

Note that this number shows the number of I/O requests, not the number of blocks read from Cell Flash Cache. Remember that Cell Flash Cache is usable both by regular block reads and cell Smart Scans. For best performance, especially if you run an OLTP database on Exadata, you should attempt to satisfy most single-block reads from either the database buffer cache or, failing that, the Cell Flash Cache. You can read more about the Exadata Flash Cache in Chapter 5. Oracle decided that starting from cell version 11.2.3.3.x and later, the cells will Smart Scan from Flash Cache and disk concurrently by default and, if possible, without any change to the configuration.

cell index scans

This statistic is incremented every time a Smart Scan is started on a B*Tree or bitmap index segment. Note that in order to use Smart Scans on index segments, the *index fast full scan* execution plan row source operator must be used together with direct path reads. This statistic is updated at the start of a Smart Scan session. As a result, if you monitor its value for a session that has been executing a long-running query for a while, you might not see this statistic incrementing for your session.

When running just a serial session with Smart Scan on a nonpartitioned index segment, this statistic would be incremented by one. However, when running a Smart Scan on a partitioned index segment, the *cell index scans* statistic would be incremented for each partition scanned using Smart Scan. The decision whether a Smart Scan is attempted is evaluated for each segment of a partitioned or subpartitioned segment. The decision is made at runtime, for each segment (table, index or partition). Since Smart Scans require direct path reads to the PGA, and the direct path reads decision in turn is made based on the scanned segment size and other factors, different partitions of the same table accessed may be scanned using different methods. You might find that some partitions in your multipartition table or index are not scanned with Smart Scan/direct path reads, as Oracle has decided to use buffered reads for them thanks to their smaller size. In this case, the *cell index scans* statistic would not increment as much, and you would see the `cell multiblock physical read` wait event pop up at the table/index scan row source path in an ASH or SQL Monitoring report.

cell IO uncompressed bytes

This statistic shows the *uncompressed* size of the data scanned in the cell and is useful when scanning HCC compressed data. The statistic is best understood with an example. Consider the following table:

```
SQL> select segment_name, segment_type, bytes/power(1024,2) m, s.blocks,
  2  t.compression, t.compress_for
  3  from user_segments s, user_tables t
  4  where s.segment_name = t.table_name
  5  and segment_name = 'BIGTAB_QH';

SEGMENT_NAME                  SEGMENT_TYPE                M     BLOCKS COMPRESS COMPRESS_FOR
----------------------------- ------------------ ---------- ---------- -------- -----------
-
BIGTAB_QH                     TABLE                10209.75    1306848 ENABLED  QUERY HIGH
```

As you can see a table, named `BIGTAB_QH` is HCC compressed using the Query High algorithm. It takes about 10GB of disc space (compressed). For reference, the uncompressed table is about 20G in size. Considering a Smart Scan against this table reveals the following statistic counters relevant to this discussion. The statistics were captured with Snapper in a five-second interval. Reduced to the minimum information required:

```
sid username     statistic                                                     delta
297 MARTIN       physical read total IO requests                               9.68k
297 MARTIN       physical read total multi block requests                      9.68k
297 MARTIN       physical read requests optimized                              9.47k
297 MARTIN       physical read total bytes optimized                            9.9G
297 MARTIN       physical read total bytes                                    10.13G
297 MARTIN       physical reads                                                1.24M
297 MARTIN       physical reads direct                                         1.24M
```

```
297 MARTIN       physical read IO requests                              9.68k
297 MARTIN       physical read bytes                                   10.13G
297 MARTIN       cell scans                                                 1
297 MARTIN       cell blocks processed by cache layer                   1.24M
297 MARTIN       cell blocks processed by txn layer                     1.24M
297 MARTIN       cell blocks processed by data layer                    1.24M
297 MARTIN       cell blocks helped by minscn optimization              1.24M
297 MARTIN       cell CUs sent uncompressed                             4.46k
297 MARTIN       cell CUs processed for uncompressed                    4.46k
297 MARTIN       cell IO uncompressed bytes                            26.57G
```

Hence, if you scan through a 10GB compressed segment, the `physical read total bytes` statistic increases by approximately 10GB, but the `cell I/O uncompressed bytes` increases by 26.57 GB, reflecting the total uncompressed size of the data scanned. This statistic is incremented only when performing a Smart Scan compression offloading, not when you read the compressed blocks directly to the database layer with block I/O. Interestingly, the statistic is populated when Smart Scanning uncompressed segments, too.

cell num fast response sessions

This statistic shows how many times Oracle started the Smart Scan code but then chose not to set up the Smart Scan session immediately. Instead, chose to do a few block I/O operations first, hoping to find enough rows to satisfy the database session. This optimization is used `for FIRST ROWS` execution plan options, either when using a `FIRST_ROWS_n` hint (or equivalent `init.ora` parameter) or a `WHERE rownum < X` condition, which may also enable the first rows option in execution plans. The idea is that if fetching only a few rows, Oracle hopes to avoid the overhead of setting up a cell Smart Scan session (with all the cells, thanks to ASM striping), but it will do a few regular block I/O operations first. Following is an example of a first-rows optimization using the `ROWNUM` predicate:

```
select * from t3 where owner like 'S%' and rownum <= 10

Plan hash value: 3128673074

-------------------------------------------------------------------------------
| Id  | Operation                             | Name | E-Rows | Cost (%CPU)|
-------------------------------------------------------------------------------
|   0 | SELECT STATEMENT                      |      |        |     4 (100)|
|*  1 |  COUNT STOPKEY                        |      |        |            |
|*  2 |   TABLE ACCESS STORAGE FULL FIRST ROWS | T3   |     11 |     4   (0)|
-------------------------------------------------------------------------------

Predicate Information (identified by operation id):
---------------------------------------------------

   1 - filter(ROWNUM<=10)
   2 - storage("OWNER" LIKE 'S%')
       filter("OWNER" LIKE 'S%')
```

If you ran Snapper at the same time as this query, you are likely to see the `cell num fast response sessions` incremented, as Oracle has tried to avoid the Smart Scan session setup:

```
NAME                                                            VALUE
--------------------------------------------------------------- ----------
cell num fast response sessions                                          1
cell num fast response sessions continuing to smart scan                 0
```

The cell fast response feature is controlled by the `_kcfis_fast_response_enabled` parameter and enabled by default.

cell num fast response sessions continuing to smart scan

This statistic shows how many times the cell Smart Scan fast response session was started, but Oracle had to switch to the real Smart Scan session because it did not find enough matching rows with the first few I/O operations. The next example builds on the previous one, but adds an additional predicate to the query:

```
select * from t3 where owner like 'S%' and object_name LIKE '%non-existent%'
and rownum <= 10

Plan hash value: 3128673074

----------------------------------------------------------------------------
| Id  | Operation                              | Name | E-Rows | Cost (%CPU)|
----------------------------------------------------------------------------
|   0 | SELECT STATEMENT                       |      |        |     9 (100)|
|*  1 |  COUNT STOPKEY                         |      |        |            |
|*  2 |   TABLE ACCESS STORAGE FULL FIRST ROWS| T3   |     10 |     9   (0)|
----------------------------------------------------------------------------

Predicate Information (identified by operation id):
---------------------------------------------------

   1 - filter(ROWNUM<=10)
   2 - storage(("OBJECT_NAME" LIKE '%non-existent%' AND "OWNER" LIKE
              'S%' AND "OBJECT_NAME" IS NOT NULL))
       filter(("OBJECT_NAME" LIKE '%non-existent%' AND "OWNER" LIKE
              'S%' AND "OBJECT_NAME" IS NOT NULL))
```

Watching the statistics with Snapper shows that the number of fast response sessions continuing to Smart Scan increased:

```
NAME                                                            VALUE
--------------------------------------------------------------- ----------
cell num fast response sessions                                          1
cell num fast response sessions continuing to smart scan                 1
```

cell num smart IO sessions using passthru mode due to *reason*

There are three related statistics counters where *reason* can be either `user`, `cellsrv`, or `timezone` to indicate how many times the Oracle database initiated a Smart Scan but then failed to execute it. In 11.2.0.4 and 12.1.0.2, you get the actual amount of data sent via passthrough mode as well. It is recorded in *cell num bytes in passthru during predicate offload*. In such a case, `cellsrv` did not start a Smart Scan and fell back entirely to block I/O mode. The blocks read are just passed through to the database, instead of processing them within the cell. This means that while you still see the `cell Smart Scan` wait events and *cell physical IO interconnect bytes returned by smart scan* increasing (which indicates that a Smart Scan is happening), the full power of Smart Scan is not utilized, as the cells just read data blocks and return the blocks back to the database layer and into the session's PGA. In other words, in passthrough mode, the cells do not open data blocks and extract only the required columns of matching rows, but return all the physical blocks of the segment as they are. Note that storage indexes can be used to eliminate I/O in passthrough mode, but remember that these indexes must first be populated by a regular Smart Scan. With the possibility that there is no Smart Scan in the first place, this will be difficult. If the segment being scanned is cached on Flash Cache, you will see it being used.

You should not see any passthrough Smart Scans happening on the latest database and Exadata cell versions unless you have problems like cells running out of memory. You can test what happens with passthrough mode in a test environment by setting `_kcfis_cell_passthru_enabled` to `TRUE` in your session and running a Smart Scan. You will still see `cell smart scan` wait events for your Smart Scans, but they are slower because they are returning all the blocks to the database for processing. The only time we saw this problem systematically was when 12c RDBMS was released and certified on Exadata, but on-cell software version did not support any offloading.

We also saw a *cell num smart IO sessions using passthru* mode due to timezone once where the timezone upgrade failed and was stuck. If `cellsrv` is almost out of memory, you will see counters increasing where the reason is `cellsrv`.

■ **Note** Cell num smart IO sessions using passthrough mode due to reason are tricky to detect. Most performance tools will show you the cell smart table scan even, and other statistics often used to work out if a Smart Scan happened are incremented just with a working Smart Scan. The Real Time SQL Monitor (covered in Chapter 12) for RDBMS 12c now shows information about passthrough mode in the "other data" column.

---

cell overwrites in flash cache

This particular session statistic has been introduced in Oracle 11.2.0.4. It is also visible in Oracle 12.1.0.2, but not in 12.1.0.1. Up until the introduction of Write-Back Flash Cache (WBFC) in 11.2.3.2.x, there was no need to worry about writes to Flash Cache. The Cell Smart Flash Cache was primarily used to speed up reads in OLTP-style workloads and, beginning with cell version 11.2.3.3.x, it was additionally and systematically used for Smart Scans as well. If you wanted to measure the benefit of Flash Cache on your workload, you could check the value for *cell flash cache read hits*, described earlier. Alternatively, you could consider *physical read requests optimized* as well as *physical read total bytes optimized*, but these two statistics would include information from storage indexes as well.

Writes are different. For quite some time after the introduction of WBFC, there was no statistic available to measure writes to Flash Cache. This changed with 11.2.0.4, and a few new statistics were introduced such as the following:

- Cell overwrites in Flash Cache
- Cell partial writes in Flash Cache
- Physical writes optimized

Considering a 12.1.0.2 system with WBFC enabled on all the cells, you can see that Oracle background processes are responsible for a lot of these writes. If you want to capture user sessions writing to WBFC, you need to do so before they disconnect. Here is an example on our 12.1.1.1.1 cell/12.1.0.2 RDBMS system:

```
SQL> select se.sid, sn.name, s.value, se.program
     from v$sesstat s natural join v$statname sn
     left join v$session se on (s.sid = se.sid)
     where sn.name in (
       'physical write requests optimized',
       'cell writes to flash cache',
       'cell overwrites in flash cache')
     and s.value <> 0
     order by s.sid,name;

       SID NAME                                   VALUE PROGRAM
---------- ----------------------------------- ---------- -----------------------------------
         1 cell overwrites in flash cache            6258 oracle@enkdb03.enkitec.com (DBW1)
         1 cell writes to flash cache               10848 oracle@enkdb03.enkitec.com (DBW1)
         1 physical write requests optimized         5405 oracle@enkdb03.enkitec.com (DBW1)
        66 cell overwrites in flash cache            9894 oracle@enkdb03.enkitec.com (DBW2)
        66 cell writes to flash cache               15218 oracle@enkdb03.enkitec.com (DBW2)
        66 physical write requests optimized         7593 oracle@enkdb03.enkitec.com (DBW2)
       132 cell overwrites in flash cache              94 oracle@enkdb03.enkitec.com (LGWR)
       132 cell writes to flash cache                 218 oracle@enkdb03.enkitec.com (LGWR)
       132 physical write requests optimized           38 oracle@enkdb03.enkitec.com (LGWR)
       197 cell overwrites in flash cache           62991 oracle@enkdb03.enkitec.com (CKPT)
       197 cell writes to flash cache               62991 oracle@enkdb03.enkitec.com (CKPT)
       197 physical write requests optimized        20997 oracle@enkdb03.enkitec.com (CKPT)
       262 cell writes to flash cache                2300 oracle@enkdb03.enkitec.com (LG00)
       262 physical write requests optimized           76 oracle@enkdb03.enkitec.com (LG00)
       392 cell writes to flash cache                   3 oracle@enkdb03.enkitec.com (LG01)
       392 physical write requests optimized            1 oracle@enkdb03.enkitec.com (LG01)
       782 cell overwrites in flash cache            3510 oracle@enkdb03.enkitec.com (MMON)
       782 cell writes to flash cache                3552 oracle@enkdb03.enkitec.com (MMON)
       782 physical write requests optimized         1184 oracle@enkdb03.enkitec.com (MMON)
       977 cell overwrites in flash cache              63 oracle@enkdb03.enkitec.com (LMON)
       977 cell writes to flash cache                  63 oracle@enkdb03.enkitec.com (LMON)
       977 physical write requests optimized           21 oracle@enkdb03.enkitec.com (LMON)
      1496 cell overwrites in flash cache           11502 oracle@enkdb03.enkitec.com (DBW0)
      1496 cell writes to flash cache               17822 oracle@enkdb03.enkitec.com (DBW0)
      1496 physical write requests optimized         8888 oracle@enkdb03.enkitec.com (DBW0)
```

```
      1498 cell overwrites in flash cache                33 oracle@enkdb03.enkitec.com (ARC0)
      1498 cell writes to flash cache                    33 oracle@enkdb03.enkitec.com (ARC0)
      1498 physical write requests optimized             11 oracle@enkdb03.enkitec.com (ARC0)
28 rows selected.
```

Note how the writes to Flash Cache are approximately twice the writes reported by RDBMS; this is caused by the ASM mirroring. The ASM disk groups on this system are created with normal redundancy.

cell physical IO bytes eligible for predicate offload

This performance counter holds one of the most important statistics for understanding Smart Scan. When you are Smart Scanning through a segment, this statistic shows how many bytes of that segment the Smart Scan would go through if returning every single bit of it. Essentially, this statistic covers all the bytes from the beginning of the segment all the way to its high water mark (as the scanning progresses through the entire segment). The catch is that this is the theoretical maximum number of bytes to scan through, but it does not account for storage indexes that potentially allow Smart Scan to skip data on disk.

Even if the storage index allows you to avoid scanning 80 percent of a 10GB segment, reducing the actual I/O amount to only 2GB, this statistic still shows the *total* size of the segment scanned, regardless of any optimizations. Experience from the field teaches that this is often the case. You need to keep an eye out on the *cell physical IO bytes saved by storage index* statistic, as shown here:

```
sid username       statistic                                                   delta
790 MARTIN         cell physical IO interconnect bytes                         3.19M
790 MARTIN         cell physical IO bytes eligible for predicate offload      21.85G
790 MARTIN         cell physical IO bytes saved by storage index                2.1M
790 MARTIN         cell physical IO interconnect bytes returned by smart scan  3.19M
790 MARTIN         cell num smartio automem buffer allocation attempts             1
790 MARTIN         cell scans                                                      1
790 MARTIN         cell blocks processed by cache layer                        2.67M
790 MARTIN         cell blocks processed by txn layer                          2.67M
790 MARTIN         cell blocks processed by data layer                         2.67M
790 MARTIN         cell blocks helped by minscn optimization                   2.67M
790 MARTIN         cell IO uncompressed bytes                                 21.84G
790 MARTIN         cell flash cache read hits                                 18.95k
```

Do not worry about the other statistics shown here—they are part of this chapter as well. Note that *cell physical IO bytes eligible for predicate offload* simply counts the physical size of the segment in the data blocks in data files and not the "eventual" data size after any decompression, filtering, or projection.

If this number does not increase for your session's V$SESSTAT (or Statspack/AWR data when looking at the whole instance), then this is another indicator that Smart Scans are not used. Any block ranges scanned through, or even skipped (thanks to storage index optimizations), by a Smart Scan session should increment this statistic. Another fact worth knowing is that when a Smart Scan falls back to passthrough (full-block shipping) mode (described earlier), the *cell physical IO bytes eligible for predicate offload* statistic is incremented regardless, although there is no predicate offloading and Smart Scan filtering done in the cell in passthrough mode.

cell physical IO bytes saved by storage index

This is another important statistic, which shows how many bytes the Smart Scan sessions could simply skip reading chunks of data from disk, thanks to the in-memory storage index in `cellsrv`. This statistic, *cell physical IO bytes saved by storage index* is closely related to *cell physical IO bytes eligible for predicate offload.* If the ratio of the two is close to 1, you have a clear indication that Smart Scans greatly benefit from storage indexes and have avoided a lot of I/O thanks to that. Remember from Chapter 4 that storage indexes are not a persistent structure: They can evolve over time and are not guaranteed to always be available.

Please also be aware that the statistic is cumulative. If you would like to investigate how many bytes could be skipped thanks to the storage index, you need to get the current value of the statistic prior to the execution of the SQL statement and right after it finished to calculate the difference between the two. The statistic is also rolled up into physical read requests optimized and physical read total bytes optimized.

cell physical IO bytes sent directly to DB node to balance CPU

If this statistic shows up—for example, during a run of Snapper—it is a sign of problems on the storage servers. Under certain conditions, such as when the cells are heavily CPU bound and there are spare CPU cycles in the RDBMS layer, the latter can take care of decompressing CUs for it. There is a certain amount of communication between the RDBMS and the storage layer, including exchanges of CPU-related information. If a cell is CPU bound, it may send columns or entire CUs back uncompressed.

Seeing counters increment for this statistic is a sign of problems on the system, and you should investigate why the cells are so CPU bound. The use of `dcli` is a good starting point to investigate CPU load. If the problem is local to a cell, it is worth connecting to it and performing additional troubleshooting. Note that this is purely a CPU problem and not necessarily disk/memory related. Different statistics exist for these.

cell physical IO interconnect bytes

This is a simple, but fundamental statistic, which shows how many bytes worth of any data have been transmitted between the storage cells and your database sessions. This includes all data—both sent and received by the database—the Smart Scan result sets, full blocks read from the cells, temporary I/O reads and writes, log writes, any supplementary iDB traffic, and so on. So, this statistic shows *all traffic (in bytes),* regardless of its direction, contents, or nature.

When measuring the write I/O metrics, it is completely normal to see the *cell physical I/O interconnect bytes* statistic two or three times higher than the *physical write total bytes* statistic. This is because the latter statistic is measured at the Oracle database level, but the *cell physical I/O interconnect bytes* is measured at the cell level, after ASM mirroring has been done. If, for example, LGWR writes 1MB to an ASM disk group with high redundancy (triple mirroring), a total of 3MB of data would be sent over the interconnect.

cell physical IO interconnect bytes returned by smart scan

This important statistic shows how many bytes of data were returned to the database layer by Smart Scans. For Smart Scans to be most efficient, the number of bytes actually returned should be far less than the bytes scanned (in other words, read from disk). This is the main point of the Exadata Smart Scan feature—the cells may read gigabytes of data every second, but as they perform early filtering thanks to predicate offloading, they may send only a small part of the rows back to the database layer. Additionally, owed to projection offloading, the Smart Scans only return the requested columns back, not full rows. Of course, if the application uses `SELECT *` for fetching all the columns of a table, projection offloading would not help, but the early filtering using predicate offloading can still be very useful.

This statistic is a subset of the *cell physical I/O interconnect bytes* statistic, but it counts only the bytes that are returned by Smart Scan sessions and no other traffic. You may see *cell physical I/O interconnect bytes* reported greater than *cell physical I/O interconnect bytes returned by smart scan* in case of sorting to disk, for example.

cell scans

This statistic is similar in nature to *cell index scans*, but *cell scans* shows the number of Smart Scans done on table and materialized view segments, including their partitions. With serial execution, this statistic is incremented once at the beginning of every segment scan. When scanning through a partitioned table, in which each partition is a separate segment, this statistic would be incremented for each partition. With parallel scans, the `cell scans` statistic will increment even more, as parallel slaves perform their scans on block ranges (PX granules) handed over to them by the query coordinator. Hence, the scan on each block range is reported as a separate `cell scan`. The presence of the *table scans (rowid ranges)* statistic indicates that PX scans on block ranges are occurring.

cell smart IO session cache hits

This statistic shows how many times a database session managed to reuse a previously initialized Smart Scan session in the cell. This statistic shows up when a single execution plan scans through multiple segments (like with partitioned tables) or revisits the same segment during a single execution.

cell smart IO session cache lookups

This statistic is incremented every time a database session tried to reuse a previously initialized Smart Scan session in the cell. If the *cell smart IO session cache hits* statistic increments, too, the lookup was successful and a previous session context can be reused. The smart I/O session caching works only within an execution (and subsequent fetches) of an open cursor. Once the execution finishes, the next executions, even of the same cursor, would have to set up new Smart Scan sessions and communicate the new consistent-read snapshot SCN to the cells, too.

cell transactions found in commit cache

This statistic is related to the consistent-read (CR) mechanism Oracle has to guarantee, even on Exadata. It shows how many times the Smart Scan sessions checked the cell commit cache to decide whether a CR rollback is needed or not, and found the transaction status information in the cell commit cache. This avoids a round trip to the database layer to check that transaction's status using undo data available there. You can read more about how the consistent reads work with Exadata Smart Scans in the *cell blocks helped by commit cache* statistic section.

chained rows processed by cell

Before explaining what this specific statistic means, let's look at what chained rows are and how Smart Scans deal with chained rows. There are a few special cases where rows move from one block to another, or "span" blocks. Oracle has to manage rows that are too big to fit into a block. And it also has to deal with rows that grow, for example, by updates on a `varchar2`-column that initially held only a few characters but is updated to a few hundred.

Row chaining implies that a row is distributed or spread across more than one block. Technically speaking, a row is divided into row pieces. In many cases, the head piece and the rest of the row are in the same block, which benefits Exadata processing. Row chaining happens most often with large rows and is the price for processing a lot of data in a row. With a chained row, the head piece is in, say, block x and the rest of the row is in blocks y and z. Each piece of the row has a pointer to the next one, called an NRID (next ROWID). This is quite logical: If you want to store 100kb-rows, then you simply cannot squeeze these into an 8k block, and row chaining is unavoidable. You can see this in a block dump. The table has been created using this statement:

```
CREATE TABLE chaines2
(
  id, a, b, c, d, e
) as
WITH v1 as (
  SELECT rownum n FROM dual CONNECT BY level <= 10000
)
SELECT  rownum id,
rpad('a',1980,'*'),
rpad('b',1980,'*'),
rpad('c',1980,'*'),
rpad('d',1980,'*'),
rpad('e',1980,'*')
FROM v1,
  v1
WHERE rownum <= 100000;
```

Checking the rows, you see that they are spread across blocks:

```
Start dump data blocks tsn: 5 file#:5 minblk 2132987 maxblk 2132987
[...]
block_row_dump:
tab 0, row 0, @0x22
tl: 7225 fb: --H-F--N lb: 0x0  cc: 5
nrid:  0x01608bfc.0
col  0: [ 2]  c1 02
col  1: [1980]
 61 2a 2a 2a 2a 2a 2a 2a 2a 2a 2a 2a 2a 2a 2a 2a 2a 2a 2a 2a 2a 2a 2a 2a 2a
[...]
col  2: [1980]
 62 2a 2a 2a 2a 2a 2a 2a 2a 2a 2a 2a 2a 2a 2a 2a 2a 2a 2a 2a 2a 2a 2a 2a 2a
[...]
col  3: [1980]
 63 2a 2a 2a 2a 2a 2a 2a 2a 2a 2a 2a 2a 2a 2a 2a 2a 2a 2a 2a 2a 2a 2a 2a 2a
[...]
col  4: [1261]
64 2a 2a 2a 2a 2a 2a 2a 2a 2a 2a 2a 2a 2a 2a 2a 2a 2a 2a 2a 2a 2a 2a 2a 2a
end_of_block_dump
```

Not all of the columns fit into the row, only up to two-thirds of column d. The row has to be continued in a different block since the remainder of column d as well as column e needs to be represented. This is expressed in the row header information, more specifically in the flag: `--H-F--N`. It translates into the (H)ead piece, the (F)irst piece and (N)ext pieces and reads: The row's head piece and first pieces are in this block, but there is another part of the row in a different block. How does Oracle find that next block? The information is encoded in the NRID, which is the block address. The NRID in this example is 0x01608bfc.0. The first bit of the hexadecimal number is the block address; the last part (.0) is the nth row in that block. `DBMS_UTILITY` has a set of functions allowing us to decode the NRID to a file and block address:

```
SQL> select
  2    dbms_utility.data_block_address_file(to_number('01608bfc','xxxxxxxxxxxxx')) fno,
  3    dbms_utility.data_block_address_block(to_number('01608bfc','xxxxxxxxxxxx')) blockno
  3  from dual;

       FNO    BLOCKNO
---------- ----------
         5    2132988
```

If you dump that block as well, you will see that the row continues:

```
Start dump data blocks tsn: 5 file#:5 minblk 2132988 maxblk 2132988
[...]
block_row_dump:
tab 0, row 0, @0x14ec
tl: 2708 fb: -----LP- lb: 0x0  cc: 2
col  0: [719]
[...]
col  1: [1980]
[...]
tab 0, row 1, @0x18
tl: 4527 fb: --H-F--N lb: 0x0  cc: 4
nrid:  0x01608bfd.0
col  0: [ 2]  c1 03
```

Row migration is a different case and has to deal with situations where an update forces a row out of its current location and into another block. Only the head piece remains in the old locations, and it has a forward pointer to the rest of the row. Very often, updates are the culprits for migrated rows. Before the update, you could see that the entire row was co-located in the block:

```
Start dump data blocks tsn: 5 file#:5 minblk 131 maxblk 131
block_row_dump:
tab 0, row 0, @0x1f7a
tl: 6 fb: --H-FL-- lb: 0x0  cc: 1
col  0: [ 2]  c1 02
tab 0, row 1, @0x1f71
```

After the update, the same block looks quite different:

```
Start dump data blocks tsn: 5 file#:5 minblk 131 maxblk 131
block_row_dump:
tab 0, row 0, @0x1f77
tl: 9 fb: --H----- lb: 0x2  cc: 0
nrid:  0x01603167.0
tab 0, row 1, @0x1f6e
```

The migrated row does not even have a single column in the original location (cc: 0); only a NRID remains.

Chained rows pose a problem for Smart Scans. The chained row's "next" row pieces may be anywhere in the segment. Thanks to ASM striping, it is not guaranteed that the next row pieces of a chained row are in the same cell where the row's head piece is located. So, a chained row may be physically split across multiple different cells. Given that cells never communicate with each other during Smart Scans, how would you be able to construct the full row when needed? The way `cellsrv` currently solves this problem is that whenever the Smart Scan hits a chained row (and realizes it has to fetch its next row piece), `cellsrv` falls back to regular block I/O for that row and sends the block back to the database layer for normal processing *if* it cannot locate the NRID in the chunk of data it is currently scanning. In this case-NRID found-the statistic *chained rows processed by cell* is incremented.

If the NRID is *not* in the current chunk of data Smart Scan is processing, the block must be sent to the RDBMS layer for processing. Once it has been received, the database layer can extract the data block address of the next row piece from the row head piece and issue the block read I/O to the appropriate cell where the ASM striping has physically put that block. The reasoning and fundamental problem behind this optimization is similar to why consistent-read rollbacks have to be done in the database layer as opposed to a cell—some of the data blocks required for this operation may just happen to be located in another cell, and cells never talk to other cells. The RDBMS layer must then issue a single block read to the block indicated with the NRID and process it further.

This behavior means that your Smart Scan performance may drop if it hits a lot of chained rows and has to fetch their next row pieces. If you get lucky and access only the columns that are present in the head piece of the row, you do not have to fall back to database block I/O mode for these blocks and your Smart Scans will be fast.

■ **Note** Remember this the next time you add a column to a table! It might be more efficient from a Smart Scan perspective to perform a table re-organization and put the most heavily accessed columns first. Alternatively, if your data is not too hot, you can consider using HCC instead where these restrictions are softened.

If you have to fetch the next row pieces constantly, then your Smart Scan will be constantly interrupted, falling back to block I/O, and the database layer starts doing logical reads (and possibly single-block physical reads as well, if these blocks are not cached in buffer cache). This means that your query ends up waiting most of its time for random single-block reads as opposed to high-performance Smart Scanning. Here is a five-second snap(er) of a session that has to fight with a lot of chained rows in a contrived and unrealistic worst-case scenario:

```
sid username    statistic                                              delta
297 MARTIN      table scan rows gotten                                22.47k
297 MARTIN      table fetch continued row                              4.95k
297 MARTIN      cell blocks processed by cache layer                  27.43k
297 MARTIN      cell blocks processed by txn layer                    27.43k
297 MARTIN      cell blocks processed by data layer                   24.73k
```

```
    297 MARTIN       cell blocks helped by minscn optimization                          27.43k
    297 MARTIN       chained rows skipped by cell                                       14.84k
    297 MARTIN       chained rows processed by cell                                         11
    297 MARTIN       chained rows rejected by cell                                          19

--------------------------------------------------------------------------------------------
Active% | INST | SQL_ID          | SQL_CHILD | EVENT                          | WAIT_CLASS
--------------------------------------------------------------------------------------------
    58% |    1 | 3bm2yp12vtyja   | 0         | cell single block physical read | User I/O
     5% |    1 | 3bm2yp12vtyja   | 0         | ON CPU                         | ON CPU
     5% |    1 | 3bm2yp12vtyja   | 0         | cell smart table scan          | User I/O
```

This chained-row performance problem applies only to regular data blocks and those compressed with regular block-level compression (BASIC or ADVANCED). Luckily, it is not a problem for HCC compressed tables at all, as in EHCC the rows and columns are physically organized differently. Also, this issue does not apply to migrated rows when full-scanning through a segment. The full scan/Smart Scan just ignores the head pieces of migrated rows, as the entire row is physically elsewhere. Note that updates can have side effects for HCC compressed tables, as explained in Chapter 3, even though chained rows are not a problem.

Another interesting case of row-chaining peculiarities is when you have over 255 columns in a table. Even when the total row size is small enough to fit inside a single block, with over 255 columns, Oracle would still do *intra-block chaining*, in which the row is chained but all the row pieces are physically inside the same block. This was needed because Oracle wanted to maintain backward compatibility when it increased the column limit from 255 to 1000 in Oracle 8.0. The "column count" byte in a row piece is just one byte, allowing 255 columns per row piece, but thanks to chaining you can have more columns in next row piece(s). Co-author Tanel Poder has an interesting case study related to this situation on his blog at `blog.tanelpoder.com`.

chained rows rejected by cell

This statistic shows how many chained rows were not processed in the cell. This statistic should be rarely incremented. In Smart Scan processing, the cells will place the result of the sliced and diced block in an output buffer before sending the result to the querying session's PGA. Whenever the result of chained row processing on the cell does not fit into this output buffer, the statistic is incremented by one.

chained rows skipped by cell

This is the most important statistic when it comes to troubleshooting chained rows processing on Exadata, together with *table fetch continued row*. A simple test can demonstrate this better. This is a SQL query against a table with row chaining in every block:

```
SQL> select id, count(e) from chaines_big where a like 'a%' and id < 11 group by id;
```

On anther session, a five-second snap has been executed specifically to include only the two statistics to be covered in this section:

```
SQL> @snapper4 all,gather=s,sinclude=fetch|chain|consistent|cell 5 1 297
```

The result can be seen here, reformatted:

```
sid username     statistic                                                   delta
297 MARTIN       cell physical IO interconnect bytes                       167.52M
297 MARTIN       consistent gets                                            45.85k
297 MARTIN       consistent gets from cache                                  7.68k
297 MARTIN       consistent gets direct                                     38.17k
297 MARTIN       cell physical IO bytes eligible for predicate offload     318.92M
297 MARTIN       cell physical IO interconnect bytes returned by smart scan 106.65M
297 MARTIN       no work - consistent read gets                              7.68k
297 MARTIN       table fetch continued row                                   7.68k
297 MARTIN       cell blocks processed by cache layer                       43.75k
297 MARTIN       cell blocks processed by txn layer                         43.75k
297 MARTIN       cell blocks processed by data layer                        38.54k
297 MARTIN       cell blocks helped by minscn optimization                  43.76k
297 MARTIN       chained rows skipped by cell                               28.03k
297 MARTIN       chained rows processed by cell                                 34
297 MARTIN       chained rows rejected by cell                                  21
297 MARTIN       cell IO uncompressed bytes                                316.74M
297 MARTIN       cell flash cache read hits                                  8.09k

--  End of Stats snap 1, end=2014-08-12 06:50:13, seconds=4.8


---------------------------------------------------------------------------------------------
Active% | INST | SQL_ID          | SQL_CHILD | EVENT                             | WAIT_CLASS
---------------------------------------------------------------------------------------------
    93% |    1 | 16srfqdur1bxg   | 0         | cell single block physical read   | User I/O
     7% |    1 | 16srfqdur1bxg   | 0         | ON CPU                            | ON CPU

--  End of ASH snap 1, end=2014-08-12 06:50:13, seconds=5, samples_taken=44
```

As you can see from the above output, Oracle has skipped about 28,000 chained rows in the cell and sent them to RDBMS for regular processing. Another indicator of the problem is the relatively high number for *table fetch continued row*.

Also note how the `consistent gets` value, which counts all CR gets done both in the database *and* in cell by Smart Scan, is a little more than 45,000. At the same time, the subcounters, *consistent gets from cache* (CR gets performed by the database layer, from buffer cache), and *consistent gets direct* (consistent gets bypassing the buffer cache) indicate how much of the CR work was done at the cell level and how much was additionally done at the database level.

As a conclusion about chained rows, the next time you see that your Smart Scan is waiting for lots of `cell single block physical reads` and is doing logical I/O inside the database layer (*consistent gets from cache*), one of the things to check is the abovementioned statistics to see whether you are hitting chained rows and have to process them in the database. Of course, do not forget that the Smart Scans offload only the large segment scan workload, but if your query plan contains other row sources, index range scans, or small, cached table scans, seeing logical I/Os and single-block physical reads is expected. You can use wait interface data in ASH, `V$SESSION`, or SQL Trace—depending on your licenses—to see against which objects these single-block reads accessed. The `current_obj#` column in ASH, and `obj#` field in raw SQL trace file refer to the `object_id` of the table (or index or partition) the session is reading from.

EHCC Related Counters

As you read in the introduction to this chapter, it is not possible to cover every single HCC related counter in this section as there are simply too many. Instead, HCC processing is put into perspective with the rest of the contents. In summary, there are two scenarios for HCC processing in Exadata. The first case is a Smart Scan where the cells take over the decompression of CUs and pass only relevant information to the RDBMS layer. In this scenario, you will find counters named *cell CU%* incremented. These are incremented on the cell level. Additionally, you will notice counters named *EHCC%* being incremented as well, which can lead to double counting as you can see later. These *EHCC%* counters are related to HCC processing on the RDBMS layer.

If you find *EHCC%* counters incremented but not *cell CU%*, your query was not offloaded. In other words, there was no Smart Scanning involved. The HCC processing, therefore, needs to happen entirely on the RDBMS layer. Oracle has instrumented the compression and decompression of HCC data quite well. Consider, for example, the creation of a HCC compressed table. Logging into a new session has reset the *EHCC%* counters.

```
SQL> create table t1_qh column store compress for query high as select * from t1;
```

A quick query reveals the result:

```
SQL> !cat hcc_stats.sql
select name, value value_bytes, round(value/power(1024,2),2)  value_mb
from v$statname natural join v$mystat
where (name like '%EHCC%' or name like 'cell CU%')
and value <> 0;
SQL> @hcc_stats

NAME                                                             VALUE_BYTES       VALUE_MB
---------------------------------------------------------------- --------------- --------------
EHCC CUs Compressed                                                         2148              0
EHCC Query High CUs Compressed                                              2148              0
EHCC Compressed Length Compressed                                       67439392          64.32
EHCC Decompressed Length Compressed                                  10709897349       10213.75
EHCC Rows Compressed                                                    10349046           9.87
EHCC CU Row Pieces Compressed                                               9899            .01
EHCC Analyzer Calls                                                            1              0

7 rows selected.
```

Translated into English, this means that 2148 CUs were compressed, all of them with the Query High algorithm. The data could be shrunk to about 64MB as opposed to 10,214MB uncompressed, which is a nice saving. The statistics indicated that a little more than one million rows were compressed into 9899 CU row pieces. The compression analyzer—explained in Chapter 3 in detail—was invoked once, because there is only one nonpartitioned table to compress.

Querying data shows a different picture as opposed to the table creation just demonstrated. Here is an example of a segment scan that was not offloaded (the *cell CU%* counters have already been discussed and will not be shown here):

```
SQL> select /* gather_plan_statistics test002 */ count(id),id
  2    from t1_qh group by id having count(id) > 100000;

no rows selected
```

```
SQL> @hcc_stats

NAME                                                             VALUE_BYTES   VALUE_MB
---------------------------------------------------------------- ----------- ----------
EHCC CUs Decompressed                                                   4129          0
EHCC Query High CUs Decompressed                                        4129          0
EHCC Compressed Length Decompressed                                130329591     124.29
EHCC Decompressed Length Decompressed                             2.0697E+10    19738.6
EHCC Columns Decompressed                                               4129          0
EHCC Total Columns for Decompression                                   24774        .02
EHCC Total Rows for Decompression                                   20000000      19.07
EHCC Pieces Buffered for Decompression                                  4161          0
EHCC Total Pieces for Decompression                                    19829        .02
EHCC Turbo Scan CUs Decompressed                                        4129          0

10 rows selected.
```

Here you can see that 4129 CUs were decompressed, all of them using the Turbo Scan decompression. There were 19,829 pieces to be decompressed, resulting in 20,000,000 rows, which is the row count of the entire table. Fewer columns were actually decompressed than there were columns in all CUs: 4129 vs. 27,774, which nicely demonstrates the capability to do less work, thanks to the column-oriented approach. You can derive the effectiveness of the decompression by comparing the *EHCC Decompressed Length Decompressed* to *EHCC Compressed Length Decompressed.*

There is one caveat to be aware of with the EHCC statistics: There is some double counting on cell and RDBMS layer. Consider the following example. It makes use of Adrian Billington's "mystats" script to capture the changes in session counters during the execution of a SQL statement. The tool can be downloaded from `oracle-developer.net`, and I recommend you have a look at it. Only the relevant information has been taken from the output:

```
SQL> @mystats start

SQL> select /* test006 */ count(id),id
  2  from BIGTAB_QH group by id having count(id) > 100000;

SQL> @mystats stop t=1

STAT    cell CUs processed for uncompressed                                     104,289
STAT    cell CUs sent uncompressed                                              104,289
STAT    cell IO uncompressed bytes                                       71,828,529,728
STAT    cell blocks helped by minscn optimization                               404,724
STAT    cell blocks processed by cache layer                                    404,724
STAT    cell blocks processed by data layer                                     404,724
STAT    cell blocks processed by txn layer                                      404,724
STAT    cell flash cache read hits                                                2,991
STAT    cell scans                                                                    1

STAT    EHCC CUs Decompressed                                                   208,578
STAT    EHCC Columns Decompressed                                               208,578
STAT    EHCC Compressed Length Decompressed                               4,744,301,064
STAT    EHCC Decompressed Length Decompressed                           143,641,134,208
STAT    EHCC Pieces Buffered for Decompression                                  208,872
```

```
STAT    EHCC Query High CUs Decompressed                                        104,289
STAT    EHCC Total Columns for Decompression                                  1,668,624
STAT    EHCC Total Pieces for Decompression                                     542,756
STAT    EHCC Total Rows for Decompression                                   512,000,000
STAT    EHCC Turbo Scan CUs Decompressed                                        104,289

------------------------------------------------------------------------------------------
3. About
------------------------------------------------------------------------------------------
- MyStats v2.01 by Adrian Billington (http://www.oracle-developer.net)
- Based on the SNAP_MY_STATS utility by Jonathan Lewis
```

In the above output, you see an example for double counting. The cell reports that it processed 104,289 CUs during this Smart Scan (*cell CUs sent uncompressed*). When the data arrives on the RDBMS layer, it is accounted for in *Turbo Scan CUs decompressed* counter, matching the number reported on the cells. Even though the data is already decompressed by the time it arrives at the RDBMS layer, it seems likely that it traverses the same code path again, causing some statistics to be incremented once more. This is visible in *EHCC CUs Decompressed* and *EHCC Columns Decompressed* as well as *EHCC Pieces Buffered for Decompression.*

Another case of double counting is visible in *cell IO uncompressed bytes* and *EHCC Decompressed Length Decompressed*, which is double the value of the former.

physical read requests optimized

This statistic shows how many I/O requests to disk were avoided either by reading the data from Flash Cache instead of disks and/or thanks to the storage index I/O elimination. This statistic is also propagated to VSQL/VSQLSTATS and V$SEGMENT_STATISTICS views.

physical read total bytes optimized

This statistic shows how many bytes worth of physical disk drive I/O was avoided either by reading it from Flash Cache and/or thanks to storage index I/O elimination. When you also see the statistic *cell physical I/O bytes saved by storage index* equally increase, this means that some I/O could be avoided completely thanks to storage indexes. If the storage index savings are smaller than the total optimized bytes, the rest of the I/O was optimized thanks to reading it from Flash Cache, instead of the good old spinning disks. In this case, you can expect to see Flash Cache read hits as well.

table fetch continued row

This statistic is not Exadata-specific, but it is relevant when troubleshooting unexpected single-block reads done by the database while a Smart Scan is used. This statistic counts how many times Oracle had to fetch a next row piece of a chained row using a regular single-block read if it cannot be found in the buffer cache. Refer to the description about chained rows earlier in the chapter for more in-depth information.

table scans (direct read)

This statistic is not Exadata-specific; it is seen in any Oracle database performing full table scans on table segments using *direct path reads*. During serial execution, this statistic is incremented at the beginning of the table or segment scan. However, with parallel execution, it is incremented each time a slave starts scanning a new ROWID-range distributed to it. Direct path reads are a prerequisite for Smart Scans to happen. One quick troubleshooting option when you do not see Smart Scan when you expected them is to check if a direct path read happened using this statistic. Another quick tip: When using Snapper to troubleshoot a query already executing that does not scan multiple partitions, you might not see an entry for this statistic. That does not imply that there was no direct path read—it might be that you started troubleshooting the session after the counter has been increased.

table scans (long tables)

This is a similar statistic to the previous one, but it shows whether the table scanned was considered to be large or not. Actually, Oracle considers this separately for each segment, so some partitions of a table may be considered small, some large. A segment that is considered small by Oracle increments the *table scans (short tables)* counter. If the segment, which is always read up to the high water mark during full scans, is bigger than 10 percent of the buffer cache, the table is considered large and direct path reads are considered even for serial full segment scans. Note that this decision logic takes other things into account, which have been explained in more detail in Chapter 2. The ten-percent-of-the-buffer-cache rule actually comes from the `_small_table_threshold` parameter. This parameter defaults to two percent of buffer cache size (in blocks), but Oracle uses 5 × `_small_table_threshold` as its direct-path-scan decision threshold (depending on the number of blocks in the buffer cache and some other factors) in early releases of Oracle 11.2. In current releases, including 11.2.0.3, a table can be eligible for a Direct Path Read/Smart Scan even if it is just a little bit larger than `_small_table_threshold`. Again, the logic is covered in Chapter 2.

It is also worth pointing out that a single-block I/O to the segment header no longer determines the size of a segment. Oracle 11.2.0.2 and later uses dictionary information about the table instead.

Understanding SQL Statement Performance

This section focuses on the SQL statement's performance metrics and understanding where a statement is spending its time and where its bottlenecks are. Metrics covered in Chapter 10 will be reviewed with a focus on how and when to use them. The bulk of the various SQL performance monitoring tools will be covered in the next chapter. Most Exadata-specific performance statistics of individual SQL statements may be monitored primarily using the following views:

- `V$SQL` and `V$SQLAREA`
- `V$SQLSTATS` and `V$SQLSTATS_PLAN_HASH`
- `V$SQL_MONITOR` and `V$SQL_PLAN_MONITOR`
- `V$ACTIVE_SESSION_HISTORY` and the `DBA_HIST_ACTIVE_SESS_HISTORY` persisted into AWR repository

Accessing the AWR-related views requires you to be properly licensed. Note that all the Exadata-specific metrics you see in `V$SQL%` views are really the same ones you can see from `V$SESSTAT` views. They originate from the same sources but are just accumulated differently. `V$SESSTAT` accumulates stats for a session, regardless of which SQL statement or command incremented them, while the views with a `V$SQL` prefix aggregate stats for different SQL statements, regardless of the sessions executing them. So, it is possible to see some Exadata metrics aggregated by a SQL statement.

Here is an example of the V$SQL% view's columns. (There are many more columns in V$SQL views; here you are shown those that matter in the context of Smart Scans.)

```
SQL> desc v$sql
 Name                                      Null?    Type
 ----------------------------------------- -------- ----------------------------
 SQL_TEXT                                           VARCHAR2(1000)
 SQL_FULLTEXT                                       CLOB
 SQL_ID                                             VARCHAR2(13)
 SHARABLE_MEM                                       NUMBER
 PERSISTENT_MEM                                     NUMBER
 RUNTIME_MEM                                        NUMBER
[...]
 IO_CELL_OFFLOAD_ELIGIBLE_BYTES                     NUMBER
 IO_INTERCONNECT_BYTES                              NUMBER
 PHYSICAL_READ_REQUESTS                             NUMBER
 PHYSICAL_READ_BYTES                                NUMBER
 PHYSICAL_WRITE_REQUESTS                            NUMBER
 PHYSICAL_WRITE_BYTES                               NUMBER
 OPTIMIZED_PHY_READ_REQUESTS                        NUMBER
 LOCKED_TOTAL                                       NUMBER
 PINNED_TOTAL                                       NUMBER
 IO_CELL_UNCOMPRESSED_BYTES                         NUMBER
 IO_CELL_OFFLOAD_RETURNED_BYTES                     NUMBER
 CON_ID                                             NUMBER
 IS_REOPTIMIZABLE                                   VARCHAR2(1)
 IS_RESOLVED_ADAPTIVE_PLAN                          VARCHAR2(1)
 IM_SCANS                                           NUMBER
 IM_SCAN_BYTES_UNCOMPRESSED                         NUMBER
 IM_SCAN_BYTES_INMEMORY                             NUMBER
```

The columns in bold typeface are specific to Exadata processing, but not specific to Exadata. If you describe V$SQL in a non-Exadata environment, you will get exactly the same columns. Table 11-1 lists the most interesting columns, explicitly excluding some of the physical read columns for readability.

Table 11-1. *V$SQL Columns and Their Meanings*

Column Name	Metric Meaning
IO_CELL_OFFLOAD_ELIGIBLE_BYTES	How many bytes worth of segment reads were offloaded to the cells. The cells either did read this data or skipped it if storage indexes helped to skip block ranges. This metric corresponds to the *cell physical IO bytes eligible for predicate offload* statistic in V$SESSTAT.
IO_INTERCONNECT_BYTES	The *total* traffic bytes (read and write) sent between the database node and cells.
OPTIMIZED_PHY_READ_REQUESTS	The number of disk I/O requests that were either completely avoided thanks to storage indexes or done against cell Flash Cache cards.

(*continued*)

Table 11-1. *(continued)*

Column Name	Metric Meaning
IO_CELL_UNCOMPRESSED_BYTES	The size of uncompressed data the cells have scanned through during a Smart Scan. Note that the cells do not have to actually decompress all the data to know the uncompressed length. The HCC compression unit headers store both the compressed and uncompressed CU length info in them. This metric is useful for estimating the I/O reduction from HCC compression. Note that this metric works for HCC segments only. For regular block-level compression, this metric just shows the compressed size of data.
IO_CELL_OFFLOAD_RETURNED_BYTES	This metric shows how much data was returned as a result from an offloaded Smart Scan access path. This is a main indicator of Smart Scan offloading efficiency when compared with IO_CELL_OFFLOAD_ELIGIBLE_BYTES (to measure the I/O reduction between cells and database) or IO_CELL_UNCOMPRESSED_BYTES when measuring the total I/O reduction thanks to offloading and compression.

Here is example output from a query on an EHCC compressed table where the table scan was offloaded to the cell. The V$SQL table output is pivoted and reduced to the relevant detail for better readability:

```
SQL_TEXT                       : select /* hccquery001 */ ...
SQL_ID                         : 5131dsd26qfc5
DISK_READS                     : 1304924
BUFFER_GETS                    : 1304934
IO_CELL_OFFLOAD_ELIGIBLE_BYTES: 10689937408
IO_INTERCONNECT_BYTES          : 84656896
PHYSICAL_READ_REQUESTS         : 10258
PHYSICAL_READ_BYTES            : 10689937408
PHYSICAL_WRITE_REQUESTS        : 0
PHYSICAL_WRITE_BYTES           : 0
OPTIMIZED_PHY_READ_REQUESTS    : 10110
LOCKED_TOTAL                   : 1
PINNED_TOTAL                   : 2
IO_CELL_UNCOMPRESSED_BYTES     : 27254591356
IO_CELL_OFFLOAD_RETURNED_BYTES: 84656896
-----------------

PL/SQL procedure successfully completed.
```

In this case, the IO_CELL_OFFLOAD_RETURNED bytes is much smaller than the IO_CELL_OFFLOAD_ELIGIBLE bytes; thus, the Smart Scan definitely did help to reduce the data flow between the cells and the database. The latter column is a good indication about how many Smart Scans have been performed in the database:

```
SQL> !cat sscan.sql
WITH offloaded_yes_no AS
  (SELECT inst_id,
    CASE
      WHEN (IO_CELL_OFFLOAD_ELIGIBLE_BYTES > 0)
```

```
      THEN 'YES'
      ELSE 'NO'
    END sscan
  FROM gv$sql
  )
SELECT COUNT(sscan),
  sscan as smart_scan,
  inst_id
FROM offloaded_yes_no
GROUP BY sscan,
  inst_id;
```

Furthermore, going back to the previous example, the `IO_CELL_UNCOMPRESSED_BYTES` is significantly larger than the `PHYSICAL_READ_BYTES`, which indicates that the HCC helped to reduce the number of bytes that had to be read from disk by the cells, thanks to compression. Note that the `IO_INTERCONNECT_BYTES` is not much greater than the `IO_CELL_OFFLOAD_RETURNED_BYTES`, which indicates that for this SQL, almost all the traffic was due to the data returned by Smart Scans. There was no extra traffic due to other reasons such as temp-tablespace reads/writes caused by non-optimal sorts, and there were no hash joins or other work-area operations or database block I/Os, caused by chained rows or in-database consistent-read processing.

■ **Note** Smart Scanning makes data *retrieval* from segments faster, but it does not magically speed up joining, sorting, and aggregate operations. These operations happen after the data has been retrieved from the segments. A notable exception is the Bloom filter pushdown to cells, which allows the cells to filter the data from the probe table using a hash bitmap built based on the driving row source's data in the hash join. Consumers can slow down producers, but that is a general truth for all storage systems.

While this example used the `V$SQL` view, which shows SQL child cursor level statistics, you could also use `V$SQL_PLAN_MONITOR` (the columns `PLAN_LINE_ID`, `PLAN_OPERATION`, and so on) to measure these metrics for each execution plan line. This is useful because a single execution plan usually accesses and joins multiple tables, and different tables may benefit from the Smart Scan offloading differently. Some more scripts and tools that use this data are introduced in Chapter 12.

Querying cellsrv Internal Processing Statistics

In earlier versions of the Exadata software, it was not always easy to gain insights into Exadata processing. In most cases, the performance analyst had to connect to the cell itself and then dump events into a trace file to gain access to these metrics. An easier way is to access the `V$CELL` family of views. This section will explain some of these and why querying them can provide you with interesting insights in the various processing steps on the cell server-without having to quit SQL*Plus! The `V$CELL` family includes these views for which Oracle provides an API. If you query `V$FIXED_VIEW_DEFINITION` for views beginning with `GV%CELL%`, you will notice that the `V$CELL` views are based on `X$` tables named `X$KCFIS%`, Kernel Cache File Intelligent Storage. Not all of these `X$` tables have a corresponding "official" `V$` view.

This section will detail the `V$CELL%` views in addition to another tool on the cell not yet covered in the book: `cellsrvstat`.

The V$CELL Family of Views

The number of V$CELL% views has steadily increased with every release, and 12c is no exception. Oracle 12.1.0.2 lists these:

```
SQL> select table_name from dict where regexp_like(table_name, 'DBA.*(ASM|CELL)|^V\$CELL');

TABLE_NAME
--------------------------------------------------------------------------------
DBA_HIST_ASM_BAD_DISK
DBA_HIST_ASM_DISKGROUP
DBA_HIST_ASM_DISKGROUP_STAT
DBA_HIST_CELL_CONFIG
DBA_HIST_CELL_CONFIG_DETAIL
DBA_HIST_CELL_DB
DBA_HIST_CELL_DISKTYPE
DBA_HIST_CELL_DISK_NAME
DBA_HIST_CELL_DISK_SUMMARY
DBA_HIST_CELL_GLOBAL
DBA_HIST_CELL_GLOBAL_SUMMARY
DBA_HIST_CELL_IOREASON
DBA_HIST_CELL_IOREASON_NAME
DBA_HIST_CELL_METRIC_DESC
DBA_HIST_CELL_NAME
DBA_HIST_CELL_OPEN_ALERTS
V$CELL
V$CELL_CONFIG
V$CELL_CONFIG_INFO
V$CELL_DB
V$CELL_DB_HISTORY
V$CELL_DISK
V$CELL_DISK_HISTORY
V$CELL_GLOBAL
V$CELL_GLOBAL_HISTORY
V$CELL_IOREASON
V$CELL_IOREASON_NAME
V$CELL_METRIC_DESC
V$CELL_OFL_THREAD_HISTORY
V$CELL_OPEN_ALERTS
V$CELL_REQUEST_TOTALS
V$CELL_STATE
V$CELL_THREAD_HISTORY

33 rows selected.
```

Quite a few more compared to 11.2.0.4:

```
SQL> select table_name from dict where regexp_like(table_name, 'DBA.*CELL|^V\$CELL');

TABLE_NAME
------------------------------
V$CELL
V$CELL_CONFIG
V$CELL_OFL_THREAD_HISTORY
V$CELL_REQUEST_TOTALS
V$CELL_STATE
V$CELL_THREAD_HISTORY

6 rows selected.
```

Since this chapter is already very long, a careful selection has been made to include only the most important of these views. The AWR versions of the views are left out as they essentially allow a longer-term archival of the information on the SYSAUX tablespace.

V$CELL

The first view that comes to mind is V$CELL. In Oracle 12.1.0.2, the view definition is as shown here:

```
SQL> desc v$cell
 Name                                      Null?    Type
 ----------------------------------------- -------- ----------------------------
 CELL_PATH                                          VARCHAR2(400)
 CELL_HASHVAL                                       NUMBER
 CON_ID                                             NUMBER
 CELL_TYPE                                          VARCHAR2(400)
```

CON_ID and CELL_TYPE are new in 12c; Oracle 11.2 only shows the cell path (an IP address) and the cell has value. You are likely to use this view to map a cellhash to a cell, as found in the Smart Scan related wait events discussed in Chapter 10.

V$CELL_OFL_THREAD_HISTORY

This interesting view records a ten-minute history of what cellsrv threads were doing, conceptually something like ASH for storage cells. This view is similar to V$CELL_THREAD_HISTORY but has additional columns allowing for an ASH-like versioning of the information. Here is the view definition for 12.1.0.2:

```
SQL> desc V$CELL_OFL_THREAD_HISTORY
 Name                                      Null?    Type
 ----------------------------------------- -------- ----------------------------
 CELL_NAME                                          VARCHAR2(1024)
 GROUP_NAME                                         VARCHAR2(1024)
 PROCESS_ID                                         NUMBER
 SNAPSHOT_ID                                        NUMBER
 SNAPSHOT_TIME                                      DATE
 THREAD_ID                                          NUMBER
 JOB_TYPE                                           VARCHAR2(32)
```

```
 WAIT_STATE                                         VARCHAR2(32)
 WAIT_OBJECT_NAME                                   VARCHAR2(32)
 SQL_ID                                             VARCHAR2(13)
 DATABASE_ID                                        NUMBER
 INSTANCE_ID                                        NUMBER
 SESSION_ID                                         NUMBER
 SESSION_SERIAL_NUM                                 NUMBER
 CON_ID                                             NUMBER
```

As you can see, the view shows the cell processes, which internally map to `cellsrv` threads. For each of these, you see job type such as `PredicateOflFilter` during a Smart Scan and a state. Even more interesting is the fact that you see the SQL ID causing the load, the database ID, and instance number as well as the session SID and serial#. Be careful though—if it is not available, the `SQL_ID` is made up of 13 white spaces, not null or the empty string:

```
SQL> select count(''''||sql_id||''''),''''||sql_id||''''
  2    from v$cell_ofl_thread_history
  3   group by ''''||sql_id||'''';

COUNT(''''||SQL_ID||'''') ''''||SQL_ID||'
------------------------- ---------------
                        2 'f254uv2p53y7j'
                   126363 '             '

2 rows selected.
```

In other words, you can see who caused how many worker threads to be busy at a given point in time. Here is an example on how to get the current information from the system:

```
SELECT CELL_NAME ,
  GROUP_NAME ,
  SNAPSHOT_ID ,
  JOB_TYPE ,
  WAIT_STATE ,
  WAIT_OBJECT_NAME ,
  SQL_ID
FROM
  (SELECT CELL_NAME ,
    GROUP_NAME ,
    SNAPSHOT_ID ,
    JOB_TYPE ,
    WAIT_STATE ,
    WAIT_OBJECT_NAME ,
    SQL_ID ,
    DATABASE_ID ,
    INSTANCE_ID ,
    SESSION_ID ,
    SESSION_SERIAL_NUM ,
    CON_ID,
    MAX (SNAPSHOT_ID) over (partition BY cell_name) max_snap
  FROM V$CELL_OFL_THREAD_HISTORY
  )
WHERE snapshot_id = max_snap;
```

As the view name suggests, historic information is available, not just a snapshot of the current state. If you correlate the session information and SQL ID with ASH monitoring information, you should be able to draw a very accurate picture of the cell's load at a given point in time.

V$CELL_STATE

This view is the source of a lot of information about the cell. Similar to V$CELL_CONFIG, it hinges on a column describing an XML field. In this case, it's STATISTICS_TYPE. The 12.1.0.2 definition of the view is shown here:

```
SQL> desc v$cell_state
 Name                                      Null?    Type
 ----------------------------------------- -------- ----------------------------
 CELL_NAME                                          VARCHAR2(1024)
 STATISTICS_TYPE                                    VARCHAR2(15)
 OBJECT_NAME                                        VARCHAR2(1024)
 STATISTICS_VALUE                                   CLOB
 CON_ID                                             NUMBER
```

The different statistics you can query very depending on the RDBMS/cell versions. For 12.1.0.2 and Exadata version 12.1.2.1.0 you can investigate the following metrics:

- IOREASON: breaks down I/O on the cell into every category imaginable
- RCVPORT: contains detail about network traffic received
- FLASHLOG: very detailed information about the use of the FLASHLOG feature
- SENDPORT: contains detail about network traffic sent
- PREDIO: contains information about how Exadata dealt with Smart Scans
- NPHYSDISKS: lists number of physical disks per cell
- CELL: similar information as in the cellsrvstat output
- THREAD: thread-related information about cellsrv's worker threads
- PHASESTAT: information about the various phases of a Smart Scan
- CAPABILITY: cell software capabilities
- LOCK: breaking down mutex waits per object type in the cell
- OFLGROUP: offload server statistics

The I/O Reasons are so interesting that Oracle decided to give them their own view in 12c, named V$CELL_IOREASON. The trick with this view is that you have to parse the output again depending on the statistic type. It helps to select just the STATISTICS_VALUE for a given type and develop a strategy on how to parse the XML data. Here is an example to list all IOREASONS on 12.1.0.2 for a given cell:

```
SELECT x.cell_name, x.statistics_type, x.object_name, stats.*
FROM  V$CELL_STATE x,
      XMLTABLE ('/ioreasongroup_stats'
        PASSING xmltype(x.STATISTICS_VALUE)
        COLUMNS ioreasons XMLTYPE PATH '*'
      ) xt,
```

```
      xmltable ('/stat'
      passing xt.ioreasons
      columns name path './@name',
              value path '/stat'
    ) stats
    where x.statistics_type = 'IOREASON'
      and stats.name <> 'reason'
      and x.cell_name = '192.168.12.8'
/
```

The output-abbreviated-is shown here:

```
CELL_NAME            STATISTICS_TYPE OBJECT_NAME          NAME           VALUE
-------------------- --------------- -------------------- -------------- --------------------
192.168.12.8         IOREASON        UNKNOWN              reads          369113
192.168.12.8         IOREASON        UNKNOWN              writes         170592
192.168.12.8         IOREASON        RedoLog Write        reads          0
192.168.12.8         IOREASON        RedoLog Write        writes         51493
192.168.12.8         IOREASON        RedoLog Read         reads          1152
192.168.12.8         IOREASON        RedoLog Read         writes         0
192.168.12.8         IOREASON        ArchLog Read         reads          0
192.168.12.8         IOREASON        ArchLog Read         writes         0
192.168.12.8         IOREASON        MediaRecovery Write  reads          0
192.168.12.8         IOREASON        MediaRecovery Write  writes         0
```

The most comprehensive output is available for the CELL statistic; it produces information that otherwise would have been available from a system state dump. Some of it is actually too complex to parse in its entirety, in which case a dump into an XML file can help. Simply cast the STATISTICS_VALUE into an XMLType and select from the dynamic performance view, paste the output into a text file, and open it with your favorite browser. The PREDIO and CELL statistics are good examples for where this really helps.

The cellsrvstat utility

For quite some time, Oracle has shipped the cellsrvstat utility as part of the cell software distribution. It is a useful tool for in-depth troubleshooting and research into how the cell software works. The tool has a built-in help, but is otherwise not really documented by Oracle. You can find several references in publications and some blogs. To give you an idea about the tool's capabilities, see the following:

```
Usage:
cellsrvstat [-stat_group=<group name>,<group name>,]
            [-offload_group_name=<offload_group_name>,]
            [-database_name=<database_name>,]
            [-stat=<stat name>,<stat name>,] [-interval=<interval>]
            [-count=<count>] [-table] [-short] [-list]

stat                    A comma separated list of short strings representing
                         the stats. Default is all. (unless -stat is specified).
                         The -list option displays all stats.
                         Example: -stat=io_nbiorr_hdd,io_nbiowr_hdd
```

```
stat_group                A comma separated list of short strings representing
                           stat groups. Default: all except database
                           (unless -stat_group is specified).
                           The -list option displays all stat groups.
                           The valid groups are: io, mem, exec, net,
                           smartio, flashcache, offload, database.
                           Example: -stat_group=io,mem
offload_group_name        A comma separated list of short strings representing
                           offload group names.
                           Default: cellsrvstat -stat_group=offload
                           (all offload groups unless -offload_group_name is specified).
                           Example: -offload_group_name=SYS_121111_130502
database_name             A comma separated list of short strings representing
                           database group names.
                           Default: cellsrvstat -stat_group=database
                           (all databases unless -database_name is specified).
                           Example: -database_name=testdb,proddb
interval                  At what interval the stats should be obtained and
                           printed (in seconds). Default is 1 second.
count                     How many times the stats should be printed.
                           Default is once.
list                      List all metric abbreviations and their descriptions.
                           All other options are ignored.
table                     Use a tabular format for output. This option will be
                           ignored if all metrics specified are not integer
                           based metrics.
short                     Use abbreviated metric name instead of
                           descriptive ones.
error_out                 An output file to print error messages to, mostly for
                           debugging.
```

When researching the mechanics of Smart Scans, it proved useful to narrow the scope to io, smartio, or offload. In best UNIX tradition, a single call to the tool prints all the stats since collection began. If you are interested in the current statistics, you should specify the interval and count parameters. An interval of five seconds proved effective with a count of at least two. Just as with vmstat and iostat, you can safely ignore the first batch of output and focus on the second one, as this one represents the current statistics on the cell. Following is an example output for the io statistics group during a single Smart Scan against an 80GB table in serial mode. The figure following the statistic name is the delta since the last snapshot; the large number following it is the cumulative number of events since the cell started recording:

```
== Input/Output related stats ==
Number of hard disk block IO read requests                    1860       47269919
Number of hard disk block IO write requests                     18        1481441
Hard disk block IO reads (KB)                              1881618    46815620582
Hard disk block IO writes (KB)                                 170      210753174
Number of flash disk block IO read requests                 135071        6106538
Number of flash disk block IO write requests                     7        2761123
Flash disk block IO reads (KB)                             8641696      372843144
Flash disk block IO writes (KB)                                188       52813784
Number of disk IO errors                                         0              4
```

```
Number of latency threshold warnings during job              0          2
Number of latency threshold warnings by checker              0          0
Number of latency threshold warnings for smart IO            0          0
Number of latency threshold warnings for redo log writes     0          0
Current read block IO to be issued (KB)                      0          0
Total read block IO to be issued (KB)                      202   42461566
Current write block IO to be issued (KB)                     0          0
Total write block IO to be issued (KB)                     249  132637393
Current read blocks in IO (KB)                               0          0
Total read block IO issued (KB)                            202   42461566
Current write blocks in IO (KB)                              0          0
Total write block IO issued (KB)                           249  132637393
Current read block IO in network send (KB)                   0          0
Total read block IO in network send (KB)                   202   42461566
Current write block IO in network send (KB)                  0          0
Total write block IO in network send (KB)                  249  132637393
Current block IO being populated in flash (KB)               0          0
Total block IO KB populated in flash (KB)                    0     401680
```

If you followed this chapter and tried the examples in your environment, the output of `cellsrvstat` looks very familiar. You get a lot of the information provided by the command line utility from the `V$CELL` views, especially from `V$CELL_STATE`.

Summary

The emphasis of this chapter was on understanding Exadata performance and the various related metrics Oracle offers the performance analyst and researcher. It is important to remember that the Exadata Smart Scan potentially speeds up your data retrieval, but Smart Scans happen only when direct path reads and full segment scans are used. Also, remember that it is not possible to determine whether a Smart Scan actually occurred by just considering the execution plan in isolation.

You should always check additional metrics, like whether you see the *cell smart table/index scan* wait events in your session and whether the `IO_CELL_OFFLOAD_ELIGIBLE_BYTES` (in `V$SQL`) or *cell physical I/O bytes eligible for predicate offload* statistic (in `V$SESSTAT`) increases while you run your SQL. Tracing on Wait Events, as explained in Chapter 10, is another method you have at your disposal to confirm if Smart Scans have been used or not. Many of the other metrics explained will hopefully be helpful for understanding and troubleshooting advanced performance issues, such as when a Smart Scan kicks in but is throttled by a multitude of special conditions like chained rows, consistent-read rollbacks, or just running out of cell server resources. In Chapter 12, we will see how to use this knowledge in monitoring and troubleshooting Exadata performance, and we will look deeper into the cell-level performance metrics from `cellsrv` and the operating system, too.

CHAPTER 12

Monitoring Exadata Performance

By now, you have learned about the key Exadata performance features and the related performance metrics. Let's see how you can use these for everyday tasks. In this chapter, you will read about standard tools available for database-layer and cell-performance monitoring, as well as how to interpret their output.

Oracle Database and the Exadata cells provide a huge variety of different metrics, but, before monitoring any metrics, you should ask yourself why you are monitoring them. Additionally, you should know what your action would be if a metric crosses some threshold. This leads to the follow-up question: Which exact threshold should prompt some action from you, and why? In other words, you should know what are you trying to achieve (good response times for users, ideally quantifiable and maybe even written down) and how performance metrics relate to that.

The monitoring tasks covered here can be divided into the following categories:

- SQL statement response-time monitoring
- Database layer utilization and efficiency monitoring
- Storage cell-layer utilization and efficiency monitoring
- Advanced metrics and monitoring for Exadata performance troubleshooting

Note that the focus will be on the Exadata-specific performance topics and not the whole wide range of other Oracle performance topics, like lock contention or general SQL performance issues. That would certainly not fit into a chapter!

A Systematic Approach

Whatever metrics you monitor, you should have a purpose in mind. In other words, do not just collect and display metrics because they are available; this will probably lead you nowhere or potentially even mislead you to fixing the wrong problem. Note that the term "performance" is vague—different people may mean different things when they use it. From an IT system user's perspective, performance is ultimately only about one thing—response time. And not some response times of individual wait events measured at a low level; the end users do not care about that. They do care about how much *they* have to wait for their *business task* to complete, like the time it takes from the report submission to actually seeing its output. This time is measured in regular wall-clock time; it's as simple as that.

If your purpose in monitoring is to ensure good response times for your application users, you should measure what matters—response time as your end user experiences it. This would be the ideal entry point to performance monitoring. In addition to this entry point, you should measure more detailed, lower-level metrics to break the end-user response time down into individual components, like time spent in an application server and database time. Your application instrumentation and monitoring tools should keep track of which database sessions were used for which end-user task, so you can report what these exact database sessions were doing when a user experienced unacceptable response times. Instrumentation in this context most often means calls to DBMS_APPLICATION_INFO, a tremendously useful package at the developer's disposal to make business processes known to the database.

■ **Note** We deliberately said "unacceptable response times" here instead of just "user experienced performance problems." Whenever users complain about a performance problem, you should try to get a clear understanding about what they actually mean and how the problem was measured. Does any user actually experience far too long response times in their application, or did some monitoring system merely raise an alarm about "too high" CPU utilization or any other secondary metric like that? Your subsequent actions would depend on the problem you are trying to solve. Ideally, you should not use a performance tool or Oracle metric for determining *whether* you have a performance problem. Your starting point should be the users (who report a problem) or application-level metrics, which see the database response time from the application perspective. No matter how good the database metrics look, if the application waits for the report completion for ages, you have a performance problem to drill down into. Conversely, no matter how "bad" your database metrics seem to be, if your application response times are satisfactory, you do not have an acute need to start fixing anything.

When examining performance metrics because of an ongoing problem (of too long response times), you should start by identifying the sessions servicing this slow application or job and then drilling down into that particular session's response time. It would be more accurate to call this performance troubleshooting, not just monitoring.

Note that there are other kinds of performance-monitoring tasks, which you may want to do—for example, proactive utilization and efficiency monitoring. Performing these tasks allows you to keep an eye on the utilization headroom left in the servers and detect any anomalies and sudden spikes in system utilization and low-level response times, possibly even before users notice a response-time difference. Yet another reason for collecting and monitoring performance and utilization data is for capacity planning. Also, because this is a database book, we cannot dive into any end-to-end performance measurement topics, which would involve identifying time spent in application servers, on the network, and so on before the database is involved.

This chapter begins with a discussion on how to identify where a long-running query is spending most of its time. You can also read more about how to tell whether a query is taking full advantage of Exadata's performance features.

Monitoring SQL Statement Response Time

Arguably, the best tool for monitoring long-running queries is Oracle's SQL Real Time Monitor. It is available either from Oracle Enterprise Manager (OEM) 12c Cloud Control, Oracle 12c OEM Express, or, alternatively, it can be produced by using a PL/SQL API. SQL Monitor is able to gather all the key performance information onto a single interactive page, even in the case of parallel execution across multiple RAC instances.

The SQL Monitoring feature requires you to have a Diagnostics and Tuning Pack license. SQL Monitoring kicks in automatically if you run your query with parallel execution or when a serial query consumes more than five seconds of I/O and CPU time in total. Additionally, you can control the monitoring feature with MONITOR and NO_MONITOR hints. If you want to monitor your frequently executed short-running queries, the best tool for this would be to use ASH data and list the top wait events and top row sources from there (using the SQL_PLAN_LINE columns in the V$ACTIVE_SESSION_HISTORY view). Accessing ASH, unfortunately, also requires you to be licensed appropriately.

If you are already aware of a performance problem (perhaps your users are already complaining of poor response times), you should use a top-down approach for monitoring. You should identify the session(s) of the problematic users' applications or reports and drill down into what these sessions are doing with ASH (which gives you the `SQL_ID`s of the top SQL statements for these sessions) and when needed. Then drill down further into the top statements with SQL Monitoring reports.

Monitoring SQL Statements with Real-Time SQL Monitoring Reports

When you click the SQL Monitoring link in the Enterprise Manager Cloud Control performance page, you will see the latest monitored queries. The SQL Monitoring reports are present since version 11g R1 or 10g R5 (10.2.0.5) of Enterprise Manager. If you are not using Enterprise Manager 12c Cloud Control, you can either use the built-in Enterprise Manager Database Express or run the SQL Monitoring reports manually from SQL*Plus, as explained shortly. Note that the SQL Monitoring feature requires Diagnostics and Tuning Pack licenses. In this chapter, you will see examples taken from Oracle Enterprise Manager 12.1.0.4 taken from a 12.1.0.2 database.

Figure 12-1 shows an excerpt of the entry page to the SQL Monitoring reports. You can get there in two ways: by clicking the SQL Monitoring link on the Performance page tab in Cloud Control, or from the Performance drop-down menu after having logged in to the database target. The database home page also shows you a quick summary of monitored statements observed during the last hour. The SQL Monitoring page, as seen in Figure 12-1, lists the currently running, queued, and recently completed monitored SQL executions, with some key performance metrics and details, such as the degree of parallelism. If parallel execution is used it shows the number of instances involved.

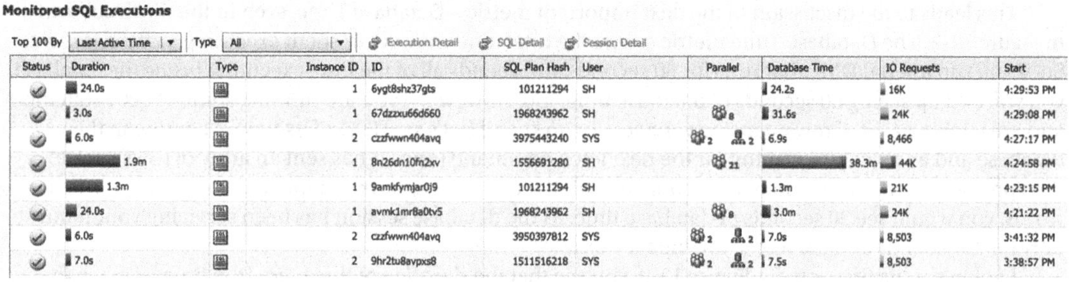
Monitored SQL Executions

Top 100 By: Last Active Time | Type: All | Execution Detail | SQL Detail | Session Detail

Status	Duration	Type	Instance ID	ID	SQL Plan Hash	User	Parallel	Database Time	IO Requests	Start
✓	24.0s	SQL	1	6ygt8shz37gts	101211294	SH		24.2s	16K	4:29:53 PM
✓	3.0s	SQL	1	67dzzxu66d660	1968243962	SH	8	31.6s	24K	4:29:08 PM
✓	6.0s	SQL	2	czzfwwn404avq	3975443240	SYS	2 2	6.9s	8,466	4:27:17 PM
✓	1.9m	SQL	1	8n26dn10fn2xv	1556691280	SH	21	38.3m	44K	4:24:58 PM
✓	1.3m	SQL	1	9amkfymjar0j9	101211294	SH		1.3m	21K	4:23:15 PM
✓	24.0s	SQL	1	avmk1mr8a0tv5	1968243962	SH	8	3.0m	24K	4:21:22 PM
✓	6.0s	SQL	2	czzfwwn404avq	3950397812	SYS	2 2	7.0s	8,503	3:41:32 PM
✓	7.0s	SQL	2	9hr2tu8avpxs8	1511516218	SYS	2 2	7.5s	8,503	3:38:57 PM

***Figure 12-1.** Enterprise Manager's overview of Monitored SQL Executions*

■ **Note** One possible explanation as to why there can be discrepancies between elapsed time and database time is that there are different sources, using different granularities. Oracle uses both of these to get this information from.

The Status column shows an icon with one of four statuses—running, done, error, or queued. When you click the status icon, the current row will be highlighted and you can use the Execution Detail button on the top of the report to take you to the SQL statement's detailed monitoring page. One of the most important pieces of information is the Duration column, showing how long a statement has been active. The duration is the wall-clock time from the start of the statement execution through the finish, or to the current time in the event the statement is still executing. Figure 12-2 illustrates the difference between duration (wall-clock) and CPU time in statement execution.

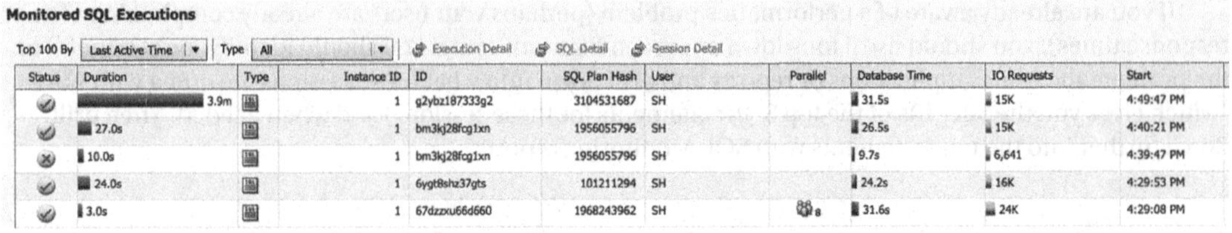
Monitored SQL Executions
Top 100 By
Last Active Time
Type
All
Execution Detail
SQL Detail
Session Detail
Status
Duration
Type
Instance ID
ID
SQL Plan Hash
User
Parallel
Database Time
IO Requests
Start
3.9m
1
g2ybz187333g2
3104531687
SH
31.5s
15K
4:49:47 PM
27.0s
1
bm3kj28fcg1xn
1956055796
SH
26.5s
15K
4:40:21 PM
10.0s
1
bm3kj28fcg1xn
1956055796
SH
9.7s
6,641
4:39:47 PM
24.0s
1
6ygt8shz37gts
101211294
SH
24.2s
16K
4:29:53 PM
3.0s
1
67dzzxu66d660
1968243962
SH
8
31.6s
24K
4:29:08 PM

***Figure 12-2.** Statement Duration compared to Database Time in the SQL Monitoring page*

The Duration column shows what users care about, which is the response time of a query since the SQL execution start. This is the time *they* have had to wait for the SQL to complete. Of course, the end users may have had to wait for much longer than the duration of the query, as the page in Figure 12-2 shows only the database response time. Time may have also been spent in the application layer or the network connection in between the user and the application server.

It is important to know that the duration measures time from SQL execution start all the way until the cursor is closed or cancelled (for example, when all data is fetched from it). This means that if your database can process the query in 30 seconds, but then millions of rows are fetched a few at a time, your query will take a long time as far as the application is concerned (caused by the network, which is used to ship packets back and forth between the database and its client to deliver the results from the query). In fact, only a little time is spent processing within the database. The Duration column still shows long query "runtime," as the cursor is still kept open for fetching of the data. Remember, the duration measures time from when the cursor is executed all the way to when it is finally closed after all the fetches are done or the application has fetched enough.

This leads to the discussion of the next important metric—Database Time, seen in the ninth column in Figure 12-2. The Database Time metric shows the total time your query spent executing *in the database*. So, if you run a serial DML that runs for 60 seconds and spends all of the time executing *inside* the database, you will end up seeing 60 seconds of database time, too. However, if you are running some SELECT statement and are fetching a lot of rows, causing your session to spend (let's say) 50% of its time executing in the database and another 50% waiting for the next fetch command (once it has sent an array of rows back to the application), you would maybe see only half of that total 60-second duration as database time. In other words, you would see 30 seconds of database time, as the database session has been servicing your request only for 30 seconds and the rest of the time it was idle.

Looking at the first entry in Figure 12-2, you see that the *duration* of the query (the time from when the execution phase started) is 3.9 minutes, the query has executed in serial (the eighth column shows that), and it has consumed only 31.5 seconds of *database time*. This indicates that the executing session has been doing something else for roughly three and a half minutes. It was either idle (probably waiting for the next fetch request) or executing some other statement (while the first statement's cursor was still open). In this particular case, the time not spent in the database was indeed spent transferring a lot of data over the network. If you see this as part of a huge report being generated, you may be able to optimize the time spent by using pagination and the new top-N query feature in Oracle 12c.

The example just discussed was about a single serial query. When you run a parallel query, you have multiple sessions executing pieces of the same query for you. Then the database time might end up being much higher than the duration (response time) of your query. If you look at the last entry in Figure 12-2, you see a statement with duration of 3 seconds, but the total time spent in the database is 31.6 seconds. When you look at the parallel column, you see that the session was executed with parallel degree 8, which means that you had multiple sessions actively working in the database for your query. All of these parallel sessions' database time plus the query coordinator's time is added into the Database Time column. This database time gives an idea of how much work was done in the database. But because the statement was parallelized, you do not have to wait that long. If you ran that same query in serial mode, the database time would be in the ballpark of how much time you might have to wait. Please take that last statement with a grain of salt since, in practice, many other things may happen in SQL execution when switching from parallel execution to serial. Consequently, you might have some pleasant or unpleasant surprises in the response time.

Note that these entries in the SQL Monitoring overview page are not SQL *statement*-specific, but SQL statement *execution*-specific. So, if two user sessions were running the same statement, you would see two separate entries in this list. You can see an example for this in figure 12-2 as well in lines two and three. This allows you to examine exactly what the problem is with a specific user (who is complaining) as opposed to looking at statement-level aggregate metrics (like those V$SQL provides) and trying to figure out *your* user's problem from there.

Real-Time Monitoring of Single Long-Running Query

Once you have identified your query of interest from the list of all the long-running queries, you can click on its "running" icon in the left side of the list to highlight the row, followed by a click on the Execution Detail button, and you will be taken to the Monitored SQL Execution Details page shown in Figure 12-3. This page has a number of sub-tabs, so feel free to explore and see all the information that is available there.

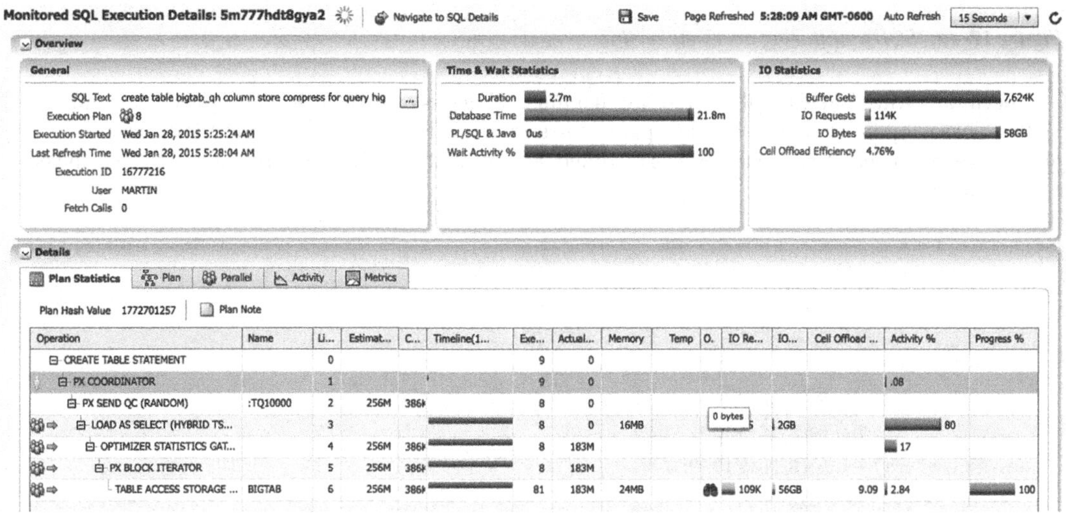

Figure 12-3. *Monitored SQL statement execution details*

The Monitored SQL Execution Details page has a lot of information in it. Thanks to good user interface design, it is fairly self-explanatory if you have read SQL execution plans before. Hence, we do not go through every single detail here, but will focus on the most important metrics. Compared to old-fashioned DBMS_XPLAN output, the SQL Monitoring page is very interactive, so make sure that you hover your mouse over and click almost everything on the screen to see the full array of functionality available to you. This can include mundane things such as a metric. As an example, try hovering your mouse pointer over the cell offload efficiency number visible in the top right in the IO Statistics.

Let's start from the top section on the page. At the top of the screen, right after the Monitored SQL Execution Details header, you see a little icon, which shows the status of the selected SQL statement's execution. The little circle implies that the statement is still being executed (the cursor has not been closed or cancelled).

The Overview section, illustrated in Figure 12-4a, will show some basic details, like an abridged version of the query text, the degree of parallelism, the time the query started, the user who started it, and so on. You can see the full SQL text when you click on the little three-dot icon to the right of the SQL Text.

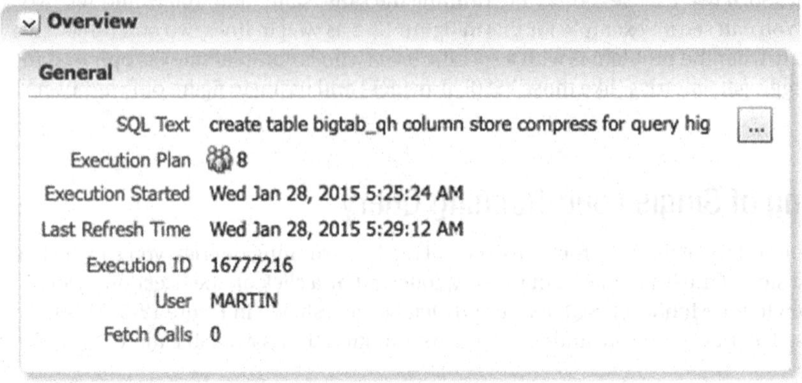

Figure 12-4a. *SQL Monitoring overivew section*

Beginning with Oracle Database 12c, another interesting piece of information is provided as well. The cost-based optimizer (CBO) has the option to use what is called Adaptive Optimization. Execution plans can evolve over time, and this is also recorded. Figure 12-4b shows the information about a resolved, adaptive plan.

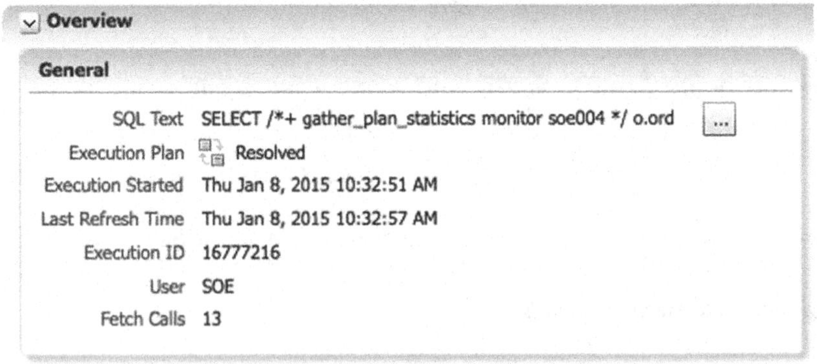

Figure 12-4b. *SQL Monitoring overivew section for an resolved apative plan*

Beginning with version 11.2.0.2, you will also see the bind variable values used for the execution. Figure 12-5 shows an example for bind variables in the query, taken from a different SQL Monitoring report.

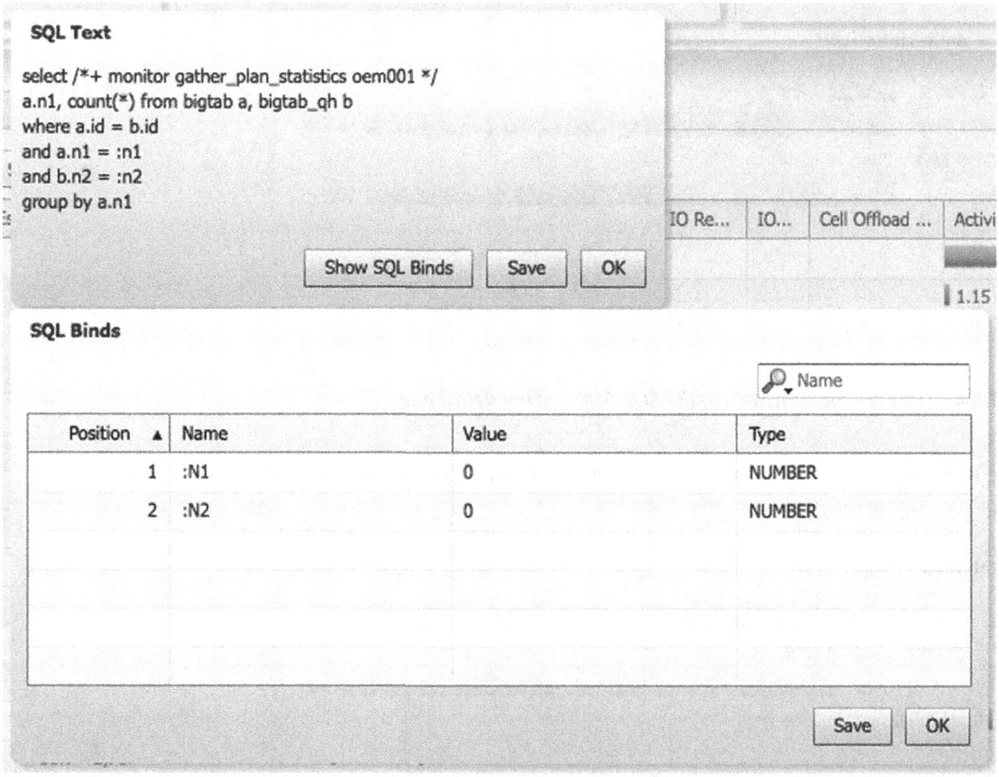

Figure 12-5. *Bind variable values in the SQL Monitoring detail page*

Of course, whether you should use bind variables for your long-running reports and DW queries is an entirely separate question. You probably should not use binds for long-running queries in your DW; you may, instead, want to sacrifice some response time for hard-parsing a new query plan for each combination of literal values and possibly get an optimal plan for each variable set. Nevertheless, monitoring bind variable values of an already-running query is easy with Oracle 11.2.0.2 and later because you no longer have to resort to the `ORADEBUG ERRORSTACK` command.

The Time & Wait Statistics section in Figure 12-6 shows the familiar metrics of Duration and Database Time of a statement. Move your mouse over the different database time components to see how much time was spent waiting inside the database compared to running on CPU. The Wait Activity % bar shows the breakdown of wait events. Note that the 100% in this bar means 100% of the *wait time* component of database time, not of the entire database time (which also includes CPU time). This statement is executing in parallel.

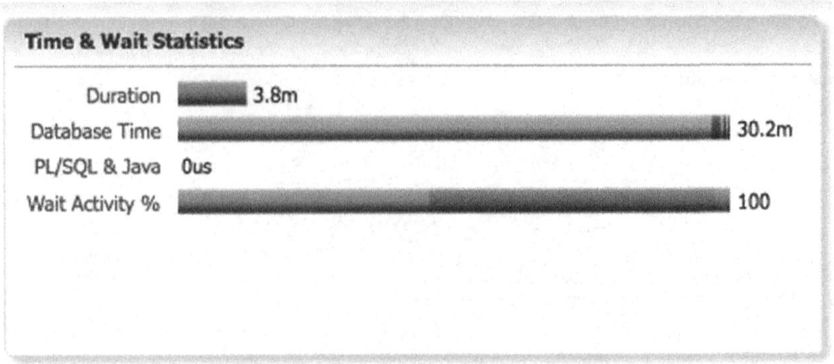

Figure 12-6. *Time & Wait Statistics in the SQL Monitoring detail page*

The IO Statistics section in Figure 12-7a shows some key I/O statistics for statement execution.

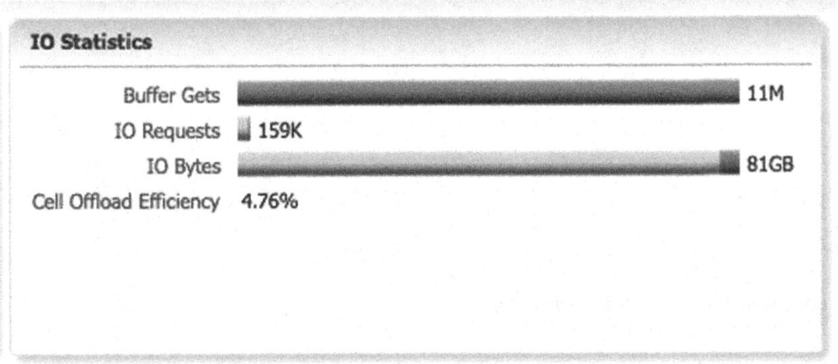

Figure 12-7a. *I/O Statistics in the SQL Monitoring detail page*

The Buffer Gets bar shows the total number of logical I/Os done in both the database layer and the cells (if Smart Scan kicked in). The IO Requests and IO Bytes statistics are self-explanatory, but note that those metrics show all I/O done for the given statement, which includes the Smart Scan I/O, any regular block I/O, and also `TEMP` tablespace I/O (done for sorting, hash joins, and any other work area operations that did not fit into allowed PGA memory). Write I/O is the reason why the Cell Offload Efficiency can be negative for a statement's execution. If, for some reason (think of Create Table as Select as the most extreme example), you perform more write I/O operations than save by offloading a query, you will see "negative savings" reported. The Cell Offload Efficiency metric should ideally show the percentage of disk-to-database-host interconnect traffic that was avoided thanks to the Smart Scans performing filtering and projection early in the cells and returning only a subset of data. However, in a complex execution plan, there is much more going on than just a Smart Scan against a single table. You have joins, aggregate operations, sorting, and direct path data loads, which all use extra I/O bandwidth, driving the offload efficiency percentage down. This is a good example of why focusing on only a single ratio is not a good idea. The single percentage value for offload efficiency hides a lot of information, such as where the percentage taken was from and the *real* values behind it. You can move your mouse over the percentage and see the underlying values used for the calculation.

When moving your mouse over the ratio (see Figure 12-7b), you can see that the cells read 81GB from disks, and (77GB) were sent back and forth over the interconnect. This makes sense since the statement monitored was a Create Table as Select operation without a where clause on the select part of the statement.

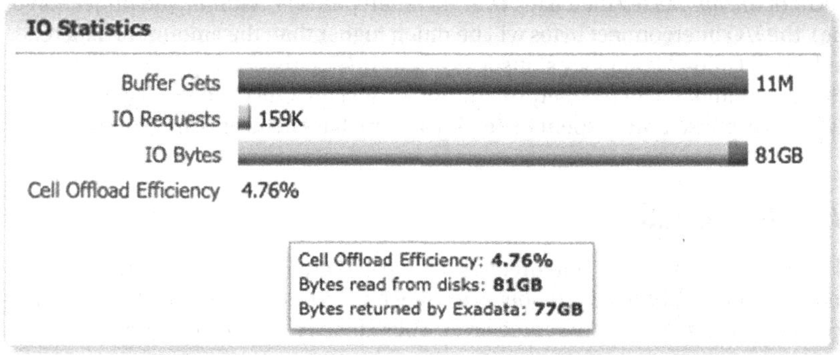

Figure 12-7b. *Cell Offload Efficiency ratio in the SQL Monitoring detail page*

In other examples, the metric explanations similar to these shown in Figure 12-7b can be misleading. Take, for example, a slow-running query. In Figure 12-7c, the cell offload efficiency turned negative!

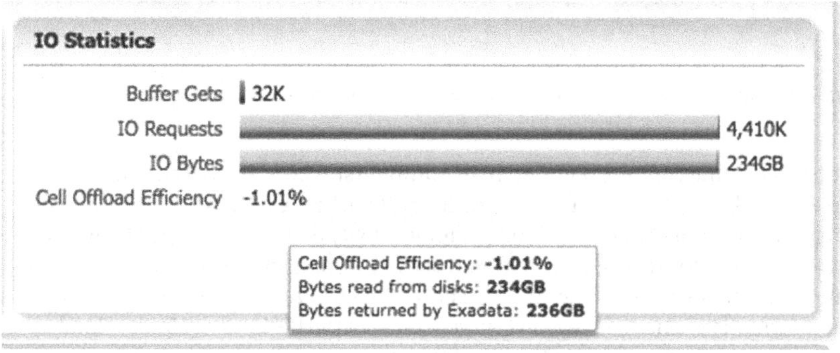

Figure 12-7c. *Cell Offload Efficiency ratio in the SQL Monitoring detail page*

The Bytes Read from Disks statistic actually represents total bytes of reads *and* writes that Oracle Database has issued, not just for Smart Scans, but for any reason. And the Bytes Returned by Exadata statistic actually shows the total interconnect traffic between the database and the cells, caused by any reason, such as block reads and writes and arrays of returned rows by Smart Scans.

If you are wondering why the I/O interconnect bytes can be larger than the actual database-issued I/O, the explanation is in how these metrics are measured. The database I/O metric (the Bytes Read from Disk statistic in Figure 12-7c) is measured by the database layer, while the I/O interconnect bytes is measured by the low-level interconnect/Oracle networking layer. And one of the layers in between is the ASM layer, which manages the software mirroring, among other things. Thus, the interconnect I/O traffic can be higher than the database traffic thanks to the write operations done by the SQL statement, which had to be mirrored by the ASM layer. Every 1MB written by the database (whether because of direct path load or some work area operation spilling to temporary tablespace) results in the writing of 2MB of data thanks to ASM normal redundancy mirroring. Users with high redundancy have an even higher write penalty to endure.

There are other reasons why the interconnect traffic may be higher than the actual amount of data read. One example is HCC compressed tables. If you have compressed your 10GB partition down to 1GB, then you will have to do 1GB worth of I/O to read it. However, if the Smart Scan decompresses this data in the cells on the fly and returns all that 10GB of *uncompressed* data back over the interconnect (assuming no projection or filtration in the cell was done), the I/O interconnect bytes will be much higher than the amount of data read from disks. This could drive the Cell Offload Efficiency statistic down to 10% for this example Smart Scan. All this is yet another reason why you should not focus solely on improving just the Cell Offload Efficiency ratio, but should rather look into where response time is spent instead. Time is what end users care about.

Execution Plan Row Source Details

Now that you have checked the key metrics of your statement execution— duration, database time, parallelism used, and how much of the database time is spent running on CPU vs. waiting—it is time to drill down into the details of the execution plan at the row source level. These details are shown in Figure 12-8.

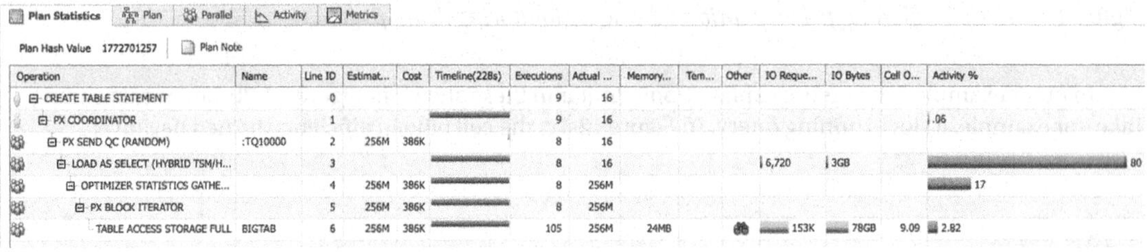

Operation	Name	Line ID	Estimat...	Cost	Timeline(228s)	Executions	Actual ...	Memory...	Tem...	Other	IO Reque...	IO Bytes	Cell O...	Activity %
CREATE TABLE STATEMENT		0				9	16							
PX COORDINATOR		1				9	16							.06
PX SEND QC (RANDOM)	:TQ10000	2	256M	386K		8	16							
LOAD AS SELECT (HYBRID TSM/H...		3				8	16				6,720	3GB		80
OPTIMIZER STATISTICS GATHE...		4	256M	386K		8	256M							17
PX BLOCK ITERATOR		5	256M	386K		8	256M							
TABLE ACCESS STORAGE FULL	BIGTAB	6	256M	386K		105	256M	24MB			153K	78GB	9.09	2.82

Figure 12-8. *Execution plan row source activity monitoring in the SQL Monitoring detail page*

Let's focus on the right-hand columns of the execution plan output first. The `Activity` column shows a breakdown of total resource usage by the statement so far. The longest bar at the `LOAD AS SELECT` line in the execution plan shows that this row source consumed 80% of total activity of that statement execution so far. In previous versions of the SQL Monitor report, CPU and wait activity were displayed in their respective separate columns. The current report, as shown in Figure 12-8, shows the information merged into a single bar. In the example, the wait information is not conveyed very well; most of the 80% activity in the "load as select" is CPU-related, but there are a few samples for other events on the very right of the bar. To make up for this (and in line with almost every part of the report), you can hover the mouse over the bar and inspect the other components. The color coding is the same as in the familiar performance home page. As you can see here, the largest part of the bar is green, indicating CPU. The session waited on compression analysis and direct path temp writes. Note that each bar for each row source only represents waits/CPU recorded for the individual row source, not of total duration or database time of the statement execution. You can examine the Time & Wait Statistics section (shown earlier, in Figure 12-6) to see how much of the total database time was consumed by CPU usage and how much by waits. Since all the data displayed in the report ultimately is taken from Active Session History, you could query that too in order to get the most detailed information.

The Cell Offload Efficiency ratio shows the aforementioned ratio between bytes eligible for Smart Scan to bytes returned over the interconnect. The efficiency in the above example must be poor since the SQL statement was a Create Table as Select statement to create a HCC compressed duplicate of the source table, `BIGTAB`. The offload efficiency is a nice additional piece of information that is added to the row source information in case a Smart Scan has happened on the segment.

The `IO Bytes` column shows how many I/O operations or bytes were read or written by a row source. Users who are familiar with earlier SQL Monitor reports might enjoy that they no longer have to right-click the chart to toggle the display of bytes or I/O operations, as there is a new column. In Figure 12-8, you see that the `TABLE ACCESS STORAGE FULL` row source has done a total of approximately 78GB worth of I/O using approximately 153,000 IO Requests. When you move your mouse over the bars, you will see the details about how much was written and how much was read (unsurprisingly, there are only reads recorded). You also see the exact figures for this row source, including the average size of an IO request. The execution plan step LOAD AS SELECT above it has written only 3GB of data to disk so far—remember the statement is still executing. Note that this 3GB of data is measured at the Oracle database level, but the lower-level ASM layer will likely mirror (or triple-mirror, depending on your configuration) these writes, so actually twice as many bytes were written physically to disks. You can check the Cell Physical IO Interconnect Bytes session statistic to see how much data was really sent (and received) over the InfiniBand network; this metric is aware of the ASM mirror write overhead and any other low-level traffic, too. If you wondered how the creation of table based on a source table of 78GB results in only 3GB worth of I/O, the answer is compression. It could otherwise have been a Create Table As Select (CTAS) statement that only took a subset of the original table. Keep in mind that the statement has not finished executing when the report was taken so the final figure can be a bit more.

Let's look at a few more items of the Real Time SQL Monitoring page.

The Plan Note, right next to the Plan Hash Value, is also of great value, especially on the Exadata platform. It can display a lot of useful, additional information such as what is shown in Figure 12-9a, where it shows an explanation for the degree of parallelism (it was set at table level). You can see that there was no in-memory execution at all.

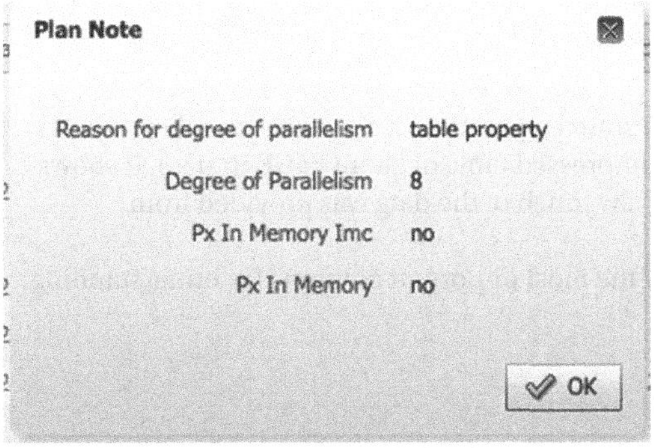

Figure 12-9a. *Plan Note for SQL ID 5m777hdt8gya2*

It will show you if the plan is an adaptive plan as well and the level that was used for dynamic sampling. An example is shown in figure 12-9b.

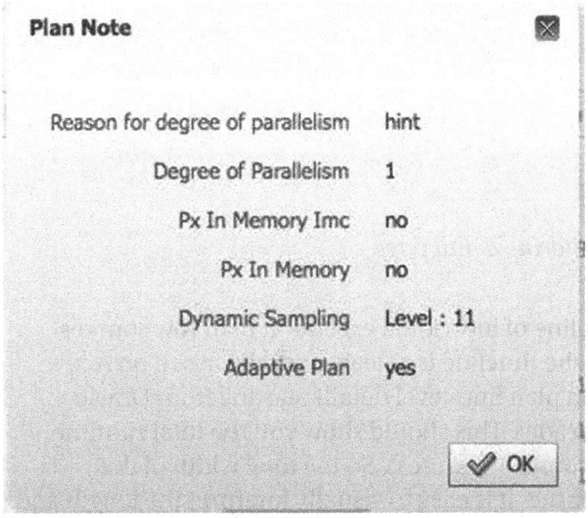

Figure 12-9b. *Plan Note for SQL ID bjbvybmu6pv9h*

Another very useful addition to the SQL Monitor reports is accessible via the binocular icon in the Other Information column. Depending on the operation, it shows valuable information to the performance analyst. For Smart Scans, it depicts the essential figures, as shown in Figure 12-10.

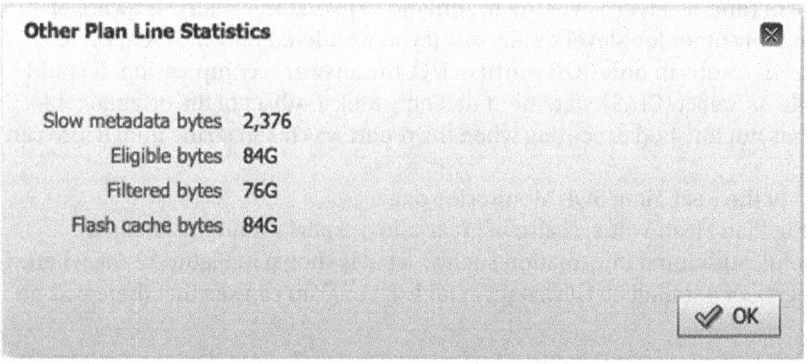
Other Plan Line Statistics
Slow metadata bytes 2,376
Eligible bytes 84G
Filtered bytes 76G
Flash cache bytes 84G
OK

Figure 12-10. *Other Plan Line statistics for the Smart Scan of BIGTAB*

Taken from the Smart Scan information in the last row source operation, it shows the number of bytes that are eligible for the Smart Scan (a nonpartitioned, uncompressed table of about 84GB in size). It shows the amount of filtering the Smart Scan could perform and how much of the data was provided from Flash Cache.

The Timeline column you see in Figure 12-11 is one of the most important columns for understanding where the SQL statement spends its time.

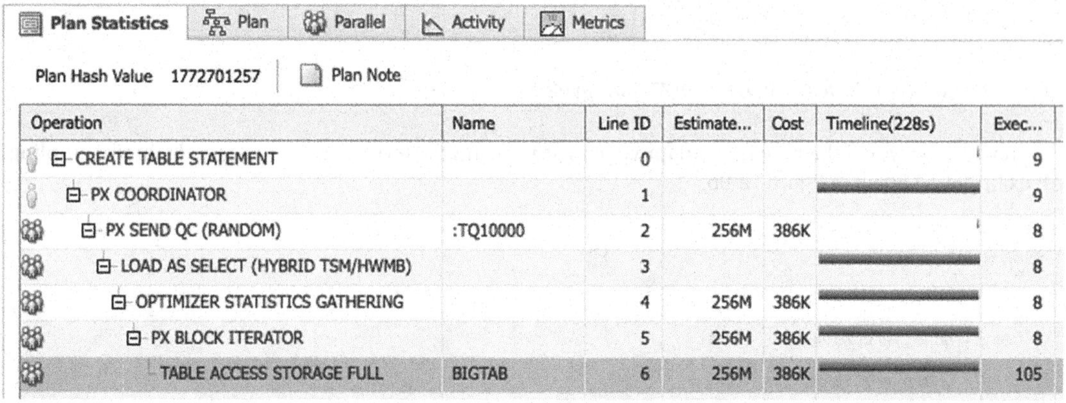
Plan Statistics
Plan
Parallel
Activity
Metrics
Plan Hash Value 1772701257
Plan Note
Operation | Name | Line ID | Estimate... | Cost | Timeline(228s) | Exec...
CREATE TABLE STATEMENT | | 0 | | | | 9
PX COORDINATOR | | 1 | | | | 9
PX SEND QC (RANDOM) | :TQ10000 | 2 | 256M | 386K | | 8
LOAD AS SELECT (HYBRID TSM/HWMB) | | 3 | | | | 8
OPTIMIZER STATISTICS GATHERING | | 4 | 256M | 386K | | 8
PX BLOCK ITERATOR | | 5 | 256M | 386K | | 8
TABLE ACCESS STORAGE FULL | BIGTAB | 6 | 256M | 386K | | 105

Figure 12-11. *Row source activity timeline in the SQL Monitoring detail page*

The Timeline column in the figure shows a visual timeline of individual execution plan row sources' activity. As with almost everything displayed in the report, the timeline is at least partially based on Active Session History (ASH) samples; ASH collects SQL execution plan line-level details starting from Oracle 11gR1. Look into the parenthesis in the Timeline column header. This should show you the total runtime duration of this SQL execution, 228 seconds in this case (around 4 minutes). So the total width of the Timeline column means about 4 minutes of wall-clock runtime. It is easy to visually interpret the length and position of these bars in each row source in the execution plan. Since there is only one set of parallel server processes, there is no dependency between consumers and producers in the above example. All operations except the PX SEND QC kicked off right at the start of the query. In longer running queries, you can use the timeline to work out which operation started when and how long it took. Hovering the mouse over the timeline bar gives more detailed information.

Oracle execution plans are trees of row source functions with strict hierarchy enforced, so a child row source can pass its results only to its direct parent. In our case, the TABLE ACCESS STORAGE FULL against BIGTAB fetched rows and passed them back to its parent operation, PX BLOCK ITERATOR, which then sent the rows back to the LOAD AS SELECT operator but not without calculating optimizer statistics (since Oracle 12c). We are not going deeper into SQL execution engine internals here, but hopefully this example illustrates the hierarchical nature of the SQL execution and how the data "flows" upward through the execution plan tree toward the root of the tree (CREATE TABLE STATEMENT in this case).

The timelines are a great tool for performance investigations since they show exactly where the time is spend in a row source. The example shown until now is not that well suited for the following discussion, which is why another one—a query—has been chosen, as shown in Figure 12-12.

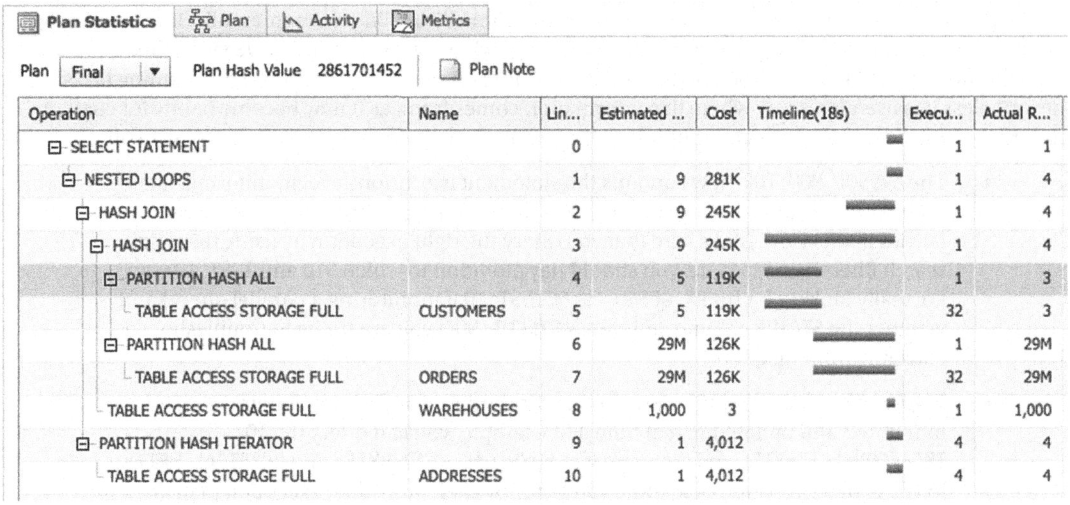

Operation	Name	Lin...	Estimated ...	Cost	Timeline(18s)	Execu...	Actual R...
SELECT STATEMENT		0				1	1
NESTED LOOPS		1	9	281K		1	4
HASH JOIN		2	9	245K		1	4
HASH JOIN		3	9	245K		1	4
PARTITION HASH ALL		4	5	119K		1	3
TABLE ACCESS STORAGE FULL	CUSTOMERS	5	5	119K		32	3
PARTITION HASH ALL		6	29M	126K		1	29M
TABLE ACCESS STORAGE FULL	ORDERS	7	29M	126K		32	29M
TABLE ACCESS STORAGE FULL	WAREHOUSES	8	1,000	3		1	1,000
PARTITION HASH ITERATOR		9	1	4,012		4	4
TABLE ACCESS STORAGE FULL	ADDRESSES	10	1	4,012		4	4

Figure 12-12. *Row source activity timeline in the SQL Monitoring detail page*

Looking at the timeline bars for the query, you notice that the PARTITION HASH ALL and TABLE ACCESS STORAGE FULL for the CUSTOMERS table were the first row sources to start shown in lines four and five. The next row sources to begin their work are the scan of the ORDERS table, both of which are hash-joined to form a new row source. This new row source is then hash-joined to WAREHOUSES, the result of which is joined to ADDRESSES in a nested loop operation.

Looking at the individual bars, you can see their individual execution time, which can serve as the starting point for the query optimization. In the above case, the scan of the ORDERS table takes longest. As with every tuning effort, the analyst should focus on the largest consumer. The optimizer is not to blame here—the cardinality estimates are very good, as you can see in the estimated and actual row columns. What is noteworthy is that around 29 million rows from the ORDERS table are processed in the query, which could potentially be reduced by a filter.

Other options to reduce the time spent in a row source operation include scanning less data, filtering more (in the cells hopefully), accessing fewer partitions, or just increasing the scanning throughput (by increasing parallelism in this case).

The timeline bars are just the first thing to check. There are lots of other useful details in the SQL Monitoring report, too. Take a SORT ORDER BY for example. Quite often in your query plans, you see that the sort operation has been active throughout the whole execution of this statement. And if you know the basics of sorting, it should make sense—the sorting row source was active for the first two-thirds of the time because it was fetching data into sort buffers and sorting it (and spilling some data to temporary tablespace). After the sort itself was complete (the child row source returned an "end of data" condition), the sorting row source function still had to be invoked. It is by invoking that function that the sort operation returns the sorted rows to its parent operation. This is why the parent row source usually becomes active only toward the end of the sort execution timeline—because *all* the rows have to be fetched and sorted first before anything can be returned for further processing. And once all the rows *are* fetched and sorted, there is no reason for the SORT ORDER BY row source to visit its child row sources again.

Manually Querying Real-Time SQL Monitoring Data

All the pretty charts in Enterprise Manager are based on some V$ or DBA_ views internally. If you do not happen to have access to Enterprise Manager, you can get what you want from the V$ views directly. You probably do not need to access the underlying V$ views for your everyday monitoring and tuning tasks, but nevertheless it is useful to know where this information comes from, as it may become handy for custom monitoring and advanced problem troubleshooting. Following are some key views to be aware of:

- The GV$SQL_MONITOR view contains the statement execution-level monitoring data. When multiple sessions are running the same statement, you will have multiple entries in this view. Make sure that you query the right execution by using the right search filters. For example, you should pay attention to which SID and INST_ID you are really looking for (or PX_QCSID, PX_QCINST_ID if monitoring a parallel query) and whether the STATUS column still shows EXECUTING if you are trying to troubleshoot a currently running query.
- The GV$SQL_PLAN_MONITOR view contains execution plan line-level metrics, monitored and updated in real time. For example, you can query the IO_INTERCONNECT_BYTES and compare it to PHYSICAL_READ_BYTES and PHYSICAL_WRITE_BYTES to determine the offloading efficiency by each individual execution plan line, instead of the whole query efficiency. Note that increasing the offloading efficiency percentage should not be your primary goal of monitoring and tuning—where you spend your response *time* matters. In Oracle 12c the view has been greatly enhanced and its data is used to populate the Other (statistics) column, an example for which is shown in figure 12-10. It appears as if a join to v$sql_monitor_statname is necessary to add labels to the OTHERSTAT% columns.
- The GV$ACTIVE_SESSION_HISTORY view contains columns like SQL_PLAN_LINE_ID, SQL_PLAN_OPERATION, and SQL_PLAN_OPTIONS starting from Oracle 11gR1. You can query these columns, in addition to SQL_ID, to find the top row sources of an SQL execution plan, too, instead of just listing the top SQL statement.

Reporting Real-Time SQL Monitoring Data with DBMS_SQLTUNE

If you do not have access to a graphical front-end for some reason, you can also extract the SQL Monitoring details using the DBMS_SQLTUNE.REPORT_SQL_MONITOR package function. You can use the following syntax, but make sure you read the related documentation to see the full power of this feature. Note that the text below is edited, as this function generates very wide output that did not fit the book pages. The tables have been wrapped around and adapted for print.

```
SQL> SELECT
       DBMS_SQLTUNE.REPORT_SQL_MONITOR(
         sql_id=> '5m777hdt8gya2',
         report_level=>'ALL',
         type => 'TEXT') as report
     FROM dual
SQL> /

SQL Monitoring Report

SQL Text
------------------------------
create table bigtab_qh column store compress for query high tablespace martin_bigfile
parallel 8 as select * from bigtab

Global Information
------------------------------
 Status              :  DONE
 Instance ID         :  1
 Session             :  MARTIN (588:34223)
 SQL ID              :  5m777hdt8gya2
 SQL Execution ID    :  16777216
 Execution Started   :  01/28/2015 05:25:24
 First Refresh Time  :  01/28/2015 05:25:24
 Last Refresh Time   :  01/28/2015 05:29:12
 Duration            :  228s
 Module/Action       :  SQL*Plus/-
 Service             :  SYS$USERS
 Program             :  sqlplus@enkdb03.enkitec.com (TNS V1-V3)

Global Stats
===========================================================================================
| Elapsed |   Cpu   |    IO    | Application | Concurrency | Cluster  | PL/SQL  |  Other   |
| Time(s) | Time(s) | Waits(s) |  Waits(s)   |  Waits(s)   | Waits(s) | Time(s) | Waits(s) |
===========================================================================================
|    1809 |    1770 |       25 |        0.00 |        0.07 |     0.01 |    0.00 |       14 |
===========================================================================================

===================================================
| Buffer | Read | Read  | Write | Write |  Cell   |
|  Gets  | Reqs | Bytes | Reqs  | Bytes | Offload |
===================================================
|    11M | 153K |  78GB |  6567 |   3GB |   4.76% |
===================================================

Parallel Execution Details (DOP=8 , Servers Allocated=8)
============================================================================================
|      Name       | Type  | Server# | Elapsed |   Cpu   |    IO    | Application |
Concurrency
|                 |       |         | Time(s) | Time(s) | Waits(s) |  Waits(s)   | Waits(s)
============================================================================================
```

```
| PX Coordinator | QC    |       |    1.04 |    0.11 |     0.00 |          0.00 |
0.00
| p000           | Set 1 |     1 |     227 |     222 |     3.20 |               |
0.00
| p001           | Set 1 |     2 |     227 |     221 |     3.26 |               |
0.01
...
| p007           | Set 1 |     8 |     225 |     222 |     3.21 |               |
0.00
=========================================================================================

===============================================================
Buffer | Read  | Read  | Write | Write | Cell    | Wait Events |
 Gets  | Reqs  | Bytes | Reqs  | Bytes | Offload | (sample #)  |
    1M | 19088 |  10GB |   811 | 399MB |   4.76% |             |
    1M | 19095 |  10GB |   822 | 398MB |   4.76% |             |
    1M | 19090 |  10GB |   828 | 399MB |   4.76% |             |
===============================================================

SQL Plan Monitoring Details (Plan Hash Value=2542114301)
==========================================================================================
| Id |              Operation              |   Name   |  Rows   | Cost |   Time    | Start
|    |                                     |          | (Estim) |      | Active(s) | Active
==========================================================================================
|  0 | CREATE TABLE STATEMENT              |          |         |      |         4 |   +225
|  1 |   PX COORDINATOR                    |          |         |      |       229 |     +0
|  2 |    PX SEND QC (RANDOM)              | :TQ10000 |    256M | 386K |         3 |   +225
|  3 |     LOAD AS SELECT (HYBRID TSM/HWMB) |          |         |      |       228 |     +1
|  4 |      OPTIMIZER STATISTICS GATHERING |          |    256M | 386K |       226 |     +2
|  5 |       PX BLOCK ITERATOR             |          |    256M | 386K |       226 |     +2
|  6 |        TABLE ACCESS STORAGE FULL    | BIGTAB   |    256M | 386K |       226 |     +2
==========================================================================================

==========================================================================================
| Execs |   Rows   | Read | Read  | Write | Write | Cell    |  Mem  | Activity | Activity   |
|       | (Actual) | Reqs | Bytes | Reqs  | Bytes | Offload | (Max) |   (%)    | Detail     |
|       |          |      |       |       |       |         |       |          |(# samples) |
==========================================================================================
|     9 |       16 |      |       |       |       |         |       |          |            |
|     9 |       16 |      |       |       |       |         |       |          |            |
|     8 |       16 |      |       |       |       |         |       |          |            |
|     8 |       16 |  153 |   2MB |  6567 |   3GB |         |       |          |            |
|     8 |     256M |      |       |       |       |         |       |          |            |
|     8 |     256M |      |       |       |       |         |       |          |            |
|   105 |     256M | 153K |  78GB |       |       |   9.09% |   25M |          |            |
==========================================================================================
```

DBMS_SQLTUNE.REPORT_SQL_MONITOR can also take HTML as a value for the TYPE parameter, instead of TEXT, in which case the output is generated as HTML. If you spool this output into an HTML file and open it in the browser, you will see much nicer output than just text. And starting with Oracle 11.2, you can also use ACTIVE as a parameter and spool that output into an HTML file. Now if you open this file in the browser, you will see the SQL Monitoring page almost exactly as it looks in the Cloud Control! And all the data required for displaying that report is self-contained in the spooled HTML file—no database access needed when opening it! This is very useful if you want to send a detailed, self-contained report with some SQL execution problem to someone via email.

Controlling SQL Monitoring

SQL Monitoring kicks in immediately for all statements executed with parallel execution—no matter how long they run. For serially executed statements, the SQL Monitoring does not kick in immediately, as it is not designed to monitor typical fast OLTP queries, which are executed many times per second. Nevertheless, if a serial query has consumed more than five seconds of total CPU and/or I/O wait time, it is considered as a long-running query and the SQL Monitoring is enabled for that statement execution. This happens seamlessly and on the fly; no re-execution of the statement is needed.

You can also use MONITOR and NO_MONITOR hints to control the SQL Monitoring for a statement. V$SQL_HINT shows all the hints available for use and the version when they were introduced. For example:

```
SQL> SELECT name, inverse, version, class, sql_feature
  2 FROM v$sql_hint WHERE name LIKE '%MONITOR%';

NAME            INVERSE         VERSION    CLASS           SQL_FEATURE
--------------- --------------- ---------- --------------- ---------------
NO_MONITORING                   8.0.0      NO_MONITORING   QKSFM_ALL
MONITOR         NO_MONITOR      11.1.0.6   MONITOR         QKSFM_ALL
NO_MONITOR      MONITOR         11.1.0.6   MONITOR         QKSFM_ALL
```

Note that the NO_MONITORING hint is something completely different despite the similar name. The NO_MONITORING hint allows you to disable the predicate usage monitoring on table columns (sys.col_usage$), and it has nothing to do with the Real-Time SQL Monitoring option introduced in Oracle 11g.

Monitoring SQL Statements Using V$SQL and V$SQLSTATS

The performance monitoring in the "old days" (before Oracle 10g ASH) was usually done using various V$ views, which showed aggregated instancewide metrics. For example, the Statspack's TOP-5 wait events report section was just a delta between two V$SYSTEM_EVENT view snapshots. The TOP SQL reports were based on V$SQL snapshots, which externalize the execution statistics and resource consumption for each child cursor still in library cache. However, in a large database system (think ERP applications), you can have tens of thousands of cursors in the library cache, so gathering and storing deltas of all of their stats is not feasible. For this reason, tools like Statspack and AWR store deltas of only some top resource-consuming statements and ignore the insignificant ones. Remember that as these tools gather instancewide data, they may end up ignoring a long-running statement if there are only a few sessions executing it. A single session running a bad SQL statement may not be "heard" in the noise of all the other sessions in the instance—potentially thousands of them. This instancewide scope performance data analysis is not as powerful as the session-level ASH data slicing and dicing. With ASH, you can drill down into any single session, regardless of how many sessions in total you have making noise in the instance.

If you use Exadata, you are running at least Oracle 11g R1 on it, so all these superior tools are technically available, assuming that you have the Diagnostics and Tuning Pack licenses for your Exadata cluster. By the way, we have not seen many Exadata-using customers without Diagnostics and Tuning Pack licenses yet, so it looks like the vast majority of Exadata users do not have to resort to old tools such as Statspack or create a custom ASH-style repository themselves (although it is not too hard to do with a few lines of PL/SQL code polling V$SESSION or its underlying X$KSUSE view in each instance).

The V$SQL and V$SQLSTATS views still do have some advantage over SQL Monitoring and ASH-style sampled data in a few cases. For example, if you want to measure metrics such as the number of executions, buffer gets, parse calls, fetches, or rows returned by the SQL child cursor, you can get this data from both Real-time SQL Monitoring (V$SQL_MONITOR) or the V$SQL/V$SQLSTATS views, but not ASH. However, the problem with SQL Monitoring is that it does not monitor short-running queries at all, hence making it unusable for keeping track of OLTP-style small queries executed many times per second. Even adding a MONITOR hint into every query of your application would not help, as the maximum number of monitored plans is limited (controlled by the _sqlmon_max_plan parameter, which defaults to 20 plans per CPU) and you would likely end up with *real-time plan statistics latch* contention as well. The SQL Monitoring feature is not meant to continuously monitor short-running queries executed many times per second.

And this leaves us with V$SQL and V$SQLSTATS. They both maintain similar data, but they are internally different. Whenever you query V$SQL without specifying an exact SQL_ID, Oracle has to traverse through every single library cache hash bucket, and all cursors under it. This may contribute to library cache mutex contention if you have a busy database and lots of cursors in the library cache due to the fact that when you traverse the library cache structure and read its objects' contents, you'll have to hold a mutex on the object. Note that starting from Oracle 11g, all library cache latches are gone and are replaced by mutexes. These same mutexes are used for parsing, looking up, and pinning cursors for execution, so if your monitoring queries poll V$SQL frequently, they may end up causing waits for other sessions.

The V$SQLSTATS view, which was introduced in Oracle 10g, does not have this problem. Starting from Oracle 10gR2, Oracle actually maintains SQL execution statistics in two places—inside the child cursors themselves (V$SQL) and in a separate cursor statistics array stored in a different location in the shared pool. This separation gives the benefit that even if a cursor is flushed out from the shared pool, its stats in this separate array may remain available for longer. Also, when monitoring tools query V$SQLSTATS, they do not have to scan through the entire library cache, thanks to the separate array where stats are stored. This means that your monitoring tools won't cause additional library cache latch (or mutex) contention when they use V$SQLSTATS instead of V$SQL. Both Statspack and AWR do use V$SQLSTATS to collect data for their top SQL reports.

Let's look into V$SQLSTATS (the V$SQL view has pretty much the same columns, by the way). Some of the output here is removed to save space:

```
SQL> @desc v$sqlstats
           Name                            Null?    Type
           ------------------------------- -------- ----------------------
    1      SQL_TEXT                                 VARCHAR2(1000)
    2      SQL_FULLTEXT                             CLOB
    3      SQL_ID                                   VARCHAR2(13)
...
    6      PLAN_HASH_VALUE                          NUMBER
...
   20      CPU_TIME                                 NUMBER
   21      ELAPSED_TIME                             NUMBER
...
   26      USER_IO_WAIT_TIME                        NUMBER
...
   33      IO_CELL_OFFLOAD_ELIGIBLE_BYTES           NUMBER
```

```
34        IO_INTERCONNECT_BYTES                      NUMBER
35        PHYSICAL_READ_REQUESTS                     NUMBER
36        PHYSICAL_READ_BYTES                        NUMBER
37        PHYSICAL_WRITE_REQUESTS                    NUMBER
38        PHYSICAL_WRITE_BYTES                       NUMBER
...
41        IO_CELL_UNCOMPRESSED_BYTES                 NUMBER
42        IO_CELL_OFFLOAD_RETURNED_BYTES             NUMBER
...
72        OBSOLETE_COUNT                             NUMBER
```

The highlighted rows starting with IO_CELL are metrics related to Exadata storage cells (although the IO_INTERCONNECT_BYTES is still populated on non-Exadata databases as well). You would want to compare these cell metrics to database metrics (such as physical_read_bytes) to understand whether this SQL statement is benefiting from Exadata Smart Scan offloading. Note that these metrics, which merely count bytes, should not be used as the primary metric of *performance*; again, the primary metric, the starting point, should always be response time, which you can then break down into individual wait events or into execution plan row source activity (with the SQL Monitoring report or ASH). You can learn more about the meaning of the metrics shown here in Chapter 11.

Note that even though the V$SQLSTATS view also contains the PLAN_HASH_VALUE column, it actually does not store separate stats for the same SQL ID with different plan hash values. It aggregates all the stats generated by different plans of the same SQL ID under a single bucket. This means that you do not really know which plan version consumed the most resources from this view. Luckily, in Oracle 11.2 there is a new view, named V$SQLSTATS_PLAN_HASH, which you should query instead. It organizes and reports the stats broken down by SQL ID *and* plan hash value instead of just SQL ID as V$SQLSTATS does.

Monitoring the Storage Cell Layer

Let's look at how to monitor the storage cell layer for utilization and efficiency. As you already know, the storage cells are industry standard servers with hard disks attached to them for storing the persistent part of the database. The systems are using Linux as their operating system. Since Exadata V2, they also have PCIe-attached Flash Drives available for use as Flash Cache and Flash Log. The Exadata X5-2 High Performance cells are the first to feature Flash memory exclusively at the expense of hard disks. You can use regular Linux OS monitoring commands and tools to keep an eye on OS metrics such as CPU usage or disk I/O activity on the cells. Due to the special nature of the communication protocol employed in Exadata, you cannot use traditional I/O monitoring tools on the compute nodes to monitor disk I/O: The grid disks are externalized only via the ASM layer. On the compute nodes, you only see a single disk used for the OS and the Oracle installation. The only catch with monitoring I/O on the cells themselves is that Oracle does not allow you to install any additional (monitoring) daemons and software on the cells—if you still want to have a supported configuration.

The good news is that Oracle cell server software and the additional OS Watcher or ExaWatcher (starting 11.2.3.3 and up) scripts do a good job of collecting detailed performance metrics in each cell. The following sections show how to extract, display, and use some of these metrics. You might also want to refer back to Chapter 11 for some additional insights into how the cells can be monitored using the V$CELL% family of views or the cellsrvstat utility.

Accessing Cell Metrics in the Cell Layer Using CellCLI

The cell-collected metrics can be accessed using the `CellCLI` utility. That is, in fact, how the Enterprise Manager Exadata storage cell plug-in retrieves its data. You have seen `CellCLI` used in earlier chapters. Following are a few examples of using `CellCLI` for retrieving performance metrics. The command names should be fairly self-explanatory—we will cover the `CellCLI` commands in more detail in Appendix A. The Oracle Exadata documentation set features `CellCli` commands in Chapter 8 of the Exadata Storage Server Software User's Guide.

```
# cellcli
CellCLI: Release 12.1.2.1.0 - Production on Wed Jan 28 09:23:26 CST 2015

Copyright (c) 2007, 2013, Oracle.  All rights reserved.
Cell Efficiency Ratio: 545

CellCLI> LIST METRICDEFINITION      ← show metric short names
         CD_BY_FC_DIRTY
         CD_IO_BY_R_LG
         CD_IO_BY_R_LG_SEC
         CD_IO_BY_R_SCRUB
         CD_IO_BY_R_SCRUB_SEC
         CD_IO_BY_R_SM

   ... lots of output removed ...

         SIO_IO_WR_HD
         SIO_IO_WR_HD_SEC
         SIO_IO_WR_RQ_FC
         SIO_IO_WR_RQ_FC_SEC
         SIO_IO_WR_RQ_HD
         SIO_IO_WR_RQ_HD_SEC

CellCLI> LIST METRICDEFINITION CL_CPUT DETAIL     ← show metric description and details
      name:                        CL_CPUT
      description:                 "Percentage of time over the previous minute that the system
                                    CPUs were not idle."
      metricType:                  Instantaneous
      objectType:                  CELL
      unit:                        %

CellCLI> LIST METRICCURRENT CL_CPUT               ← list the latest metric snapshot value
CL_CPUT      enkcel01      5.3 %
```

```
CellCLI> LIST METRICCURRENT CL_CPUT DETAIL         ← list latest snapshot in detail
         name:                    CL_CPUT
         alertState:              normal
         collectionTime:          2015-01-28T09:24:46-06:00
         metricObjectName:        enkcel04
         metricType:              Instantaneous
         metricValue:             1.4 %
         objectType:              CELL

CellCLI> LIST METRICHISTORY CL_CPUT                ← show historical metric snapshots

         CL_CPUT          enkcel04        1.6 %    2015-01-23T12:05:42-06:00
         CL_CPUT          enkcel04        4.5 %    2015-01-23T12:06:42-06:00
         CL_CPUT          enkcel04        4.1 %    2015-01-23T12:07:42-06:00
         CL_CPUT          enkcel04        4.3 %    2015-01-23T12:08:42-06:00
         CL_CPUT          enkcel04        4.2 %    2015-01-23T12:09:42-06:00
         CL_CPUT          enkcel04        1.6 %    2015-01-23T12:10:56-06:00
... a lot of output skipped ...

CellCLI> LIST METRICHISTORY CL_CPUT -
> where collectiontime < "2015-01-23T12:09:00-06:00" -
> and collectiontime > "2015-01-23T12:06:00-06:00"

         CL_CPUT          enkcel04        4.5 %    2015-01-23T12:06:42-06:00
         CL_CPUT          enkcel04        4.1 %    2015-01-23T12:07:42-06:00
         CL_CPUT          enkcel04        4.3 %    2015-01-23T12:08:42-06:00
```

Accessing Cell Metrics Using the Enterprise Manager Exadata Storage Server Plug-In

The Exadata plug-in version 12.1.0.6 was introduced with the release of OEM 12c R4 and offers significant user interface and instrumentation improvements. This enables the DBA to have more visibility on the detailed breakdown of I/O metrics by resource components and consumers that is critical to ensuring the entire cluster is still within capacity, running optimally, and within service levels.

On the previous versions of the Exadata plug-in, the installation is a somewhat tedious process. You have to customize some of the monitoring charts and align them in a specific way to have a meaningful performance dashboard. With the new plug-in release, the Exadata Database Machine Discovery is a much more streamlined procedure where you can configure all the related components easily. The plug-in installation is out of the scope of this book, but it is well documented in the plug-in's installation guide. Also in this section, we will focus only on the critical improvements of the Exadata plug-in in terms of performance monitoring. There is a more elaborate Maximum Availability Architecture white paper titled "Exadata Health and Resource Usage Monitoring" published at Oracle Technology Network that discusses a wide variety of monitoring methodologies using OEM12c R4.

To give you a high-level aggregate IO performance, let's start by accessing the Exadata Storage Server Grid home. To access the page, from the OEM12c R4 home page, select Targets tab, then Exadata, and then the Exadata Grid environment. Figure 12-13 shows the drop-down menu.

Figure 12-13. ***Targets tab ➤ Exadata***

Once you navigate to the list of Exadata targets, you are going to see all the database machines that have been discovered. Figure 12-14 shows one of these. A click on the little triangle next to the database machine name breaks the system down into storage and compute nodes, as shown in Figure 12-14. Clicking the Grid will lead you to the main performance page for the Exadata grid, shown in figure 12-15.

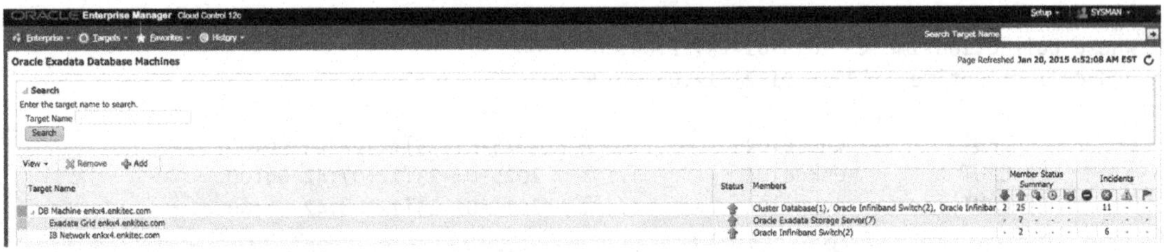

Figure 12-14. ***Discovered Exadata Database Machines ➤ Exadata Grid***

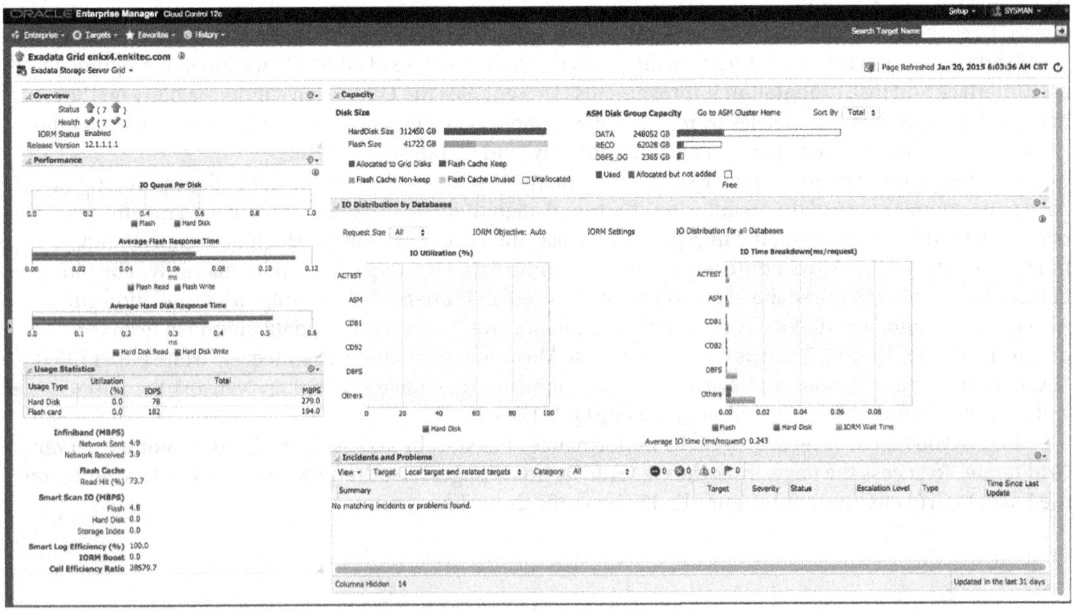

Figure 12-15. ***Exadata Storage Server Grid home page***

The Exadata Storage Server Grid landing page is very useful for the Exadata administrator. It provides a wealth of information that the Oracle database administrator is not normally used to being exposed to. In many cases, different teams tend to play a ping-pong game of blame, helping no one. The database administrator does not normally have visibility of the full stack's components—but with Exadata there is.

The Exadata Storage Server Grid home page provides a high-level overview performance of the Exadata Database Machine. The page is broken down by cell server state, efficiency and usage statistics, capacity, IO breakdown, and incidents/problems. From here, you will be able to highlight any issues that require immediate attention. In case of suspected I/O performance problems, this is the first and key page you need to look at to see the overall health of the environment.

The next step is to drill down on the breakdown of IO by resource component (Flash vs. Hard disk) and by database. From the home page, select Performance, as shown in Figure 12-16.

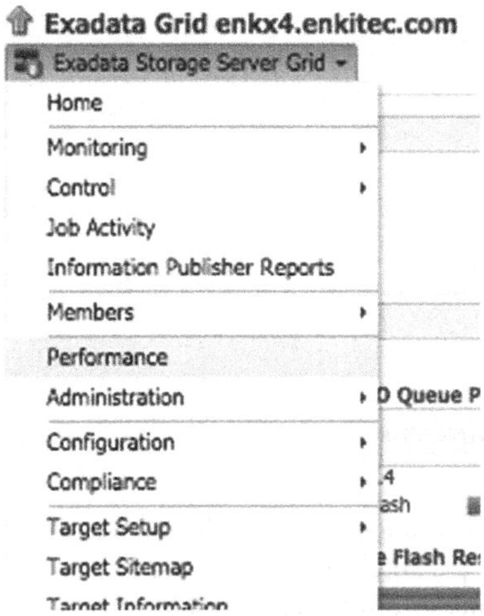

Figure 12-16. *Exadata Storage Server Grid home Performance tab*

As soon as the page finishes loading, you will see a page similar to the one shown in Figure 12-17. The initial load might take a couple of seconds to populate the various graphs.

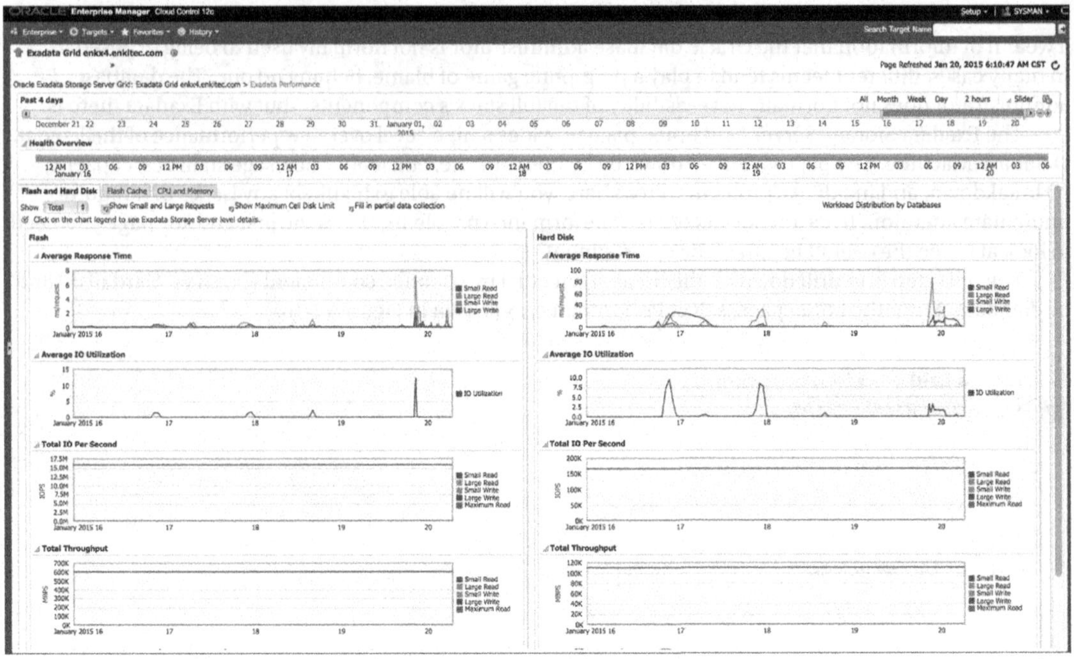

Figure 12-17. Exadata Storage Server Performance view—Flash and Hard Disk

Here you can observe the current and historical high-level I/O performance separately for flash and hard disk. On the top of the page is the time dimension from which you are able to drill down and filter up to the oldest historical data that exists in the OEM repository. A feature introduced in Exadata plug-in 12.1.0.4 is the "Show Maximum Cell Disk Limit," which is the red line that you see on the metrics "Total IO Per Second" and "Total Throughput" that corresponds to the performance capacity line on both flash and hard disk. Whenever you make use of the "Cell Disk Limit," make sure to toggle show to "Total" instead of "Average" so that all IOs happening will sum up and be shown against the total performance capacity. Also the "Show Small and Large Requests" will present the breakdown of small and large IOs across flash and hard disk. Figure 12-18 shows an example for history Flash Cache performance.

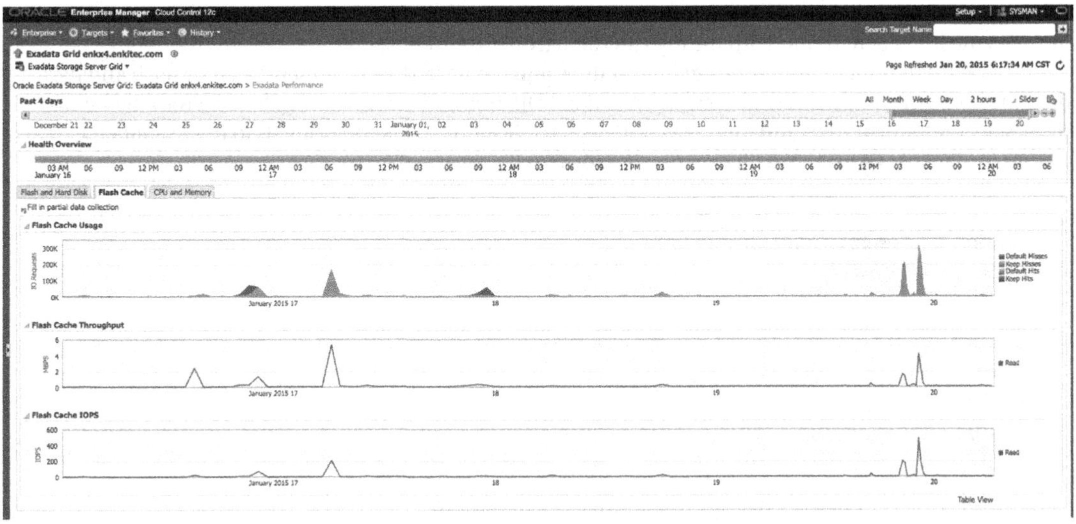

Figure 12-18. *Exadata Storage Server Performance view—Flash Cache*

The Flash Cache tab contains metrics about the Flash Cache efficiency (hits vs. misses) and flash I/O usage. Moving on to the next tab, CPU and memory shows these statistics as well, as demonstrated in Figure 12-19.

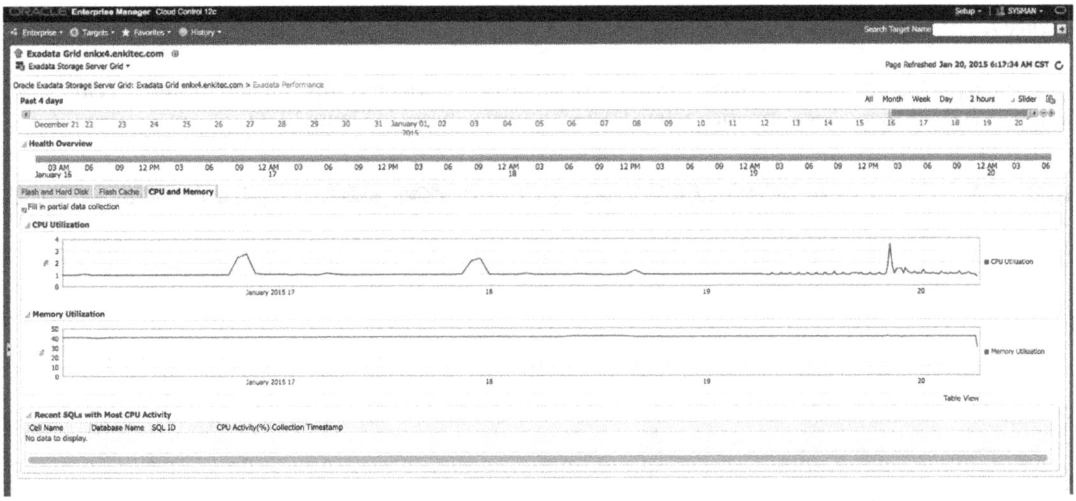

Figure 12-19. *Exadata Storage Server Performance view—CPU and Memory*

The CPU and Memory tab displays metric data for Storage Server CPU and memory utilization, and it includes the list of SQL scripts with the top CPU activity up to seven days.

After we determined the periods of high activity and the IO performance separated by flash and hard disk, the next thing to do is to drill down by Workload Distribution across the databases. From the home page, select Administration **and** then select Manage IO Resource. This will bring us to the Exadata IO Resource Manager (IORM) page. The menu is shown in Figure 12-20.

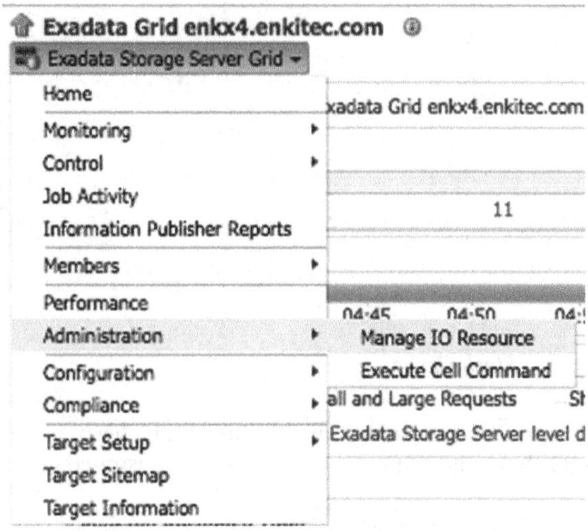

***Figure 12-20.** Exadata Storage Server Grid home ➤ Administration ➤ Manage IO Resource tab*

The IORM settings page is too large to fit into a single figure, which is why you find the top part in Figures 12-21 and actual performance-related data for the databases in Figure 12-22.

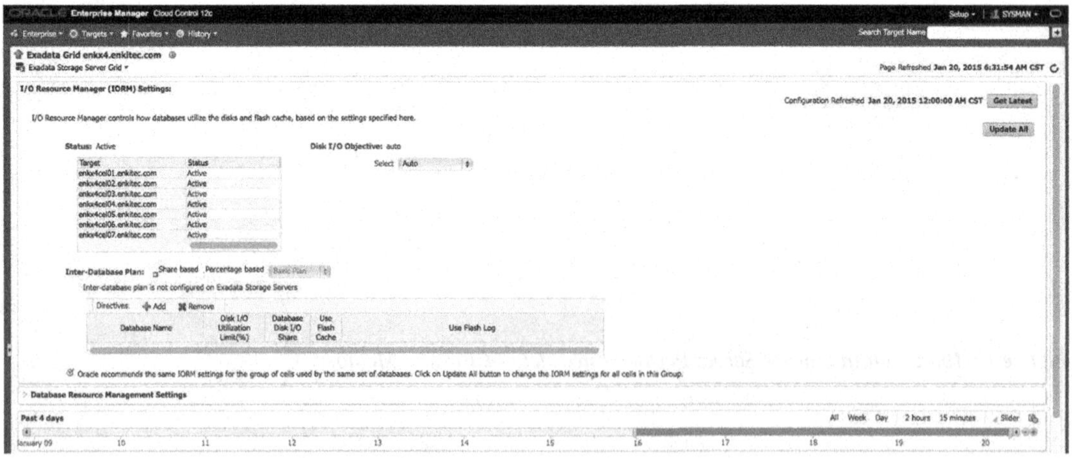

***Figure 12-21.** Exadata IORM page*

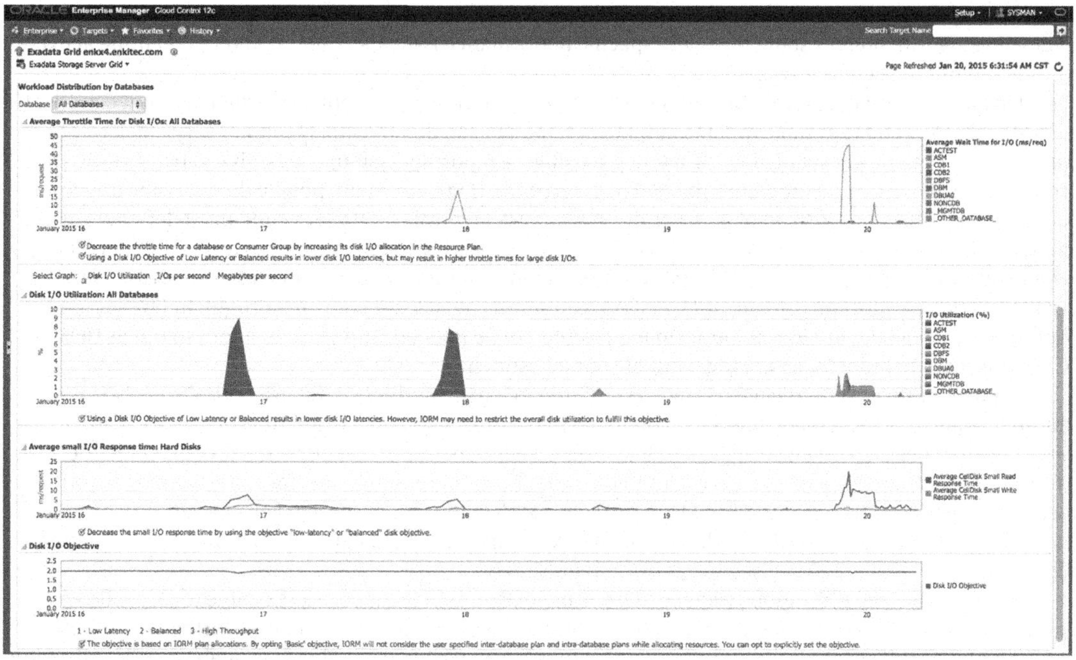

Figure 12-22. *Exadata IORM page—Workload Distribution by Databases*

Performance data for the databases hosted on the Exadata system is available when scrolling down, as shown in Figure 12-22.

The Exadata IORM page can be used to simply monitor the time series workload distribution by database or to configure the IO resource management settings. This page is well laid out, giving you an idea of the average throttle time, utilization, small IO latency, and disk IO objective across the databases, which are the key information to have when setting up a general Resource Management and IORM plan. This, together with the two previous pages (Storage Server Grid home page and Performance view), makes it easier to validate if the cause of the performance degradation is due to resource contention, capacity, or a problem just within the database. I/O Resource Manager is covered in more detail in Chapter 7.

Which Cell Metrics to Use?

Which cell metrics to use is an important question. Oracle provides a huge variety of different metrics—from the database level, the host server level, and the Exadata cell level. Not only is the number huge already as of 12.1.2.1, but it keeps growing. Therefore, it is very easy to get lost in the metrics or, even worse, get misled and troubleshoot a wrong or nonexistent problem. In performance troubleshooting, the rule is to start with what matters—user response time—and drill down from there, as explained in the previous sections of this chapter. But general efficiency monitoring, utilization overview, and capacity planning are sometimes good reasons for examining cell-level aggregated metrics.

This may come as a surprise if you have expected more, but there is no long list of secret and special Exadata metrics you should monitor in your cells. A cell is just a server, with RAM, CPUs, and disks, sending data out over a network link. The fundamental metrics you would want to monitor at the cell level are the same you would use in any server: CPU utilization, system load, memory utilization and disk utilization, and I/O throughput and latency. The most important metrics are available in the OEM Exadata Storage Server

Plug-in, and the rest can be extracted from ExaWatcher log files. The advanced metrics come into play only when dealing with bugs or some rare, very specific performance issues, so they should not really be actively monitored unless there is a problem.

One topic deserves some elaboration—the CPU usage monitoring, both in the database and cells. The data warehouses and reporting systems, unlike OLTP databases, do not usually require very quick response times for user queries. Instead of being latency sensitive, a reporting system is sensitive to bandwidth. Of course, the faster a query completes, the better, but in a DWH environment, people do not really notice if a query ran in 33 seconds instead of 30 seconds. In contrast, a typical OLTP user would most definitely notice if their one-second query took six seconds occasionally. That is one of the reasons why, in OLTP servers, you would not want to constantly run at 100% CPU utilization. You cannot do that and also expect to maintain stable, reliable performance. In an OLTP system, you simply must leave some headroom. In DW servers, however, the small fluctuations in performance would not be noticed, and you can afford to run at 100% of CPU utilization in order to get the most out of your investment.

However, Exadata complicates things. In addition to having multiple database nodes, you also have another whole layer of servers: the cells. Things get interesting, especially when running Smart Scans with high degrees of parallelism against EHCC tables. Remember from Chapters 3 and 11 that offloaded decompression requires a lot of CPU cycles in the cells. Thus, it is possible that for some workloads your cells' CPUs will be 100% busy and unable to feed data back to the database layer fast enough. The database layer CPUs may be half idle, while cells could really use some extra CPU capacity. To remedy the situation, Oracle compute nodes and cell servers perform handshakes.

The risk from cell utilization reaching 100% is the reason Oracle made `cellsrv` able to skip offload processing for some data blocks and pass these blocks straight back to the database (starting in `cellsrv` 11.2.2.3.0). The cell checks whether its CPU utilization is over 90% and whether the database CPU utilization (it is sent in based on resource manager stats from the database) is lower than that. If so, some blocks are not processed in the cells, but passed through to the database directly. The database then will decrypt (if needed, this processing model is not strictly related to HCC) and decompress the blocks and perform projection and filtering in the database layer. This allows you to fully utilize all your CPU capacity in both layers of the Exadata cluster. However, this automatically means that if some blocks are suddenly processed in the database layer (instead of being offloaded to cells), you may see unexpected CPU utilization spikes in the database layer when cells are too busy. This should not be a problem on most DW systems, especially with properly configured resource manager settings, but you would want to watch out for this when running OLTP or other low-latency systems on Exadata.

As usual, Oracle provides good metrics about this passthrough feature. Whenever the offload processing is skipped for some blocks during a Smart Scan and these blocks are sent back to the database layer for processing, the statistic "cell physical IO bytes pushed back due to excessive CPU on cell" or more recently "cell physical IO bytes sent directly to DB node to balance CPU" is incremented in `V$SESSTAT/V$SYSSTAT` and AWR reports. Read more about this feature and statistic in Chapter 11.

Monitoring Exadata Storage Cell OS-Level Metrics

The Oracle Database and the `cellsrv` software do a good job of gathering performance metrics, but there are still cases where you would want to use an OS tool instead. One of the reasons is that usually the V$ views in Oracle tell you what Oracle *thinks* it's doing. However, this may not necessarily be what is really happening if you hit a bug or some other limitation of Oracle's built-in instrumentation. One of the limitations is low-level I/O measurement.

Monitoring the Storage Cell Server's I/O Metrics with iostat

Both the Oracle Database and the storage cells do measure the I/O completion time; in other words, the response time of I/Os. With synchronous I/O operations, Oracle's I/O wait time is merely the system call (like `pread`) completion time. With asynchronous I/O, the response time measurement is trickier, as an asynchronous I/O submit system call will not block and wait; it will return immediately in microseconds and some I/O reaping system call will be executed later, which will mark the I/O operation as complete. The Exadata storage cells keep track of each asynchronous I/O request (for example, when it was submitted), and once the I/O is successfully reaped, they will check the reaping timestamp against that I/O's submit timestamp and know its duration.

Regardless of this extra `cellsrv`-level I/O monitoring, the cells still do not break the I/O response time into the two important components: how much time this I/O request spent uselessly *waiting* in the OS I/O queue before it was even sent out to the SCSI device, and how long the actual hardware *service time* was once the I/O request was sent out to the hardware. We noticed quite a few new cell metrics that include "wait time" and "service time" in their names in Exadata 12.1.2.1.0 but these were related to the IO Resource Manager and not individual grid disks. Therefore, it is still useful to compare the I/O service time to waiting time. This comparison gives an important clue about whether the storage hardware itself responds slowly, in which case the service time is higher than you would expect from a modern disk drive.

■ **Note** So what is this normal I/O service time to expect from disks? That depends on which disks you have, what their seek latency is, how far the disk read/write head has to seek from its previous location, what the rotational latency of the disk is, how fast it spins (RPM), and how fast it can transfer the bits just read over the wires (or fiber). There is no magic in calculating what a good service time should be for a disk; it's all based on the physical capabilities of the disk, and these capabilities are documented in the vendor's disk specs. You can read more about the various latencies involved from Wikipedia: `http://en.wikipedia.org/wiki/Hard_disk_drive#Access_time`.

Of course, there may be other overhead, like SAN storage network roundtrip times and any extra latency caused by storage controllers, switches, and so on. But remember, Exadata is not connected to SAN storage; the disks are attached directly to the storage cells. Each storage cell with the exception of the X5-2 High Performance server has a little LSI MegaRaid controller in it, and the disks are attached to that controller. This is owed to the fact that there are no hard disks available in that server type either so the discussion about mechanical specifics on hard disks does not apply.

Furthermore there are no complex network components such as intermediary fabric switches between the disks and storage (cells), which might drive up latency or fail. More importantly, there are no "outsider" databases or applications connected to the storage, which you have no control over, but which could suddenly start saturating the disks without a warning. All you would be able to see in that case is that the disk I/O service times suddenly go up as the storage array gets overloaded.

Anyway, a small I/O request (up to 256KB) against a modern 15000RPM disk drive should ideally have average service time of 5-7 milliseconds per I/O request. This comes from a 3.5ms average seek latency, 2ms average rotational latency, plus 0.4ms for transferring the 256KB over SAS channels. In theory, this average seek latency is a pessimistic figure, assuming that the whole disk is full and the disk read/write heads have to do random seeks across tracks from end to end of the disk cylinders. But you probably have a configuration where your disks are carved into hotter and colder regions, which is commonly referred to as *short-stroking*. Such a setup is created by the default Exadata install, in which the DATA disk group is on the faster outer regions of the platters across the hard disks; the RECO disk group on the middle region of the platters across the disks, which is visited much less frequently; and the `DBFS_DG` is on the inner region of the platters, except for the first to disks, on which at this place the operating system partitions are placed, mirrored via software

RAID. In effect, this data placement reduces the real average seek times. So, while you may get these low 2-3ms service times when your disk heads do not have to seek too far; in practice, 10ms average I/O service times are completely OK once you run real production workloads.

■ **Note** This discussion about short-stroking disks for best performance does not apply to the all-flash X5-2 High Performance cells because these servers do not have any spinning disks.

The whole point of this explanation so far is really that it *is* possible to know what the ideal disk *service* times should be for an Exadata cell's disk drives If the service times are constantly much higher than that, there is some problem with the storage hardware and it could be a mix of controller issues, disk failure, or degrading performance due to data fragmentation. With SAN storage, high OS-level service times could also mean that there is some queueing going on inside the SAN network or the storage array (for example, if a thousand other servers are hammering the same storage array with I/O). But, as said above, Exadata storage cells have dedicated storage in them; only the current cell OS can access this storage, and all IOs are visible in `iostat`. Starting with version 11.2.3.2, Exadata cells try to detect underperforming disks and remove them from the disk group if possible. All of these operations are tracked in the cell alert log file and alerts will be sent out if the cells are configured appropriately. In most cases, a spike in the workload causes the disk to be temporarily taken offline and checked, entering a confined state. If the thorough checking results in a predictable poor performance of the disk, it can be dropped. Otherwise, it is added back to the configuration as if nothing had ever happened. The fine print to this can be found in MOS note 1509105.1.

What if the service time is OK, but Oracle (`cellsrv`) still sees bad I/O performance? Well, this may mean there is still *queueing* going on inside the cell Linux servers—and `iostat` can show this information, too. You can have only a limited number of outstanding I/Os in the "on-the-fly" state against your storage controller LUNs. The storage controller needs to keep track of each outstanding I/O (for example, it has to remember where in the host RAM to write the block once it is read from disk and arrives at the controller), and these I/O slots are limited. The Linux kernel does not allow sending out more I/Os than the storage controller can handle; otherwise, a SCSI reset would occur. These throttled I/Os will have to wait in the OS disk device I/O queue— and they are *uselessly* waiting there; they are not even sent out to the storage controller yet. Only when some previously outstanding I/O operation completes will the first item in the queue be sent to the disks (assuming that the I/O latency deadline has not been reached for some request; `cellsrv` uses the Linux "deadline" I/O scheduler).

The good news is that beginning with the X5-2, the PCIe Flash devices use the NVMe (NVM Express or Non Volatile Memory Host Controller) Interface, which has the potential to vastly increase the number of IO queues as well as the queue depth per queue. But that only applies to the Flash devices; hard disks are still bound to the limits just described. Over time, the flash devices have taken a lot more responsibility for shouldering the I/O workload. In the case of the X5-2 High Performance cells, this is driven to the extreme. But even in the mixed hard-disk/flash memory configurations, you can enable Write-Back Flash Cache to help out in the rare cases where disks are a bottleneck for writes. Smart Flash Log helps you with commits. And since Exadata 11.2.3.3, reads are automatically cached in Smart Flash Cache for small and large I/O requests anyway. In summary, a large portion of your I/O requests will ideally be satisfied from flash instead of disk. Small, random I/O requests benefit from flash memory a lot.

Circling back to the discussion of hard disks. If you observe I/O waiting (queueing time), the `await` (average I/O completion time) column in `iostat` will be significantly higher than the `svctm` (estimated I/O service time) column. Note that the name "await" is somewhat misleading, as it does not show only the wait (queueing) time—it shows the total wait plus service time. Similarly, the `avgqu-sz` column does not show just the average I/O wait queue length, but rather the average *total* number of not completed I/Os in the I/O request queue, regardless of whether they have already been sent out to storage hardware (are already being serviced) or still waiting in the I/O queue (not yet serviced).

Linux iostat shows statistics for the disk partition and the cell software RAID device (used for cell OS partition mirroring). We can filter out those lines so that only the physical disk stats would be listed; LVM and partitions information is excluded. The next example works for all but the X5-2 High Performance cells; these do not have any spinning disks.

```
$ iostat -xm 5 | egrep -v "sd.[0-9]|^md"
avg-cpu:  %user   %nice %system %iowait  %steal   %idle
          56.38    0.03   18.65   15.33    0.00    9.61

Device:
       rrqm/s  wrqm/s      r/s   w/s   rMB/s  wMB/s  avgrq-sz  avgqu-sz   await  svctm  %util
sdd      0.00    0.00   156.20  0.20   78.10   0.00   1022.69     20.78  116.79   5.77  90.20
sde      0.00    0.00   165.40  0.00   82.70   0.00   1024.00     27.96  163.97   5.69  94.08
sdh      0.00    0.00   163.20  3.20   81.34   0.01   1001.18     24.67  148.05   5.82  96.92
sdi      0.00    0.00   154.40  0.20   77.20   0.00   1022.68     12.81   82.68   5.75  88.82
sdj      0.00    0.00   163.20  0.00   81.31   0.00   1020.39     20.27  124.22   5.58  91.12
sdk      0.00    0.00   157.60  0.40   78.51   0.01   1017.76     30.54  168.64   5.91  93.42
sdc      0.00    0.00   166.80  3.60   80.96   0.03    973.48     30.23  169.08   5.70  97.20
sdf      0.00    0.00   161.80  0.00   80.51   0.00   1019.08     30.66  177.49   6.08  98.44
sdl      0.00    0.00   147.40  0.00   73.70   0.00   1024.00     17.52  119.09   6.01  88.64
sda      0.00   15.40   166.00  8.40   83.00   0.09    975.71     37.20  209.58   5.73 100.00
sdg      0.00    0.00   172.40  0.00   86.20   0.00   1024.00     32.10  171.85   5.75  99.18
sdn     83.00    0.00  2850.00  0.60  183.90   0.00    132.13     18.18    6.37   0.33  93.12
sdr     76.00    0.00  2788.20  0.40  179.60   0.01    131.91     16.43    5.89   0.33  92.12
sdv    108.60    0.00  2797.60  0.40  182.40   0.00    133.51     19.04    6.79   0.33  91.82
sdz    130.00    0.00  3119.80  0.80  203.63   0.00    133.64     35.88   11.47   0.30  95.12
sds     72.80    0.00  2969.60  0.60  190.57   0.00    131.40     21.37    7.19   0.32  94.46
sdo     88.80    0.00  2847.80  1.20  184.19   0.01    132.41     18.22    6.40   0.33  93.22
sdw     95.20    0.00  2711.40  0.40  176.20   0.00    133.07     16.79    6.18   0.33  90.14
sdaa    70.00    0.00  2556.40  0.60  164.43   0.00    131.71     14.96    5.85   0.34  87.42
sdq     56.00    0.00  2565.80  0.40  164.14   0.00    130.99     12.27    4.78   0.35  89.34
sdm     79.20    0.00  2863.00  1.20  184.33   0.01    131.81     18.99    6.62   0.33  93.64
sdp     91.20    0.00  2863.40  4.40  185.18   0.04    132.28     18.82    6.56   0.33  93.54
sdu    100.60    0.00  2774.20  0.40  180.51   0.00    133.24     18.84    6.78   0.33  91.88
sdy    105.60    0.00  2830.00  0.80  184.05   0.01    133.16     21.14    7.46   0.32  91.26
sdt    160.40    0.00  3054.40  0.80  201.74   0.01    135.24     35.70   11.64   0.32  96.48
sdx    111.60    0.00  2752.00  0.40  179.93   0.00    133.88     17.63    6.39   0.33  91.12
sdab    85.60    0.00  2828.80  0.40  182.62   0.00    132.20     20.28    7.15   0.32  90.88
sdb      0.00   15.40   162.80  7.80   81.40   0.09    978.27     23.15  132.24   5.63  96.04
sdac     0.00    0.00     0.00  0.00    0.00   0.00      0.00      0.00    0.00   0.00   0.00
```

Bu wait a minute! Shouldn't you see fewer disks, as each cell has only 12 hard drives in it? You see so many disks because, in addition to the 12 hard disks, cells also have their flash cards presented as separate SCSI "disks." The output above is from an X3-2 cell, showing 4 SCSI devices per flash card in addition to the hard disks. The X5-2 output is very similar except that the devices are accessed via NVMe and thus have different names. They also have fewer FMODs, as you read in Chapter 5.

Finally, there is also one USB disk for system recovery that is not known to the cell software. You can use the lsscsi command or cellcli in the cell to see all disks detected by the OS again with an exception: Since the Flash devices in the X5-2 cells are not SCSI devices, you cannot see them there. In the above example, we hit the particular Exadata X3-2 cell really hard with multiple Smart Scans issued by 50 users for demonstration purposes. The figures are for illustration only; the current generation of Exadata hardware is more powerful than the model used here. Looking at the following output and correlating it with the previous iostats listing, you will see that the disks that are really busy providing best throughput are the Flash disks—most of the data returned to the database sessions is cached in Flash Cache.

```
CellCLI> list lun attributes deviceName,diskType,status
         /dev/sda         HardDisk         normal
         /dev/sdb         HardDisk         normal
         /dev/sdc         HardDisk         normal
         /dev/sdd         HardDisk         normal
         /dev/sde         HardDisk         normal
         /dev/sdf         HardDisk         normal
         /dev/sdg         HardDisk         normal
         /dev/sdh         HardDisk         normal
         /dev/sdi         HardDisk         normal
         /dev/sdj         HardDisk         normal
         /dev/sdk         HardDisk         normal
         /dev/sdl         HardDisk         normal
         /dev/sdq         FlashDisk        normal
         /dev/sdr         FlashDisk        normal
         /dev/sds         FlashDisk        normal
         /dev/sdt         FlashDisk        normal
         /dev/sdy         FlashDisk        normal
         /dev/sdz         FlashDisk        normal
         /dev/sdaa        FlashDisk        normal
         /dev/sdab        FlashDisk        normal
         /dev/sdm         FlashDisk        normal
         /dev/sdn         FlashDisk        normal
         /dev/sdo         FlashDisk        normal
         /dev/sdp         FlashDisk        normal
         /dev/sdu         FlashDisk        normal
         /dev/sdv         FlashDisk        normal
         /dev/sdw         FlashDisk        normal
         /dev/sdx         FlashDisk        normal
```

The LSI disks here are the hard disks presented to the host by the LSI SCSI RAID controller (from devices sda to sdl); the other disks are the flash cards. Up until Exadata X5-2, each physical flash card is subdivided into four different "domains" reported as individual device to the OS. Furthermore, such a so-called FMOD is addressed just like any other SCSI device, as indicated by the device name starting with sd. If you compare the average I/O service times (svctm) in iostat, you will see that the devices belonging to flash cards have a service time an order of magnitude lower than hard disk devices. So, if you want to monitor only the hard-disk devices, you can filter iostat output by appending the device names to filter to it. The iostat utility provided with Exadata 12.1.2.1 even recognizes regular expressions. The output below was created using iostat -x -m 5 1 /dev/sd[a-l]:

```
Device:
    rrqm/s  wrqm/s     r/s     w/s   rMB/s   wMB/s  avgrq-sz  avgqu-sz   await  svctm  %util
sdd   0.00    0.00    9.54    0.39    3.49    0.05    729.81      0.05    5.29   3.18   3.16
sde   0.00    0.00    9.56    0.44    3.49    0.05    725.00      0.06    5.51   3.29   3.29
sdh   0.00    0.00    9.54    0.42    3.49    0.05    727.57      0.05    5.43   3.17   3.16
sdi   0.00    0.00    9.56    0.41    3.49    0.05    727.11      0.05    5.37   3.25   3.24
sdj   0.00    0.00    9.62    0.43    3.52    0.05    729.15      0.05    5.22   3.13   3.15
sdk   0.00    0.00    9.56    0.92    3.49    0.06    693.37      0.05    5.10   3.07   3.22
```

```
sdc  0.00   0.00  12.83  3.21  3.49  0.07  454.96   0.06  4.05  2.52  4.04
sdf  0.00   0.00   6.97  0.38  3.35  0.05  948.27   0.05  7.11  4.17  3.06
sdl  0.00   0.00   9.63  0.37  3.49  0.05  725.13   0.05  5.41  3.24  3.24
sda  0.01  17.61  10.35  8.22  3.49  0.15  400.95   0.07  3.85  1.80  3.34
sdg  0.00   0.00   8.20  0.43  3.42  0.05  822.55   0.05  6.25  3.70  3.20
sdb  0.01  17.61  10.34  8.10  3.49  0.15  404.44   0.08  4.26  1.83  3.38
```

One of the nice aspects when working with Exadata is that, despite every new hardware generation adding new features, the concepts remain the same. In the example above, it does not matter at all if the devices are accessed as block devices or Flash disk—what changes is the device name. You can adapt the `iostat` output just shown by limiting the devices to be reported.

Advanced Cell Monitoring With ExaWatcher

While the database-level wait profile and SQL Monitoring should be used as a starting point for performance monitoring and troubleshooting, sometimes these approaches are not enough and you want to drill deeper. This section explains one additional data source for that. Exadata compute nodes and storage cells come with a preinstalled tool called ExaWatcher, which replaces OSWatcher starting with Exadata software versions 11.2.3.3 and up. It is located under the `/opt/oracle.ExaWatcher` directory. This tool is just a set of shell scripts, which then run standard OS tools, such as `vmstat`, `iostat`, and `netstat`, to collect their data at regular intervals. ExaWatcher's benefit is that it runs at OS level, not inside a database, so it is not affected by database hangs and performance issues or cases where the database's `V$` views don't show the truth or have enough detail. Additionally, the high-frequency ExaWatcher collectors sample data every few seconds, allowing it to detect short "hiccups," or bursts of activity.

ExaWatcher is started automatically when the machine boots. You can check whether the ExaWatcher is running by simply searching for any processes with "ExaWatcher" in their name:

```
# pgrep -lf "ExaWatcher"
4372 /bin/bash ./ExaWatcher.sh --fromconf
4500 sh -c /usr/bin/mpstat -P ALL  5  720 2>/dev/null >>
   /opt/oracle.ExaWatcher/archive/Mpstat.ExaWatcher/2015_01_19_03_02_48_
   MpstatExaWatcher_enkx3cel01.enkitec.com.dat
4734 sh -c /usr/bin/iostat -t -x  5  720 2>/dev/null >>
  /opt/oracle.ExaWatcher/archive/Iostat.ExaWatcher/2015_01_19_03_03_13_
  IostatExaWatcher_enkx3cel01.enkitec.com.dat
5116 /usr/bin/perl /opt/oracle.ExaWatcher/ExecutorExaWatcher.pl
  /opt/oracle.ExaWatcher/ExaWatcher.execonf
5571 sh -c /opt/oracle.ExaWatcher/ExaWatcherCleanup.sh 1417968473 1733501253 3600
  /opt/oracle.ExaWatcher/archive/ 614400 2>>/dev/null
5572 /bin/bash /opt/oracle.ExaWatcher/ExaWatcherCleanup.sh 1417968473 1733501253 3600
  /opt/oracle.ExaWatcher/archive/ 614400
5578 /usr/bin/perl /opt/oracle.ExaWatcher/ExecutorExaWatcher.pl
  /opt/oracle.ExaWatcher/ExaWatcher.execonf
6171 sh -c /opt/oracle/cell/cellsrv/bin/cellsrvstat -interval=5 -count=720 2>/dev/null >>
  /opt/oracle.ExaWatcher/archive/CellSrvStat.ExaWatcher/2015_01_19_03_04_23_
  CellSrvStatExaWatcher_enkx3cel01.enkitec.com.dat
8202 sh -c /usr/bin/vmstat  5  2 >>
  /opt/oracle.ExaWatcher/archive/Vmstat.ExaWatcher/2015_01_19_03_04_58_
  VmstatExaWatcher_enkx3cel01.enkitec.com.dat
16614 sh -c /usr/bin/top -b -d 5 -n 720 2>/dev/null >>
  /opt/oracle.ExaWatcher/archive/Top.ExaWatcher/2015_01_19_02_09_22_
  TopExaWatcher_enkx3cel01.enkitec.com.dat
```

If you want to see the hierarchy of the ExaWatcher process daemons, on Linux you can use either the `ps -H` command or the `pstree` command, as shown here:

```
[root@enkcel04 oracle.ExaWatcher]# pstree -Ahlup $(pgrep ExaWatcher.sh)
ExaWatcher.sh(19804)---perl(20519)-+-perl(20995)---sh(20996)---ExadataDiagColl(20999)
    ---sleep(20311)
                                   |-sh(4960)---mpstat(4961)
                                   |-sh(4993)---iostat(4994)
                                   |-sh(5690)---cellsrvstat(5691)
                                   |-sh(9208)-+-grep(9211)
                                   |          |-sed(9210)
                                   |          `-top(9209)
                                   |-sh(9214)---FlexIntervalMod(9215)---sleep(20129)
                                   |-sh(11658)---FlexIntervalMod(11659)---sleep(20310)
                                   |-sh(14104)---FlexIntervalMod(14105)---sleep(20306)
                                   |-sh(20312)---vmstat(20313)
                                   |-sh(20987)---ExaWatcherClean(20988)---sleep(4294)
                                   |-{perl}(20581)
                                   |-{perl}(20584)
                                   |-{perl}(20587)
                                   |-{perl}(20604)
                                   |-{perl}(20630)
                                   |-{perl}(20647)
                                   |-{perl}(20651)
                                   |-{perl}(20660)
                                   |-{perl}(20672)
                                   |-{perl}(20700)
                                   |-{perl}(20723)
                                   |-{perl}(20743)
                                   |-{perl}(20749)
                                   |-{perl}(20755)
                                   |-{perl}(20758)
                                   |-{perl}(20789)
                                   |-{perl}(20986)
                                   `-{perl}(20994)
[root@enkcel04 oracle.ExaWatcher]#
```

The ExaWatcher daemons store their collected data in the `/opt/oracle.ExaWatcher/archive` directory. It does not use any special format for storing the data; it just stores the text output of the standard OS tools it runs. This makes it easy to use regular text-processing utilities, such as grep, AWK, or Perl/python scripts to extract and present the information you need.

Each data collection command has its own directory, and each directory contains archive files of the command output:

```
# ls -l /opt/oracle.ExaWatcher/archive/
total 616
drwxr----- 2 root root 45056 Jan 19 03:04 CellSrvStat.ExaWatcher
drwxr----- 2 root root 40960 Jan 19 03:07 Diskinfo.ExaWatcher
drwxr----- 3 root root  4096 Jan 17 02:11 ExtractedResults
drwxr----- 2 root root 45056 Jan 19 03:08 FlashSpace.ExaWatcher
drwxr----- 2 root root 40960 Jan 19 03:03 IBCardInfo.ExaWatcher
drwxr----- 2 root root 32768 Jan 19 03:02 IBprocs.ExaWatcher
```

```
drwxr----- 2 root root 40960 Jan 19 03:03 Iostat.ExaWatcher
drwxr----- 2 root root 40960 Jan 19 03:06 Lsof.ExaWatcher
drwxr----- 2 root root  4096 Jan 18 04:02 MegaRaidFW.ExaWatcher
drwxr----- 2 root root 45056 Jan 19 03:04 Meminfo.ExaWatcher
drwxr----- 2 root root 45056 Jan 19 03:02 Mpstat.ExaWatcher
drwxr----- 2 root root 45056 Jan 19 02:15 Netstat.ExaWatcher
drwxr----- 2 root root 36864 Jan 19 03:14 Ps.ExaWatcher
drwxr----- 2 root root 40960 Jan 19 03:04 RDSinfo.ExaWatcher
drwxr----- 2 root root 45056 Jan 19 03:08 Slabinfo.ExaWatcher
drwxr----- 2 root root 36864 Jan 19 03:09 Top.ExaWatcher
drwxr----- 2 root root 40960 Jan 19 03:04 Vmstat.ExaWatcher
```

Changing directory to the IOstat monitoring (IOstat.ExaWatcher) shows that data captured is archived using the bzip2 tool after an interval:

```
# ls -tr  | tail
2015_01_18_18_02_56_IostatExaWatcher_enkx3cel01.enkitec.com.dat.bz2
2015_01_18_19_02_58_IostatExaWatcher_enkx3cel01.enkitec.com.dat.bz2
2015_01_18_20_03_00_IostatExaWatcher_enkx3cel01.enkitec.com.dat.bz2
2015_01_18_21_03_02_IostatExaWatcher_enkx3cel01.enkitec.com.dat.bz2
2015_01_18_22_03_04_IostatExaWatcher_enkx3cel01.enkitec.com.dat.bz2
2015_01_18_23_03_06_IostatExaWatcher_enkx3cel01.enkitec.com.dat.bz2
2015_01_19_00_03_08_IostatExaWatcher_enkx3cel01.enkitec.com.dat.bz2
2015_01_19_01_03_10_IostatExaWatcher_enkx3cel01.enkitec.com.dat.bz2
2015_01_19_02_03_11_IostatExaWatcher_enkx3cel01.enkitec.com.dat.bz2
2015_01_19_03_03_13_IostatExaWatcher_enkx3cel01.enkitec.com.dat
```

There is a separate bzipped file saved for each hour, making it easy to manually investigate past performance data or write a quick AWK, grep, or Perl script, which extracts only the data of interest. The configuration file ExaWatcher.conf is located under the /opt/oracle.ExaWatcher directory so you can alter or check the collection interval for each data collection command. On the output below, each group of data collection command sums up to 3,600 seconds worth of data (Interval x Count) before the ExaWatcher zips the current data collection file and generates a new one:

```
# cat ExaWatcher.conf | sed -e '/^\#/d' -e '/^$/d'
<ResultDir> /opt/oracle.ExaWatcher/archive
<ZipOption> bzip2
<SpaceLimit> 600
<Group>
<Start> 01/23/2015 18:25:03
<End> 01/22/2025 18:24:43
<Interval:s> 3
<Count> 1200
<CommandMode> SELECTED
<Command> Diskinfo
<Group>
<Start> 01/23/2015 18:25:03
<End> 01/22/2025 18:24:43
<Interval:s> 5
<Count> 720
<CommandMode> ALL
<Command> Iostat;;"/usr/bin/iostat -t -x"
```

```
<Command> IBprocs
<Command> Top;;"/usr/bin/top -b"
<Command> Vmstat;;"/usr/bin/vmstat"
<Command> Ps;;"/opt/oracle.ExaWatcher/FlexIntervalMode.sh '/bin/ps -eo flags,s,ruser,pid,ppi
d,c,psr,pri,ni,addr,sz,wchan,stime,tty,time,cmd'"
<Command> Netstat;;"/opt/oracle.ExaWatcher/FlexIntervalMode.sh '/opt/oracle.ExaWatcher/
NetstatExaWatcher.sh'"
<Command> RDSinfo
<Command> Mpstat;;"/usr/bin/mpstat -P ALL"
<Command> Lsof
<Command> IBCardInfo
<Command> Meminfo
<Command> Slabinfo
<RunEnd>
```

Whenever an issue comes up, you will be particularly interested on the before-and-after state of the performance data. On the same directory, the `GetExaWatcherResults.sh` script can be used to get all the ExaWatcher archived command output all at once. The command below extracts the data two hours before and after the specified timestamp and places it under the default archive directory `/opt/oracle.ExaWatcher/archive/ExtractedResults`. The other script options can be used to specify a more precise time range and different archive location. The script expects the date to be formatted mm/dd/yyyy:

```
[root@enkcel04 oracle.ExaWatcher]# ./GetExaWatcherResults.sh --at '01/30/2015 09:00:00'
\> --range 2
```

In Exadata 12.1.2.1.0, there is no further output on the screen. If you want to learn what happened, you need to visit the log and trace files in `/var/log/cellos/ExaWatcher.log` or `/var/log/cellos/ExaWatcher.trc`. The output will have been saved to `/opt/oracle.ExaWatcher/archive/ExtractedResults`. The compressed file contains information from all subsystems monitored by ExaWatcher for the time period specified. Invoking the script with the `--help` option displays a useful online help.

The next example extracts `iostat` I/O statistics from a 9 a.m. bzipped file:

```
# bzcat 2015_01_17_09_02_39_IostatExaWatcher_enkx3cel01.enkitec.com.dat.bz2 | head -20
############################################################
# Starting Time:         01/17/2015 09:02:39
# Sample Interval(s):    5
# Archive Count:         720
# Collection Module:     IostatExaWatcher
# Collection Command:    /usr/bin/iostat -t -x  5  720
############################################################
zzz <01/17/2015 09:02:39> Count:720
Linux 2.6.39-400.128.17.el5uek (enkx3cel01.enkitec.com)          01/17/2015

Time: 09:02:39 AM
avg-cpu:  %user   %nice %system %iowait  %steal   %idle
           0.54    0.00    0.89    0.22    0.00   98.34
```

```
Device:
         rrqm/s   wrqm/s   r/s   w/s    rsec/s    wsec/s avgrq-sz avgqu-sz   await  svctm  %util
sda        0.48    17.27  1.52  5.31   1074.19    181.77   183.93     0.03    3.97   0.95   0.65
sda1       0.00     0.00  0.00  0.00      0.44      0.00    93.97     0.00    4.47   0.38   0.00
sda2       0.00     0.00  0.00  0.00      0.00      0.00     2.55     0.00    0.77   0.76   0.00
sda3       0.47     0.00  0.47  0.45    956.01      4.74  1038.28     0.01    5.69   5.67   0.52
sda4       0.00     0.00  0.00  0.00      0.00      0.00     1.79     0.00    1.16   1.16   0.00
```

The ExaWatcher output samples are prefixed by a timestamp line, which starts with "zzz," as you see above. This shows you the exact time, up to the second, when the OS command was executed. Note that this "zzz" line will only show you when the monitoring command was executed. Some commands are executed only once per hour, but they keep collecting and dumping data samples throughout that hour. In such case, there are monitoring command-specific timestamps printed for each data sample. The following example shows how the `cellsrvstat` command uses `===Current Time===` to indicate the exact time the performance data below it is from. You can use this prefix in your custom scripts. Here is an example:

```
# bzcat 2015_01_17_09_02_55_CellSrvStatExaWatcher_enkx3cel01.enkitec.com.dat.bz2 \
> | head -30
zzz <01/17/2015 09:02:55> Count:720
===Current Time===                                          Sat Jan 17 09:02:55 2015

== Input/Output related stats ==
Number of hard disk block IO read requests                         0      167987444
Number of hard disk block IO write requests                        0      150496829
Hard disk block IO reads (KB)                                      0   111186344274
Hard disk block IO writes (KB)                                     0    25224016152
Number of flash disk block IO read requests                        0       67230332
Number of flash disk block IO write requests                       0       15528794
Flash disk block IO reads (KB)                                     0      870806808
Flash disk block IO writes (KB)                                    0      347337424
Number of disk IO errors                                           0              0
Number of reads from flash cache                                   0       57890992
Number of writes to flash cache                                    0       13119701
Flash cache reads (KB)                                             0      870014160
Flash cache writes (KB)                                            0      347236056
Number of flash cache IO errors                                    0              0
Size of eviction from flash cache (KB)                             0              0
Number of outstanding large flash IOs                              0              0
Number of latency threshold warnings during job                    0          13400
Number of latency threshold warnings by checker                    0              0
Number of latency threshold warnings for smart IO                  0              0
Number of latency threshold warnings for redo log writes           0           6568
Current read block IO to be issued (KB)                            0              0
Total read block IO to be issued (KB)                              0     9066623802
Current write block IO to be issued (KB)                           0              0
Total write block IO to be issued (KB)                             0    25054696317
Current read blocks in IO (KB)                                     0              0
Total read block IO issued (KB)                                    0     9066623802
.... a lot of output removed ....
```

This output is just the first of each five-second sample dumped by `cellsrvstat` every hour. The first column shows the cell metric name, and the second column (all zeros) shows the metric value in the *current metric interval* (snapshot). Because the command was just executed (and took its first sample), it shows zero for each metric, as the delta computation starts only after the second snapshot is taken. If you navigate downward in the ExaWatcher dump file, you will see nonzero values for many metrics, starting from the second snapshot. The last column shows the cumulative value (since the `cellsrv` process started) for each metric. You probably should just ignore this cumulative value, as it contains information from the `cellsrv` start (which may be months ago). Looking at a single cumulative value, accumulating information from such a long time would not tell you much about what is happening right now or what was happening last Friday at 8 a.m. Metric deltas over shorter time periods are the way to go, and this is what you see in the second column: the current interval value as of sampling the metrics. The `cellsrvstat` tool is described in more detail in Chapter 11.

Analyzing IO metrics with metric_iorm.pl

Another very useful tool available to the performance analyst is an Oracle-provided script named `metric_iorm.pl`. It is available from My Oracle Support note 1337265.1 as a perl script and needs to be deployed to a cell to gather information. This sort of violates the rule that you are not allowed to deploy any software to a storage cell, but since it is a perl script and Oracle-provided, it is probably ok.

Once deployed, the script can be invoked without parameters to display a wealth of information. Under the covers, it uses `cellcli` to gather metrics but combines this with elegant arithmetic to provide useful output. It is not limited to presenting I/O Resource Manager information for non-CDBs or 11.2 instances. It also captures I/O Resource Manager information for 12c Pluggable Databases. To keep the output manageable the following example uses a 12c non-Container Database, or non-CDB. Before going into any further detail, let's review the output from an X2-2 cell that has been worked a little bit by a series of Smart Scans against the exact same segment (a little unrealistic use case in reality, but good example to stress I/O):

```
[root@enkcel04 ~]# ./metric_iorm.pl
Database: _OTHER_DATABASE_
Utilization:     Small=0%    Large=0%
Flash Cache:     IOPS=98.7
Disk Throughput: MBPS=0
Small I/O's:     IOPS=0.4    Avg qtime=0.0ms
Large I/O's:     IOPS=0.0    Avg qtime=0.0ms
        Consumer Group: _ORACLE_BACKGROUND_GROUP_
        Utilization:     Small=0%    Large=0%
        Flash Cache:     IOPS=98.7
        Disk Throughput: MBPS=0
        Small I/O's:     IOPS=0.3    Avg qtime=0.0ms
        Large I/O's:     IOPS=0.0    Avg qtime=0.0ms
...
Database: DBM01
Utilization:     Small=0%    Large=86%
Flash Cache:     IOPS=42595
Disk Throughput: MBPS=962
Small I/O's:     IOPS=1.4    Avg qtime=0.0ms
Large I/O's:     IOPS=919    Avg qtime=1611ms
        Consumer Group: HIGHPRIO_GROUP
        Utilization:     Small=0%    Large=82%
        Flash Cache:     IOPS=40501
        Disk Throughput: MBPS=915
```

```
        Small I/O's:       IOPS=0.0     Avg qtime=0.0ms
        Large I/O's:       IOPS=874     Avg qtime=913ms
        Consumer Group: _ORACLE_BACKGROUND_GROUP_
        Utilization:       Small=0%     Large=0%
        Flash Cache:       IOPS=4.6
        Disk Throughput: MBPS=0
        Small I/O's:       IOPS=1.4     Avg qtime=0.0ms
        Large I/O's:       IOPS=0.0     Avg qtime=0.0ms
        Consumer Group: LOWPRIO_GROUP
        Utilization:       Small=0%     Large=3%
        Flash Cache:       IOPS=2090
        Disk Throughput: MBPS=47
        Small I/O's:       IOPS=0.0     Avg qtime=0.0ms
        Large I/O's:       IOPS=45.5     Avg qtime=15027ms
        Consumer Group: _ORACLE_LOWPRIBG_GROUP_
        Utilization:       Small=0%     Large=0%
        Flash Cache:       IOPS=0.2
        Disk Throughput: MBPS=0
        Small I/O's:       IOPS=0.0     Avg qtime=0.0ms
        Large I/O's:       IOPS=0.0     Avg qtime=0.0ms
...
CELL METRICS SUMMARY

Cell Total Utilization:     Small=0%    Large=86%
Cell Total Flash Cache:     IOPS=42730.9
Cell Total Disk Throughput: MBPS=965
Cell Total Small I/O's:     IOPS=39.1
Cell Total Large I/O's:     IOPS=919

Cell Avg small read latency:  76.17 ms
Cell Avg small write latency: 32.64 ms
Cell Avg large read latency:  52.82 ms
Cell Avg large write latency: 0.00 ms
```

As you can see from the above output, the script breaks the information down into sections per database and a summary for the entire cell. If your scope is the entire Grid, you will need to execute the script via `dcli` and perhaps consolidate the output into a file for further processing. Half and full racks, otherwise, will provide too much output. In this particular example, the database DBM01 was the sole target of I/O activities. You can see that the utilization is primarily on large I/O requests and on the Flash devices. In fact, there is very little recorded disk throughput, thanks to the transparent caching introduced in 11.2.3.3.0 and later. The figures should be self-explanatory. What is interesting is that the script reports the breakdown per consumer group as well. What you seen in the above output is the work of IO Resource Manager. For the purpose of the example, an intra-database plan was activated favoring all activities of `HIGHPRIO` group over `LOWPRIO` group.

Summary

There are thousands of metrics that Oracle Database and the cells provide us. We have only touched on a small set of them in this chapter. Some more have been discussed in Chapter 11. This leads to the obvious questions: Are all these metrics important? What should be their "good" values? Which ones should we act on? And so on. The general answer to all these questions is that no, you do not need to learn, memorize, and "tune" all of these metrics (it is impossible). You should always measure what matters—and usually it is response time. Ideally, you should start by measuring the *end-user* response time and drill down where needed from there, sometimes to the database, sometimes to the application server or network metrics. It is not always the database that is causing the trouble, as you know. However, thanks to the complexity of modern multi-tier applications, this end-to-end diagnosis may not be available and not feasible to implement or retrofit.

In such cases, you would take a step downward and monitor the response time of your database queries and transactions. You just start the top-down approach from a little lower in the application stack, keeping in mind that the problem may still actually be happening somewhere in the application layer or higher. When monitoring the response times of your user reports and DW queries, you should probably start from the SQL Monitoring page (or ASH data) if you have the appropriate licenses and identify the problem user's query from there so you can drill down into it. Using the top-down approach and following the biggest time consumers in the SQL plan from there is much easier than the opposite bottom-up approach, where you might look at some databasewide top SQL report and hope to figure out what is wrong with your specific user's workload.

Of course, there are cases where you will be monitoring systemwide aggregated *anonymous* performance data (not tied to any specific user or session), as in capacity planning and utilization monitoring. However, questions such as "Is my database performing well?" should never be answered by looking at some system utilization report. None of these tools can tell you whether your database system performs well; only your users can. And if the users are unhappy, you can start from an unhappy user and drill down into the response time from there. Oracle provides all the metrics you need!

CHAPTER 13

Migrating to Exadata

Finally, the big day is here. Your Exadata Database Machine is installed, configured, tuned, tweaked, and ready to go. By now, you have probably invested many, many hours learning about Exadata, proving its value to the company, and planning how you will make the most of this powerful database platform. No doubt, it has been a long road to travel, but you are not there quite yet. Now the real work begins—migration. After all, the budget owners need to be shown that all that money invested is invested well and pays off!

This was a much more difficult chapter to write than expected since is nearly impossible to count all the migrations Enkitec has done over the years. But when you consider all the various versions of Oracle, the migration tools available, and the change they have undergone from one version to the next, it became clear that the scope had to be narrowed somewhat. So, to keep this interesting and save trees, the focusing will be on versions 11.2 and 12.1 (Enterprise Edition) for the majority of this chapter. Along the way, you can learn more about how to make the most of the features available in previous versions of the Oracle database. "Previous versions of Oracle" is always in relation to the currently supported version. At the time of writing, 11.2.0.3+ and 12.1.0.1+ were in error correction support, although you should check Doc ID 742060.1 for a more accurate overview. You can also check My Oracle Support Note 888828.1 for the support status of Oracle releases as well as the Certification Matrix on My Oracle Support.

There are many methods, tools, and techniques for migrating your database from legacy hardware to Exadata, but, generally speaking, they fall into two broad categories: physical migration and logical migration, and these can be combined. While there are several factors that determine which method is best, the decision-making process is usually dominated by one factor: the available downtime to complete the move. A secondary factor is the skill set of your team. Some of the content covered in this chapter is beyond what would be expected as business as usual from a database administrator. It might require a little time to upskill team members to be able to work with some of these tools confidently.

The good news is that there are several strategies to help you get to Exadata. Each method comes with its own pros and cons. In this chapter, you can read plenty about each of these methods. You will read about reasons why you might use one over the other, the relative advantages and disadvantages, and common pitfalls you should watch out for.

Note Migrating your applications to Oracle Exadata from non-Oracle platforms is out of the scope of this chapter.

Migration Strategies

Once you have a good understanding what Exadata is and how it works, you are ready to start thinking about how you are going to get your database moved. Let's circle back to the two general categories-logical migration and physical migration. Logical migration involves extracting the data from one database and loading it into another. Physical migration refers to lifting the database, block by block, from one database server and moving it to another. The data access characteristics of your database are a key consideration when deciding which migration method is best, primarily because of the way the data is accessed on Exadata. OLTP databases tend to use single block reads and update data across all tables, whereas Data Warehouse (DW) databases are typically optimized for full table scans and only update current data, if any.

Exadata uses Smart Flash Cache on the storage cells to optimize single-block reads and improve the overall performance for OLTP databases. For DW databases, Exadata uses Smart Scan technology to optimize full table scans. Beginning with Exadata version 11.2.3.3.x, Smart Scans scan flash and disk storage concurrently for higher throughput. The details of Smart Scans and Flash Cache optimization methods are covered in Chapters 2 and 5 as well as Chapter 16. A logical migration gives you the opportunity to make changes to your database and optimize it for the Exadata platform. Such changes might include resizing extents, implementing or redesigning your current partitioning schemes, and compressing tables using Hybrid Columnar Compression (HCC). These are all very important storage considerations for large tables and especially so for DW databases.

Because OLTP applications tend to update data throughout the database, HCC compression might not be a good fit depending on the implementation of your partitioning schema. In worst-case scenarios, HCC could actually degrade performance. And while large extents are beneficial for DW databases, there are fewer benefits for OLTP databases, which use mostly index-based access and "random" single-block reads. Beginning with 11.2.0.2, Oracle creates partitions as 8MB extents to allow better full-segment scan performance (documented in My Oracle Support Doc ID 1295484.1).

Physical migration, by its very nature, allows no changes to be made to the storage parameters for tables and indexes in the database, while logical migration allows much more flexibility in redefining storage, compression, partitioning, and more.

The most impressive way to migrate your database to Exadata is a combination of logical and physical migration, as described in various white papers on the Oracle web site. One example involving Golden Gate for a near-zero downtime migration between a big endian platform and Exadata describes how you can make use of an intermediate database as a staging area. If you roll the intermediary database forward to a known SCN, you can start the extraction of transactions on the source at that very same SCN. While the Golden Gate extract process is capturing changes on the source, you convert the intermediary database to Exadata using the Transportable Tablespace Technology, described later in this chapter. After the endianness conversion is complete and the tablespaces are plugged into an otherwise empty database on Exadata, you start the transfer and application of captured transactions Golden Gate was mining at the source. The Golden Gate apply process will update the Exadata database with all changes that happened on the source while the intermediary database has been migrated. Before getting too deep into technical aspects of a combined logical and physical migration, let's start by covering the essentials first.

Logical Migration

Regardless of the technology used, logical migration consists of extracting objects from the source database and reloading them into a target database. Even though logical migration strategies tend to be more complicated than physical strategies, they are often preferable because of the following advantages:

Staged Migration: Tables and partitions that are no longer taking updates can be moved outside of the migration window, reducing the volume to be moved during the final cut over.

Selective Migration: Often the source database has obsolete user accounts and database objects that are no longer needed. With the logical method, these objects may be simply omitted from the migration. The old database may be kept around for some time in case you later decide you need something that did not migrate.

Platform Differences: Data is converted to target database block size automatically. Big-endian to little-endian conversion is handled automatically.

Exadata Hybrid Columnar Compression (HCC) can be configured before data is moved. That is, the tables may be defined with HCC in the Exadata database so that data is compressed as it is loaded into the new database.

Extent Sizing: Target tables, partitions, and indexes may be pre-created with optimal extent sizes (Oracle uses 8MB by default since 11.2.0.2 for partitions, for example) before the data is moved. Refer to Chapter 16 for a discussion about the relevance of extent sizes for Smart Scans.

Allows Merging of Databases: This feature is particularly important when Exadata is used as a consolidation platform. If your Exadata is model V2 or X2-2, memory on the database servers may be a somewhat limiting factor. V2 database servers are configured with 72G of RAM each, while X2-2 comes with 96G of RAM per server (upgradable). This might be sufficient memory when dealing with 10 or fewer moderate- to large-sized databases, but it is becoming fairly common to see 15 or more databases on a server in Oracle 11.2. For example, Enkitec worked on a project where Exadata was used to host PeopleSoft HR and Financials databases. The implementer requested 15 databases for this effort. Add to this the 10 databases in their plan for other applications, and SGA memory became a real concern. The solution, of course, is to merge these other separate databases together, allowing them to share memory more efficiently. The problem of merging databases is addressed with Oracle 12c and Pluggable Databases. These can be the perfect vehicle for merging and consolidating databases. Memory shortage is less of an issue with the X3 and later compute nodes. They are equipped with 256GB of RAM by default, upgradable to 768GB per node. The X3-8 and X4-8 have 2TB of DRAM per server. Each X4-8 compute node can be equipped with up to 6TB of DRAM for a total of 12TB of RAM per cluster.

Pre-ordering: If using the Create Table as Select method or Insert into as Select method (CTAS or IAS) over a database link, the data may also be sorted as it is loaded into the target database to improve index efficiency, optimize for Exadata Storage Indexes, and achieve better compression ratios.

There are basically two approaches for logical migration. One involves extracting data from the source database and loading it into the target database. This is often referred to as the "Extract and Load method." Tools commonly used in this approach are Data Pump, Export/Import, and Create Table as Select (CTAS) (or Insert ... as Select-IAS) through a database link. The other method is to replicate the source database during normal business operations. When the time comes to switch to the new database, replication is cancelled and client applications are redirected to the new database. This technique is often referred to as the "Replication-Based method." Tools commonly used in the Replication-Based method are Oracle Streams, Oracle Data Guard (Logical Standby), and Oracle Golden Gate. It is also possible to use a combination of physical and logical migration, such as copying (mostly) read-only tablespaces over well ahead of the final cutover and applying changes to them via some replication method like Streams. Note that Oracle Streams is deprecated in 12c and did not receive any enhancements.

Extract and Load

Generally speaking, the Extract and Load method requires the most downtime of all the migration strategies because once the extract begins and for the duration of the migration, all DML activity must be brought to a stop. Data warehouse environments are the exception to the rule because data is typically organized in an "age-in/age-out" fashion. Since data is typically partitioned by date range, static data is separated from data that is still undergoing change. This "read-only" data may be migrated ahead of time, outside the final migration window, perhaps even during business hours. The biggest advantage of the Extract and Load strategy is its simplicity. Most DBAs have used Data Pump or CTAS for one reason or another, so the tool set is familiar. Another big advantage is the control it gives you. One of the great new features Exadata brings to the table is Hybrid Columnar Compression (HCC). Since you have complete control over how the data is loaded into the target database, it is a relatively simple task to employ HCC to compress tables as they are loaded in. Extract and Load also allows you to implement partitioning or change partitioning strategies. Loading data using CTAS allows you to sort data as it is loaded, which improves the efficiency of Exadata's storage indexes. One could argue that all these things could be done post migration, and that is true, but why move the data twice when it can be incorporated into the migration process itself? In some situations, it may not even be possible to fit the data onto the platform without applying compression. In the next few sections, you can read about several approaches for performing Extract and Load migrations.

Data Pump

Data Pump is an excellent tool for moving large quantities of data between databases. Data Pump consists of two programs, `expdp` and `impdp`. Both are documented in the Utilities Guide. The `expdp` command is used to extract database objects out of the source database. It can be used to dump the contents of an entire database or, more selectively, by schema or by table. Like its predecessor Export (`exp`), Data Pump extracts data and saves it into a portable data file. This file can then be copied to Exadata and loaded into the target database using the `impdp` command. Data Pump made its first appearance in Oracle 10g, so if your database is version 9i or earlier, you will need to use the old Export/Import (`exp`/`imp`) instead. Export and Import have been around since Oracle 7, and, although they are getting a little long in the tooth, they are still very effective tools for migrating data and objects from one database to another. Even though Oracle has been talking about dropping `exp` and `imp` for years now, they are still part of the base 12c install.

First, you can read about Data Pump and how it can be used to migrate to Exadata. After covering the new tool set, you can have a look at ways to migrate older databases using Export and Import. Keep in mind that new features and parameters are added to Data Pump with each major release. Check the Oracle documentation for capabilities and features specific to your database version.

From time to time in this chapter, you will see reference to tests and timings we saw in our lab. Table 13-1 shows some of the relevant characteristics of the servers and databases we used for these tests. The LAB112 database is the source database and not on Exadata. DB12C is the target (Exadata) database.

Table 13-1. *Lab Configuration*

Database	DB Version	Platform
LAB112	11.2.0.4	Oracle Linux 6, 64 bit
DB12C	12.1.0.2	Oracle Linux 6, 64 bit

Before continuing, let's take a look at some of the most relevant Data Pump parameters to know about. Here are some of the key parameters that are useful for migrating databases.

`COMPRESSION`: Data Pump compression is a new 11g feature. In 10g you had the ability to compress metadata, but in 11g this capability was extended to table data as well. Valid options are `ALL`, `DATA_ONLY`, `METADATA_ONLY`, and `NONE`. Using the `COMPRESSION=ALL` option Data Pump reduced the size of a test export from 13.4G to 2.5G, a compression ratio of over five times. That is a very significant saving in storage. When testing with compression turned on, we fully expected it to slow down the export, but instead it actually reduced our export time from 39 minutes to just over 9 minutes. This cannot be expected to always be the case, of course. Compression effectiveness is highly dependent on the actual data. On our test system, the export was clearly I/O-bound. But it does point out that compression can significantly reduce the storage requirements for exporting your database without necessarily slowing down the process. Unfortunately, the ability to compress table data on the fly was not introduced until release 11gR1. If your database is 10g and you need to compress your dump files before transferring them to Exadata, you will need to do that using external tools like gzip, zip, or compress. Note that the use of the data `COMPRESSION` option in Data Pump requires Oracle Advanced Compression licenses.

`COMPRESSION_ALGORITHM`: Oracle 12c gives you finer granularity about the algorithm used when compressing dump files. You can choose between basic, low, medium, and high compression. As with any compression, you trade file size for (CPU) time. You should test if compressing your dump files more aggressively is worth the effort. The use of this parameter requires the Advanced Compression Option.

`FLASHBACK_TIME`, `FLASHBACK_SCN`: It may come as a surprise that Data Pump does not guarantee the read consistency of your export by default. To export a read-consistent image of your database, you must use either the `FLASHBACK_SCN` or the `FLASHBACK_TIME` parameter. If you use `FLASHBACK_TIME`, Data Pump looks up the nearest System Change Number (SCN) corresponding to the time you specified and exports all data as of that SCN. `FLASHBACK_TIME` can be passed in to Data Pump as follows:

```
FLASHBACK_TIME="to_timestamp('05-JUN-2014 21:00:00','DD-MON-YYYY HH24:MI:SS')"
```

If you choose to use `FLASHBACK_SCN`, you can get the current SCN of your database by running the following query:

```
SQL> select current_scn from v$database;
```

FULL, SCHEMAS, TABLES: These options are mutually exclusive and specify whether the export will be for the full database, a selection of schemas, or a selection of individual tables. Note that certain schemas, such as SYS, MDSYS, CTXSYS, and DBSNMP, are never exported when doing a full database export. The FULL keyword has been enhanced in 12c and allows you to incorporate transportable tablespace technology where applicable.

PARALLEL: The PARALLEL parameter instructs Data Pump to split the work up into multiple parts and run them concurrently. PARALLEL can vastly improve the performance of the export process. If you are planning on using the PARALLEL keyword, do not forget to specify multiple output files using the %U identifier in the dump file name.

NETWORK_LINK: This parameter specifies a database link in the target database to be used for the export. It allows you to export a database from a remote server, pulling the data directly through the network via database link (defined in the target database). According to the Utilities Guide, there is no dump file involved when using the parameter with impdp. The network link is used by Grid Control to automate the migration process using the Import from Database process as well as for the Transportable Tablespaces with Cross-Platform Backups and the new 12c Full Transportable import.

When exporting, it might be a good idea to create a number of export dump files. The first one could be the metadata-only export dump you take off the whole database. This way you can create a valid DDL file (SQLFILE=...) of the database or a subset. A clever combination of the SQLFILE and INCLUDE/EXCLUDE parameters, for example, allows you to create the DDL for all users and their grants without extracting that information using DBMS_METADATA. This is also useful for removing hints from views: The LONG data type used for the column TEXT in DBA_VIEWS requires some clever coding to read the full text in 11.2 (if the view's code fits into 4,000 characters, you can retrieve it from DBA_VIEWS.TEXT_VC in 12.1). Dumping the DDL of all views of a schema in a single file allows you to use perl, awk or sed to globally search and replace text. Another export could be a small sample of the schema(s) you want to import. The SAMPLE keyword can be used during the export to limit the amount of data in the dump file. You could use such a file on a development system to hone the procedure. The final export file would then contain everything you need to get across to the Exadata system.

■ **Note** When using a dump file on Exadata, either during export or import, you should consider using the Database File System (DBFS) to store the file. The number of disks available in the DBFS_DG greatly surpasses the number of internal disks on the compute node. Beginning with Grid Infrastructure 12.1.0.2, you also have the option to use the ASM Cluster File System (ACFS).

Now let's turn our attention to the import process. Schema-level import is usually preferable when migrating databases. It allows you to break the process up into smaller, more manageable parts. This is not always the case, and there are times when a full database import is the better choice. Most of the tasks you already read about here apply to both schema-level and full-database imports. Throughout this section, you should see notes about any exceptions you will need to be aware of. If you choose not to do a full database import, be aware that system objects including roles, public synonyms, profiles, public database links, system privileges, and others will *not* be imported. You will need to extract the DDL for these objects using the SQLFILE parameter and a FULL=Y import. The required export can be performed as a metadata-only export. You can then execute the DDL against the target database to create the missing objects. Let's take a look at some of the impdp parameters useful for migrating databases.

REMAP_SCHEMA: As the name implies, this parameter tells Data Pump to change the ownership of objects from one schema to another during the course of the import. This is particularly useful for resolving schema conflicts when merging multiple databases into one Exadata database. When importing into a 12c PDB, this might not even be required.

REMAP_DATAFILE: Data files can be renamed dynamically during the import process using this parameter. This allows ASM to automatically organize and name the data files according to Oracle Managed Files (OMF) rules.

REMAP_TABLESPACE: This option changes the tablespace name reference for segments from one tablespace to another. It is useful when you want to physically relocate tables from one tablespace to another during the import.

SCHEMAS: Lists schemas to import.

SQLFILE: Instead of importing anything into the database, Object definitions (DDL) are written to an SQL script. This can be quite useful for pre-building objects if you want to make changes to their physical structure, such as partitioning or using HCC compression. Note that beginning with Oracle 12c, you can use the TRANSFORM parameter (described later) to change further physical structure, most notably the compression level.

TABLE_EXISTS_ACTION: The action to take if the imported object already exists. Valid keywords are APPEND, REPLACE, SKIP, and TRUNCATE. Skip is the default.

TABLES: A list of tables to import. For example, TABLES=MARTIN.T1,MARTIN.T2

TRANSFORM: This parameter allows you to make changes to segment attributes in object-creation DDL statements, like storage attributes. This provides a convenient way to optimize extent sizes for tables when they are created in Exadata. Oracle 12c greatly enhances the potential of the parameter. You can now request that the logging attribute of the segment you are importing is set to NOLOGGING using the DISABLE_ARCHIVE_LOGGING parameter. Be careful in environments where you already implemented a physical standby database—the NOLOGGING operation will corrupt data files on the standby.

Additional new parameters allow you to change the compression level of a segment using the TABLE_COMPRESSION_CLAUSE as well as a change of the LOB type (basic/secure file) on the fly using the LOB_STORAGE keyword. There are other parameters that might be useful in your situation, so have a look at the specifics in the documentation.

LOGTIME: a very useful addition in Oracle 12c allows you to request timestamps to be emitted in the Data Pump log files. This is a very convenient way to forecast the time the process will take in case it is repeated.

NETWORK_LINK: This parameter has already been covered in the previous section.

Before you begin importing schemas into your Exadata database, be aware that Data Pump only creates tablespaces automatically when a full database import is done. If you are importing at the schema or table level, you have to create your tablespaces manually. To do this, generate the DDL for tablespaces using the import Data Pump parameters FULL=yes and SQLFILE={your_sql_script}. This produces a script with the DDL for all objects in the SQL file (including data files). You may notice that in the CREATE TABLESPACE DDL the data-file file names are fully qualified. This is not at all what you want because it circumvents OMF and creates hard-coded file names that cannot easily be managed. The REMAP_DATAFILE parameter allows you to rename your data files to reflect the ASM disk groups in your Exadata database. The syntax looks like this:

```
REMAP_DATAFILE='/u02/oradata/LAB112/example01.dbf':'+DATA'
```

An alternative is to use REMAP_TABLESPACE. One final note before moving on to Export/Import. Character set translation between the source and target databases is done automatically with Data Pump. Please make sure the character set of the source database is a subset of the target database, or something may be lost in translation. For example, it is OK if your source database is US7ASCII (7 bit) and the target database is WE8ISO8859P15 (8 bit). However, migrating between different 8-bit character sets or going from 8 bit to 7 bit may cause special characters to be dropped.

Another reference that matters is version compatibility. When in doubt, consult Doc ID 553337.1, which explains the compatibility of Data Pump for the different Oracle versions out there.

Export and Import

If the database you are migrating to Exadata is a release prior to version 10g, Data Pump is not an option. Instead you need to work with its predecessors, Export (exp) and Import (imp). Export/Import features have not changed much since Oracle 9.2, but if you are migrating from a previous release, you will notice that some features may be missing. Hopefully, you are not still supporting 8i databases, or even 7.x, but not to worry. Even though some options such as FLASHBACK_SCN and PARALLEL are not options in these older releases, there are ways to work around these missing features. Speaking of releases, MOS Doc ID 132904.1 has a compatibility matrix for the different versions of the export and import tools as well as some other background information we take for granted in this section.

PARALLEL is strictly a Data Pump feature, but you can still parallelize database exports by running concurrent schema exports. This is a much less convenient way of "parallelizing" your export process. If you have to parallelize your export process in this way, you have to do the work of figuring out which schemas, grouped together, are fairly equal in size to minimize the time it takes for all of them to complete.

COMPRESSION is another feature missing from Export. This has never been much of an issue for DBAs supporting Unix/Linux platforms. These systems provide the ability to redirect the output from Export through the compress or gzip commands by means of a named pipe, something like this (the $ sign is the shell prompt, of course):

```
oracle@solaris:~$ mkfifo exp.dmp
oracle@solaris:~$ ls -l exp.dmp
prw-r--r--   1 oracle   oinstall       0 Jun 20 20:08 exp.dmp
oracle@solaris:~$ cat exp.dmp | gzip > exp_compressed.dmp.gz &
[1] 5140
oracle@solaris:~$ exp system file=exp.dmp owner=martin consistent=y statistics=none \
> log=exp_compressed.dmp.log

[...]

oracle@solaris:~$ ls -lh *exp_compressed*
-rw-r--r--   1 oracle   oinstall     16M Jun 20 20:12 exp_compressed.dmp.gz
-rw-r--r--   1 oracle   oinstall    1.4K Jun 20 20:12 exp_compressed.dmp.log
```

The REMAP_TABLESPACE parameter is not available in Export/Import. To work around this, you have to generate a SQL file using the INDEXFILE parameter, which produces a SQL script like Data Pump's SQLFILE parameter. You can then modify tablespace references and pre-create segments in the new tablespace as needed. Using the IGNORE parameter will allow Import to simply perform an insert into the tables you manually created ahead of time. The REMAP_SCHEMA parameter takes on a slightly different form in Import. To change the name of a schema during import, use the FROMUSER and TOUSER parameters.

There is one limitation with Export/Import that cannot be escaped. Import does not support Exadata HCC. Our tests show that when importing data using Import, the best table compression you can expect to get is about what you would get with tables compressed for OLTP (also known in 11g as "Advanced Compression"), an extra licensable feature. It does not matter if a table is configured for any one of the four HCC compression modes available on Exadata (Query Low/High and Archive Low/High). This is because HCC compression can only occur if the data is direct-path inserted, using syntax like `insert /*+ APPEND */`, for example. According the Exadata User's Guide, conventional inserts and updates work, but do not allow you to achieve the same compression savings. This "reduced compression ratio" is actually the same as the OLTP compression provided by the Advanced Compression option, which HCC falls back to for normal inserts. By the way, Import will not complain or issue any warnings to this effect. It will simply import the data at a much lower compression rate, silently eating up far more storage than you planned or expected. There is nothing you can do about it other than rebuild the affected tables after the import is complete. The important bit to understand is that you cannot exploit Exadata's HCC compression using Export/Import.

The Export/Import approach also does not support Transparent Data Encryption (TDE). If your database uses TDE, you need to use Data Pump to migrate this data. If you are importing at the schema level, system objects such as roles, public synonyms, profiles, public database links, and system privileges will not be imported. System objects like these can be extracted by doing a full database import and with the INDEXFILE parameter to extract the DDL to create these objects. This step is where the most mistakes are made. It is a tedious process and careful attention must be given so that nothing falls through the cracks. Fortunately, there are third-party tools that do a very good job of comparing two databases and showing you where you missed something. Most of these tools also provide a feature to synchronize the object definitions across to the new database.

If you are still thinking about using Export/Import, note that as the data loading with Import does not use direct-path load inserts, it will have a much higher CPU usage overhead due to undo and redo generation and buffer cache management. You would also have to use a proper BUFFER parameter for array inserts (you will want to insert thousands of rows at a time) and COMMIT=Y (which will commit after every buffer insert) so you do not fill up the undo segments with one huge insert transaction.

When to Use Data Pump or Export/Import

Data Pump and Export/Import are volume-sensitive operations. That is, the time it takes to move your database will be directly tied to its size and the bandwidth of your network. For OLTP applications, there can be a fair bit of downtime. As such, it is better suited for smaller-sized databases. It is also well suited for migrating large DW databases, where read-only data is separated from read-write data. Take a look at the downtime requirements of your application and run a few tests to determine whether Data Pump is a good fit. Another benefit of Data Pump and Export/Import is that they allow you to copy over all the objects in your application schemas easily, relieving you from manually having to copy over PL/SQL packages, views, sequence definitions, and so on. It is not unusual to use Export/Import for migrating small tables and all other schema objects, while the largest tables are migrated using a different method.

In cases where Transportable Database or Transportable Tablespace is not applicable, (in other words, objects that cannot be transported and/or converted) you might end up with a two-pronged approach. In the first move, you ensure that the data files are converted and plugged in. In the second part of the migration, you move the non-transportable components across. Interestingly, in Oracle 12c, the Transportable Tablespace option is combined with the logical export in a new feature name Full Transportable Export/Import.

What to Watch Out for When Using Data Pump or Export/Import

Character-set differences between the source and target databases are supported, but if you are converting character sets, make sure the character set of the source database is a subset of the target. If you are importing at the schema level, check to be sure you are not leaving behind any system objects, like such as roles and public synonyms, or database links and grants. Remember that HCC is only effectively applied with Data Pump. Be sure you use the consistency parameters of Export (`CONSISTENT=Y`) or Data Pump (`FLASHBACK_SCN/FLASHBACK_TIME`) to ensure that your data is exported in a read-consistent manner. Do not forget to take into account the load you might be putting on the network.

Data Pump and Export/Import methods also might require you to have some temporary disk space (both in the source and target server) for holding the dumpfiles. Note that using Data Pump's table data compression option requires you to have Oracle Advanced Compression licenses both for the source and target database (only the `metadata_only` compression option is included in the Enterprise Edition license).

Copying Data over a Database Link

When extracting and copying very large amounts of data—many terabytes—between databases, database links may be a very useful option. Unlike with the default Data Pump option (that is, not using the network link clause), with database links you read your data once (from the source), transfer it immediately over the network, and write it once (into the target database). With traditional Data Pump, Oracle would have to read the data from source and then write it to a dumpfile. Then you need to transfer the file with some file-transfer tool (or do the network copy operation using NFS) and then read the data from the dumpfile before writing it into the target database tables. In addition to the extra disk I/O done for writing and reading the dumpfiles, you would need extra disk space for holding these files during the migration. Now you might say "Hold on." Data Pump does have the `NETWORK_LINK` option and the ability to transfer data directly over database links, but there is a slight caveat.

Data Pump in Oracle 12c allows for a few optimizations, but there is a very important downside to the network link method: You cannot import a table with parallelism. With Data Pump and the network link option, each segment has its own (and only) worker process for writing data. Now, before discarding Data Pump, you should read about what it has to offer.

Very importantly for Exadata, `impdp` in 12c allows you to use direct path inserts. This is crucial for HCC compressed data. Remember from the HCC chapter that, in order to achieve compression, you need to use direct path inserts. With traditional inserts, you create blocks flagged for OLTP compression, resulting in segments larger than they need to be. Here is a demonstration showing that HCC compression works with `impdp`. The first step is to create a database link in the destination database.

```
CREATE DATABASE LINK sourcedb
    CONNECT TO source:user
    IDENTIFIED BY source:password
    USING 'tns_alias';
```

Before launching `impdp`, you could now make use of your DDL file to pre-create the tables you want to import. With a little editing, you can add HCC compression to specific segments before starting the import. In 12c this has become easier using the `TABLE_COMPRESSION_CLAUSE` of the `TRANSFORM` option to `impdp`.

■ **Note** When creating the database link, you can specify the database link's TNS connect string directly with a USING clause, like this:

```
CREATE DATABASE LINK ... USING '(DESCRIPTION = (ADDRESS = (PROTOCOL = TCP)(HOST = source-host)
(PORT = 1521)) (CONNECT_DATA = (SERVER = DEDICATED) (SERVICE_NAME = ORA10G)))'
```

That way, you do not have to set up `tnsnames.ora` entries in the database server.

Once the setup is completed, execute `impdp` like so:

```
[oracle@enkdb03 ~]$ impdp network_link=dplink remap_schema=martin:imptest \ > schemas=martin
directory=imptest logfile=nlimp.log
```

When examining the sessions on the system you will see the master as well as the import slaves. In one particular instance the following was recorded:

```
IMPTEST@DB12C1:1> @as

  SID    SERIAL# USERNAME      PROG       SQL_ID        SQL_TEXT
----- ---------- ------------- ---------- ------------- -----------------------------
 1240      59677 IMPTEST       udi@enkdb0 7wn3wubg7gjds BEGIN :1 := sys.kupc$que_int...
  264      16273 IMPTEST       oracle@enk 9qhxsv2smtyw9 INSERT /*+    APPEND
 1499       9287 IMPTEST       oracle@enk bjf05cwcj5s6p BEGIN :1 := sys.kupc$...
```

As you can see from the little SQL snippet and its output direct path inserts are possible with Data Pump. If you do not use a Data Guard standby database or similar redo-based replication tool you might even consider operating this in `NOLOGGING` mode. Another 12c enhancement allows you to specify the operation in that fashion without modifying the table DDL:

```
[oracle@enkdb03 ~]$ impdp network_link=dplink remap_schema=martin:imptest schemas=martin \
> directory=imptest logfile=nlimp2.log table_exists_action=replace \
> transform=disable_archive_logging:Y
```

Just be careful when you have any kind of redo-based standby database. All loads using `NOLOGGING` will not make it across to the standby database and you have to take a backup from SCN to get it back in sync. The important downside with the Data Pump approach using a network link is that you cannot make use of intra-segment parallelism. Read on if you want to know more about intra-segment parallelism.

Achieving High-Throughput CTAS or IAS over a Database Link

While the previous examples are simple, they may not give you the expected throughput, especially when the source database server is not in the same network segment as the target. The database links and the underlying TCP protocol must be tuned for high-throughput data transfer. The data transfer speed is limited, obviously, by your networking equipment throughput and is also dependent on the network roundtrip time (RTT) between the source and target database.

When moving tens of terabytes of data in a short time, you obviously need a lot of network throughput capacity. You must have such capacity from end to end, from your source database to the target Exadata cluster. This means that your source server must be able to send data as fast as your Exadata cluster has to receive it, and any networking equipment (switches, routers) in between must also be able to handle that (in addition to all other traffic that has to flow through them). Dealing with corporate network topology and network hardware configuration is a very wide topic and out of the scope of this book, but it is very important to touch on the subject of the network hardware built in to Exadata database servers here.

In addition to the InfiniBand ports, Exadata clusters also have built-in Ethernet ports. Table 13-2 lists all the Ethernet and InfiniBand ports.

Table 13-2. *Exadata Ethernet and InfiniBand Ports in Each Database Server*

Exadata Version	Hardware	Ethernet Ports	InfiniBand Ports
V2	Sun	4 × 1 Gb/s	2 × 40 Gb/s QDR
X2-2	Sun	4 × 1 Gb/s 2 × 10 Gb/s	2 × 40 Gb/s
X2-8	Sun	8 × 1 Gb/s 8 × 10 Gb/s	8 × 40 Gb/s
X3-2	Sun	4 x 1 or 10 Gb/s 2 x 10 Gb/s	2 x 40 Gb/s
X3-8	Sun	8 × 1 Gb/s 8 × 10 Gb/s	8 × 40 Gb/s
X4-2	Sun	4 x 1 or 10 Gb/s 2 x 10 Gb/s	2 x 40 GB/s x 40 Gb/s (active/active)
X4-8	Sun	10 x 1 Gb/s 8 x 10 Gb/s	8 x 40 Gb/s (active/ active)
X5-2	Sun	4 x 1 or 10 Gb/s 2 x 10 Gb/s	2 x 40 GB/s x 40 Gb/s (active/active)

The database servers and cells each have one more administrative Ethernet port for server management (ILOM). Note that there was no X5-8 at the time of writing.

Note that the X2 and earlier generations use PCIe version 2.0, while the X3 and later use PCIe version 3 for higher throughput per PCI lane. However, up to the X3 generation the InfiniBand cards are capable of using PCIe version 2.0 and 8 lanes, which means the maximum bandwidth of the InfiniBand card communicating with its PCI bus is limited to 8 x 500MB = 4000MB (roughly 4GB). Quadruple Data Rate (QDR) InfiniBand throughput with a four times link aggregate as used with Exadata has a maximum data rate of 40Gb/s, or 5GB/s. This might explain the active/passive configuration of InfiniBand up to the X3 generation.

Table 13-2 shows the number of network ports per database server. While Exadata V2 does not have any 10GbE ports, it still has 4 × 1GbE ports per database server. With eight database servers in a full rack, this would add up to 32 × 1 GbE ports, giving you a maximum theoretical throughput of 32 gigabits per second when using only Ethernet ports. With various overheads, three gigabytes per second of transfer speed would theoretically still be achievable if you manage to put all of the network ports equally into use and there are no other bottlenecks. This would mean that you have to either bond the network interfaces in an all-active configuration or route the data transfer of different datasets via distinct different network interfaces. Different dblinks' connections can be routed via different IPs or `Data Pump` dumpfiles transferred via different routes. Thankfully, current Exadata systems can use 10Gb/s Ethernet either using the built-in ports with a copper connection or, alternatively, make use of the two optical ports for the same theoretical bandwidth. On the dash-8 systems, you are really spoiled for network ports.

Because this is rather complicated, companies migrating to Exadata often used the high-throughput bonded InfiniBand links for migrating large datasets with low downtime. Unfortunately, the existing database networking infrastructure in most companies does not include InfiniBand (in old, big, iron servers). The standard usually is a number of switched and bonded 1GbE Ethernet ports or 10GbE ports in some cases. That is why, for Exadata V1/V2 migrations, you would have had to either install an InfiniBand card into your source server or use a switch capable of both handling the source Ethernet traffic and flowing it on to the target Exadata InfiniBand network.

Luckily, the Exadata X2 and newer releases both have 10GbE ports included in them, so you do not need to go through the hassle of getting your old servers InfiniBand-enabled anymore and can resort to 10GbE connections (if your old servers or network switches have 10GbE Ethernet in place).

If you are going to migrate your system to Exadata using a network link as the primary means of getting data across, you might consider checking the bandwidth with `iperf`, an open source tool for measuring throughput. The tool is prominently featured in a MOS note: How to use `iperf` to test network performance, ID: 1507397.1 detailing how to troubleshoot the RAC interconnect traffic and lost packets. In our opinion, it is well worth using.

This leads us to software configuration topics for high network throughput for database migrations. This chapter does not aim to be a network tuning reference, but we would like to explain some challenges we have seen. Getting the Oracle database links throughput right involves changing multiple settings and requires manual parallelization. Hopefully, this section will help you avoid reinventing the wheel when dealing with huge datasets and low downtime requirements. Before starting to tune the database for best throughput, you should ensure that the network connection provides enough throughout and lower-enough latency for the migration.

In addition to the need for sufficient throughput capacity at the network hardware level, there are three major software configuration settings that affect Oracle's data transfer speed:

- Fetch array size (`arraysize`)
- TCP send and receive buffer sizes
- Oracle Net Session Data Unit (SDU) size

With regular application connections, the fetch array size has to be set to a high value, ranging from hundreds to thousands, if you are transferring lots of rows. Otherwise, if Oracle sends too few rows out at a time, most of the transfer time may end up being spent waiting for SQL*Net packet ping-pong between the client and server.

However, with database links, Oracle is smart enough to automatically set the fetch array size to the maximum—it transfers 32,767 rows at a time. As a result, we do not need to tune it ourselves.

Tuning TCP Buffer Sizes

The TCP send and receive buffer sizes are configured at the operating-system level, so every O/S and hardware device has different settings for it. In order to achieve higher throughput, the TCP buffer sizes might have to be increased in both ends of the connection. You can read about a Linux example here; for other operating systems, please refer to your networking documentation. The Pittsburgh Supercomputing Center's "Enabling High Performance Data Transfers" page is used as a reference (`http://www.psc.edu/networking/projects/tcptune/`) here.

As a first step, you have to determine the maximum buffer size TCP (per connection) in your system. On the Exadata servers, just keep the settings for TCP buffer sizes as they were set during standard Exadata install. On Exadata, the TCP stack has already been changed from generic Linux defaults. Please do not configure Exadata servers settings based on generic database documentation (such as the "Oracle Database Quick Installation Guide for Linux").

Many non-Exadata systems are configured conservatively for networking in the 100Mbit/s or 1Gbit/s range. The use of 10Gbit/s Ethernet can be optimized by setting parameters in the operating system to enlarge send and receive buffers. A useful figure in this context is the Bandwidth Delay Product (BDP). The BDP is the maximum amount of data "on the wire" at a given point in time, and your non-Exadata systems network configuration should take it into account. Some time ago, starting with the 2.6.18 kernel used in Red Hat Linux 5.x, Linux introduced automatic tuning of the send and receive buffers. Tuning of the buffers can be checked in `/proc/sys/net/ipv4/tcp_moderate_rcvbuf`; it should be set to a value of 1. The recommendations commonly found when researching the topic state that you should not try to outsmart Linux and stick with the default.

The optimal buffer sizes are dependent on your network roundtrip time (RTT) and the network link maximum throughput (or desired throughput, whichever is lower). The optimal buffer size value can be calculated using the BDP formula, also explained in the "Enabling High Performance Data Transfers" document mentioned earlier in this section. Note that changing the kernel parameters shown earlier means a global change within the server. If your database server has a lot of processes running, the memory usage may rise thanks to the increased buffer sizes. Hence, you might not want to increase these parameters until the actual migration happens.

Before you change any of the socket buffer settings mentioned above at the O/S level, there is some good news if your source database is Oracle 10g or newer. Starting from Oracle 10g, it is possible to make Oracle request a custom buffer size itself when a new process is started. You can do this by changing the `listener.ora` configuration file on the server side (source database) and `tnsnames.ora` (or the raw TNS connect string in database link definition) in the target database side. The target database acts as the client in the database link connection pointing from target to source. This is well documented in the Optimizing Performance section of the Oracle Database Net Services Administrator's Guide, section "Configuring I/O Buffer Space."

Additionally, you can reduce the number of system calls Oracle uses for sending network data by increasing the SDU size. This requires a change in `listener.ora` and setting the default SDU size in server-side `sqlnet.ora`. You should also edit your client configuration files accordingly. Please refer to the Oracle documentation for more details. Note that in Oracle 12c, the maximum size of the SDU has been increased from 32kb to 2MB for 12c-to-12c communication.

Following is an example that shows how to enable the large SDU on the source database. First of all, you need a listener. Thinking about the migration, you might want to use a new listener instead of modifying an existing one. This also means you do not interfere with your regular listener, which can be a burden if you use dynamically registered databases. In the example, you will see the listener defined as `SDUTEST` on the *source* database:

```
$ cat listener.ora
LISTENER_sdutest =
  (DESCRIPTION_LIST =
    (DESCRIPTION =
      (SDU = 2097152)
      (ADDRESS =
        (PROTOCOL = TCP)
        (HOST = sourcehost)
        (PORT = 2521)
        (SEND_BUF_SIZE=4194304)
        (RECV_BUF_SIZE=1048576)
      )
    )
  )

SID_LIST_listener_sdutest =
  (SID_DESC=
    (GLOBAL_DBNAME=source)
    (ORACLE_HOME = /u01/app/oracle/product/12.1.0.2/dbhome_1)
    (SID_NAME = source1)
  )
```

In addition to the listener.ora file you need to set the default SDU to 2M as well in sqlnet.ora:

```
DEFAULT_SDU_SIZE=2097152
```

You might want to store the listener.ora and the sqlnet.ora files in their proper `TNS_ADMIN` directory and not interfere with the other listeners. If you plan on modifying the networking parameters for the duration of the migration only then it is of course fine to modify the default listeners.

The `tnsnames.ora` file on Exadata (as client) would refer to a database similar to this example:

```
$ cat tnsnames.ora
source =
  (DESCRIPTION =
    (SDU=2097152)
    (ADDRESS =
      (PROTOCOL = TCP)
      (HOST = sourcehost)
      (PORT = 2521)
      (SEND_BUF_SIZE=1048576)
      (RECV_BUF_SIZE=4194304)
    )
    (CONNECT_DATA =
      (SERVER = DEDICATED)
      (SERVICE_NAME = source)
    )
  )
```

With these settings, when the database link connection is initiated in the target (Exadata) database, the `tnsnames.ora` connection string additions will make the target Oracle database request a larger TCP buffer size for its connection. Thanks to the SDU setting in the target database's `tnsnames.ora` and the source database's `sqlnet.ora`, the target database will negotiate the maximum SDU size possible.

■ **Note** If you have done SQL*Net performance tuning in old Oracle versions, you may remember another SQL*Net parameter: `TDU` (Transmission Data Unit size). This parameter is obsolete and is ignored starting with Oracle Net8 (Oracle 8.0).

Additionally, when this book goes to print, it is more likely that you are migrating a non-12c database into Exadata, so please be advised that the jumbo SDU is not available in these releases.

It is possible to ask for different sizes for send and receive buffers. This is because, during the data transfer, the bulk of data will move from source to target direction. Only some acknowledgement and "fetch more" packets are sent in the other direction. That is why you see the send buffer larger in the source database (`listener.ora`) as the source will do mostly sending. On the target side (`tnsnames.ora`), the receive buffer are configured to be larger as the target database will do mostly receiving. Note that these buffer sizes are still limited by the O/S-level maximum buffer size. As you read in the previous section, that number is automatically tuned on Linux. Other operating systems may be different.

Parallelizing Data Load

If you choose the extract-load approach for your migration, there is one more bottleneck to overcome in case you plan to use EHCC. You probably want to use EHCC to save the storage space and also get better data-scanning performance (compressed data means fewer bytes to read from disk). Note that faster scanning may not make your queries significantly faster if most of your query execution time is spent in operations other than data access, such as sorting, grouping, joining, and any expensive functions called either in the SELECT list or filter conditions. However, EHCC compression requires many more CPU cycles than the classic block-level de-duplication, since the final compression in EHCC is performed with CPU intensive algorithms (currently LZO, Zlib, or BZip, depending on the compression level). Also, while decompression can happen either in the storage cell or database layer, the compression of data can happen only in the database layer. Thus, if you load lots of data into an EHCC compressed table using a single session, you will be bottlenecked by the single CPU (core) you are using. Therefore, you will almost definitely need to parallelize the data load to take advantage of all the database layer's CPUs for more efficient and faster compression.

This sounds very simple—just add a PARALLEL flag to the target table or a PARALLEL hint into the query, and you should be all set, right? Or maybe use the PARALLEL keyword in impdp to get the work done in parallel? Unfortunately, things are a little more complex than that. There are a couple of issues to solve; one of them is easy, but the other one requires some effort.

The next few sections will not reference imdp for a simple reason: When importing using imdp over a network link, the tool cannot perform intra-segment parallelism. It will import segments in parallel—respecting the parallel clause—but none of the segments will be imported in parallel. Instead, the focus is on how to use your own DIY intra-segment parallelism with insert statements across the database link.

Issue 1: Making Sure the Data Load Is Performed in Parallel

The problem here is that while parallel query and Data Definition Language (DDL) statements are enabled by default for any session, parallel execution of Data Manipulation Language (DML) statements is not. Therefore, parallel CTAS statements will run in parallel from end to end, but the loading part of parallel IAS statements will be done in serial! The query part (SELECT) will be performed in parallel, as the slaves pass the data to the single Query Coordinator (QC) and it is the single process, which is doing the data loading (including the CPU-intensive compression).

This problem is simple to fix, though; you will just need to enable parallel DML in your session. Let's check the parallel execution flags in the session first:

```
SQL> SELECT pq_status, pdml_status, pddl_status, pdml_enabled
  2> FROM v$session WHERE sid = SYS_CONTEXT('userenv','sid');

PQ_STATUS PDML_STATUS PDDL_STATUS PDML_ENABLED
--------- ----------- ----------- ---------------
ENABLED   DISABLED    ENABLED     NO
```

The parallel DML is disabled in the current session. The PDML_ENABLED column is there for backward compatibility. Let's enable PDML:

```
SQL> ALTER SESSION ENABLE PARALLEL DML;

Session altered.

SQL> SELECT pq_status, pdml_status, pddl_status, pdml_enabled
  2> FROM v$session WHERE sid = SYS_CONTEXT('userenv','sid');
```

```
PQ_STATUS PDML_STATUS PDDL_STATUS PDML_ENABLED
--------- ----------- ----------- ---------------
ENABLED   ENABLED     ENABLED     YES
```

After enabling parallel DML, the INSERT AS SELECTs are able to use parallel slaves for the loading part of the IAS statements.

There is another important aspect to watch out for regarding parallel inserts. In the next example, a new session has been started (thus the PDML is disabled), and the current statement is a parallel insert. You can see a "statement-level" PARALLEL hint was added to both insert and query blocks, and the explained execution plan output (the DBMS_XPLAN package) shows us that parallelism is used. However, this execution plan would be very slow loading into a compressed table, as the parallelism is enabled only for the query (SELECT) part, not the data loading part!

How can that be? Pay attention to where the actual data loading happens—in the LOAD AS SELECT operator in the execution plan tree. This LOAD AS SELECT, however, resides above the PX COORDINATOR row source (this is the row source that can pull rows and other information from slaves into QC). Also, in line 3, you see the P->S operator, which means that any rows passed up the execution plan tree from line 3 are received by a serial process (QC).

```
---------------------------------------------------------------------------------------------
| Id  | Operation                     | Name      | Rows |  Bytes | Cost (%CPU)| Time       |
---------------------------------------------------------------------------------------------
|   0 | INSERT STATEMENT              |           |      |        | 6591 (100) |            |
|   1 |  LOAD AS SELECT               |           |      |        |            |            |
|   2 |   PX COORDINATOR              |           |      |        |            |            |
|   3 |    PX SEND QC (RANDOM)        | :TQ10000  | 10M  |  1268M | 6591    (1)| 00:00:01   |
|   4 |     PX BLOCK ITERATOR         |           | 10M  |  1268M | 6591    (1)| 00:00:01   |
|*  5 |      TABLE ACCESS STORAGE FULL| T1        | 10M  |  1268M | 6591    (1)| 00:00:01   |
---------------------------------------------------------------------------------------------

... continued from previous output:

----------------------------
    TQ  |IN-OUT| PQ Distrib |
----------------------------
        |      |            |
        |      |            |
  Q1,00 | P->S | QC (RAND)  |
  Q1,00 | PCWP |            |
  Q1,00 | PCWC |            |
  Q1,00 | PCWP |            |
----------------------------

Predicate Information (identified by operation id):
---------------------------------------------------

   5 - storage(:Z>=:Z AND :Z<=:Z)

Note
-----
   - Degree of Parallelism is 8 because of hint
```

The output of the plan table was too wide to put it into a single row; therefore, the remaining information (which is very important!) has been wrapped around.

The message "Degree of Parallelism is 8 because of hint" means that a request for running some part of the query with parallel degree 8 was understood by Oracle, and this degree was used in CBO calculations when optimizing the execution plan. However, as explained above, this does not mean that this parallelism was used throughout the whole execution plan. It's important to check whether the actual data loading work (LOAD AS SELECT) is done by the single QC or by PX slaves.

Let's see what happens with parallel DML enabled:

```
SQL> alter session enable parallel dml;

Session altered.

SQL> insert /*+ monitor append parallel(8) */ into t1 select /*+ parallel(8) */ * from t2

SQL Plan Monitoring Details (Plan Hash Value=3136303183)
=================================================================================
| Id |          Operation                   |   Name    |  Rows   | Cost |   Time    |
|    |                                      |           | (Estim) |      | Active(s) |
=================================================================================
|  0 | INSERT STATEMENT                     |           |         |      |         1 |
|  1 |   PX COORDINATOR                     |           |         |      |         1 |
|  2 |    PX SEND QC (RANDOM)               | :TQ10000  |     10M | 3764 |         1 |
|  3 |     LOAD AS SELECT                   |           |         |      |         3 |
|  4 |      OPTIMIZER STATISTICS GATHERING  |           |     10M | 3764 |         3 |
|  5 |       PX BLOCK ITERATOR              |           |     10M | 3764 |         2 |
|  6 |        TABLE ACCESS STORAGE FULL     | T2        |     10M | 3764 |         3 |
=================================================================================
```

The requested DOP in this case is eight, just as before, but compare the two plans. The execution plan is taken from a SQL Monitor report from a 12c database. You can see an extra step—gathering statistics. This is a new feature ensuring that you have accurate statistics in a newly created or populated segment.

You will need to see the parallel distribution as well to follow the discussion. Here it is—this time taken from DBMS_XPLAN.DISPLAY_CURSOR from an 11.2 database:

```
-------------------------------------------------------------------------------------------
| Id  | Operation                     | Name     | Rows  | Bytes ||    TQ  |IN-OUT| PQ Distrib |
-------------------------------------------------------------------------------------------
|   0 | INSERT STATEMENT              |          |       |       ||        |      |            |
|   1 |  PX COORDINATOR               |          |       |       ||        |      |            |
|   2 |   PX SEND QC (RANDOM)         | :TQ10000 |   10M|  1268M|| Q1,00 | P->S | QC (RAND)  |
|   3 |    LOAD AS SELECT             |          |       |       || Q1,00 | PCWP |            |
|   4 |     PX BLOCK ITERATOR         |          |   10M|  1268M|| Q1,00 | PCWC |            |
|*  5 |      TABLE ACCESS STORAGE FULL| T1       |   10M|  1268M|| Q1,00 | PCWP |            |
-------------------------------------------------------------------------------------------
```

In this second case represented by the two execution plans on this page, the LOAD AS SELECT operator has moved down the execution plan tree; it is not a parent of PX COORDINATOR anymore. How you can read this simple execution plan is that the TABLE ACCESS STORAGE FULL sends rows to PX BLOCK ITERATOR (which is the row source who actually calls the TABLE ACCESS and passes it the next range of data blocks to read). PX BLOCK ITERATOR then sends rows back to LOAD AS SELECT, which then immediately loads the rows to the inserted table, without passing them to QC at all. All the `SELECT` and `LOAD` work is done within the same slave—there is no inter-process communication needed. How can you tell? It is because the `IN-OUT` column says `PCWP` (Parallel operation, Combined With Parent) for both operations, and the `TQ` value for both of the operations is the same (`Q1,00`). This indicates that parallel execution slaves do perform all these steps under the same Table Queue node, without passing the data around between slave sets.

The actual execution plan when reading data from a database link looks like this:

```
SQL_ID  0pla8qhhymj4d, child number 0
-------------------------------------
insert /*+ append parallel(8) */ into fact select /*+ parallel(8) */ *
from fact@srcdb

Plan hash value: 1680854865

-----------------------------------------------------------------------------------------------------------------------
| Id  | Operation                          | Name     | Rows  | Bytes | Cost (%CPU)| Time     | TQ/Ins |IN-OUT| PQ Distrib |
-----------------------------------------------------------------------------------------------------------------------
|   0 | INSERT STATEMENT                   |          |       |       |  4376 (100)|          |        |      |            |
|   1 |  PX COORDINATOR                    |          |       |       |            |          |        |      |            |
|   2 |   PX SEND QC (RANDOM)              | :TQ10001 |  1000K|   126M|  4376   (1)| 00:00:01 |  Q1,01 | P->S | QC (RAND)  |
|   3 |    LOAD AS SELECT                  |          |       |       |            |          |  Q1,01 | PCWP |            |
|   4 |     OPTIMIZER STATISTICS GATHERING |          |  1000K|   126M|  4376   (1)| 00:00:01 |  Q1,01 | PCWP |            |
|   5 |      BUFFER SORT                   |          |       |       |            |          |  Q1,01 | PCWC |            |
|   6 |       PX RECEIVE                   |          |  1000K|   126M|  4376   (1)| 00:00:01 |  Q1,01 | PCWP |            |
|   7 |        PX SEND RANDOM LOCAL        | :TQ10000 |  1000K|   126M|  4376   (1)| 00:00:01 |        | S->P | RANDOM LOCA|
|   8 |         REMOTE                     | FACT     |  1000K|   126M|  4376   (1)| 00:00:01 |  SRCDB | R->S |            |
-----------------------------------------------------------------------------------------------------------------------

Remote SQL Information (identified by operation id):
----------------------------------------------------

   8 - SELECT /*+ OPAQUE_TRANSFORM SHARED (8) SHARED (8) */
       "ID","T_PAD","ORDER_DATE","DATE_COMPLETED","STATE","SPCOL" FROM "FACT" "FACT" (accessing 'SRCDB' )


Note
-----
   - Degree of Parallelism is 8 because of hint
```

In this example, because parallel DML is enabled at the session level, the data loading is done in parallel; the `LOAD AS SELECT` is a parallel operation (the `IN-OUT` column shows `PCWP`) executed within PX slaves and not the QC.

Note that `DBMS_XPLAN` shows the SQL statement for sending to the remote server over the database link (in the Remote SQL Information section above). Instead of sending `PARALLEL` hints to the remote server, an undocumented `SHARED` hint is sent, which is an alias of the `PARALLEL` hint. Note the output is from 12c, where this load as select operation triggers a stats-gathering operation.

This was the easier issue to fix. If your data volumes are really big, there is another problem to solve with database links, which we will now explain.

Issue 2: Achieving Fully Parallel Network Data Transfer

Another issue with database links and parallel execution is that even if you manage to run parallel execution on both ends of the link, it is the QCs that actually open the database link and manage the network transfer. The Parallel Execution (PX) slaves cannot somehow magically open their own database link connections to the other database—all traffic flows through the single query coordinator of a query. So you can run your CTAS/IAS statement with hundreds of PX slaves; however, you still only have one single database link connection for the network transfer. While you can optimize the network throughput by increasing the TCP buffer and SDU sizes, there is still a limit of how much data the QC process (on a single CPU) is able to ingest.

Figure 13-1 illustrates how the data flows through a single QC despite all the parallel execution.

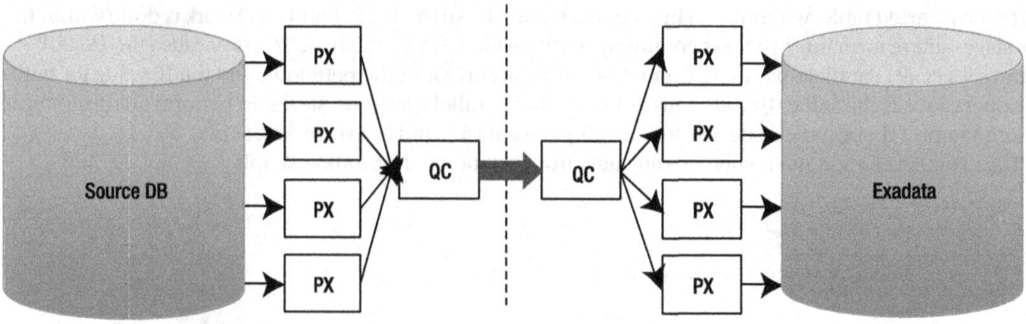

***Figure 13-1.** Data flow is single-threaded through query coordinators*

In addition to the single QC database link bottleneck, sending data (messages) between the QC and PX slaves takes some extra CPU time. This is where fine-tuning the `parallel_execution_message_size` parameter has helped a little in the past. However, starting from Oracle 11.2, its value defaults to 16KB anyway, so there probably will not be any significant benefit in adjusting this further. If you are doing parallel data loads across multiple nodes in a RAC instance, there will still be a single QC per query with a single network connection. So, if the QC runs in node 1 and the parallel slaves in node 2, the QC will have to send the data it fetches across the database link to the PX slaves over the RAC interconnect as PX messages.

Should you choose to use database links with parallel slaves, you should run multiple separate queries in different instances and force the PX slaves to be in the same instance as the QC, using the following command:

```
SQL> ALTER SESSION SET parallel_force:local = TRUE;

Session altered.
```

This way, you will avoid at least the RAC inter-instance traffic and remote messaging CPU overhead, but the QC to PX slave intra-instance messaging (row distribution) overhead still remains here.

Despite all these optimizations and migration of different large tables using parallel queries in different instances, you may still find that a single database link (and query coordinator) does not provide enough throughput to migrate the largest fact tables of your database within your downtime. As stated earlier, the database links approach is best used for the few huge tables in your database, and all the rest can be exported/imported with Data Pump. Perhaps you only have a couple of huge fact tables, but if you have eight RAC instances in the full rack Exadata cluster, how could you make all the instances transfer and load data efficiently? You would want to have at least one parallel query with its query coordinator and database link per instance and likely multiple such queries if a single QC process cannot pull and distribute data fast enough.

The obvious solution here is to take advantage of partitioning, as your large multi-terabyte tables are likely partitioned in the source database anyway. You simply copy the huge table as multiple independent separate parts. However, there are a couple of problems associated with this approach.

The first issue is that when performing the usual direct path load insert (which is needed for HCC and for `NOLOGGING` loads where applicable), your session would lock the table it inserts into exclusively for itself. Nobody else can modify or insert into that table while there is an uncommitted direct path load transaction active against that table. Note that others can still read that table, as `SELECT` statements do not take enqueue locks on tables they select from.

How do you work around this concurrency issue? Luckily, the Oracle INSERT syntax allows you to specify the exact partition or subpartition where you want to insert by name:

```
INSERT /*+ APPEND */
INTO
    fact PARTITION ( Y20080101 )
SELECT
    *
FROM
    fact@sourcedb
WHERE
    order_date >= TO_DATE('20080101 ', 'YYYYMMDD ')
AND order_date  < TO_DATE('20080102', 'YYYYMMDD ')
```

With this syntax, the direct-path insert statement would lock only the specified partition, and other sessions could freely insert into other partitions of the same table. Oracle would still perform partition key checking to ensure that data is not be loaded into wrong partitions. If you attempt to insert an invalid partition key value into a partition, Oracle returns the error message

```
ORA-14401: inserted partition key is outside specified partition.
```

Note that you cannot use the PARTITION (partition_name) syntax in the SELECT part of the query. The problem here is that the query generator (unparser), which composes the SQL statement to be sent over the database link, does not support the PARTITION syntax. If you try it, you will get an error:

```
ORA-14100: partition extended table name cannot refer to a remote object.
```

That is why you have to rely on the partition pruning on the source database side—for example, by adding filter predicates to the WHERE condition so that only the data in the partition of interest is returned. In the example just shown, the source table is range-partitioned by order_date column. Thanks to the WHERE clause passed to the source database, the partition pruning optimization in that database will only scan through the required partition and not the whole table.

Note the absence of the BETWEEN clause in this example, as it includes both values in the range specified in the WHERE clause, whereas Oracle Partitioning option's "values less than" clause excludes the value specified in DDL from the partition's value range.

It is also possible to use subpartition-scope insert syntax to load into a single subpartition (thus locking only a single subpartition at time). This is useful when even a single partition of data is too large to be loaded fast enough via a single process/database link, allowing you to split your data into even smaller pieces. Just be careful not to have too many (small) subpartitions—you may not be able to Smart Scan them later. Here is the above example again, this time for a subpartition insert:

```
INSERT /*+ APPEND */
INTO
    fact SUBPARTITION ( Y20080101_SP01 )
SELECT
    *
FROM
    fact@sourcedb
WHERE
    order_date >= TO_DATE('20080101 ', 'YYYYMMDD ')
AND order_date  < TO_DATE('20080102', 'YYYYMMDD ')
AND ORA_HASH(customer_id, 63, 0) + 1 = 1
```

In this example, the source table is still range-partitioned by `order_date`, but it is hash-partitioned to 64 subpartitions. As it is not possible to send the `SUBPARTITION` clause through the database link either, you have used the `ORA_HASH` function to fetch only the rows belonging to the first hash subpartition of 64 total subpartitions. The `ORA_HASH SQL` function uses the same `kgghash()` function internally, which is used for distributing rows to hash partitions and subpartitions. If there were 128 subpartitions, you would need to change the 63 in the SQL syntax to `127 (n - 1)`.

As you would need to transfer all the subpartitions, you can copy other subpartitions in parallel, depending on the server load of course, by running slight variations of the above query and changing only the target subpartition name and the `ORA_HASH` output to corresponding subpartition position:

```
INSERT /*+ APPEND */
INTO
    fact SUBPARTITION ( Y20080101_SP02 )
SELECT
    *
FROM
    fact@sourcedb
WHERE
    order_date >= TO_DATE('20080101 ', 'YYYYMMDD ')
AND order_date  < TO_DATE('20080102', 'YYYYMMDD ')
AND ORA_HASH(customer_id, 63, 0) + 1 = 2
```

At the end of the day, you need to execute 64 slight variations of that script:

```
... INTO fact SUBPARTITION ( Y20080101_SP03 )  ... WHERE ORA_HASH(customer_id, 63, 0) + 1 = 3  ...
... INTO fact SUBPARTITION ( Y20080101_SP04 )  ... WHERE ORA_HASH(customer_id, 63, 0) + 1 = 4  ...
...
... INTO fact SUBPARTITION ( Y20080101_SP64 )  ... WHERE ORA_HASH(customer_id, 63, 0) + 1 = 64 ...
```

If your table's hash subpartition numbering scheme in the subpartition name does not correspond to the real subpartition position (the `ORA_HASH` return value), you will need to query `DBA_TAB_SUBPARTITIONS` and find the correct `subpartition_name` using the `SUBPARTITION_POSITION` column.

There is one more catch. While the `order_date` predicate will be used for partition pruning in the source database, the `ORA_HASH` function won't; the query execution engine just does not know how to use the `ORA_HASH` predicate for subpartition pruning. In other words, the above query will read all 64 subpartitions of a specified range partition, and then the `ORA_HASH` function will be applied to every row fetched and the rows with non-matching `ORA_HASH` result will be thrown away. So, if you have 64 sessions, each trying to read one subpartition with the above method, each of them would end up scanning through all subpartitions under this range partition, meaning 64 × 64 = 4096 subpartition scans.

It is possible to work around this problem by creating views on the source table in the source database. Start by creating a view for each subpartition, using a script, of course, to generate the create view commands. The view names would follow a naming convention such as `V_FACT_Y2008010_SP01`, and each view would contain the `SUBPARTITION ( xyz )` clause in the view's `SELECT` statement.

Remember, these views have to be created in the source database to avoid an issue with database links syntax restriction. When it is time to migrate, the insert-into-subpartition statements executed in the target Exadata database would reference appropriate views depending on which subpartition is required. This means that some large fact tables would have thousands of views on them. The views may be in a separate schema as long as the schema owner has select privileges on the source table. Also, you probably do not have to use this trick on all partitions of the table since, if your largest tables are time-partitioned by some `order_date` or similar, you can probably transfer much of the old partitions before the downtime window. Consequently, you do not need to use such cunning but time-consuming workarounds.

The techniques just discussed may seem quite complicated and time-consuming, but if you have tens or hundreds of terabytes of raw data to extract, transfer, and compress (all of which has to happen very fast), such measures are going to be useful. We have used these techniques for migrating VLDB data warehouses up to 100TB in size (compressed with old-fashioned block compression) with raw data sets exceeding a quarter of a petabyte. You might ask yourself now if the approach just shown is worth it. Read more in the next section about when it is feasible to go with database links and when it is not.

When to Use CTAS or IAS over Database Links

If you have allocated plenty of downtime, the database to be migrated is not too big, and you do not want or need to perform a major reorganization of your database schemas, you probably do not have to use data load (IAS/CTAS) over database links. A full Data Pump export/import is much easier if you have the time; everything can potentially be exported and imported with a simple command.

However, if you are migrating VLDBs with low downtime windows, database links can provide one performance advantage—with database links you can create your own intra-table parallelism that is not available with Data Pump import over a network link. Compared to the "classic" Data Pump export with a dump file, both the network link option as well as the database link technique offer the significant advantage that no disk space is needed for the exported data. You do not have to dump the data to a disk file just to copy it over and reload it back in the other server. Also, you do not need any intermediate disk space for keeping dumps when using database links. With database links, you read the data from disk once (in the source database), transfer it over the network, and write it to disk once in the target.

Transferring lots of small tables (or table partitions) may actually be faster with the Export/Import or Data Pump method. Also, the other schema objects (views, sequences, PL/SQL, and so on) have to be migrated anyway. From that point of view, it might be a good idea to transfer only the large tables over database links and use Export/Import or Data Pump for migrating everything else. Clever use of the `INCLUDE` (or, depending on use case, `EXCLUDE`) parameter in Data Pump can make the migration a lot less problematic. Also remember that the `SQLFILE` option can be used to create scripts for specific database objects. If you needed all the grants from a database before a schema import, you could use the following example (assuming that the dump is a metadata-only dumpfile from a full database export):

```
[oracle@enkdb03 ~]> impdp sqlfile=all_grants.sql dumpfile=metadata.dmp \
> directory=migration_dir logfile=extract_grants.log include=GRANT
```

You can query the dictionary views `DATABASE_EXPORT_OBJECTS`, `SCHEMA_EXPORT_OBJECTS`, and `TABLE_EXPORT_OBJECTS` respectively, depending on the mode (`FULL`, `SCHEMA`, or `TABLE`) chosen, for objects to be included or excluded.

What to Watch Out for When Copying Tables over Database Links

Copying tables during business hours can impact performance on the source database. It can also put a load on the network, sometimes even when dedicated network hardware is installed for reducing the impact of high-throughput data transfer during production time. Table 13-3 shows a summary of the capabilities of each of these Extract and Load methods.

Table 13-3. *When to Use Extract and Load*

Requirement	Data Pump	Export/Import	Database Link
Schema Changes	Yes	Yes	Yes
Table/Index Storage Changes	Yes	Yes (1)	Yes
Tablespace Changes	Yes	No	Yes
Data Is Encrypted (TDE)	Yes	No	Yes
Database Version <9i	No	Yes	Yes (2)
Hybrid Columnar Compression	Yes	No	Yes
Direct path load	Yes	No	Yes

1. It is possible to change the object creation DDL by running imp with show=y option to extract the DDL statements, modifying the script and creating the objects manually in Sqlplus. Data Pump has made such tasks much easier thanks to its `TRANSFORM` *parameter.*
2. Support for connections to old clients is described in Client / Server Interoperability Support Matrix for Different Oracle Versions (Doc ID 207303.1).

Replication-Based Migration

Generally speaking, replication-based migration is done by creating a copy of the source database and then keeping it in sync by applying changes to the copy, or "target database." There are two very different methods for applying these changes.

Physical replication ships redo information to the target where it is applied to the database using its internal recovery mechanisms. This is called "Redo Apply." You can read more about how that works in the "Physical Migration" section later in this chapter. With logical replication, changes to the source database are extracted as SQL statements from the redo stream and executed on the target database. The technique of using SQL statements to replicate changes from source to target is called "SQL Apply." Back in the nineties when Oracle 7 and 8 were all the rage, it was common practice among DBAs to use snapshots to keep tables in a remote database in sync with master tables in the source database. These snapshots used triggers to capture changes to the master table and execute them on the target. Snapshot logs were used to queue up these changes when the target tables were unavailable so they could be executed at a later time. It was a simple form of logical replication. Of course, this was fine for a handful of tables, but it became unwieldy when replicating groups of tables or entire schemas. In later releases, Oracle wrapped some manageability features around this technology and branded it "Simple Replication." Its next evolution step, "Advanced Replication," was hot in 8, but is now deprecated in 12c and slated for a replacement with Oracle Golden Gate.

Even back in the early days of database replication, there were companies that figured out how to mine database redo logs to capture DML more efficiently and less intrusively than triggers could. Today there are several products on the market that do a very good job of using this "log-mining" technique to replicate databases. The advantage logical replication has over physical replication is in its flexibility. For example, logical replication allows the target to be available for read access. In some cases, it also allows you to implement table compression and partitioning in the target database. In the next few sections, we will introduce several tools that support replication-based migration.

Oracle Streams and Golden Gate

Oracle Streams is included in the base RDBMS product and was introduced as a new feature in version 9i. Although still present in 12.1—the current production release of the database software at the time of writing—it has been deprecated. Deprecation of a feature means that developers and administrators alike should try to remove dependencies on it as it will disappear at some stage in the future.

Golden Gate started out as an independent product but has been acquired by Oracle. Both products—Streams and Golden Gate—replicate data in much the same way by mining redo information, although their implementations are different. For the purpose of the database migration, a copy of the source database is created (the target) and started up. This may be done from a full database backup using Recovery Manager or by using Data Pump to instantiate a select number of schemas if it is not the entire database that you want to migrate. Then changes in the source database are extracted, or mined, from the redo logs. The changes are then converted to equivalent DML and DDL statements and executed in the target database. Oracle calls these steps Capture, Propagation, and Apply.

Regardless of which product you use, the target database remains online and available for applications to use while replication is running. New tables may be created in the target schema or in other schemas, although that is not recommended by Oracle. Any restrictions on the target are limited to the tables being replicated. This is particularly useful when your migration strategy involves consolidation—taking schemas from multiple source databases and consolidating them into one (pluggable?) database. Because of its extremely high performance and scalability, most companies use Exadata for database consolidation to at least some degree, so this is a very useful feature. If you read between the lines, you realize that this means you can migrate multiple databases concurrently.

Another capability of both Streams and Golden Gate is the ability to transform data on the fly. This is not something normally associated with database migration, but it is available should it be needed. Since both tools use SQL Apply to propagate data changes to the target, you can implement changes to the target tables to improve efficiencies. For example, you can convert conventional target tables to partitioned tables. You can also add or drop indexes and change extent sizes to optimize for Exadata. Be aware that even though replication provides this capability, it can get messy, especially if the number of changes is high. If you are planning a lot of changes to the source tables, consider implementing them before you begin replication.

Tables in the target database may be compressed using Exadata HCC. Be prepared to test performance when inserting data and using HCC compression. As you saw in Chapter 3, compressing is a CPU-intensive process, much more so than Basic and OLTP compression. However, the rewards are usually significant in terms of storage savings and query performance, depending on the nature of the query of course. Please remember that if conventional inserts or updates are executed on HCC compressed tables, Oracle switches to OLTP compression (for the affected rows) and your compression ratio drops significantly. Direct path inserts can be done by implementing the insert append hint as follows:

```
SQL> insert /*+ append */ into my_hcc_table select ...;

SQL> insert /*+ append_values */ into my_hcc_table values ( <array of rows> );
```

Note that the `append_values` hint only works from Oracle 11gR2 onward. Unlike mentioned in the first edition of this book, Golden Gate now supports reading from compressed tables, it does so now. The only way to add support for Basic, Advanced (OLTP), and EHCC is to configure the new integrated capture mechanism. Unlike the classic capture, which mines online redo logs, integrated capture interacts directly with the log-mining server to receive changes to data in form of a Logical Change Record (LCR).

■ **Note** You cannot use classic capture for use with an Oracle 12c Multi-Tenant database.

As for Streams, the documentation reads that direct path inserts are not supported in 10g databases. 11g does provide limited support through the Direct Path API. Once again, make sure you check the Oracle documentation to see what is supported for your database version. If in doubt, run a few tests to see whether you do get the level of compression you expect. However, a big improvement is that Oracle 11.2 allows Streams to capture data from tables compressed with basic table compression and OLTP compression. From Oracle 11.2.0.2 patchset onward, Streams/XStream can also capture changes made to HCC compressed tables. The Oracle Streams Concepts and Administration Guide explains this in more detail in Appendix B.

Streams has supported most of Oracle's data types, and the list increased with every release. The following is a quick summary of the benefits common to both Oracle Streams and Golden Gate:

- Support for failover (Oracle RAC environments)
- Support for multi-tenant databases
- Support for table partitioning (target tables)
- Support for HCC compression although you may not get the best loading compression ratio compared to CTAS or IAS
- Support for storage changes for tables and indexes (target tables)
- Ability to change indexing strategy (target tables)
- Read access to the target tables during migration
- Support for endian differences between source and target
- Support for (some) character set differences between source and target
- Support for different database block sizes between source and target
- Support for change capture on the target server, reducing the performance impact on the source system
- Not difficult to set up
- Database version-agnostic
- Very little downtime to switch over
- Support exists in Oracle Enterprise Manager.

Disadvantages common to both Streams and Golden Gate include the following:

- Replicated tables must have a primary or unique key. If there is no primary key on the source table, you must provide a list of columns that provide uniqueness. If no such combination exists, the table cannot be replicated.
- Some data types are not supported for replication.
- Log mining on the source system can impact performance. Consider moving the change capture to the target system.
- Logical replication in general is more complex than other migration strategies.

Disadvantages of Streams compared to Golden Gate:

- Streams is deprecated in Oracle 12c. It is still available (unlike Change Data Capture—CDC) but cannot support multi-tenant databases as documented in Appendix B of the Streams Concepts and Administration Guide. Golden Gate is generally seen as the replacement for Streams.
- Data mining can heavily impact performance on the source database.
- It is more complex to set up and maintain.
- DDL is supported but problematic.
- If replication breaks, fixing it can be messy. It is often easier to rebuild the target from scratch.
- SQL Apply is more prone to falling behind the source than Golden Gate.
- Streams tends to require much more CPU resources than Golden Gate.

Advantages of Streams over Golden Gate:

- Streams is included with your database license, while Golden Gate is sold separately.
- All process information is stored in the database, providing convenient remote access.

So which should you use, Streams or Golden Gate? On the one hand, there is the technical aspect. We have spoken with clients and colleagues who have used both products. In every case, they are using the product for simple replication to a remote site much like you would for database migration. The feedback we get is overwhelmingly in favor of Golden Gate. These users cite Golden Gate's ease of use, stability, and performance as the most important reasons. In addition to this, Golden Gate supports non-Oracle database sources. Streams runs inside the Oracle database and has not been ported to any other database platform. As mentioned, Streams is included in your Oracle database license. Golden Gate is not, and the cost based on the total number of cores on the source and target servers is not trivial. If you have need for data replication beyond your Exadata migration, the investment may be well worth it. If you are faced with a one-time migration, Streams may be a better fit for cost (neglecting the fact that the team needs to familiarize itself with the tool). But then, on the other hand, Streams has been dropped in favor of Golden Gate. Many readers will still be on 11g Release 2, so the fact that Streams has been deprecated might not affect you straight away. However, the time will come where lack of support of some of the more interesting 12c features in Streams becomes a limiting factor.

When to Use Streams or Golden Gate

Streams and Golden Gate both provide a lot of flexibility with near-zero downtime. They are well suited for migrations that require changes to the target tables. This includes resizing table and index extents, implementing partitioning strategies, and compressing tables. They also allow you to change schemas, tablespaces, and disk groups, among other things.

What to Watch Out for with Streams and Golden Gate

Since Streams and Golden Gate propagate database changes by means of redo, you must prevent `NOLOGGING` operations at the source database. This can be done at the tablespace level using `alter tablespace force logging` or at the database level using `alter database force logging`. Here are a few examples of `NOLOGGING` operations that you must prevent:

- `CREATE TABLE newtab NOLOGGING AS select * from ...`
- `insert /*+ append */` ... (for tables in nologging mode) or
- `insert /*+ append nologging */`(specifically overriding the default logging operation)
- Direct path SQL*Loader (for tables in nologging mode)

Note that some large DW databases are designed to use `NOLOGGING` for large data loads to save CPU and disk space (fewer archive logs generated). These databases rely on incremental backups plus data reloads as a recovery strategy. In such databases, forcing redo logging for everything may cause unacceptable performance degradation and archive log generation. In those cases, it makes sense to configure the ETL engine to perform loads to both the old and new DW system during the transition period. Although it appears trivial to change from nologging to logging load operations, it can prove impossible to change, especially in silo'd organizations. Instead, you may have to use `alter database force logging` if you use a replication method that relies on mining the redo logs.

Logical Standby

Another type of replication potentially useful for database migration is a logical standby database. Logical standby is a built-in feature of the Oracle database. It was introduced in version 9i release 2 as an extension or additional feature of Data Guard (formerly Standby Database). On the surface, this strategy sounds a lot like Streams and Golden Gate in that it is basically performing the same task. Changes to the source database are mined from the redo (or archived redo) and converted to SQL statements and executed on the target database. As in other logical replication methods, the database is open and available while replication is running.

Logical standby is far more restrictive than Streams or Golden Gate. Because the logical standby is actually instantiated from a physical, block-for-block copy of the source database, several rules come into play. The database version must be the same for the source and the target databases, even down to the patch level.

Oracle supports heterogeneous configurations for primary and logical standby database in the same Data Guard configuration. The master note can be found on My Oracle Support: Data Guard Support for Heterogeneous Primary and Logical Standbys in Same Data Guard Configuration (Doc ID 1085687.1). Reading this note reveals a matrix of supported combinations of operating systems for Oracle Data Guard. Before you get your hopes too high, however, there are only a precious few exceptions to the rule that you cannot have Data Guard between different platforms or even endiannesses.

It might surprise you to know that while indexes and materialized views can easily be created in the target database, implementing a partitioning strategy is more difficult. You have to pause replication, recreate the table with partitions, and then resume replication. If your replicated table is out of sync with the primary, you are in trouble. The `DBMS_LOGSTDBY.INSTANTIATE_TABLE` procedure normally used to get things back in order removes the existing table on the standby and replaces it with the table as it exists on the primary.

Table compression is not 100% supported, either. Remember that HCC compression only works with direct path load, and logical standby applies changes using conventional inserts. Worse, a bulk update is replicated using row-by-row updates. Implementing EHCC is often a very important performance strategy for Exadata. The lack of support for this feature is a significant downside for logical standby and a one-shot approach to migrating. You can, of course, issue a number of alter table move commands once the cutover is complete to achieve the correct compression ratio.

The list of unsupported data types is found in Appendix C in the Data Guard Concepts and Administration Guide.

Creating a logical standby database is more involved than creating its cousin, the physical standby database. There are a lot of steps in configuring and instantiating a logical standby. Listing all of them would extend the chapter even further. The high-level steps have to suffice:

1. Create a physical standby database (note that this is covered a little later in the "Physical Standby" section).
2. Stop redo apply on the physical standby database.
3. Configure Log Miner in the primary database.
4. Convert the physical standby database to a logical standby.
5. Open the logical standby database and restart redo apply.
6. Verify that the logical standby database is applying changes from the source.

Logical standby uses the SQL Apply instead of Redo Apply technology to replicate changes from the source database to the target. As mentioned earlier, changes in the source database are converted to SQL statements and shipped to the target for execution. Although this may sound fairly straightforward, there are some interesting implications because of how it is implemented. Here are a few things to keep in mind for DML statements:

- Batch updates are executed one row at a time. So, if you are updating 100,000 records with just one command, you will apply 100,000 individual commands on the standby.
- Direct path inserts are performed in conventional manner.
- Parallel DML is not executed in parallel.

DDL statements are replicated without any special configuration requirements. However, there are some considerations for DDL statements:

- Parallel DDL is not executed in parallel.
- CTAS is executed as create table, insert, insert, insert.

You should keep a close eye on your apply process on the standby database to ensure that bulk operations do not interfere with performance too much. When a massive bulk insert into a table is replicated on the logical standby database, you will see quite a bit of overhead and performance of the queries on the logical standby will suffer due to undo application and block cleanouts.

When to Use Logical Standby

Logical standby has a very narrow list of benefits that set it apart from other, more likely, migration methods. It provides full database replication and allows read access to the standby database during replication. As such, the standby may be used to offload resource-intensive reporting operations from the production database until the time you are ready to make the final switch. Tables and materialized views may be created on the standby database, and indexes may be created or dropped to improve performance.

What to Watch Out for with Logical Standby

`NOLOGGING` operations do not generate enough redo, which means they will not be replicated to the standby database. As with any Data Guard setup, be sure to prevent `NOLOGGING` operations using the `alter database force logging` command in SQL*Plus on the primary and logical standby database. Considering its lack of support for modifying storage of target tables, compression, and partitioning, you might opt to use the physical standby approach instead. If you do not require full database replication, Streams and Golden Gate are excellent alternatives providing support for many of the capabilities lacking in a logical standby database.

Parallel Load

This is a bit of "roll-your-own" method for migration. In this strategy, data changes are fed to the database through an in-house developed application. As such, it is a small task to configure the application to update Exadata tables in parallel with the current production database. Historical data is then migrated over to Exadata during normal business hours. Depending on the volume, this may take several days to several weeks. Once all tables have been migrated to Exadata, the feed to the old production system is cut and Exadata becomes the new production database.

Logical Migration Wrap Up

In most cases logical migration provides the most flexibility for reconfiguring extent sizes, implementing or modifying partitioning strategies, and compressing tables using HCC. This flexibility comes at the cost of complexity and restrictions that should be weighed and measured against the simplicity of some of the physical migration strategies presented in this chapter. At the end of the day, you want to properly size extents for large tables, implement a good partitioning strategy, and compress read-only tables using HCC compression. This can be done before you switch over to Exadata using most of the logical migration strategies discussed here.

Physical Migration

Physical database migration, as the name implies, is the process of creating a block-for-block copy of the source database (or parts of the database) and moving it to Exadata. Physical migration is a much simpler process than some of the logical migration strategies discussed earlier in this chapter. As you might expect, it does not allow for any changes to be made to the target database, other than choosing not to migrate some unnecessary tablespaces. This means that you will not be able to modify extent sizes for tables and indexes, alter your indexing strategy, implement partitioning, or apply HCC table compression. Furthermore, if your database saw the light of the day in the 7.x or 8i days, chances are that you have hundreds or even thousands of data files due to restrictions of the file systems at the time. Do you still remember the 2GB file size limit?

All tasks to simplify or "exadatarize" your database must be done post-migration. However, physical migration is, hands down, the fastest way to migrate your database to Exadata. For all physical migration strategies, except Transportable Tablespaces (TTS), the new Exadata database starts out as a single-instance database. Post-migration steps are needed to register the database and all its instances with Cluster Ready Services (Grid Infrastructure). Because physical migration creates an exact copy of the source database, the list of restrictions is very short:

- The source database version must be 11.2 or later.
- One option is to upgrade the production database to version 11.2 or later before copying it to Exadata. Upgrading is usually a quick process and is not dependent on the size of the database tables, but rather on the number of objects in the database and the options configured. (The post-upgrade recompilation of PL/SQL packages and views may take a while however.)

- The source platform must be certified for running Oracle 11.2 or later. You can check the My Oracle Support Certification Matrix to see which Linux distribution is certified for Oracle 11.2 and 12.1 respectively.
- The source platform must be little-endian. When using a hybrid solution creating a new database on Exadata and using cross-platform transportable tablespaces, the source database can be on different platforms with different endianness (supported platforms are listed in `v$transportable_platform` view.)

There are three strategies for performing a physical migration: backup and restore, physical standby, and Cross Platform Transportable Tablespaces with incremental backups. In this section, we will discuss these strategies, how they work, and what they are best suited for.

Backup and Restore

The backup and restore strategy uses Oracle's Recovery Manager (RMAN) to create a full backup of the source database and then restore it to the Exadata platform. Unless you plan to shut down the database during this process, the source database must be running in Archivelog mode. The backup and restore process can be done in one pass using a full backup. This is the best way to move smaller databases to Exadata since smaller databases take much less time. Larger databases may take hours to back up and restore. For these databases, the process can be done in two passes by taking a full backup followed by an incremental backup.

Full backup and restore are well understood processes and are not listed in detail here. One of the rules with RMAN backup and restore/recovery was that you could not cross platforms with it. There were a few exceptions, documented in MOS Doc ID 1079563.1 "RMAN DUPLICATE/RESTORE/RECOVER Mixed Platform Support," but they are hardly worth mentioning since there are so few of them. What is more interesting is a new 12c feature where you create cross-platform backups using backup sets and offload the conversion to the destination database. The current implementation does not support moving to a different endiannes, which makes the feature less attractive for migrations to Exadata and, for the same reason, is not covered here.

Please note that unless your source database is a 12c database, you will not immediately be able to make use of the new multi-tenant database architecture. An 11.2 database will first have to be migrated to 12c before you can convert it into a Pluggable Database (PDB). If you are happy to keep using the database as a non-CDB, then no further action is needed. If, however, you are consolidating multiple databases into a single Container Database as PDBs, then further steps are needed.

Full Backup and Restore

RMAN is used to create a full backup of the database to be migrated. The backup files are staged in a file system or otherwise made accessible to Exadata. The backup is then restored to the Exadata platform. Note that this is the section about the full restore, which cannot overcome a difference in the database endianness. You can, however, perform cross-platform conversion as long as the endianness stays the same. This involves extra steps not covered in this chapter. In other words, you cannot convert the database from big endian (for example, SPARC) to little endian (for example, Intel = Exadata), but you can convert from Windows to Linux. The high-level steps restoring a backup on Exadata are as follows:

1. Perform pre-migration tasks:
   a. Create an entry in the `tnsnames.ora` file for your database on Exadata (optional).
   b. Copy the password file and parameter file (`init.ora` or `spfile`) to Exadata.

2. Restrict user and application access to the database.
3. Take a full database backup.
4. Copy the files to Exadata (not required if backup resides on a shared file system or NFS).
5. On Exadata, start the database into nomount mode using the adapted server parameter file.
6. Restore the control file.
7. Mount the database.
8. Restore the database.
9. Recover the database.
10. Perform post-migration tasks:
    a. Convert the database to RAC and create service names.
    b. Reconfigure client `tnsnames.ora` files, configuration files for connecting to the Exadata database.
11. Make the database available to users and applications.

As you can see, this is a fairly straightforward process. After following these, you have an exact copy of your production database running on Exadata. There are a few things to keep in mind, though. If your source database uses file systems for database storage or if you are using ASM but the disk group names are different on Exadata, you may redirect the restored files to the new disk group names by changing the `db_create_file_dest` and `db_recovery_file_dest` parameters in the `init.ora` file before starting the restore process. Table 13-4 shows how these parameters can be used to remap disk group names from the source database to Exadata.

***Table 13-4.** Remap Disk Groups*

Init.ora Parameters	Source Database	Exadata Database
`db_create_file_dest`	`'+DATA_FILES'`	`'+DATA'`
`db_recovery_file_dest`	`'+RECOVERY_FILES'`	`'+RECO'`

If your database uses multiple ASM disk groups to store your database files, use the RMAN `db_file_name_convert` clause—part of the restore command—to remap the file names to ASM disk groups. For example:

```
db_file_name_convert= \
  ('+DATA_FILES/exdb/datafile/system.737.729723699','+DATA')
db_file_name_convert= \
  ('+DATA_FILES1/exdb/datafile/sysaux.742.729723701','+DATA')
```

The attentive reader will now undoubtedly point out that the use of the RMAN duplicate command can achieve the exact same thing, and that is, of course, correct. However, in our experience, management is notoriously cautious about access to production, even for a (non-active) duplication process. The extra steps just explained in the procedure above are often worth it—the backup may even exist already and only needs to be rolled forward with the use of archived logs. And, as an added benefit, it was not even necessary to "touch" the production system, an action that normally requires elaborate change control processes.

Incremental Backup

If the database you need to migrate is large and the time to migrate is limited, you might consider using the incremental backup and restore strategy to reduce downtime for the final switch to Exadata. Alas, the incremental method does not support endian format conversion either (but there is a way around that which you will read about later). Here are the basic steps:

1. Perform pre-migration tasks:
    a. Create an entry in the `tnsnames.ora` file for your database on Exadata (optional).
    b. Copy the password file and parameter file (`init.ora` or `spfile`) to Exadata.
2. Create a level 0 backup of the database.
3. Copy the backup files to Exadata (not required if backup resides on a shared file system or NFS).
4. On Exadata, start the database in nomount mode.
5. Restore the control file.
6. Mount the database.
7. Restore the database.
8. Restrict user and application access to the database.
9. Create an incremental level 1 backup of the source database.
10. Copy the incremental backup files to Exadata.
11. Recover the database (applying incremental backup and archived redo logs) until the cutover date.
12. Perform post-migration tasks:
    a. Convert the database to RAC and create service names.
    b. Reconfigure client `tnsnames.ora` files.
13. Make the database available to users and applications.

You certainly noticed that the steps for the incremental backup method are almost identical to the full backup method. The important difference is the downtime required. The bulk of the time for migrating the database is in the full backup itself. This could take hours to complete and, with the full backup method, that is all database downtime. The incremental backup method uses a level 0 backup instead of a full backup. Actually, the level 0 backup is the same as the full backup except that it has special properties that allow it to be used as a baseline to which incremental backups can be applied. Thus, using the incremental method, the database remains online for users during the longest part of the migration.

Block change tracking (BCT) should really be activated on the source database before the incremental level 0 is taken. When block change tracking is turned on, Oracle keeps track of all the blocks that have changed since the last level 0 backup by flipping a bit in a small bitmap file. This means that when you take an incremental level 1 backup, Oracle does not have to scan every block in the database to see which ones have changed. It simply looks them up in the block change tracking file instead. The use of a block change tracking file is almost guaranteed to reduce the time an incremental backup takes. We have seen cases where a 13TB data warehouse could be backed up incrementally using a BCT file in 15 minutes, down from 9 hours. To see if block change tracking is active, execute the following query in SQL*Plus:

```
SQL> SELECT status FROM v$block_change_tracking;

STATUS
----------
DISABLED
```

You do not have to shut down the database to activate block change tracking. It can be done at any time. To enable block change tracking, execute the following command:

```
SQL> ALTER DATABASE ENABLE BLOCK CHANGE TRACKING;

Database altered.
```

By default, the block change tracking file is created in the `db_create_file_dest` location. If this parameter is not set, you will need to set it or specify the file name for the block change tracking file:

```
ALTER DATABASE ENABLE BLOCK CHANGE TRACKING
  USING FILE '/u01/app/oracle/admin/<ORACLE_SID>/bct/bct.dat';
```

Post-migration tasks are necessary to convert your single-instance Exadata database to a multi-instance RAC database. In order to do so, you need to add mappings for instances to online redo log threads and also add additional undo tablespaces, one per instance. It is also a very sound idea to register the new RAC database in Clusterware. Once the database is recovered and running on Exadata, you should take a full database backup. Assuming the database is running in Archivelog mode, you can do this after the database is back online and servicing end users and applications.

■ **Note** A slight variation of the incremental backup is to automate the process of rolling the copy forward using the Exadata database as a Data Guard physical standby. This will be covered later in the chapter.

When to Use Backup and Restore

Executing a simple database backup and recovery using RMAN is something all DBAs should be able to do in their sleep. This makes the backup and restore a very attractive strategy. It is best suited for OLTP databases that do not require partitioning and HCC compression straight away. It is also suitable for data warehouse databases that already run on a little-endian, 64-bit platform, post-migration steps notwithstanding.

What to Watch Out for When Considering the Backup and Restore Strategy

Incremental backup and restore does not support endianness conversion. If this is a requirement, you might be better off using the Transportable Tablespace migration strategy or revisiting some of the logical migration strategies you read about earlier in this chapter. Objects will need to be rebuilt after migration to take advantage of Exadata storage features such as HCC. The same goes for data files. If your database has a lot of version history in it then you may have lots of small data files. In the days of Solaris 2.5 and early AIX versions the file system limits mandated that you could not create data files larger than 2GB. In the Exadata age it makes sense to reorganize these fragmented data files and the segments stored on them.

Related to these points are questions about materialized views, micro-partitioning tables, block fragmentation, and so on, which could be revisited in an effort to simplify and optimize the database on the new Exadata platform. It is also likely that rows are chained across multiple blocks when a database has a lot of history to it and has never been physically been reorganized.

Transportable Tablespaces

Transportable tablespaces (TTS) can be used to migrate subsets of the source database to Exadata. To do this, you need a running database on Exadata to host these subsets of your database. We often describe TTS as a sort of "Prune and Graft" procedure. This method allows a set of tablespaces to be copied from a source database and installed into a live target database. Unlike the full backup and restore procedure described earlier, you can plug in individual tablespaces into a 12c Pluggable Database. This way, you save yourself a bit of work converting a non-CDB to a PDB. This task is further simplified if you implemented schema-level consolidation in your source database. Assume for a moment that your schemas are all nicely self-contained on their own (bigfile) tablespaces. Migrating them to Exadata is a very elegant way of migrating, isn't it?

The standard TTS method is based on image copies of the data files. The process is fairly simple, especially if there is no Data Guard physical standby database, but there are a few things you need to be aware of before beginning. The important restrictions around the process are these, as mentioned in Chapter 15:

- Tablespaces to be migrated must be put in read-only mode during the process.
- Character sets will, ideally, be the same for the source and target databases. There are exceptions to this rule. See the Oracle documentation if you plan to change character sets during migration.
- Objects with underlying dependencies like materialized views and table partitions are not transportable unless they are contained in the same set. A tablespace set is a way of moving a group of related tablespaces together in one operation.
- Before transporting encrypted tablespaces, you must first copy the Oracle wallet to the target system and enable it for the target database. A database can only have one Oracle wallet for TDE. If the database you are migrating to already has a wallet, you will need to use Data Pump to export and import table data.
- Tablespaces that do not use block-level encryption but have tables that use column encryption cannot be transported with TTS. In this case, Data Pump is probably the best alternative.
- Tablespaces that contain XML data types are supported by TTS as of 10g Release 2. In that release, you need to use the original exp/imp utilities to extract the metadata. From 11.1 onward, you have to use expdp/impdp. There are other restrictions and caveats to transporting XML data. Refer to the Oracle XML DB Developer's Guide for a complete listing. To list tablespaces with XML data types, run the following query:

```
SQL> select distinct p.tablespace:name
       from dba_tablespaces p,
            dba_xml:tables  x,
            dba_users       u,
            all_all_tables  t
     where t.table_name=x.table_name
       and t.tablespace:name=p.tablespace:name
       and x.owner=u.username;
```

- Opaque types such as RAW and BFILE are supported by TTS but are not converted cross-platform. The structure of these types is only known to the application, and any differences in endian format must be handled by the application. Types and objects are subject to this limitation whether their use of opaque types is direct or indirect.
- Database version differences are supported as long as the target database is of the same or higher version than the source database.

Cross-Platform Transportable Tablespaces (XTTS) supports conversion between most but not all platforms. To determine whether your platform is supported, run the following query:

```
SQL>SELECT * FROM V$TRANSPORTABLE_PLATFORM ORDER BY PLATFORM_NAME;

PLATFORM_ID PLATFORM_NAME                        ENDIAN_FORMAT
----------- ------------------------------------ --------------
          6 AIX-Based Systems (64-bit)           Big
         16 Apple Mac O/S                        Big
         21 Apple Mac O/S (x86-64)               Little
         19 HP IA Open VMS                       Little
         15 HP Open VMS                          Little
          5 HP Tru64 UNIX                        Little
          3 HP-UX (64-bit)                       Big
          4 HP-UX IA (64-bit)                    Big
         18 IBM Power Based Linux                Big
          9 IBM zSeries Based Linux              Big
         10 Linux IA (32-bit)                    Little
         11 Linux IA (64-bit)                    Little
         13 Linux x86 64-bit                     Little
          7 Microsoft Windows IA (32-bit)        Little
          8 Microsoft Windows IA (64-bit)        Little
         12 Microsoft Windows x86 64-bit         Little
         17 Solaris Operating System (x86)       Little
         20 Solaris Operating System (x86-64)    Little
          1 Solaris[tm] OE (32-bit)              Big
          2 Solaris[tm] OE (64-bit)              Big
```

Exadata is little-endian, 64-bit Linux (or Solaris x86-64), so if the source database is also little-endian, tablespaces may be transported as if the platform were the same. If the source platform is big-endian, an additional step is required. To convert a tablespace from one platform to another, use the RMAN CONVERT TABLESPACE or CONVERT DATAFILE command. You may convert the endian format of files during the backup using the following command:

```
RMAN> CONVERT TABLESPACE payroll_data,payroll_mviews
           TO PLATFORM 'Linux x86 64-bit'
              FORMAT '/u01/shared_files/%U';
```

In this example, RMAN converts the data files to an endian format compatible with Exadata. The converted data files are uniquely named automatically (%U) and saved in the /u01/shared_files directory. This conversion can alternatively be performed on the source system as just demonstrated or the target (Exadata). The following command converts the endian format during the restore operation on Exadata:

```
RMAN> CONVERT DATAFILE payroll_data.dbf, payroll_mviews.dbf
        FROM PLATFORM 'Solaris[tm] OE (64-bit)'
        DB_FILE_NAME_CONVERT
          '/u01/shared_files/payroll_data.dbf','+DATA',
          '/u01/shared_files/payroll_mviews.dbf','+DATA';
```

This gives you the additional advantage of moving the files into ASM at the same time. A tablespace can be transported individually or as part of a transport set. Transport sets are more common because, more often than not, object dependencies exist across tablespaces. For example, there may be tables in one tablespace and dependent materialized views or indexes in another. In order to transport a tablespace, you must first put it in read-only mode. Tablespace metadata is then exported using Data Pump with the transportable_tablespaces parameter. You should also specify the TRANSPORT_FULL_CHECK parameter to ensure strict containment of the tablespaces being transported. This ensures that no dependent objects (like indexes) exist outside of the transport set. RMAN is then used to take a backup of the tablespaces in the transport set. Conversion between endian formats may be done during the RMAN backup or during the restore on the target system. Here are the steps for transporting tablespaces to Exadata:

1. Identify tablespace object dependencies.
2. Set tablespaces to read-only mode.
3. Export metadata for the transport set using Data Pump.
4. Take an RMAN backup of the tablespaces in the transport set.
5. Copy the export files along with the data file backups to Exadata.
6. Restore the data files from the RMAN backup to your Exadata database. If endian conversion is needed, use the CONVERT DATAFILE command to restore and convert the data files simultaneously.
7. Make the tablespaces read/write again.
8. Using Data Pump, import the tablespace metadata into the Exadata database using the transport_datafiles parameter. You can optionally remap the schema of the tablespace contents using the remap_schema parameter.

When to Use Transportable Tablespaces

TTS and XTTS are useful for migrating portions of the source database using the speed of RMAN. If parts of your database are ready to move to Exadata but others are not, TTS may be a good fit. Be careful, though, that some objects in the data dictionary are not migrated along—grants, privileges, PL/SQL code—, and so must be exported separately. And you also have to pre-create accounts before you can plug the tablespaces into the database. Remember the metadata-only Data Pump export? This could be a good strategy to create a SQLFILE and execute the necessary DDL commands.

What to Watch Out for with the Transportable Tablespace Strategy

Check your Oracle documentation for specific restrictions or caveats that may apply to your database. Watch out for tablespace and schema name collisions on the target (Pluggable) database. Tablespaces must be put in read-only mode for the move, so this will incur downtime for applications requiring read-write access to the tablespaces. This downtime window should not be underestimated! The tablespaces have to remain read-only for as long as it takes to migrate the copy into Exadata. For a multi-TB database, that duration can be very significant and range days, if not weeks (all depending on network throughput or alternative means of getting data to the Exadata system). You can run an RMAN backup of the tablespaces while they are in read/write mode to see how long this operation will take before deciding whether TTS is an appropriate method or not for your migration. One option to shorten the downtime window without having to resort to logical replication tools is the use of Cross-Platform Transportable Tablespaces with Incremental Backups. This will not completely eliminate the downtime window, but has the potential to shorten it considerably. If you truly require no downtime migrations, you need to use logical migration tools capturing any changes to the system while the endianness conversion to Exadata is ongoing. Only after the transportable tablespace set is completely imported into Exadata can the floodgates be opened and the replication of the changes on Exadata begin.

Cross-Platform TTS with Incremental Backups

Another option to physically migrate a subset of the database is to use a little known My Oracle Support note and the steps documented in it. There is nothing really new to this procedure as it builds on top of features already within the database—you just read about XTTS, for example. The MOS document is titled "11G - Reduce Transportable Tablespace Downtime using Cross Platform Incremental Backup" and has a Doc ID of 1389592.1. The procedure described in it applies to Oracle 11.2. The MOS document has been updated for 12c very recently, referring to another Doc ID: 2005729.1. The procedure for 12c as just mentioned requires that the source database and destination have their initialization parameter `compatible` set to 12.1.0 or higher. Since it is quite likely that you are moving off old hardware, it is unrealistic to assume that you upgrade your source system in place to 12c before migrating to Exadata. This section, therefore, focuses on the procedure for 11.2. Once the database is safely on the Exadata system, further steps to bring it up to a higher version can be taken.

As the name suggests, the whole idea is based on cross-platform transportable tablespaces. XTTS are not new—so why this section about incremental backups? While indeed XTTS are well known, what is new is the way you use incremental backups to roll the image copies of the data files forward. That is nothing new, either, because that is exactly what happens when you recover a database. What *is* truly new, however, is that you take the incremental backup on your source system and apply it on your destination Exadata database. If you consider that your source system is most likely Big Endian such as Power, or SPARC, or Itanium-based, you will start appreciating the elegance of the proposed solution.

In summary, x-platform TTS plus incremental backups allow you to migrate your big-endian database from your old hardware into Exadata, potentially at very little expense (of downtime). The amount of downtime you will incur is expected to be roughly proportional to the amount of metadata you will need to import as part of the transportable tablespace move. The procedure you are reading about is focused around these steps, most of which are initiated using a perl script named `xttdriver.pl`:

- Begin with a setup phase in which you set up all the needed structures, databases, and scripts.
- During the preparation phase, you create the initial image copies of the data files to migrate and transfer them to the Exadata system.
- During the roll-forward phase, you take incremental backups of the source system and apply them on the image copies of the destination system.

- When the cutover weekend has finally arrived, you put the tablespace(s) to be migrated into read-only mode, create a last incremental backup, apply it, and plug the tablespace in.
- You can verify the data file in the Exadata database before flipping the switch and making it read-write.

If you read the above bullets attentively, you will have noticed that the source system stays online and available until the cutover date. This is a huge advantage compared to the "traditional" TTS approach, where you place the tablespace into read-only mode for as long as it takes to convert all its data files.

Before Christmas 2013 (and Oracle 11.2.0.4), the procedure you read about now was slightly more involved. Instead of just a source and destination database, you had to have a conversion instance. If your destination database is 11.2.0.4 or higher, you no longer need that instance. If you want to migrate to 11.2.0.3, which we hope you do not have to do, an additional "conversion" instance is required. Furthermore, the procedure used to be supported when you migrated to Exadata only. This restriction has now been lifted as well and you can use it to migrate to 64-bit Oracle Linux.

■ **Warning** The X-platform TTS + incremental backup procedure cannot perform any magic and work around the limitations of TTS. Make sure to read the previous section of this chapter and the Oracle documentation set to understand the limitations of TTS.

Setup and Configuration

For this section, please assume that the source database resides on Solaris on SPARC (meaning big endian) and will be migrated to Exadata (meaning little endian). The source database with the `ORACLE_SID` "solaris" uses Oracle 11.2.0.3, while the destination database "EXA" is 11.2.0.4. A conversion instance, therefore, is not required. Be careful in Data Guard environments—the new data files are not automatically copied to the standby databases. It is your responsibility to ensure the files are physically present on all the standby databases in addition to the primary.

You start the preparation by looking up DOC ID 1389592.1 and downloading the attached zip file. At the time of writing, the file was named `rman_xttconvert_2.0.zip`. Stage the zip file on the source host. In the following example, we will use a new directory named `xtt` in the oracle user's home directory to keep the scripts and configuration files.

With version 2 of the scripts, you have the option to transfer the files either using `DBMS_FILE_TRANSFER` or `RMAN`. The advantage of the first is that you do not need to worry how to get the data files into Exadata. On the other hand, there is a restriction with regards to the maximum file size, which cannot exceed 2 TB. That restriction renders the `DBMS_FILE_TRANSFER` procedure problematic, especially with bigfile tablespaces. For that reason, the `RMAN` method is chosen in this example.

When using the `RMAN` approach, you have to think about how the files can be transferred physically between the source and destination systems. For systems in clos(er) proximity, NFS might be an option. But firewalls and routing issues to the various VLAN settings often times prevent NFS from being used. The fallback alternative—especially for longer distances—is SCP. Depending on your network bandwidth, you can start multiple SCP sessions in parallel, and even compress data as it flows through the pipe. The downside to using the RMAN approach should not be concealed either: You will require a staging area on the source and destination side to hold the image copies as well as any incremental backups. Thankfully for those Exadata users that always looked for a purpose for their `DBFS_DG`, here is one in form of using the database filesystem option with a database in the `DBFS_DG` disk group as the staging area! And Oracle 12.1.0.2 Grid Infrastructure allows you to use ACFS as an alternative to DBFS.

As part of the preparation, you need to edit the `xtt.properties` file. It contains all the information about source and target databases, data file backup locations, and a lot more, all of which is needed for the next steps. Here is an example of the configuration file stripped of all comments:

```
oracle@solaris:~/xtt$ grep -i '^[a-z]' xtt.properties
tablespaces=DATA_TBS
platformid=2
dfcopydir=/u01/stage/src
backupformat=/u01/stage/src
stageondest=/u01/stage/dest
storageondest=+DATA/EXA/datafile/
backupondest=+RECO
asm_home=/u01/app/11.2.0.4/grid
asm_sid=+ASM1
parallel=8
rollparallel=4
```

Here, `tablespaces` list the tablespace to be migrated. Multiple tablespaces can be listed, but they need to be comma separated. The platform ID is the source database's `v$database.platform_id`. The directory indicated by `dfcopydir` is the location where the image copies of the tablespaces will be placed during the prepare phase (more on that later). Likewise, `backupformat` takes the directory where the incremental backups are created. On the Exadata, `stageondest` is where the process expects the initial image copies. The converted data files will then be stored in `storageondest`. The location indicated by `backupondest` instructs the driver script to write the incremental backups during the roll-forward phase. The ASM parameters are self-describing. You can take advantage of parallel execution of some steps as well: Parallel is the degree of parallelism during the data file conversion, and roll parallel defines the level of parallelism rolling the image copies forward using the incremental backups from the source. Adjust the parameters to suit your needs. You will have to set a few other parameters should you decide to use the `DBMS_FILE_TRANSFER` method. These parameters are not shown here to keep it simple.

■ **Note** Yes, that is correct—you can take incremental backups on the source (big endian) platform and apply them on image copies in Exadata. That is why we like the process so much.

With the configuration completed on the source system, copy the `xtt` directory to the driving Exadata compute node into the Oracle user's home directory. Ensure that all the directories exist. You could, of course, make use of NFS as well—your directories indicated by `dfcopydir`, `backupformat`, `stageondest` will be the same in that case.

Implementation

Once the step completes, transfer the image copies to the Exadata system to the `stageondest` directory. This step is optional if you are using NFS. You also need to copy the newly created metadata files and scripts to the `~/xtt` directory on Exadata. After the data files have made it across, convert them to 64-bit Linux x86-64. Note that it does not matter how long this takes. The tablespace has been online read-write all the time on the source database, so there is no impact on application availability on the source at all.

The next phase is named roll-forward. You take an incremental backup of the tablespace you want to migrate with the intention to roll the image copies previously taken forward. Again, this is the biggest selling point of this technique: You take a backup on a big-endian system to roll a data file already converted to little-endian forward. The backup files alongside their meta-information and scripts need to be transferred to Exadata where they are applied. This process can be repeated many times until the next phase starts: the transport phase.

The transport phase is not really different from the traditional x-platform TTS technique: You change the tablespaces to be migrated to read-only mode on the source and take a last incremental backup, transfer, and apply it on Exadata. As soon as you set the source tablespaces to read-only mode, you incur the outage on the source. The difference compared to regular x-platform TTS is that you do not need to transfer the data files to Exadata and convert them, potentially a huge time saver. The last incremental backup ensures that your image copies in the Exadata database are 100% current. If the data owners of the tablespaces you want to import do not exist yet, create them now including grants, roles, and privileges. As soon as the final roll-forward command finishes, you can import the tablespace metadata into the Exadata database.

Once the import finished—the time for it to finish is proportional to the amount of dictionary metadata associated with the tablespaces you are importing—you can validate the tablespaces for integrity and make them read-write on the destination.

Physical Standby

In the physical standby strategy, the target database is instantiated from a full backup of the source database. The backup is restored to Exadata in the same way you would for the backup and restore strategy. Once the database is restored to Exadata, it is started in mount mode and kept in a continual state of recovery. As changes occur in the source database, redo information is generated and transmitted to the standby database, where changes are written to the standby redo logs before they are applied (Redo Apply). Unlike the backup and restore strategy, this database is kept in recovery mode for a period of time. Because redo information is constantly being applied to the standby database, conversion from big-endian to little-endian format is not supported. Standby databases have been around since version 7 of Oracle. The capability is inherent in the database architecture. Of course, back then you had to write scripts to monitor the archive log destination on the source system and then copy them (usually via FTP) to the standby system, where another script handled applying them to the standby database. In version 9i, Oracle introduced a new product called Data Guard to manage and automate many of those tedious tasks of managing and monitoring the standby environment. Today Data Guard provides the following services:

- Redo Transport Services
    - Handles the transmission of redo information to the target system
    - Resolves gaps in archive redo logs due to network failure
    - Detects and resolves missing or corrupt archived redo logs by retransmitting replacement logs
- Apply Services
    - Automatically applies redo information to the standby database in real time, whenever possible
    - Can allow read-only access to the standby database during redo apply, which requires a license for the Active Data Guard option
    - Provides role transition management: The role of the source and standby databases may be switched temporarily or permanently
    - Switchover: gracefully switches the roles of the source and standby databases. Does not have any impact on the databases in the Data Guard configuration. Useful for undoing a migration to the old hardware if no version changes are involved

    - Failover: change in roles, usually as a consequence of a site failure. Requires a re-instantiation of the former primary database either by means of Flashback Database, where applicable, or a complete rebuild. Not normally used for migrations

- Data Guard Broker:
    - Simplifies the configuration and management of the standby database
    - Oracle Enterprise Manager offers a graphical user interface that can assist in creating a Data Guard configuration
    - Centralized console for monitoring and managing the standby database environment
    - Simplifies switchover/failover of the standby database
    - A very versatile command line interface exists as well.

Data Guard provides three modes of protection of the standby database:

Maximum Availability: A good compromise between the *laissez-faire* approach employed by the maximum performance mode and the very strict maximum performance setting. For transactions to commit on the primary, at least one synchronized standby database must have received the relevant redo information in one of its standby redo logs. If that is not possible, the primary will still carry on. With 12c, it is possible to configure maximum availability in `FASTSYNC` mode. In this mode, the standby database acknowledges to the primary that it received the redo information without having to wait for I/O to complete, writing the information to disk. The slightly higher performance this mode offers might expose you to a higher risk of data loss.

Maximum Performance: The default protection mode in Data Guard. It does not impact the availability of the primary database at all, primary and standby database operate independently of each other. The standby database can still be completely in synch with the primary using real-time redo apply.

Maximum Protection: the only Data Guard configuration that can guarantee zero data loss. Now that sounds like a very desirable feature, but it comes at the cost of potential loss of service. If the primary standby database cannot write redo information to the standby, it will shut down. Few customers implement this protection mode. Operating in this protection mode can imply a performance penalty on the primary database.

Keep in mind that although Data Guard is an excellent tool for database migration, it is not its only purpose. Data Guard's force is protecting databases from media corruption, catastrophic media failure, and site failure. It is an integral component in Oracle's Maximum Availability Architecture. So, it is no surprise that some of the replication modes mentioned above make no sense in the context of database migration. Maximum performance is the replication mode most appropriate for migrating databases because it has no impact on the performance of the source database. In maximum performance mode, the source database continues to function as it always has. Transactions are not delayed by network issues or downstream replication problems. It is also worth mentioning that Data Guard fully supports either a single-instance standby or an Oracle RAC standby. And as of 11gR1, redo can be applied while the standby database is open in read-only mode provided you paid for the Active Data Guard option. There is also strong integration with Enterprise Manager Grid Control.

Interesting new features in Data Guard 12c include the Far-Sync standby configuration, allowing the database to send redo to really remote locations more easily. Support for cascading standby databases has also been greatly enhanced, but these do not add value for the average database migration and will not be covered here.

When to Use Physical Standby

The physical standby database does not allow any changes to the database (other than data file name changes). As a result, it is best suited for database migrations where no changes to the target database are required. In that respect, it is very similar to the full backup and restore you read about earlier in the chapter. If changes need to be made, they will have to be done post-migration. Generally speaking, this is less of an issue with OLTP databases because changes such as migrating to large table extent sizes, implementing partitioning, and implementing HCC are not as beneficial as they are for larger DW databases. If getting to Exadata as quickly and safely as possible is your goal, physical standby may be a good fit. With Exadata's performance and scalability, post-migration tasks may take far less time to implement than you might expect.

What to Watch Out for When Considering the Physical Standby Strategy

There aren't many twists or turns with the physical standby strategy. You should keep an eye on network stability and performance. While it is possible to use Oracle's cross-platform physical standby feature for low-downtime migrations between some platforms, you have no opportunity to do such migrations across platforms with different byte order (endian orientation). There are also some Oracle version specific limitations. (Read more from My Oracle Support note 413484.1 "Data Guard Support for Heterogeneous Primary and Physical Standbys in Same Data Guard Configuration.") If a low-downtime migration between incompatible platforms is required, you should consider the Logical Standby, Streams, or Golden Gate strategies instead.

Wrap Up Physical Migration Section

Physical migration may prove to be an easy migration option if your application schema is complex enough that you do not want to take any logical migration path. It is also very suited for the migration of lots of databases into Exadata. If you need quick results, a physical migration—"lift and shift"—is the way to go, but do not forget to simplify and optimize when you have a chance.

Also, physical migration can potentially be done with very low downtime by restoring a production copy to the Exadata database as a physical standby database and applying production archivelogs until it is time to switch over and make standby the new production database. However, this approach cannot be used between platforms with different endianness, and there are a few more Oracle version specific restrictions.

Dealing with Old Initialization Parameters

When migrating from an older version of Oracle, you might be tempted to keep all the old (undocumented) `init.ora` parameters for "tuning" or "stability." The fact is that Oracle has very good default values for its parameters since 10g, especially so in 11.2 and later, which likely runs on your Exadata cluster. Whatever problems were solved by setting these undocumented parameters years ago are probably already fixed in the database code. Also, moving to Exadata brings a much bigger change than any parameter adjustment can introduce, so the stability point is also moot. As such, it is recommended not to carry over any undocumented parameters from the old databases, unless your application (such as Oracle Siebel, SAP) documentation clearly states it as a requirement for the new Oracle release you are migrating to.

Planning VLDB Migration Downtime

When you are estimating the downtime or data migration time, you should only rely on actual measurements in your environment, with your data, your network connection, database settings, and compression options. While it is possible to load raw data to a full rack at 5TB/hour (Exadata V2) or even 21.5 TB/hour (Exadata X5-2) according to Oracle, you probably are unlikely to get such loading speeds when the target tables are compressed with `ARCHIVE` or `QUERY HIGH`. No matter which numbers you find from this book or official specs, you will have to test everything out yourself, end to end. There are some temporary workarounds for improving loading rates. For example, if you have enough disk space, you can first load to non-compressed or `EHCC QUERY LOW`-compressed tables during the downtime window and, once in production, recompress individual partitions with higher compression rates.

Summary

In this lengthy chapter, you read a lot about the wide range of tools available for migrating your data to Exadata. You should choose the simplest approach you can as this reduces risk and can also save your own time. You might consider evaluating Data Pump as well; it is often overlooked, but it can transfer the whole database or just a schema. In 12c, the Full Transportable Export/Import leverages Transportable Tablespaces under the covers. And it can do the job fast and is even flexible when you want to adjust the object DDL metadata in the process. Often, however, this approach is not fast enough (network bandwidth!) or requires too much temporary disk space. It all depends on how much data you have to transfer and how much downtime you are allowed. When moving VLDBs that are tens or even hundreds of terabytes in size, you may have to get creative and use less straightforward approaches like database links, copying read-only data in advance, or perhaps doing a completely incremental migration using one of the replication approaches. The cross-platform transportable tablespaces plus incremental backup method is very useful, helping you with a low downtime window if the metadata export does not consume too much time.

Every enterprise's database environments and business requirements are different, but you can use the methods explained in this chapter as building blocks. You may need to combine multiple techniques if the migrated database is very large and the allowed downtime is small. No matter which techniques you use, the most important thing to remember is to test everything—the whole migration process from end to end—preferably multiple times to iron out any problems along the way. You will likely find and fix many problems in advance thanks to systematic testing. Good luck!

CHAPTER 14

Storage Layout

In Oracle 10gR1, Oracle introduced Automatic Storage Management (ASM) and changed the way we think of managing database storage. Exadata is the first Oracle product to rely completely on ASM to provide database storage. Without ASM, databases would not be capable of utilizing the Exadata storage servers at all. Because of this, ASM is a hard requirement for running Exadata. While ASM may not be a new technology, the storage servers are a concept that had not been used prior to Exadata.

Looking at all the various intricacies of cell storage can be a little daunting at first. There are several layers of abstraction between physical disks and the ASM disk groups many DBAs are familiar with. If you've never worked with Oracle's ASM product, there will be a lot of new terms and concepts to understand there as well. In Chapter 8, we discussed the underlying layers of Exadata storage from the physical disks up through the cell disk layer. This chapter will pick up where Chapter 8 left off and discuss how cell disks are used to create grid disks for ASM storage. We'll briefly discuss the underlying disk architecture of the storage cell and how Linux presents physical disks to the application layer. From there, we'll take a look at the options for carving up and presenting Exadata grid disks to the database tier. The approach Oracle recommends is to create a few large "pools" of disks across all storage cells. While this approach generally works well from a performance standpoint, there are reasons to consider alternative strategies. Sometimes, isolating a set of storage cells to form a separate storage grid is desirable. This provides separation from more critical systems within the Exadata enclosure so that patches may be installed and tested before they are implemented in production. Along the way, we'll take a look at how ASM provides fault resiliency and storage virtualization to databases. Lastly, we'll take a look at how storage security is implemented on Exadata. The storage cell is a highly performant, highly complex, and highly configurable blend of hardware and software. This chapter will take a close look at how all the various pieces work together to provide flexible, high-performance storage to Oracle databases.

Exadata Disk Architecture

When Linux boots up, it runs a scan to identify disks attached to the server. When a disk is found, the operating system determines the device driver needed and creates a block device called a LUN for application access. While it is possible for applications to read and write directly to these block devices, it is not a common practice. Doing so subjects the application to changes that are complicated to deal with. For example, because device names are dynamically generated on bootup, adding or replacing a disk can cause all of the disk device names to change. ASM and databases need file permissions to be set that will allow read/write access to these devices as well. In earlier releases of ASM, system administrators managed disk name persistency via native Linux utilities such as ASMLib and `udev`. Exadata shields system administrators and DBAs from these complexities through various layers of abstraction. Cell disks provide the first abstraction layer for LUNs. Cell disks are used by `cellsrv` to manage I/O resources at the storage cell. Grid disks are the next layer of abstraction and are the disk devices presented to the database servers as ASM disks. Figure 14-1 shows how cell disks and grid disks fit into the overall storage architecture of an Exadata storage cell.

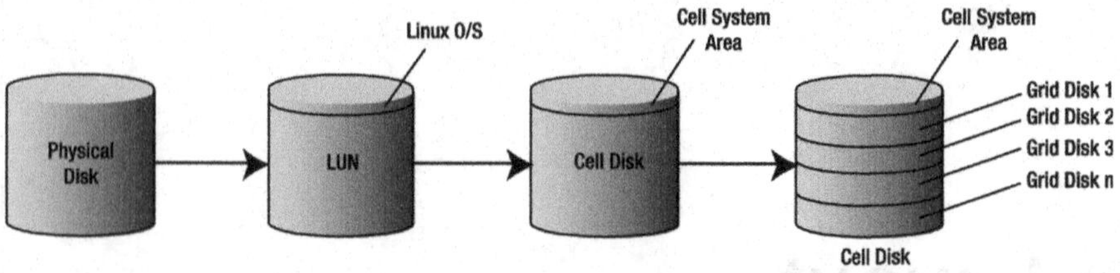

Figure 14-1. *The relationship between physical disks and grid disks*

With the introduction of ASM, Oracle provided a way to combine many physical disks into a single storage volume called a *disk group*. Disk groups are the ASM replacement for traditional file systems and are used to implement Oracle's SAME (Stripe and Mirror Everything) methodology for optimizing disk performance. As the name implies, the goal of SAME is to spread I/O evenly across all physical disks as visible from the ASM instance. Virtualizing storage in this way allows multiple databases to share the same physical disks. It also allows physical disks to be added or removed without interrupting database operations. If a disk must be removed, ASM migrates its data to the other disks in the disk group before it is dropped. When a disk is added to a disk group, ASM automatically rebalances data from other disks onto the new disk to ensure that no single disk contains more data than the others. In a very basic ASM configuration, LUNs are presented to ASM as ASM disks. ASM disks are then used to create disk groups, which in turn are used to store database files such as data files, control files, and online redo logs. The Linux operating system presents LUNs to ASM as native block devices such as `/dev/sda`. Exadata virtualizes physical storage through the use of grid disks and ASM disk groups. Grid disks are used for carving up cell disks similar to the way partitions are used to carve up physical disk drives. Figure 14-2 shows the relationship between cell disks, grid disks, and ASM disk groups. It is important to remember that ASM disks on Exadata are different from ASM disks on a standard system in that they are not physically mounted on the database server. All ASM disks on Exadata are accessed via the iDB protocol.

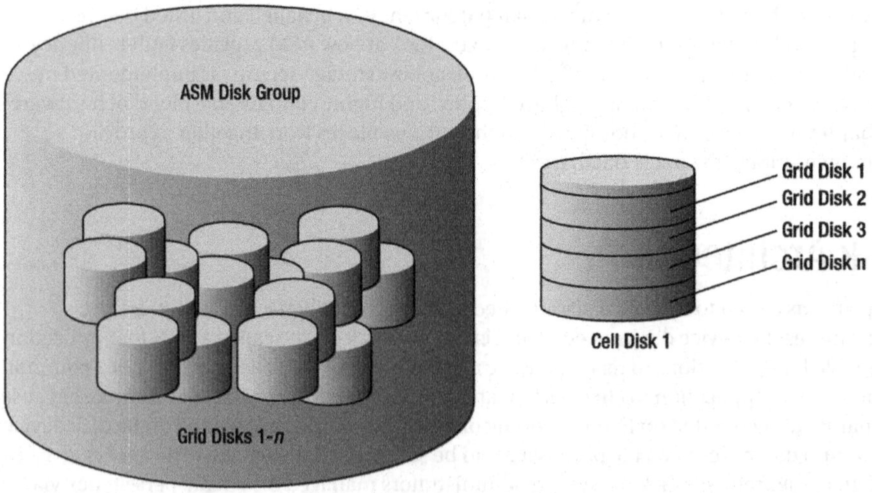

Figure 14-2. *ASM disk group with its underlying grid disks and cell disks*

Failure Groups

Before we talk in more detail about grid disks, let's take a brief detour and talk about how disk redundancy is handled in the ASM architecture. ASM uses redundant sets of ASM disks called *failure groups* to provide mirroring. Traditional RAID1 mirroring maintains a block-for-block duplicate of the original disk. ASM failure groups provide redundancy by assigning ASM disks to failure groups and guaranteeing that the original and any mirror copies of a block do not reside within the same failure group. It is critically important to separate physical disks into separate failure groups. Because each of the storage servers is an independent Linux system (that could fail at any moment), Exadata breaks each of the disks from a storage server into a fail group. This ensures that two disks on a single storage server will never contain two copies of the same block. For example, the following listing shows the fail groups and grid disks for storage cells 1-3. As the names imply, these fail groups correspond to storage cells 1–3. These fail groups were created and named automatically by ASM when the grid disks were created.

```
SYS:+ASM1> select failgroup, name from v$asm_disk order by 1,2

FAILGROUP   NAME
----------- ----------------------
CELL01      DATA_CD_00_CELL01
CELL01      DATA_CD_01_CELL01
CELL01      DATA_CD_02_CELL01
CELL01      DATA_CD_03_CELL01
...
CELL02      DATA_CD_00_CELL02
CELL02      DATA_CD_01_CELL02
CELL02      DATA_CD_02_CELL02
CELL02      DATA_CD_03_CELL02
...
CELL03      DATA_CD_00_CELL03
CELL03      DATA_CD_01_CELL03
CELL03      DATA_CD_02_CELL03
CELL03      DATA_CD_03_CELL03
```

Figure 14-3 shows the relationship between the DATA disk group and the failure groups, CELL01, CELL02, and CELL03. Note that this does not indicate which level of redundancy is being used, only that the DATA disk group has its data allocated across three failure groups.

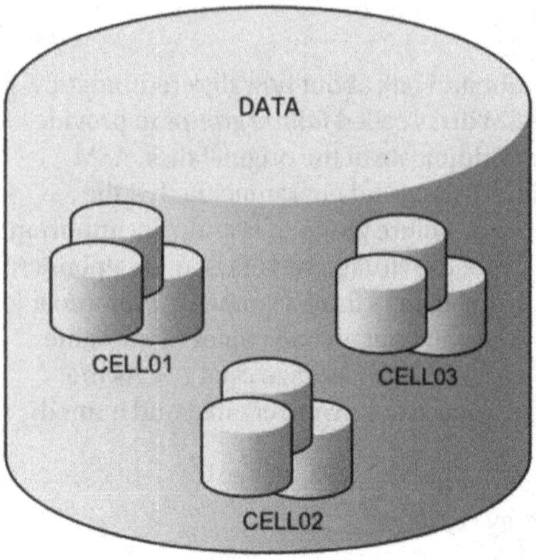

***Figure 14-3.** ASM failure groups CELL01-CELL03*

There are three types of redundancy in ASM: External, Normal, and High:

External Redundancy: No redundancy is provided by ASM. It is assumed that the storage array, usually a SAN, is providing adequate redundancy—in most cases, RAID1, RAID10, or RAID5. This has become the most common method where large storage area networks are used for ASM storage. In the Exadata storage grid, ASM provides the only mechanism for mirroring. If External Redundancy were used on Exadata, the loss of a single disk drive would mean a catastrophic loss of the entire ASM disk group using that disk. It also means that even the temporary loss of a storage cell (reboot, crash, or the like) would make all disk groups using storage on the failed cell unavailable for the duration of the outage and possibly require a database recovery.

Normal Redundancy: Normal Redundancy maintains two copies of data blocks in separate failure groups. Until Oracle 12c, databases will always attempt to read from the primary copy of a data block first. Secondary copies are only read when the primary blocks are unavailable or corrupted. At least two failure groups are required for Normal Redundancy, but many more may be used. For example, an Exadata full rack configuration has 14 storage cells, and each storage cell constitutes a failure group. When data is written to the database, the failure group used for the primary copy of every other block rotates from failure group to failure group in a round-robin fashion. This ensures that disks in all failure groups participate in read operations.

High Redundancy: High Redundancy is similar to Normal Redundancy except that three copies of data blocks are maintained in separate failure groups.

In order for ASM to maintain sanity regarding where the primary and secondary copies of data reside, each disk has a set number of partners where the redundant copy could be. By default, each disk will have eight partners. This number is the same regardless of whether Normal or High Redundancy is used. The partner relationship between disks can be seen by querying the `x$kfdpartner` view inside of the ASM instance. For example, looking at disk 0 in the DATA disk group, we can see the eight partner disks:

```
SQL> select g.name "Diskgroup", d.disk_number "Number", d.name "Disk"
  2  from v$asm_diskgroup g, v$asm_disk d
  3  where g.group_number=d.group_number
  4  and g.name='DATA'
  5  and d.name='DATA_CD_00_ENKCEL01'
  6  /

Diskgroup                          Number  Disk
------------------------------ ----------- -------------------
DATA                                     0 DATA_CD_00_ENKCEL01

SQL> select g.name "Diskgroup", d.name "Disk", p.number_kfdpartner "Partner", d.FAILGROUP
"Failgroup"
  2    from x$kfdpartner p, v$asm_disk d, v$asm_diskgroup g
  3  where p.disk = 0
  4  and g.name='DATA'
  5  and p.grp=g.group_number
  6  and d.group_number = g.group_number
  7  and p.number_kfdpartner=d.disk_number
  8  ORDER BY p.number_kfdpartner
  9  /

Diskgroup                      Disk                              Partner  Failgroup
------------------------------ ------------------------------ ----------- ---------
DATA                           DATA_CD_02_ENKCEL02                     13 ENKCEL02
DATA                           DATA_CD_03_ENKCEL02                     14 ENKCEL02
DATA                           DATA_CD_06_ENKCEL02                     17 ENKCEL02
DATA                           DATA_CD_07_ENKCEL02                     18 ENKCEL02
DATA                           DATA_CD_05_ENKCEL03                     28 ENKCEL03
DATA                           DATA_CD_06_ENKCEL03                     29 ENKCEL03
DATA                           DATA_CD_08_ENKCEL03                     31 ENKCEL03
DATA                           DATA_CD_11_ENKCEL03                     34 ENKCEL03
```

The partner disks are balanced evenly across the remaining two storage cells on the quarter rack shown above. Whenever ASM places a primary copy of data on DATA_CD_00_ENKCEL01, the secondary (or tertiary copy in High Redundancy disk groups) will be placed on one of the eight disks listed by the second query above. From a disk failure standpoint, the partner disks are crucial. In a Normal Redundancy disk group, only one disk that contains portions of the data can be offline. In a High Redundancy disk group, a disk and one of its eight partners can be offline because a third copy of the data exists. If ASM is unable to reach any of the copies of data, the entire disk group will be taken offline in an attempt to prevent possible data loss or corruption.

No matter the number of copies of data, Oracle ASM in version 11g will only read from the primary copy of data. If a disk fails, ASM will look for the redundant copy. In Oracle 12c, an "even read" feature has been introduced. In the event of a disk failure, ASM will attempt to keep disk I/O balanced by reading both primary and secondary copies of all data, regardless of the status of the primary copy.

Grid Disks

Grid disks are created within cell disks, which you may recall are made up of physical disks. Grid disks can either reside on hard-disk-based or flash-based cell disks. In a simple configuration, one grid disk can be created per cell disk. Typical configurations have multiple grid disks per cell disk. The `CellCLI` command `list griddisk` displays the various characteristics of grid disks. For example, the following output shows the relationship between grid disks and cell disks, the type of device on which they are created, and their size:

```
 [enkcel03:root] root
> cellcli
CellCLI: Release 11.2.1.3.1 - Production on Sat Oct 23 17:23:32 CDT 2010

Copyright (c) 2007, 2009, Oracle. All rights reserved.
Cell Efficiency Ratio: 20M

CellCLI> list griddisk attributes name, celldisk, disktype, size
         DATA_CD_00_cell03        CD_00_cell03     HardDisk        1282.8125G
         DATA_CD_01_cell03        CD_01_cell03     HardDisk        1282.8125G
   ...
         FLASH_FD_00_cell03       FD_00_cell03     FlashDisk       4.078125G
         FLASH_FD_01_cell03       FD_01_cell03     FlashDisk       4.078125G
   ...
```

ASM doesn't know anything about physical disks or cell disks. Grid disks are what the storage cell presents to the database servers (as ASM disks) to be used for Clusterware and database storage. ASM uses grid disks to create disk groups in the same way conventional block devices are used on a non-Exadata platform. To illustrate this, the following query shows what ASM disks look like on a non-Exadata system:

```
SYS:+ASM1> select path, total_mb, failgroup
             from v$asm_disk
            order by failgroup, group_number, path;

PATH                  TOTAL_MB FAILGROUP
--------------- ---------- ---------
/dev/sdd1            11444 DATA01
/dev/sde1            11444 DATA02
...
/dev/sdj1             3816 RECO01
/dev/sdk1             3816 RECO02
...
```

The same query on Exadata reports grid disks that have been created at the storage cell:

```
SYS:+ASM1> select path, total_mb, failgroup
             from v$asm_disk
            order by failgroup, group_number, path;
```

```
PATH                                                          TOTAL_MB  FAILGROUP
------------------------------------------------------------  --------  ----------
o/192.168.12.9;192.168.12.10/DATA_CD_00_CELL01                 3023872   CELL01
o/192.168.12.9;192.168.12.10/DATA_CD_01_CELL01                 3023872   CELL01
o/192.168.12.9;192.168.12.10/DATA_CD_02_CELL01                 3023872   CELL01
...
o/192.168.12.9;192.168.12.10/RECO_CD_00_CELL01                 756160    CELL01
o/192.168.12.9;192.168.12.10/RECO_CD_01_CELL01                 756160    CELL01
o/192.168.12.9;192.168.12.10/RECO_CD_02_CELL01                 756160    CELL01
...
o/192.168.12.11;192.168.12.12/DATA_CD_00_CELL02                3023872   CELL02
o/192.168.12.11;192.168.12.12/DATA_CD_01_CELL02                3023872   CELL02
o/192.168.12.11;192.168.12.12/DATA_CD_02_CELL02                3023872   CELL02
...
o/192.168.12.11;192.168.12.12/RECO_CD_00_CELL02                756160    CELL02
o/192.168.12.11;192.168.12.12/RECO_CD_01_CELL02                756160    CELL02
o/192.168.12.11;192.168.12.12/RECO_CD_02_CELL02                756160    CELL02
...
o/192.168.12.13;192.168.12.14/DATA_CD_00_CELL03                3023872   CELL03
o/192.168.12.13;192.168.12.14/DATA_CD_01_CELL03                3023872   CELL03
o/192.168.12.13;192.168.12.14/DATA_CD_02_CELL03                3023872   CELL03
...
o/192.168.12.13;192.168.12.14/RECO_CD_00_CELL03                756160    CELL03
o/192.168.12.13;192.168.12.14/RECO_CD_01_CELL03                756160    CELL03
o/192.168.12.13;192.168.12.14/RECO_CD_02_CELL03                756160    CELL03
...
o/192.168.12.15;192.168.12.16/DATA_CD_00_CELL04                3023872   CELL04
o/192.168.12.15;192.168.12.16/DATA_CD_01_CELL04                3023872   CELL04
o/192.168.12.15;192.168.12.16/DATA_CD_02_CELL04                3023872   CELL04
...
o/192.168.12.15;192.168.12.16/RECO_CD_00_CELL04                756160    CELL04
o/192.168.12.15;192.168.12.16/RECO_CD_01_CELL04                756160    CELL04
o/192.168.12.15;192.168.12.16/RECO_CD_02_CELL04                756160    CELL04
...
o/192.168.12.17;192.168.12.18/DATA_CD_00_CELL05                3023872   CELL05
o/192.168.12.17;192.168.12.18/DATA_CD_01_CELL05                3023872   CELL05
o/192.168.12.17;192.168.12.18/DATA_CD_01_CELL06                3023872   CELL05
...
o/192.168.12.17;192.168.12.18/RECO_CD_00_CELL05                756160    CELL05
o/192.168.12.17;192.168.12.18/RECO_CD_01_CELL05                756160    CELL05
o/192.168.12.17;192.168.12.18/RECO_CD_02_CELL05                756160    CELL05
...
```

Tying it all together, Figure 14-4 shows how the layers of storage fit together, from the storage cell to the ASM disk group. Note that the Linux operating system partitions on the first two cell disks in each storage cell are identified by a darkened partition. We'll talk a little more about the operating system partitions later in this chapter and in much more detail in Chapter 8.

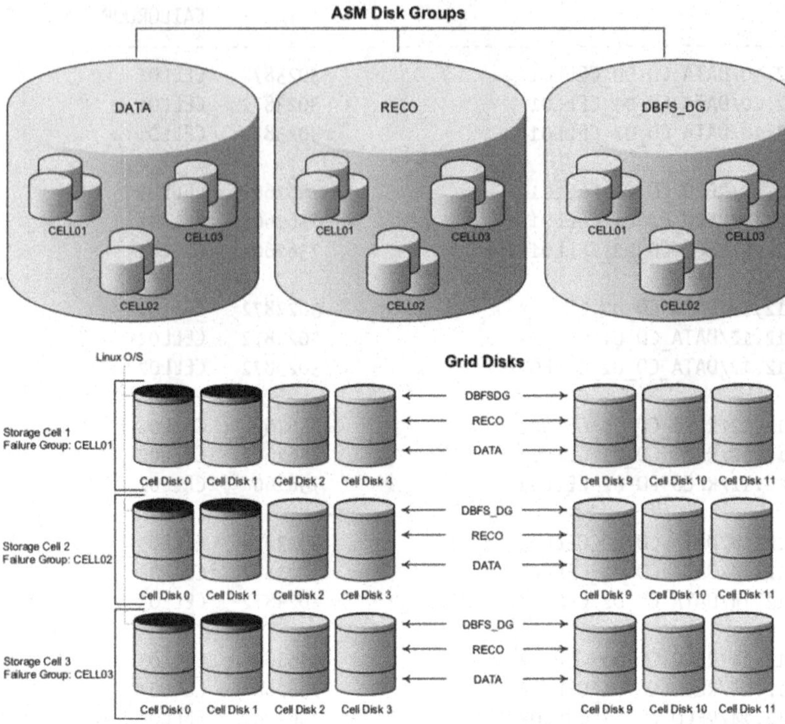

Figure 14-4. *Storage on Exadata*

Storage Allocation

Disk drives store data in concentric bands called *tracks*. Because the outer tracks of a disk have more surface area, they are able to store more data than the inner tracks. As a result, data transfer rates are higher for the outer tracks and decline slightly as you move toward the innermost track. Figure 14-5 shows how tracks are laid out across the disk surface from fastest to slowest.

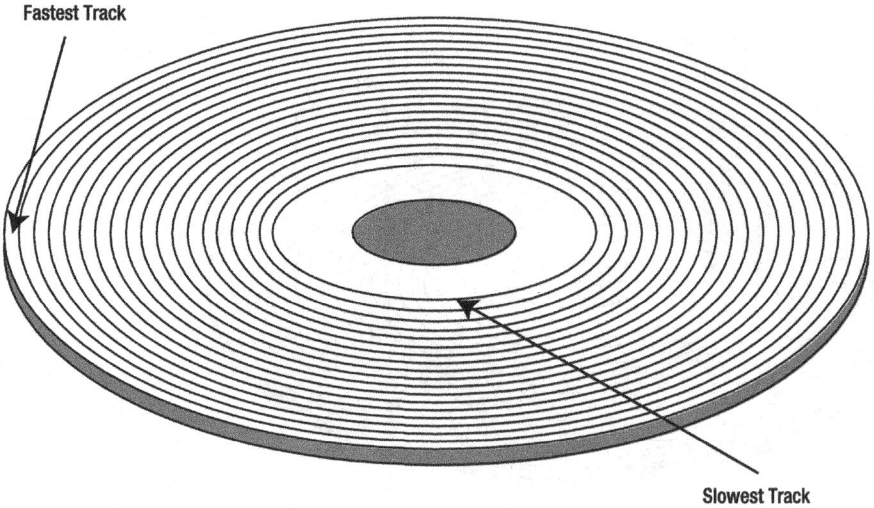

Figure 14-5. *Disk tracks*

Exadata provides two policies for allocating grid disk storage across the surface of disk drives. The first method is the default behavior for allocating space on cell disks. It has no official name so, for purposes of this discussion, I'll refer to it as the *default policy*. Oracle calls the other allocation policy *interleaving*. These two allocation policies are determined when the cell disks are created. Interleaving must be explicitly enabled using the `interleaving` parameter of the `create celldisk` command. For a complete discussion on creating cell disks, refer to Chapter 8.

Fastest Available Tracks First

The default policy simply allocates space starting with the fastest available tracks first, moving inward as space is consumed. Using this policy, the first grid disk created on each cell disk will be given the fastest storage, while the last grid disk created will be relegated to the slower, inner tracks of the disk surface. When planning your storage grid, remember that grid disks are the building blocks for ASM disk groups. These disk groups will, in turn, be used to store tables, indexes, online redo logs, archived redo logs, and so on. To maximize database performance, frequently accessed objects (such as tables, indexes, and online redo logs) should be stored in the highest priority grid disks. Low priority grid disks should be used for less performance-sensitive objects such as database backups, archived redo logs, and flashback logs. Figure 14-6 shows how grid disks are allocated using the default allocation policy.

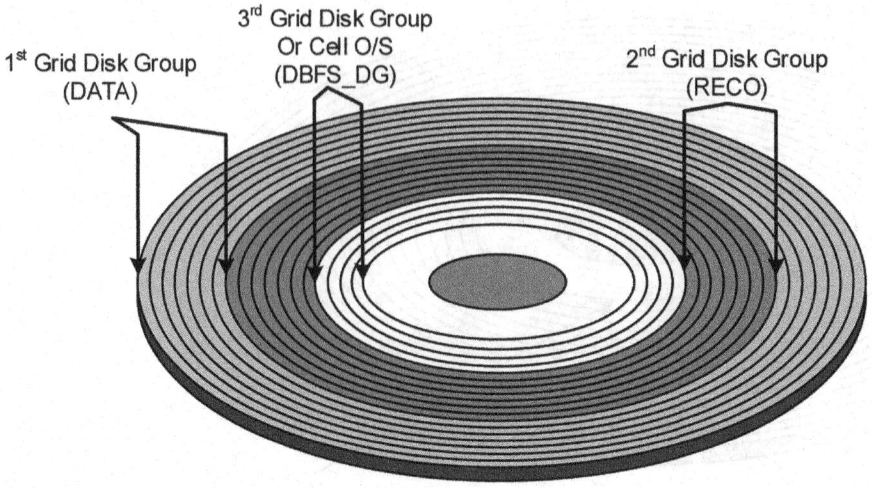

Figure 14-6. *The default allocation policy*

Table 14-1 shows the performance effect on the ASM disk groups from the first to the last grid disk created when using the default allocation policy. You won't find the term "I/O Performance Rating" in the Oracle documentation. It's a term I'm coining here to describe the relative performance capabilities of each disk group due to its location on the surface of the physical disk drive.

Table 14-1. *I/O Performance—Default Allocation Policy*

ASM Disk Group	I/O Performance Rating
DATA	1
RECO	2
DBFS_DG	3

Interleaving

The other policy, interleaving, attempts to even out performance of the faster and slower tracks by allocating space in an alternating fashion between the slower and faster tracks of the disks. This is achieved by splitting each cell disk into two regions—an outer region and an inner region. Grid disks are slices of cell disks that will be used to create ASM disk groups. For example, the following command creates 12 grid disks (one per physical disk; see Figure 14-4) on Cell03 to be used for the DATA disk group:

```
CellCLI> CREATE GRIDDISK ALL HARDDISK PREFIX=DATA, size=744.6813G
```

These grid disks were used to create the following DATA disk group. Notice how each grid disk was created on a separate cell disk:

```
SYS:+ASM2> select dg.name diskgroup,
                  substr(d.name, 6,12) cell_disk,
                  d.name grid_disk
```

```
         from v$asm_diskgroup dg,
              v$asm_disk d
        where dg.group_number = d.group_number
          and dg.name ='DATA'
          and failgroup = 'CELL03'
        order by 1,2;

DISKGROUP   CELL_DISK     GRID_DISK
----------  ------------  --------------------
DATA        CD_00_CELL03  DATA_CD_00_CELL03
DATA        CD_01_CELL03  DATA_CD_01_CELL03
DATA        CD_02_CELL03  DATA_CD_02_CELL03
DATA        CD_03_CELL03  DATA_CD_03_CELL03
...
DATA        CD_10_CELL03  DATA_CD_10_CELL03
DATA        CD_11_CELL03  DATA_CD_11_CELL03
```

Using interleaving in this example, DATA_CD_00_CELL03 (the first grid disk) is allocated to the outer most tracks of the outer (fastest) region of the CD_00_CELL03 cell disk. The next grid disk, DATA_CD_01_CELL03, is created on the outermost tracks of the slower, inner region of cell disk CD_01_CELL03. This pattern continues until all 12 grid disks are allocated. When the next set of grid disks is created for the RECO disk group, they start with the inner region of cell disk 1 and alternate from inner to outer region until all 12 grid disks are created. Figure 14-7 shows how the interleaving policy would look if two grid disk groups were created.

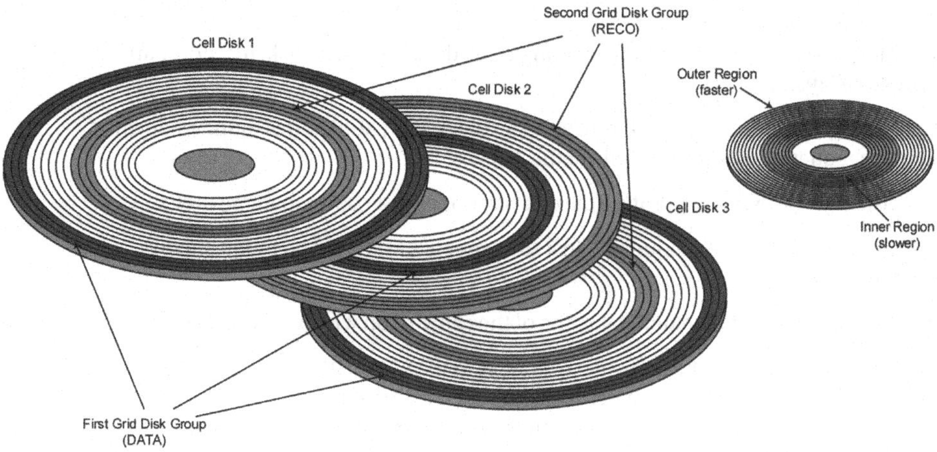

Figure 14-7. *The interleaving allocation policy*

Table 14-2 shows the performance effect on the ASM disk groups from the first to the last grid disk created when the interleaving allocation policy is used.

Table 14-2. I/O Performance—Interleaving Policy

ASM Disk Group	I/O Performance Rating
DATA	1
RECO	1
DBFS_DG	2

As you can see, the main difference between the default policy and the interleaving policy is that default provides finer-grained control over ASM disks. With the default policy you have the ability to choose which set of grid disks will be given the absolute fastest position on the disk. The interleaving policy has the effect of evening out the performance of grid disks. In practice, this gives the first two sets of grid disks (for DATA and RECO) the same performance characteristics. This may be useful if the performance demands of the first two disk groups are equal. In our experience, this is rarely the case. Usually there is a clear winner when it comes to the performance demands of a database environment. Tables, indexes, and online redo logs (the DATA disk group) have much higher performance requirements than database backups, archived redo logs, and flashback logs, which are usually stored in the RECO disk group. Unless there are specific reasons for using interleaving, we recommend using the default policy.

Creating Grid Disks

Before we run through a few examples of how to create grid disks, let's take a quick look at some of their key attributes:

- Multiple grid disks may be created on a single cell disk, but a grid disk may not span multiple cell disks.
- Storage for grid disks is allocated in 16M Allocation Units (AUs) and is rounded down if the size requested is not a multiple of the AU size.
- Grid disks may be created one at a time or in groups with a common name prefix.
- Grid disk names must be unique within a storage cell and should be unique across all storage cells.
- Grid disk names should include the name of the cell disk on which they reside.

Once a grid disk is created, its name is visible from ASM in the V$ASM_DISK view. In other words, grid disks = ASM disks. It is very important to name grid disks in such a way that they can easily be associated with the physical disk to which they belong in the event of disk failure. To facilitate this, grid disk names should include both of the following:

- The name of the ASM disk group for which it will be used
- The cell disk name (which includes the name of the storage cell)

Figure 14-8 shows the properly formatted name for a grid disk belonging to the TEST disk group, created on cell disk CD_00_cell03.

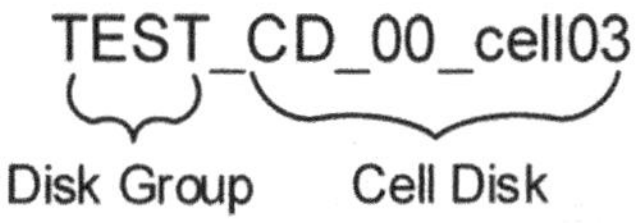

Figure 14-8. *Grid disk naming*

Creating Grid Disks

The CellCLI command create griddisk is used to create grid disks. It may be used to create individual grid disks one at a time or in groups. If grid disks are created one at a time, it is up to you to provide the complete grid disk name. The following example creates one properly named 400GB grid disk on cell disk CD_00_cell03. If we had omitted the size=400GB parameter, the resulting grid disk would have consumed all free space on the cell disk:

```
CellCLI> create griddisk TEST_CD_00_cell03 -
         celldisk='CD_00_cell03', size=400G

GridDisk TEST_CD_00_cell03 successfully created

CellCLI> list griddisk attributes name, celldisk, size -
         where name='TEST_CD_00_cell03'

        TEST_CD_00_cell03        CD_00_cell03     400G
```

There are 12 drives per storage cell, and the number of storage cells varies from 3, for a quarter rack, to 14, for a full rack. That means you will be creating a minimum of 36 grid disks for a quarter rack, and up to 168 grid disks for a full rack. Fortunately, CellCLI provides a way to create all the grid disks needed for a given ASM disk group in one command. For example, the following command creates all the grid disks for the ASM disk group TEST:

```
CellCLI> create griddisk all harddisk prefix='TEST', size=400G

GridDisk TEST_CD_00_cell03 successfully created
GridDisk TEST_CD_01_cell03 successfully created
...
GridDisk TEST_CD_10_cell03 successfully created
GridDisk TEST_CD_11_cell03 successfully created
```

When this variant of the create griddisk command is used, CellCLI automatically creates one grid disk on each cell disk, naming them with the prefix you provided in the following manner:

{prefix}_{celldisk_name}

The optional size parameter specifies the size of each individual grid disk. If no size is provided, the resulting grid disks will consume all remaining free space of their respective cell disk. The all harddisk parameter instructs CellCLI to use only disk-based cell disks. Just in case you are wondering, Flash Cache modules are also presented as cell disks (of type FlashDisk) and may be used for creating grid disks as well. We'll discuss flash disks later on in this chapter. The following command shows the grid disks created:

```
CellCLI> list griddisk attributes name, cellDisk, diskType, size -
         where name like 'TEST_.*'
```

```
TEST_CD_00_cell03          CD_00_cell03       HardDisk         96M
TEST_CD_01_cell03          CD_01_cell03       HardDisk         96M
 ...
TEST_CD_10_cell03          CD_10_cell03       HardDisk         96M
TEST_CD_11_cell03          CD_11_cell03       HardDisk         96M
```

Grid Disk Sizing

As we discussed earlier, grid disks are equivalent to ASM disks. They are literally the building blocks of the ASM disk groups you will create. The DBFS_DG disk group is created when Exadata is installed on a site. It is primarily used to store the OCR and voting files used by Oracle Clusterware (Grid Infrastructure). However, there is no reason DBFS_DG cannot be used to store other objects such as tablespaces for the Database File System (DBFS). In addition to the DBFS_DG, (formerly SYSTEMDG) disk group, Exadata is also delivered with DATA and RECO disk groups to be used for database files and Fast Recovery Areas. But these disk groups may actually be created with whatever names make the most sense for your environment. For consistency, this chapter uses the names DBFS_DG, DATA, and RECO. If you are considering something other than the "factory defaults" for your disk group configuration, remember that a main reason for using multiple ASM disk groups on Exadata is to prioritize I/O performance. The first grid disks you create will be the fastest, resulting in higher performance for the associated ASM disk group.

■ **Note** When Exadata V2 rolled out, SYSTEMDG was the disk group used to store OCR and voting files for the Oracle Clusterware. When Exadata X2 was introduced, this disk group was renamed to DBFS_DG, presumably because there was quite a bit of usable space left over that made for a nice location for a moderately sized DBFS file system. Also, the other default disk group names changed somewhat when X2 came out. The Exadata Database Machine name was added as a postfix to the DATA and RECO disk group names. For example, the machine name for one of our lab systems is ENK. So DATA became DATA_ENK, and RECO became RECO_ENK.

By the way, Oracle recommends you create a separate database for DBFS because it requires instance parameter settings that would not be optimal for typical application databases.

Following are some of the most common ASM disk groups:

> DBFS_DG: This disk group is typically the location for Clusterware's OCR and voting files, along with the spfile for ASM. It may also be used for other files with similar performance requirements. For OCR and voting files, Normal Redundancy is the minimum requirement. Normal Redundancy will create three voting files and three OCR files. The voting files must be stored in separate ASM failure groups. Recall that on Exadata, each storage cell constitutes a failure group. This means that only Normal Redundancy may be used for an Exadata eighth or quarter rack configuration (three storage cells/failure groups). Only in half rack and full rack configurations (seven or fourteen storage cells/failure groups) are there a sufficient number of failure groups to store the required number of voting and OCR files required by High Redundancy. Table 14-3 summarizes the storage requirements for OCR and voting files at various levels of redundancy. Note that External Redundancy is not supported on Exadata. We've included it in the table for reference only. If a High Redundancy disk group with a suitable number of fail groups is available, the scripted installation process will move the OCR and voting disks to that disk group.

Table 14-3. OCR and Voting File Storage Requirements

Redundancy	Min # of Disks	OCR	Voting	Total
External	1	400 MB	300 MB	700 MB
Normal	3	800 MB	900 MB	1.7 GB
High	5	1.2 GB	1.5 GB	2.7 GB

> DATA: This disk group is used for storing files associated with the `db_create_file_dest` database parameter. These include datafiles, online redo logs, control files, and spfiles.
>
> RECO: This disk group is what used to be called Flash Recovery Area (FRA). Some time after 11gR1, Oracle renamed it to the "Fast Recovery Area"; rumor has it that the overuse of "Flash" was causing confusion among the marketing team. So to clarify, this disk group will be used to store everything corresponding to the `db_recovery_file_dest` database parameter. It includes online database backups and copies, copies of the online redo log files, mirror copies of the control file, archived redo logs, flashback logs, and Data Pump exports.

Recall that Exadata storage cells are actually finely tuned Linux servers with 12 internal disk drives. Oracle could have dedicated two of these internal disks to run the operating system, but doing so would have wasted a lot of space. Instead, they carved off several small partitions on the first two disks in the enclosure. These partitions, about 33GB each, create a slight imbalance in the size of the cell disks. The DBFS_DG grid disks even out this imbalance. Figure 14-9 illustrates the size imbalance.

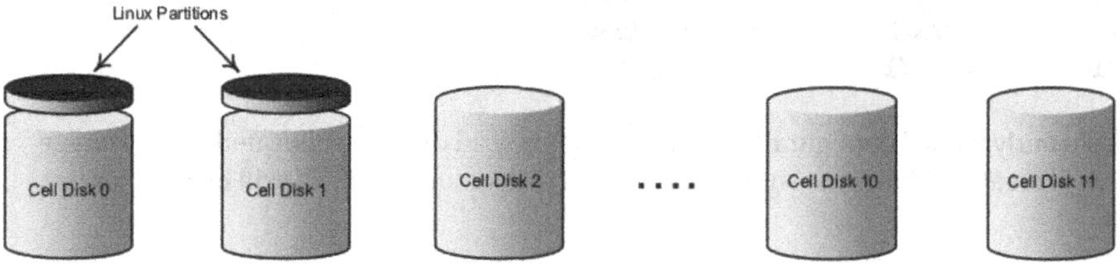

Figure 14-9. *Cell disk layout*

This reserved space can be seen by running `parted` on one of the storage cells. The `/dev/sda3` partition in the listing is the location of the cell disk. All other partitions are used by the Linux operating system:

```
[root@enkx3cel01 ~]# parted /dev/sda print

Model: LSI MR9261-8i (scsi)
Disk /dev/sda: 3000GB
Sector size (logical/physical): 512B/512B
Partition Table: gpt
```

```
Number  Start   End     Size    File system  Name     Flags
 1      32.8kB  123MB   123MB   ext3         primary  raid
 2      123MB   132MB   8225kB  ext2         primary
 3      132MB   2964GB  2964GB               primary
 4      2964GB  2964GB  32.8kB               primary
 5      2964GB  2975GB  10.7GB  ext3         primary  raid
 6      2975GB  2985GB  10.7GB  ext3         primary  raid
 7      2985GB  2989GB  3221MB  ext3         primary  raid
 8      2989GB  2992GB  3221MB  ext3         primary  raid
 9      2992GB  2994GB  2147MB  linux-swap   primary  raid
10      2994GB  2995GB  732MB                primary  raid
11      2995GB  3000GB  5369MB  ext3         primary  raid
```

You can see the smaller cell disks in the `size` attribute when you run the `list celldisk` command:

```
CellCLI> list celldisk attributes name, devicePartition, size -
    where diskType = 'HardDisk'
         CD_00_cell01     /dev/sda3           2760.15625G
         CD_01_cell01     /dev/sdb3           2760.15625G
         CD_02_cell01     /dev/sdc            2793.953125G
         CD_03_cell01     /dev/sdd            2793.953125G
         CD_04_cell01     /dev/sde            2793.953125G
         CD_05_cell01     /dev/sdf            2793.953125G
         CD_06_cell01     /dev/sdg            2793.953125G
         CD_07_cell01     /dev/sdh            2793.953125G
         CD_08_cell01     /dev/sdi            2793.953125G
         CD_09_cell01     /dev/sdj            2793.953125G
         CD_10_cell01     /dev/sdk            2793.953125G
         CD_11_cell01     /dev/sdl            2793.953125G
```

Let's take a look at a fairly typical configuration to illustrate how grid disks are allocated in the storage cell. In this example, we'll create grid disks to support three ASM disk groups. `DBFS_DG` will be used for the OCR and Voting files:

- `DATA`
- `RECO`
- `DBFS_DG`

This storage cell is configured with 3TB sized, high-capacity disks, so the raw space per storage cell is 33.45 terabytes. Newer models with larger disk sizes distribute the additional space between the `DATA` and `RECO` grid disks. Table 14-4 shows what the allocation would look like.

Table 14-4. *I/O Grid Disk Space Allocation (All Sizes Expressed in Gigabytes)*

Cell Disk	OS	DATA	DBFS_DG	RECO	Total Grid Disk Space
CD_00_cel01	33.796875	2607	N/A	1084.4375	3691.4375
CD_01_cel01	33.796875	2607	N/A	1084.4375	3691.4375
CD_02_cel01	N/A	2607	33.796875	1084.4375	3725.234375
CD_03_cel01	N/A	2607	33.796875	1084.4375	3725.234375
CD_04_cel01	N/A	2607	33.796875	1084.4375	3725.234375
CD_05_cel01	N/A	2607	33.796875	1084.4375	3725.234375
CD_06_cel01	N/A	2607	33.796875	1084.4375	3725.234375
CD_07_cel01	N/A	2607	33.796875	1084.4375	3725.234375
CD_08_cel01	N/A	2607	33.796875	1084.4375	3725.234375
CD_09_cel01	N/A	2607	33.796875	1084.4375	3725.234375
CD_10_cel01	N/A	2607	33.796875	1084.4375	3725.234375
CD_11_cel01	N/A	2607	33.796875	1084.4375	3725.234375
Total Per Cell	**67.59**	**31,284**	**337.97**	**13,013.25**	**44,635.22**

Creating a configuration like this is fairly simple. The following commands create grid disks according to the allocation in Table 14-4:

```
CellCLI> create griddisk all prefix='DATA' size=2607G

CellCLI> create griddisk all prefix='RECO' size=1084.4375G
CellCLI> create griddisk all prefix='DBFS_DG'
```

Notice that no size was specified for the `DBFS_DG` grid disks. When size is not specified, `CellCLI` automatically calculates the size for each grid disk so they consume the remaining free space on the cell disk. For example:

```
CellCLI> list griddisk attributes name, size
         DATA_CD_00_cell01       2607G
         DATA_CD_01_cell01       2607G
         DATA_CD_02_cell01       2607G
         ...
         RECO_CD_00_cell01       1084.4375G
         RECO_CD_01_cell01       1084.4375G
         RECO_CD_02_cell01       1084.4375G
         ...
         DBFS_DG_CD_02_cell01    33.796875G
         DBFS_DG_CD_03_cell01    33.796875G
         DBFS_DG_CD_04_cell01    33.796875G
         ...
```

Creating FlashDisk-Based Grid Disks

Exadata uses offloading features like Smart Scan to provide strikingly fast I/O for direct path reads typically found in DSS databases. These features are only activated for very specific data access paths in the database. To speed up I/O performance for random reads, Exadata V2 introduced *Flash Cache*, a solid-state, storage-backed cache. In an X4-2 model, each storage cell comes configured with four 3.2T Flash Cache cards (2,978G usable) to augment I/O performance for frequently accessed data. When configured as Exadata Smart Flash Cache, these devices act like a large, database-aware disk cache for the storage cell. We discussed this in detail in Chapter 5. Optionally, some space from the Flash Cache may be carved out and used like high-speed, solid-state disks. The Flash Cache is configured as a cell disk of type `FlashDisk`, and just as grid disks are created on `HardDisk` cell disks, they may also be created on `FlashDisk` cell disks. When `FlashDisks` are used for database storage, it's primarily to improve performance for highly write-intensive workloads when disk-based storage cannot keep up. The need for flash-based grid disks has diminished greatly with the advent of write-back Flash Cache. `FlashDisk` cell disks may be seen using the CellCLI `list celldisk` command, as in the following example:

```
CellCLI> list celldisk attributes name, diskType, size
         CD_00_cel01    HardDisk         3691.484375G
         CD_01_cel01    HardDisk         3691.484375G
         CD_02_cel01    HardDisk         3725.28125G
         ...
         CD_11_cel01    HardDisk         3725.28125G
         FD_00_cel01    FlashDisk        186.25G
         FD_01_cel01    FlashDisk        186.25G
         ...
         FD_15_cel01    FlashDisk        186.25G
```

`FlashDisk` type cell disks are named with a prefix of FD and a `diskType` of `FlashDisk`. It is not recommended to use all of your Flash Cache for grid disks. When creating the Flash Cache, use the `size` parameter to hold back some space to be used for grid disks. The following command creates a Flash Cache of 512GB, reserving the remaining space for grid disks (example below from an X3-2 Exadata):

```
CellCLI> create flashcache all size=512G
Flash cache cel01_FLASHCACHE successfully created
```

Note that the `create flashcache` command uses the `size` parameter differently than the `create griddisk` command. When creating the flash cache, the `size` parameter determines the total size of the cache:

```
CellCLI> list flashcache detail
         name:                    cel01_FLASHCACHE
         cellDisk:                FD_11_cel01,FD_03_cel01,FD_07_cel01, ...
         ...
         size:                    512G
         status:                  normal

CellCLI> list celldisk attributes name, size, freespace -
        where disktype='FlashDisk'
         FD_00_cel01    22.875G          4.078125G
         FD_01_cel01    22.875G          4.078125G
         ...
         FD_15_cel01    22.875G          4.078125G
```

Now we can create 16 grid disks with the remaining free space on the Flash Disks, using the familiar `create griddisk` command. This time we'll specify `flashdisk` for the cell disks to use:

```
CellCLI> create griddisk all flashdisk prefix='RAMDISK'
GridDisk RAMDISK_FD_00_cel01 successfully created
...
GridDisk RAMDISK_FD_14_cel01 successfully created
GridDisk RAMDISK_FD_15_cel01 successfully created

CellCLI> list griddisk attributes name, diskType, size -
       where disktype='FlashDisk'

         RAMDISK_FD_00_cel01    FlashDisk       4.078125G
         RAMDISK_FD_01_cel01    FlashDisk       4.078125G
         ...
         RAMDISK_FD_15_cel01    FlashDisk       4.078125G
```

Once the grid disks have been created, they may be used to create ASM disk groups used to store database objects just as you would any other disk-based disk group. The beauty of Flash Cache configuration is that all this may be done while the system is online and servicing I/O requests. All of the commands we've just used to drop and reconfigure the Flash Cache were done without the need to disable or shut down databases or cell services.

Storage Strategies

Each Exadata storage cell is an intelligent mini-SAN, operating somewhat independently of the other cells in the rack. Now this may be stretching the definition of SAN a little, but with the Cell Server software intelligently controlling I/O access we believe it is appropriate. Storage cells may be configured in such a way that all cells in the rack provide storage for all databases in the rack. This provides maximum I/O performance and data transfer rates for each database in the system. Compute nodes may also be configured to communicate with specific cell servers using the `cellip.ora` file. In addition, cell security may be used to restrict access to specific databases or ASM instances through use of storage realms. In this section, I'll discuss strategies for separating cells into groups that service certain database servers or RAC clusters. To borrow a familiar term from the SAN world, this is where we will talk about "zoning" a set of storage cells to service development, test, and production environments. While both of these options are available to Exadata administrators, the methodology described in "Isolating Storage Cell Access" has been seen much more frequently across Exadata environments.

Configuration Options

Exadata represents a substantial investment for most companies. For one reason or another, we find that many companies want to buy a full or half rack for consolidating several database environments. Exadata's architecture makes it a very good consolidation platform. These are some of the most common configurations we've seen:

- A full rack servicing development, test, and production
- A full rack servicing several, independent production environments
- A half rack servicing development and test
- Isolating a scratch environment for DBA testing and deploying software patches

For each of these configurations, isolating I/O to specific database servers may be a key consideration. For example, your company may be hosting database environments for external clients that require separation from other database systems. Or your company may have legal requirements to separate server access to data. Another reason for segmenting storage at the cell level may be to provide an environment for DBA training, or testing software patches. There are two ways to isolate Exadata storage cells—by network access and by storage realm. Based on experience seen in the field, the most common method for restricting access between database servers and storage cells is via the first method described below.

Isolating Storage Cell Access

Recall that ASM gains access to grid disks through the InfiniBand network. This is configured by adding the IP address of storage cells in the `cellip.ora` file. For example, in a full rack configuration, all 14 storage cells are listed as follows:

```
[enkdb02:oracle:EXDB2] /home/oracle
> cat /etc/oracle/cell/network-config/cellip.ora
cell="192.168.10.17;192.168.10.18"
cell="192.168.10.19;192.168.10.20"
cell="192.168.10.21;192.168.10.22"
cell="192.168.10.23;192.168.10.24"
cell="192.168.10.25;192.168.10.26"
cell="192.168.10.27;192.168.10.28"
cell="192.168.10.29;192.168.10.30"
cell="192.168.10.31;192.168.10.32"
cell="192.168.10.33;192.168.10.34"
cell="192.168.10.35;192.168.10.36"
cell="192.168.10.37;192.168.10.38"
cell="192.168.10.39;192.168.10.40"
cell="192.168.10.41;192.168.10.42"
cell="192.168.10.43;192.168.10.44"
```

The example above is from a full rack X4-2 Exadata with active - active InfiniBand links. Each line defines a single storage cell. When ASM starts up, it interrogates the storage cells on each of these IP addresses for grid disks it can use for configuring ASM disk groups. We can easily segregate storage cells to service specific database servers by removing the IP address of cells that should not be used. Obviously, this is not enforced by any kind of security, but it is an effective, simple way of pairing up database servers with the storage cells they should use for storage. Table 14-5 illustrates a configuration that splits a full rack into two separate database and storage grids. Production is configured with six database servers and eleven storage cells, while Test is configured for two database servers and three storage cells.

Table 14-5. *A Storage Network Configuration*

Production Database Servers, 1-6	Production Storage Cells, 1-11	
/etc/oracle/cell/network-config/cellip.ora		
cell="192.168.10.17;192.168.10.18"	dm01cel01	192.168.10.17;192.168.10.18
cell="192.168.10.19;192.168.10.20"	dm01cel02	192.168.10.19;192.168.10.20
cell="192.168.10.21;192.168.10.22"	dm01cel03	192.168.10.21;192.168.10.22
cell="192.168.10.23;192.168.10.24"	dm01cel04	192.168.10.23;192.168.10.24
cell="192.168.10.25;192.168.10.26"	dm01cel05	192.168.10.25;192.168.10.26
cell="192.168.10.27;192.168.10.28"	dm01cel06	192.168.10.27;192.168.10.28
cell="192.168.10.29;192.168.10.30"	dm01cel07	192.168.10.29;192.168.10.30
cell="192.168.10.31;192.168.10.32"	dm01cel08	192.168.10.31;192.168.10.32
cell="192.168.10.33;192.168.10.34"	dm01cel09	192.168.10.33;192.168.10.34
cell="192.168.10.35;192.168.10.36"	dm01cel10	192.168.10.35;192.168.10.36
cell="192.168.10.37;192.168.10.38"	dm01cel11	192.168.10.37;192.168.10.38
Test Database Servers, 7-8	**Test Storage Cells, 12-14**	
/etc/oracle/cell/network-config/cellip.ora		
cell="192.168.10.39;192.168.10.40"	dm01cel12	192.168.10.39;192.168.10.40
cell="192.168.10.41;192.168.10.42"	dm01cel13	192.168.10.41;192.168.10.42
cell="192.168.10.43;192.168.10.44"	dm01cel14	192.168.10.43;192.168.10.44

Database servers and storage cells can be paired in any combination that best suits your specific needs. Remember that the minimum requirements for Oracle RAC on Exadata requires two database servers and three storage cells, which is basically a quarter rack configuration. Table 14-6 shows the storage and performance capabilities of Exadata storage cells in quarter rack, half rack, and full rack configurations.

Table 14-6. *Performance Capabities of Exadata Storage Cells (Exadata X4-2)*

MBPS & IOPS by Device Type	Eighth Rack	Quarter Rack	Half Rack	Full Rack
Disk Transfer Bandwidth				
High Perf	2.6 GB/s	5.2 GB/s	12 GB/s	24 GB/s
High Cap	2.25 GB/s	4.5 GB/s	10 GB/s	20 GB/s
Flash Disk Transfer Bandwidth	10.7 GB/s	21.5 GB/s	50 GB/s	100 GB/s
Disk IOPS				
High Perf	5,400	10,800	25,000	50,000
High Cap	3,500	7,000	16,000	32,000
Flash Disk IOPS	210,000	570,000	1,330,000	2,660,000

If some of your environments do not require Oracle RAC, there is no reason they cannot be configured with stand alone (non-RAC) database servers. If this is done, then a minimum of one storage cell may be used to provide database storage for each database server. In fact, multiple standalone database servers may even share a single storage cell. Once again, Exadata is a highly configurable system. But just because you can do something doesn't mean you should. Storage cells are the workhorse of Exadata. Each cell supports a finite data transfer rate (MBPS) and number of I/Os per second (IOPS). Reducing the storage cell footprint of your database environment directly impacts the performance your database can yield. Finally, if a single storage cell services multiple database clusters, there are certain components that cannot be segmented (Flash Cache, Flash Log).

■ **Note** Over time, Oracle has changed types of storage available to Exadata. Prior to the X4-2 release, high-performance disks had a rotational speed of 15,000 RPM. X4 storage cells (including X3-8 racks purchased after December 2013) included 10,000RPM high-density drives, and the X5 storage server replaced the high-performance disks with NVMe flash cards. The only change to the high-capacity disks has been the size, ranging from 2TB to 4TB, depending on when the Exadata was purchased.

Cell Security

In addition to isolating storage cells by their network address, Exadata also provides a way to secure access to specific grid disks within the storage cell. An access control list (ACL) is maintained at the storage cell, and grid disks are defined as being accessible to specific ASM clusters and, optionally, databases within the ASM cluster. If you've already logged some time working on your Exadata system, chances are you haven't noticed any such access restrictions. That is because, by default, cell security is open, allowing all ASM clusters and databases in the system access to all grid disks. Cell security controls access to grid disks at two levels—by ASM cluster and by database:

> **ASM-Scoped Security**: ASM-scoped security restricts access to grid disks by ASM cluster. This is the first layer of cell security. It allows all databases in the ASM cluster to have access to all grid disks managed by the ASM instance. For example, an Exadata full rack configuration can be split so that four database servers and seven storage cells can be used by Customer-A, and the other four database servers and seven storage cells can be used by Customer-B.
>
> **Database-Scoped Security**: Once ASM-scoped security is configured, access to grid disks may be further controlled at the database level using database-scoped security. Database-scoped security is most appropriate when databases within the ASM cluster should have access to a subset of the grid disks managed by the ASM instance. In the earlier example, Customer-A's environment could use database-scoped security to separate database environments from one another within its half rack configuration.

Cell Security Terminology

Before we get too far along, let's take a look at some of the new terminology specific to Exadata's cell security:

> **Storage realm**: Grid disks that share a common security domain are referred to as a *storage realm*.
>
> **Security key**: A security key is used to authenticate ASM and database clients to the storage realm. It is also used for securing messages sent between the storage cells and the ASM and database clients. The security key is created using the CellCLI command `create key`. The key is then assigned to grid disks using the CellCLI `assign key` command.
>
> **`cellkey.ora`**: The `cellkey.ora` file is stored on the database servers. One `cellkey.ora` file is created for ASM-scoped security and another `cellkey.ora` file is created for each database requiring database-scoped security. The `cellkey.ora` files are used to identify security keys, the storage realm, and the unique name of the ASM cluster or database.

Table 14-7 shows the definitions for the fields in the `cellkey.ora` file.

***Table 14-7.** The Contents of the cellkey.ora File*

Field	Description
`key`	This is the security key generated at the storage cell with the `create key` command. This key is used to authenticate the ASM cluster and database to the storage realm. For ASM-scoped security, this value must match the key assigned to the ASM cluster using the `assign key` command. For database-scoped security, this value must match the security key assigned to the database using the `assign key` command.
`asm`	This is the unique name of the ASM cluster found in the `DB_UNIQUE_NAME` parameter of the ASM instance. It is used to associate the ASM cluster with the `availableTo` attribute of the grid disks in the storage realm. Grid disks are assigned this value using the CellCLI `create griddisk` and `alter grid disk` commands.
`realm`	This field is optional. If used, the value must match the `realmName` attribute assigned to the storage cells using the CellCLI command `alter cell realmName`.

Cell Security Best Practices

Following Oracle's best practices is an important part of configuring cell security. It will help you avoid those odd situations where things seem to work some of the time or only on certain storage cells. Following these best practices will save you a lot of time and frustration:

- If database-scoped security is used, be sure to use it for all databases in the ASM cluster.
- Make sure the ASM `cellkey.ora` file is the same on all servers for an ASM cluster. This includes contents, ownership, and permissions.
- Just as you did for the ASM `cellkey.ora` file, make sure contents, ownership, and permissions are identical across all servers for the database `cellkey.ora` file.

- Ensure the cell side security settings are the same for all grid disks belonging to the same ASM disk group.
- It is very important that the cellkey.ora files and cell commands are executed consistently across all servers and cells. Use the dcli utility to distribute the cellkey.ora file and reduce the likelihood of human error.

Configuring ASM-Scoped Security

With ASM-scoped security, the ASM cluster is authenticated to the storage cell by its DB_UNIQUE_NAME and a security key. The security key is created at the storage cell and stored in the cellkey.ora file on the database server. An access control list (ACL) is defined on the storage cell that is used to verify the security key it receives from ASM. The availableTo attribute on each grid disk dictates which ASM clusters are permitted access.

Now let's take a look at the steps for configuring ASM-scoped security:

1. Find the DB_UNIQUE_NAME for your ASM cluster using the show parameter command from one of the ASM instances:

```
SYS:+ASM1>show parameter db_unique_name

NAME             TYPE        VALUE
---------------- ----------- -----
db_unique_name   string      +ASM
```

2. Shut down all databases and ASM instances in the ASM cluster.
3. Create the security key using the CellCLI create key command:

```
CellCLI> create key
         3648e2a3070169095b799c44f02fea9
```

   This simply generates the key, which is not automatically stored anywhere. The create key command only needs to be run once and can be done on any storage cell. This security key will be assigned to the ASM cluster in the key field of the cellkey.ora file.

4. Next, create a cellkey.ora file and install it in the /etc/oracle/cell/network-config directory for each database server on which this ASM cluster is configured. Set the ownership of the file to the user and group specified during the ASM software installation. Permissions should allow it to be read by the owner of the file. For example:

```
key=3648e2a3070169095b799c44f02fea9
asm=+ASM
realm=customer_A_realm

> chown oracle:dba cellkey.ora
> chmod 600 cellkey.ora
```

Note that if a realm is defined in this file, it must match the realm name assigned to the storage cells using the `alter cell realm=` command. Using a storage realm is optional.

5. Use the CellCLI `assign key` command to assign the security key to the ASM cluster being configured. This must be done on each storage cell to which you want the ASM cluster to have access:

```
CellCLI> ASSIGN KEY -
            FOR '+ASM'='3648e2a3070169095b799c44f02fea9'
```

6. Using the CellCLI `create griddisk` command, set the `availableTo` attribute for each grid disk to which you want this ASM cluster to have access. This can be done for all grid disks on the cell as follows:

```
CellCLI> create griddisk all prefix='DATA' -
                size= 1282.8125G availableTo='+ASM'
```

7. For existing grid disks, use the `alter grid disk` command to set up security:

```
CellCLI> alter griddisk all prefix='DATA' -
               availableTo='+ASM'
```

8. A subset of grid disks may also be assigned, as follows:

```
CellCLI> alter griddisk DATA_CD_00_cell03, -
                        DATA_CD_01_cell03, -
                        DATA_CD_02_cell03, -
                        ...
               availableTo='+ASM'
```

This completes the configuration of ASM-scoped cell security. The ASM cluster and all databases can now be restarted. When ASM starts up, it will check for the `cellkey.ora` file and pass the key to the storage cells in order to gain access to the grid disks. Keep in mind that when you use ASM scoped security, each cluster will need a different name for identification purposes.

Configuring Database-Scoped Security

Database-scoped security locks down database access to specific grid disks within an ASM cluster. It is useful for controlling access to grid disks when multiple databases share the same ASM cluster. Before database-scoped security may be implemented, ASM-scoped security must be configured and verified.

When using database-scoped security, there will be one `cellkey.ora` file per database, per database server, and one ACL entry on the storage cell for each database. The following steps may be used to implement simple database-scoped security for two databases, called HR (Human Resources) and PAY (Payroll). Each database has its own respective disk group (`DATA_HR` and `RECO_HR` for the Human Resources database, `DATA_PAY` and `RECO_PAY` for the Payroll database) in this example.

1. Retrieve the DB_UNIQUE_NAME for each database being configured using the show parameter command from each of the databases:

```
SYS:+HR>show parameter db_unique_name

NAME             TYPE        VALUE
---------------- ----------- -----
db_unique_name   string      HR

SYS:+PAY>show parameter db_unique_name

NAME             TYPE        VALUE
---------------- ----------- -----
db_unique_name   string      PAY
```

2. Shut down all databases and ASM instances in the ASM cluster.

3. Create the security key using the CellCLI create key command:

```
CellCLI> create key
        7548a7d1abffadfef95a53185aba0e98

CellCLI> create key
        8e7105bdbd6ad9fa53d41736a533b9b1
```

The create key command must be run once for each database in the ASM cluster. It can be run from any storage cell. One security key will be assigned to each database within the ASM cluster in the key field of the database cellkey.ora file.

4. For each database, create a cellkey.ora file using the keys created in step 2. Install these cellkey.ora files in the ORACLE_HOME/admin/{db_unique_name}/pfile directories for each database server on which database-scoped security will be configured. Just as you did for ASM-scoped security, set the ownership of the file to the user and group specified during the ASM software installation. Permissions should allow it to be read by the owner of the file. For example:

```
# -- Cellkey.ora file for the HR database --#
key=7548a7d1abffadfef95a53185aba0e98
asm=+ASM
realm=customer_A_realm
# --

> chown oracle:dba $ORACLE_HOME/admin/HR/cellkey.ora
> chmod 600 $ORACLE_HOME/admin/HR/cellkey.ora

# -- Cellkey.ora file for the PAY database --#
key=8e7105bdbd6ad9fa53d41736a533b9b1
asm=+ASM
realm=customer_A_realm
# --

> chown oracle:dba $ORACLE_HOME/admin/PAY/cellkey.ora
> chmod 600 $ORACLE_HOME/admin/PAY/cellkey.ora
```

Note that if a realm is defined in this file, it must match the realm name assigned to the storage cells using the `alter cell realm=` command.

5. Use the CellCLI `assign key` command to assign the security keys for each database being configured. This must be done on each storage cell you want the HR and PAY databases to have access to. The following keys are assigned to the `DB_UNIQUE_NAME` of the HR and PAY databases:

```
CellCLI> ASSIGN KEY -
   FOR HR='7548a7d1abffadfef95a53185aba0e98', -
      PAY='8e7105bdbd6ad9fa53d41736a533b9b1'

Key for HR successfully created
Key for PAY successfully created
```

6. Verify that the keys were assigned properly:

```
CellCLI> list key
         HR       d346792d6adea671d8f33b54c30f1de6
         PAY      cae17e8fdce7511cc02eb7375f5443a8
```

7. Using the CellCLI `create disk` or `alter griddisk` command, assign access to the grid disks to each database. Note that the ASM unique name is included with the database unique name in this assignment.

```
CellCLI> create griddisk DATA_HR_CD_00_cell03, -
                         DATA_HR_CD_01_cell03  -
                size=1282.8125G                -
                availableTo='+ASM,HR'

CellCLI> create griddisk DATA_PAY_CD_00_cell03, -
                         DATA_PAY_CD_01_cell03  -
                size=1282.8125G                -
                availableTo='+ASM,PAY'
```

8. The `alter griddisk` command may be used to change security assignments for grid disks. For example:

```
CellCLI> alter griddisk DATA_HR_CD_00_cell03, -
                        DATA_HR_CD_01_cell03  -
               availableTo='+ASM,HR'

CellCLI> alter griddisk DATA_PAY_CD_00_cell03, -
                        DATA_PAY_CD_01_cell03  -
               availableTo='+ASM,PAY'
```

This completes the configuration of database-scoped security for the HR and PAY databases. The ASM cluster and databases may now be restarted. The human resources database now has access to the `DATA_HR` grid disks, while the payroll database has access to the `DATA_PAY` grid disks.

Removing Cell Security

Once implemented, cell security may be modified as needed by updating the ACL lists on the storage cells and changing the availableTo attribute of the grid disks. Removing cell security is a fairly straightforward process of backing out the database security settings and then removing the ASM security settings.

The first step in removing cell security is to remove database-scoped security. The following steps will remove database-scoped security from the system:

1. Before database security may be removed, the databases and ASM cluster must be shut down.

2. Remove the databases from the availableTo attribute of the grid disks using the CellCLI command alter griddisk. This command doesn't selectively remove databases from the list. It simply redefines the complete list. Notice that we will just be removing the databases from the list at this point. The ASM unique name should remain in the list for now. This must be done for each cell you want to remove security from.

```
CellCLI> alter griddisk DATA_HR_CD_00_cell03, -
                        DATA_HR_CD_01_cell03  -
                 availableTo='+ASM'

CellCLI> alter griddisk DATA_PAY_CD_00_cell03, -
                        DATA_PAY_CD_01_cell03  -
                 availableTo='+ASM'
```

3. Optionally, all the databases may be removed from the secured grid disks with the following command:

```
CellCLI> alter griddisk all availableTo='+ASM'
```

Assuming that these databases have not been configured for cell security on any other grid disks in the cell, the security key may be removed from the ACL list on the storage cell as follows:

```
CellCLI> assign key for HR='', PAY=''

Key for HR successfully dropped
Key for PAY successfully dropped
```

4. Remove the cellkey.ora file located in the ORACLE_HOME/admin/{db_unique_name}/pfile directory for the database client.

5. Verify that the HR and PAY databases are not assigned to any grid disks with the following CellCLI command:

```
CellCLI> list griddisk attributes name, availableTo
```

Once database-scoped security has been removed, you can remove ASM-scoped security. This will return the system to default open security status. The following steps remove ASM-scoped security. Once this is done, the grid disks will be available to all ASM clusters and databases on the storage network.

1. Before continuing with this procedure, be sure that database-scoped security has been completely removed. The `list key` command should display the key assignment for the ASM cluster only. No databases should be assigned keys at this point. The `list griddisk` command should show all the names of the grid disks assignments for the ASM cluster `'+ASM'`.

   ```
   CellCLI> list griddisk attributes name, availableTo
   ```

2. Next, remove the ASM unique name from the `availableTo` attribute on all grid disks.

   ```
   CellCLI> list griddisk attributes name, availableTo
   ```

3. Now, remove the ASM security from the ACL by running the following command:

   ```
   CellCLI> alter griddisk all assignTo=''
   ```

4. The following command removes the ASM cluster assignment for select grid disks:

   ```
   CellCLI> alter griddisk DATA_CD_00_cell03, -
                           DATA_CD_01_cell03  -
                           DATA_CD_02_cell03  -
                           DATA_CD_03_cell03  -
                  availableTo=''
   ```

5. The `list griddisk` command should show no assigned clients. Verify this by running the `list griddisk` command.
6. The ASM cluster key may now be safely removed from the storage cell using the CellCLI `assign key` command:

   ```
   CellCLI> list key detail
            name:      +ASM
            key:       196d7983a9a33fccae276e24e7a9f89

   CellCLI> assign key for +ASM=''
   Key for +ASM successfully dropped
   ```

7. Remove the `cellkey.ora` file from the `/etc/oracle/cell/network-config` directory on all database servers in the ASM cluster.

This completes the removal of ASM-scoped security. The ASM cluster may now be restarted as well as all the databases it services.

Summary

Understanding all the various layers of the Exadata storage architecture and how they fit together is a key component to properly laying out storage for databases. In most cases, using Oracle's default layout will be sufficient, but understanding the relationship between physical disks, LUNs, cell disks, grid disks, and ASM disk groups is absolutely necessary if you need to carve up disk storage for maximum performance and security. In this chapter, we've discussed what grid disks are, what they are made up of, and how they fit into the ASM storage grid. We've taken a look at how to create disk groups so that I/O is prioritized for performance critical data files. Carving up storage doesn't end at the disk, so we also discussed methods for partitioning storage by cell and by grid disk within the cell.

CHAPTER 15

Compute Node Layout

The term *node* is a fairly generic one that has many different meanings in the IT industry. For example, network engineers call any addressable device attached to their network a node. Unix administrators commonly use the term interchangeably with *host* or *server*. Oracle DBAs often refer to a database server that is a member of an RAC cluster as a node. Oracle's documentation uses the term *compute node* when referring to the database server tier of the platform. In this chapter, we will discuss the various ways in which you can configure your Exadata compute nodes, whether they are members of an RAC cluster (nodes) or nonclustered (database servers).

It's a common misconception that an Exadata rack must be configured as a single Oracle RAC cluster. This couldn't be further from the truth. In its simplest form, the Exadata database tier can be described as a collection of independent database servers hardwired into the same storage and the same management networks. Each of these servers can be configured to run stand-alone databases completely independent of the others. However, this is not commonly done for two reasons—scalability and high availability. Oracle RAC has historically been used to provide node redundancy in the event of node or instance failure, but Oracle marketing has made it clear all along that the ability to scale-out has been an equally important goal. Traditionally, if we needed to increase database performance and capacity, we did so by upgrading server hardware. This method became so commonplace that the industry coined the phrase *hardware refresh* to describe it. This term can mean anything from adding CPUs, memory, or I/O bandwidth to a complete replacement of the server itself. Increasing performance and capacity in this way is referred to as *scale-up*. With Exadata's ability to provide extreme I/O performance to the database server, bus speed is now the limiting factor for scale-up. So, what happens when you reach the limits of single-server capacity? The obvious answer is to add more servers. To continue to scale your application, you must scale-out, using Oracle RAC. Nonetheless, understanding that the database servers are not tied together in some proprietary fashion clarifies the highly configurable nature of Exadata.

In Chapter 14, we discussed various strategies for configuring Exadata's storage subsystems to service specific database servers. In this chapter, we will take a look at ways the database tier may be configured to create clustered and nonclustered database environments that are well suited to meet the needs of your business.

Provisioning Considerations

Exadata is an extremely configurable platform. Determining the best configuration for your business will involve reviewing the performance and uptime demands of your applications as well as ensuring adequate separation for development, test, and production systems. Here are a few of the key considerations for determining the most suitable compute node layout to support your database environments:

CPU Resources: When determining the optimal node layout for your databases, keep in mind that Exadata handles the I/O workload very differently from traditional database platforms. On non-Exadata platforms, the database server is responsible for retrieving all data blocks from storage to satisfy I/O requests from the applications. Exadata offloads a lot of this work to the storage cells. This can significantly reduce the CPU requirements of your database servers. Figuring out how much less CPU your databases will require is a difficult task because it depends, in part, on how much your database is utilizing parallel query and HCC compression, as well as how suitable your application SQL is to offloading. Some of the Smart Scan optimizations, such as decryption, predicate filtering, and HCC decompression, will reduce CPU requirements regardless of the type of application. (We covered these topics in detail in Chapters 2–6.)

Systems requiring thousands of dedicated server connections can overwhelm the resources of a single machine. Spreading these connections across multiple compute nodes reduces the burden on the system's process scheduler and allows the CPU to spend its time more effectively servicing client requests. Load-balancing connections across multiple compute nodes also improves the database's capacity for handling concurrent connection requests.

Memory Resources: Systems that require thousands of dedicated server connections can also put a burden on memory resources. Each dedicated server connection requires a slice of memory, whether or not the connection is actively being used. Spreading these connections across multiple RAC nodes allows the database to handle more concurrent connections than a single compute node can manage.

I/O Performance and Capacity: Each compute node and storage cell is equipped with one 40Gbps QDR, dual-port InfiniBand card through which, in practicality, each compute node can transmit/receive a maximum of 3.2 gigabytes per second (6.4 gigabytes per second for X4-2 and X5-2 compute nodes). If this is sufficient bandwidth, the decision of moving to a multi-node RAC configuration may be more of an HA consideration. If you have I/O-hungry applications that require more throughput than one compute node can provide, RAC may be used to provide high availability as well as additional I/O capacity.

Patching and Testing: Another key consideration in designing a stable database environment is providing a separate area where patches and new features can be tested before rolling them into production. For non-Exadata platforms, patching and upgrading generally involves O/S patches and Oracle RDBMS patches. Exadata is a highly complex database platform, consisting of several additional hardware and software layers that must be patched periodically, such as Cell Servers, ILOM firmware, InfiniBand switch firmware, InfiniBand network card firmware, and OFED drivers. As such, it is absolutely crucial that a test environment be isolated from critical systems to be used for testing patches.

Non-RAC Configuration

Compute nodes may be configured in a number of ways. If your application does not need the high availability or scale-out features of Oracle RAC, then Exadata provides an excellent platform for delivering high performance for stand-alone database servers. You can manage I/O service levels between independent databases (be it single instance or Oracle RAC) by configuring IORM (See Chapter 7 for more information about IORM). In a non-RAC configuration, the Oracle Grid Infrastructure is still configured for a cluster, but the Oracle database homes are linked for single-instance databases only. Because the Exadata storage servers provide shared storage for all of the compute nodes, a clustered set of ASM disk groups can be used to provide storage to all of the compute nodes. This configuration gives database administrators the flexibility of a cluster while still maintaining licensing requirements for single-instance databases.

It may seem counterintuitive to use a cluster for single-instance databases, but users running this configuration gain many benefits of running across shared storage while cutting down on the drawbacks of segmenting resources to an extreme. Even though your database servers may run stand-alone databases, they can still share Exadata storage (cell disks). This allows each database to make use of the full I/O bandwidth of the Exadata storage subsystem. Database placement is determined by strain placed on the compute node, not the ASM disk group that belongs to that compute node. Because ASM disk groups are shared, databases can be moved within the cluster with minimal effort. Also, migration to a full-fledged RAC configuration is very simple from this configuration—just relink the database homes and convert the database to support RAC.

For example, let's say you have three databases on your server called `SALES`, `HR`, and `PAYROLL`. All three databases can share the same disk groups for storage. To do this, all three databases would have instance parameters as follows:

```
db_create_file_dest='+DATA'
db_recovery_file_dest='+RECO'
local_listener='<connect string of local host listener>'
remote_listener='<SCAN_HOSTNAME:1521>'
```

In Figure 15-1, we see all eight compute nodes in an Exadata full rack configuration running stand-alone databases. You will notice that storage is allocated exactly the same as in a clustered configuration. All nodes use the `+DATA` and `+RECO` disk groups, which are serviced by the clustered ASM instances. Each ASM instance shares the same set of ASM disk groups, which consist of grid disks from all storage cells. Because the ASM disk groups are shared across all of the compute nodes, the loss of a single node does not mean that the databases it serves must stay down. If adequate resources are available on the surviving compute nodes, single-instance databases can easily be migrated to those nodes to restore service. Clients connecting over the SCAN interface need no reconfiguration to connect.

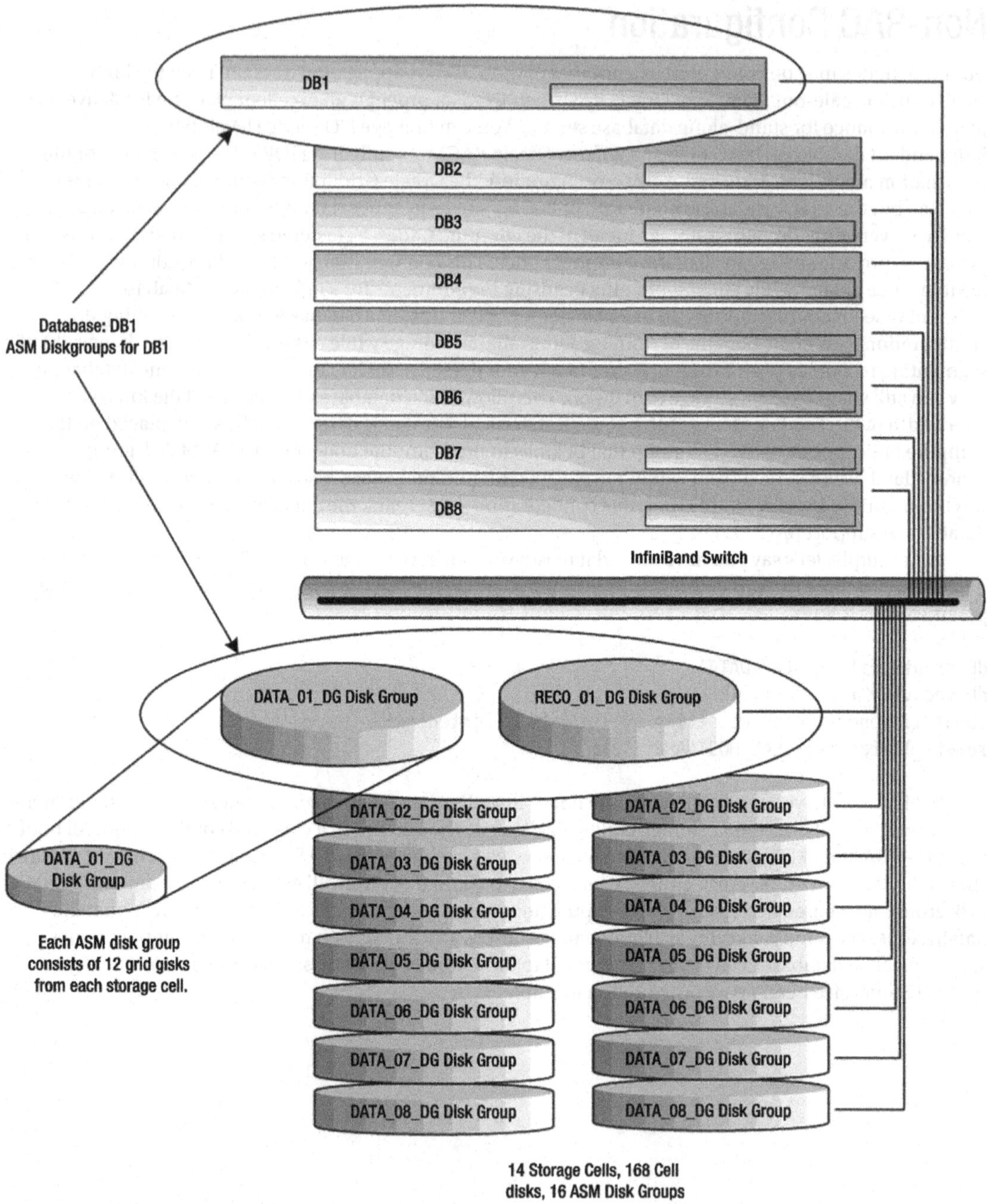

Figure 15-1. *Example of a non-RAC Exadata configuration*

If separate disk groups were created for each compute node, administrators would have to choose database placement based on both compute node resources and the disk space available to that cluster. Because reconfiguration of storage on Exadata is not a quick process, splitting disk groups between nodes forces much more early planning. Also, individual storage servers would be forced to manage Flash Cache and resource management plans across multiple clusters, leading to extra overhead needed to manage resources. Finally, the number of grid disks created in a configuration utilizing separate disk groups makes the cluster much more difficult to manage—a full rack utilizing separate +DATA and +RECO ASM disk groups would require 2,688 grid disks. The configuration described above creates no additional grid disks apart from the standard 476.

Split-Rack Clusters

Now that we've discussed how to run Exadata in a non-RAC configuration, let's take a look at how a single rack can be carved into multiple clusters. But before we do that, we'll take a brief detour and establish what high availability and scalability are.

High availability (HA) is a fairly well-understood concept, but it often gets confused with fault tolerance. In a truly fault-tolerant system, every component is redundant. If one component fails, another component takes over without any interruption to service. High availability also involves component redundancy, but failures may cause a brief interruption to service while the system reconfigures to use the redundant component. Work in progress during the interruption must be resubmitted or continued on the redundant component. The time it takes to detect a failure, reconfigure, and resume work varies greatly in HA systems. For example, active/passive Unix clusters have been used extensively to provide graceful failover in the event of a server crash. Now, you might chuckle to yourself when you see the words *graceful failover* and *crash* used in the same sentence (unless you work in the airline industry), so let me explain. *Graceful failover*, in the context of active/passive clusters, means that when a system failure occurs or a critical component fails, the resources that make up the application, database, and infrastructure are shut down on the primary system and brought back online on the redundant system automatically with as little downtime as possible. The alternative, and somewhat less graceful, type of failover would involve a phone call to your support staff at 3:30 in the morning. In active/passive clusters, the database and possibly other applications only run on one node at a time. Failover using this configuration can take several minutes to complete, depending on what resources and applications must be migrated. Oracle RAC uses an active/active cluster architecture. Failover on an RAC system commonly takes less than a minute to complete. True fault tolerance is generally very difficult and much more expensive to implement than high availability. The type of system and impact (or cost) of a failure usually dictates which is more appropriate. Critical systems on an airplane, space station, or a life-support system easily justify a fault-tolerant architecture. By contrast, a web application servicing the company's retail storefront usually cannot justify the cost and complexity of a fully fault-tolerant architecture. Exadata is a high-availability architecture providing fully redundant hardware components. When Oracle RAC is used, this redundancy and fast failover is extended to the database tier.

When CPU, memory, or I/O resource limits for a single server are reached, additional servers must be added to increase capacity. The term *scalability* is often used synonymously with *performance*. That is, increasing capacity equals increasing performance. But the correlation between capacity and performance is not a direct one. Take, for example, a single-threaded, CPU-intensive program that takes 15 minutes to complete on a two-CPU server. Assuming the server isn't CPU-bound, installing two more CPUs is not going to make the process run any faster. If it can only run on one CPU at a time, it will only execute as fast as one CPU can process it. Performance will only improve if adding more CPUs allows a process to have more uninterrupted time on the processor. Neither will it run any faster if we run it on a four-node cluster. However, scaling out to four servers could mean that we can run four copies of our program concurrently and get roughly four times the amount of work done in the same 15 minutes. To sum it up, scaling out adds capacity to your system. Whether or not it improves performance depends on how scalable your application is and how heavily loaded your current system is. Keep in mind that Oracle RAC scales extremely well for well-written applications. Conversely, poorly written applications tend to scale poorly.

Exadata can be configured as multiple RAC clusters to provide isolation between environments. This allows the clusters to be managed, patched, and administered independently. At the database tier, this is done in the same way you would cluster any ordinary set of servers using Oracle Clusterware. To configure storage cells to service-specific compute nodes, the `cellip.ora` file on each compute node lists the storage cells it will use. For example, the following `cellip.ora` file lists seven of the fourteen storage cells by their network address (remember that beginning with X4-2, compute nodes support active/active InfiniBand connections):

```
[db01:oracle:EXDB1] /home/oracle
> cat /etc/oracle/cell/network-config/cellip.ora
cell="192.168.10.17;192.168.10.18"
cell="192.168.10.19;192.168.10.20"
cell="192.168.10.21;192.168.10.22"
cell="192.168.10.23;192.168.10.24"
cell="192.168.10.25;192.168.10.26"
cell="192.168.10.27;192.168.10.28"
cell="192.168.10.29;192.168.10.30"
```

When ASM starts up, it searches the storage cells on each of these IP addresses for grid disks it can use for configuring ASM disk groups. Alternatively, cell security can be used to lock down access so that only certain storage cells are available for compute nodes to use. The `cellip.ora` file and cell security are covered in detail in Chapter 14.

To illustrate what a multi-RAC Exadata configuration might look like, let's consider an Exadata X5-2 full rack configuration partitioned into three Oracle RAC clusters. A full rack gives us eight compute nodes and fourteen storage cells to work with. Consider an Exadata full rack configured as follows:

- One Production RAC cluster with four compute nodes and seven storage cells
- One Test RAC cluster with two compute nodes and three storage cells
- One Development RAC cluster with two compute nodes and four storage cells

Table 15-1 shows the resource allocation of these RAC clusters, each with its own storage grid. As you read this table, keep in mind that hardware is a moving target. These figures are from an Exadata X5-2. In this example, we used the high-capacity, 4TB disk drives.

Table 15-1. *Cluster Resources*

Cluster	Db Servers	Db Memory	Db CPU	Storage Cell	Cell Disks	Raw Storage
PROD_CLUSTER	Prod1-Prod4	256G × 4	36 × 4	1-7	84	336T
TEST_CLUSTER	Test1, Test2	256G × 2	36× 2	8-10	36	144T
DEV_CLUSTER	Dev1, Dev2	256G × 2	36 × 2	11-14	48	192T

These RAC environments can be patched and upgraded completely independently of one another. The only hardware resource they share is the InfiniBand fabric. If you are considering a multi-RAC configuration like this, keep in mind that patches to the InfiniBand switches will affect all storage cells and compute nodes. Figure 15-2 illustrates what this cluster configuration would look like.

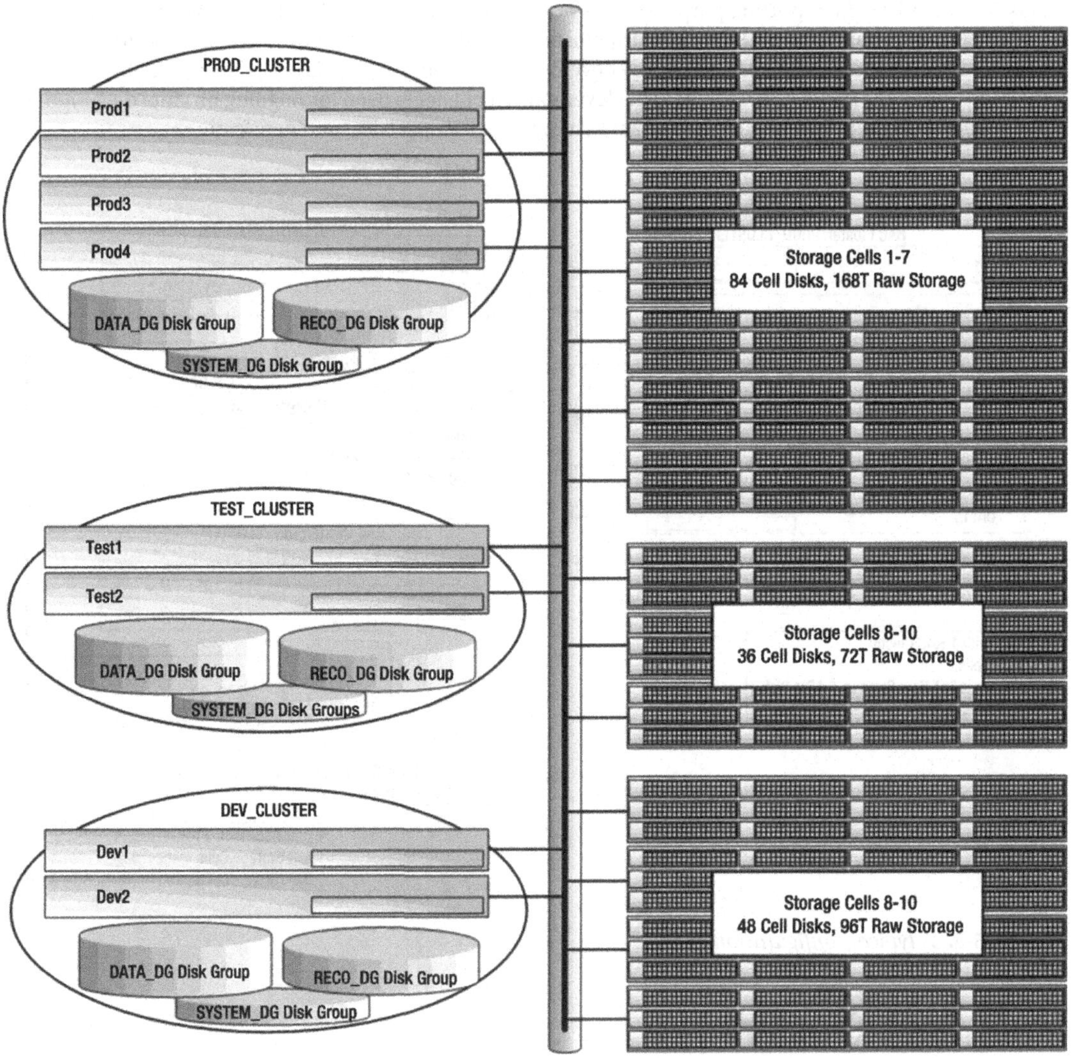

Figure 15-2. *An Exadata full rack configured for three RAC clusters*

Typical Exadata Configuration

The two configuration strategies we've discussed so far are fairly extreme examples. The non-RAC database configuration illustrated how Exadata can be configured without Real Application Clusters, creating a true consolidation platform. The second example, Split-RAC Clusters, showed how Clusterware can be used to create multiple, isolated RAC clusters. Neither of these configurations is typically found in the real world, but they illustrate the configuration capabilities of Exadata. Now let's take a look at a configuration we commonly see in the field. Figure 15-3 shows a typical system with two Exadata half racks. It consists of a production cluster (PROD_CLUSTER) hosting a two-node production database and a two-node UAT database. The production and UAT databases share the same ASM disk groups (made up of all grid disks across all storage cells). I/O resources are regulated and prioritized using Exadata I/O Resource Manager (IORM), discussed in Chapter 7. The production database uses Active Data Guard to maintain a physical standby for disaster recovery and reporting purposes. The UAT database is not considered business-critical, so it is not protected with Data Guard. On the standby cluster (STBY_CLUSTER), the STBY database uses four of the seven storage cells for its ASM storage. On the development cluster (DEV_CLUSTER), the Dev database uses the remaining three cells for its ASM storage. The development cluster is used for ongoing product development and provides a test bed for installing Exadata patches, database upgrades, and new features.

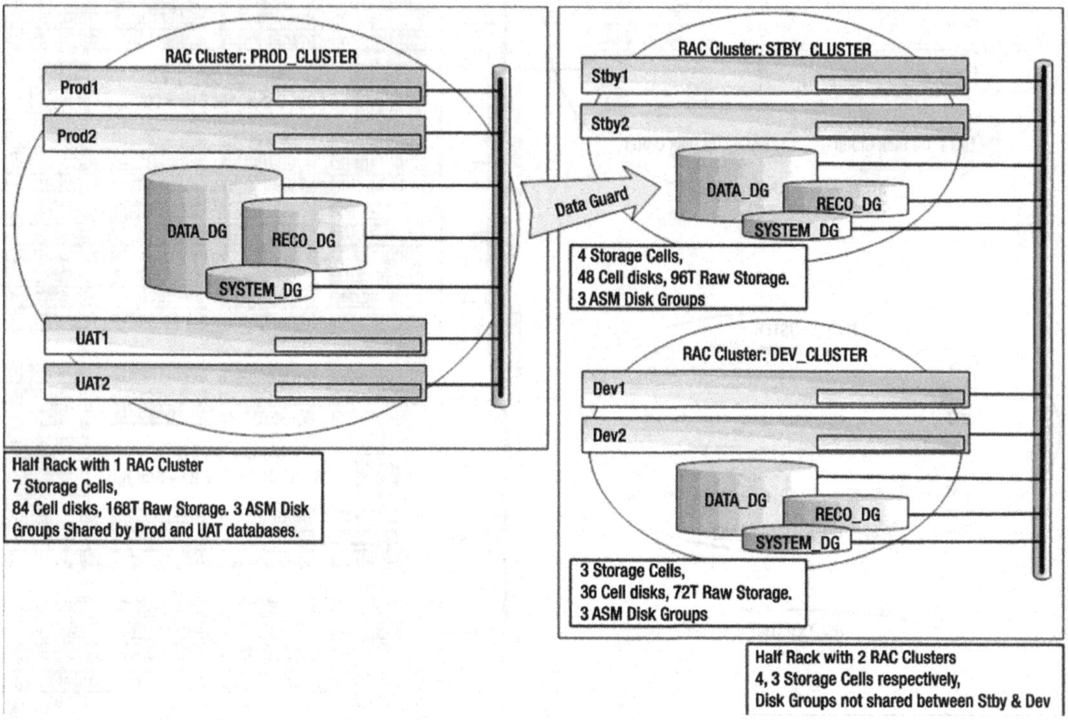

Figure 15-3. *A typical configuration*

Multi-Rack Clusters

Exadata's ability to scale out doesn't end when the rack is full. When one Exadata rack doesn't quite get the job done for you, additional racks may be added to the cluster, creating a large-scale database grid. Up to 18 racks may be cabled together to create a massive database grid, consisting of 144 database servers and over 12 petabytes of raw disk storage. Actually, Exadata will scale beyond 18 racks, but additional InfiniBand switches must be purchased to do it. Exadata utilizes a spine switch to link cabinets together (compute and storage servers connect directly to the leaf switches). The spine switch was included with all half rack and full rack X2-2 and X3-2 configurations. Beginning with the X4-2 model, the spine switch is an additional purchase. Unless a spine switch is purchased, quarter rack configurations can only be linked with one other Exadata rack. In a full rack configuration, the ports of a leaf switch are used as follows:

- Eight links to the database servers
- Fourteen links to the storage cells
- Seven links to the redundant leaf switch
- Seven ports open

Figure 15-4 shows an Exadata full rack configuration that is not linked to any other Exadata rack. It's interesting that Oracle chose to connect the two leaf switches together using the seven spare cables. Perhaps it's because these cables are preconfigured in the factory—patching them into the leaf switches simply keeps them out of the way and makes it easier to reconfigure later. The leaf switches certainly do not need to be linked together.

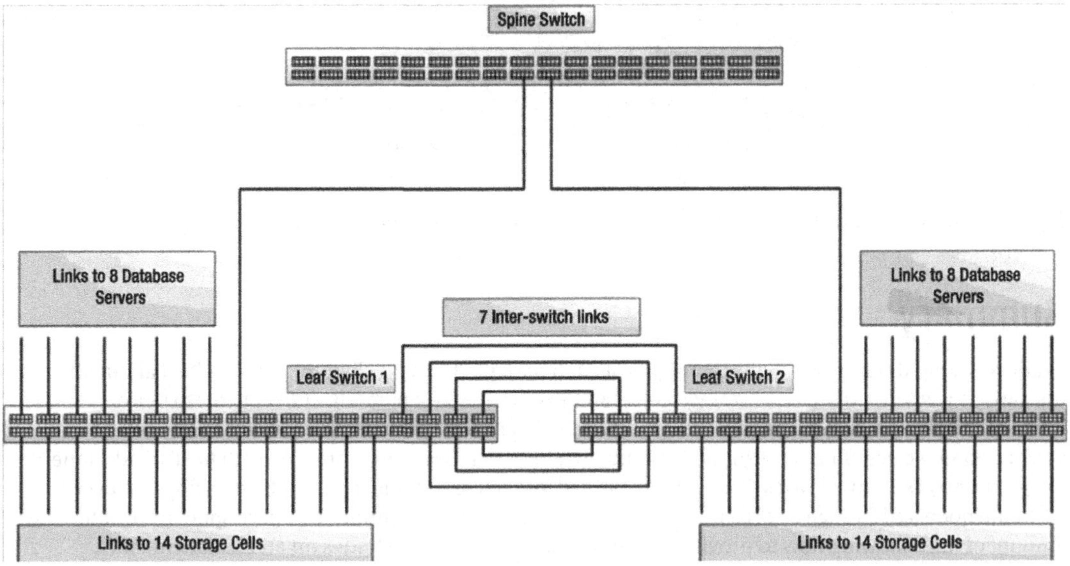

Figure 15-4. *An Exadata full rack InfiniBand network*

The spine switch is just like the other two InfiniBand switches that service the cluster and storage network, with one exception. The spine switch serves as the subnet manager master for the InfiniBand fabric. Redundancy is provided by connecting each leaf switch to every spine switch in the configuration (from two to eighteen spine switches).

To cable two Exadata racks together, the seven inter-switch cables, seen in Figure 15-4, are redistributed so that four of them link the leaf switch with its internal spine switch, and four of them link the leaf switch to the spine switch in the adjacent rack. Figure 15-5 shows the network configuration for two Exadata racks networked together. When eight Exadata racks are linked together, the seven inter-switch cables seen in Figure 15-4 are redistributed so that each leaf-to-spine-switch link uses one cable (eight cables per leaf switch). When you're linking from three to seven Exadata racks together, the seven inter-switch cables are redistributed as evenly as possible across all leaf-to-spine-switch links. Leaf switches are not linked to other leaf switches, and spine switches are not linked to other spine switches. No changes are ever needed for the leaf switch links to the compute nodes and storage cells. This network topology is typically referred to as *fat tree topology*.

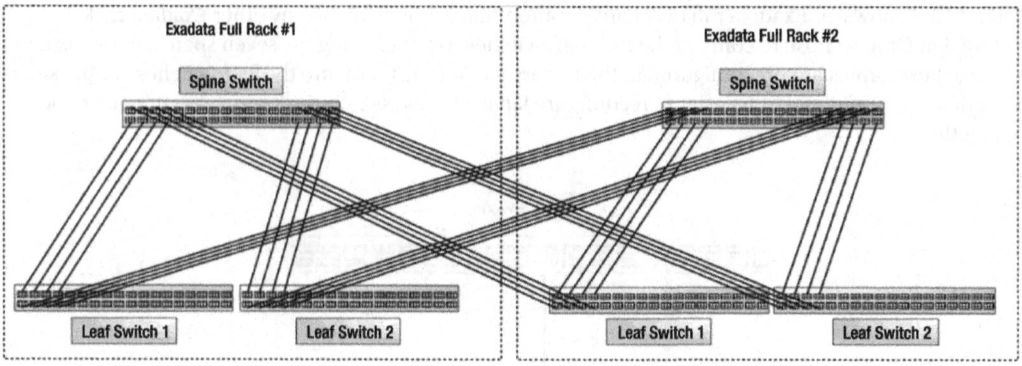

***Figure 15-5.** A switch configuration for two Exadata racks, with one database grid*

Summary

Exadata is a highly complex, highly configurable database platform. In Chapter 14, we talked about all the various ways disk drives and storage cells can be provisioned separately or in concert to deliver well-balanced, high-performance I/O to your Oracle databases. In this chapter, we turned our attention to provisioning capabilities and strategies at the database tier. Exadata is rarely used to host stand-alone database servers. In most cases, it is far better suited for Oracle RAC clusters. Understanding that every compute node and storage cell is a fully independent component is important, so we spent a considerable amount of time showing how to provision eight stand-alone compute nodes on an Exadata full rack configuration. From there, we moved on to an Oracle RAC provisioning strategy that provided separation between three computing environments. And, finally, we touched on how Exadata racks may be networked together to build massive database grids. Understanding the concepts explored in Chapters 14 and 15 of this book will help you make the right choices when the time comes to architect a provisioning strategy for your Exadata database environment.

CHAPTER 16

Patching Exadata

One of the biggest drawbacks of running a custom-built Oracle system is that it may be a one-of-a-kind configuration. Even in environments with tight standards, it is very difficult to maintain consistency between hardware, firmware, and operating system configurations. Most organizations do not have the time needed to ensure that every build has the exact same Fibre Channel HBAs, internal RAID controllers, and network cards running the same firmware level, much less go through a testing plan to upgrade each of these components in a single maintenance window. Over the course of a year, it is atypical to find exactly matching components all the way across the stack. With Exadata, Oracle has a standard build that provides the exact same hardware, firmware, and operating system configuration for each release. Every Exadata customer with an X3-2 rack running storage server version 11.2.3.3.0 has an LSI RAID controller running version 12.12.0-178, Sun Flash F40 cards with firmware version UI5P, Oracle Unbreakable Kernel version 2.6.39-400.126.1, and so on. If an update is needed, Oracle releases a single patch that upgrades all of those components in one shot. This standardization allows Exadata administrators to apply bug fixes and firmware updates that most system administrators would not be willing to apply for fear of unexpected changes to their unique configuration. Testing these changes is much easier on Exadata due to the standardized configurations within each generation. This chapter will look at Exadata patching in depth, starting with the various types of patches to be applied on Exadata, the ways each of the patches are applied, and options to make patching as painless as possible.

Before any patches should be applied, check Oracle support note number 888828.1. This note is a living document for Oracle Exadata patching and is known as the patching note or, more formally, *Exadata Database Machine and Exadata Storage Server Supported Versions.* Covering software versions 11g and 12c, this note encompasses the entire scope of Exadata patching, including references to various kernel and firmware versions for each storage server software release, links to information regarding patches for other Oracle products running on Exadata such as Database Filesystem (DBFS), and a full history of all major patch releases for the product. When looking for important updates, check the “Latest Releases and Patching News” section of the note, as shown in Figure 16-1.

Latest Releases and Patching News

Before upgrading, see the *Requirements for Exadata Feature Usage* section in this document for software requirements that may necessitate pre-upgrade patch application to other software in order to support specific Exadata features or patch application methods.

- New OneCommand release - Patch 18905676 - Supports 12.1.0.1 (GI PSU1-PSU3), 11.2.0.4 (BP1-BP8), and 11.2.0.3 (BP3-BP23)
- New 11.2.0.4 Database release - Patch 18632316 - 11.2.0.4 Database Patch for Exadata June 2014 - 11.2.0.4.8
- New Exadata Storage Server 11g release - Patch 17636228 - Exadata Storage Server software 11.2.3.3.1 (Note 1667414.1)
- New 11.2.0.3 Database release - Patch 18342655 - 11.2.0.3 recommended Quarterly Database Patch for Exadata Apr 2014 - 11.2.0.3.23
- New 12.1.0.1 Database release - Patch 18139660 - 12.1.0.1.3 (Apr 2014) recommended Grid Infrastructure Patch Set Update (GI PSU)
- New QFSDP release - Quarterly Full Stack Download Patch (QFSDP)Apr 2014
  - Patch 18370223 - contains 12.1 and 11.2 quarterly database patches
  - Patch 18370227 - contains only 11.2.0.4 quarterly database patches
  - Patch 18370231 - contains only 11.2.0.3 quarterly database patches
- New Exadata Storage Server 11g release - Patch 17953347 - Exadata Storage Server software11.2.3.2.2 (Note 1608581.1)
  - This is a bug fix release only intended to improve availability and stability for customers currently using Exadata 11.2.3.2. If any of the following one-off Exadata patches are planned for install on top of 11.2.3.2.1, then 11.2.3.2.2 should be installed instead: patch 17878822, patch 16360464, patch 18031908.
  - New deployments and customers targeting new Exadata features should use Exadata 11.2.3.3 or 12.1. Default shipping version remains Exadata 11.2.3.3.
- New Exadata Storage Server 12c release - Patch 16980054 - Exadata Storage Server software 12.1.1.1.0 (Note 1571789.1)
  - This is the recommended Exadata version to use with Database 12c
  - Provides full Exadata offload functionality for Oracle Database 12c and 11g, and IORM support for 12c container databases and pluggable databases
  - Default shipping version remains Exadata 11.2.3.3
- Final 11.2.0.2 Database release - Patch 17380185 - 11.2.0.2 Bundle Patch 22 for Exadata

***Figure 16-1.** Latest releases and patching news*////*

Types of Exadata Patches

Exadata patches can be broken down in to two main categories—Exadata storage server patches and Quarterly Database Patches for Exadata. The Exadata storage server patches contain many different components, all bundled in to one single patch. In addition to the version of `cellsrv` running on the storage servers, Exadata storage server patches contain operating system updates, new versions of the Linux kernel, and firmware updates for many of the hardware components inside the compute and storage servers. The Exadata storage server patch level is commonly referred to as the version of software running on the Exadata. An example version of a storage server patch release is 11.2.3.3.1, as illustrated in Figure 16-2. This version tells the major and minor release versions for both database compatibility and the `cellsrv` version. Keep in mind that these rules are not hard and fast, as version 11.2.3.3.1 does support 12c databases but does not contain the ability to perform offload processing for 12c—that functionality is introduced in a 12c version of the cellsrv software.

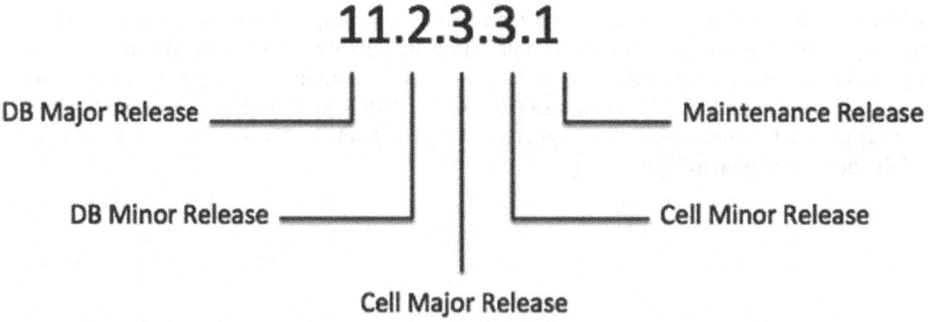

***Figure 16-2.** Exadata storage server version numbering*

Typically, Oracle releases two or three Exadata storage server patches throughout the calendar year. As with most software releases, changes to the final digit are maintenance releases, which may only contain a few bug fixes or firmware updates. Changes to the cell major or minor release traditionally include new features at the storage server level. Examples of Exadata storage server patches including new features are Exadata Smart Flash log (11.2.2.4.0), write-back Flash Cache (11.2.3.2.0), and Flash Cache compression (11.2.3.3.0).

While the name may imply that an Exadata storage server patch is only applied to the storage servers, there are also corresponding patches that are applied to the compute nodes and (in some cases) InfiniBand switches. Because the Exadata storage server patches include operating system and kernel updates, there is an additional component that must be applied to the compute nodes. This ensures that all components in the stack are running the same version of the Linux kernel, which now includes the OpenFabrics Alliance (OFA) drivers for the InfiniBand stack. Starting with Exadata storage server version 11.2.3.3.0, Oracle began to include any firmware updates for the InfiniBand switches as well in the Exadata storage server patch. This helped to streamline the process of applying patches to those components, even though updates are typically few and far between.

In addition to the Exadata storage server patches, Oracle releases a Quarterly Database Patch for Exadata, or QDPE. The QDPE is released in the same time frame as the quarterly PSU (January, April, July, October). Beginning with Oracle Database 12c, a single PSU is issued for both Exadata and non-Exadata platforms. Previously, there was a separate patch release for Exadata. In addition, Oracle releases monthly interim "bundle patches" for the latest database release, allowing customers to have fixes for any critical bugs that may need to be fixed outside of the standard quarterly release cycle. While these patches were applied as standard practice with older versions (Exadata administrators running 11.2.0.1 will remember monthly bundle patches fondly), Oracle recommends customers to stick with the QDPE releases. The monthly bundle patches should only be applied if specific bugs are affecting the system. The term "bundle patch" was used because it is just that—a bundle of patches released together. QDPEs and bundle patches contain two separate patches—one for the database component and one for cluster ready services. Before 11.2.0.4, there was also a diskmon component, but that has since been rolled into the cluster-ready services patch.

Quarterly Database Patch for Exadata

There are several different components of the Exadata "stack" that should be considered when looking at Exadata patching. The first component is what most database administrators are familiar with—the Oracle binaries that comprise the various Oracle homes on each of the compute nodes. In Oracle Database 11g, the Quarterly Database Patch for Exadata (QDPE) is the equivalent to the standard quarterly Patch Set Update (PSU) that is released by Oracle. This patch is applied to both the database and grid infrastructure homes on each compute node.

■ **Note** The QDPE has been retired in Oracle Database 12c. Database administrators need only apply the quarterly Grid Infrastructure Patch Set Update (PSU) for Engineered Systems and Database In-Memory. This allows patches for the Oracle stack on Exadata to fall in line with a normal RAC system running Oracle Database 12c.

Because the QDPE is similar to the PSU in structure and contents, patches are applied using the same tools. Oracle's patching utility, OPatch, does all of the heavy lifting. In order to find out what QDPE is installed on the system, administrators can use OPatch. OPatch has an `lspatches` command, which easily shares this information:

```
[oracle@enkx3db01 ~]$ $ORACLE_HOME/OPatch/opatch lspatches
Patch description:  "ACFS Patch Set Update : 11.2.0.4.2 (18031731)"
Patch description:  "CRS PATCH FOR EXADATA (APR2014 - 11.2.0.4.6) : (18497417)"
Patch description:  "DATABASE PATCH FOR EXADATA (APR2014 - 11.2.0.4.6) : (18293775)"
```

In the above example, this 11.2.0.4 home has the April 2014 QDPE applied. From the version number, you can derive that it is bundle patch 6 for 11.2.0.4. ACFS patch #18031731 is included but has not been updated since bundle patch 2 (there were apparently no necessary bug fixes since then). The patch numbers listed are for each of the components. All that needs to be applied is the single QDPE, which can be found in the Exadata supported versions note.

Applying a QDPE in Place

Applying a QDPE is no different than applying a quarterly PSU on any other Oracle RAC system running version 11.2 or higher. Due to the complexity of patching a Grid Infrastructure home in version 11.2, Oracle introduced the *auto* functionality to the OPatch utility. Because the Grid Infrastructure home itself is owned by the root account, the software owner cannot create new directories without going through an unlock process. There are also prepatch and postpatch scripts that must be run for each database home. Finally, there are several patches contained within a single bundle patch or PSU that must be applied. Using OPatch's auto feature, database administrators need only issue a single OPatch command to patch all Oracle homes on a single node. This allows for true rolling patches that are applied to vertical silos rather than horizontally across the cluster. Figure 16-3 shows a list of the commands run by the OPatch utility in auto mode for an 11gR2 cluster.

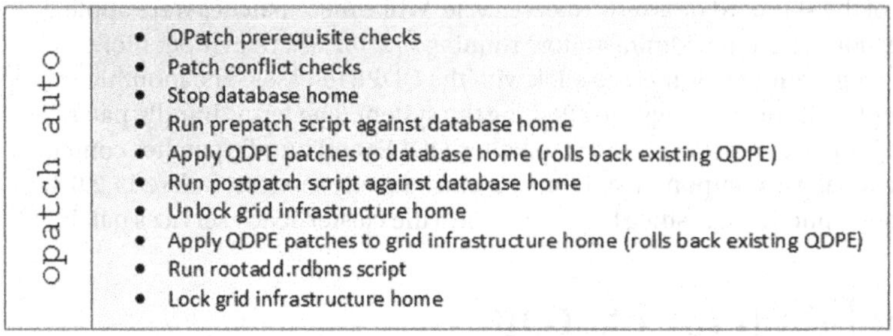

opatch auto
OPatch prerequisite checks
Patch conflict checks
Stop database home
Run prepatch script against database home
Apply QDPE patches to database home (rolls back existing QDPE)
Run postpatch script against database home
Unlock grid infrastructure home
Apply QDPE patches to grid infrastructure home (rolls back existing QDPE)
Run rootadd.rdbms script
Lock grid infrastructure home

Figure 16-3. *Steps run by OPatch auto*

Before applying a QDPE, the OPatch utility should be updated in each Oracle home that will receive the patch. Minimum version requirements can be found in the README for the actual patch, but it is generally a good idea to download the latest version of OPatch (patch 6880880) from My Oracle Support and stage it in each Oracle home directory. When the QDPE is applied, a minimum version check will be performed. You should do this beforehand in order to save time during a maintenance window. It is safe to stage the OPatch binaries and run prerequisite checks while cluster resources are still running on the system.

Because the OPatch auto functionality runs scripts that require root privileges, the `opatch` command must be invoked with those privileges. This can either be performed directly as the root user or via the `sudo` command. As the software owner, unzip the patch file. It is recommended to unzip this file as the software owner to ensure that all required access is allowed. In the case of a role separated environment, with separate grid and Oracle users, ensure that the common oinstall group has permissions on all files. Change to the directory where the patches are unzipped and run the command `opatch auto`. On 12cR1 clusters, the command to issue is `opatchauto apply`. The command can be run with either the full path or via environment variables if `$ORACLE_HOME` is set. If multiple Oracle homes are installed, the home to be patched must be specified with the `-oh` switch. When running in auto mode, the OPatch utility checks with the Oracle Cluster Registry (OCR) to determine which Oracle homes contain cluster-managed resources. OPatch will skip a home if an Oracle home does not have any targets registered to it unless directly specified with the `-oh` switch. The exercise below breaks down the process of applying a QDPE on an 11gR2 Exadata cluster.

APPLYING A QDPE IN PLACE

This exercise demonstrates the application of the July 2014 QDPE for 11.2.0.4 (patch #18840215) using the in-place method. This example demonstrates installing this patch on an Exadata cluster containing Oracle homes running 11.2.0.3 and 11.2.0.4. Because multiple homes are installed, `opatch auto -oh` must be used to specify the database homes to be patched.

1. Download patch 18840215 and unzip in directory `/u01/app/oracle/patches`
2. As the Oracle user, generate an Oracle Configuration Manager response file. In a role-separated environment, create the file in a directory that both accounts can access.

```
$ /u01/app/11.2.0.4/grid/OPatch/ocm/bin/emocmrsp
OCM Installation Response Generator 10.3.4.0.0 - Production
Copyright (c) 2005, 2010, Oracle and/or its affiliates. All rights reserved.

Provide your email address to be informed of security issues, install and
initiate Oracle Configuration Manager. Easier for you if you use your My
Oracle Support Email address/User Name.
Visit http://www.oracle.com/support/policies.html for details.
Email address/User Name:

You have not provided an email address for notification of security issues.
Do you wish to remain uninformed of security issues ([Y]es, [N]o) [N]:  y
The OCM configuration response file (ocm.rsp) was successfully created.
```

3. Unzip the patch file as the Oracle account.

```
$ unzip -oq p18840215_112040_Linux-x86-64.zip -d /u01/app/oracle/patches
```

4. On the first compute node as the root user, run `opatch auto`, specifying the Grid Infrastructure home. When asked for the OCM response file, enter the full path to the file created in step 2.

```
# /u01/app/11.2.0.4/grid/OPatch/opatch auto -oh /u01/app/11.2.0.4/grid
Executing /u01/app/11.2.0.4/grid/perl/bin/perl /u01/app/11.2.0.4/grid/OPatch/
crs/patch11203.pl -patchdir /u01/app/oracle/patches -patchn 18840215 -oh /u01/
app/11.2.0.4/grid -paramfile /u01/app/11.2.0.4/grid/crs/install/crsconfig_params

This is the main log file: /u01/app/11.2.0.4/grid/cfgtoollogs/
opatchauto2014-08-23_15-50-24.log

This file will show your detected configuration and all the steps that opatchauto
attempted to do on your system:
/u01/app/11.2.0.4/grid/cfgtoollogs/opatchauto2014-08-23_15-50-24.report.log

2014-08-23 15:50:24: Starting Clusterware Patch Setup
Using configuration parameter file: /u01/app/11.2.0.4/grid/crs/install/crsconfig_params
OPatch  is bundled with OCM, Enter the absolute OCM response file path:
/home/oracle/ocm.rsp
```

```
Stopping CRS...
Stopped CRS successfully

patch /u01/app/oracle/patches/18840215/18825509  apply successful for home  /u01/
app/11.2.0.4/grid
patch /u01/app/oracle/patches/18840215/18522515  apply successful for home  /u01/
app/11.2.0.4/grid
patch /u01/app/oracle/patches/18840215/18522514  apply successful for home  /u01/
app/11.2.0.4/grid

Starting CRS...
Using configuration parameter file: /u01/app/11.2.0.4/grid/crs/install/crsconfig_params
Installing Trace File Analyzer
CRS-4123: Oracle High Availability Services has been started.

opatch auto succeeded.
```

5. On the first compute node as the root user, run `opatch auto`, specifying the 11.2.0.4 database homes to be patched. If multiple homes are to be patched, use a comma-separated list.

```
# /u01/app/11.2.0.4/grid/OPatch/opatch auto -oh /u01/app/oracle/product/11.2.0.4/
dbhome_1
Executing /u01/app/11.2.0.4/grid/perl/bin/perl /u01/app/11.2.0.4/grid/OPatch/crs/
patch11203.pl -patchdir /u01/app/oracle/patches -patchn 18840215 -oh /u01/app/oracle/
product/11.2.0.4/dbhome_1 -paramfile /u01/app/11.2.0.4/grid/crs/install/crsconfig_params

This is the main log file: /u01/app/11.2.0.4/grid/cfgtoollogs/
opatchauto2014-09-04_09-01-55.log

This file will show your detected configuration and all the steps that opatchauto
attempted to do on your system:
/u01/app/11.2.0.4/grid/cfgtoollogs/opatchauto2014-09-04_09-01-55.report.log

2014-09-04 09:01:55: Starting Clusterware Patch Setup
Using configuration parameter file: /u01/app/11.2.0.4/grid/crs/install/crsconfig_params
OPatch  is bundled with OCM, Enter the absolute OCM response file path:
/home/oracle/ocm.rsp

Stopping RAC /u01/app/oracle/product/11.2.0.4/dbhome_1 ...
Stopped RAC /u01/app/oracle/product/11.2.0.4/dbhome_1 successfully

patch /u01/app/oracle/patches/18840215/18825509  apply successful for home  /u01/app/
oracle/product/11.2.0.4/dbhome_1
patch /u01/app/oracle/patches/18840215/18522515/custom/server/18522515  apply
successful for home  /u01/app/oracle/product/11.2.0.4/dbhome_1

Starting RAC /u01/app/oracle/product/11.2.0.4/dbhome_1 ...
Started RAC /u01/app/oracle/product/11.2.0.4/dbhome_1 successfully

opatch auto succeeded.
```

6. Repeat steps 1-5 on the remaining compute nodes, one at a time.

7. Run the `catbundle.sql` script as the Oracle user on any newly patched database that is not a data guard physical standby. Physical standby databases will receive the catalog update when the script is run on the primary database. Only run the script against one instance in a database. Note that in Oracle database 12c, the `catbundle.sql` script has been replaced with the `datapatch` script. For more information, consult the specific patch README.

```
$ cd $ORACLE_HOME
$ sqlplus / as sysdba

SYS@dbm1> @?/rdbms/admin/catbundle.sql exa apply
```

After all of the nodes have been patched, there is one final step that must be run against all databases with newly patched homes. On any database that is not a data guard physical standby, run the `catbundle.sql` script from SQL*Plus. The script must be run from the Oracle home due to additional scripts that are called out in `$ORACLE_HOME/rdbms/admin`. Running from outside of the Oracle home directory will prevent those scripts from being properly called. Databases running 12cR1 will use the `datapatch` script. For more information on `datapatch`, consult the specific patch README.

Applying a QDPE by Cloning Homes

In order to save downtime associated with patching, it is possible to clone an Oracle home and apply patches in an out-of-place upgrade. While less commonly used, this method can save time by prebuilding an Oracle home with the new patches applied and then moving the database instances to it. While this process does reduce the amount of time needed to put a patch in place, it requires additional filesystem space and contains more steps than an in-place QDPE application. This process is useful when multiple database instances share a home and only a subset of those databases require a patch upgrade or one off fix. My Oracle Support note #1136544.1 details this process for 11gR2 Oracle homes. The following exercise will detail the process for cloning an 11.2.0.4 database home and applying the July 2014 QDPE.

APPLYING A QDPE OUT OF PLACE

This exercise demonstrates the application of the July 2014 QDPE for 11.2.0.4 (patch #18840215) using the out of place method, with /u01/app/oracle/product/11.2.0.4/dbhome_1 as the original and /u01/app/oracle/product/11.2.0.4/db_july2014 as the new home.

1. As the Oracle user, create the new Oracle home and clone the existing home using the `tar` command. Any errors about the `nmb`, `nmhs`, and `nmo` executables can be ignored.

```
$ export ORACLE_HOME=/u01/app/oracle/product/11.2.0.4/db_july2014
$ dcli -g ~/dbs_group -l oracle mkdir -p $ORACLE_HOME
$ dcli -g ~/dbs_group -l oracle "cd /u01/app/oracle/product/11.2.0.4/dbhome_1;
\tar cf - . | ( cd $ORACLE_HOME ; tar xf - )"
```

2. After the home has been cloned, use the `clone.pl` script to complete the clone and relink the Oracle home.

```
$ export ORACLE_HOME=/u01/app/oracle/product/11.2.0.4/db_july2014
$ dcli -g ~/dbs_group -l oracle "cd $ORACLE_HOME/clone/bin; \
./clone.pl ORACLE_HOME=$ORACLE_HOME \
ORACLE_HOME_NAME=OraDB_home_july2014 ORACLE_BASE=/u01/app/oracle"
```

3. On each compute node, update the inventory to reflect the new Oracle home.

```
$ export ORACLE_HOME=/u01/app/oracle/product/11.2.0.4/db_july2014
$ $ORACLE_HOME/oui/bin/runInstaller \
-updateNodeList ORACLE_HOME=$ORACLE_HOME "CLUSTER_NODES={db01,db02}"
```

4. Relink the database executable for RDS. Note that the Oracle installer will relink a new home for RDS upon installation, but this method does not perform that relink automatically.

```
$ export ORACLE_HOME=/u01/app/oracle/product/11.2.0.4/db_july2014
$ dcli -g ~/dbs_group -l oracle "cd $ORACLE_HOME/rdbms/lib; \
ORACLE_HOME=$ORACLE_HOME make -f ins_rdbms.mk ipc_rds ioracle"
```

5. Run the `root.sh` script to complete the upgrade.

```
# export ORACLE_HOME=/u01/app/oracle/product/11.2.0.4/db_july2014
# dcli -g ~/dbs_group -l root $ORACLE_HOME/root.sh
```

6. Verify that the version of OPatch matches the minimum version required by the QDPE.

```
$ export ORACLE_HOME=/u01/app/oracle/product/11.2.0.4/db_july2014
$ dcli -l oracle -g ~/dbs_group $ORACLE_HOME/OPatch/opatch version
```

7. Apply the patch to the new home. Download patch 18840215 and place in directory `/u01/app/oracle/patches`.

8. As the Oracle user, generate an Oracle Configuration Manager response file. In a role-separated environment, create the file in a directory that both accounts can access.

```
$ /u01/app/11.2.0.4/grid/OPatch/ocm/bin/emocmrsp
OCM Installation Response Generator 10.3.4.0.0 - Production
Copyright (c) 2005, 2010, Oracle and/or its affiliates.  All rights reserved.

Provide your email address to be informed of security issues, install and
initiate Oracle Configuration Manager. Easier for you if you use your My
Oracle Support Email address/User Name.
Visit http://www.oracle.com/support/policies.html for details.
Email address/User Name:

You have not provided an email address for notification of security issues.
Do you wish to remain uninformed of security issues ([Y]es, [N]o) [N]:  y
The OCM configuration response file (ocm.rsp) was successfully created.
```

9. Unzip the patch file as the Oracle account.

```
$ unzip -oq p18840215_112040_Linux-x86-64.zip -d /u01/app/oracle/patches
```

10. On the first compute node as the root user, run `opatch auto`, specifying the new 11.2.0.4 database home to be patched.

```
# /u01/app/11.2.0.4/grid/OPatch/opatch auto -oh /u01/app/oracle/product/11.2.0.4/
db_july2014
Executing /u01/app/11.2.0.4/grid/perl/bin/perl /u01/app/11.2.0.4/grid/OPatch/crs/
patch11203.pl -patchdir /u01/app/oracle/patches -patchn 18840215 -oh /u01/app/
oracle/product/11.2.0.4/ db_july2014 -paramfile /u01/app/11.2.0.4/grid/crs/install/
crsconfig_params

This is the main log file: /u01/app/11.2.0.4/grid/cfgtoollogs/
opatchauto2014-09-04_09-01-55.log

This file will show your detected configuration and all the steps that opatchauto
attempted to do on your system:
/u01/app/11.2.0.4/grid/cfgtoollogs/opatchauto2014-09-04_09-01-55.report.log

2014-09-04 09:01:55: Starting Clusterware Patch Setup
Using configuration parameter file: /u01/app/11.2.0.4/grid/crs/install/
crsconfig_params
OPatch  is bundled with OCM, Enter the absolute OCM response file path:
/home/oracle/ocm.rsp

Stopping RAC /u01/app/oracle/product/11.2.0.4/ db_july2014 ...
Stopped RAC /u01/app/oracle/product/11.2.0.4/ db_july2014 successfully

patch /u01/app/oracle/patches/18840215/18825509  apply successful for home  /u01/app/
oracle/product/11.2.0.4/ db_july2014
patch /u01/app/oracle/patches/18840215/18522515/custom/server/18522515  apply
successful for home  /u01/app/oracle/product/11.2.0.4/ db_july2014

Starting RAC /u01/app/oracle/product/11.2.0.4/ db_july2014 ...
Started RAC /u01/app/oracle/product/11.2.0.4/ db_july2014 successfully

opatch auto succeeded.
```

11. Repeat steps 7-10 on the remaining compute nodes, one at a time.

12. Ensure that the database is using the old Oracle home.

```
$ srvctl config database -d dbm -a
Database unique name: dbm
Database name: dbm
Oracle home: /u01/app/oracle/product/11.2.0.4/dbhome_1
Oracle user: oracle
Spfile: +DATA/dbm/spfiledbm.ora
Domain:
Start options: open
Stop options: immediate
Database role: PRIMARY
```

```
Management policy: AUTOMATIC
Server pools: dbm
Database instances: dbm1,dbm2
Disk Groups: DATA,RECO
Mount point paths:
Services:
Type: RAC
Database is enabled
Database is administrator managed
```

13. Relocate the database using the `srvctl` utility.

```
$ srvctl modify database -d dbm -o /u01/app/oracle/product/11.2.0.4/db_july2014
```

14. Modify instance and database entries in the `/etc/oratab` file on each node.

```
dbm1:/u01/app/oracle/product/11.2.0.4/ db_july2014:N              # line added by Agent
dbm:/u01/app/oracle/product/11.2.0.4/ db_july2014:N               # line added by Agent
```

15. Perform a rolling restart of the database instances, one at a time.

```
$ srvctl stop instance -d dbm -i dbm1
$ srvctl start instance -d dbm -i dbm1
$ srvctl stop instance -d dbm -i dbm2
$ srvctl start instance -d dbm -i dbm2
```

16. Run the `catbundle.sql` script as the Oracle user on any newly patched database that is not a data guard physical standby. Physical standby databases will receive the catalog update when the script is run on the primary database. Only run the script against one instance in a database.

```
$ cd $ORACLE_HOME
$ sqlplus / as sysdba

SYS@dbm1> @?/rdbms/admin/catbundle.sql exa apply
```

As you can see, the process for applying a QDPE out of place can include many more steps than a traditional in-place patch application. This method is typically reserved for cases where multiple database instances share a home and only a subset of those databases require a patch upgrade or one-off fix.

Exadata Storage Server Patches

The term *Exadata storage server patch* encompasses a wide breadth of components that reside throughout the stack of an Exadata environment. These patches contain updates for not only the storage servers, but also the compute nodes and InfiniBand switches. In addition to new features and operating system upgrades, updates may include firmware for the RAID controller, flash cards, BIOS, ILOM, and even the disk drives themselves.

Before digging into how the patches are applied, it is good to get an understanding of the architecture of the storage server operating system. Because Exadata storage servers run Oracle Enterprise Linux, Oracle has been able to tailor the operating system layout with patching in mind. On an Exadata storage server, the first two hard disks have a small amount of space carved off to house the operating system. These partitions are then used to build software RAID devices using the standard Linux kernel md RAID driver:

```
[root@enkx3cel01 ~]# parted /dev/sda print

Model: LSI MR9261-8i (scsi)
Disk /dev/sda: 3000GB
Sector size (logical/physical): 512B/512B
Partition Table: gpt

Number  Start   End     Size    File system  Name     Flags
 1      32.8kB  123MB   123MB   ext3         primary  raid
 2      123MB   132MB   8225kB  ext2         primary
 3      132MB   2964GB  2964GB               primary
 4      2964GB  2964GB  32.8kB               primary
 5      2964GB  2975GB  10.7GB  ext3         primary  raid
 6      2975GB  2985GB  10.7GB  ext3         primary  raid
 7      2985GB  2989GB  3221MB  ext3         primary  raid
 8      2989GB  2992GB  3221MB  ext3         primary  raid
 9      2992GB  2994GB  2147MB  linux-swap   primary  raid
10      2994GB  2995GB  732MB                primary  raid
11      2995GB  3000GB  5369MB  ext3         primary  raid

Information: Don't forget to update /etc/fstab, if necessary.

[root@enkx3cel01 ~]# cat /proc/mdstat
Personalities : [raid1]
md4 : active raid1 sda1[0] sdb1[1]
      120384 blocks [2/2] [UU]

md5 : active raid1 sda5[0] sdb5[1]
      10485696 blocks [2/2] [UU]

md6 : active raid1 sda6[0] sdb6[1]
      10485696 blocks [2/2] [UU]

md7 : active raid1 sda7[0] sdb7[1]
      3145664 blocks [2/2] [UU]

md8 : active raid1 sda8[0] sdb8[1]
      3145664 blocks [2/2] [UU]

md2 : active raid1 sda9[0] sdb9[1]
      2097088 blocks [2/2] [UU]

md11 : active raid1 sda11[0] sdb11[1]
      5242752 blocks [2/2] [UU]

md1 : active raid1 sda10[0] sdb10[1]
      714752 blocks [2/2] [UU]

unused devices: <none>
```

```
[root@enkx3cel01 ~]# df -h
Filesystem            Size  Used Avail Use% Mounted on
/dev/md6              9.9G  6.7G  2.8G  72% /
tmpfs                  32G     0   32G   0% /dev/shm
/dev/md8              3.0G  797M  2.1G  28% /opt/oracle
/dev/md4              114M   51M   58M  47% /boot
/dev/md11             5.0G  255M  4.5G   6% /var/log/oracle
```

Looking at the output of /proc/mdstat, there are a total of eight RAID devices, but only five are mounted by the operating system at a given time. Looking closer at the sizes of each device, /dev/md5 and /dev/md6 have matching sizes, along with /dev/md7 and /dev/md8. This becomes apparent when running the imageinfo command to see what version of the Exadata storage server software is running:

```
[root@enkx3cel01 ~]# imageinfo

Kernel version: 2.6.39-400.126.1.el5uek #1 SMP Fri Sep 20 10:54:38 PDT 2013 x86_64
Cell version: OSS_11.2.3.3.0_LINUX.X64_131014.1
Cell rpm version: cell-11.2.3.3.0_LINUX.X64_131014.1-1

Active image version: 11.2.3.3.0.131014.1
Active image activated: 2013-12-22 23:48:05 -0600
Active image status: success
Active system partition on device: /dev/md6
Active software partition on device: /dev/md8

In partition rollback: Impossible

Cell boot usb partition: /dev/sdm1
Cell boot usb version: 11.2.3.3.0.131014.1

Inactive image version: 11.2.3.2.1.130109
Inactive image activated: 2013-12-22 22:44:01 -0600
Inactive image status: success
Inactive system partition on device: /dev/md5
Inactive software partition on device: /dev/md7

Boot area has rollback archive for the version: 11.2.3.2.1.130109
Rollback to the inactive partitions: Possible
```

The imageinfo command gives a wealth of information about the storage server in question. From looking at the "Active image version" line, we can see that it is currently running release 11.2.3.3.0. The / filesystem is listed in the "Active system partition on device" line, and the /opt/oracle partition is defined in the "Active software partition on device" line. The lines that begin with "Inactive" refer to the previous version of the Exadata storage server software that was installed on this cell. As you can see, the system and software partitions are located on /dev/md5 and /dev/md7, respectively. This reflects the out-of-place patching mechanism used by the Exadata storage server process. In the storage server shown above, /dev/md6 and /dev/md8 are used for the operating system. When a new patch is applied, the /dev/md5 and /dev/md7 devices will be wiped out and receive a new image of the operating system. After the image has been deployed and the newly imaged devices will be made active, the storage server will reboot and use the new image, leaving the former image untouched. This allows a rollback of the patch either from the patch administrator or an automatic rollback in the event of a failure during the patching cycle.

Applying an Exadata Storage Server Patch

Exadata storage server patches are applied using the patchmgr utility. Unlike the opatch utility, which is downloaded separately from the actual patch files, patchmgr is included with each release. This utility relies on SSH and the dcli utility to patch all storage servers in a cluster with a single command. Because of this, the user who is running patchmgr must have passwordless access to the root account on all storage servers during the patch. Because of these requirements, storage server patches are typically applied from one of the compute nodes in the cluster, but they can also be applied from any system with SSH keys set up. This could be either a host running Oracle Enterprise Manager or Oracle's platinum services gateway server. SSH keys can be temporarily configured and removed using the -k and --unkey options in dcli. There are two main modes to the patchmgr utility—a prerequisite check and the actual patch. Even though the patch mode runs the prerequisite check, it is recommended to run the prerequisite check first in a separate run.

Before upgrading a storage server, the patch must be downloaded and unpacked on the host that will be driving the patch session. In addition to the patch itself, it is important to check MOS note #888828.1 for any additional plug-ins that are recommended. Because the patch application involves several reboots, it must be run outside of the hosts that are actually being patched. The patch archive contains several scripts including patchmgr, supporting shell scripts to obtain status updates, and an ISO file that contains the entire Exadata storage server operating system. Releases beyond 11.2.3.3.0 also may contain an update for the InfiniBand switches, which will be discussed later. Before running the patchmgr script, a cell_group file must either be created or copied into the patch directory. This file contains the hostnames of the storage servers that are going to be patched by patchmgr.

Now that the patch contents have been unpacked, it is important to run the prerequisite check to ensure that the system is ready to be patched. The syntax to run patchmgr in prerequisite mode is the following:

```
patchmgr -cells cell_group -patch_check_prereq
```

The output below shows the output of a prerequisite check. This check can be run while Clusterware is up and running. It will verify that the current image status of the storage servers reports successful, that there is sufficient disk space for the upgrade, and that there are no open alerts on the storage servers. This is very important to ensure that a failed patch does not leave any of the storage servers in an unbootable state:

```
[root@enkx3db01 patch_11.2.3.3.1.140708]# ./patchmgr -cells cell_group -patch_check_prereq

2014-10-22 18:37:41 -0500        :Working: DO: Initialize files, check space and state of
cell services. Up to 1 minute ...

2014-10-22 18:38:00 -0500        :SUCCESS: DONE: Initialize files, check space and state of
cell services.
2014-10-22 18:38:00 -0500        :Working: DO: Copy, extract prerequisite check archive to
cells. If required start md11 mismatched partner size correction. Up to 40 minutes ...

2014-10-22 18:38:14 -0500        :SUCCESS: DONE: Copy, extract prerequisite check archive to
cells. If required start md11 mismatched partner size correction.
2014-10-22 18:38:14 -0500        :Working: DO: Check prerequisites on all cells. Up to 2 minutes ...
2014-10-22 18:39:17 -0500        :SUCCESS: DONE: Check prerequisites on all cells.
2014-10-22 18:39:17 -0500        :Working: DO: Execute plugin check for Patch Check Prereq ...
2014-10-22 18:39:17 -0500 :INFO: Patchmgr plugin start: Prereq check for exposure to bug
17854520 v1.1. Details in logfile /tmp/patch_11.2.3.3.1.140708/patchmgr.stdout.
```

```
2014-10-22 18:39:17 -0500 :INFO: This plugin checks dbhomes across all nodes with oracle-
user ssh equivalence, but only for those known to the local system. dbhomes that exist only
on remote nodes must be checked manually.
2014-10-22 18:39:17 -0500 :SUCCESS: No exposure to bug 17854520 with non-rolling patching
2014-10-22 18:39:17 -0500        :SUCCESS: DONE: Execute plugin check for Patch Check Prereq.
```

At this point, Clusterware is either left running (for a rolling patch) or taken down (for an offline patch). Either way, the patchmgr script is called in the same fashion. The syntax to apply the patch is the following:

```
./patchmgr -cells cell_group -patch [-rolling] [-smtp_from "address"] [-smtp_to "address1
address2"]
```

Just like with the prerequisite check, the file containing the list of cells to patch is included. The "-patch" switch tells patchmgr to perform a patch operation. Adding "-rolling" to the command will instruct patchmgr to apply the patch to each of the storage servers in a rolling fashion.

The final switches enable e-mail alerting for each portion of the patching process. Enabling the e-mail option will send alerts when patchmgr starts, along with updates when the patch state for a storage server changes. These states can be any of "Started," "Patching," "Waiting," "Succeeded," or "Failed." This can be useful during rolling patches, which may run for a long time. Separate multiple e-mail addresses with a space when specifying the smtp_to switch. Figure 16-4 shows a sample email that is sent from patchmgr. You can see that it has completed patching the first storage server, and is beginning to patch host dm01cel02.

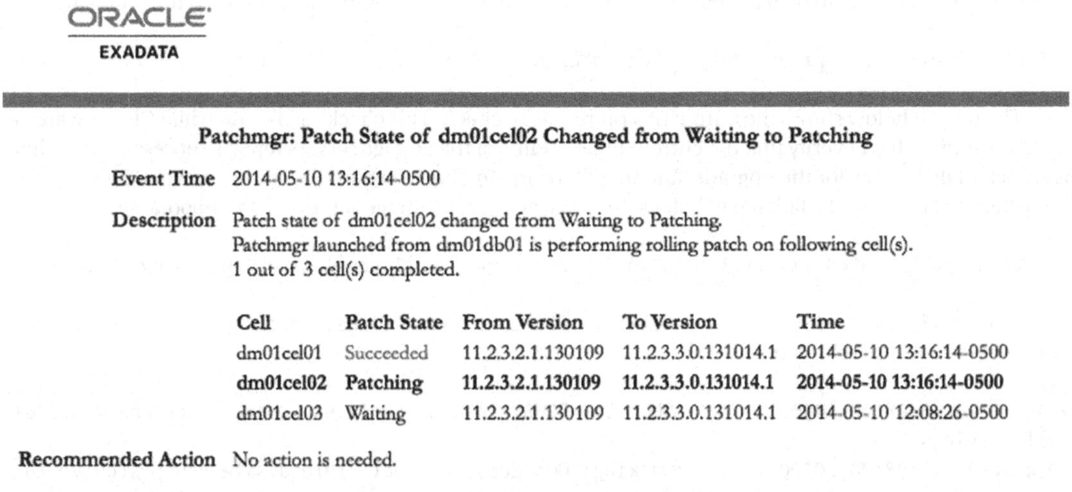
ORACLE
EXADATA

Patchmgr: Patch State of dm01cel02 Changed from Waiting to Patching

Event Time 2014-05-10 13:16:14-0500

Description Patch state of dm01cel02 changed from Waiting to Patching.
Patchmgr launched from dm01db01 is performing rolling patch on following cell(s).
1 out of 3 cell(s) completed.

Cell	Patch State	From Version	To Version	Time
dm01cel01	Succeeded	11.2.3.2.1.130109	11.2.3.3.0.131014.1	2014-05-10 13:16:14-0500
dm01cel02	**Patching**	**11.2.3.2.1.130109**	**11.2.3.3.0.131014.1**	**2014-05-10 13:16:14-0500**
dm01cel03	Waiting	11.2.3.2.1.130109	11.2.3.3.0.131014.1	2014-05-10 12:08:26-0500

Recommended Action No action is needed.

Figure 16-4. *Exadata storage server patch alerts*

It is important to run patchmgr using a utility such as screen or VNC due to the potential length of a single run. If a patch is applied using the rolling method, patchmgr will not complete until all storage servers have completed the patch process.

After patchmgr has completed successfully and all storage servers are upgraded, it is important to clean up the installation on the storage servers. This is done with the "-cleanup" switch. The full syntax is as follows:

```
./patchmgr -cells cell_group -cleanup
```

Storage Server Patching In Depth

There are three distinct phases to a storage server patch: the prerequisite phase, the pre-reboot phase, and the reboot phase. As mentioned previously, the prerequisite phase is executed whenever `patchmgr` is run, regardless of the mode. During this phase, `patchmgr` will check for open alerts, available space, and general health of the storage server. The prerequisite phase runs in parallel across all of the storage servers whether the patch is being applied rolling or with a full outage. This is the quickest of all of the phases.

The pre-reboot phase also occurs in parallel, regardless of the patching mode. During the pre-reboot phase, several additional checks are run on the storage servers. First, the file containing the operating system image is copied to all of the storage servers, and the recovery USB media is updated to the latest copy via the `make_cellboot_usb.sh` script. This step is very important because the USB recovery media may be called upon in the event of a failed patch. After the recovery media is recreated, `patchmgr` will instruct the cells to destroy the inactive operating system and software partitions and recreate them. The contents of the new operating system image are then copied to the newly created partitions, and the BIOS boot order is validated. Once these steps have completed, the patch will enter a standby state. Once all of the storage servers have completed the pre-reboot phase, `patchmgr` moves on to the reboot phase. It is at this point where the actions for rolling and non-rolling patches differ.

For non-rolling patches, all storage servers execute the reboot phase in parallel. Because Clusterware must be shut down during a non-rolling patch, there are no negative consequences in applying the patch to all storage servers at once. For a rolling patch, one cell at a time goes through the reboot phase. Before a cell can begin the reboot phase during a rolling patch, the grid disks must be taken offline first. The reboot phase begins with a final validation of all of the components, and critical files that are needed to rebuild the cell are copied to the new partitions. These files include home directories of the root, celladmin, and cellmonitor user accounts, the contents of the `/etc` directory, and any other necessary files. Finally, the grub bootloader is instructed to boot off of the newly created partitions and ignore the partitions that were previously used to host the operating system and `cellsrv` application. These now inactive partitions will be left alone in the event that a rollback is needed. Through this method, Oracle ensures that there will always be an installation of the operating system to fall back to, whether that is the previously active partitions or through the bootable USB recovery media. After all of these actions have completed, the storage server will reboot.

During the first reboot of this phase, the storage server will boot up to an incomplete version of the operating system and install a handful of additional RPM packages. These packages reside in a temporary `/install/post` directory that contains enumerated directories named `10commonos`, `30kernel`, `40debugos`, `50ofed`, `60cellrpms`, `70sunutils`, and `90last`. Inside each of these directories is an `install.sh` script that installs the packages inside of the directory. Upon completion of the installation script in the `90last` directory, the `/install` directory is deleted and the host is rebooted. During the next reboot, firmware components are upgraded. As part of the boot process for each storage server, the `/opt/oracle.cellos/CheckHWnFWProfile` script is run in upgrade mode. This script will check all of the hardware components in the storage server and validate if their firmware version matches the expected version for the new image. If the current version does not match, it is upgraded to the supported version. This script checks the BIOS, ILOM, RAID controller, InfiniBand HCA, flash cards, and disk drives. Depending on the number of firmware updates that need to be applied, this process can take up to two hours. On older patch releases, the SSHD process was disabled during firmware updates, but this has been removed on some releases. For updates on the status of the firmware upgrade process, log in to the storage server and look at the output of the `/var/log/cellos/CheckHWnFWProfile.log` file. When all of the hardware components have been upgraded, the storage server will reboot for a final time. If the patch includes a BIOS upgrade, the final reboot could take a significantly longer period of time than what is usually seen. During the final reboot, validation checks will take place to ensure that the new image matches the expected configuration. Results of the validation checks can be found in the `/var/log/cellos/validations` directory and, specifically, the `/var/log/cellos/validations.log` file. Upon successful completion of the validation checks, the storage server enters a state of "success," and `patchmgr` will either complete or instruct the cell to activate its grid disks (if the patch is being applied rolling). If the patch is being applied rolling, then after the grid disks have been activated, patchmgr will check for the status of the grid disks within ASM. This is checked via the asmmodestatus attribute for each grid disk. During the time that the grid disks are being brought online in ASM, they will show a status of "SYNCING" in V$ASM_DISK (or via the asmmodestatus attribute for the grid disk). This means that the disks are catching up on any writes that they missed while they were offline due to the patch. After the disks have finished the resync process, patchmgr will move on to the next cell, and the reboot phase will begin there. The process repeats until all storage servers have been patched successfully. Recent storage server patches have shown to take slightly over one hour to complete the reboot phase of the patch. Assuming that it takes 30 minutes for each storage server to resync its disks, the reboot phase alone will take approximately 21 hours on a full rack (14 storage servers x 1.5 hour reboot and resync). The amount of time needed for the resync is completely dependent on the activity level of the system. Systems that are not busy during the patch may take between three and five minutes for a resync. In extreme cases where the cluster is very busy, we have seen resync times upward of six hours.

When looking to troubleshoot a storage server patch failure, it helps to know where the log files for the patch reside. When patchmgr is run, it copies the patch contents and runs out of the /root/_patch_hctap_/_p_ directory on each of the storage servers. During a patch session, there are two log files that detail everything that the patchmgr script does: wait_out and wait_out_tmp. The wait_out log file records each time that patchmgr logs in and gives general messages, such as the patch state. For the detail of what exactly patchmgr is doing, look inside the wait_out_tmp file. This log records everything that is going on during the pre-reboot phase. More recent versions of patchmgr also include a log file on the controlling host named for each of the storage servers. These files can be useful to look at, but may not give the full picture that the wait_out and wait_out_tmp files can give.

Much has been said in this section about patchmgr, but not how it works. The patchmgr utility is a bash script that drives the patching process on a set of storage servers designated at runtime. Whether running an upgrade or rollback, rolling or not, the functionality of patchmgr is the same—it pushes scripts and files to the nodes that will be patched and interacts with them via SSH keys and the dcli utility. When patching multiple hosts, patchmgr does not return to a prompt until all of the hosts are patched or there is a failure in the process. Most of the time, the output of patchmgr will look like a pinwheel. During the various phases, patchmgr will report a number of minutes left. This is not an estimate, but a timeout. If the phase does not complete in this amount of time, the patch will be marked as failed. While this is going on in the foreground, patchmgr wakes up every minute and logs in to each cell and runs a patch status script. Based on what the script returns, patchmgr will sleep for another minute, move on to the next phase, or complete the patch. Figure 16-5 shows the output of a patchmgr session.

```
2014-04-06 20:29:36        :Working: DO: Check space and state of Cell services on target cells. Up to 1 minute ...
2014-04-06 20:29:58        :SUCCESS: DONE: Check space and state of Cell services on target cells.
2014-04-06 20:29:58        :Working: DO: Copy, extract prerequisite check archive to cells. If required start md11 mismatched partner size correction. U
p to 40 minutes ...
2014-04-06 20:30:12 Wait correction of degraded md11 due to md partner size mismatch. Up to 30 minutes.


2014-04-06 20:30:13        :SUCCESS: DONE: Copy, extract prerequisite check archive to cells. If required start md11 mismatched partner size correction.
2014-04-06 20:30:13        :Working: DO: Check prerequisites on all cells. Up to 2 minutes ...
2014-04-06 20:30:45        :SUCCESS: DONE: Check prerequisites on all cells.
2014-04-06 20:30:45        :Working: DO: Copy the patch to all cells. Up to 3 minutes ...
2014-04-06 20:31:34        :SUCCESS: DONE: Copy the patch to all cells.
2014-04-06 20:31:36 1 of 5 :Working: DO: Initiate patch on cells. Cells will remain up. Up to 5 minutes ...
2014-04-06 20:31:38 1 of 5 :SUCCESS: DONE: Initiate patch on cells.
2014-04-06 20:31:38 2 of 5 :Working: DO: Waiting to finish pre-reboot patch actions. Cells will remain up. Up to 45 minutes ...
2014-04-06 20:32:38 Wait for patch pre-reboot procedures


2014-04-06 20:44:54 2 of 5 :SUCCESS: DONE: Waiting to finish pre-reboot patch actions.
2014-04-06 20:44:54 3 of 5 :Working: DO: Finalize patch on cells. Cells will reboot. Up to 5 minutes ...
2014-04-06 20:45:09 3 of 5 :SUCCESS: DONE: Finalize patch on cells.
2014-04-06 20:45:09 4 of 5 :Working: DO: Wait for cells to reboot and come online. Up to 120 minutes ...
2014-04-06 20:46:09 Wait for patch finalization and reboot

||||| Minutes left 101
```

Figure 16-5. *Exadata storage server patch*

Rolling vs. Non-rolling Patches

Exadata storage server patches can be installed in parallel during a full cluster outage or sequentially with no downtime. As with any choice involving Oracle, there are benefits and drawbacks to both approaches. While rolling patches do have a certain allure, the extended nature of them tends to dissuade Exadata administrators. Another factor to consider with rolling patches is the ASM redundancy level of your ASM disk groups. If you remember from Chapter 14, disk groups can either have two (Normal Redundancy) or three (High Redundancy) copies of data. When a storage server is being patched, the data that it stores is offline throughout the reboot phase. For an Exadata running high redundancy, this is not an issue because two more copies of data are offline. However, most Exadata customers seem to be running their Exadata racks with normal redundancy for disk groups. This means that throughout the reboot phase of the patch process, a cluster with disk groups configured for normal redundancy has a partial degradation of the ASM disk groups, leaving only one copy of data online throughout. If a partner disk of a currently offline disk was lost during the patching process, there would most likely be a failure of the ASM disk groups, potentially leading to data loss. Due to these factors, patching with a full outage is the method most frequently chosen. While there is an argument to patching the servers sequentially rather than in parallel in order to mitigate risk more effectively, the storage servers are all individual machines. A failure on one cell will not affect the remaining cells. With all of the safeguards put in place through the patch process, a storage server that fails to patch successfully will boot back to the state that it was in before the patch started. If this happens, simply determine the issue that caused the cell to not patch successfully, modify the `cell_group` file to contain the hostname of the cell that failed the patch, and run the patch process again. It goes without saying—when choosing between rolling patches and taking an outage, consider the redundancy level of the ASM disk groups and the estimated amount of time that a rolling patch will take. In some cases, it's easier to take the short outage or switch to a disaster recovery system and apply the patch in a non-rolling manner.

Rolling Back Storage Server Patches

The method used for rolling back storage server patches is exactly the same as what was used to apply the patch in the first place. By giving the "-rollback" switch to `patchmgr`, a rollback process is initiated. When invoked, the rollback process sets the inactive partitions to activate on the next reboot. This will leave the version you are rolling back from as the inactive version. As with an upgrade action, the USB recovery media is recreated in order to ensure that there will be no issues from the rollback operation. Typically, firmware is left at the newer level.

UPGRADING AN EXADATA STORAGE SERVER

This exercise demonstrates upgrading Exadata storage servers to version 12.1.1.1.1 via the full outage patching method.

1. Download desired storage server patch file, as found in MOS note #888828.1. In this example, version 12.1.1.1.1 is available as patch number 18084575, and the patch will be run out of the `/u01/stage/patches` directory. According to the supplemental README note (#1667407.1), additional plug-ins (patch # 19681939) should be downloaded as well. Unzip the patch, followed by the plug-ins. The plug-ins should be copied to the plug-ins directory where the storage server patch is unzipped. Ensure that all plug-in scripts are executable. Patches should be run from the first compute node or a host that is able to access the storage servers via SSH keys.

```
# cd /u01/stage/patches
# unzip p18084575_121111_Linux-x86-64.zip
# unzip -o -d patch_12.1.1.1.1.140712/plugins p19681939_121111_Linux-x86-64.zip -x
Readme.txt
# chmod +x patch_12.1.1.1.1.140712/plugins/*
```

2. Create a `cell_group` file that contains the hostnames of the storage servers to be patched. On older releases, this file will exist within `/root`. After creating the file, verify the connectivity using `dcli`.

```
# cp /root/cell_group /u01/stage/patches/patch_12.1.1.1.1.140712
# cd /u01/stage/patches/patch_12.1.1.1.1.140712
# dcli -l root -g cell_group hostname
```

3. Stop Oracle Clusterware across all of the nodes in the cluster.

```
# $GRID_HOME/bin/crsctl stop cluster -all
# dcli -l root -g <dbs_group> $GRID_HOME/bin/crsctl stop crs
```

4. Run the patch prerequisite check.

```
# cd /u01/stage/patches/patch_12.1.1.1.1.140712
# ./patchmgr -cells cell_group -patch_check_prereq [-rolling]
```

5. Check to ensure that there aren't any processes running.

```
# dcli -l root -g <dbs_group> "ps -ef | grep grid"
# dcli -g dbs_group -l root "ps -ef | grep grid"
enkdb01: root      11483   9016  0 05:46 pts/0    00:00:00 python /usr/local/bin/dcli
-g dbs_group -l root ps -ef | grep grid
enkdb01: root      11500  11495  0 05:46 pts/0    00:00:00 /usr/bin/ssh -l root
enkdb02 ( ps -ef | grep grid) 2>&1
enkdb01: root      11501  11496  0 05:46 pts/0    00:00:00 /usr/bin/ssh -l root
enkdb01 ( ps -ef | grep grid) 2>&1
enkdb01: root      11513  11502  0 05:46 ?        00:00:00 bash -c ( ps -ef | grep
grid) 2>&1
enkdb01: root      11523  11513  0 05:46 ?        00:00:00 bash -c ( ps -ef | grep
grid) 2>&1
enkdb01: root      11525  11523  0 05:46 ?        00:00:00 grep grid
enkdb02: root      61071  61069  0 05:46 ?        00:00:00 bash -c ( ps -ef | grep
grid) 2>&1
enkdb02: root      61080  61071  0 05:46 ?        00:00:00 bash -c ( ps -ef | grep
grid) 2>&1
enkdb02: root      61082  61080  0 05:46 ?        00:00:00 grep grid
```

6. Run the patch.

```
# cd /u01/stage/patches/patch_12.1.1.1.1.140712
# ./patchmgr -cells cell_group -patch [-rolling]
```

7. Wait for all of the storage servers to finish patching and run the cleanup phase.

```
# cd /u01/stage/patches/patch_12.1.1.1.1.140712
# ./patchmgr -cells cell_group -cleanup
```

Remember to check the README for the patch along with the supplemental note found via MOS note #888828.1 before applying any Exadata storage server patch. These documents will contain known issues and workarounds that could prove valuable during your patching.

Upgrading Compute Nodes

Another component that is included in the Exadata storage server patch is the corresponding patch for the compute nodes. Because the compute and storage servers should both be running the same kernel and operating system versions, Oracle releases a separate patch that includes a yum repository containing all of the Linux packages required to upgrade the host. Because the compute nodes are not a closed system that can easily be reimaged, Oracle provides operating system and firmware updates via the standard Linux method of a yum update. Early patches that utilized the yum updated method offered a plethora of ways to perform the update—over the Internet with Oracle's Unbreakable Enterprise Linux Network, from a local yum repository, or through the use of an ISO image file provided by Oracle support through a separate patch download. Oracle now has a helper script named `dbnodeupdate.sh` that makes the upgrade process very straightforward. The most common patch application method used with `dbnodeupdate.sh` is via an ISO image file containing the yum repository. One of the biggest benefits to using the repository based on the patch file is that it guarantees consistency between updates. If you are like most people, your nonproduction machines are patched before your production systems. This allows time for the patches to "bake in," and any issues can be discovered through testing. When you are using a public repository for your patches, you cannot control which versions of patches are applied. The repository file created by Oracle support is a static file that is not updated without a change to the patch version number. Also, by using a repository local to the host, there is no need to download patches multiple times or have servers directly connected to the Internet.

Applying Patches with dbnodeupdate.sh

The `dbnodeupdate.sh` script is available to assist with the process of upgrading the operating system and firmware on a compute node. As mentioned earlier, Oracle support periodically releases a new version of the `dbnodeupdate.sh` script. This script is available through patch # 16486998. While primarily used to upgrade the operating system, `dbnodeupdate.sh` performs several additional tasks. Because "best practices" change, as new practices are better than their predecessors, `dbnodeupdate.sh` will routinely check to make sure that your compute nodes are following along with the guidelines with MOS note # 757552.1. One example of these checks is when Oracle changed the recommendation for the minimum amount of memory to be allocated to the Linux operating system (the kernel parameter `vm.min_free_kbytes`). In many early deployments, only ~50MB was allocated. After customers began to see node evictions due to the operating system being starved for memory, the recommendation increased to ~512MB. Because many customers may never see the recommendation in the middle of a very long note, the `dbnodeupdate.sh` script will check this and change the setting during the next run. This is just one example of the fixes that `dbnodeupdate.sh` can put in place when needed. Other versions will include security fixes for various vulnerabilities that have been discovered after the version was released (in particular, the BASH "Shellshock" exploit).

Another key feature of the `dbnodeupdate.sh` script is its use of Linux's native logical volume management (LVM) functionality. Due to the filesystem layout on Exadata — / is a 30GB logical volume, and `/u01` is a 100GB logical volume—it is easy to take backups of the root filesystem before making any changes. While this option has been available since the X2-2 was released, many customers did not take snapshot backups before upgrading the operating system. With `dbnodeupdate.sh`, backups are automatically taken. While different from the methodology used by the Exadata storage servers, the concepts are similar. Exadata storage servers utilize an out-of-place patching mechanism. On Exadata compute nodes, the inactive volume is only used in the event of a rollback—the patches are applied in place unless there is a failure. The default root filesystem resides on the `VGExaDb-LVDbSys1` logical volume. When `dbnodeupdate.sh` is run for the first time, a new logical volume, `VGExaDb-LVDbSys2`, will be created. If `dbnodeupdate.sh` has been run before, the volume will be overwritten on the next run. This volume will be used to create a full backup of the original active volume at the time that the script is run. First, a snapshot of the root filesystem is taken, and that snapshot is mounted in `/mnt_snap`. After the inactive root volume has been created (typically VGExaDb-LVDbSys2), it is mounted to `/mnt_spare` and the contents of the snapshot are copied to `/mnt_spare` using the tar utility. After everything has been copied to `/mnt_spare`, the volume is unmounted and the snapshot volume is removed. Now is probably a good time to note that if you increase the size of the root filesystem, the backups will certainly take longer. Also, additional space will need to be reserved in the volume group to accommodate the larger root volume. Keep in mind that only the root filesystem is backed up by `dbnodeupdate.sh` because the script does not modify any files on `/u01`. A copy of the `/boot` filesystem is created as well, in the event that a backup is needed. Table 16-1 describes the available flags to be used with dbnodeupdate.sh.

***Table 16-1.** Flags Used with dbnodeupdate.sh*

Flag	Description
-u	Updates a compute node to a new release
-r	Rolls a compute node back to the previous release
-c	Performs post-patch or post-rollback operations
-l	URL or location of zip file containing the ISO file
-s	Shut down Clusterware stack before running
-q	Quiet mode—used with -t
-n	Disable filesystem backup
-p	Bootstrap phase, used when updating from version
-v	11.2.2.4.2
-t	Dry run—verify prerequisites only
-V	Used with -q to specify which release to patch to
	Print the version number

Before running `dbnodeupdate.sh`, download the patch containing the ISO that corresponds to the desired patch level. Place that file and the patch containing the `dbnodeupdate.sh` script on each compute node. While `dbnodeupdate.sh` can pull from a yum repository via HTTP, the ISO method has shown to be much more straightforward. There are two stages to every run of `dbnodeupdate.sh`—the upgrade/rollback stage and the closing stage. Just like the auto functionality of OPatch, `dbnodeupdate.sh` performs many different tasks that would otherwise have to be executed separately. First, `dbnodeupdate.sh` will shut down and unlock the grid infrastructure home, followed by a backup of the root filesystem. Next, `dbnodeupdate.sh` will unpack the zip file containing the patch repository to a temporary location, mount that ISO, and update the `/etc/yum.repos.d/Exadata-computenode.repo` file to utilize the location of the RPM packages. A yum update is performed, and the system reboots. While the host reboots, firmware components are upgraded. Typically, firmware updates include the InfiniBand HCA, RAID controller, BIOS, and ILOM. The upgrade process is the same methodology used on the storage servers—the `/opt/oracle.cellos/CheckHWnFWProfile` script is run to compare the firmware versions with the registry of supported versions. If a component does not match, it is flashed to the expected version. After all of the firmware updates have been applied, the host will reboot.

After the host reboots, and the imageinfo command shows a successful upgrade, the dbnodeupdate.sh script must be run again to "close" the upgrade. This mode will validate that the yum update was successful, clean out the yum cache, relink the Oracle homes for the RDS protocol, and start Clusterware and enable it at boot time. When this step has competed, the host is ready to be put back in to service.

UPGRADING AN EXADATA COMPUTE NODE

This exercise demonstrates upgrading an Exadata compute node to version 12.1.1.1.1.

1. Download the latest version of the dbnodeupdate.sh utility and desired patch ISO, as found in MOS note #888828.1. In this example, dbnodeupdate.sh is available as patch number 16486998, and the ISO file is in patch number 18889969. In this example, both of the files are downloaded into the /u01/stage/patches directory. Unzip the patch file containing dbnodeupdate.sh.

```
# cd /u01/stage/patches
# unzip p16486998_121111_Linux-x86-64.zip
```

2. Run the dbnodeupdate.sh script, specifying the patch file location.

```
# ./dbnodeupdate.sh -u -l /u01/stage/patches/p18889969_121111_Linux-x86-64.zip -s
```

3. After the compute node has rebooted and imageinfo shows a successful status, close the upgrade using dbnodeupdate.sh.

```
# imageinfo

Kernel version: 2.6.39-400.128.17.el5uek #1 SMP Tue May 27 13:20:24 PDT 2014 x86_64
Image version: 12.1.1.1.1.140712
Image activated: 2014-12-08 04:42:43 -0500
Image status: success
System partition on device: /dev/mapper/VGExaDb-LVDbSys1

# cd /u01/stage/patches
# ./dbnodeupdate.sh -c
```

These steps can be executed one node at a time for a rolling patch, or they can be executed on each node in parallel for a full outage.

Rolling Back Patches with dbnodeupdate.sh

The process of rolling back a compute node is very similar to that of an upgrade. Call the dbnodeupdate.sh script with the -r flag to roll back to the previous version of the compute node operating system. Doing this will change the filesystem label of the inactive logical volume (the backup that was created when the update was run) and reconfigure the GRUB bootloader to utilize this volume. The host is rebooted and, when it comes back, it will be running in the state that it was before the patch was issued. Because of this, it is important to not let too many changes occur on the host before you decide to roll back. Any passwords or configuration settings will match the system at the time of the patch.

Upgrading InfiniBand Switches

While updates are seldom released, the InfiniBand switches in an Exadata environment must be updated periodically. These updates have been so infrequent that nearly each release has contained a different installation method. Oracle seems to have standardized on bundling the switch firmware with an Exadata storage server patch release and using the `patchmgr` utility to apply the update. This makes sense because the InfiniBand switch patches have typically been released in conjunction with a storage server release. By using `patchmgr`, the syntax will be familiar, and the methods will stabilize.

Just like with a storage server patch, upgrading an InfiniBand switch is a two-step process. First, there is a prerequisite check, followed by the actual upgrade of the switches. While the steps are the same, the syntax is a little bit different. Storage server patches use the `-patch_check_prereq` flag, whereas InfiniBand patches use the `-ibswitch_precheck` flag. Patches on the storage servers are applied using the `-patch` flag, and `-upgrade` is used for applying updates to the InfiniBand switches. The `patchmgr` script still uses a file containing the names of the InfiniBand switches, just like when patching a storage server. InfiniBand switch updates are always applied in a rolling fashion, one switch at a time. When applying these patches using `patchmgr`, verification tests are performed both before and after each switch is patched. These patches can be applied while the Clusterware stack is online and require no systemwide downtime.

UPGRADING EXADATA INFINIBAND SWITCHES

This exercise demonstrates upgrading the Exadata InfiniBand switches to version 2.1.3-4, included in Exadata storage server version 12.1.1.1.1.

1. On the same node that was used to apply the Exadata storage server patch, gather the names of the InfiniBand switches. Note that with environments that contain other Oracle-engineered systems, not all InfiniBand switches need to be upgraded. (Exalogic and Big Data Appliance contain "gateway" switches that use different firmware.) Look for switches labeled "SUN DCS 36P" These are the switches that need to be patched.

```
[root@enkx3db01 ~]# ibswitches
Switch : 0x002128ac ports 36 "SUN DCS 36P QDR enkx3sw-ib3 x.x.x.x" enhanced port 0
lid 1 lmc 0
Switch : 0x002128ab ports 36 "SUN DCS 36P QDR enkx3sw-ib2 x.x.x.x" enhanced port 0
lid 2 lmc 0
```

2. Create a text file named `ibswitches.lst` that contains the names of the InfiniBand switches that are to be patched.

```
# cd /u01/stage/patches/patch_12.1.1.1.1.140712
# cat ibswitches.lst
enkx3sw-ib2
enkx3sw-ib3
```

3. Run `patchmgr` with the `-ibswitch_precheck` flag to ensure that everything is ready to be patched. The `patchmgr` script will ask for the root password for all of the switches and verify connectivity, along with other tests (available free space, verify-topology output, and so on). If the script returns successfully, you are ready to apply the patch.

```
# cd /u01/stage/patches/patch_12.1.1.1.1.140712
# ./patchmgr -ibswitches ibswitches.lst -upgrade -ibswitch_precheck
```

4. Apply the patch using the `patchmgr` script. Each switch will be patched sequentially, as `patchmgr` would with a rolling Exadata storage server patch. The script will not return to a prompt until all switches have been patched or an error occurs.

```
# cd /u01/stage/patches/patch_12.1.1.1.1.140712
# ./patchmgr -ibswitches ibswitches.lst -upgrade
```

Unlike the Exadata storage server patches, there is no cleanup needed on the InfiniBand switches. Once the patch has completed, you are ready to move along to the next piece in the process.

Applying Patches to Standby Systems

Looking at all of the patches described in this chapter, it's easy to think, "I'll never get the downtime approved to apply all of these!" One feature that Oracle offers in order to cut actual downtime related to patching is that every Exadata patch since database version 11.2.0.2 supports standby-first patching. Using this method, the only database downtime is the amount of time needed to perform a Data Guard switch to your standby. Simply apply all patches to your standby system ahead of time, switch the databases to the newly patched system, and patch the original primary system. At that point, you can either switch back to the original primary system or continue to run with the roles reversed. Upon the next patch cycle, simply repeat the process. Using this method can show two things that auditors love—successful disaster recovery testing and up-to-date databases. The steps to apply patches in standby-first mode are very simple:

1. Apply quarterly patches to the standby system via rolling or full outage method. Patches can include Exadata storage server, compute node, QDPE, and InfiniBand switch upgrades. Grid Infrastructure patch set upgrades can be performed as well, as they do not affect Oracle Data Guard. Do not run post-patch scripts (`catbundle.sql` or `datapatch`) on the standby databases, as those scripts need to be run after all Oracle homes have been patched.

2. Perform testing against the standby database using Active Data Guard, snapshot standby, or other means.

3. Perform Data Guard role switch of all databases on the primary cluster to the secondary cluster.

4. Apply quarterly patches to the primary system via rolling or full outage method. These patches should be the same patches applied to the standby system in step 1.

5. Perform post-patch steps (`catbundle.sql` or `datapatch`) on the primary database instance as instructed in the patch README.

6. Switch databases back to the original primary cluster, if desired.

The only patch type that cannot be applied with the standby-first method is a database patchset upgrade. These upgrades involve changing the version number (11.2.0.3 to 11.2.0.4, or from any version to Oracle database 12c). These upgrades cannot be done through the standby-first method because they require an upgrade of the database catalog. This is not a limitation of Exadata, but the Oracle database itself. At a high level, upgrading a database within a Data Guard configuration requires starting the standby database in a home with the new version and running the upgrade scripts from the primary. This would apply for patchset upgrades within a major version (11.2.0.3 to 11.2.0.4 or 12.1.0.1 to 12.1.0.2), or between major versions (for example, 11.2.0.3 to 12.1.0.2). Components within the database are upgraded, and changes propagate via Data Guard. For more details on this process, look in the MOS notes mentioned in Appendix B. They are actually very thorough and methodically walk through the process from end to end.

Summary

Hopefully, this chapter helped to alleviate some of the anxiety many people feel when patching their Exadata for the first time. Like anything else, the process will be more familiar as more patches are applied. Despite being a hit-or-miss proposition in the early stages of Exadata, patch releases have been much more stable over the course of the past few years. This can be attributed to many factors—the maturation of the platform, better testing, and a growing customer base. The best advice to be given when applying Exadata patches is to read the documentation several times and be very patient. Taking a close look at the OPatch logs when applying a QDPE will reveal warnings when the previously installed patches are rolled back. When looking under the covers during an Exadata storage server patch, you may see what look like errors. Trust that the `patchmgr` script will be able to filter through what can be ignored and what is an actual error. If there is really a failure, `patchmgr` will give proper warnings that a failure has occurred. As with any other software release, it's a good idea to wait a little bit before applying the patches after they have been released. The ability for the platform to provide a single set of patches for every component in the stack is something that no other vendor can offer in terms of the Oracle database.

CHAPTER 17

Unlearning Some Things We Thought We Knew

Oracle can do some things very differently when running on Exadata than when running on non-Exadata platforms. The optimizations provided by Exadata are designed to take a different approach than Oracle has traditionally followed. This change means that you need to attack some problems with a different mindset. That is not to say that everything is different—quite the contrary. In fact, most of the fundamental principles remain unchanged. After all, the same database software runs on Exadata that runs on other platforms. But there are some things that are just different. As you read in Chapter 13, you can just take your database and deploy it 1:1 on Exadata. Depending on the type of deployment, this might be OK. However, if you are interested in getting the most out of your investment, you should probably take a step back and review what you can do to further optimize the database on Exadata. Since there are a few things that are different on Exadata compared to a standard, non-Exadata deployment, this chapter is worth reading for phase 2 of your migration. In this chapter, we will focus on how we should change our approach when running databases on Exadata.

A Tale of Two Systems

The way we think about systems running on Exadata largely depends on the workload being executed. Online-Transaction-Processing (OLTP)-oriented workloads tend to focus us on using Smart Flash Cache for speeding up small physical reads. But frankly, this type of workload is not able to take advantage of most of the performance advantages provided by Exadata. Data-Warehouse (DW)-oriented workloads tend to focus on making use of Smart Scans at every opportunity and trying to use all the available resources (CPU resources on the storage and database tiers, for example). This is where Exadata's built-in advantages can have the most impact. Unfortunately, most systems exhibit characteristics of both DW and OLTP workloads. These "mixed workloads" are the most difficult and, ironically, the most common. They are the most common because it is rare to see an OLTP-oriented system that does not have some reporting component that produces long-running, throughput-sensitive queries. It is also quite common to see DW-oriented workloads that have OLTP-like trickle feeds or similar Extraction, Load, Transformation (ELT) processing needs. These combination systems require the most difficult thought process because, depending on the issue at hand, you will have to be constantly resetting your approach to managing performance. They are also difficult because DW workloads are generally constrained by the data-flow dynamics that control throughput, while OLTP systems are usually constrained by latency issues. Hence, for mixed workloads, you basically need to train yourself to evaluate each scenario and categorize it as either latency-sensitive or throughput-sensitive. This evaluation of workload characteristics should be done prior to beginning any analysis.

If you thought that was an interesting challenge, a third variable can be thrown into the equation. Very few Exadata systems deployed today are home to just one single application. Whereas it used to be quite common to place *the critical application* on Exadata when the first two generations were made available, the increase in capacity for both Smart Flash Cache as well as disk and the ever-increasing CPU power offered by Intel make Exadata an interesting consolidation platform. This has been recognized by many users and, instead of *one* database with mixed workload requirements, you quite often have to arrange the needs of multiple databases—potentially with mixed workload requirements—on your hardware. Thankfully, Oracle offers tools to deal with this situation.

OLTP-Oriented Workloads

Even though there is little to say about running OLTP workloads on Exadata, there are a handful of points to keep in mind with this type of system. Since Exadata runs standard Oracle database software, you should not have to adjust your basic approach significantly.

Exadata Smart Flash Cache (ESFC)

The key component of Exadata when it comes to OLTP workloads is Exadata Smart Flash Cache (ESFC), which can significantly reduce disk-access times for small reads. For that reason, it is important to verify that ESFC is working correctly. For this type of workload, you should also expect that a large percentage of physical I/O operations are being satisfied by ESFC. This can be inferred fairly easily by looking at the average single-block read times. A single-block read should take approximately 0.5 ms if it is satisfied by Flash Cache. By contrast, single-block reads take on average approximately 5 ms if they are satisfied by actual disk reads. Standard AWR reports provide both average values and a histogram of wait events. If the average single-block read times are well above the 1 ms range, you should be looking for a systemic problem—such as flash cards that are not working or a critical table has been defined to never be cached—using the `CELL_FLASH_CACHE NONE` syntax. I/O Resource Management should also be checked. The histograms should be used as well to verify that the average is not covering up a significant number of outliers. Here is the `cellcli` syntax to check the status of the flash cards:

```
CellCLI> list flashcache detail
         name:                   dm01cel03_FLASHCACHE
         cellDisk:               FD_00_dm01cel03,FD_01_dm01cel03,FD_02_dm01cel03,
                                 FD_03_dm01cel03,FD_04_dm01cel03,FD_05_dm01cel03,
                                 FD_06_dm01cel03,FD_07_dm01cel03,FD_08_dm01cel03,
                                 FD_09_dm01cel03,FD_10_dm01cel03,FD_11_dm01cel03,
                                FD_12_dm01cel03,FD_13_dm01cel03,FD_14_dm01cel03,FD_15_dm01cel03
         creationTime:           2010-03-22T17:39:46-05:00
         id:                     850be784-714c-4445-91a8-d3c961ad924b
         size:                   365.25G
         status:                 critical
```

Note that the `status` attribute on this cell is `critical`. As you might expect, this is not a good thing. On this particular system, the Flash Cache had basically disabled itself. We noticed it because the single-block read times had slowed down. This example is from an early version of `cellsrv`. The later versions include a little more information. Here is an example from `cellsrv` 12.1.2.1.0:

```
CellCLI> list flashcache detail
         name:                    enkx4cel01_FLASHCACHE
         cellDisk:                FD_04_enkx4cel01,FD_06_enkx4cel01,FD_11_enkx4cel01,
                                  FD_02_enkx4cel01,FD_13_enkx4cel01,FD_12_enkx4cel01,
                                  FD_00_enkx4cel01,FD_14_enkx4cel01,FD_03_enkx4cel01,
                                  FD_09_enkx4cel01,FD_10_enkx4cel01,FD_15_enkx4cel01,
                                  FD_08_enkx4cel01,FD_07_enkx4cel01,FD_01_enkx4cel01,
                                  FD_05_enkx4cel01
         creationTime:            2015-01-19T21:33:37-06:00
         degradedCelldisks:
         effectiveCacheSize:      5.8193359375T
         id:                      3d415a32-f404-4a27-b9f2-f6a0ace2cee2
         size:                    5.8193359375T
         status:                  normal
```

Notice the new attribute `degradedCelldisks`. Also notice that the Flash Cache on this cell shows a `status` of `normal`. Monitoring storage software behavior is covered in more detail in Chapter 12.

Scalability

Another thing to keep in mind when dealing with OLTP workloads is that the Exadata platform provides exceptional scalability. Upgrading from a half rack to full rack doubles the number of CPUs at both the database layer and the storage layer. The amount of ESFC is also doubled, as is the available memory. This allows Exadata to scale in a nearly linear fashion for many systems.

To add to this point, we can share a little anecdote. When presenting Exadata Smart Scan capabilities during workshops, we used to run a query against a table with all Exadata optimizations disabled, purely hard-disk access at first against an X2-2 quarter rack. When the X4-2 was introduced, we were lucky to have access to an X4-2 half rack. CPU differences aside, the difference between using three cells vs. seven cells was staggering. Add to the mix that most of the table was served via ESFC and you can imagine response times dropping drastically. In order to get back to the timings we were used to, we had to significantly increase the size of the table. This is just one example where Exadata scales very nicely, without any change to the application itself.

Write-Intensive OLTP Workloads

Write-intensive workloads are a subset of OLTP-oriented systems. There are some systems that just constantly perform single-row inserts followed by a commit or, using different words, employing the slow-by-slow (row-by-row) approach. These systems are often limited by the speed at which commits can be done, which often depends on the speed with which writes to the log files can be accomplished. This is one area where Exadata competes with other platforms on a fairly even playing field when operating ESFC in the default write-through mode. There are no major enhancements that make Exadata run orders of magnitudes faster for systems that are bottlenecked on write operations. Flash Logging can help here. Beginning with `cellsrv` 11.2.2.4, Exadata performs redo writes to disk and Flash devices simultaneously. The one that completes first "wins," allowing the log writer to continue processing while the other write is completed. Additionally, the cache on the disk controllers has doubled to 1GB with the X5 hardware generation.

Smart Flash Logging is no magic bullet, and established methods of tuning— such as minimizing commits—are much more appropriate for these types of systems. You would be amazed what changing from row-by-row processing to set-based processing can do in terms of performance, without even having to think about hardware! Many web sites, most prominently perhaps Tom Kyte's, Ask Tom have lots of references showing how row-by-row processing followed by commits every time some work has been performed are suboptimal for performance.

Log Writer is not the only component that longs for low latency I/O performance. Until Exadata version 11.2.3.2.1, using the Smart Flash Cache in write-through mode was the only available option. Beginning with 11.2.3.2.1, it is possible to use Flash Cache in write-back mode. Switching to write-back mode does not remove the need for Flash Log, by the way—after the switch you will still find it defined. Enabling write-back mode can improve performance for write-intensive workloads, as you saw in Chapter 5. However, you should assess carefully if using Write Back Cache is worth it, using the information provided in the aforementioned Chapter 5 on Flash Cache.

DW-Oriented Workloads

Exadata was initially designed to speed up long-running queries against large volumes of data. Therefore, it should come as no surprise that data warehousing is where it is important to change some of our basic thought processes. Of course, one of the major techniques is to be constantly looking for opportunities to allow Exadata optimizations to kick in. This means making sure that the application can take advantage of Smart Scans.

Enabling Smart Scans

The most important concept to keep in mind when dealing with DW-oriented workloads is that long-running statements should usually be offloaded. Here are the steps to follow:

1. Determine whether Smart Scans are being used.
2. If Smart Scans are not being used, fix things so that they will be used.

These points seem so obvious that it should not really be necessary to repeat them. A large portion of the optimizations built into Exadata work only when Smart Scans are used. One of the first changes you need to make in the way you think is to train yourself to be constantly considering whether Smart Scans are being used appropriately or not. This means you need to have a good understanding of which statements (or parts of statements) can be offloaded and be able to determine whether statements are being offloaded or not. The requirements for Smart Scans and some of the techniques that can be used to verify whether they are being performed or not have been covered extensively throughout the book. But at the risk of being repetitive, here you go again.

Essentially, there are two main prerequisites that must be met in order for Smart Scans to occur. The first is that the optimizer must choose to do a full scan of a table or a materialized view, or the optimizer must choose to do a fast full scan of an index. Note that Smart Scans are not limited to queries or even to sub-queries. The optimizer can also choose to use full scans for `DELETE`s and `UPDATE`s when a large percentage of the rows will be affected. However, if your application is doing this, you might want to consider modifying it to do something like a truncate and rebuild. As the saying goes, "it depends".

The second requirement for Smart Scans is that the scans must be performed using the direct path read mechanism. Note that the optimizer was not mentioned intentionally in the description of the second requirement. This is because the optimizer does not make the decision about whether to use direct path reads or not. It is a heuristic decision that is made after the plan has been determined. As such, it is not directly exposed by any of the tools like `explain plan` or other performance-related utilities. What this means in practice is that it is easy to verify that the first requirement has been met, but more challenging to verify the second requirement.

On most Exadata implementations, a fairly high percentage of long-running queries are offloaded. You can check to see what percentage of your long-running SQL statements have been offloaded by selecting all the statements from v$sql (or from the AWR table DBA_HIST_SQLSTAT provided you have the license for it) that have an average run time of over some number of seconds, or that have an average logical I/O value that is greater than some reasonable value. Actually, the logical I/O is a better metric to use, as some of the offloaded statements will run very quickly and may not meet your minimum time criteria, which will give you a distorted perspective on the percentage of statements that are being offloaded. Here is an example (note that the scripts are included in the online code repository):

```
SQL> @offload_percent
Enter value for sql_text:
Enter value for min_etime:
Enter value for min_avg_lio: 500000

     TOTAL  OFFLOADED OFFLOADED_%
-------------------------------
        13         11      84.62%

SQL> /
Enter value for sql_text: SELECT%
Enter value for min_etime:
Enter value for min_avg_lio: 500000

     TOTAL  OFFLOADED OFFLOADED_%
-------------------------------
        11         11        100%
```

The listing makes use of the offload_percent.sql script, which calculates a percentage of statements currently in the shared pool that have been offloaded. It was initially used to evaluate all statements that had over 500,000 logical I/Os. It was run a second time where the investigation was limited to statements that begin with the word SELECT. In the next listing, you can see the output of a different script (fsxo.sql) that allows you to see the actual statements that contribute to the OFFLOAD_% calculated in the previous listing:

```
SQL> @fsxo
Enter value for sql_text:
Enter value for sql_id:
Enter value for min_etime:
Enter value for min_avg_lio: 500000
Enter value for offloaded:

SQL_ID          EXECS  AVG_ETIME OFFLOAD IO_SAVED_% SQL_TEXT
----------------------------------------------------------------------------------
0bvt5z48t18by       1        .10 Yes         100.00 select count(*) from skew3 whe
0jytfr1y0jdr1       1        .09 Yes         100.00 select count(*) from skew3 whe
12pkwt8zjdhbx       1        .09 Yes         100.00 select count(*) from skew3 whe
2zbt555tg123s       2       4.37 Yes          71.85 select /*+ parallel (a 8) */ a
412n404yughsy       1        .09 Yes         100.00 select count(*) from skew3 whe
5zruc4v6y32f9       5      51.13 No             .00 DECLARE job BINARY_INTEGER :=
6dx247rvykr72       1        .10 Yes         100.00 select count(*) from skew3 whe
6uutdmqr72smc       2      32.83 Yes          71.85 select /* avgskew3.sql */ avg(
7y09dtyuc4dbh       1       2.87 Yes          71.83 select avg(pk_col) from kso.sk
```

```
b6usrg82hwsa3      5      83.81 No          .00 call dbms_stats.gather_databas
fvx3vOwpvxvwt      1      11.05 Yes       99.99 select count(*) from skew3 whe
gcq9a53z7szjt      1        .09 Yes      100.00 select count(*) from skew3 whe
gs35v5t21d9yf      1       8.02 Yes       99.99 select count(*) from skew3 whe

13 rows selected.
```

The `fsxo.sql` script provides the same limiting factors as the `offload_percent.sql` script, namely a minimum average elapsed time and a minimum average logical I/O. It also optionally allows you to limit the statements to only those that are offloaded or those that are not offloaded. Please refer to the scripts for further details and keep in mind that these techniques can also be applied to the data recorded by AWR for a historical perspective.

In the next section, we will discuss some issues that can complicate your efforts to enable Smart Scans.

Things That Can Cripple Smart Scans

There are several common coding "techniques" that either disable Smart Scans completely or cause them to be much less effective than they could be. Some of the techniques are just bad practices, regardless of whether you are on the Exadata platform or not. Others do not carry as significant a penalty on non-Exadata platforms, but, when run on Exadata, they can prevent the storage software from doing all that it could do. That is a common observation that can be made when development is located on a non-Exadata platform. Such a system makes developing a well-performing application difficult at best. Ensuring that an application performs on a non-Exadata system will most likely use techniques that do not lend themselves for best performance on the Exadata platform, and additional work is needed to optimize the code once on Exadata.

Many of these issues have been discussed throughout this book. Here are a few that you should keep in mind because of the fundamentally different behavior on the Exadata platform.

Functions in WHERE Clauses

Oracle provides a large set of functions that can be applied directly in SQL statements. As discussed in Chapter 2, not all of those functions are offloadable. Knowing which functions are not offloadable is important because the use of those functions in `WHERE` clauses disables predicate filtering that may otherwise provide a massive reduction in the amount of data to be transferred back to the database layer. Obviously, custom-written PL/SQL functions fall into the category of "non-offloadable" functions as well.

This issue is somewhat counterintuitive since you are often doing full table scans anyway with data warehouse systems. On non-Exadata platforms, applying a function in a `WHERE` clause of a statement that is executed via a full table scan does not impose much of a penalty with regard to the amount of data that must be returned because the database must already return all blocks from the table to the database server. With Exadata, though, applying a function that can disable predicate filtering can impose a huge performance penalty. By the way, using custom PL/SQL functions in a `WHERE` clause is generally also a bad idea on non-Exadata platforms because additional CPU will be required to process PL/SQL for each row, as opposed to the optimized functions, based on C code, provided by Oracle.

■ **Note** You can query `V$SQLFN_METADATA` to see which functions are offloadable.

Furthermore, "offloadable" functions can also impose large performance penalties. Here is a very simple example showing the negative effect of an offloadable function in a WHERE clause:

```
SQL> select /* example001 */ count(*) from SALES where prod_id < 1;

  COUNT(*)
----------
         0

Elapsed: 00:00:00.75
SQL> select /* example001 */ count(*) from SALES where abs(prod_id) < 1;

  COUNT(*)
----------
         0

Elapsed: 00:00:34.26
SQL> @fsx4
Enter value for sql_text: %example001%
Enter value for sql_id:

SQL_ID          CHILD OFFLOAD IO_SAVED_%  AVG_ETIME SQL_TEXT
------------- ------ ------- ---------- ---------- ----------------------------------------
7ttw461bngzn0      0 Yes         100.00        .75 select /* example001 */ count(*) from SA
fktc9145xy6qg      0 Yes          99.98      33.81 select /* example001 */ count(*) from SA

Elapsed: 00:00:00.08
SQL> select name, offloadable from v$sqlfn_metadata
  2  where name = 'ABS';

NAME                           OFF
------------------------------ ---
ABS                            YES
ABS                            YES
ABS                            YES

3 rows selected.
```

ABS() is an offloadable function, yet when used in the WHERE clause of this particular statement, the result was a large degradation in performance. If you have been following this example on your own environment, you may already have a pretty good idea why. Here is the solution:

```
SQL> select name,value from v$statname natural join v$mystat
  2  where name like '%storage index%';

NAME                                                                  VALUE
---------------------------------------------------------------- ----------
cell physical IO bytes saved by storage index                              0

SQL> set timing on
SQL> select /* example001 */ count(*) from SALES where abs(prod_id) < 1;
```

```
  COUNT(*)
----------
         0

Elapsed: 00:00:33.90
SQL> select name,value from v$statname natural join v$mystat where name like '%storage
index%';

NAME                                                                  VALUE
---------------------------------------------------------------- ----------
cell physical IO bytes saved by storage index                             0

Elapsed: 00:00:00.00
SQL> select /* example001 */ count(*) from SALES where prod_id < 1;

  COUNT(*)
----------
         0

Elapsed: 00:00:00.76
SQL> select name,value from v$statname natural join v$mystat where name like '%storage
index%';

NAME                                                                  VALUE
---------------------------------------------------------------- ----------
cell physical IO bytes saved by storage index                    1.4517E+11

Elapsed: 00:00:00.00
```

Storage indexes are disabled by functions, just like regular indexes. This is not too surprising, but, again, it can easily be missed. When we see a full scan, we have trained ourselves to not worry about functions in the `WHERE` clause that could disable indexes. Exadata is different.

Chained Rows

This is a very broad generalization, but basically any Oracle processing that requires reading an extra block to complete a row causes the Exadata storage software to revert to block shipping or *passthrough* mode. You read about this in several places in the previous chapters-Chapter 11 specifically provides most details. A simple example is a chained row, but there are other situations that can cause Oracle to revert to passthrough mode. What this means in practice is that some operations that cause slight delays on non-Exadata platforms can potentially have a more severely impact performance on Exadata. The primary diagnostic symptom of this issue is the presence of many single-block-read wait events in combination with cell Smart Scan wait events. In such situations, you may find that you are better off not using offloading for the statements in question as an immediate remedy before addressing the problem more thoroughly. Here is an example showing where Oracle spends its time when selecting from a table with chained rows during the first execution. The example is specifically engineered to exaggerate the problem and make it reproducible, as the dictionary information about the table shows.

```
SQL> select num_rows,chain_cnt,avg_row_len from tabs where table_name = 'CHAINS';

  NUM_ROWS  CHAIN_CNT AVG_ROW_LEN
---------- ---------- -----------
    600000     600000       20005

1 row selected.

SQL> select segment_name,partition_name,round(bytes/power(1024,3),2) gb
  2   from user_segments
  3  where segment_name = 'CHAINS';

SEGMENT_NAME                   PARTITION_NAME                         GB
------------------------------ ------------------------------ ----------
CHAINS                                                             12.75

SQL> alter system flush buffer_cache;

System altered.

SQL> select /*+ gather_plan_statistics monitor */ avg(length(col2)) from chains;

AVG(LENGTH(C))
--------------
          3990

1 row selected.
```

An investigation into where the execution time is spent could see the following commands being used:

```
SQL> select * from table(dbms_xplan.display_cursor);

PLAN_TABLE_OUTPUT
-----------------------------------------------------------------------------------------
--
SQL_ID  6xpsmzknmkutw, child number 0
-------------------------------------
select /*+ gather_plan_statistics monitor */ avg(length(col2)) from chains

Plan hash value: 1270987893

---------------------------------------------------------------------------------
| Id  | Operation                  | Name   | Rows  | Bytes | Cost (%CPU)| Time     |
---------------------------------------------------------------------------------
|   0 | SELECT STATEMENT           |        |       |       |   450K(100)|          |
|   1 |  SORT AGGREGATE            |        |     1 |  3990 |            |          |
|   2 |   TABLE ACCESS STORAGE FULL| CHAINS |   600K|  2283M|   450K  (1)| 00:00:18 |
---------------------------------------------------------------------------------
```

Please note that the above output shows the *estimates* for time and number of rows returned by the query. If you want the *actual* statistics, either use SQL Monitor (provided you have the license to) or provide ALLSTATS LAST as the format parameter in DBMS_XPLAN.DISPLAY_CURSOR. Other useful tools include session snapper and fsx- family of scripts mentioned in Chapter 2. Querying Active Session History (which also requires a license) can also provide interesting insights into what is currently happening, but make sure you filter appropriately. Ultimately, a trace will reveal every single wait that occurred. After processing the raw trace file, the following information has been gathered. The actual processing time is prolonged due to the large number of entries in the trace file:

```
SQL ID: 6xpsmzknmkutw Plan Hash: 1270987893

select /*+ gather_plan_statistics monitor */ avg(length(col2)) from chains

call     count       cpu    elapsed       disk      query    current        rows
------- ------  -------- ---------- ---------- ---------- ----------  ----------
Parse        1      0.00       0.00          0          0          0           0
Execute      1      0.00       0.00          0          0          0           0
Fetch        2     95.91     497.32    2321346    2321394          0           1
------- ------  -------- ---------- ---------- ---------- ----------  ----------
total        4     95.91     497.32    2321346    2321394          0           1

Misses in library cache during parse: 1
Optimizer mode: ALL_ROWS
Parsing user id: 65
Number of plan statistics captured: 1

Rows (1st) Rows (avg) Rows (max) Row Source Operation
---------- ---------- ---------- ---------------------------------------------------
         1          1          1 SORT AGGREGATE (cr=2321394 pr=2321346 pw=0 time=497324130 us)
    600000     600000     600000  TABLE ACCESS STORAGE FULL CHAINS (cr=2321394 pr=2321346 pw=0
                                     time=484769611 us cost=450678 size=2394000000 card=600000)

 Elapsed times include waiting on following events:
   Event waited on                             Times   Max. Wait  Total Waited
   ----------------------------------------   Waited  ----------  ------------
   row cache lock                                  5        0.00          0.00
   Disk file operations I/O                        2        0.00          0.00
   SQL*Net message to client                       2        0.00          0.00
   cell single block physical read            660743        0.42        448.04
   enq: KO - fast object checkpoint                3        0.00          0.00
   reliable message                                1        0.00          0.00
   cell smart table scan                        1681        0.00          0.45
   latch: redo allocation                          1        0.00          0.00
   SQL*Net message from client                     2       16.25         16.25
********************************************************************************
```

In this example, a query was executed against a table in which every row was chained (again a bit of an extreme, but a 100%-reproducible example). Before starting the execution of the main query, a 10046/SQL Trace was started, which ran throughout the execution of the statement. You saw the output of `tkrprof` on the trace file, which produced the list of wait events just shown. Notice that the statement had an elapsed time of about 8 minutes (497 seconds), of which the vast majority was spent doing single-block physical reads. The statement used a full table scan and was clearly offloaded in parts, as indicated by the cell smart table scan wait events, but it spent most of its time doing single-block reads. Of course, the single-block reads were a result of the chained rows. The next listing shows the difference between running the query with offloading and without offloading. First, the example with all Exadata features disabled:

```
SQL> alter session set "_serial_direct_read"=always;

Session altered.

Elapsed: 00:00:00.01
SQL> alter session set cell_offload_processing=false;

Session altered.

Elapsed: 00:00:00.00
SQL> alter system flush buffer_cache;

System altered.

Elapsed: 00:00:01.99
SQL> select /*+ gather_plan_statistics monitor */ avg(length(col2)) from chains;

AVG(LENGTH(COL2))
-----------------
             3990

Elapsed: 00:00:50.10
```

As you can see with all offloading disabled and direct path reads, the execution time is 50 seconds. The rows are still chained—nothing has happened to the table. In the next example, direct path reads are disabled as well:

```
SQL> alter session set "_serial_direct_read"=never;

Session altered.

Elapsed: 00:00:00.01
SQL> alter system flush buffer_cache;

System altered.

Elapsed: 00:00:00.14
SQL> select /*+ gather_plan_statistics monitor */ avg(length(col2)) from chains;

AVG(LENGTH(COL2))
-----------------
             3990

Elapsed: 00:00:28.33
```

And, finally, everything back to default—cell offloading enabled and Smart Scans:

```
SQL> alter session set "_serial_direct_read"=always;

Session altered.

Elapsed: 00:00:00.00
SQL> alter session set cell_offload_processing=true;

Session altered.

Elapsed: 00:00:00.00
SQL> alter system flush buffer_cache;

System altered.

Elapsed: 00:00:00.08
SQL> select /*+ gather_plan_statistics monitor */ avg(length(col2)) from chains;

AVG(LENGTH(COL2))
-----------------
             3990

Elapsed: 00:07:02.29
```

Ouch—the last example clearly showed severe performance degradation. However, it is very important at this stage to point out that this is the most extreme example, as every row was chained. In fact, many of the records spanned three blocks. In this extreme case, it is clear that avoiding offloading actually improves the performance significantly. Of course, eliminating the chained rows where possible would be the best solution.

Very Busy Cells

When a storage cell becomes very busy with CPU operations, it is possible for the storage software to begin refusing to perform offload activities on some portion of the requests. That is, if a particular cell becomes extremely busy and is getting offloadable requests from a database server that is not particularly busy, it may decide to send some data back to the database server that has not been processed or has only partially been processed. In some cases, column projection may be done but not filtering; in other cases, `cellsrv` may revert to shipping entire blocks back to the database layer. While this issue does not result in a complete shutdown of offloading, it can reduce the amount of work that is done on the storage tier.

This is an extremely complex topic, and it is difficult to observe the behavior directly. The goal of the feature is to utilize available CPU resources, regardless of whether they are on the database tier or the storage tier. This behavior was introduced in `cellsrv` version 11.2.2.3.1 with databases running 11.2.0.2 with bundle patch 6 or later. There is a statistic called `cell physical IO bytes pushed back due to excessive CPU on cell` in 11.2.0.2 with BP 6 and later that shows this is happening. Note that the statistic name later changed to `cell physical IO bytes sent directly to DB node to balance CPU`. The feature is designed to improve throughput on very busy systems, but it may also cause some degree of instability in the performance of certain statements. It is possible to disable this feature if your `cellsrv` is erroneously deciding it is too busy to take on additional work; however, in general, if you observe this behavior, you are probably getting close to the limits of the system. Adding additional resources at the storage layer (more storage cells) may be a viable option if reducing the load created is not possible.

Hinted Code

Hints are very useful for coercing the optimizer to do what you want it to do. Unfortunately, hints are not well documented and even less well understood. In many cases, hints are used to resolve a problem that is caused by some misconfiguration of the database (and then forgotten during the upgrade, potentially causing problems with the new major release). Their intended purpose is to allow humans to help the optimizer make the right choices in situations where it just cannot do the job effectively (or consistently) on its own. This happens in situations where the optimizer is just not smart enough (yet) to arrive at the best execution plan in a specific situation. However, even when hints are used appropriately and are generating the expected behavior, they can prevent Exadata from taking advantage of some of its built-in abilities. When migrating to Exadata, the best approach is to allow ample time for testing. If your application makes use of hints, one of the important steps in the test plan should be to test its behavior without the hints. This can easily be accomplished by setting the hidden parameter `_optimizer_ignore_hints` to "true" in a session for the upgrade/regression test. Only after the unnecessary hints have been weeded out should the system go into production on Exadata. Ultimately, it is far easier to remove hints when the migration testing is performed than after the system is live. You simply have more resources and time dedicated to testing!

Indexes

This may seem like a strange topic, but indexes can work against Smart Scans as well. The optimizer will try to use indexes if they are available. In a pure data warehouse environment, analytic indexes may not be necessary at all. You are about to read more about indexes in the next section on mixed workloads, but it is important to understand that index usage often means that offloading is less likely to occur.

Row-at-a-Time Processing

It is amazing how often we see row-at-a-time processing in very large data sets. This type of coding is rarely a good idea on non-Exadata platforms, and it is definitely not a good idea on Exadata. In fact, the differences in performance can be even more dramatic on Exadata because of the optimizations built into the platform.

Other Things to Keep in Mind

There are a few other things that you should keep in mind when working with DW systems: the use of Exadata Smart Flash Cache, compression, and partitioning.

Exadata Smart Flash Cache: To Keep or Not to Keep

Exadata Smart Flash Cache (EFSC) is thought of primarily as providing benefit to latency-sensitive SQL statements, satisfying single-block reads from faster Flash devices. What is good for single-block I/O cannot be bad for multi-block I/O. In this context, it is important to remember that scanning from Flash can dramatically improve scan performance as well. Up until Exadata version 11.2.3.3.0, Smart Scans ignore ESFC and only scan using hard disks by default. In version 11.2.3.3.0 and later, Smart Scans can and will transparently cache data in the Flash Cache, too. That particular Exadata feature had a radical effect on the way scans were performed on the platform. From that release onward, scan performance has improved by many magnitudes. Transparently storing entire segments or parts thereof in ESFC will benefit both Smart Scans as well as non-offloaded single- and multi-block reads. The new feature largely eliminates the fine-tuning of which objects may use Flash Cache by using the segment's storage clause for those segments critical for processing.

If you want to demonstrate the usefulness of ESFC for table scans in current Exadata versions, you have to reverse the situation from before 11.2.3.3.0: Instead of pinning segments to Flash Cache to enable Smart Scans from benefiting from ESFC, you specifically have to forbid segments from using it. The following two tables are 100% identical, with the exception that table T1_NOCOMPRESS_NOESFC is forbidden to benefit from ESFC.

```
SQL> select table_name, num_rows, compression, partitioned, cell_flash_cache
  2  from tabs where table_name like 'T1_NOCOMPRESS%';

TABLE_NAME                          NUM_ROWS COMPRESS PAR CELL_FL
------------------------------ ------------- -------- --- -------
T1_NOCOMPRESS_NOESFC                10000000 DISABLED NO  NONE
T1_NOCOMPRESS                       10000000 DISABLED NO  DEFAULT

2 rows selected.

SQL> select segment_name, bytes/power(1024,2) m, blocks
  2  from user_segments where segment_name like 'T1_NOCOMPRESS%';

SEGMENT_NAME                            M     BLOCKS
------------------------------ ---------- ----------
T1_NOCOMPRESS                       13056    1671168
T1_NOCOMPRESS_NOESFC                13056    1671168

2 rows selected.
```

In preparation for the demonstration, a number of full scans were executed against T1_NOCOMPRESS so as to ensure that the table contents are largely found in Flash Cache. Remember from Chapter 5 that you can use cellcli's list flashcachecontents command to see what is actually cached on a cell. A Smart Scan against T1_NOCOMPRESS will set the baseline for the comparison:

```
SQL> select count(*) from T1_NOCOMPRESS;

  COUNT(*)
----------
  10000000

Elapsed: 00:00:01.24
```

The query has deliberately been chosen to not feature a WHERE clause to rule out any optimization by storage indexes. There are no indexes involved either, as you can see from the execution plan:

```
SQL> select * from table(dbms_xplan.display_cursor)
  2  /

PLAN_TABLE_OUTPUT
-------------------------------------------------------------------------------------
SQL_ID  38ttfy95yg3sd, child number 0
-------------------------------------
select count(*) from T1_NOCOMPRESS
```

```
Plan hash value: 3825536868

-----------------------------------------------------------------------------------
| Id  | Operation                  | Name           | Rows  | Cost (%CPU)| Time     |
-----------------------------------------------------------------------------------
|   0 | SELECT STATEMENT           |                |       |   452K(100)|          |
|   1 |  SORT AGGREGATE            |                |     1 |            |          |
|   2 |   TABLE ACCESS STORAGE FULL| T1_NOCOMPRESS  |   10M|   452K  (1)| 00:00:18 |
-----------------------------------------------------------------------------------

14 rows selected.
```

Digging into the execution statistics using session snapper or `mystats.sql`, you can see that lots of the read requests are optimized. The output below is taken from `mystats`; statistics not necessary for this discussion have been removed:

```
------------------------------------------------------------------------------------------
2. Statistics Report
------------------------------------------------------------------------------------------

Type    Statistic Name                                                         Value
------  ----------------------------------------------------------------  ---------------
STAT    cell IO uncompressed bytes                                         13,653,352,448
STAT    cell blocks helped by minscn optimization                               1,666,679
STAT    cell flash cache read hits                                                 11,576
STAT    cell physical IO bytes eligible for predicate offload              13,653,336,064
STAT    cell physical IO interconnect bytes returned by smart scan            269,067,552
STAT    cell scans                                                                      1
STAT    physical read IO requests                                                  13,048
STAT    physical read bytes                                                13,653,336,064
STAT    physical read requests optimized                                           11,576
STAT    physical read total IO requests                                            13,048
STAT    physical read total bytes                                          13,653,336,064
STAT    physical read total bytes optimized                                12,111,839,232
STAT    physical read total multi block requests                                   13,037
STAT    physical reads                                                          1,666,667
STAT    physical reads direct                                                   1,666,667

------------------------------------------------------------------------------------------
3. About
------------------------------------------------------------------------------------------
- MyStats v2.01 by Adrian Billington (http://www.oracle-developer.net)
- Based on the SNAP_MY_STATS utility by Jonathan Lewis
```

You can see that out of all these, approximately 13GB read using 13,048 I/O requests, a large portion was satisfied via Flash Cache, namely 11,576. You can put this into perspective by comparing physical read total bytes optimized to physical read total bytes. And, by the way, once the data is in Flash Cache, traditional single-block and multi-block reads will benefit from the fact that the segment is on faster storage, too, at no extra penalty.

On the other hand, if a table cannot benefit from ESFC such as T1_NOCOMPRESS_NOESFC, things look a little different:

```
SQL> select count(*) from T1_NOCOMPRESS_NOESFC;

  COUNT(*)
----------
  10000000

Elapsed: 00:00:11.27
```

Repeated executions of the statement cannot have an effect: There will not be any caching on Flash Cache as this operation is administratively prohibited. The execution plan is identical to the first one shown:

```
PLAN_TABLE_OUTPUT
-----------------------------------------------------------------------------------------------
SQL_ID  9gdnw7yk14mpw, child number 0
-------------------------------------
select count(*) from T1_NOCOMPRESS_NOESFC

Plan hash value: 4286875364

----------------------------------------------------------------------------------------------
| Id  | Operation                   | Name                 | Rows  | Cost (%CPU)| Time     |
----------------------------------------------------------------------------------------------
|   0 | SELECT STATEMENT            |                      |       |   452K(100)|          |
|   1 |  SORT AGGREGATE             |                      |     1 |            |          |
|   2 |   TABLE ACCESS STORAGE FULL| T1_NOCOMPRESS_NOESFC |   10M|   452K  (1)| 00:00:18 |
----------------------------------------------------------------------------------------------

14 rows selected.
```

Interestingly, the optimizer assumes the same elapsed time for the scan, namely 18 seconds. The difference in the execution time can be found in the execution statistics:

```
------------------------------------------------------------------------------------------
2. Statistics Report
------------------------------------------------------------------------------------------

Type    Statistic Name                                                     Value
------  --------------------------------------------------------  ---------------
STAT    cell IO uncompressed bytes                                   13,653,336,064
STAT    cell physical IO bytes eligible for predicate offload        13,653,336,064
STAT    cell physical IO interconnect bytes returned by smart scan      269,067,184
STAT    cell scans                                                                1
STAT    physical read IO requests                                            13,046
STAT    physical read bytes                                          13,653,336,064
STAT    physical read total IO requests                                      13,046
STAT    physical read total bytes                                    13,653,336,064
STAT    physical read total multi block requests                             13,037
STAT    physical reads                                                    1,666,667
STAT    physical reads direct                                             1,666,667
```

```
--------------------------------------------------------------------------------
3. About
--------------------------------------------------------------------------------
- MyStats v2.01 by Adrian Billington (http://www.oracle-developer.net)
- Based on the SNAP_MY_STATS utility by Jonathan Lewis
```

The effect of Flash Cache is visible in the I/O-related statistics in `V$SQL`, you can query `physical_read_requests` and `optimized_phy_read_requests`. The output is rearranged for better readability:

```
SQL> @fsx4.sql
Enter value for sql_text: %esfc_example%
Enter value for sql_id:

SQL_ID         CHILD OFFLOAD IO_SAVED_% AVG_ETIME SQL_TEXT
------------- ------ ------- ---------- ---------- ------------------------------------- ...
aqmusjaqj5yy6      0 Yes          98.03       9.23 select /* esfc_example */ count(*) from ...
g85ux15kbh9hr      0 Yes          98.03       1.23 select /* esfc_example */ count(*) from ...

... SQL_ID        PHYSICAL_READ_REQUESTS OPTIMIZED_PHY_READ_REQUESTS
... ------------- ---------------------- ---------------------------
... aqmusjaqj5yy6                  13046                           0
... g85ux15kbh9hr                  13046                       11576

2 rows selected.
```

Thankfully, a lot of the complexity around pinning segments to Flash Cache has been resolved with the introduction of Exadata 11.2.3.3. And you do not even have to spend too much time thinking about it. In the output of the query against `user_tables` shown earlier, you will notice that the attributes to `cell_flash_cache` are `NONE` and `DEFAULT`, but none of them is set to `KEEP`. For the transparent caching of data for Smart Scans alone, it was worth upgrading to 11.2.3.3.

Compression

Exadata's Hybrid Columnar Compression (HCC) is a big step forward in its ability to reduce the size of data stored inside of Oracle databases. The compression ratios that are achievable with HCC turn the traditional concept of information life-cycle management on its head. HCC makes it practical to consider using compression instead of tiered storage or archiving and purging strategies. Because partitions of a table can be defined to use different compression methods, the combination of partitioning and compression can provide a much more robust solution for "archiving" data than actually purging it from the database.

You should remember, though, that HCC is not appropriate for data that is being subject to DML. A better approach is to partition data such that HCC can be applied to data that is no longer being changed. This leads us to the next topic—partitioning.

Partitioning

Partitioning has been and still is a very key component for data warehousing systems. The optimizations provided by Exadata do not alleviate the need for a well thought-out partitioning strategy. Of course, date-based strategies are very useful from a management standpoint. Being able to use more aggressive compression on older data is often a good approach. But partition elimination is still a technique that you will want to use. And, of course, storage indexes can work well with partitioning, providing behavior comparable to partition elimination on additional columns.

You should keep in mind that the sizes of partitions can affect Oracle's decision to use Smart Scans. When performing a serial scan on a partitioned object, the decision to do direct path reads is based on the individual segment (table, partition, subpartition) size, not the overall size of the object. This can result in situations where scans of some partitions are offloaded, while scans of others are not. This is particularly relevant for colder partitions that have been compressed. Consider a table created with a number of random dates, range partitioned by date using monthly intervals:

```
SQL> select segment_name, partition_name, bytes/power(1024,2) m
  2  from user_segments where segment_name= 'SMARTSCANHCC';

SEGMENT_NAME                   PARTITION_NAME                         M
------------------------------ ------------------------------ ---------
SMARTSCANHCC                   SYS_P9676                            944
SMARTSCANHCC                   SYS_P9677                            968
SMARTSCANHCC                   SYS_P9678                            384

3 rows selected.

SQL> select partition_name, high_value from user_tab_partitions
  2  where table_name = 'SMARTSCANHCC'

PARTITION_NAME                 HIGH_VALUE
------------------------------ --------------------------------------------------
P_START                        TO_DATE(' 1995-01-01 00:00:00', 'SYYYY-MM-DD HH24:
SYS_P9676                      TO_DATE(' 2014-05-01 00:00:00', 'SYYYY-MM-DD HH24:
SYS_P9677                      TO_DATE(' 2014-09-01 00:00:00', 'SYYYY-MM-DD HH24:
SYS_P9678                      TO_DATE(' 2014-10-01 00:00:00', 'SYYYY-MM-DD HH24:

SQL> select partition_name, last_analyzed, num_rows from user_tab_partitions
  2  where table_name = 'SMARTSCANHCC';

PARTITION_NAME                 LAST_ANALYZED         NUM_ROWS
------------------------------ ------------------- ----------
P_START                        2015-03-15:16:31:52          0
SYS_P9676                      2015-03-15:16:31:55     837426
SYS_P9677                      2015-03-15:16:31:58     863109
SYS_P9678                      2015-03-15:16:31:59     335539

4 rows selected.
```

The table is interval-partitioned, partition P_START is empty, and—thanks to deferred segment creation—has not even be created. The size of the partitions enables Smart Scans. The SQL Monitor report has been cut down to fit the page, and only relevant information is shown:

```
SQL Monitoring Report

SQL Text
------------------------------
select /*+ monitor gather_plan_statistics */ count(*) from smartscanhcc partition (SYS_P9676)
```

```
Global Information
------------------------------
 Status              :  DONE (ALL ROWS)
 Instance ID         :  1
 Session             :  MARTIN (591:27854)
 SQL ID              :  76yr0u2rhkqq8
 SQL Execution ID    :  16777217
 Execution Started   :  03/15/2015 16:32:52
 First Refresh Time  :  03/15/2015 16:32:52
 Last Refresh Time   :  03/15/2015 16:32:53
 Duration            :  1s
 Module/Action       :  SQL*Plus/-
 Service             :  SYS$USERS
 Program             :  sqlplus@enkdb03.enkitec.com (TNS V1-V3)
 Fetch Calls         :  1

Global Stats
=========================================================================================
| Elapsed |   Cpu   |    IO    | Application | Fetch | Buffer | Read | Read  |  Cell   |
| Time(s) | Time(s) | Waits(s) |  Waits(s)   | Calls |  Gets  | Reqs | Bytes | Offload |
=========================================================================================
|    0.33 |    0.13 |     0.21 |        0.00 |     1 |   120K |  940 | 935MB |  97.64% |
=========================================================================================
```

Imagine next that the partition undergoes maintenance and is HCC compressed:

```
SQL> alter table smartscanhcc modify partition SYS_P9676 column store compress for query
high;

Table altered.

SQL> alter table smartscanhcc move partition SYS_P9676;

Table altered.

SQL> select segment_name, partition_name, bytes/power(1024,2) m
  2  from user_segments where segment_name= 'SMARTSCANHCC';

SEGMENT_NAME                   PARTITION_NAME                          M
------------------------------ ------------------------------ ----------
SMARTSCANHCC                   SYS_P9677                             968
SMARTSCANHCC                   SYS_P9678                             384
SMARTSCANHCC                   SYS_P9676                              16

3 rows selected.
```

As expected, the compressed size of this partition smaller than it was before. If a user now executes a query against the segment, it is most likely not Smart Scanned. And, indeed, this can be confirmed, for example by using a SQL Monitor report (alternatively if you do not have the license to use it, you can query V$SQL):

```
SQL Monitoring Report

SQL Text
------------------------------
select /*+ monitor gather_plan_statistics */ count(*) from smartscanhcc partition (SYS_P9676)

Global Information
------------------------------
 Status              :  DONE (ALL ROWS)
 Instance ID         :  1
 Session             :  MARTIN (1043:51611)
 SQL ID              :  76yr0u2rhkqq8
 SQL Execution ID    :  16777216
 Execution Started   :  06/09/2015 11:02:38
 First Refresh Time  :  06/09/2015 11:02:38
 Last Refresh Time   :  06/09/2015 11:02:38
 Duration            :  .123527s
 Module/Action       :  SQL*Plus/-
 Service             :  SYS$USERS
 Program             :  sqlplus@enkdb03.enkitec.com (TNS V1-V3)
 Fetch Calls         :  1

Global Stats
=========================================================================================
| Elapsed |   Cpu   |    IO    | Cluster  |  Other   | Fetch | Buffer | Read | Read  |
| Time(s) | Time(s) | Waits(s) | Waits(s) | Waits(s) | Calls |  Gets  | Reqs | Bytes |
=========================================================================================
|    0.12 |    0.02 |     0.09 |     0.00 |     0.01 |     1 |   1245 |   11 |  10MB |
=========================================================================================
```

The missing column about cell offload efficiency is an indicator for a traditional read and the absence of a Smart Scan. There are cases when the absence of a Smart Scan does not matter when partitions are small. In the above example the data set was reduced from 944MB to 16MB. These can be read very quickly if you looked at the elapsed time.

Mixed Workloads

There is a third type of system that is a combination of the other two. In fact, one could argue that the pure form of the other two (OLTP and DW) rarely exist in the real world. There are many systems that do not fall neatly into the two main categories already described. In fact, most systems display characteristics of both. Consider, for example, the case where an "OLTP" system is performing short, distinct little transactions during the day with a lot of reporting during the evening hours. Or take the point of view of the data warehouse where you run lots of reports but have a scheduled ELT (Extraction Load Transform) process that makes generous use of the merge clause, which of course requires a lookup.

Combining long-running, throughput-sensitive queries with fast, latency-sensitive statements definitely introduces some additional issues that must be dealt with. One of the main issues in systems of this type is how to deal with indexes.

To Index or Not to Index?

One of the biggest debates we have had during Exadata implementations is whether to drop indexes or not. The problem has somewhat been exacerbated by claims that you do not need any indexes on Exadata. Access paths that use indexes are generally not able to take advantage of Exadata-specific optimizations. Yes, you read that right—it is generally because offloading can occur in cases where the optimizer chooses to execute a fast full scan on an index, but this is not the most common usage pattern for indexes. The more common pattern is to use them for retrieving relatively few records from a table using an index range scan, and this operation is not currently offloadable. Generally speaking, you will want to use index range scans on selective predicates. However, since Exadata is so effective at scanning disks, in many cases the index-based access paths are no longer faster than the scan-based access operations. The frequency of how many times this query is executed starts to play an important role. If you are scanning a multi-million-row table in a couple of seconds, then this is undoubtedly fast. However, if you need to do this 10,000 times during a merge an index on the lookup might speed things up. It is really a case of getting our bearings all over again with respect to when we want to use indexes and when we would expect a full scan to perform better.

One of the things we commonly heard when Exadata was first starting to appear at customer sites was that indexes were no longer necessary and that they should be dropped. For pure data warehouse workloads, this may actually be reasonably good advice for analytical indexes. However, we rarely see anything you could call a “pure data warehouse” workload. Most systems have a mix of access patterns, with one set of statements hoping for low latency and another set hoping for high throughput. In these cases, dropping all indexes just will not work. This is why this discussion was saved for this section. The problem with mixed workloads, where it is necessary to keep indexes for specific sets of statements, is that the optimizer is not as well equipped to choose between using and ignoring them as one might hope. However there might be a way around this situation by making creative use of invisible indexes. This 11g feature allows you to hide indexes from the optimizer when it comes to developing an execution plan. The indexes are still there and will also be maintained, so you might want to review index use. Not every index needs to be dropped, but, likewise, not every analytical index needs to be kept.

The following example is a relatively simple implementation on how to have indexes in the database but make only selective use of them. The `dbm01` database has been modified, and two services have been created and started. DSSSRV, as the name implies, is a service users should use when performing decision support queries or those with high demand on throughput and less need for low latency. As you would imagine, the opposite is true for the OLTPSRV. Users connecting through that service care a lot for low latency but less for bandwidth. A small PL/SQL procedure can be written to check which service a session used to connect and change the parameter `optimizer_use_invisible_indexes`. The index on table `T1_WITH_INDEX` is invisible:

```
SQL> select index_name, visibility
  2  from user_indexes
  3  where index_name = 'I_T1_WITH_INDEXES_1';

INDEX_NAME                     VISIBILIT
------------------------------ ---------
I_T1_WITH_INDEXES_1            INVISIBLE
```

The little procedure being used here just checks for the service name and changes the optimizer’s visibility of the index:

```
SQL> create procedure check_service is
  2  begin
  3   if lower(sys_context('userenv','service:name')) = 'dsssrv' then
  4    execute immediate 'alter session set optimizer_use_invisible_indexes = false';
  5   elsif lower(sys_context('userenv','service:name')) = 'oltpsrv' then
```

```
    execute immediate 'alter session set optimizer_use_invisible_indexes = true';
  end if;
end;
/

Procedure created.
```

The following execution plans show that the index is used based on the service the session connects through. The first example uses the OLTPSRV connection:

```
SQL> select sys_context('userenv','service:name') from dual;

SYS_CONTEXT('USERENV','SERVICE_NAME')
------------------------------------------------------------------------------------------
oltpsrv

SQL> exec check_service

SQL> select /* oltpsrv */ count(*) from t1_with_index where id between 200 and 400;

  COUNT(*)
----------
       201

SQL> select * from table(dbms_xplan.display_cursor);

PLAN_TABLE_OUTPUT
------------------------------------------------------------------------------------------
SQL_ID  46auh11c8ddts, child number 0
-------------------------------------
select /* oltpsrv */ count(*) from t1_with_index where id between 200
and 400

Plan hash value: 2861271559

------------------------------------------------------------------------------------------
| Id  | Operation          | Name                 | Rows  | Bytes | Cost (%CPU)| Time     |
------------------------------------------------------------------------------------------
|   0 | SELECT STATEMENT   |                      |       |       |     3 (100)|          |
|   1 |  SORT AGGREGATE    |                      |     1 |     6 |            |          |
|*  2 |   INDEX RANGE SCAN| I_T1_WITH_INDEXES_1 |   202 |  1212 |     3   (0)| 00:00:01 |
------------------------------------------------------------------------------------------

Predicate Information (identified by operation id):
---------------------------------------------------

   2 - access("ID">=200 AND "ID"<=400)

20 rows selected.
```

Notice the index-driven execution plan. When connecting via DSSSRV, the situation changes:

```
SQL> select sys_context('userenv','service:name') from dual;

SYS_CONTEXT('USERENV','SERVICE_NAME')
------------------------------------------------------------------------------------------
dsssrv

Elapsed: 00:00:00.00
SQL> exec check_service

PL/SQL procedure successfully completed.

Elapsed: 00:00:00.01
SQL> select /* dsssrv */ count(*) from t1_with_index where id between 200 and 400;

  COUNT(*)
----------
       201

Elapsed: 00:00:00.56
SQL> select * from table(dbms_xplan.display_cursor);

PLAN_TABLE_OUTPUT
------------------------------------------------------------------------------------------
SQL_ID  0ym2m0whwsn1y, child number 0
-------------------------------------
select /* dsssrv */ count(*) from t1_with_index where id between 200
and 400

Plan hash value: 1131101492

------------------------------------------------------------------------------------------
| Id  | Operation                    | Name          | Rows  | Bytes | Cost (%CPU)| Time     |
------------------------------------------------------------------------------------------
|   0 | SELECT STATEMENT             |               |       |       |   452K(100)|          |
|   1 |  SORT AGGREGATE              |               |     1 |     6 |            |          |
|*  2 |   TABLE ACCESS STORAGE FULL| T1_WITH_INDEX |   202 |  1212 |   452K  (1)| 00:00:18 |
------------------------------------------------------------------------------------------

Predicate Information (identified by operation id):
---------------------------------------------------

   2 - storage(("ID"<=400 AND "ID">=200))
       filter(("ID"<=400 AND "ID">=200))

21 rows selected.
```

Unlike the previous example, you do not see any index in the execution plan. If you consider putting the little PL/SQL block into a nicer format, you can easily embed it in a login trigger and control index usage that way. Further optimizer limitations in the context of Exadata are discussed in the next section.

The Optimizer Doesn't Know

You have read several times in this book that the optimizer is not aware that it is running on Exadata. In general, the principles that guide the optimizer decisions are sound, regardless of the storage platform. The fact that the code on the database tier is identical—regardless of whether it is running on Exadata or not—means that an application will behave similarly on Exadata in terms of plan selection. So, you should not expect any application to experience a large number of changes in the plans caused simply by moving to Exadata if you remain on the same version and same memory settings. Having the same software generating the execution plans help a lot toward stability! The situation might be different if you are migrating to Exadata from a lower Oracle version, such as during a 11.2 to 12.1 migration, or from single instance to RAC, but you would expect similar changes outside the Exadata platform, too.

The downside is that the optimizer is not aware that Exadata has optimizations that can cause full scans to perform much better than on other platforms, apart from the EXADATA system statistics you will read about in the next section. So mixed-workload systems that have many indexes make the optimizer's job more challenging. In fact, as you might expect, the optimizer will tend to pick index-oriented plans in preference to full scan-based plans in situations where indexes are available, despite the fact that the full scan-based plans are often much faster.

There are several ways to deal with the optimizer's tendency to prefer index access over full table scans. System statistics, optimizer parameters, and hints all come to mind as potential solutions. You can read more about these in the following sections.

System Statistics

System statistics provide the optimizer with additional information about the "system," including how long it takes to do a single-block read (typical of index lookups) and how long it takes to do a multi-block read (typical of full table scans). This may appear to be an ideal mechanism to manipulate the optimizer by giving it the additional information it needs to make the right decisions. Unfortunately, Smart Scans are not based on traditional multi-block reads and, in fact, Smart Scans can be orders of magnitude faster than multi-block reads. Hence, modifying System Statistics is probably not the best option in this case.

In fact, the question whether or not to gather system statistics in WORKLOAD mode comes up quite often during discussions about Exadata deployments. For the reasons outlined above, it is probably not a wise idea to gather them, as it potentially introduces plan regression. Introducing WORKLOAD statistics can also have far-reaching effects.

Another alternative exists, however, for database version 11.2.0.2 BP18 and 11.2.0.3 BP8 and newer, according to DOC ID 1274318.1: gathering statistics the Exadata way. The Document on My Oracle Support specifically states that this is not a generic recommendation, but should be assessed carefully. To enable Exadata system statistics, you can use the following command:

```
SQL> exec DBMS_STATS.GATHER_SYSTEM_STATS('EXADATA')
```

As a result of this call, the database engine is told that it can read more data in a single request on Exadata, thus lowering the cost of full scans. It does not prevent the optimizer from selecting an index though. The change in the costing model is the reason why you should only introduce the change after careful testing! The aforementioned note also recommends that if the application is developed from the ground up on Exadata, the effect of gathering Exadata-statistics can be controlled more easily and any adverse side effects can be caught in testing, before going live. Whichever way-careful testing is needed.

Optimizer Parameters

There are a couple of initialization parameters that can push the optimizer toward or away from index usage. The parameters OPTIMZER_INDEX_CACHING and OPTIMIZER_INDEX_COST_ADJ can both be used for this purpose. While these are big knobs that can affect the core functionality of the optimizer, they were designed for the very purpose of making indexes more or less attractive to the optimizer. Using the parameters in a limited way, such as with an `alter session` command, before running large batch processes is a viable approach in some cases. These parameters can also be set at the statement level using the OPT_PARAM hint. Here is a very simple example:

```
SQL> show parameter optimizer_index

NAME                                 TYPE        VALUE
------------------------------------ ----------- ------------------------------
optimizer_index_caching              integer     0
optimizer_index_cost_adj             integer     100

SQL> select /*+ parallel(2) gather_plan_statistics monitor chap17-f */
  2  count(*), a.state
  3  from bigt a, t1_sml b
  4  where a.id = b.id
  5  and b.state = 'RARE'
  6  group by a.state
  7  /

no rows selected

Elapsed: 00:00:25.46

SQL> select * from table(dbms_xplan.display_cursor);

PLAN_TABLE_OUTPUT
-------------------------------------------------------------------------------------------
SQL_ID  4q6vqy2r1yn5w, child number 0
-------------------------------------
select /*+ parallel(2) gather_plan_statistics monitor chap17-f */
count(*), a.state from bigt a, t1_sml b where a.id = b.id and b.state =
'RARE' group by a.state

Plan hash value: 1484706486
```

```
-------------------------------------------------------------------------------------------
| Id  | Operation                                   | Name          | Rows  | Bytes |
-------------------------------------------------------------------------------------------
|   0 | SELECT STATEMENT                            |               |       |       |
|   1 |  PX COORDINATOR                             |               |       |       |
|   2 |   PX SEND QC (RANDOM)                       | :TQ10003      |     1 |    32 |
|   3 |    HASH GROUP BY                            |               |     1 |    32 |
|   4 |     PX RECEIVE                              |               |     1 |    32 |
|   5 |      PX SEND HASH                           | :TQ10002      |     1 |    32 |
|   6 |       HASH GROUP BY                         |               |     1 |    32 |
|*  7 |        HASH JOIN                            |               |     1 |    32 |
|   8 |         JOIN FILTER CREATE                  | :BF0000       |     8 |   128 |
|   9 |          PX RECEIVE                         |               |     8 |   128 |
|  10 |           PX SEND BROADCAST                 | :TQ10001      |     8 |   128 |
|  11 |            TABLE ACCESS BY INDEX ROWID BATCHED| T1_SML      |     8 |   128 |
|  12 |             SORT CLUSTER BY ROWID           |               |     8 |       |
|  13 |              BUFFER SORT                    |               |       |       |
|  14 |               PX RECEIVE                    |               |     8 |       |
|  15 |                PX SEND HASH (BLOCK ADDRESS) | :TQ10000      |     8 |       |
|  16 |                 PX SELECTOR                 |               |       |       |
|* 17 |                  INDEX RANGE SCAN           | T1_SML_STATE  |     8 |       |
|  18 |         JOIN FILTER USE                     | :BF0000       |  100M|  1525M|
|  19 |          PX BLOCK ITERATOR                  |               |  100M|  1525M|
|* 20 |           TABLE ACCESS STORAGE FULL         | BIGT          |  100M|  1525M|
-------------------------------------------------------------------------------------------

Predicate Information (identified by operation id):
---------------------------------------------------

   7 - access("A"."ID"="B"."ID")
  17 - access("B"."STATE"='RARE')
  20 - storage(:Z>=:Z AND :Z<=:Z AND SYS_OP_BLOOM_FILTER(:BF0000,"A"."ID"))
       filter(SYS_OP_BLOOM_FILTER(:BF0000,"A"."ID"))

Note
-----
   - dynamic statistics used: dynamic sampling (level=AUTO)
   - Degree of Parallelism is 2 because of hint

SQL> alter session set optimizer_index_cost_adj=10000;

Session altered.

SQL> select /*+ parallel(2) gather_plan_statistics monitor chap17-f */
  2  count(*), a.state
  3  from bigt a, t1_sml b
  4  where a.id = b.id
  5  and b.state = 'RARE'
  6  group by a.state
  7  /

no rows selected
```

```
Elapsed: 00:00:15.40

SQL> select * from table(dbms_xplan.display_cursor);

PLAN_TABLE_OUTPUT
---------------------------------------------------------------------------------
SQL_ID  4q6vqy2r1yn5w, child number 1
-------------------------------------
select /*+ parallel(2) gather_plan_statistics monitor chap17-f */
count(*), a.state from bigt a, t1_sml b where a.id = b.id and b.state =
'RARE' group by a.state

Plan hash value: 3199786897

---------------------------------------------------------------------------------
| Id  | Operation                          | Name     | Rows  | Bytes | Cost (%CPU)|
---------------------------------------------------------------------------------
|   0 | SELECT STATEMENT                   |          |       |       | 2510K(100)|
|   1 |  PX COORDINATOR                    |          |       |       |           |
|   2 |   PX SEND QC (RANDOM)              | :TQ10001 |     1 |    32 | 2510K   (1)|
|   3 |    HASH GROUP BY                   |          |     1 |    32 | 2510K   (1)|
|   4 |     PX RECEIVE                     |          |     1 |    32 | 2510K   (1)|
|   5 |      PX SEND HASH                  | :TQ10000 |     1 |    32 | 2510K   (1)|
|   6 |       HASH GROUP BY                |          |     1 |    32 | 2510K   (1)|
|*  7 |        HASH JOIN                   |          |     1 |    32 | 2510K   (1)|
|   8 |         JOIN FILTER CREATE         | :BF0000  |     8 |   128 |   137   (4)|
|*  9 |          TABLE ACCESS STORAGE FULL | T1_SML   |     8 |   128 |   137   (4)|
|  10 |         JOIN FILTER USE            | :BF0000  |  100M|  1525M| 2510K   (1)|
|  11 |          PX BLOCK ITERATOR         |          |  100M|  1525M| 2510K   (1)|
|* 12 |           TABLE ACCESS STORAGE FULL| BIGT     |  100M|  1525M| 2510K   (1)|
---------------------------------------------------------------------------------

Predicate Information (identified by operation id):
---------------------------------------------------

   7 - access("A"."ID"="B"."ID")
   9 - storage("B"."STATE"='RARE')
       filter("B"."STATE"='RARE')
  12 - storage(:Z>=:Z AND :Z<=:Z AND SYS_OP_BLOOM_FILTER(:BF0000,"A"."ID"))
       filter(SYS_OP_BLOOM_FILTER(:BF0000,"A"."ID"))
Note
-----
   - dynamic statistics used: dynamic sampling (level=AUTO)
   - Degree of Parallelism is 2 because of hint
```

In this simple example, pushing the optimizer away from indexes with the `alter session` caused the optimizer to pick a plan that was considerably faster. The plans show that the improvement in elapsed time was a result of doing a full table scan, instead of using the index.

Hints

Of course, hints can also be used to help the optimizer make the right choices, but that is somewhat of a slippery slope. This is especially true with the aforementioned mixed-workload scenarios. Nevertheless, telling Oracle that you would prefer to do a hash join or ignore a specific index is an option. As mentioned in the previous section, the `OPT_PARAM` hint can also prove useful for setting some initialization parameters that can influence the optimizer's decisions. SQL patches can help you by injecting hints into code outside of your control. Until a fix is available, Oracle 12c should reduce the necessity to use hints to influence join methods with the introduction of adaptive optimization.

Using Resource Manager

Unfortunately, it is still a commonly held belief that Oracle databases cannot be configured to adequately handle both DW and OLTP workloads at the same time. And, in truth, keeping them on separate systems does make them easier to manage. The downside of this approach is that it is expensive. Many companies dedicate the majority of their computing resources to moving data between platforms. The power of Exadata makes it tempting to combine these environments. Keep in mind that Exadata has additional capabilities for dividing resources between multiple databases that are not available on other platforms. I/O Resource Manager can prevent long-running DW queries from crippling latency-sensitive statements that are running on the same system. Having a good understanding of Oracle's resource management capabilities should change the way you think about what is possible in a mixed-workload or consolidated environment. Resource management is covered in depth in Chapter 7.

Summary

Exadata is different from traditionally deployed Oracle database. To make the best use of it, you will need to think differently. This does not imply that you have to rewrite your application when moving it to Exadata, but it is a good opportunity to perform a general review of it. Quite often, in today's world, DBAs look after tens or hundreds of databases. "Know your data" is becoming wishful thinking in such situations. The DBA might be assigned a problem ticket to be closed, and the sheer number of tickets to handle often does not allow any deeper analysis of the root cause for as long as the system "ticks along" nicely.

When it is decided that a database is migrated to Exadata, this decision frequently implies an update to a newer Oracle version. Platform changes and database release changes are the most opportune moments to review a database environment for further performance gains. If it is possible and you are not facing massive time constraints when moving to Exadata, we would like to encourage you not to stop working on the system after the migration completed successfully, but to continue to push the boundaries of what is possible. The Exadata system is very powerful when using Smart Scans, and you should harness that performance where you can and where it makes sense.

APPENDIX A

CELLCLI and DCLI

You have already seen many references to dcli and cellcli in the previous chapters. Although the syntax appears quite intuitive, a more thorough discussion of what you can do with the tools is certainly in order. You probably ended up here following a reference in another chapter. This appendix is not meant to be a comprehensive discussion of what you can do with the tools. You have the Exadata Storage Server Software User's Guide Chapter 8 (Using the CellCLI Utility) and Chapter 9 (Using the dcli Utility) for this. The appendix is rather your guide to getting started and understanding two of the most useful configuration tools available for the Exadata system. The cellcli part is a bit longer, paying tribute to the more powerful of the two utilities.

cellcli is a command interpreter through which you can manage a storage cell. Understandably, it is not available on the compute nodes. cellcli is to a cell what SQL*Plus is to a database instance. The other utility to introduce in more detail in this appendix is dcli. It is a utility that sends a single command to all your database servers and/or storage cells in one go. Other functionality includes copying files to multiple locations and copying SSH keys. Everyone who has been a RAC administrator before supporting Exadata will probably join the author in thinking that dcli is something that every RAC system should have available. It may not sound so useful in the eighth or quarter rack case, but as soon as you manage half racks or full racks, you will start to appreciate the ability to execute a command once across all cluster nodes.

An Introduction to CellCLI

As the name implies, Exadata storage software uses the cellcli utility as its command-line interface. We complained about the lack of syntax reference about cellcli in the first edition of the book. At the time, the only help you had was the online help or this appendix. Things have thankfully changed for the better, and the Exadata Storage Administrator's Guide has a chapter dedicated to the use of cellcli. However, since you may not be reading this book on an electronic device (or may not have one nearby), we decided to include a little reference anyway. When writing this appendix, we also found out that the documentation is lagging behind in some places, so we thought we would include a few of the things we learned while working with it.

It is interesting that Oracle chose to write an entirely new command-line tool for managing the storage cell. Oracle could have used SQL*Plus, which has become the most well-known tool for managing databases and ASM. Be that as it may, cellcli is the tool you will use for managing the storage cells. The syntax is somewhat different from SQL*Plus, but there are similarities, particularly with the LIST command. LIST is used to execute queries, and it looks very similar to the SELECT command that DBAs have become accustomed to. Like SELECT, it has WHERE and LIKE keywords that allow you to filter out unwanted information from the output.

Following is our top-ten list of things you should know about `cellcli`:

1. `cellcli` does implement a handful of SQL*Plus commands (`START (@), SET ECHO ON`, `SPOOL`, `DESCRIBE, REM`, and `HELP`).
2. `SELECT` is replaced by `LIST`, and it must be the first keyword on the command line.
3. There is no `FROM` keyword (the `LIST` keyword must be immediately followed by the `ObjectType`, which is equivalent to a table name).
4. Column names are specified with the `ATTRIBUTES` keyword followed by the columns you wish to be displayed.
5. There is a `DESCRIBE` command, which displays the attributes (columns) that make up an `ObjectType` (table).
6. There is a default set of columns for each `ObjectType` that will be returned if the `ATTRIBUTES` keyword is not specified.
7. There is a `WHERE` clause that can be applied to any attribute and multiple conditions can be `AND`ed together; however, there is no support for `OR`.
8. Unlike in the first edition of this book, there is an `ORDER BY` equivalent in 12.1.2.1.0 and later, and you can limit the output to a maximum of 200 lines.
9. The `DETAIL` keyword can be appended to any `LIST` command to change the output from column-oriented to row-oriented.
10. The `LIKE` operator works, but instead of the standard SQL wildcard, `%`, `cellcli` uses a simple form of regular expressions, so the `%` we know from SQL*Plus becomes the `.*`, matching any character zero or more times.

After a little bit of practice, you will feel at ease with `cellcli`. For the most part, you will use the `LIST` command to query different (performance) aspects of the cell.

Invoking cellcli

When you execute `cellcli` on the command line, you actually launch a bash script. The script is a wrapper with sanity checks, sourcing in environment variables and eventually executing Java code. By default, you will be dropped into an interactive session when entering `cellcli` on the command line while connected to the cell. The privileges you enjoy in your session depends on the account you used to connect to the cell. You have the option to connect as root, celladmin, or cellmonitor, where root has most privileges (careful!) and cellmonitor the least.

When invoking it, you can pass a few command line options. The most relevant ones are "`-e`" to execute a command in a non-interactive session and "`-xml`" to generate XML output. If you are running into problems, you can use "`-v`" to "`-vvv`" to generate more verbose logging. Other options exist but are of no relevance for this chapter.

Since `cellcli` creates output on `STDOUT`, you can use your favorite UNIX tools as well: just pipe the output of `cellcli` to `sed`, `awk`, `grep`, `sort`, `uniq`, `nl`, or any other of the myriad of UNIX tools helping you to process text. These provide a great way to perform data slicing and dicing for pre 12.1.2.1.0 storage cells. Here is an example on how to simulate the missing order by clause—first on 12.1.2.1.0, to show you how you can do this with a current Exadata software release:

```
# cellcli -e list metriccurrent where objectType = 'SMARTIO' order by metricValue limit 30
         SIO_IO_EL_OF_SEC                SMARTIO         0.000 MB/sec
         SIO_IO_RD_FC_HD_SEC             SMARTIO         0.000 MB/sec
         SIO_IO_RD_RQ_FC_HD_SEC          SMARTIO         0.0 IO/sec
         SIO_IO_RD_RQ_FC_SEC             SMARTIO         0.0 IO/sec
         SIO_IO_OF_RE_SEC                SMARTIO         0.000 MB/sec
         SIO_IO_RD_RQ_HD_SEC             SMARTIO         0.0 IO/sec
         SIO_IO_RV_OF                    SMARTIO         0.000 MB
         SIO_IO_RV_OF_SEC                SMARTIO         0.000 MB/sec
         SIO_IO_RD_FC_SEC                SMARTIO         0.000 MB/sec
         SIO_IO_SI_SV_SEC                SMARTIO         0.000 MB/sec
         SIO_IO_PA_TH                    SMARTIO         0.000 MB
         SIO_IO_WR_FC_SEC                SMARTIO         0.000 MB/sec
         SIO_IO_RD_HD_SEC                SMARTIO         0.000 MB/sec
         SIO_IO_WR_HD_SEC                SMARTIO         0.000 MB/sec
         SIO_IO_PA_TH_SEC                SMARTIO         0.000 MB/sec
         SIO_IO_WR_RQ_FC_SEC             SMARTIO         0.0 IO/sec
         SIO_IO_WR_RQ_HD_SEC             SMARTIO         0.0 IO/sec
         SIO_IO_RD_FC_HD                 SMARTIO         577 MB
         SIO_IO_RD_RQ_FC_HD              SMARTIO         582 IO requests
         SIO_IO_WR_FC                    SMARTIO         106,126 MB
         SIO_IO_WR_RQ_FC                 SMARTIO         106,564 IO requests
         SIO_IO_OF_RE                    SMARTIO         128,723 MB
         SIO_IO_WR_HD                    SMARTIO         225,426 MB
         SIO_IO_WR_RQ_HD                 SMARTIO         226,354 IO requests
         SIO_IO_SI_SV                    SMARTIO         235,694 MB
         SIO_IO_RD_FC                    SMARTIO         408,460 MB
         SIO_IO_RD_RQ_FC                 SMARTIO         412,032 IO requests
         SIO_IO_RD_HD                    SMARTIO         573,819 MB
         SIO_IO_RD_RQ_HD                 SMARTIO         574,816 IO requests
         SIO_IO_EL_OF                    SMARTIO         1,481,339 MB
```

In an older version of the cell software you will notice that the syntax is not supported. On the other hand, the UNIX sort command can be used instead, as you see in the second example.

```
# cellcli -e cellcli -e list metriccurrent where objectType = 'SMARTIO' order by metricValue
CELL-01504: Invalid command syntax.

# cellcli -e list metriccurrent where objectType = 'SMARTIO' | sort -n -k 3 | head -n30
         SIO_IO_EL_OF_SEC                SMARTIO         0.000 MB/sec
         SIO_IO_OF_RE_SEC                SMARTIO         0.000 MB/sec
         SIO_IO_PA_TH_SEC                SMARTIO         0.000 MB/sec
         SIO_IO_PA_TH                    SMARTIO         0.000 MB
         SIO_IO_RD_FC_HD_SEC             SMARTIO         0.000 MB/sec
         SIO_IO_RD_FC_SEC                SMARTIO         0.000 MB/sec
```

```
SIO_IO_RD_HD_SEC               SMARTIO         0.000 MB/sec
SIO_IO_RD_RQ_FC_HD_SEC         SMARTIO         0.0 IO/sec
SIO_IO_RD_RQ_FC_SEC            SMARTIO         0.0 IO/sec
SIO_IO_RD_RQ_HD_SEC            SMARTIO         0.0 IO/sec
SIO_IO_RV_OF_SEC               SMARTIO         0.000 MB/sec
SIO_IO_RV_OF                   SMARTIO         0.000 MB
SIO_IO_SI_SV_SEC               SMARTIO         0.000 MB/sec
SIO_IO_WR_FC_SEC               SMARTIO         0.000 MB/sec
SIO_IO_WR_HD_SEC               SMARTIO         0.000 MB/sec
SIO_IO_WR_RQ_FC_SEC            SMARTIO         0.0 IO/sec
SIO_IO_WR_RQ_HD_SEC            SMARTIO         0.0 IO/sec
SIO_IO_RD_FC_HD                SMARTIO         577 MB
SIO_IO_RD_RQ_FC_HD             SMARTIO         582 IO requests
SIO_IO_WR_FC                   SMARTIO         106,126 MB
SIO_IO_WR_RQ_FC                SMARTIO         106,564 IO requests
SIO_IO_OF_RE                   SMARTIO         128,723 MB
SIO_IO_WR_HD                   SMARTIO         225,426 MB
SIO_IO_WR_RQ_HD                SMARTIO         226,354 IO requests
SIO_IO_SI_SV                   SMARTIO         235,694 MB
SIO_IO_RD_FC                   SMARTIO         408,460 MB
SIO_IO_RD_RQ_FC                SMARTIO         412,032 IO requests
SIO_IO_RD_HD                   SMARTIO         573,819 MB
SIO_IO_RD_RQ_HD                SMARTIO         574,816 IO requests
SIO_IO_EL_OF                   SMARTIO         1,481,339 MB
```

Use the UNIX tools and be creative! This could be a good moment to review the `sed`, `awk`, and `perl` tutorials.

Getting Familiar with cellcli

As any good command-line utility, `cellcli` comes with an online help. This built-in help was more accurate than the official documentation, and, as a tip, you should check the official HTML documentation against the output of the help command. To show you what you can do with `cellcli` in Exadata 12.1.2.1.0, here is the output:

```
CellCLI> help

 HELP [topic]
   Available Topics:
        ALTER
        ALTER ALERTHISTORY
        ALTER CELL
        ALTER CELLDISK
        ALTER FLASHCACHE
        ALTER GRIDDISK
        ALTER IBPORT
        ALTER IORMPLAN
        ALTER LUN
        ALTER PHYSICALDISK
        ALTER QUARANTINE
        ALTER THRESHOLD
```

```
ASSIGN KEY
CALIBRATE
CREATE
CREATE CELL
CREATE CELLDISK
CREATE FLASHCACHE
CREATE FLASHLOG
CREATE GRIDDISK
CREATE KEY
CREATE QUARANTINE
CREATE THRESHOLD
DESCRIBE
DROP
DROP ALERTHISTORY
DROP CELL
DROP CELLDISK
DROP FLASHCACHE
DROP FLASHLOG
DROP GRIDDISK
DROP QUARANTINE
DROP THRESHOLD
EXPORT CELLDISK
IMPORT CELLDISK
LIST
LIST ACTIVEREQUEST
LIST ALERTDEFINITION
LIST ALERTHISTORY
LIST CELL
LIST CELLDISK
LIST DATABASE
LIST FLASHCACHE
LIST FLASHCACHECONTENT
LIST FLASHLOG
LIST GRIDDISK
LIST IBPORT
LIST IORMPLAN
LIST KEY
LIST LUN
LIST METRICCURRENT
LIST METRICDEFINITION
LIST METRICHISTORY
LIST PHYSICALDISK
LIST QUARANTINE
LIST THRESHOLD
SET
SPOOL
START
```

Each command can be further described using the HELP command, as in HELP LIST or HELP LIST CELL, for example.

```
CellCLI> help list

  Usage: LIST <object_type> [<name> | <filters>] [<attribute_list>] [DETAIL] \
         [ORDER BY <order_by_attribute_list>] [LIMIT integer]
  Purpose: The LIST command displays attributes for Oracle Exadata Server Software objects.
           Objects displayed are identified by name or by filters.
           The attributes displayed for each object are determined by the specified attribute
           list.

  Arguments:
    <object_type>:  The type of existing object to be displayed.
    <name>:  The name of the active request to be displayed.
    <filters>:  an expression which determines which active requests should
               be displayed.
    <attribute_list>: The attributes that are to be displayed.
                      ATTRIBUTES {ALL | attr1 [, attr2]... }
    <order_by_attribute_list>: The attributes that are to be ordered by.
                               {attr1 [asc|desc] [, attr2 [asc|desc]]}

  Options:
    [DETAIL]: Formats the display as an attribute on each line, with
              an attribute descriptor preceding each value.
    [ORDER BY]: Orders the objects by attributes in ascending or descending order.
                The default is ascending.
    [LIMIT]: Sets the number of displayed objects.

  Enter HELP LIST <object_type> for specific help syntax.
    <object_type>:  {ACTIVEREQUEST | ALERTHISTORY | ALERTDEFINITION | CELL
                    | CELLDISK | DATABASE | FLASHCACHE | FLASHLOG | FLASHCACHECONTENT
                    | GRIDDISK | IBPORT | IORMPLAN | KEY | LUN
                    | METRICCURRENT | METRICDEFINITION | METRICHISTORY
                    | PHYSICALDISK | QUARANTINE | THRESHOLD }

CellCLI> help list cell

  Usage: LIST CELL [<attribute_list>] [DETAIL]

  Purpose: Displays specified attributes for the cell.

  Arguments:
    <attribute_list>: The attributes that are to be displayed.
                      ATTRIBUTES {ALL | attr1 [, attr2]... }

  Options:
    [DETAIL]: Formats the display as an attribute on each line, with
              an attribute descriptor preceding each value.
```

```
  Examples:
    LIST CELL attributes status, cellnumber
    LIST CELL DETAIL
```

The output shown in the previous listing is taken from a cell with Exadata software version 12.1.2.1.0. As you can see, the help system allows you to see the syntax for each command. You may also have noticed a couple of SQL*Plus carryovers. SET, SPOOL, and START work pretty much as expected. Note that the @ character is equivalent to the SQL*Plus START command and that the only things you can use SET for are ECHO and DATEFORMAT. Now, here are a few examples of queries using the LIST command:

```
CellCLI> describe metriccurrent
        name
        alertState
        collectionTime
        metricObjectName
        metricType
        metricValue
        objectType

CellCLI> list metriccurrent where objectType = 'FLASHCACHE' and name not like '.*SEC' -
> attributes name, metricType, metricValue
         FC_BYKEEP_OVERWR                         Cumulative      0.000 MB
         FC_BYKEEP_USED                           Instantaneous   0.062 MB
         FC_BY_ALLOCATED                          Instantaneous   337,591 MB
         FC_BY_DIRTY                              Instantaneous   166,816 MB
         FC_BY_STALE_DIRTY                        Instantaneous   373 MB
         FC_BY_USED                               Instantaneous   363,063 MB
[many more skipped]
         FC_IO_RQ_W_SKIP_NCMIRROR                 Cumulative      0 IO requests

CellCLI> list metriccurrent where objectType = 'FLASHCACHE' and name not like '.*SEC' -
> and metricValue not like '0.*' attributes name, metricType, metricValue -
> order by metricValue desc limit 20
         FC_IO_RQ_W                         Cumulative      1,325,800,847 IO requests
         FC_IO_RQ_R                         Cumulative      1,323,518,596 IO requests
         FC_IO_RQ_W_OVERWRITE               Cumulative      1,288,444,158 IO requests
         FC_IO_RQ_W_SKIP                    Cumulative      545,358,635 IO requests
         FC_IO_RQ_W_FIRST                   Cumulative      35,716,955 IO requests
         FC_IO_BY_W                         Cumulative      11,196,640 MB
         FC_IO_BY_W_OVERWRITE               Cumulative      10,702,060 MB
         FC_IO_BY_R                         Cumulative      10,518,906 MB
         FC_IO_RQ_R_SKIP                    Cumulative      4,422,859 IO requests
         FC_IO_RQ_REPLACEMENT_ATTEMPTED     Cumulative      4,051,159 IO requests
         FC_IO_RQ_R_SKIP_NCMIRROR           Cumulative      4,029,287 IO requests
         FC_IO_RQ_R_DW                      Cumulative      2,614,954 IO requests
         FC_IO_RQ_W_SKIP_LG                 Cumulative      2,558,104 IO requests
         FC_IO_BY_W_SKIP                    Cumulative      2,467,692 MB
         FC_IO_RQ_W_POPULATE                Cumulative      1,639,734 IO requests
         FC_IO_RQ_R_MISS                    Cumulative      1,581,764 IO requests
         FC_IO_BY_W_SKIP_LG                 Cumulative      989,725 MB
```

```
         FC_IO_RQ_DISK_WRITE             Cumulative       800,551 IO requests
         FC_IO_RQ_REPLACEMENT_FAILED     Cumulative       455,425 IO requests
         FC_IO_BY_R_DW                   Instantaneous    404,121 MB

CellCLI> list metriccurrent where objectType = 'FLASHCACHE' and name not like '.*SEC' -
> and metricValue not like '0.*' attributes name, metricType, metricValue -
> order by metricType, metricValue desc limit 20
         FC_IO_RQ_W                      Cumulative       1,325,801,132 IO requests
         FC_IO_RQ_R                      Cumulative       1,323,520,259 IO requests
         FC_IO_RQ_W_OVERWRITE            Cumulative       1,288,444,442 IO requests
         FC_IO_RQ_W_SKIP                 Cumulative       545,359,973 IO requests
         FC_IO_RQ_W_FIRST                Cumulative       35,716,956 IO requests
         FC_IO_BY_W                      Cumulative       11,196,644 MB
         FC_IO_BY_W_OVERWRITE            Cumulative       10,702,065 MB
         FC_IO_BY_R                      Cumulative       10,518,931 MB
         FC_IO_RQ_R_SKIP                 Cumulative       4,424,593 IO requests
         FC_IO_RQ_REPLACEMENT_ATTEMPTED  Cumulative       4,051,159 IO requests
         FC_IO_RQ_R_SKIP_NCMIRROR        Cumulative       4,030,357 IO requests
         FC_IO_RQ_R_DW                   Cumulative       2,614,954 IO requests
         FC_IO_RQ_W_SKIP_LG              Cumulative       2,558,201 IO requests
         FC_IO_BY_W_SKIP                 Cumulative       2,467,735 MB
         FC_IO_RQ_W_POPULATE             Cumulative       1,639,734 IO requests
         FC_IO_RQ_R_MISS                 Cumulative       1,581,764 IO requests
         FC_IO_BY_W_SKIP_LG              Cumulative       989,754 MB
         FC_IO_RQ_DISK_WRITE             Cumulative       800,551 IO requests
         FC_IO_RQ_REPLACEMENT_FAILED     Cumulative       455,425 IO requests
         FC_IO_BY_W_FIRST                Cumulative       378,110 MB
```

The DESCRIBE verb works similarly to the way it does in SQL*Plus, but it must be fully spelled out; you cannot use the familiar DESC as an abbreviation. Notice that there are no headings for column-oriented output. Many of the LIST commands were strung across multiple lines by using the continuation operator (-). The LIST commands look a lot like SQL, except for LIST being used instead of SELECT and the regular expressions for matching when using the LIKE keyword. You can see that the ATTRIBUTES and WHERE keywords can be anywhere on the command line after the LIST ObjectType keywords. In other words, these two keywords are not positional; either one can be used first.

The first example in the previous listings can be executed on any Exadata cell version. The LIST command is used to display a certain set of attributes related to the cell's FLASHCACHE performance metrics. More specifically, those metrics that calculate values "per second" are excluded.

The second example expands on the previous one by specifying an ORDER BY, which is new for 12.1.2.1.0 and later. Very often when an ORDER BY is specified, a LIMIT clause has to be provided as well, or else an error similar to this one is raised:

```
CellCLI> list metriccurrent where objectType = 'FLASHCACHE' and name not like '.*SEC' -
> and metricValue not like '0.*' attributes name, metricType, metricValue -
> order by metricValue desc
CELL-02026: The LIMIT parameter is mandatory for "LIST METRICCURRENT" command when using the
ORDER BY option.
```

One alternative to circumvent the limit would be to pipe the output into the UNIX sort command as shown earlier. Note that you can order by in ascending (ASC, the default) or descending (DESC) order. You are not limited to order by just one column. The last example shows you can sort by more than one column.

Sending Commands from the Operating System

In addition to running cellcli interactively you just saw in these examples, you read in the introduction that you can specify the -e option to pass in cellcli commands from your operating system prompt (even via dcli as you will see in a minute). For example, the following listing shows how the -e option can be used to query the status of cellsrv directly from the OS command line:

```
[root@enkcel04 ~]# cellcli -e "list cell detail"
         name:                       enkcel04
         bbuStatus:                  normal
         cellVersion:                OSS_12.1.2.1.0_LINUX.X64_141206.1
         cpuCount:                   24
         diagHistoryDays:            7
         fanCount:                   12/12
         fanStatus:                  normal
         flashCacheMode:             WriteBack
[...]
         usbStatus:                  normal
         cellsrvStatus:              running
         msStatus:                   running
         rsStatus:                   running
```

Among other things, the -e option is helpful when you want to invoke cellcli from within an operating system shell script. You need to be careful when passing commands to cellcli using the -e argument—escaping quotes can become very important, as you will see later in the chapter.

Using cellcli XML Output in the Database

Parsing the output of cellcli in tabular form can be a bit of a challenge. Thankfully, another output method—XML—is available to the performance analyst. Combining the -e and -xml flags allows you to read the cellcli output into the database and process it using SQL. Here is an example how to load cellcli information in XML format into the database.

The first step is to create a directory object in the database, using the create directory command in SQL*Plus. The directory used in the following paragraphs is ORADIR. With the directory in place, you can create a table of XMLType. There are alternative ways of storing the XML information but this one works for the author.

```
SQL> create table metrics_xmltab of xmltype;

Table created.
```

This particular table will hold the XML representation of cellcli performance data. Before XML information can be loaded, it needs to be extracted from the cell first. In order to keep the example simple, just a single cell's performance data will be loaded. You could alternatively use dcli to capture the information simultaneously. The XML file with performance metrics related to the SMARTIO category can be read using SSH and placed into the directory ORADIR. This is just an example. You can fire off any query against the cell:

```
ssh cellmonitor@enkcel04 "cellcli -xml -e list metriccurrent where objectType = \'SMARTIO\'" \
> > oradir/metrics.xml
```

The XML file will have the following contents; the important bits to be displayed later are found in the <metric> tags:

```
[oracle@enkdb03 ~]$ head -n20 oradir/metrics.xml
<?xml version="1.0" encoding="utf-8" ?>
<cli-output>
<context cell="enkcel04" realm="" ossStartTimestamp="1430673687318"
iormResetTimestamp="782230633"/>
<metric> <name>SIO_IO_EL_OF</name>
 <alertState>normal</alertState>
 <collectionTime>1431455744000</collectionTime>
 <metricObjectName>SMARTIO</metricObjectName>
 <metricType>Cumulative</metricType>
 <metricValue>634659.296875</metricValue>
 <objectType>SMARTIO</objectType>

</metric>

<metric> <name>SIO_IO_EL_OF_SEC</name>
 <alertState>normal</alertState>
```

Well-formed XML—all you need. In the next step, this can be loaded into the database:

```
SQL> insert into metrics_xmltab values (xmltype
  2   (bfilename('ORADIR','metrics.xml'), nls_charset_id('AL32UTF8')));

1 row created.

SQL> commit;

Commit complete.

SQL> select count(*) from metrics_xmltab;

  COUNT(*)
----------
         1
```

All that remains to do now is to use some XMLDB magic to transform the XML information into something tabular for easier digestion by the human eye. The XMLTABLE construct can be used to generate a report. Later on, when inserting more data, you can distinguish records based on the collection time. The XML document reports the time in UNIX epoch time.

```
SQL> select x.name, TO_DATE('1970-01-01', 'YYYY-MM-DD') + x.collectionTime/86400000
  2    as collectedAt, x.metricType, x.metricValue, x.objectType
  3   from metrics_xmltab m,
  4  xmltable('//metric'
  5   passing object_value
  6   columns
  7    name           varchar2(25)          path 'name',
  8    collectionTime number                path 'collectionTime',
  9    metricType     varchar2(20)          path 'metricType',
```

```
 10     metricValue     number              path 'metricValue',
 11     objectType      varchar2(50)        path 'objectType') x;

NAME                      COLLECTEDAT         METRICTYPE          METRICVALUE OBJECTTYPE
------------------------- ------------------- ------------------- ----------- -------------
SIO_IO_EL_OF              12.05.2015 18:35:44 Cumulative           634659.297 SMARTIO
SIO_IO_EL_OF_SEC          12.05.2015 18:35:44 Rate                          0 SMARTIO
SIO_IO_OF_RE              12.05.2015 18:35:44 Cumulative           14336.6719 SMARTIO
SIO_IO_OF_RE_SEC          12.05.2015 18:35:44 Rate                          0 SMARTIO
SIO_IO_PA_TH              12.05.2015 18:35:44 Cumulative                    0 SMARTIO
SIO_IO_PA_TH_SEC          12.05.2015 18:35:44 Rate                          0 SMARTIO
SIO_IO_RD_FC              12.05.2015 18:35:44 Cumulative           60078.5391 SMARTIO
SIO_IO_RD_FC_HD           12.05.2015 18:35:44 Cumulative           3831.76563 SMARTIO
```

You can extend the example by creating another XML table with the metric names and their definition taken from the metricdefinition found on every cell and then joining both to get more easily readable output. Views help reduce the amount of typing to extract the same information.

Configuring and Managing the Storage Cell

cellcli is also used in a number of ways for configuring everything from disk storage to cell alerts. You can also use cellcli for management tasks such as startup and shutdown. Following are a few examples of how to use cellcli to configure and manage the storage cell.

Cell services can be shut down one at a time or all at once. The following commands are used to shut down cell services:

```
-- Shutdown cell services one at a time --
CellCLI> alter cell shutdown services cellsrv
CellCLI> alter cell shutdown services ms
CellCLI> alter cell shutdown services rs

-- Shutdown all cell services --
CellCLI> alter cell shutdown services all
```

Cell services may also be started up one-by-one or all at once. Note that the RS process must be started first or cellcli will throw an error such as the following:

```
CellCLI> alter cell startup services cellsrv

Starting CELLSRV services...
CELL-01509: Restart Server (RS) not responding.
```

The following commands are used to start up cell services:

```
-- Startup cell services one at a time --
CellCLI> alter cell startup services rs
CellCLI> alter cell startup services ms
CellCLI> alter cell startup services cellsrv

-- Startup all cell services --
CellCLI> alter cell startup services all
```

To show the current status of cellsrv, use the LIST CELL command:

```
CellCLI> list cell attributes name,cellsrvStatus,cellVersion,flashCacheMode,-
> msStatus,rsStatus,status detail
         name:                       enkcel04
         cellVersion:                OSS_12.1.2.1.0_LINUX.X64_141206.1
         flashCacheMode:             WriteBack
         status:                     online
         cellsrvStatus:              running
         msStatus:                   running
         rsStatus:                   running
```

Several of the settings you see in the output of list cell detail can be changed using the ALTER CELL command. These settings may be configured one at a time or together by separating them with a comma. For example:

```
-- Configure notification level for alerts --
CellCLI> ALTER CELL notificationPolicy='critical,warning,clear'

-- Configure the cell for email notifications --
CellCLI> ALTER CELL smtpServer='smtp.example.com', -
                    smtpFromAddr='exa01@example.com', -
                    smtpFrom='exa01', -
                    smtpToAddr='all_dba@example.com', -
                    notificationPolicy='critical,warning,clear', -
                    notificationMethod='mail'
```

By the way, if you have not already stumbled across this feature, cellcli stores a command history similar to the bash shell. You can scroll up and down through your history and edit commands using the arrow keys. And thanks to the regular expression support in queries, you have a very powerful pattern-matching capability at your disposal. The cellcli syntax will be something new to system administrators and DBAs alike, but once you understand the logic, it really is not difficult to master at all.

An Introduction to dcli

dcli is a tool by which you can execute a single command across all cells or compute nodes. Having worked on various clustered systems over the years, we have come to appreciate the importance of keeping scripts (and some configuration files) identical across all nodes. It is also very handy to have a facility for executing the same command consistently across all nodes of a cluster. Oracle provides the dcli command to do just that—unfortunately, not on ordinary clustered systems. Among other things, the dcli command allows you to do the following:

- Configure SSH equivalency across all storage cells and/or database servers
- Distribute a file to the same location on all servers/cells in the cluster
- Distribute and execute a script on servers/cells in the cluster
- Execute commands and scripts on servers/cells in the cluster

dcli uses SSH equivalency to authenticate your session on the remote servers. If you do not have SSH equivalency established across servers/cells, you can still use it, but it will prompt you for a password for each remote system before executing the command. dcli executes all commands in parallel, aggregates the output from each server into a single list, and displays the output on the local machine.

Unlike cellcli just discussed, dcli is not a bash script. It is still a script but written in python. The script can take the following command line options, taken from a 12.1.2.1.0 compute node:

```
[oracle@enkdb03 ~]$ dcli -h

Distributed Shell for Oracle Storage
[...]
Usage: dcli [options] [command]

Options:
  --version             show program's version number and exit
  --batchsize=MAXTHDS   limit the number of target cells on which to run the
                        command or file copy in parallel
  -c CELLS              comma-separated list of cells
  -d DESTFILE           destination directory or file
  -f FILE               files to be copied
  -g GROUPFILE          file containing list of cells
  -h, --help            show help message and exit
  --hidestderr          hide stderr for remotely executed commands in ssh
  -k                    push ssh key to cell's authorized_keys file
  -l USERID             user to login as on remote cells (default: celladmin)
  --maxlines=MAXLINES   limit output lines from a cell when in parallel
                        execution over multiple cells (default: 100000)
  -n                    abbreviate non-error output
  -r REGEXP             abbreviate output lines matching a regular expression
  -s SSHOPTIONS         string of options passed through to ssh
  --scp=SCPOPTIONS      string of options passed through to scp if different
                        from sshoptions
  --serial              serialize execution over the cells
  --showbanner          show banner of the remote node in ssh
  -t                    list target cells
  --unkey               drop keys from target cells' authorized_keys file
  -v                    print extra messages to stdout
  --vmstat=VMSTATOPS    vmstat command options
  -x EXECFILE           file to be copied and executed
```

In most cases, you will find yourself executing commands against either all the cells or all compute nodes. The tool relies on a simple text file with names of machines, delimited by carriage returns, and passed using the -g parameter. Usually the files are called cell_group, dbs_group, and all_group respectively, which is what the onecommand tool leaves after installation. These files may be described as follows:

> dbs_group: This file contains the management hostnames for all database servers in your Exadata configuration. It provides a convenient way to execute dcli commands on the database servers.
>
> cell_group: This file contains the management hostnames for all storage cells in your Exadata configuration. It provides a convenient way to execute dcli commands limited to the storage cells.
>
> all_group: This file is a combination of the dbs_group and cell_group files and contains a list of the management hostnames for all database servers and storage cells in your Exadata configuration. Using this file, you can execute dcli commands on all database servers and storage cells with care.

Here is an example for a quarter rack:

```
[root@enkdb03 ~]# cat cell_group
enkcel04
enkcel05
enkcel06
```

In addition to the -g parameter, you will most often provide the user ID using the -l argument to dcli to specify which user should connect against the systems specified in the group file. Remember that you can use root, celladmin, and cellmonitor when connecting to a cell. When invoking dcli to interact with other compute nodes, root and oracle are the most obvious candidates for user IDs.

dcli is particularly useful when you want to collect information from all storage cells using the cellcli commands. The following example shows how dcli and cellcli commands can be used together to report the status of all storage cells in a quarter rack cluster:

```
[oracle@enkdb03 ~] $ dcli -g cell_group -l cellmonitor cellcli -e list cell
enkcel04: enkcel04       online
enkcel05: enkcel05       online
enkcel06: enkcel06       online
```

Any of the cellcli commands discussed in this appendix may be executed from a central location using dcli. In fact, the only restriction is that the command cannot be interactive, (such as requiring user input during execution). For example, the following listing illustrates collecting current performance metrics from the storage cells:

```
[oracle@enkdb03 ~]$ dcli -l cellmonitor -g cell_group \
> cellcli -e "LIST METRICCURRENT  ATTRIBUTES name,metricValue, \
> collectionTime where objecttype=\'FLASHLOG\' and name like \'.*FIRST\'"
enkcel04: FL_DISK_FIRST          525,232,661 IO requests        2015-05-12T14:33:45-05:00
enkcel04: FL_FLASH_FIRST         11,914,368 IO requests         2015-05-12T14:33:45-05:00
enkcel05: FL_DISK_FIRST          555,655,999 IO requests        2015-05-12T14:34:06-05:00
enkcel05: FL_FLASH_FIRST         12,418,630 IO requests         2015-05-12T14:34:06-05:00
enkcel06: FL_DISK_FIRST          555,696,351 IO requests        2015-05-12T14:34:08-05:00
enkcel06: FL_FLASH_FIRST         12,086,961 IO requests         2015-05-12T14:34:08-05:00
```

Using cellcli from dcli requires creative quoting in the where clause as you can see.

Summary

There are many more uses for dcli and cellcli than what we cover here. System administrators will find it useful for creating new user accounts on the database servers using the useradd and groupadd commands, for example. DBAs will find dcli useful for distributing scripts and other files to other servers in the cluster. And using dcli and cellcli together provides a convenient way of managing, extracting, and reporting key performance metrics from the storage cells. Scheduling these as cron jobs and loading them into the database as shown in the little example allows you to keep a nice repository of performance-related information for later analysis.

APPENDIX B

Online Exadata Resources

This appendix details some helpful online resources for DBAs managing Exadata. Oracle Support creates a good many of what are termed *support notes*. You will see references to some of those we consider most helpful, and you can read them—if you are a licensed user—by going to Oracle's support site. In addition to the My Oracle Support notes, we would like to point you to the online resources provided by the authors. You should check these resources for additional background information about the book and other Exadata-related topics. There is a mind-blowing number of great Exadata-related blogs out there worth reading as well—too many, in fact, to list here.

My Oracle Support Notes

Listed in Table B-1 are several good online notes for managing the Exadata platform on My Oracle Support (MOS). Some of these notes are living documents, meaning they are continually updated as new software versions and patches become available. MOS Note 888828.1 is a must-read for anyone responsible for administering the system. It contains critical information about supported software releases. Some of the MOS notes listed here, such as 757552.1, are simply placeholders for dozens of other important documents you will want to be aware of. Obviously, this is not a comprehensive or exhaustive list, and there are many more good technical documents for Exadata on MOS, but we hope you find this list helpful in getting you started off in the right direction.

Table B-1. *Useful, Nonexhaustive List of Documents for the Exadata Administrator on My Oracle Support*

Category	Doc ID	Title
Generic Database	565535.1	Flashback Database Best Practices & Performance
	1053147.1	11gR2 Clusterware and Grid Home—What You Need to Know
	887522.1	Grid Infrastructure Single Client Access Name (SCAN) Explained
Migration	1152016.1	Master Note For Oracle Database Upgrades and Migrations
	1389592.1	11G—Reduce Transportable Tablespace Downtime Using Cross Platform Incremental Backup
	2005729.1	12C—Reduce Transportable Tablespace Downtime Using Cross Platform Incremental Backup

(*continued*)

Table B-1. (*continued*)

Category	Doc ID	Title
	762540.1	Consolidated Reference List of Notes for Migration / Upgrade Service Requests
Exadata Configuration, Setup, and Diagnostics	888828.1	Exadata Database Machine and Exadata Storage Server-Supported Versions
	1389191.1	Get Proactive with Exadata
	1346612.2	Information Center: Troubleshooting Oracle Exadata Database Machine
	1270094.1	Exadata Critical Issues
	757552.1	Oracle Exadata Best Practices
	1306791.2	Information Center: Oracle Exadata Database Machine
	1274324.1	Oracle Sun Database Machine X2-2/X2-8, X3-2/X3-8, and X4-2 Diagnosability and Troubleshooting Best Practices
	1070954.1	Oracle Exadata Database Machine exachk or HealthCheck
	761868.1	Oracle Exadata Diagnostic Information Required for Disk Failures and Some Other Hardware Issues
	1901729.1	SRDC—Oracle Engineered Systems (ES) Sosreport Data Collection for Linux Servers
	330364.1	Remote Diagnostic Agent (RDA) - Main Man Page
	314422.1	Remote Diagnostic Agent (RDA) - Getting Started
	391983.1	Remote Diagnostic Agent (RDA) - Profile Manual Pages
InfiniBand	1538237.1	Gathering Troubleshooting Information for the Infiniband Network in Engineered Systems
	1286263.1	Troubleshooting InfiniBand Switch Problems on Exadata
	745616.1	Oracle Reliable Datagram Sockets (RDS) and InfiniBand (IB) Support for RAC Interconnect and Exadata Storage
Powering Off	1188080.1	Steps to Shut Down or Reboot an Exadata Storage Cell without Affecting ASM
	1093890.1	Steps to Shut Down / Start Up the Exadata & RDBMS Services and Cell / Compute Nodes on an Exadata Configuration
Patching	1364356.2	Information Center: Upgrading Oracle Exadata Database Machine
	1553103.1	dbnodeupdate.sh: Exadata Database Server Patching Using the DB Node Update Utility

(*continued*)

Table B-1. (*continued*)

Category	Doc ID	Title
	1681467.1	11.2.0.2, 11.2.0.3, 11.2.0.4 or 12.1.0.1 to 12.1.0.2 Grid Infrastructure and Database Upgrade on Exadata Database Machine Running Oracle Linux
	1565291.1	Exadata Database Machine 11.2.0.4 Grid Infrastructure and Database Upgrade for 11.2.0.2 BP12 and later
	1262380.1	Exadata Patching Overview and Patch Testing Guidelines

The Authors' Blogs

In addition to the My Oracle Support notes, you should check the blogs of the authors of this book for updates, potentially errata, and other interesting Exadata-related material. The very first link to present, though, is the official page to this book, proudly hosted at `www.expertoracleexadata.com`

The original authors' blogs are up next, in alphabetical order:

- Andy Colvin: `http://blog.oracle-ninja.com`
- Randy Johnson: `https://dallasdba.wordpress.com`
- Kerry Osborne: `http://kerryosborne.oracle-guy.com`
- Tanel Poder: `http://blog.tanelpoder.com`

The authors of the second edition blog here:

- Karl Arao: `https://karlarao.wordpress.com`
- Martin Bach: `http://martincarstenbach.wordpress.com`
- Andy Colvin `http://blog.oracle-ninja.com`
- Frits Hoogland: `https://fritshoogland.wordpress.com`

We wish you happy reading!

APPENDIX C

Diagnostic Scripts

Throughout this book, you have witnessed a plethora of useful diagnostic scripts. While the contents of many of them are displayed in the body of the book, some of them are lengthy enough that we decided not to print their contents in the listings. These scripts are all available online at `www.expertoracleexadata.com`. Always make sure you understand what a particular script does, and test thoroughly before using it. This includes a check against the licenses.

Table C-1 contains a list of the scripts along with a brief description of each one.

Table C-1. *Diagnostic Scripts Used in This Book*

Script Name	Description
`as.sql` `cdb_as.sql`	*AS* is short for *Active SQL*. This script shows all active SQL statements on the current instance as shown by `V$SESSION`. Note that you may need to execute it several times to get an idea of what's happening on a system, as fast statements may not be "caught" by this quick-and-dirty approach.
`calibrate_io.sql`	This script provides a simple wrapper for the `DBMS_RESOURCE_MANAGER.CALIBRATE_IO` procedure. The procedure must be run before Oracle will allow you to enable Auto DOP on versions prior to Oracle 12cR1.
`check_px.sql`	This script contains a simple query of `V$PX_PROCESS_SYSSTAT` to show how many parallel server processes are currently in use.
`comp_ratio.sql`	This is a simple script that computes a compression ratio based on an input value (the original table size).
`create_display_raw.sql`	This script creates the `display_raw()` function in the ENKITEC schema, which translates raw-data-type values into various other data-types (originally written by Greg Rahn).
`dba_tables.sql`	This is a simple script to query `DBA_TABLES`. It shows the number of rows, number of blocks, and default degree of parallelism.
`cdb_tables.sql`	This is a simple script to query `CDB_TABLES`. It shows the number of rows, number of blocks, and default degree of parallelism for the entire CDB or limited to a specific PDB.
`display_raw.sql`	This is a simple script to translate a raw value into a specified data-type format such as `NUMBER` or `VARCHAR2`. It depends on the `display_raw()` function created by the `create_display_raw.sql` script.

(*continued*)

Table C-1. *(continued)*

Script Name	Description
dplan.sql	This script shows the actual execution plan for a SQL statement in the shared pool. This is a very simple script that prompts for a SQL_ID and CHILD_NO and then calls dbms_xplan.display_cursor.
dump_block.sql	This script dumps a data block to a trace file using ALTER SYSTEM DUMP DATAFILE. It prompts for fileno and blockno.
esfc_keep_tables.sql	This script displays objects that have the CELL_FLASH_CACHE attribute set to KEEP. Modifying the storage clause should not be necessary since Exadata 11.2.3.3; this script helps you identify the segments in need for a change.
flush_pool.sql	This script uses ALTER SYSTEM FLUSH SHARED_POOL to flush all SQL statements from the shared pool. Use this script with great care in production as it can cause a (hard) parse storm.
flush_sql.sql	This script uses DBMS_SHARED_POOL.PURGE to flush a single SQL statement from the shared pool. It only works with 10.2.0.4 and later.
fs.sql	This script allows you to search through V$SQL using a bit of SQL text or a SQL_ID. (*FS* is short for *Find SQL*.) The script reports some statistical information such as average elapsed time and average LIOs.
fsx.sql	*FSX* stands for *Find SQL eXadata*. This script searches the shared pool (V$SQL) based on the SQL statement text or a specific SQL_ID and reports whether statements were offloaded or not and, if offloaded, what percentage of I/O was saved. Note that there are several alternate versions of this script used in the book (fsx2.sql, fsx3.sql, and fsx4.sql). These versions reduce the width of the output to something more easily printed in the limits imposed by the printed book format.
fsxo.sql	This script is similar to the fsx.sql script but lists only those statements that have been offloaded. It can be used in conjunction with the offload_percent.sql script to drill into the individual statements contributing to its calculated offload percentage.
gather_table_stats.sql	This is a simple script to gather table statistics using the DBMS_STATS.GATHER_TABLE_STATS procedure.
get_compression_ratio.sql get_compression_ratio_12c.sql	This script is a wrapper for the built in compression advisor functionality (DBMS_COMPRESSION.GET_COMPRESSION_RATIO). It prompts for a table name and a compression type and then estimates the expected compression ratio by actually compressing a subset of the table's rows.
get_compression_type.sql	This script provides a wrapper for the DBMS_COMPRESSION.GET_COMPRESSION_TYPE procedure. It can be used to identify the actual compression type used for a specific row. It prompts for a table name and a ROWID and returns the actual compression type for that row as opposed to the compression type assigned to the table.

(continued)

Table C-1. *(continued)*

Script Name	Description
mystat.sql	This is a simple script for querying V$MYSTATS, not to be confused with Adrian Billington's mystats script described later.
mystats.sql	Extensively covered in Chapter 11 Adrian Billington's myststs.sql allows you to capture the change in session statistics during the execution of a SQL statement. Download from www.oracle-developer.net
old_rowid.sql	This script creates the old_rowid() function. The old_rowid() function accepts a rowid and returns the fileno, blockno, and rowno (the old rowid format).
obj_by_hex.sql	This script translates an object_id in hex format into an object name. The hex value is contained in block dumps.
offload_percent.sql	This script can be used to provide a quick check on whether statements are being offloaded or not on Exadata platforms. It allows all statements over a minimum time or a minimum number of LIOs to be evaluated and calculates a percentage of statements that have been offloaded.
parms.sql	This script displays database parameters and their current values. Includes a switch to show or suppress display of hidden parameters. Requires you to log in as SYSDBA.
parmsd.sql	This script displays database parameters and their descriptions. Includes a switch to show or suppress display of hidden parameters. Requires a login as SYSDBA.
part_size2.sql	This script shows the sizes of partitions as reported by DBA_SEGMENTS.
pool_mem.sql	This script provides a simple query against V$SGASTAT, showing memory assigned to various "pools."
queued_sql.sql	This simple script queries V$SQL_MONITOR for statements that are queued by the parallel statement queuing feature.
report_sql_monitor.sql	This is a script to call DBMS_SQLTUNE.REPORT_SQL_MONITOR.
si.sql	This script displays the current value for the statistic Cell Physical IO Bytes Saved by Storage Index from V$MYSTATS. It provides a quick way to check storage index usage.
snapper.sql	This is far and away the most robust script used in the book. It is really more like a monitoring program that can report on an extremely wide range of information about active sessions. The script and documentation can be found on Tanel Poder's blog http://blog.tanelpoder.com
ss_off.sql	This script turns off Smart Scans via alter session (that is, it sets CELL_OFFLOAD_PROCESSING=FALSE).
ss_on.sql	This script turns on Smart Scans via alter session (that is, it sets CELL_OFFLOAD_PROCESSING=TRUE).

(continued)

Table C-1. *(continued)*

Script Name	Description
table_size.sql	This script shows sizes of objects as reported by DBA_SEGMENTS. There is another version (table_size2.sql) that is basically the same script with a reduced number of output columns.
valid_events.sql	This script displays a list of wait events that match a text string. Requires you to connect as SYSDBA.
whoami.sql whoami_12c.sql	This script displays current session information, including SID, Serial#, Previous SQL Hash Value, and OS Shadow Process ID. The 12c version also reports the thread ID in case you operate with threaded_execution = true.

APPENDIX D

exachk

The term "best practice" has long drawn the ire of database professionals. As the saying goes, "They are only best practices until a better one comes along." The My Oracle Support site contains several exhaustive notes regarding best practices on Exadata. The central "Oracle Exadata Best Practices" support note links to 12 other notes that include best practices for running an Exadata environment. These notes cover many different aspects of managing an Exadata environment: setup, performance, high availability, migration, OLTP, data warehouse, and more. Keeping up with the changes would be a daunting task (MOS note #1274318.1, "Oracle Sun Database Machine Setup/Configuration Best Practices" consumes an astounding 127 pages when printed out). Thankfully, Oracle provides a standard health-check utility, known as `exachk`, which checks your Exadata system against all of these recommendations.

The `exachk` script is available from MOS note #1070954.1, and it is generally updated on a quarterly basis. As the checks that it runs are changed with every version, you should always ensure you are on the latest version before running `exachk`. It initially began as a script specifically written for Exadata environments, but is now the standard script used to validate the configuration of many of Oracle's other engineered systems. It will perform exhaustive checks against the hardware in the rack, as well as against the Oracle software binaries and databases themselves. `exachk` is a flexible tool that can be run against a subset of targets, or the system as a whole.

An Introduction to exachk

Once the `exachk` bundle has been downloaded from My Oracle Support, it is commonly placed in the `/opt/oracle.SupportTools/exachk` directory on the first compute node in the cluster. This directory should be owned by the operating system account that was used to install the Grid Infrastructure software (typically oracle or grid). This is especially important on Exadata systems that utilize role separation between different databases or pieces of the software stack. On some consolidated environements, administrators may only have access to a single-user account that runs a subset of the databases across the entire cluster. The `exachk` script utilizes local connections to the database, relying on operating system authentication to run database checks. Imagine that you have two teams of database administrators, each with separate operating system accounts, orahr and oradw. The orahr account is used to run the databases associated with the HR application, and the oradw account is used to run the data warehouse databases. If the administrators only have access to their respective software accounts, they can run a database-level `exachk` report against the databases that they administer without impacting or accessing any part of the stack that they are restricted from. For a full overview of the system, `exachk` would either need to be run with root priviliges or the root passwords would need to be entered.

As the check will execute across all of the nodes in the cluster, it is recommended to only install `exachk` on the first compute node in the cluster. A complete `exachk` run creates a zip file containing all of the raw data collected across the cluster and an HTML report that can be reviewed for detailed information regarding every check that was run. The reports include a system score, cluster summary, Maximum Availability Architecture scorecard, and full references to all of the checks that were passed or failed during the run.

The bundle available from My Oracle Support includes exachk documentation, sample reports, and a zip file containing the script and the driver files. Unzipping the exachk.zip file will give you everything needed to run exachk against your Exadata cluster. The following example shows how to unzip the archive to the recommended exachk directory:

```
$ unzip -q exachk.zip -d /opt/oracle.SupportTools/exachk
$ ls -al /opt/oracle.SupportTools/exachk/
total 50036
drwxr-xr-x 3 oracle oinstall      4096 Jul 11 15:31 .
drwxr-xr-x 8 root   root     4096 Jan 26 20:43 ..
drwxrwxrwx 3 oracle oinstall      4096 Jul  2 14:56 .cgrep
-rw-r--r-- 1 oracle oinstall   4114714 Jul  2 14:54 CollectionManager_App.sql
-rw-r--r-- 1 oracle oinstall  39700004 Jul  2 14:56 collections.dat
-rwxr-xr-x 1 oracle oinstall   2209024 Jul  2 14:54 exachk
-rw-r--r-- 1 oracle oinstall      2533 Jul  2 14:56 readme.txt
-rw-r--r-- 1 oracle oinstall   5071756 Jul  2 14:56 rules.dat
-rw-r--r-- 1 oracle oinstall     39612 Jul  2 14:54 sample_user_defined_checks.xml
-rw-r--r-- 1 oracle oinstall      2758 Jul  2 14:54 user_defined_checks.xsd
-rw-r--r-- 1 oracle oinstall       291 Jul  2 14:56 UserGuide.txt
```

Running exachk

Now that the files have been staged, you are ready to execute your first exachk run. Launch exachk in interactive mode by executing ./exachk as the root user on the first compute node. Upon starting, exachk will first query across the cluster for all running databases. You can choose all of the running databases, none of the running databases, or a subset of the databases. exachk will run configuration and parameter checks against whichever databases you specify when queried. These database checks will be run in parallel across the cluster in order to minimize the time needed to run the script. The following text shows the database selection text from a recent exachk run. As you can see, the default is to check all databases on the cluster:

```
Searching for running databases . . . . .

. . . . . . . . . . . . . . . . . . . . . . . . . . . . . . . . . . . . . . . .
List of running databases registered in OCR
1. ACSTBY
2. BDT
3. BIGDATA
4. dbfs
5. dbm
6. demo
7. All of above
8. None of above

Select databases from list for checking best practices. For multiple databases, select 7 for
All or comma separated number like 1,2 etc [1-8][7].
```

Remember that exachk runs many configuration checks against the hardware and operating system. Because of this, the script requires root privilieges for all of the nodes that will be checked. In fact, Oracle changed its previous recommendation and now asks that exachk be run as root (beginning with version 12.1.0.2.2). Older Exadata systems were automatically configured to allow passwordless access between compute and storage serves as root. That restriction changed in 2014 when Exadata's configuration scripts were rewritten to remove this functionality. Some customers see this passwordless access as a security risk, so Oracle has removed it from the default configuration. If your system does not have SSH equivalence configured, exachk will need a way to execute with root privileges. When it comes to handling root passwords, there are several options that are provided to users when exachk is run in interactive mode:

1. Manually enter the root password for all hosts.
2. Utilize sudo privileges if the user account running exachk is not root.
3. Skip root checks for the run.

If you choose to enter the root password, it will be saved in memory for the exachk process and not written to disk. The password is only stored in memory during the run—when the script completes, the passwords will no longer be saved. If SSH-user equivalence is already configured between the hosts in the cluster, exachk will not ask for a password at all. When run without SSH-user equivalence, exachk will separately ask for the passwords for the storage cells, compute nodes, and then the InfiniBand switches. If you would prefer to only run the checks against a subset of hosts within the cluster, Table D-1 lists some of the parameters that can be included in the exachk command to customize the run.

Table D-1. *exachk Command Parameters*

Configuration Parameter	Description
`-clusternodes`	Runs checks against the hosts in a comma-separated list. By default, exachk will run checks against all hosts returned by the `olsnodes` command.
`-cells`	Runs checks against the storage servers in a comma-separated list. By default, exachk executes against all hosts listed in the `cellip.ora` file.
`-ibswitches`	Runs checks against the specified InfiniBand switches. By default, exachk executes against the switches listed by the `ibswitches` command.
`-dbnames`	Runs checks against the comma-separated list of databases.
`-dball`	Runs checks against all databases running on the cluster.
`-dbnone`	Skips all database checks.

If we wanted to run exachk against none of the database, but execute checks for the first compute node, storage server, and InfiniBand switch, we would start exachk using the following options:

```
# ./exachk -clusternodes enkx4db01 -cells enkx4cel01 -ibswitches enkx4sw-iba -dbnone
```

When exachk has completed, it will give the location of the HTML report as well as a compressed archive that contains all of the files generated during the run. Typically, the report file is all that is needed, but the zip file contains other useful information, including patch inventory files for each Oracle software home and the raw data from all of the checks. Figure D-1 shows an example of the summary seen in an exachk report. The exachk HTML report is a comprehensive configuration check of the system. These checks include, but are not limited to the following:

- Operating system kernel versions
- Oracle database homes, patch levels, and databases registered within them
- Exadata software image version
- Maximum Availability Architecture (MAA) comparisons

- Firmware version for all hardware components on each host
- Operating system configuration files
- ASM disk group adherence to best practices
- Oracle clusterware parameters
- Database parameter checks
- Exadata storage server alert checks
- InfiniBand switch configuration

Oracle Exadata Assessment Report

System Health Score is 98 out of 100 (detail)

Cluster Summary

Cluster Name	xd02
OS/Kernel Version	LINUX X86-64 OELRHEL 6 2.6.39-400.248.3.el6uek.x86_64
CRS Home - Version	/u01/app/11.2.0.4/grid - 11.2.0.4.0
DB Home - Version - Names	/u01/app/oracle/product/11.2.0.4/dbhome_1 - 11.2.0.4.0 - None Selected
Exadata Version	12.1.2.1.1
Number of nodes	7
Database Servers	2
Storage Servers	3
IB Switches	2
exachk Version	12.1.0.2.3_20150305
Collection	exachk_xd02db01_061215_175217.zip
Duration	8 mins, 28 seconds
Executed by	root
Collection Date	12-Jun-2015 17:54:34

***Figure D-1.** exachk report summary*

The first section includes a system summary and overall score for the Exadata rack. While everyone likes to compare scores, remember that the score itself is not as important as the details surrounding the checks that have failed. Immediately following the system summary is the "Findings Needing Attention" section. This is where you will find any of the important messages in the report. Findings are broken down by host type and include a brief description of the problem, what components failed the check, and a link to further in the report with more details. Clicking that link will take you to a detailed overview of the check: a reference to the My Oracle Support note that describes the finding, what is required to remediate the failure, and, most importantly, the results of that check on each component that was investigated.

After the "Findings Needing Attention" section, you will see the MAA scorecard section. This scorecard validates databases against Oracle's Maximum Availability Architecture. These checks include looking at each database for Data Guard configurations, whether flashback is enabled, as well as the presence of block corruptions and various database parameters. While many customers will not fully pass the MAA checks, they provide valuable insight into what Oracle recommends from a high availability perspective. Finally, an "Infrastructure and Software Configuration Summary" is provided. This section details the configuration of the hosts, including network settings, ASM storage utilization, and Exadata Storage Server configurations.

Oracle also provides several profiles that can be used with exachk to execute a specific subset of checks. These profiles can be selected by adding the `-profile` parameter to the command used to launch exachk. Table D-2 defines the profiles available in exachk version 12.1.0.2.4.

Table D-2. *exachk Profiles*

Profile	Description
`asm`	ASM specific checks
`clusterware`	Validation checks for Oracle Clusterware
`dba`	Database configuration checks
`maa`	Maximum Availability Architecture checks and scorecard
`storage`	Exadata Storage Server checks
`switch`	InfiniBand switch checks
`sysadmin`	Checks specific for system administrators

Saving Passwords for exachk

Many organizations protect the root password for their Exadata racks (as they should). Restrictions on giving out the root password can make running exachk in interactive mode very difficult, as it will request root passwords on every run. Other organizations will not allow DBAs to run commands directly as root. Oracle has resolved these issues by allowing exachk to store the passwords and run in daemon mode. When the host boots up, an administrator must run the exachk script in interactive mode with a specific switch, -d. The prompts will be the same as a normal interactive exachk run, but the checks will not execute. Instead, a process is left running that stores the passwords that were entered. The process does not write any files to disk, so the passwords are only saved in memory. As long as the daemon process is running, administrators can run exachk as many times as they would like without having to enter a single password. If the host reboots, the exachk daemon must be started back up and the passwords entered again. The following shows launching exachk in daemon mode. In this example, only the dbm01 database will be checked by exachk:

```
# ./exachk -d start

Checking ssh user equivalency settings on all nodes in cluster

Node enkx4db02 is configured for ssh user equivalency for root user
Node enkx4db03 is configured for ssh user equivalency for root user
Node enkx4db04 is configured for ssh user equivalency for root user
```

```
Searching for running databases . . . . .
. . . . . . . . . . . . . . . . . . . . . . . . . . . . . . . . . . . . . . . . .
List of running databases registered in OCR
1. dbm01
2. demo
3. db12c
4. All of above
5. None of above

Select databases from list for checking best practices. For multiple databases, select 4 for
All or comma separated number like 1,2 etc [1-5][4].1

Searching out ORACLE_HOME for selected databases.
. . . . . . . . . . . . . . . . . . . . . . . . . .

Checking Status of Oracle Software Stack - Clusterware, ASM, RDBMS
. . . . . . . . . . . . . . . . . . . . . . . . . . . . . . . . . . . . . . . . . . . . . . .
. . . . . . . . . . . . . . . . . . . . . . . . . . . . . . .
-------------------------------------------------------------------------------------------
                                                Oracle Stack Status
-------------------------------------------------------------------------------------------
Host Name  CRS Installed  RDBMS Installed  CRS UP    ASM UP    RDBMS UP  DB Instance Name
-------------------------------------------------------------------------------------------
enkx4db01  Yes              Yes              Yes         Yes        Yes        dbm011
enkx4db02  Yes              Yes              Yes         Yes        Yes        dbm012
enkx4db03  Yes              Yes              Yes         Yes        Yes        dbm013
enkx4db04  Yes              Yes              Yes         Yes        Yes        dbm014
-------------------------------------------------------------------------------------------

Skipping version checks merge as RAT_SKIP_MERGE_INTERNAL is set

Copying plug-ins
. . . . . .
root user equivalence is not setup between enkx4db01 and STORAGE SERVER enkx4cel02
(192.168.12.12).

1. Enter 1 if you will enter root password for each STORAGE SERVER when prompted.
2. Enter 2 to exit and configure root user equivalence manually and re-run exachk.
3. Enter 3 to skip checking best practices on STORAGE SERVER.

Please indicate your selection from one of the above options for STORAGE SERVER[1-3][1]:-1

Is root password same on all STORAGE SERVER[y/n][y]y

Enter root password for STORAGE SERVER :-
Verifying root password.
. . . . . . . . . . . . . . . . . . . . . . . . . .

9 of the included audit checks require root privileged data collection on INFINIBAND SWITCH .
```

```
1. Enter 1 if you will enter root password for each INFINIBAND SWITCH when prompted
2. Enter 2 to exit and to arrange for root access and run the exachk later.
3. Enter 3 to skip checking best practices on INFINIBAND SWITCH

Please indicate your selection from one of the above options for INFINIBAND SWITCH[1-3][1]:- 1

Is root password same on all INFINIBAND SWITCH ?[y/n][y]n

. Enter root password for INFINIBAND SWITCH enkx4sw-ibb :-
Verifying root password.
. . . . Enter root password for INFINIBAND SWITCH enkx4sw-ibs :-
Verifying root password.
. . . . Enter root password for INFINIBAND SWITCH enkx4sw-iba :-
Verifying root password.
. . .
exachk daemon is started with PID : 53208
```

exachk was instructed to start daemon mode, as seen by the -d start option. If you would like to run exachk and take advantage of the credentials stored by the exachk daemon, simply add -daemon to your exachk command. Execute exachk with either -d status or -d info if you would like to see information about the running daemon:

```
# ./exachk -d status
exachk daemon is running. Daemon PID : 53208

# ./exachk -d info

----------------------------------------------------------
exachk daemon information
----------------------------------------------------------

install node = enkx4db01

exachk daemon version = 12.1.0.2.4_20150702

Install location = /tmp/exachk

Started at = Mon Jul 06 21:30:34 CDT 2015
```

Automating exachk Executions

It is recommended to run exachk monthly in order to assess the overall health of your Exadata system. When using the exachk daemon, it is possible to schedule periodic exachk executions specific to your needs. This auto-run functionality allows for scheduling utility similar to the standard Linux cron utility, with multiple schedules for various needs. Execute exachk and specify the AUTORUN_SCHEDULE parameter to define a schedule. Figure D-2 shows the options that are used to schedule the auto-run functionality.

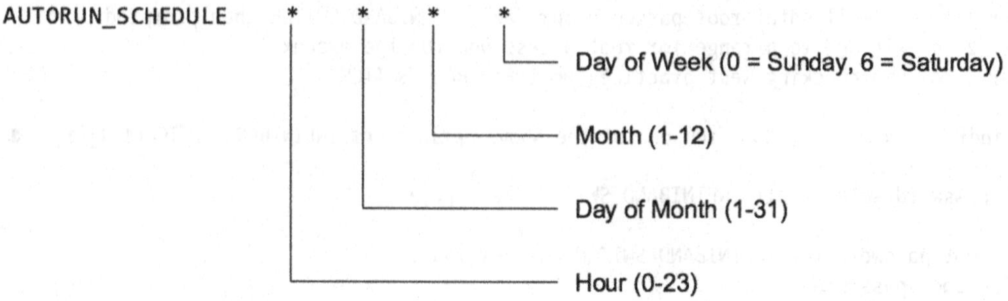

Figure D-2. *AUTORUN_SCHEDULE options*

As you can see, the AUTORUN_SCHEDULE is similar to cron, but doesn't allow you to specify the minute that the exachk script will be executed. When using AUTORUN_SCHEDULE, exachk always executes at the top of the hour. In addition to AUTORUN_SCHEDULE, Oracle recommends to include a NOTIFICATION_EMAIL and PASSWORD_CHECK_INTERVAL. The PASSWORD_CHECK_INTERVAL parameter defines how often the exachk daemon will validate that the passwords stored in memory are still valid. In the event that a password changes, the daemon process will send an e-mail to the address defined by NOTIFICATION_EMAIL. Also, when the scheduled exachk run has completed, the final HTML report will be sent to the address listed in the NOTIFICATION_EMAIL parameter. The following example shows how to create an auto-run schedule that executes every Monday night at 10 p.m.:

```
# ./exachk -id Monday_Night -set "AUTORUN_SCHEDULE=22 * * 1;\
NOTIFICATION_EMAIL=user@example.com;\
PASSWORD_CHECK_INTERVAL=1"

Created autorun_schedule for ID[Monday_Night]

Created notification_email for ID[Monday_Night]

Created password_check_interval for ID[Monday_Night]
```

Schedules can be named by using the -id parameter. This allows for multiple schedules with different options or profiles for each schedule. For example, DBAs could get a specific exachk run that runs against a subset of databases, while system administrators could receive an exachk report monthly that outlines the status of the storage cells. Launch exachk with the -get all parameters if you want to see all of the schedules configured with the exachk daemon. In the following example, there are two schedules, Monday_Night and Tuesday_Night. The Tuesday_Night schedule executes the "storage" profile that only checks against the storage servers:

```
# ./exachk -get all

ID: Monday_Night
----------------------------------
autorun_schedule = 22 * * 1
notification_email = user@example.com
password_check_interval = 1
```

```
ID: Tuesday_Night
----------------------------------
autorun_schedule = 22 * * 2
notification_email = sysadmin@example.com
password_check_interval = 1
autorun_flags = -profile storage
```

Finally, you can query the exachk daemon to see when the next automatic run will occur. Querying the exachk daemon and adding the nextautorun argument will declare when the next exachk automatic run will occur, as well as the schedule that will be calling it:

```
# ./exachk -d nextautorun

ID: Monday_Night

Next auto run starts on Jul 13, 2015 22:00:00
```

Previous exachk reports will be saved in the directory that the exachk daemon was launched (typically /opt/oracle.SupportTools/exachk). When automatic runs are scheduled, the e-mail notification that is sent will compare the current run to the previous one. The e-mail will give the number of checks passed, failed, and skipped, along with a comparison between the runs. Also, a report detailing the differences between the two runs is created and referenced in the e-mail. If further investigation is needed, this report must be downloaded from the server.

Summary

Best practices are not static recommendations that are set in stone once they are written. Oracle understands that Exadata is a moving target from this perspective. Whether recommendations change due to more powerful hardware and software being developed or due to issues discovered with existing software, the tool that is used to validate the environment must change as well. While certainly not being a tool that will catch every possible issue before it occurs, exachk is able to take advantage of the standardized nature of Exadata to run a host of validation checks that would take months to develop on a build-your-own system.

Index

E

F

G

H

I, J, K

Q

R

S

Printed in the United States
By Bookmasters